The ‘Legal Pluriverse’ Surrounding Multinational Military Operations

The 'Legal Pluriverse' Surrounding Multinational Military Operations

Edited by

ROBIN GEIß AND HEIKE KRIEGER

Assistant Editor

HENNING LAHMANN

OXFORD
UNIVERSITY PRESS

OXFORD
UNIVERSITY PRESS

Great Clarendon Street, Oxford, OX2 6DP,
United Kingdom

Oxford University Press is a department of the University of Oxford. It furthers the University's objective of excellence in research, scholarship, and education by publishing worldwide. Oxford is a registered trade mark of Oxford University Press in the UK and in certain other countries

First Edition published in 2020
Impression: 1

Published in the United States of America by Oxford University Press
198 Madison Avenue, New York, NY 10016, United States of America

British Library Cataloguing in Publication Data
Data available

Library of Congress Control Number: 2019947242

ISBN 978–0–19–884296–5

Printed and bound by
CPI Group (UK) Ltd, Croydon, CR0 4YY

Preface and Acknowledgements

The global security environment and the humanitarian landscape are rapidly evolving. Many of today's protracted crises and conflict situations require integrated and increasingly multi-dimensional responses. As a result, multinational military operations with complex multi-functional mandates have increasingly become the rule. These operations can take many forms and they often involve and interact with various actors. They come with different command structures and their mandates and functions, tailored and adjusted to the particular operational contexts, may differ considerably. But a common feature they all share is that they are governed and surrounded by a multiplicity of rules and legal regimes that partly overlap, i.e. they operate in a 'legal pluriverse'. Indeed, the more complex, multi-functional, multi-dimensional, and protection-oriented contemporary multinational military operations are, and the more actors are involved, the more intricate the surrounding legal environment becomes. Left unaddressed, such a level of legal complexity can contribute to (a perception) of legal uncertainty; it can affect the predictability and transparency of governance decisions as well as the division of powers and allocation of responsibility. These complexities have the potential to undermine the legitimacy and effectiveness of these operations and can thereby detrimentally affect the international rule of law. It is against this backdrop that the present book aims at the rationalization of the 'legal pluriverse' surrounding contemporary multinational military operations and thereby to make a contribution to their legitimacy and effectiveness.

This book is one of the outputs of a broader research project on security governance in areas of limited statehood which the editors pursued at the Collaborative Research Centre 700 – a coordinated research programme funded by the German Research Foundation (DFG) and hosted by the Freie Universität Berlin. The book brings together a diverse group of renowned scholars and practitioners, all of whom are experts in the field of international humanitarian law, human rights law, and public international law generally. Most of the authors participated in a workshop on 'The Legal Pluriverse Surrounding Military Operations in Areas of Limited Statehood', which was funded by the German Research Foundation (DFG) and organized in collaboration with the International Law Association's (ILA) Study Group on 'The conduct of hostilities and international humanitarian law: challenges of 21st century warfare'. In this regard we owe special thanks to the members of Study Group and especially its Rapporteurs Terry Gill and Robert Heinsch as well as other participants whose inputs and expert opinions have helped to inform and shape this book, namely Robert Cryer, Charles Garraway, Wolff Heintschel von Heinegg, Kirsten Schmalenbach, and, as a representative from the ICRC, Laurent Gisel.

A special debt of gratitude goes to our assistant editor Dr. Henning Lahmann for his invaluable work on this book and to Jeanne Gillet und Pia Wolski who supported him throughout the editing process. We are also grateful for the meticulous work done by the publication team at Oxford University Press, in particular Merel Alstein, Jack McNichol, and Jordan Burke, as well as the project manager Mohith Singh and the various proof readers. Last but not least, we wish to thank the anonymous OUP reviewers for their helpful comments and constructive feedback on our proposal for this book.

Robin Geiß and Heike Krieger, Glasgow/Berlin, UK/Germany,
August 2019

Contents

List of Abbreviations xi
List of Contributors xv

Introduction: The History of Multinational Military Operations and Contemporary Legal Challenges 1
Robin Geiß, Heike Krieger, and Henning Lahmann

PART I: THE APPLICATION AND INTEROPERABILITY OF THE LAWS OF ARMED CONFLICT TO MULTINATIONAL MILITARY OPERATIONS

1. Multinational Military Operations and the Geographical Scope of the Laws of Armed Conflict in Non-International Armed Conflict 27
Katja Schöberl

2. The Temporal Scope of the Laws of Armed Conflict in Multinational Military Operations 49
Christian Schaller

3. The Legal Interoperability of the Laws of Armed Conflict 70
Michael Newton

PART II: LAWS OF ARMED CONFLICT AND INTERNATIONAL HUMAN RIGHTS LAW IN THE CONTEXT OF MULTINATIONAL MILITARY OPERATIONS: A MATTER OF PERSPECTIVE?

4. An Operational Perspective 91
Hans Boddens Hosang

5. A North American Perspective: The Overlap of the Laws of Armed Conflict and International Human Rights Law 109
Kenneth Watkin

6. A European Perspective on the International Human Rights and Humanitarian Law Relationship in the Context of Multinational Military Operations 126
Gentian Zyberi and Anna Andersson

PART III: LAWS OF ARMED CONFLICT AND INTERNATIONAL HUMAN RIGHTS LAW IN THE CONTEXT OF MULTINATIONAL MILITARY OPERATIONS: LAW ENFORCEMENT, DETENTION, HOSTILITIES, AND PRECAUTIONS IN ATTACK AS RELEVANT CASES IN POINT

7. Law Enforcement Activities in Peacekeeping and Multinational Military Operations: The Cases of Haiti and Afghanistan 151
Héctor Olásolo, Felipe Tenorio-Obando, Sergio Andrés Díaz, and Antonio Varón

8. Detention in the Context of Multinational Military Operations 163
Jacques Hartmann

9. An Exercise in Defragmentation: The Grand Chamber Judgment in *Hassan v UK* 179
Andreas von Arnauld

10. International Human Rights Law and Extraterritorial Hostilities 198
Yaël Ronen

11. The Invaluable Civilian Risk Mitigation Contribution of Recognizing the Value of Precautionary Measures 223
Geoffrey Corn

12. European Partners in Multinational Military Operations—Extended Legal Restraints: The ECtHR's Rights-based Conception of Precautions in and against the Effects of Attacks 239
Tilmann Altwicker

PART IV: THE ROLE OF PERTINENT SUBFIELDS OF PUBLIC INTERNATIONAL LAW IN RELATION TO MULTINATIONAL MILITARY OPERATIONS

13. UN Security Council Resolutions as a Legal Framework for Multinational Military Operations 267
Pia Hesse

14. The Coordinating and Steering Function of Status of Forces Agreements 287
Dieter Fleck

15. Accountability and Multinational Military Operations 300
Paulina Starski

16. Protecting the Environment during Multinational Military Operations 322
Onita Das

17. Multinational Military Operations at Sea 345
Anna Petrig

PART V: COMPLEX OPERATIONAL ENVIRONMENTS: DIVERSITY OF ACTORS AND ITS IMPACT ON THE LEGAL PLURIVERSE SURROUNDING MULTINATIONAL MILITARY OPERATIONS

18. Receiving States, Sending States, and the Impact of Their Domestic Laws 373
Aurel Sari

19. Legal Challenges in Multinational Military Operations: The Role of National Caveats 393
Jochen Katze and Maral Kashgar

20. The Involvement of Private Security Companies in Multinational Military Operations 406
Hin-Yan Liu

21. Asymmetric Actors in Asymmetric Conflicts 424
Robert Frau

22. Human Rights Obligations of Armed Groups 444
Andreas Th Müller

Index 463

List of Abbreviations

ACHR	American Convention on Human Rights
ACLU	American Civil Liberties Union
AFISMA	African-led International Support Mission in Mali
AfrChHPR	African Charter on Human and Peoples' Rights
AMIB	African Mission in Burundi
AMIS	African Union Mission in Sudan
AMISOM	African Union Mission in Somalia
ANSAs	armed non-state actors
AP II	Additional Protocol II
ARIO	ILC Articles on the Responsibility of International Organizations
ARSIWA	Articles on Responsibility of States for Internationally Wrongful Acts
ASR	ILC Articles on the Responsibility of States for Internationally Wrongful Acts
ATT	Arms Trade Treaty
CCS	Combined Chiefs of Staff
CCW	Certain Conventional Weapons Convention
CDE	Collateral Damage Estimation
CFSP	Common Foreign and Security Policy
CIHL	customary international humanitarian law
CMC	Convention on Cluster Munitions
CoE	Council of Europe
CSDP	Common Security and Defence Policy
CSTC-A	Combined Security Transition Command for Afghanistan
CWC	Chemical Weapons Convention
DFS	Department of Field Support
DoD	US Department of Defense
DPKO	UN Department of PKOs
DRC	Democratic Republic of the Congo
ECHR	European Convention on Human Rights
ECOWAS	Economic Community of West African States
ECtHR	European Court of Human Rights
ENMOD	Convention on the Prohibition of Military or Any Other Hostile Use of Environmental Modification Techniques
ESDP	European Security and Defence Policy
EUNAVFOR	EU-led naval forces
EUPOL	European Union Police Mission
EUTM Mali	European Union Training Mission in Mali
FARC	Revolutionary Armed Forces of Colombia

FIB	Force Intervention Brigade
FRY	former Yugoslavia
GC	Geneva Convention
GWOT	Global War on Terror
IACs	international armed conflicts
ICC	International Criminal Court
ICCPR	International Covenant on Civil and Political Rights
ICCSt	Rome Statute of the International Criminal Court
ICJ	International Court of Justice
ICL	international criminal law
ICoC	International Code of Conduct
ICRC	International Committee of the Red Cross
ICTR	International Criminal Tribunal for Rwanda
ICTRSt	Statute of the International Criminal Tribunal for Rwanda
ICTY	International Criminal Tribunal for the Former Yugoslavia
IDPs	internally displaced persons
IEL	International Environmental Law
IFOR	Implementation Force
IHL	international humanitarian law
IHRL	international human rights law
ILA	International Law Association
ILC Articles	Articles on the Responsibility of States for Internationally Wrongful Acts
ILC	International Law Commission
ISAF	International Security Assistance Force
ISIL	Islamic State of Iraq and the Levant
JCHR	Joint Committee on Human Rights
JFIT	Joint Forward Interrogation Team
JTAC	Joint Terminal Attack Controller
KFOR	Kosovo Force
LCBC	Lake Chad Basin Commission
LEAs	law enforcement activities
LRA	Lord's Resistance Army
LTTE	Liberation Tigers of Tamil Eelam
MEJA	Military Extraterritorial Jurisdiction Act 2000
MINUSCA	United Nations Multidimensional Integrated Stabilization Mission in the Central African Republic
MINUSMA	United Nations Multidimensional Integrated Stabilization Mission in Mali
MIO	Maritime Interdiction Operation
MMOs	multinational military operations
MNFI	*Multi-National Force Iraq*
MNJTF	Multinational Joint Task Force
MoA	Memorandum of Arrangement

MONUSCO	United Nations Organization Stabilization Mission in the Democratic Republic of the Congo
MSO	Maritime Security Operation
NATO	North-Atlantic Treaty Organization
NCC	National Contingent Commanders
NIACs	non-international armed conflicts
OMLT	Operational Mentoring and Liaison Teams
OPCOM	operational command
OPCON	operational control
OPLAN	Operation Plan
OSCE	Organization for the Security and Cooperation in Europe
PACE	Parliamentary Assembly of the Council of Europe
PCIJ	Permanent Court of International Justice
PID	personal identification
PKK	Kurdistan Workers' Party
PKOs	peacekeeping operations
PoC	protection of civilians
POW	prisoners of war
PSC AU	African Union Peace and Security Council
PSCs	Private Security Companies
RCA	riot control agents
RoE	Rules of Engagement
RPF	Regional Protection Force
RSM	Resolute Support Mission
RUF	Revolutionary United Front
SCSLSt	Statute of the Special Court for Sierra Leone
SFOR	Stabilisation Force
SHADE	Shared Awareness and Deconfliction
SOFAs	status of forces agreements
SOMAs	status of mission agreements
SPMs	special political missions
SROE	Standing RoE
STANAG	Standardization Agreement
SUA Convention	Convention for the Suppression of Unlawful Acts Against the Safety of Maritime Navigation
TCN	troop-contributing nation
TOA	transfer of authority
UCDP	Uppsala Conflict Data Program
UDHR	Universal Declaration of Human Rights
UNAMID	United Nations
UNAMSIL	United Nations Mission in Sierra Leone
UNCLOS	United Nations Convention on the Law of the Sea
UNHCR	United Nations High Commissioner for Refugees
UNMEE	UN missions in Ethiopia and Eritrea

UNMIK	United Nations Interim Administration Mission in Kosovo
UNMISS	United Nations Mission in the Republic of South Sudan
UNOCI	United Nations Operation in Côte d'Ivoire
UNOMIG	United Nations Observer Mission in Georgia
UNPKM	UN peacekeeping mission
UNPROFOR	United Nations Protection Force
UNSC	United Nations Security Council
VCLT	Vienna Convention on the Law of Treaties

List of Contributors

Tilmann Altwicker
Professor Tilmann Altwicker holds a Swiss National Science Foundation (SNSF) Professorship at the Institute for International Law and Foreign Constitutional Law at the University of Zurich. His main research areas are Public Law, International Law, Legal Philosophy, and Empirical Legal Research.

Anna Andersson
Anna Andersson is a PhD candidate at the Norwegian Centre for Human Rights, Faculty of Law, University of Oslo. She holds a bachelor's and a master's degree with a major in law from Örebro Universitet, Sweden, and a master's degree (LLM) from the Geneva Academy of International Humanitarian Law and Human Rights, Switzerland.

Andreas von Arnauld
After positions as professor at Helmut Schmidt University of the Federal Armed Forces in Hamburg and at Münster University, Dr Andreas von Arnauld has been professor at the Chair of Public Law, Public International and European Law at Kiel University and has been serving as Co-director of the Walther Schücking Institute of International Law since 2013. He is the Co-editor of the *German Yearbook of International Law* and of *Die Friedens-Warte: Journal of International Peace and Organization*.

Geoffrey Corn
Geoffrey Corn is the Vinson & Elkins Professor of Law at South Texas College of Law in Houston and a retired US Army Lieutenant Colonel. His Army career included service as the Army's Senior Law of War Expert Adviser, as tactical intelligence officer in Panama, and as a supervisory defence counsel for the Western United States. He also served as the Chief of International Law for US Army Europe. He is co-author of 'The Law of Armed Conflict: An Operational Perspective', 'The Laws of War and the War on Terror', 'National Security Law and Policy: Principles and Policy', 'U.S. Military Operations: Law, Policy, and Practice', and 'National Security Law and the Constitution, and Law in War: A Concise Overview' (with K Watkin and J Williamson).

Onita Das
Dr Onita Das is a Senior Lecturer in Law at the University of the West of England, Bristol. She studied for her LLM in International Law at the University of Bristol and subsequently completed her PhD in International Law at the University of the West of England in 2010. She currently teaches Environmental Law at undergraduate level and contributes to teaching on the International Environmental Law module at postgraduate level. Her principal research area is on Environmental Protection relevant to Security and Armed Conflict. She is also currently the Head of the Environmental Law Research Unit at the University of the West of England.

Sergio Andrés Díaz

Sergio Andrés Díaz obtained a degree in Law at the Universidad del Rosario in Bogotá, Colombia, and completed advanced studies on Environmental Law at the Universidad Externado de Colombia (Colombia). He currently serves as Legal Adviser for the Treaty Section of the Ministry of Foreign Affairs of the Republic of Colombia and has held a position as Adjunct Professor of International Law at Universidad del Rosario.

Dieter Fleck

Dr Dieter Fleck is Honorary President of the International Society for Military Law and the Law of War, Member of the Advisory Board of the Amsterdam Center for International Law, and Rapporteur of the Committee on Nuclear Weapons, Non-Proliferation and Contemporary International Law of the International Law Association. He has served as legal adviser in various commands of the German armed forces, the German Chancellors Office, and the Federal Ministry of Defence, where he was last Director International Agreements & Policy. He is widely published on issues of international law and security.

Robert Frau

Dr Robert Frau studied law at the European University Viadrina in Frankfurt/Oder, Germany. After his legal clerkship at the Kammergericht Berlin (2008–10), he obtained a PhD in 2010. He was visiting professor at the Universities of Leipzig, Potsdam, and the Free University of Berlin, and has been an associate Professor ('Privatdozent') at the European University Viadrina since 2019.

Jacques Hartmann

Dr Jacques Hartmann is Reader at the School of Law, University of Dundee, United Kingdom. Prior to joining Dundee University, he worked as Legal Adviser at the Danish Ministry of Foreign Affairs. He has taught international and human rights law at various universities around the world. He holds a PhD from Cambridge University, where he also worked as a Research Associate at the Lauterpacht Centre for International Law. His research interests focus on general issues of public international law, particularly relating to security and human rights.

Pia Hesse

Pia Hesse is a doctoral candidate at Universität Potsdam and a junior lawyer at the Kammergericht Berlin. In her PhD research project, she examines law enforcement operations by external actors as a response to transnational security threats. Pia Hesse completed the UN Staff Officer Course at the Senior Military Academy of the German armed forces in Hamburg and worked as a Tutor for the MOOC 'Right vs Might in International Relations' at the University of Glasgow. In 2014, she obtained an LLM degree in International Law and International Security from the University of Glasgow.

Hans Boddens Hosang

Dr JFR (Hans) Boddens Hosang is Deputy Director of Legal Affairs of the Netherlands Ministry of Defence and head of the international law section of the directorate. He completed his master's degree in international law at the University of Utrecht and gained a PhD in international law at the University of Amsterdam. Apart from his work at the MoD, he is co-lecturer at the University of Leiden, a regular guest lecturer at the University of

Amsterdam and the Netherlands Defence Academy, and Senior External Researcher of the LACMO Research Group, Amsterdam Center for International Law, University of Amsterdam.

Maral Kashgar

Oberregierungsrätin Maral Kashgar, LLM (Ottawa) is a legal instructor at the German Army Officers School. After studying law in Münster and working as a research assistant at the Human Rights Centre of the University of Potsdam besides her doctorate studies, she joined the German Armed Forces Legal Service in 2016 and has served as Legal Adviser at the German Army Headquarters Operational Law Division.

Jochen Katze

Regierungsdirektor Jochen Katze is the head of branch for operational law in the legal office of the German Army Headquarters. After studying law in Münster, Westphalia, and a first practice as an attorney at law, he joined the German Armed Forces Legal Service in 1999 and served in different functions as a legal adviser, legal instructor, and desk officer in the Ministry of Defence. He completed his military service as a reserve officer in the armoured infantry and has been deployed to missions in Afghanistan and Kosovo as legal adviser staff officer.

Hin-Yan Liu

Dr Hin-Yan Liu is the author of *Law's Impunity* (Hart 2015), which explores and explicates the myriads of ways in which the Private Military Company confounds ordinary legal principles and processes. He has published on the legal challenges raised by the Private Military Companies in the *Journal of Conflict and Security Law*, and more recently to challenge the strength of the anti-mercenary norm in the *Journal of Global Security Studies*. Dr Liu is Associate Professor at the Faculty of Law, University of Copenhagen, having previously worked at the European University Institute, NYU Florence, King's College London, and the University of Westminster, United Kingdom.

Andreas Th Müller

Andreas Th Müller is Full Professor at the Department of European Law and Public International Law of the University of Innsbruck, Austria. He studied law and philosophy at the Universities of Innsbruck, Strasbourg, and Yale Law School. He has been a regular Visiting Professor at the University of Alcalá, Spain, the Universidad Panamericana, Mexico, as well as Addis Ababa University, Ethiopia. His research focuses on international human rights law, international humanitarian law, international criminal law, international and European migration and asylum law, EU constitutional law, and questions of legal philosophy and legal theory.

Michael Newton

Michael Newton is Professor of the Practice of Law and of the Practice of Political Science at Vanderbilt University in Nashville, Tennessee. He is an expert on terrorism, accountability, transnational justice, and conduct of hostilities issues. Over the course of his career, he has published more than ninety books, articles, op-eds, and book chapters. Most recently, he edited the volume *The United States Department of Defense Law of War Manual: Commentary and Critique*, published by Cambridge University Press. Professor

Newton served as the senior adviser to the Ambassador-at-Large for War Crimes Issues in the US State Department from January 1999 to August 2002, and has been on the executive council of the American Society of International Law. He served in the US Army for more than twenty-one years.

Héctor Olásolo

Professor Dr Héctor Olásolo obtained a Law Degree at the University of Salamanca, an LLM at Columbia University, and a PhD in Law at the University of Salamanca. Professor Olásolo holds the Chair in International Law at the Universidad del Rosario, Bogotá, Colombia, and is chairman of the Ibero-American Institute of The Hague for Peace, Human Rights and International Justice (the Netherlands). He is also director of the 'Anuario Iberoamericano de Derecho Internacional Penal' (*Ibero-American Yearbook of International Law*). Professor Olásolo previously held the Chair in International Criminal Law at the University of Utrecht (2010–12) and served as Legal Officer in Chambers of the International Criminal Court (2004–09) and the Office of the Prosecutor of the International Criminal Tribunal for the former Yugoslavia (2002–04). He was Legal Adviser to the Spanish Delegation to the Preparatory Commission for the International Criminal Court (1999–2002) and expert witness before the Inter-American Court of Human Rights.

Anna Petrig

Dr Anna Petrig is a Professor of International Law and Public Law at the University of Basel (Switzerland). She is an expert on the law of the sea and widely published in the field of maritime security, notably on piracy, human rights at sea, and private maritime security companies. Dr Petrig is Co-Editor-in-Chief of the Maritime Safety and Security Law Journal and regularly advises governmental and non-governmental bodies on maritime security-related matters. Her broad legal experience includes work in private practice, the courts, and the Legal Division of the International Committee of the Red Cross in Geneva.

Yaël Ronen

Professor Yaël Ronen is a faculty member at the Academic Center for Science and Law in Hod Hasahron, Israel. She is also a research fellow at the Minerva Center for Human Rights at the Hebrew University in Jerusalem and academic editor of the *Israel Law Review*, published by Cambridge University Press. Her areas of interest include issues of territorial status, particularly as they intersect with questions of human rights, humanitarian law, and international criminal law.

Aurel Sari

Dr Aurel Sari is an Associate Professor of Public International Law at the University of Exeter. He is the Director of the Exeter Centre for International Law, a Fellow of Supreme Headquarters Allied Powers Europe, and a Fellow of the Allied Rapid Reaction Corps. His scholarship focuses primarily on international conflict and security law and the law relating to military operations, including the law of visiting forces.

Christian Schaller

Dr Christian Schaller is Deputy Head of the Global Issues Division at the German Institute for International and Security Affairs (Stiftung Wissenschaft und Politik, SWP) in Berlin. He has more than fifteen years of experience in advising the Federal Government, the

Bundestag, and various national and international institutions on matters of international law. Before joining SWP in 2003, he was a Senior Research Fellow at the Max Planck Institute for Comparative Public Law and International Law in Heidelberg where he specialized in the law of armed conflict.

Katja Schöberl

Dr Katja Schöberl is a Legal Adviser for the German Red Cross in Berlin. She previously worked for the Geneva Academy of International Humanitarian Law and Human Rights, the International Committee of the Red Cross, and the Institute for International Law of Peace and Armed Conflict. She holds a BA in International Relations, an LLM in International Humanitarian Law and Human Rights, and a Doctorate in Law. Her current research focuses on the geographical scope of the application of international humanitarian law. Previous publications on the subject include a chapter in the *Commentary on the 1949 Geneva Conventions* (OUP 2015).

Paulina Starski

Dr Paulina Starski is Senior Research Fellow at the Max Planck Institute for Comparative Public Law and International Law in Heidelberg and Visiting Professor at the Humboldt University Berlin. Dr Starski earned degrees from Bucerius Law School, Hamburg (LLB and PhD (*summa cum laude*)). In 2017, she was Hauser Global Fellow at the NYU School of law and in 2018 Senior Visiting Fellow at the University of Sydney Law School and Kathleen Fitzpatrick Postdoctoral Visiting Fellow at the University of Melbourne Law School taking part in the Laureate Project in International Law 'Civil War, Intervention and International Law', directed by Anne Orford. Her main research project focuses on the 'Unwilling or Unable State as a Challenge to International Law'.

Felipe Tenorio-Obando

Felipe Tenorio-Obando, who has a Law Degree from the Universidad del Rosario in Bogotá, Colombia, an LLM in International Criminal Law from Granada University, Spain, and an LLM in Legal Theory from Goethe-Universität in Frankfurt/Main, Germany, is currently a PhD candidate at Goethe-Universität of Frankfurt on a scholarship from the DAAD. Felipe Tenorio-Obando held a position as a lecturer on Legal Theory and International Criminal Law at the Universidad del Rosario (2016–17) and served as Legal Adviser to the International Committee of the Red Cross in Colombia (2016–17).

Antonio Varón

Antonio Varón Mejía LLM (Université Paris 2 Panthéon-Assas) is a Law Professor at the Universidad del Rosario in Bogotá, Colombia. Professor Varón has been National Director of the Protection Section of the Colombian Institute for Family Well-Being. He has also been National Director of the Section on Restorative Juvenile Justice of the NGO *Terre des Hommes*.

Kenneth Watkin

Kenneth Watkin served for thirty-three years in the Canadian Forces, including as the Judge Advocate General (2006–10), as a Foreign Observer to the Israeli Independent Commission investigating the 31 May 2010 Gaza blockade incident, as the Charles H Stockton Professor of International Law at the United States Naval War College (2011–12), and more recently as a national security/counterterrorism consultant. He has written extensively about contemporary conflict and counterterrorism, including the book *Fighting at the Legal Boundaries: Controlling the Use of Force in Contemporary Conflict* (OUP 2016), and co-authored *Law in War: A Concise Overview* (Routledge 2018).

Gentian Zyberi

Professor Dr Gentian Zyberi is the Head of the Norwegian Centre for Human Rights, Faculty of Law, University of Oslo, and a member of the UN Human Rights Committee (2019–22). He holds a bachelor's degree (LLB) from Tirana University, Albania, and a Master's degree (LLM) and a PhD in International Law from Utrecht University, the Netherlands. Professor Zyberi's research interests include the contribution of the International Court of Justice and other international courts and tribunals to interpreting and developing rules and principles of international human rights and humanitarian law; the protection of community interests under international law; the operationalization of the responsibility to protect doctrine; and transitional justice issues with a focus in the Balkans.

Introduction

The History of Multinational Military Operations and Contemporary Legal Challenges

Robin Geiß, Heike Krieger, and Henning Lahmann

1. Concept and Challenges

'There is only one thing worse than fighting with allies, and that is fighting without them.'[1] Ascribed to Winston Churchill, who was reflecting on the fraught and complicated Alliance that nevertheless managed to liberate Europe from Nazi Germany, the famous quote might have turned into a cliché by now. Yet Churchill's sentiment still rings true decades later. Today, when states decide to deploy their militaries, they usually do so in concert with other states. Multinational military operations have become the default mode for administering global security governance in the twenty-first century. As one author has observed, they are so common now that they might well be the only ones most states have conducted at all in recent years.[2]

At the same time—as Churchill's witticism illustrates—going to combat jointly with another sovereign's forces is anything but a novelty.[3] Indeed, as far back as in ancient Greece, different communities with not always entirely aligned interests, and with sometimes vastly uneven powers, have come together in order to achieve a common purpose by military means. But it perhaps has never made more sense than today: in an ever-shifting global threat environment, the reasons for multinational military operations are manifold and range from aiming to increase efficiency and cost-effectiveness of missions to augmenting their legitimacy.[4] The more matters of transnational security have become a multilateral concern since the end of the Second World War, the more military operations have become multinational. Accordingly, the United Nations or regional organizations often play a crucial role, not only mandating missions but frequently also assuming command and control.[5] The trend towards ever more military integration has been

[1] Quoted from K Harris, 'Wartime Lies' *The New York Times* (New York, 27 April 1997).
[2] V Bernard, 'Editorial: Multinational Operations and the Law—Great Expectations, Great Responsibilities' (2013) 95 International Review of the Red Cross 475, 475.
[3] M Zwanenburg, 'International Humanitarian Law Interoperability in Multinational Operations' (2013) 95 International Review of the Red Cross 681, 681.
[4] ibid.
[5] Bernard (n 2) 475.

Robin Geiß, Heike Krieger, and Henning Lahmann, *Introduction* In *The 'Legal Pluriverse' Surrounding Multinational Military Operations*. Edited by Robin Geiß and Heike Krieger, Oxford University Press (2020). © The Several Contributors.
DOI: 10.1093/oso/9780198842965.003.0001

conspicuous at least since the end of the Cold War, with some organizations now even commencing to properly institutionalize the multinational approach.[6]

The more complex, multifunctional, multidimensional, and protection-oriented contemporary multinational military operations become, and the more actors are involved, the more intricate the surrounding legal questions inevitably become as well. Whether operating under the command of a single hegemonic state, or a regional or international organization, a multitude of partly distinct, partly overlapping legal regimes apply to each mission. These regimes stem from various sources: bi- and multilateral international agreements or customary international law; but also soft law has an important role to play, be it through national or multinational codes of conduct, best-practice recommendations, or mission-specific rules of engagement.

Against this backdrop, the present book aims to conceptualize and rationalize *The 'Legal Pluriverse' Surrounding Multinational Military Operations*. This term is used to describe the multiplicity of rules that apply to and regulate contemporary multinational missions and the diversity of actors involved. The book intends to systematically compile and take stock of the various legal regimes which make up this pluriverse, to assess how these rules interact, and to expose norm conflicts, areas of legal uncertainty, or protective loopholes. Taken together, the book's individual contributions identify and evaluate approaches to better streamline the different applicable legal frameworks with a view to enhancing cooperation and thereby to ensure the long-term success of multinational military operations.

As its premise, *The 'Legal Pluriverse' Surrounding Multinational Military Operations* takes up the trend towards ever-more robust mandates, not least within the United Nations framework.[7] Thus, without failing to acknowledge that holistic approaches are necessary in order to achieve and secure peace and security on the international level, as the military alone is inherently incapable of solving any conflict, this book nevertheless focuses on military operations.

[6] See for the European Union's discussion regarding a common joint multinational force Council of the European Union, 'Defence Cooperation: Council Establishes Permanent Structured Cooperation' (PESCO) (Press Release, 11 December 2017) <https://www.consilium.europa.eu/en/press/press-releases/2017/12/11/defence-cooperation-pesco-25-member-states-participating/>, all URLs accessed 27 December 2018; see more recently the call by French President Emmanuel Macron and German Chancellor Merkel's approval, 'France's Macron Pushes for "True European Army"' (*BBC*, 6 November 2018) <https://www.bbc.com/news/world-europe-46108633>; 'Merkel Joins Macron in Calling for EU Army to Complement NATO' (*Politico*, 13 November 2018) <https://www.politico.eu/article/angela-merkel-emmanuel-macron-eu-army-to-complement-nato/>.

[7] See United Nations, 'Force Commanders Outline Challenges Facing United Nations Peacekeeping Efforts in Briefing to Security Council' (Press Release, 23 May 2017) <https://www.un.org/press/en/2017/sc12834.doc.htm>.

1.1 Multinational military operations: a preliminary approximation

There has not emerged a clear and universally agreed upon legal or political definition of the concept of multinational military operations to date. For the purpose of this book, it will be understood in a broad sense as any mission involving armed forces relying on contributions of a number of states and other actors such as international organizations. Those operations typically, but by no means exclusively, take place in zones of armed conflict and in areas of limited statehood with deficient or partially absent governance structures. One significant characteristic of such areas is a prevalence of organized crime and other, similarly destabilizing, factors. As a consequence, multinational military operations frequently find themselves in a situation in which they do not just have to fulfil more traditional military functions, but at the same time—often even more importantly—engage in policing and other governance functions in the territory that they control or in which they operate.

Often comprising a considerable range of troop-contributing states, the objectives of such military operations are just as varied as their mandates, and regularly multidimensional. Depending on the context, they engage in conflict management, the protection of civilians, disarmament and demobilization efforts in the aftermath of internal conflict; they conduct specific law enforcement missions or attempt to implement the rule of law[8] or reform and train the security sector.[9] Multinational forces can be found in transnational counter-terrorism endeavours[10] as well as in post-conflict situations[11] or major disaster relief operations.[12] And not only the diversity of actors on the operation's part is crucial to reckon with. Just as significant is the range of stakeholders on the target area's side that interact, cooperate, and engage with the foreign troops such as regional states, local authorities, or a number of different non-state actors ranging from armed groups to humanitarian NGOs. All this shows that while there are certain characteristics that all multinational military operations have in common, the differences are just as significant and thus need to be considered by any overarching treatment of the topic.

As any military commander will readily attest to, multinational operations can easily be more time-consuming, cumbersome, and overall more limiting than

[8] See eg the EU Mission in Kosovo EULEX, <https://www.eulex-kosovo.eu>.

[9] Eg as part of Operation Inherent Resolve in Iraq, <http://www.inherentresolve.mil>.

[10] Eg the Combined Task Force 150: Maritime Security, based in Bahrain, which was established to monitor, board, inspect, and stop suspect vessels as part of the 'war on terrorism'.

[11] Eg the United Nations Transitional Administration in East Timor (UNTAET) from 1999 to 2002, <https://peacekeeping.un.org/mission/past/etimor/etimor.htm>.

[12] Eg in reaction to the 2010 monsoon floods in Pakistan, see JDP Moroney and others, 'Lessons from Department of Defense Disaster Relief Efforts in the Asia-Pacific Region' (*RAND*, 2013) <https://www.rand.org/content/dam/rand/pubs/research_reports/RR100/RR146/RAND_RR146.pdf>, 74 et seq.

pursuing sensitive missions with only one's own capacities.[13] This observation, of course, begs the question why this form of military engagement became so prevalent in the twentieth century that it can only be described as being the norm at the outset of the twenty-first century. Historically, the most important reason for setting up multinational operations was the aggregation of military capabilities. After the French Empire under Napoleon had conquered large parts of the European continent, the opposing states concluded that the only chance they had to beat the French troops was to build an uneasy coalition and thus combine their respective military powers.[14] But this rationale does not always hold up today. Otherwise a powerful nation such as the United States, with a military capacity that eclipses that of every other state, would virtually never have a true incentive to build a coalition in order to pursue its geostrategic goals.[15] However, as could be witnessed during the prelude to the internationally contentious war in Iraq against Saddam Hussein's regime in 2003, the United States made a serious effort to convince other nations to join in. The goal, of course, was to gain legitimacy, a motive especially consequential in an international system that has outlawed war as a legitimate means of politics.[16]

For other states, however, the burden and cost sharing argument continues to be an important factor when deciding whether to participate in a multinational operation. Further advantages such as facilitated access to resources, intelligence, and other strategic gains come up as well.[17] Still, it is the question of legitimacy that most pointedly reveals why most nations and internationally mandated operations make an attempt to gather allies in order to achieve a certain political goal by means of military might:[18] when no legitimacy is expected or sought, the issue of joint military missions appears to become less urgent. An example of a state that decided to act on its own is the Russian Federation in its armed conflict with Georgia in 2008. The Russian Federation had apparently concluded that its own strength would be sufficient to prevail whereas the legal justification for intervention on behalf of Georgia's separatist regions Abkhazia and South Ossetia remained doubtful.[19] A comparable situation occurred in 2014 with regard to the

[13] KJ McInnis, 'Lessons in Coalition Warfare: Past, Present and Implications for the Future' (2013) 1 International Politics Reviews 78, 81.

[14] ibid.

[15] ibid.

[16] K Hald Galster, 'Introduction' in Niels Bo Poulsen and others (eds), *Coalition Warfare: An Anthology of Scholarly Presentations at the Conference on Coalition Warfare at the Royal* (Danish Defence College, 2011) 13 et seq; RC Gross and I Henderson, 'Multinational Operations' in Geoffrey S Corn and others (eds), *U.S. Military Operations: Law, Policy, and Practice* (OUP 2015) 341, 341.

[17] Galster (n 16) 14.

[18] In some states such as Germany, constitutional provisions in some instances require military operations that are typically joint military operations under a mandate of an international organization that qualifies as a system of collective security, see Article 24(2) of the Basic Law for the Federal Republic of Germany.

[19] See N Higgins and K O'Reilly, 'The Use of Force, Wars of National Liberation and the Right to Self-Determination in the South Ossetian Conflict' (2009) 9 International Criminal Law Review 567.

Russian Federation's intervention in Eastern Ukraine. In both cases, Russia had decided not to pursue coalition warfare. Thus, if increased legitimacy is not expected and burden sharing is considered unnecessary to achieve their goals, states are apparently still willing to proceed on their own.

1.2 Legal justifications and mandates

A broad spectrum of mandates is possible when it comes to establishing multinational military operations, relying on virtually all conceivable legal justifications. Most strikingly, the UN Charter itself envisages joint military engagements, explicitly providing for the collective use of force in situations that involve a threat to international peace and security,[20] and acknowledging the important role of regional arrangements in Chapter VIII.

Some forms of collective engagement involve armed contingents without comprising a clear military component, for instance missions with the purpose of monitoring a ceasefire agreement in a post-conflict situation or capacity building missions. Examples include the UN verification mission in Colombia in the aftermath of the country's decades-long civil war[21] or the European Union Training Mission in Mali (EUTM Mali).[22] Such operations are not the focus of this book. Instead, the contributions zoom in on operations that were mandated in such a way as to at least imply the authorization of a resort to force, such as in Afghanistan, the Democratic Republic of the Congo, Libya, Somalia, or Mali.

Concerning possible justifications for such missions, a wide array of legal bases is conceivable. Over the course of the past decade, multinational military operations have often operated with UN Security Council authorization under Chapter VII of the Charter, for example the United Nations Multidimensional Integrated Stabilization Mission in the Central African Republic (MINUSCA), mainly involving troops from other African countries;[23] or arguably the 2011 intervention during the uprising in Libya, claiming to enforce UN Security Council Resolution 1973.[24] It was led by NATO and principally conducted by France and the United Kingdom but involved in total the forces of seventeen states, including four non-NATO nations.[25]

[20] Bernard (n 2) 475.

[21] See UNSC Res 2381 (6 October 2017) UN Doc S/RES/2381.

[22] See European Council Decision on a European Union military mission to contribute to the training of the Malian Armed Forces (EUTM Mali) (17 January 2013) 2013/34/CFSP.

[23] See <https://peacekeeping.un.org/en/mission/minusca>; established by UNSC Res 2149 (10 April 2014) UN Doc S/RES/2149.

[24] UNSC Res 1973 (17 March 2011) UN Doc S/RES 1973.

[25] M Payandeh, 'The United Nations, Military Intervention, and Regime Change in Libya' (2012) 52 Virginia Journal of International Law 355.

In other instances, states have acted in concert upon invitation of a beleaguered government, as for example concerning Operation Astute in Timor-Leste from 2006 to 2013, led by Australia with considerable contributions from New Zealand, Portugal, and Malaysia;[26] in Mali in early 2012, when France and a few other European states cooperated with the Economic Community of West African States (ECOWAS) in order to fight different Islamist factions in the northern part of the state,[27] or against the Islamic State of Iraq and the Levant (ISIL) in Iraq.[28] Regional organizations have intervened in member states in the course of internal armed conflict or other serious turmoil, as for example the African Union in Darfur from 2004 (the African Union Mission in Sudan (AMIS), later dissolved in the United Nations/African Union Hybrid Operation in Darfur (UNAMID)),[29] or ECOWAS in the Gambia since the occurrence of a post-election insurgency and the breakdown of public order in January 2017 (Operation Restore Democracy or ECOMIG).[30]

As for further legal justifications for more recent multinational military operations, partaking states have invoked the right to collective self-defence pursuant to Article 51 of the UN Charter, as for instance regarding the intervention in Afghanistan against the Taliban regime in the aftermath of the terrorist attacks of September 11, 2001;[31] or, more recently, in the case of the US-led coalition strikes against ISIL in Syria, an operation that was justified as a collective self-defence action on behalf of Iraq.[32] Humanitarian grounds in accordance with the 'Responsibility to Protect' doctrine have also been cited on several occasions, as by some participants in the case of the multinational intervention in Libya in 2011,[33] but also in the multinational fight against ISIL in Iraq and Syria.[34]

[26] DR Rothwell and others, *International Law. Cases and Materials with Australian Perspectives* (3rd edn, CUP 2018) 716.

[27] K Bannelier and T Christakis, 'Under the UN Security Council's Watchful Eyes: Military Intervention by Invitation in the Malian Conflict' (2013) 26 Leiden Journal of International Law 855.

[28] See JA Green, 'The "Additional" Criteria for Collective Self-Defence: Request but not Declaration' (2017) 4 Journal on the Use of Force and International Law 4; O Gross, 'Unresolved Legal Questions Concerning Operation Inherent Resolve' (2017) 52 Texas International Law Journal 1; K Bannelier and T Christakis, 'Military Interventions Against ISIL in Iraq, Syria and Libya and the Legal Basis of Consent' (2016) 29 Leiden Journal of International Law 743.

[29] UNSC Res 1769 (31 July 2007) UN Doc S/RES/1769.

[30] I Akwei, 'ECOWAS Okays Military Intervention in Gambia, Joint Troops Stationed at Border' (*AfricaNews*, 18 January 2017) <http://www.africanews.com/2017/01/18/ecowas-okays-military-intervention-in-gambia-joint-troop-stationed-at-border/>.

[31] See eg House of Commons, 'The Legal Basis for the Invasion of Afghanistan' (Standard Note, 26 February 2010) SN/IA/5340.

[32] MP Scharf, 'How the War Against ISIS Changed International Law' (2016) 48 Case Western Reserve Journal of International Law 1, 3.

[33] S Chesterman, '"Leading from Behind": The Responsibility to Protect, the Obama Doctrine, and Humanitarian Intervention after Libya' (2011) 25 Ethics & International Affairs 279.

[34] Scharf (n 32) 48.

1.3 Forms of cooperation

Just as multinational military operations may be conducted under many different mandates relying on varying legal foundations, the possible forms of cooperation between the troop-contributing states and other participating actors are just as manifold. To a certain degree, it is often the mandate that determines the organizational modalities of the mission. What is more, the legal justifications invoked for intervening may change over time, so that different mandates apply to different phases of one and the same multinational mission, correspondingly affecting the modes of cooperation between the individual forces.[35]

While regional organizations assuming a leading role is continuing to become more common, a considerable number of recent multinational missions have operated within the framework of the United Nations. But here, too, vastly different forms of implementation exist. On the one hand, direct UN command is the standard model for traditional peacekeeping missions. Established as subsidiary bodies of the United Nation's principal organs, states allocate their troops to the peacekeeping mission by way of contractual agreements.[36] Examples are the United Nations Operation in Côte d'Ivoire,[37] the United Nations Stabilisation Mission in Haiti,[38] or the United Nations Interim Administration Mission in Kosovo.[39]

If the UN Security Council merely provides a mandate to a multinational operation by authorizing the use of military means with a Chapter VII resolution, on the other hand, the subsequent mission will usually not act within the UN institutional framework. In these cases, the actors that actually carry out the peace enforcement mission, that is either a coalition of states or a regional organization such as the African Union or NATO, retain all command responsibilities.[40] A long-running instance is the ongoing African Union Mission to Somalia,[41] which was established in 2007 by Security Council Resolution 1744.[42] Operating under AU command, six member states have provided troops that are each responsible for different geographic sectors of Somalia. Another significant example for this variant was the International Security Assistance Force in Afghanistan between 2001 and 2014,[43] a NATO-led operation authorized by Security Council Resolution 1386.[44]

35 A case in point is the mission in Mali, which started with a French-led military intervention in 2012 on the basis of a Security Council resolution and an invitation by the Malian government, before it gradually transformed into a United Nations peacekeeping mission (MINUSMA) and a European Union Training Mission (EUTM Mali) from 2013, see <https://minusma.unmissions.org/en/history>.

36 P Starski, 'Zurechnungsfragen bei multinationalen militärischen Einsätzen' in S Kielmansegg, H Krieger, and S Sohm (eds), *Multinationalität und Integration im militärischen Bereich—Eine rechtliche Perspektive* (Nomos 2018) 163–208.

37 ONUCI, see <https://onuci.unmissions.org/en>.

38 MINUSTAH, see <https://minustah.unmissions.org/>.

39 UNMIK, see <https://unmik.unmissions.org/>.

40 Starski (n 36) 17.

41 AMISOM, see <http://amisom-au.org/>.

42 UNSC Res 1744 (21 February 2007) UN Doc S/RES/1744.

43 ISAF, see <https://www.nato.int/cps/en/natohq/topics_69366.htm>.

44 UNSC Res 1386 (20 December 2001) UN Doc S/RES/1386.

A third modality are hybrid or co-led operations that are based on command structures involving both the United Nations and military representatives of a regional organization, such as for example in the already mentioned UNAMID.[45]

On a more granular, operational level, more noteworthy distinctions can be observed. The actual cooperation between states' military organizations in multinational operations will always be tailored to meet the specific circumstances of the respective mission. In some cases, partnered states will in fact combine their forces on the battlefield in joint operations, as during the first months of the 2003 invasion of Iraq by the so-called 'Coalition of the Willing', which involved fighting troops from the United States and the United Kingdom as well as Australia and Poland. Other states provided military contingents without taking an active role in combat, mostly for the purpose of post-invasion stabilization of Iraq.[46] In the Multinational Joint Task Force (MNJTF) Nigeria, Cameroon, Chad, and Niger combined their forces in order to fight the terrorist organization Boko Haram. MNJTF has been acting under the auspices of the Lake Chad Basin Commission (LCBC) since March 1994 and has been endorsed by the African Union Peace and Security Council.[47] When several Arab states started intervening in the civil war in Yemen in 2015 after a joint statement by the Gulf Cooperation Council, the Saudi-led coalition comprised fighter jets from Egypt, Morocco, Jordan, Sudan, Kuwait, the United Arab Emirates, Qatar, and Bahrain.[48]

In other instances, one or a number of states are merely providing logistical support while the forces of one or more allied nations conduct the actual military operations. This approach was followed during Opération Serval. The military operation against Islamic militant groups in northern Mali was principally conducted by France but relied on military transport capabilities by several co-operating states including the United States, the United Kingdom, Canada, and Germany.[49]

The above cases shall merely serve as a rough overview in order to illustrate the spectrum of contemporary multinational military operations, without aiming to provide a full picture of all possible variations. This preliminary mapping shows a

[45] Bernard (n 2) 476.

[46] C Dale, 'Operation Iraqi Freedom: Strategies, Approaches, Results, and Issues for Congress', CRS Report for Congress, updated 28 March 2008, 32.

[47] W Assanvo and others, 'Assessing the Multinational Joint Task Force against Boko Haram, West Africa Report' (Institute for Security Studies, September 2016) <https://issafrica.s3.amazonaws.com/site/uploads/war19.pdf>.

[48] B Nußberger, 'Military Strikes in Yemen in 2015: Invitation by Invitation and Self-Defence in the Course of Yemen's "Model Transitional Process"' (2017) 4 Journal on the Use of Force in International Law 110; for an assessment of plans to institutionalize the cooperation among Arab states see J Noll and S Roll, 'From Yemen War to Joint Army? Egyptian-Saudi Differences over Arab Military Cooperation' (May 2015) 31 SWP Comments.

[49] Bannelier and Christakis (n 27); A Seyedfarshi, 'French Interventionism in the Age of R2P: A Critical Examination of the Case of Mali' (2015) 7 Creighton International and Comparative Law Journal 2.

landscape of possible missions that is both fragmented and fluid. The modalities of each individual case depend on factors such as mandate, operational design, the capabilities of the cooperating states, or their political or strategic willingness to commit to a certain degree of involvement. As no two missions are ever exactly alike, the notion of 'multinational military operations' that underlies the present book should be considered an overarching, intentionally loose and only minimally defined concept. Such a broad approach is necessary, as the great variety that can be observed indicates legal complexity, the analysis of which is the purpose of the present selection of contributions on the topic. This complexity, framed as the eponymous 'legal pluriverse', will briefly be outlined below after a cursory look at the history of multinational military operations.

2. Multinational Military Operations over Time

2.1 Historic development

Military coalitions have been a defining characteristic of much of human history all the way back to antiquity. That being said, what one considers the starting point of the history of multinational military operations strongly depends on one's view as regards the requirements of actual military cooperation on the ground. Already in ancient Greek mythology, the Trojan War was told as a story of a campaign of an alliance of Greek communities against a coalition of their Trojan adversaries. A few centuries later, the Greek city states built various alliances during the wars against the invading troops of the Persian Empire—which in itself should be considered an assemblage of different nations rather than a coherent 'nation'[50]—with wavering endurance and success, culminating in the devastating defeat at the pass of Thermopylae in the late summer of 480 BC.[51]

More to the point, coalition warfare gained traction after the middle ages at the outset of the modern period.[52] However, although a number of European powers were heavily involved in the Thirty Years War, the operations mostly amounted to battles of one entity against another. If collaborations existed at all, they were very limited in time and purpose. Therefore, historians have suggested that it was not until after the establishment of the Westphalian system in 1648 that coalition warfare in the modern sense came into being. As a starting point for the novel

[50] RL DiNardo, 'Coalition and Alliance War' (*Oxford Bibliographies Online*, 22 April 2013) <http://www.oxfordbibliographies.com/view/document/obo-9780199791279/obo-9780199791279-0108.xml>.

[51] Galster (n 16) 1.

[52] See for an attempt to exhaustively and systematically compile all relevant alliances since 1648 (not limited to, but with a heavy focus on the West) DM Gibler, 'International Military Alliances 1648–2008' (CQ Press 2009).

modus operandi of warfare, one may look at the Dutch War in the second half of the seventeenth century, when France's Louis XIV, Britain's Charles II, Münster, and Cologne formed a coalition against the Dutch Republic, which was then assisted by the Habsburg Monarchy, Brandenburg-Prussia, and Spain.[53] A few years later, a pan-European alliance led by King John III Sobieski of Poland broke the Ottoman Empire's siege of Vienna.[54]

The already mentioned wars against Napoleon at the beginning of the nineteenth century serve as another cornerstone for the history of multinational operations. Considering the emerging nationalist currents in the decades after the French Revolution in 1789, they might even count as the first ones to justify the notion 'multinational'. Between 1803 and 1815, seven military coalitions in total were formed in order to eventually defeat the French Empire.[55] Still, it has been pointed out that frequent and severe disagreements between the partnered states long prevented success against Napoleon, which even led him to assert that he preferred to lead war against coalitions.[56] Even at the Battle of Waterloo in 1815, despite fighting as an alliance, Prussia's General Blücher and Britain's Wellington acted separately rather than jointly, so that both partners could assert their own victory against the French army.[57]

Another important event in the history of multinational military operations was the Crimean War in the middle of the century, in which a coalition mainly consisting of the Ottoman, British, and French Empires and the Kingdom of Sardinia fought against the Russian Empire, with contingents from a few smaller European powers on both sides.[58] Moreover, the conflict is noteworthy for serving as the theatre for one of the first deliberate combined forces campaigns as an integral part of a multinational expedition.[59]

Over the course of the nineteenth century, the zenith of the colonial age saw a number of armed conflicts involving military coalitions. Those sometimes engaged in wars between settler-colonial states and metropolitan colonial powers as in the Second Boer War from 1899 and 1902. The war was conducted between the Orange Free State and the South African Republic on the one side, and the British Empire on the other. Britain fought in alliance with troops from some of its colonial subjects such as Australia, New Zealand, India, and Ceylon, but also with a significant contribution by recently independent Canada.[60] Other joint campaigns

[53] *Encyclopaedia Britannica*, 'Dutch War 1672–1678' <https://www.britannica.com/event/Dutch-War>.
[54] DiNardo (n 50).
[55] GE Rothenberg and J Keegan, *The Napoleonic Wars* (Cassell 1999) 16.
[56] OR Holsti and others, *Unity and Disintegration in International Alliances* (Wiley 1973) 22.
[57] Galster (n 16) 11.
[58] JB Agnew, 'The Great War That Almost Was: The Crimea 1853–1856' (1973) 3 Parameters 46.
[59] J Black, *Combined Operations. A Global History of Amphibious and Airborne Warfare* (Rowman & Littlefield 2018) 97.
[60] R Foot and C Miller, 'Canada and the South African War' (*The Canadian Encyclopedia*, 2006) <https://www.thecanadianencyclopedia.ca/en/article/south-african-war>; RG Haycock, 'The Alliance Proving Grounds: Canada in the Anglo-Boer War and the Great War' in RS Rush and WW Epley (eds),

in colonial contexts are even more historically fraught, as for instance the highly problematic suppression of the Boxer Rebellion in northern China between 1899 and 1901, conducted by an alliance of no fewer than eight colonial powers against the insurgent Yìhéquán and the declining Qing Dynasty's forces.[61]

While the United States remained a decidedly reluctant co-belligerent, not entering the First World War before 1917,[62] the war proved to be a test case for coalitions between Europe's main powers. On the side of the western alliance, early German advances made concerted action necessary, resulting in the foundation of the Supreme War Council in 1917 which comprised military representatives from the United Kingdom, France, Italy, and the United States.[63] In the view of prevalent scholarship, adopting a united and centralized framework for the military campaign ultimately assured victory despite differences among the allies.[64] During the Second World War, the efforts by the leaders of the United Kingdom, the Soviet Union, and the United States to come together in the Grand Alliance after 1941—despite virtually irreconcilable ideological disparities—proved crucial in order to defeat the Axis Powers. Britain and the United States went as far as to fully integrate their respective armed forces in the Combined Chiefs of Staff (CCS) in Washington DC in January of 1942, the body through which the allies subsequently jointly made all relevant decisions for the war.[65]

In contrast to the two World Wars, some of the most noteworthy armed conflicts of the Cold War period were characterized by states conducting military campaigns largely on their own despite being members of collective defence organizations. Some of these armed conflicts fall into the category of ideological proxy wars along the East/West divide, such as the Soviet Union's intervention into Afghanistan in 1979.[66] Others marked the end of the colonial era, when European powers were confronted with independence wars in their overseas territories. The Algerian war from 1954 until 1962 may serve as the most striking example in this regard.[67] The war in Vietnam, by contrast, while mostly remembered as principally a solo campaign by the United States, is an important case in point for the legitimizing function of coalition building. Being acutely aware of the shaky moral, legal,

Multinational Operations, Alliances, and International Military Cooperation. Past and Future (Center for Military History, US Army 2006) 39.

---

[61] DJ Silbey, *The Boxer Rebellion and the Great Game in China* (Hill and Wang 2012).

[62] SJ Cimbala and PK Forster, *Multinational Military Intervention. NATO Policy, Strategy and Burden Sharing* (Ashgate Publishing 2010) 193 et seq.

[63] JB Agnew, 'Coalition Warfare: A Successful Experiment in Combined Command, 1914–1918' (1971) 1 Parameters 50, 56.

[64] ibid 63 et seq.

[65] M Matloff, *Strategic Planning for Coalition Warfare, 1943–1944* (Office of the Chief of Military History Department of the Army 1959) 5.

[66] G Feifer, *The Great Gamble: The Soviet War in Afghanistan* (Harper Perennial 2010).

[67] G Merom, *How Democracies Lose Small Wars. State, Society, and the Failures of France in Algeria, Israel in Lebanon, and the United States in Vietnam* (CUP 2003) 83 et seq.

and political grounds on which the decision to intervene on behalf of the Saigon government stood, the decision-makers in Washington DC made a serious effort to convince allied nations in the region, mainly Australia and New Zealand, to participate in the conduct of hostilities in Vietnam, chiefly out of political rather than military considerations.[68]

Also during the post-Second World War period, a series of armed conflicts in the Middle East saw an effectively solitary Israel threatened and attacked by a number of Arab coalitions,[69] starting on the day after Israel's declaration of independence in May 1948.[70] Within the context of multinational military operations, these conflicts are notable for the repeated, decisively premature dissolution of the wartime coalitions between the Arab nations despite a similar cultural and religious background and the shared goal of defeating the Israeli state.[71]

Since the end of the Cold War and the bipolar world order, multinational military operations have vastly increased not only in number, but also in overall geo-political significance. A first test of the new multilateral reality came in 1991 with Operation Desert Storm, the coalition campaign to end Iraq's occupation of Kuwait.[72] At the same time, however, it laid bare frictions among the involved parties, in particular the five permanent members of the UN Security Council which had mandated the Chapter VII operation with Resolution 678.[73] While the United States advocated a further invasion of Iraq with the aim of removing Saddam Hussein, the Soviet Union and France, in accordance with the Arab members of the warring coalition, were strongly in favour of sticking to the more limited objectives as stated in the resolution. Ultimately, the United States did not follow through.[74] Over the course of the 1990s, the armed conflicts triggered by the dissolution of the Socialist Federal Republic of Yugoslavia gave rise to increasingly institutionalized, long-term engagements of multinational forces. These forces were led by international organizations such as the United Nations or NATO and endowed with progressively robust mandates. Still, failures and shortcomings could not be prevented[75]—most momentously the United Nations Protection Force's (UNPROFOR) inaptitude to prevent the genocide in the Bosnian town of

[68] J Colman, 'The Challenges of Coalition-Building: The Vietnam Experience, 1964–1969' (*RUSI*, 15 March 2010) <https://rusi.org/commentary/challenges-coalition-building-vietnam-experience-1964-1969>.

[69] *Encyclopaedia Britannica*, 'Arab-Israeli Wars' <https://www.britannica.com/event/Arab-Israeli-wars>.

[70] A Shlaim, 'Israel and the Arab Coalition in 1948' in E Rogan and A Shlaim (eds), *The War for Palestine: Rewriting the History of 1948* (2nd edn, CUP 2007) 79.

[71] See in detail A Kober, *Coalition Defection: The Dissolution of Arab Anti-Israeli Coalitions in War and Peace* (Praeger 2002).

[72] H Mashhud *Choudhry, Coalition Warfare—Can the Gulf War-91 Be the Model for Future?* (US Army War College 1992).

[73] UNSC Res 678 (29 November 1990) UN Doc SC/RES/678.

[74] Cimbala and Forster (n 62) 4.

[75] ibid 5.

Srebrenica in 1995, which was traced back to a number of factors, inter alia the lack of a clear mandate and a lack of coordination between political leaders and military commanders.[76]

The terrorist attacks of September 11, 2001 turned out to become yet another watershed in the evolution of multinational military operations. Not only did NATO for the first time in the alliance's history invoke Article 5 of the North Atlantic Treaty, which determines that an attack against one member is considered an attack against all,[77] for the subsequent intervention in Afghanistan against the Taliban regime, the United States could count on the support of a wide-ranging coalition of states, not only consisting of NATO members. After the UN Security Council had established the International Security Assistance Force (ISAF) in order to assist the transition towards a democratic government in Kabul, no fewer than forty-three states were involved in the operation.[78] However, for the invasion of Iraq in 2003 which lacked UN authorization, the United States were compelled to form a 'Coalition of the Willing' of concurring states. It eventually comprised troops from the United Kingdom, Australia, and Poland, with other states joining after the initial phase of armed conflict in order to provide assistance during the transition.[79] Just like a few decades earlier in Vietnam, building a coalition mainly served the purpose of enhancing legitimacy for a legally and politically fraught endeavour.

The rich and well-documented history of peacekeeping and peace enforcement operations under the auspices of the United Nations and regional organizations, finally, calls for a treatment of its own.[80] It represents a prevalent yet clearly distinct category of multinational military operations. Arguably having their beginnings as early as in the 1920s in the form of delimitation commissions to redraw certain frontiers in Europe in the aftermath of the First World War[81] these missions were initially mostly confined to small-scale observer missions.[82] Over time peacekeeping and peace enforcement missions have become a staple of international

[76] The Hague Institute for Global Justice, 'International Decision-Making in the Age of Genocide: Srebrenica 1993–1995' (Rapporteur Report, The Hague 2015) 2 et seq.

[77] S Daley, 'After the Attacks: The Alliance; For First Time, NATO Invokes Joint Defense Pact with U.S.' *The New York Times* (New York, 13 September 2001) A00017.

[78] AJ Rubin, 'NATO Chief Promises to Stand by Afghanistan' *The New York Times* (New York, 22 December 2009) A14; Cimbala and Forster (n 62) 149 et seq.

[79] S Schifferes, 'US Names "Coalition of the Willing"' (*BBC News*, 18 March 2003) <http://news.bbc.co.uk/2/hi/americas/2862343.stm>.

[80] See only R Hatto, 'From Peacekeeping to Peacebuilding: The Evolution of the Role of the United Nations in Peace Operations' (2013) 95 International Review of the Red Cross 495; JT O'Neill and N Rees, *United Nations Peacekeeping in the Post-Cold War Era* (Routledge Chapman & Hall 2005); A Adebajo, *UN Peacekeeping in Africa: From the Suez Crisis to the Sudan Conflicts* (Lynne Rienner Publishers 2011); for an examination of the applicable law see T Gill and others (eds), *Leuven Manual on the International Law Applicable to Peace Operations* (CUP 2017).

[81] See M Goulding, 'The Evolution of United Nations Peacekeeping' (1993) 69 International Affairs 451, 452.

[82] Bernard (n 2) 478.

security governance. In particular after the end of the Cold War, they not only vastly increased in number, as already mentioned, but also became much broader in scope, with a growing focus on the protection of civilians in armed conflicts and post-conflict stabilization.[83] Since 1948, there have been seventy-one peacekeeping operations within the UN framework, with 124 states contributing uniformed personnel.[84] The most troops have been sent by India, Bangladesh, and Pakistan.[85]

Since the 1990s, regional organizations have increasingly taken on a more prominent role in peacekeeping and peace enforcement, more often than not in concert with the United Nations.[86] The three organizations that stand out are the African Union, the European Union, and NATO. In 2003, the African Union, which superseded the Organisation of African Unity in 2002, conceived its Peace and Security Council (PSC AU), whose mission statement is to actively promote stability on the continent. That same year, it oversaw the first operation, the African Mission in Burundi (AMIB),[87] made up of forces from South Africa, Ethiopia, and Mozambique, before the United Nations assumed primary operational responsibility in 2004.[88] Since then, missions have been conducted in Sudan (AMIS, 2004–06),[89] Comoros (AMISEC, 2006; MAES, 2007–08),[90] Mali (AFISMA, 2013; subsequently transformed into the already mentioned UN-led MINUSMA),[91] and the Central African Republic (MISCA, 2013–14; subsequently transformed into UN-led MINUSCA).[92]

The Amsterdam Treaty, concluded in 1999, legally enabled the European Union to conduct multinational operations on the basis of its Common Foreign and Security Policy (CFSP) and the European Security and Defence Policy (ESDP), the latter of which has since been transformed into the Common Security and Defence Policy (CSDP). Since the EU started conducting military and civilian crisis management operations in 2003, roughly thirty such missions have been undertaken.[93]

[83] Gill (n 80) 6 et seq.
[84] United Nations Peacekeeping, 'Peacekeeping Operations Fact Sheet' (30 April 2018) <https://peacekeeping.un.org/sites/default/files/pk_factsheet_04_18_eng_0.pdf>.
[85] Bernard (n 2) 477.
[86] Gill (n 80) 8.
[87] IA Badmus, 'The African Mission in Burundi (AMIB): A Study of the African Union's Peacekeeping Success and "Triangular Area of Tension in African Peacekeeping"' (2017) 73 India Quarterly: A Journal of International Affairs 1.
[88] Gill (n 80) 20.
[89] Human Rights Watch, 'Sudan: Imperatives for Immediate Change. The African Union Mission in Sudan' (19 January 2006) <https://www.hrw.org/report/2006/01/19/sudan-imperatives-immediate-change/african-union-mission-sudan>.
[90] E Svensson, 'The African Union's Operations in the Comoros. MAES and Operation Democracy, Defence Analysis' (*Swedish Defence Research Agency*, Stockholm 2008) <http://www.operationspaix.net/DATA/DOCUMENT/5040~v~The_African_Union__8217s_Operations_in_the_Comoros.pdf>.
[91] M Caparini, 'The Mali Crisis and Responses by Regional Actors, NUPI Working Paper 849' (*Norwegian Institute of International Affairs*, Oslo 2015) <https://brage.bibsys.no/xmlui/bitstream/id/366213/NUPI_WP_849+Marina+Caparini.pdf>.
[92] <http://www.misca.peaceau.org/en/>.
[93] See European Union External Action, 'Military and Civilian Missions and Operations' <https://eeas.europa.eu/headquarters/headquarters-homepage/430/military-and-civilian-missions-and-operations_en>.

As already hinted at, NATO started transforming from the mutual defence arrangement that it had been conceived of during the Cold War into a more multipurpose collective security organization. Taking on more diverse tasks, the alliance conducted its first multinational operation with the aim of keeping and enforcing peace in Bosnia and Herzegovina in 1995 (Implementation Force, IFOR), followed a year later by the Stabilisation Force (SFOR).[94] Conduct in former Yugoslavia (FRY) was completed with the 1999 KFOR mission in Kosovo, which was deployed in the aftermath of NATO's air campaign against the FRY.[95] Since June 2007, the alliance has been assisting the AU Mission in Somalia (AMISOM), providing airlift duties.[96]

2.2 Trends and changes concerning the nature of multinational operations

The historic development of multinational military operations over the course of the last centuries has shown a clear evolution from ad hoc alliances, formed for rather limited purposes in the context of military campaigns or certain theatres of conflict, to institutionalized and multi-purpose tools of international security governance in the post-Cold War global order that often run over the course of a number of years.

For a number of years after 1990, the most important factor for this observed change was the increased role of international and regional organizations as collective security arrangements in not only mandating, but more and more also leading and conducting multinational military operations. Save a few prominent exceptions, military missions towards the end of the twentieth century and at the beginning of the twenty-first were performed within the framework of larger associations of states, more often than not on the basis of a mandate issued by an international organization. This trend both boosted legitimacy of such operations in the eyes of the global constituency and helped—at least to some degree—to more evenly distribute their costs and burdens.[97] At the same time, a growing perception of the global institutionalized system as an administrator of world peace and security made military solutions more likely, ever so often treating the combined states' armed forces as a globally deployable, transnational police force.[98] However, it bears mentioning that over the past couple of years, the mentioned trend has slowly started to reverse. Marking yet another shift, this time diverging from

94 ibid 23.
95 <https://www.nato.int/cps/en/natolive/topics_48818.htm>.
96 Gill (n 80) 24.
97 Galster (n 16) Preface; see already the National Security Strategy of the U.S. 1994, available at <http://nssarchive.us/NSSR/1994.pdf>, 6 et seq.
98 Cimbala and Forster (n 62) 9.

internationally mandated missions, more states have started to conduct military operations unilaterally and within the framework of ad hoc coalitions with other willing allies again. In legal terms, those states have been more likely to invoke the right to self-defence or the doctrine of humanitarian intervention rather than to rely on a Security Council authorization—as seen above in the cases of Iraq, Syria, or Eastern Ukraine.

This redefined function of multinational missions has become particularly apparent in the so-called global 'war on terrorism', a genuinely borderless conflict involving a great number of states in varying constellations, engaged in different missions, operating with shifting mandates, and embedded in various institutional frameworks. One noteworthy feature of most of these missions is their clear military mandate. At the same time, the objectives vary, ranging from administering post-conflict transition in Afghanistan to suppression of piracy off the East African coast and on the Somalian mainland,[99] or active counter-terrorism operations against ISIL in Syria and Iraq.[100] And even though the so-called 'war on terrorism' after September 11, 2001 has mostly been performed under leadership of the United States, there is a general understanding that pursuing a broad international alliance of states is indispensable if any kind of long-term successful outcome is to be achieved.[101]

Regional organizations' more recent shift from constituting collective defence alliances to functioning as collective security arrangements has entailed considering ever more global issues as being matters of security. This shift broadened not only the organizations' operative scope but crucially also increased the number of situations which are deemed fit to be treated with a combination of multinational armed forces, police, and civilian administrators.[102] At the same time, it has been observed that multilateralism has made it easier for states to commit troops or other officials to such operations. Heightened legitimization, in combination with functional control by an international organization, in many states fulfils the high legal requirements set up by their constitutional arrangements and leads to more acceptance by the troop-sending states' populations.[103]

This trend has been expedited by further efforts to properly institutionalize multinational operations. As mentioned, the United Nations now routinely works in concert with other international organizations. As for regional consolidation, it

[99] R Geiß and A Petrig, *Piracy and Armed Robbery at Sea: The Legal Framework for Counter-Piracy Operations in Somalia and the Gulf of Aden* (OUP 2011); M Sterio, 'Fighting Piracy in Somalia (and Elsewhere): Why More is Needed' (2009) 33 Fordham International Law Journal 372; Eric A Heinze, 'A "Global War on Piracy?" International Law and the Use of Force against Sea Pirates' in MJ Struett and others (eds), *Maritime Piracy and the Construction of Global Governance* (Routledge 2013) 47.

[100] Bannelier and Christakis (n 28); MP Scharf, 'How the War against ISIS Changed International Law' (2016) 48 Case Western Reserve Journal of International Law 16.

[101] Cimbala and Forster (n 62) 207.

[102] ibid 14.

[103] ibid 28.

is noteworthy to point to recent attempts by the African Union to set up permanent standby brigades with military, police, and civilian components for five defined regions on the continent. Two of those have been operational since the autumn of 2016.[104]

3. Contemporary Multinational Military Operations

3.1 Stocktaking

Most current multinational military operations have been mentioned in the sections above. At the time of writing, there are fourteen active UN peacekeeping operations. Seven of those are set on the African continent, two in Europe, one in the Caribbean, one in South Asia, and three in the Middle East.[105] UNAMID, the UN mission in Darfur, is conducted jointly with the African Union. The other ongoing African Union operation is AMISOM, deployed to Somalia since 2007.

Outside the peacekeeping context, multinational missions of note are—with or without UN mandate—the Saudi-led intervention in Yemen and the multiforce conduct against ISIL in Iraq and Syria, which consists both of an air campaign by various nations and special forces operations on the ground. Operation Atalanta, the EU-led mission to fight piracy in the Western Indian Ocean that includes capacities from a couple of non-EU states, has been active since 2008.[106]

3.2 Legal questions and challenges

A look at the list of current multinational military operations, noting their phenotypical differences, leads to the issue of the legal questions and other challenges connected to them today. As a direct result of the mentioned diversity of mandates, setups, and general operational activities, multinational military operations are subject to a multitude of partly distinct, partly overlapping legal regimes. In this context, it has already been alluded to that necessarily, a mission's underlying mandate and legal justification to some degree determines the relevant applicable rules. Yet as there is no 'standard model' for multinational operations given the spectrum of possible engagements and modalities, few universal norms can be derived in the abstract. While for a field as established as peace operations under the auspices of the United Nations it is instructive to compile some kind of rulebook of recurring legal standards,[107] for multinational military operations more generally

[104] Gill (n 80) 17.
[105] See Peacekeeping Operations Fact Sheet (n 84).
[106] <http://eunavfor.eu/>.
[107] See generally Gill (n 80).

it seems at least equally important to approach the topic by way of focusing on the different relevant subject matters. Those include, inter alia, the law governing the *jus ad bellum*, international humanitarian law, international human rights law,[108] international environmental law, the law of the sea, the law of state jurisdiction, state immunity, or the law governing state responsibility.[109] That is the approach of the present book.

Of course, not all challenges are matters of international—or indeed national[110]—law. Quite the contrary: many of the peculiar intricacies concerning the interoperability of the different parts of recent or current multinational missions can be explained by looking at cultural and related discrepancies,[111] or problems caused by the sheer dimension of the undertaking. The more states contribute to a single operation, the more obvious the drawbacks of collaboration become. To be mentioned here are differences in strategic or cultural leadership approaches, diverging ethical guidelines that are sometimes heavily informed by varying religious backgrounds,[112] or different cultural attitudes towards casualties among one's own troops.[113] To name an example, the participation of women soldiers in multinational operations, in particular in commanding ranks, might trigger complications with contingents from nations whose cultures are not accustomed to this practice, or perhaps even reject it outright on the grounds of cultural or religious principle.[114] A crucial difference with potentially serious ramifications in the field has been observed between troops from individualist and collectivist cultures as regards the communication process. While armed forces members from individualist societies tend to communicate more directly, groups with a collectivist cultural approach are inclined 'to deliver inborn, ambiguous, context-sensitive messages' that may be hard to fully grasp by individuals from outside such groups.[115] There are also more practical downsides such as logistical challenges, capability or training deficiencies among some of the involved actors as compared to their partners. Probably above all else, there are the pitfalls of speaking different languages that invariably need to be taken into account when planning the operation or individual tasks in the operation's course.[116] In fact, the language problem

[108] S Hill and D Lemétayer, 'Legal Issues of Multinational Military Operations: An Alliance Perspective' (2016) 55 Military Law and the Law of War Review 13, 17.

[109] Starski (n 36); P Palchetti, 'The Allocation of Responsibility for Internationally Wrongful Acts Committed in the Course of Multinational Operations' (2013) 95 International Review of the Red Cross 727.

[110] See for an overview eg G Nolte (ed), *European Military Law Systems* (De Gruyter 2003).

[111] N Leonhard, 'Multinational Co-operation within the MNTF SE in Mostar—General Conclusions' in N Leonhard and others (eds), *Military Co-operation in Multinational Missions: The Case of EUFOR in Bosnia and Herzegovina* (SOWI 2008) 241, 244 et seq.

[112] Galster (n 16) 10.

[113] ibid 13 et seq.

[114] M Smolarek, 'Challenges for Leading Multinational and Multicultural Military Units' (2016) 2 Journal on Baltic Security 183, 191.

[115] I Goldbach and F Rapan, 'The Effects of Cultural Interactions in Multinational Military Missions' (International Conference RCIC'17, Bucharest 2018) 420, 423.

[116] McInnis (n 13) 83.

is most often cited as one of the principal causes of inefficiency and shortcomings of multinational military operations.[117]

What is more, even if states agree to engage in a joint military mission, that does not necessarily mean that their strategic political interests or long-term goals are aligned. Individual states frequently arrive with vastly differing understandings of what the operation is supposed to achieve. More to the point, several scholars have argued that an actual unity of purpose, one that is beneficial to the functioning of the coalition, requires a grave and imminent threat to the involved actors. Only in such cases, as for instance in the campaign to defeat Napoleon, can the overwhelming pressure of having to collaborate for success overcome the negative aspects of cooperation.[118]

Where such an incentive is missing, a clear and agreed-upon legal framework can in fact not only constrain the actors but may rather serve as a stable ground from which the mission is then able to achieve its objectives. By circumscribing each contributing military's possible conduct, the applicable body of law can conceal existing strategic or cultural differences and thus contribute to a multinational military operation's ultimate success. This consideration only further shows why it is crucial to examine and appraise the legal pluriverse surrounding these missions, and why a coherent legal framework which takes their factual complexities into account is necessary.[119]

To be sure, that is neither an easy nor obvious task. While practical challenges regarding multinational operations certainly haunt many military commanders and political decision-makers, it seems fair to say that sifting through the legal pluriverse in the attempt to provide systematic coherence is still in its infancy. It starts with identifying the legal situations a multinational military operation engages in: the determination whether it constitutes an international or a non-international armed conflict, or even an armed conflict in the first place,[120] has wide-ranging implications for the rules applicable to the mission, stemming from international humanitarian law, international human rights law, or domestic law.[121] Yet even this often less than straightforward assessment only solves part of the calculus. To some extent depending on the mandate, multilateral agreements such as the International Covenant on Civil and Political Rights or specifications comprised in a UN Security Council resolution shape the mission's outlines and influence the applicable legal framework.

[117] Galster (n 16) 8; A van Dijk, 'Tough Talk: Clear and Cluttered Communication during Peace Operations' in J Soeters and P Manigart (eds), *Military Cooperation in Multinational Peace Operations. Managing Cultural Diversity and Crisis Response* (Routledge 2008) 70.

[118] McInnis (n 13) 88.

[119] Bernard (n 2) 479.

[120] E David and O Engdahl, 'How Does the Involvement of a Multinational Peacekeeping Force Affect the Classification of a Situation?' (2013) 95 International Review of the Red Cross 659.

[121] Bernard (n 2) 480.

But even then, it will still likely be the case that the different troop-contributing states and other actors involved are subject to widely different international obligations. While some legal regimes such as the Geneva Conventions or the UN Charter will apply to all,[122] the individual states may commit to diverging status-of-forces agreements with the host state; they may not be party to the same international treaties that are applicable to the situation *ratione materiae*, such as the Protocols to the Geneva Conventions; they likely have varying rules of engagement, and their domestic laws or court decisions may impose irreconcilable national caveats on the respective missions. For example, during the KFOR operation in Kosovo, German forces could not be deployed to counter ongoing riots as they were legally prevented from using tear gas.[123] This imperfect list shows the crucial importance of identifying and clarifying the applicable legal framework for all involved stakeholders, if possible, prior to the operation's beginning—not least because the failure to meet the given legal standards may have a serious negative impact on the legitimacy and the prospects of success. If certain issues cannot be resolved beforehand, some states might be inclined to back out before committing forces to a legally fraught undertaking.[124]

At the same time, a number of legal questions will probably not arise before the troops of the multinational mission start operating on the ground. In such a case, there will be the need to find and establish specific solutions ad hoc under time pressure. Moreover, in the case that the dispatched troops have violated international law, the contentious question of attribution and (state) responsibility becomes pertinent. Depending on the mission's operational and institutional design, numerous legal issues remain to be solved regarding this particular subject matter.[125]

To take stock of this legal pluriverse and to help make sense of it in order to gradually move towards a more coherent regime is the subject of the present book. The following section briefly outlines its five main parts and the legal problems that are dealt with by the contributing authors in their individual chapters.

4. The Structure of this Book

The book is divided into five main parts. Part I deals with the geographical and temporal scope of the laws of armed conflict, before the examination turns towards different perspectives on the relationship between international humanitarian law and human rights law (Part II). The contributions in this section are followed by an

122 Gross and Henderson (n 16) 342.
123 See Chapter 19 by Katze and Kashgar in this book.
124 Gross and Henderson (n 16) 343.
125 Starski (n 36) 3.

analysis of the specific interaction of the laws of armed conflict and human rights law in a core area of the laws of armed conflict, namely the conduct of hostilities, with regard to detention, law enforcement, and precautions in attack in particular (Part III). Part IV tackles the role of public international law in relation to military operations, before Part V concludes the book with an investigation of the diversity of actors and its impact on the legal pluriverse surrounding multinational military operations.

4.1 Part I: The application and interoperability of the laws of armed conflict to multinational military operations

The application of the law of armed conflict to multinational military operations basically determines the legal framework on the basis of which the operation proceeds. Part I commences by analysing the legal implications of the application of international humanitarian law to multinational military operations.

Katja Schöberl considers the still contentious issue of the geographical scope of international humanitarian law in non-international armed conflicts, with particular attention to the challenges for multinational military operations. *Christian Schaller* explores the temporal scope of application of the laws of armed conflict in multinational military operations considering that determining the end of an armed conflict may not always be a straightforward exercise in situations of persistent instability. For that purpose, the chapter identifies and categorizes classes of rules with varying temporal dimensions. *Michael Newton*'s contribution closes the chapter with an in-depth analysis of the legal interoperability of the laws of armed conflict.

4.2 Part II: Laws of armed conflict and international human rights law in the context of multinational military operations: a matter of perspective?

Drawing on the findings of the first section, Part II is devoted to the long-standing discussion on the relationship between the laws of armed conflict and international human rights law. Typically, multinational military operations will operate at the very intersection of the two bodies of law. The section thus critically considers the increasingly prevalent albeit controversial presumption that given the fluidity and fragmentation of modern conflicts, a move towards further convergence of applicable standards is the appropriate way ahead.

While *Hans Boddens Hosang* examines the relationship from an operational viewpoint, *Kenneth Watkin* offers a North American perspective on the debate and explains in detail why exclusionary approaches are, in general, favoured in the

United States and Canada. In the subsequent chapter, *Gentian Zyberi* and *Anna Andersson* take the opposite view from a European standpoint. Arguing in favour of defragmentation, the authors carry out a comprehensive survey of the various instances of international humanitarian law (IHL) and international human rights law (IHRL) substantially influencing each other in contexts in which multinational military operations typically operate.

4.3 Part III: Laws of armed conflict and international human rights law in the context of multinational military operations: law enforcement, detention, hostilities, and precautions in attack as relevant cases in point

Part III further illustrates the proposition of substantive convergence and considers three crucial fields of significant operational importance in contemporary missions in which the fraught interplay between the laws of armed conflict and international human rights law becomes particularly relevant, namely law enforcement, detention, and the obligation to take precautions in attack.

Héctor Olásolo and his colleagues devote their case study to the legal difficulties that military missions face when fighting crime in times of armed conflict. When multinational military forces are, as is frequently the case, simultaneously engaged in genuine military operations as well as traditional law enforcement and policing tasks, they operate at the intersection of the laws of armed conflict and human rights law.

Detention in the context of multinational military operations is the focus of *Jacques Hartmann*'s contribution. Discussing a variety of recent court decisions regarding the issue—most prominently by the ECtHR—as well as relevant norm-finding efforts such as the Copenhagen process, and recent global state practice, the author analyses applicable legal bases, procedures, and constraints concerning detentions.

Marking one of the most discussed and critical cases regarding the relationship between the laws of armed conflict and human rights law, *Andreas von Arnauld* takes another look at the ECtHR's decision in the case *Hassan v UK*. The author evaluates the decision with a focus on its prospective influence on the global debate regarding the relationship between the two bodies of law. Conversely, representing the exclusionary camp, *Yaël Ronen* offers an innovative line of argumentation against the application of human rights law to the extraterritorial conduct of hostilities by military operations.

Geoffrey Corn then zooms in on the potential of precautionary measures for the effective protection of civilians from the perspective of IHL, with novel attention on the planning stage of military operations and the training of soldiers. As opposed to Corn, *Tilmann Altwicker* takes a progressive human rights approach to precautions. Analysing the ECtHR's jurisprudence in this regard, the contribution compares precautions under IHL and IHRL, illustrating the mutual impact of both regimes.

4.4 Part IV: The role of pertinent subfields of public international law in relation to multinational military operations

The next part identifies the various other legal regimes that are part of the legal pluriverse surrounding multinational military operations, such as environmental law or the law of the sea, but also potentially mission-defining status-of-forces agreements.

While *Pia Hesse* examines UN Security Council resolutions as a legal framework for multinational military operations, *Dieter Fleck* devotes his contribution to an analysis of status-of-forces agreements, proposing policy guidelines on indispensable core elements of such agreements. *Paulina Starski*'s analysis focuses on the conditions under which wrongful conduct committed during multinational military operations can be attributed to international organizations or troop- and other contributing states. Furthermore, the prerequisites of multiple attribution and responsibility are examined.

The protection of the environment during multinational military operations is the focus of the subsequent chapter. *Onita Das* considers the ILC's recent work regarding the issue but goes beyond these developments, exploring how multinational military operations are influenced more generally by international environmental law. The fourth part is concluded by *Anna Petrig*'s contribution on the law of the sea in relation to multinational military operations. Taking counter-piracy, counter-terrorism, and security interventions in the context of illegal fishing, drug- and weapons-trafficking as relevant examples, her chapter examines the rules applicable to maritime law enforcement operations.

4.5 Part V: Complex operational environments: diversity of actors and its impact on the legal pluriverse surrounding multinational military operations

Part V turns to the diversity of actors involved in or affected by multinational military operations. In particular, non-state armed groups may be subject to legal and factual asymmetries in relation to the multinational military operation. In light of this, the section explores the extent of said asymmetry, and analyses its effects on the practice of the multinational mission.

In his contribution, *Aurel Sari* examines the additional legal dimensions brought into the legal pluriverse by the domestic laws of the territorial state on the one hand

and the troop-contributing state on the other, which have the tendency to magnify conflicts between the different applicable legal regimes. Diverging domestic legal standards of troop-contributing states are frequently addressed by so-called national caveats, as *Jochen Katze* and *Maral Kashgar* show in their chapter. They explain the legal framework for such caveats, assess their significance, and analyse relevant recent jurisprudence.

In view of the fact that it is common practice to outsource various tasks to private security companies, *Hin-Yan Liu* analyses how this practice and the involvement of private actors affects the contracting state, the home state, and the territorial state in relation to the complexity of the legal framework of a multinational mission. *Robert Frau* exposes the various dimensions and implications of asymmetry in armed conflicts, particularly when multinational military operations are involved. Three aspects of asymmetry—legal, factual, and methodological—are identified. Finally, *Andreas Müller* highlights one especially material legal asymmetry, the question of human rights obligations of non-state armed groups. The contribution traces the evolution of international legal practice in this regard over the past decade.

PART I

THE APPLICATION AND INTEROPERABILITY OF THE LAWS OF ARMED CONFLICT TO MULTINATIONAL MILITARY OPERATIONS

1

Multinational Military Operations and the Geographical Scope of the Laws of Armed Conflict in Non-International Armed Conflict

Katja Schöberl

1. Introduction

Current military operations against organized non-state armed groups are frequently conducted in areas of limited statehood, including through third-party (multilateral) interventions. Concomitant asymmetries in warfare become apparent not only in the means and methods of warfare available and of avail to unequal conflict parties, but also in the location of battlefields.[1] States increasingly engage in combat in far-away locations while their own territory and civilian population remain unaffected by hostilities—albeit not by armed conflict in general considering, for example, the effects of casualties on next-of-kin and societies at large. Recent examples include the United Nations Multidimensional Integrated Stabilization Mission (MINUSMA) in Mali, which was established in 2013.[2] These military operations raise not only political questions about the democratic control of armed forces as fighting occurs removed from capitals and constituencies.[3] They also pose challenges to the legal classification of armed conflicts, in particular to the definition of their geographical boundaries.

This chapter aims to contribute to the ongoing debate[4] about the geographical scope of application of international humanitarian law (IHL) by setting out

[1] See further E Benvenisti, 'The Legal Battle to Define the Law on Transnational Asymmetric Warfare' (2010) 20 Duke Journal of Comparative and International Law 339, 344.

[2] UNSC Res 2100 (25 April 2013) UN Doc S/RES/2100; UNSC Res 2100 (ibid) transferred authority from a previous ECOWAS/AU-mandated African-led International Support Mission in Mali (AFISMA) to the newly established MINUSMA.

[3] See generally H Wulf, 'Good Governance Beyond Borders: Creating a Multi-Level Public Monopoly of Legitimate Force' (Geneva Centre for the Democratic Control of Armed Forces, Occasional Paper Series 10, 2006) <https://www.files.ethz.ch/isn/17430/occasional_10.pdf>. All URLs last accessed 27 December 2018.

[4] See eg Study Group, 'Interim Report on the Conduct of Hostilities and International Humanitarian Law Challenges of 21st Century Warfare' (International Law Association, London 2014). The notion of a 'geographical scope of application of international humanitarian law' was first addressed systematically

Katja Schöberl, *Multinational Military Operations and the Geographical Scope of the Laws of Armed Conflict in Non-International Armed Conflict* In *The 'Legal Pluriverse' Surrounding Multinational Military Operations.* Edited by Robin Geiß and Heike Krieger, Oxford University Press (2020).
DOI: 10.1093/oso/9780198842965.003.0002

for discussion some reflections on the internal and external geographical scope of non-international armed conflicts (NIACs) involving multinational military operations successively.

For the purpose of this chapter, NIACs are understood as armed conflicts between armed forces of a state and organized non-state armed groups, or between such groups, provided a certain threshold of violence is met and a sufficient degree of organization of the conflict parties is fulfilled.[5] They need to be distinguished from internal disturbances and tensions, such as riots, isolated and sporadic acts of violence, and other acts of a similar nature, to which IHL does not apply.[6]

2. Internal Geographical Scope of NIACs

The internal geographical scope of NIACs has recently become the subject of attention and debate with respect to Syria. Several statements of the International Committee of the Red Cross (ICRC) between May and July 2012 seemed to suggest that while the ICRC was publicly classifying the situation as an NIAC, it was considering it to be limited to certain parts of the Syrian territory. Most prominently,[7] its former President Jakob Kellenberger is reported to have told *Reuters* that since the conflict in the city of Homs and province of Idlib had met the criteria of intensity, duration, and level of organization of organized non-state armed groups, 'a situation of internal armed conflict in certain areas' had come into existence—which was described as 'a localized civil war'.[8] Following a debate among commentators,[9]

by the International Criminal Tribunal for the Former Yugoslavia (ICTY) with respect to the various armed conflicts having taken place within the territory of the former Socialist Federal Republic of Yugoslavia. Most of the debate was, however, generated through later cross-border military operations, such as those initially labelled as being part of the so-called 'Global War on Terror' in response to the attacks against the United States on September 11, 2001.

[5] *Prosecutor v Duško Tadić a/k/a 'Dule'* (Appeal Chamber Decision on the Defence Motion for Interlocutory Appeal on Jurisdiction) ICTY-94-1-AR7 (2 October 1995) para 70 (*Tadić*). For a summary of the ICTY's interpretation of both criteria, see ICTY, *Prosecutor v Ramush Haradinaj, Idriz Balaj and Lahi Brahimaj* (Trial Chamber Judgment) IT-04-84-T (3 April 2008) para 39. For an overview of current issues regarding the material and temporal scopes of application of IHL (of both IACs and NIACs), see J Grignon, 'The Beginning of Application of International Humanitarian Law: A Discussion of a Few Challenges' (2014) 96 International Review of the Red Cross 139.

[6] Protocol Additional to the Geneva Conventions of 12 August 1949 and relating to the protection of victims of non-international armed conflicts (entered into force 7 December 1978) 1125 UNTS 609, Art 1, para 2 (AP II) makes an express distinction between NIACs and 'internal disturbances and tensions'. This distinction is considered to also apply to situations to which Common Article 3 is applicable.

[7] For an overview, see K Fortin, 'Syria and the Geographical Scope of International Humanitarian Law: Moving Towards a Localised Approach?' (*Armed Groups and International Law Blog* 2 October 2012) <http://armedgroups-internationallaw.org/2012/10/02/syria-and-the-geographical-scope-of-international-humanitarian-law-moving-towards-a-localised-approach>.

[8] S Nebehay, 'Some Syrian Violence Amounts to Civil War: Red Cross' (*Reuters* 8 May 2012) <https://www.reuters.com/article/us-syria-redcross/some-syria-violence-amounts-to-civil-war-red-cross-idUSBRE8470D920120508>.

[9] See especially R Chesney, 'The War in Syria and LOAC: Some Key Issues' (*Lawfare Blog* 15 July 2012) <https://www.lawfareblog.com/war-syria-and-loac-some-key-issues>; R Chesney, 'Heller Responds

the ICRC published an operational update in which it clarified that, according to its evaluation, 'there is currently [ie in July 2012] a non-international (internal) armed conflict occurring in Syria opposing Government Forces and a number of organised armed opposition groups operating in several parts of the country (including, but not limited to, Homs, Idlib and Hama)', and that 'hostilities between these parties *wherever they may occur in Syria* are subject to the rules of international humanitarian law'[10] (emphasis added). Subsequent statements issued by the ICRC regarding Syria have been in line with this updated position.[11]

The issue is of particular relevance for multinational military operations as troop-contributing nations not only share tasks, but also divide areas of operation within a country in armed conflict. While certain contingents may be actively involved in hostilities with a party to the conflict in one part of the country, others might not be in different parts.

Considering IHL treaty law, neither Common Article 3 to the Geneva Conventions nor Additional Protocol II (AP II) defines the geographical scope of NIACs. Common Article 3, which requires each party to the conflict to apply certain minimum guarantees and which prohibits certain conduct 'at any time and in any place whatsoever', contains an important reference to the 'territory of one of the High Contracting Parties', but does not govern the geographical scope within such territory. According to Article 1 AP II, the Protocol, which further develops Common Article 3, only applies to NIACs in which an organized non-state armed group exercises control over a part of the High Contracting Party's territory. This, however, serves as a restriction of AP II's material scope of application—and not as a definition of its geographical one. Conflicts within the meaning of AP II are thus

to my Post on Syria and LOAC' (*Lawfare Blog* 16 July 2012) <https://www.lawfareblog.com/heller-responds-my-post-syria-and-loac>; and R Chesney, 'Rona Responds to my Post on Syria and LOAC' (*Lawfare Blog* 17 July 2012) <https://www.lawfareblog.com/rona-responds-my-post-syria-and-loac>.

[10] ICRC, 'Syria: ICRC and Syrian Arab Red Crescent Maintain Aid Effort Amid Increased Fighting' (17 July 2012) <https://www.icrc.org/eng/resources/documents/update/2012/syria-update-2012-07-17.htm>. See also R Chesney, 'Guest Post from the ICRC's Daniel Cahen Responding to my Post on Syria/LOAC' (*Lawfare Blog* 17 July 2012) <https://www.lawfareblog.com/guest-post-icrcs-daniel-cahen-responding-my-post-syrialoac> in which he provided insight into the ICRC's legal classification approach and assumed that 'the reason why my colleague [referring to the ICRC's spokesperson Hicham Hassan having expressed similar positions as Kellenberger] insisted on particular flashpoints of armed violence such as Homs, Idlib and Hama was to indicate that IHL/LOAC is not the *only* legal framework applicable in Syria' (emphasis in original) and that measures taken against civilian protesters (which were still continuing at the time) would need to comply with the stricter IHRL standards governing the use of force in law enforcement operations.

[11] See especially P Maurer, 'Statement' (High Level Syria Crisis Ministerial Event, UN General Assembly 72nd session, 21 September 2017) <https://www.icrc.org/en/document/supporting-future-syria-and-region-icrc-statement-un-general-assembly-high-level-event> in which he notes with respect to the ongoing armed conflict in Syria which is subject to a 'shift in dynamics' with people being forced to flee the fighting in one place and others being able to move back to rebuild their lives in another place: 'In the cities of Raqqa and Deir Ezzor, as conflict continues, parties must respect and protect civilians trapped by the violence. Inhabitants must be spared, and allowed free and safe passage if they want to leave. And, of course, this principle applies throughout Syria.'

not geographically limited to those areas over which the non-state armed group exercises control.[12]

Common Article 3's and AP II's geographical scopes are thus commonly analysed based on the general rules of public international law regarding treaties, today codified in the Vienna Convention on the Law of Treaties (VCLT).[13] According to Article 29 VCLT, with a view to creating legal certainty, a treaty is binding upon each (state) party in respect of its entire territory—unless a different intention appears from the treaty or is otherwise established. In case of NIACs, the equality of belligerents, according to which all conflict parties have the same rights and obligations under IHL,[14] seems to demand that non-state armed groups be bound to this same geographical extent, even though they have not formally ratified IHL treaties.[15]

The 'entire territory' for the purposes of treaty application comprises not only a state's land territory, internal waters, and territorial sea, but also its superjacent airspace.[16] This aspect seems worth recalling given that NIACs might comprise air and naval operations where the non-state armed group possesses the necessary military capacities.[17]

A crucial question hence seems to be whether 'a different intention appears from the treaty or is otherwise established' which would justify a deviation from the

[12] For example, the application of AP II (n 6) within Nigeria has recently been suggested based on the ongoing NIAC between Nigerian armed forces and Boko Haram, which exercises control over at least certain northern parts of Nigeria; see A Bellal (ed), *The War Report—Armed Conflict in 2014* (OUP 2015) 212.

[13] While the Vienna Convention on the Law of Treaties (adopted 23 May 1969, entered into force 27 January 1980) 115 UNTS 331, Art 4 (VCLT) bars the retroactive application of the Convention to treaties concluded by states before the entry into force of the Convention for those states, it can nevertheless be argued that Art 29 VCLT (ibid) may be applied to the Geneva Conventions (1949) since the rule on non-retroactivity is without prejudice to the application of any of its rules having constituted customary international law prior to the Convention's entry into force—which arguably is the case for Art 29 VCLT (ibid) (Geneva Convention (I) for the Amelioration of the Condition of the Wounded and Sick in Armed Forces in the Field (entered into force 21 October 1950) 75 UNTS 31; Convention (II) for the Amelioration of the Wounded, Sick and Shipwrecked Members of Armed Forces at Sea (entered into force 21 October 1950) 75 UNTS 85; Geneva Convention (III) Relative to the Treatments of Prisoners of War (entered into force 21 October 1950) 75 UNTS 135; Geneva Convention (IV) Relative to the Protection of Civilian Persons in Time of War (entered into force 21 October 1950) 75 UNTS 287). See ILC, 'Draft Articles on the Law of Treaties with Commentaries—Report on the Work of its eighteenth session' (4 May–19 July 1966) (1996) 2 Yearbook of the International Law Commission 213.

[14] Note that the equality of belligerents-principle's application in NIACs has been challenged especially with regard to the lack of combatant privilege of NSA who, unlike members of state armed forces, may be prosecuted for taking part in hostilities under domestic law. For an analysis of the notions of 'equality of belligerents', 'reciprocity', and 'asymmetry' in NIAC, see S Sivakumaran, *The Law of Non-International Armed Conflict* (OUP 2012) 242.

[15] The reasons for which NSA are considered bound by IHL treaty law remain controversial. See JM Henckaerts, 'Binding Armed Opposition Groups through Humanitarian Treaty Law and Customary Law' (2003) 27 Proceedings of the Bruges Colloquium: Relevance of International Humanitarian Law to Non-State Actors, 123.

[16] I Brownlie, *Principles of Public International Law* (6th edn, OUP 2003) 115.

[17] See eg the former NIAC between the Sri Lankan Government and Liberation Tigers of Tamil Eelam (LTTE), including its 'Air Tigers' and 'Sea Tigers' units.

general rule of Article 29 VCLT. Within the law of treaties, it remains rather unsettled how such an intention is best identified.[18] IHL commentators frequently refer to the object and purpose of IHL in this regard—the meaning of which remains similarly controversial. At least two competing approaches have emerged: The first focuses on the effects of armed conflict which IHL seeks to govern. Accordingly, it is sensible to assume that IHL applies to a state's whole territory given that such consequences cannot always be confined to a certain area. A second approach stresses IHL's positioning within the international legal order. Consequently, the possible 'crowding-out' of international human rights law (IHRL) standards speaks against a comprehensive geographical scope of IHL which is meant to only provide minimum guarantees where the more protective rules of IHRL cannot be applied.[19] The (controversial) assumption that IHL not only prohibits and prescribes conduct (eg the treatment of detainees or of the wounded and sick), but also authorizes acts (eg the killing or detention of members of organized armed groups)[20] has caused even more concerns about its geographically unlimited application—both internally and externally. While the relationship between IHL and IHRL norms deserves and has received particular attention once both bodies of law apply,[21] the suitability of considering IHRL arguments in establishing the application of IHL may be challenged.

[18] M Milanovic, 'The Spatial Dimension: Treaties and Territory' in CJ Tams, A Tzanakopoulos, and A Zimmermann (eds), *Research Handbook on the Law of Treaties* (Edward Elgar Publishing 2014) 186.

[19] Note, however, that arguments based on IHRL being the 'default regime' (see D Kretzmer, 'Rethinking the Application of IHL in Non-International Armed Conflicts' (2009) 42 Israel Law Review 8 and D Kretzmer, A Ben-Yehuda, and M Furth, '"Thou Shall Not Kill": The Use of Lethal Force in Non-International Armed Conflicts (2014) 47 Israel Law Review 191) frequently do not sufficiently take the different addresses of IHL and IHRL rights and obligations into account. While it may be warranted to claim that states should primarily be bound by IHRL in NIAC (and IHL thus only be applied 'on the battlefield'), the extent to which NSA are and/or should be bound by IHRL (treaty) law remains disputed (see A Clapham, *Human Rights Obligations of Non-State Actors* (OUP 2006) Ch 7).

[20] For a recent expression of this position, see Office of General Counsel Department of Defense, 'Law of War Manual' (United States Department of Defense, June 2015, updated December 2016) < https://dod.defense.gov/Portals/1/Documents/pubs/DoD%20Law%20of%20War%20Manual%20-%20June%202015%20Updated%20Dec%202016.pdf?ver=2016-12-13-172036-190>, para 17.17.1, which argues that '[a] State's authority to conduct detention operations has often been understood as incident to the legal basis of the State to engage in operations against the non-State armed group'. See further K Mačák, 'A Needle in a Haystack? Locating the Legal Basis for Detention in Non-International Armed Conflict' (2015) 45 Israel Yearbook on Human Rights 87; G Rona, 'Is There a Way Out of the Non-International Armed Conflict Detention Dilemma?' (2015) 91 US Naval War College Series International Law Studies 32; L Hill-Cawthorne and D Akande, 'Does IHL Provide a Legal Basis for Detention in Non-International Armed Conflicts?' (*EJIL: Talk Blog* 7 May 2014) <https://www.ejiltalk.org/does-ihl-provide-a-legal-basis-for-detention-in-non-international-armed-conflicts/>.

[21] For some recent comment, see TD Gill, 'Some Thoughts on the Relationship between International Humanitarian Law and International Human Rights Law: A Plea for Mutual Respect and a Common-Sense Approach' (2013) 16 Yearbook of International Humanitarian Law 251 or M Milanovic, 'The Lost Origins of Lex Specialis: Rethinking the Relationship between Human Rights and International Humanitarian Law' in JD Ohlin (ed), *Theoretical Boundaries of Armed Conflict and Human Rights* (CUP 2016).

Instead of venturing into an examination of IHL's 'intention' within the meaning of Article 29 VCLT, an analysis of the internal geographical scope of NIACs should reveal the suitability and feasibility of possible limiting criteria.

Different approaches seem possible. First, the application of IHL could be limited to places where hostilities take place. Yet, despite containing numerous references to 'hostilities', conventional IHL does not define which acts or omissions qualify as such.[22] A too narrow interpretation would lead to unreasonable results, for example if deprivation of liberty was not included. Furthermore, the approach is not convincing given that hostilities in contemporary warfare are usually not limited to specific areas, but (sporadically) take place all over a state's territory. In NIACs in particular, hostilities frequently move around a state's territory, not least because organized non-state armed groups often have a strategic interest in dispersing military operations instead of fighting unified frontlines in order to overcome asymmetries in the means of warfare.[23] Where multinational military operations are involved, their intervention might lead to the diffusion of hostilities across a country.[24] The International Criminal Tribunal for the Former Yugoslavia (ICTY) thus rightly rejected an approach to armed conflict covering only the precise time and place of hostilities.[25]

Secondly, in view of the ICTY's finding that IHL applies 'in the whole territory of the warring States or, in the case of internal conflicts, the whole territory under the control of a party, whether or not actual combat takes place there',[26] the geographical scope of NIACs could be limited to territories under the control of either the government or a non-state armed group—to the detriment of those areas outside of any established control. However, such limitation would not only be nonsensical for the rules on the conduct of hostilities whose application is warranted especially in areas where territorial control is being disputed. It would also be incompatible with Common Article 3's material scope, which, unlike Additional Protocol II, does not require non-state armed groups to exercise any territorial control. The ICTY's finding is hence better understood as a reminder of the possible parties to an NIAC, that means as a substitution of the term 'warring States' used within its definition of the geographical scope of IACs, and of the fact that in the case

[22] N Melzer, *Interpretative Guidance on the Notion of Direct Participation in Hostilities Under International Humanitarian Law* (ICRC 2009) 43 (ICRC 'Notion of Direct Participation').

[23] T Pfanner, 'Asymmetrical Warfare from the Perspective of Humanitarian Law and Humanitarian Action' (2005) 87 International Review of the Red Cross 149, 154.

[24] See eg the development of the NIACs in Yemen, most notably the NIAC between the government armed forces and Houthis, originally mainly within the north of Yemen since 2004, but extended to Yemen's capital Sana'a in 2014 and to other regions since the intervention of the Saudi-led coalition in 2015.

[25] *Tadić* (n 5) para 67. In its *Tadić* decision, the ICTY was asked to address the geographical scope of application because the defendant argued, inter alia, that no legally cognizable armed conflict, either 'internal' or international, existed at the time and place the alleged offences were committed since the conflict in the region was limited to a political assumption of power and did not involve armed combat.

[26] Ibid, para 70.

of NIACs, territory may be not under state control but the control of a non-state armed group.[27]

Thirdly, the geographical scope could be determined for each rule, depending on whether it has an intrinsic link to hostilities or not. The ICTY suggested this to be a possibility for the determination of the geographical scope of IACs when noting that 'some of the provisions are clearly bound up with the hostilities and the geographical scope of those provisions should be so limited' while '[o]thers, particularly those relating to the protection of prisoners of war and civilians, are not so limited'.[28] Not only would this approach lead to a fragmentation of applicable norms. It also remains to be argued why the geographical scope of norms having an intrinsic link to hostilities should be limited if the material conditions triggering the application of the provisions are not met in areas without hostilities anyhow.

Instead of focusing on a factual link to hostilities, commentators have interpreted the ICTY's observation to having introduced (admittedly without success for lack of use in the ICTY's own later jurisprudence) a distinction between the geographical scopes of permissive and protective rules of IHL. According to this argument, the protective rules of IHL (eg governing the treatment of detainees) should apply within the entire state whereas the permissive rules (ie governing the conduct of hostilities) should be restricted to locations where hostilities take place.[29] Let alone the definitional challenges associated with the concepts of 'protective' and 'permissive' rules, the approach is not persuasive as it neglects the careful balance between the notions of 'military necessity' and 'humanity' inherent in IHL. While it might seem appealing to limit the application of permissive rules to 'the battlefield' to some, it seems equally improbable that conflict parties will accept such proposition. The location of a permissive act inside or outside a combat zone might be considered relevant for establishing military necessity under IHL,[30]

[27] See also N Lubell and N Derejko, 'A Global Battlefield? Drones and the Geographical Scope of Armed Conflict' (2013) 11 Journal of International Criminal Justice 65, 69. See *contra* Fortin (n 7) who asserts that consistently with the ICTY's decision in case of NIACs between NSA IHL 'will only apply to the territory under the control of those groups but it will not apply to areas outside their control'.

[28] *Tadić* (n 5) para 68.

[29] See Fortin (n 7).

[30] In its Interpretive Guidance on the Notion of Direct Participation in Hostilities, the ICRC argued that '[i]n addition to the restraints imposed by international humanitarian law on specific means and methods of warfare, and without prejudice to further restrictions that may arise under other applicable branches of international law, the kind and degree of force which is permissible against persons not entitled to protection against direct attack must not exceed what is actually necessary to accomplish a legitimate military purpose in the prevailing circumstances', see ICRC 'Notion of Direct Participation' (n 22) Ch IX. See also the criticism expressed in particular regarding Ch IX, for example MN Schmitt, 'The Interpretive Guidance on the Notion of Direct Participation in Hostilities: A Critical Analysis' (2010) 1 Harvard Law School National Security Journal 5; MN Schmitt, 'Deconstructing Direct Participation in Hostilities: The Constitutive Elements' (2010) 42 New York University Journal of International Law and Politics 697; W Hays Parks, 'Part IX of the ICRC 'Direct Participation in Hostilities' Study: No Mandate, No Expertise, and Legally Incorrect' (2010) 42 New York University Journal of International Law and Politics 769 and N Melzer, 'Keeping the Balance between Military Necessity and Humanity: A Response to Four Critiques of the ICRC's Interpretive Guidance on the Notion of Direct Participation in Hostilities' (2010) 42 New York University Journal of International Law and Politics 831. On the relationship between the geographical scope of IHL of NIACs and Ch IX, see also J Pejic, 'Extraterritorial

for preferring a law enforcement over a conduct of hostilities-paradigm[31] and/or for determining the interplay between IHL and IHRL. It is currently not regarded as being legally constrained to areas of hostilities because of a restricted geographical scope of application of IHL, however.

Finally, in accordance with the ICTY's jurisprudence,[32] IHL should therefore apply to the entire territory, but only to acts or omissions having a sufficient nexus to the armed conflict. This approach, which is in line with Article 29 VCLT, certainly deserves further consideration and elaboration. Regarding NIACs, the ICTY has argued that both Common Article 3 and Article 2 AP II apply respectively to those taking no or no longer active part in hostilities 'outside the narrow geographical context of the actual theatre of combat operations',[33] and to those affected by armed conflict and deprived of their liberty for reasons related to armed conflict, requiring only 'a relationship between the conflict and the deprivation of liberty, not that the deprivation occurred in the midst of battle'.[34] It applied this nexus-doctrine more generally when holding that for prosecution purposes '[t]he armed conflict need not have been causal to the commission of the crime, but the existence of an armed conflict must, at a minimum, have played a substantial part in the perpetrator's ability to commit it, his decision to commit it, the manner in which it was committed or the purpose for which it was committed'.[35] According to the ICTY, it is sufficient to establish that 'the perpetrator acted in furtherance of or

Targeting by Means of Armed Drones: Some Legal Implications' (2014) 96 International Review of the Red Cross 67.

[31] See especially ICRC, 'Report on the Expert Meeting on the Use of Force in Armed Conflicts: Interplay between the Conduct of Hostilities and Law Enforcement Paradigms' (ICRC November 2013) 8 <https://www.icrc.org/eng/assets/files/publications/icrc-002-4171.pdf> in which experts were requested to discuss the application of a law enforcement- or conduct of hostilities-paradigm in five case studies (ie (1) sleeping fighter, (2) riots, (3) criminality, (4) escape attempts and rioting detainees, as well as (5) checkpoints). Especially regarding (1) experts were asked if the location of a military operation against a sleeping fighter inside or outside a conflict zone was relevant for determining which paradigm applied. The majority of experts concluded, by a small margin, that the use of force against a legitimate target (eg sleeping fighter) is governed by the conduct of hostilities-paradigm. Regardless of which paradigm they favoured, experts vastly agreed that the location of a military operation should not be considered a legal criterion as it is 'too subjective', 'too open to debate and misinterpretation or disagreement' raising issues such as: 'Who decides what is the immediate theatre of operations? Would that imply that an encampment of fighters outside the conflict zone could not be targeted? Would that not constitute an incitement for fighters to operate from outside the conflict zone? If a fighter is targeted in a zone where there are no hostilities, does that zone become a conflict zone? What if a civilian is directly participating in hostilities in an area where there are no confrontations at all? Would this area be considered as a conflict zone?' 'Report on the Expert Meeting on the Use of Force in Armed Conflicts: Interplay between the Conduct of Hostilities and Law Enforcement Paradigms' (ibid) 22. For further, critical discussion of the ICRC's case studies, see also Kretzmer, Ben-Yehuda and Furth (n 19) 191.

[32] *Tadić* (n 5) para 70.

[33] Ibid, para 69.

[34] Ibid.

[35] *The Prosecutor v Dragoljub Kunarac, Radomir Kovač, Zoran Vuković* (Appeals Chamber Judgment) ICTY-96-23 & 23/1-A (12 June 2002) para 58 (*Kunarac*).

under the guise of the armed conflict'[36] in order to conclude that acts are closely related to an armed conflict. It has therefore identified certain criteria based on which a nexus can be established. They include 'the fact that the perpetrator is a combatant; . . . the victim is a non-combatant; . . . the victim is a member of the opposing party; . . . the act may be said to serve the ultimate goal of a military campaign; and . . . that the crime is committed as part of or in the context of the perpetrator's official duties'.[37] If developed and operationalized, these criteria may help to distinguish to which acts and omissions IHL applies. The nexus-criterion seems to make sense also in cases of multiple armed conflicts occurring on the territory of a single state, the possibility of which is by now accepted[38] and currently the case in Syria,[39] for example. This way, relations between parties to different armed conflicts can be disentangled despite them occurring within the same territory and the geographical scope of each armed conflict extending to the entire state.[40] Already existing, different approaches to defining a nexus should thus be reviewed and examined for their suitability. The criteria developed under international criminal law[41] or elements established to define 'direct participation in hostilities'[42] might not necessarily be fit for purpose.

3. External Geographical Scope of NIACs

The applicability of the laws of NIACs outside 'traditional' NIACs, that is armed conflicts fought exclusively on the territory of a single High Contracting Party between the territorial state and an organized armed group or between such groups, remains controversial yet highly relevant, as states have progressively been engaged in armed hostilities with organized non-state armed groups operating

[36] Ibid.
[37] Ibid, para 59.
[38] Military and Paramilitary Activities in and against Nicaragua (*Nicaragua v US*) (Merits) [1986] ICJ Rep 14, para 219 (Nicaragua case) and ICC, *Prosecutor v Germain Katanga* (Trial Chamber Judgment) [2014] ICC-01/04-01/07, para 1197.
[39] S Casey-Maslen (ed), *The War Report 2012* (OUP 2013) 60, 165; S Casey-Maslen (ed), *The War Report—Armed Conflict in 2013* (OUP 2014) 35, 81, and 207 and A Bellal (ed), *The War Report—Armed Conflict 2014* (OUP 2015) 57, 107, and 265.
[40] Note, however, that the multitude of conflict parties in Syria (caused, inter alia, by the split within the armed opposition and intervention of foreign states) leads to a situation in which 'some of the conflictual relations are barely comprehensible': ICRC, 'International Humanitarian Law and the Challenges of Contemporary Armed Conflicts' (32nd International Conference of the Red Cross and Red Crescent, 32IC/15/11, Geneva October 2015) 6 <https://reliefweb.int/report/world/international-humanitarian-law-and-challenges-contemporary-armed-conflicts-32ic1511>.
[41] See H van der Wilt, 'War Crimes and the Requirement of a Nexus with an Armed Conflict' (2012) 10 Journal of International Criminal Justice 1113 who analyses the nexus criterion to distinguish war crimes not only from ordinary crimes but also from other international crimes, especially from genocide (based on the *Mpambara* case before Dutch courts).
[42] ICRC 'Notion of Direct Participation' (n 22).

outside of the state's own territory.[43] For example, the US-led 'Global Coalition against Daesh'/'Anti-IS Coalition' formed in September 2014 has conducted a military campaign to degrade and destroy Daesh in Iraq and Syria.

Based on its wording, Common Article 3 was traditionally understood to be limited to armed conflicts occurring within the territory of one High Contracting Party only, that is to 'internal' armed conflicts. The provision's reference to the 'territory of *one* of the High Contracting Parties' was read in contradistinction to 'two', 'three', or 'several' High Contracting Parties' territories (emphasis added). However, it is now increasingly interpreted to refer to the territory not of 'one' but of 'a' state party to the Geneva Conventions—mainly based on the argument that Common Article 3 required a territorial link to 'a' High Contracting Party because it equally binds non-state armed groups.[44] Given the Conventions' universal ratification, it is moreover argued that any armed conflict today takes place on the territory of a High Contracting Party and that the territorial reference within Common Article 3 has lost importance in practice.[45]

A contextual approach to interpreting Common Article 3, as taken by the United States Supreme Court,[46] furthermore suggests that, in order to avoid a gap in legal regulation,[47] NIACs may be defined negatively as armed conflicts not covered by Common Article 2—regardless of their geographical extent and contrary to their denotation as 'non-international armed conflicts'. Accordingly, the Geneva Conventions comprehensively govern all types of armed conflict and classify them as either 'international' (Common Article 2) or 'non-international' (Common Article 3).

Much of the current debate about the external geographical scope of NIACs focuses on the object and purpose of Common Article 3. Proponents and opponents of its extraterritorial application can now be found on both sides of the classic IHL

[43] This trend can be explained, inter alia, by an increase in non-state armed groups' ability to conduct operations across borders and technological advances, eg in the development of armed drones, enabling states to engage such groups in remote areas on foreign territory without military ground presence and danger to own personnel.

[44] N Melzer, *Targeted Killing in International Law* (OUP 2008) 258.

[45] ICRC, 'How is the Term "Armed Conflict" Defined in International Humanitarian Law?' (Opinion Paper March 2008) 3 <https://www.icrc.org/eng/assets/files/other/opinion-paper-armed-conflict.pdf>. Nevertheless, the possibility of an NIAC occurring on the territory of a newly created state not (yet) party to the Conventions continues to exist.

[46] US Supreme Court, *Salim A Hamdan v Donald H Rumsfeld et al*, No 05-184, 29 June 2006, 6. In the *Hamdan* case (involving a Yemeni national captured during hostilities between the US and Taliban forces in Afghanistan), the US Supreme Court supported the application of Common Article 3 to the conflict with Al-Qaeda without explicitly limiting the armed conflict's geographical scope to Afghanistan.

[47] M Sassòli, 'Transnational Armed Groups and International Humanitarian Law' [2006] Series 9, Program on Humanitarian Policy and Conflict Research, Harvard Occasional Paper. See also D Jinks, 'September 11 and the Laws of War' (2003) 28 Yale Journal of International Law 1. Jinks notes that 'Common Article 3 was revolutionary because it purported to regulate wholly internal matters as a matter of international humanitarian law' and argues that '[i]f the provision governs wholly internal conflicts, as the "one state" interpretation recognizes, then the provision applies *a fortiori* to armed conflicts with international or transnational dimensions' (at 41).

range between 'humanitarians' and 'military lawyers'. Following the 9/11 attacks, the debate was at first driven from a humanitarian perspective, and aimed to extend protection to Guantánamo detainees. It was considered 'inconceivable'[48] that persons captured in relation to an NIAC could be deprived of Common Article 3's safeguards because its application ceases at a border. The debate has shifted with the increasing resort to targeted killings by means of armed drones.[49] It is now argued from a military perspective that, if Common Article 3 is to govern the effects of armed conflict, 'fighters'[50] may be directly targeted regardless of their location unless having disengaged from the fighting or having been placed *hors de combat*.[51] According to this argument, they should not be able to escape the reach of IHL by using third country 'safe havens' which are unable or unwilling to respond to the threat they pose.[52] In return, especially international human rights lawyers assert that the laws of NIACs should be applied only with territorial constraints to the benefit of IHRL[53]—whose extraterritorial application continues to be challenged, however.[54]

The wording, context, as well as the object and purpose of Common Article 3 have therefore been described as 'rather ambiguous'[55] regarding its extraterritorial application. Supplementary means of treaty interpretation, such as Common Article 3's preparatory work,[56] which may hence be resorted to (Article 32 VCLT),

[48] J Pejic, 'The Protective Scope of Common Article 3: More than Meets the Eye' (2011) 93 International Review of the Red Cross 1, 15.

[49] A missile was first test-fired from a drone in February 2001, the first known US drone strike killed Abu Ali Al-Harithi, the alleged plotter of the USS Cole bombing and head of Al-Qaeda in Yemen in November 2002. Different databases on the use of armed drones in various regions of the world exist, see eg J Serle and J Purkiss, 'Drone Wars: the Full Data' (*The Bureau of Investigative Journalism* 1 January 2017) <https://www.thebureauinvestigates.com/stories/2017-01-01/drone-wars-the-full-data>; The New America Foundation, 'International Security Data Site', <http://securitydata.newamerica.net> or The Long War Journal, 'Drone Strikes Data', <https://www.longwarjournal.org/us-airstrikes-in-the-long-war>.

[50] Note that whereas IHL treaty law of NIAC does not provide for a 'fighter' status similar to a 'combatant' status in IAC, the ICRC has argued (in defining the concept of 'civilian' in NIAC) and received support for the proposition that 'organized armed groups constitute the armed forces of a non-State party to the conflict and consist only of individuals whose continuous function it is to take a direct part in hostilities ("continuous combat function")'; ICRC 'Notion of Direct Participation' (n 22) 27. For references expressing criticism on the ICRC's position, see *supra* (n 30).

[51] R Chesney, 'Who May Be Killed? Anwar al-Awlaki as a Case Study in the International Legal Regulation of Lethal Force' in T McCormack, M Schmitt, and L Arimatsu (2010) 13 Yearbook of International Humanitarian Law 3, 37.

[52] Ibid.

[53] ME O'Connell, 'The Choice of Law Against Terrorism' (2010) 4 Journal of National Security Law and Policy 343.

[54] For an overview see eg M Milanovic, *Extraterritorial Application of Human Rights Treaties. Law, Principles, and Policy* (OUP 2011). Also note the increased (scholarly) attention being paid to the territorial state's IHRL obligations which arguably prevent it from providing consent for 'targeted killings' of individuals present on its territory. See eg J Horowitz, 'Ending the Global War: The Power of Human Rights in a Time of Unrestrained Armed Conflict' in Ohlin (n 21).

[55] R Bartels, 'Timelines, Borderlines and Conflicts. The Historical Evolution of the Legal Divide between International and Non-International Armed Conflicts' (2009) 91 International Review of the Red Cross 35, 60.

[56] The preparatory work of Common Article 3 is usually considered to have commenced with the gathering of National Red Cross and Red Crescent Societies at the invitation of the International

are however also of limited assistance. Early proposals made by the ICRC, according to which '[i]n all cases of armed conflict which are not of an international character ..., which may occur *in the territory of one or more of the High Contracting Parties* [emphasis added], the implementing of the principles of the present Convention shall be obligatory on each of the adversaries',[57] were not adopted—the reasons, however, remain unclear.[58]

(State) practice shows support for the general possibility of applying Common Article 3 extraterritorially, but currently seems to distinguish between different kinds of 'extraterritorial' NIACs, or 'NIAC[s] with an extraterritorial element'[59] alongside the majority of commentators.[60]

In cases in which an NIAC spills over into the territory of one or more adjacent, non-belligerent state(s),[61] it is increasingly accepted that the laws of NIACs apply in such territory, while a renewed assessment of the threshold of NIACs is not required, otherwise establishing a separate NIAC.[62] The ICRC has argued that, in such instances, conflict parties remain at a minimum bound by Common Article

Committee of the Red Cross in 1946 (see ICRC, *Report on the Work of the Preliminary Conference of National Red Cross Societies for the Study of the Conventions and of Various Problems Relative to the Red Cross*, Geneva, 26 July–3 August 1946 (ICRC 1947) Series I, No 3a)—though efforts to extend the Geneva Conventions' application had already been undertaken before (see eg Draft Convention on the Role of the Red Cross during Civil War submitted to the IXth International Conference of the Red Cross and Red Crescent in Washington DC in 1912, Resolution XIV adopted at the Xth International Conference in Geneva in 1921, and Resolution XIV adopted at the XVIth International Conference in London in 1938).

[57] ICRC, *Draft Revised or New Conventions for the Protection of War Victims* (ICRC 1948) 5. In its comments on the Draft Conventions, the ICRC did not address the geographical scope of the proposed article.

[58] See Bartels (n 55) 63 and *contra* Melzer (n 44) 258.

[59] ICRC (n 40) 14.

[60] For a classification of various forms of NIACs, see S Vité, 'Typology of Armed Conflicts in International Humanitarian Law: Legal Concepts and Actual Situations' (2009) 91 International Review of the Red Cross 69.

[61] While the ICRC limits the description of 'spill-over armed conflicts' to 'an armed conflict originating within the territory of a State that is waged between government armed forces and one or more organized armed groups, which spills over into the territory of one or more neighbouring States' (ICRC (n 40) 15), it should arguably encompass NIACs solely between organized non-state armed group spilling over.

[62] Uganda's military operations against members of the Lord's Resistance Army (LRA) on Sudanese territory, military clashes between Colombian armed forces and Revolutionary Armed Forces of Colombia (FARC) members on Ecuadorian territory, and the spilling-over of the Rwandan armed conflict onto the territory of the Democratic Republic of the Congo, for example, were widely considered covered by Common Article 3. The International Criminal Tribunal for Rwanda (ICTR) was thus given the power to prosecute persons responsible for serious violations of IHL committed in the territory of Rwanda, and Rwandan citizens responsible for such violations committed in the territory of neighbouring states between 1 January 1994 and 31 December 1994 (Art 1 Statute of the International Criminal Tribunal for the Prosecution of Persons Responsible for Genocide and Other Serious Violations of International Humanitarian Law Committed in the Territory of Rwanda and Rwanda Citizens Responsible for Genocide and Other Such Violations Committed in the Territory of Neighbouring States, between 1 January 1994 and 31 December 1994—Adopted by UNSC Res 55 (8 November 1994) amended by UNSC Res 1165 (30 April 1998), UN Res 1329 (30 November 2000), UNSC Res 1411 (17 May 2002) and UNSC Res 1431 (14 August 2002).

3 and customary IHL[63] because 'the spill over of an NIAC into adjacent territory cannot have the effect of absolving the parties of their IHL obligations simply because an international border has been crossed'.[64] What remains to be settled however is to what extent the laws of NIACs apply within the entire neighbouring country. Some argue that they should be geographically confined to a 'spill-over' area,[65] but do not offer guidance on how to determine the limits of such an area. Most therefore maintain that the laws of NIACs should apply to the neighbouring country's entire territory (and cover all acts or omissions having a sufficient nexus to the pre-existing NIAC in analogy to the internal geographical scope of NIACs).

The increasing acceptance of the applicability of the laws of NIACs to 'spill-over armed conflicts' raises the question whether the application of IHL is and/or should be dependent on geographical proximity.[66] It is pertinent not only for the delimitation of 'spill-over' areas in border regions within neighbouring countries, but also—and maybe more importantly—for the applicability of IHL to the territory of a non-neighbouring, non-belligerent state. Whereas 'spill-over armed conflicts' are currently frequently presented as constituting an 'exceptional and *sui generis* basis'[67] for extending IHL's geographical scope to non-belligerent countries,[68] legal scholars and practitioners rightly question their distinctiveness.

Significant disagreement thus exists with respect to the legality of targeting 'fighters' and civilians directly participating in hostilities who are located on the territory of a non-neighbouring, non-belligerent state. Some argue that such

[63] Note that some authors are ready to also accept the applicability of AP II (n 6) to 'spill-over' armed conflicts if some part of the hostilities take place on the HCP's territory whose armed forces are fighting a NSA (and continue to do so in neighbouring territory), see E Crawford and A Pert, *International Humanitarian Law* (CUP 2015) 82.

[64] ICRC, 'International Humanitarian Law and the Challenges of Contemporary Armed Conflicts' (31st International Conference of the Red Cross and Red Crescent 31IC/11/5.1.2, October 2011) 9 <https://www.icrc.org/eng/assets/files/red-cross-crescent-movement/31st-international-conference/31-int-conference-ihl-challenges-report-11-5-1-2-en.pdf>.

[65] See eg S Breau, M Aronsson, and R Joyce, 'Drone Attacks, International Law, and the Recording of Civilian Casualties of Armed Conflict' (Oxford Research Group Discussion Paper 2, June 2011) 12 <https://www.files.ethz.ch/isn/138987/ORG%20Drone%20Attacks%20and%20International%20Law%20Report.pdf> who argue that the law of NIACs applies to drone strikes conducted in relation to the Afghan conflict only if carried out within the Afghan-Pakistani border regions of the Federally Administered Tribal Areas (FATA) and the North-West Frontier Province (NWFP).

[66] Lubell and Derejko (n 27) 82. Consider also the argument that 'the geographical contiguity between belligerent States could facilitate the remote exercise of effective control' for the purposes of establishing the end of occupation under the laws of IAC; ICRC (n 40) 12.

[67] ICRC (n 40) 15.

[68] The ICRC argues (ibid) that 'there are cogent reasons to link the geographical extension of IHL to the neighbouring country depending on the extent of control that a party to an NIAC has over the territory of the neighbouring country or over the places where hostilities are taking place in such country' by referring to ICTY case law (*Prosecutor v Ramush Haradinaj, Idriz Balaj and Lahi Brahimaj* (Trial Chamber Retrial Judgment) ICTY-04-84*bis*-T (29 November 2012) para 396)—however, without developing the argument or explaining how the Court's general statement quoting *Tadić* (n 5) and *Kunarac* (n 35) ('The armed conflict is seen to extend to the entire territory of the warring states or, in case of a non-international conflict, the entire territory controlled by a party, irrespective of whether actual combat takes place there') may be used as authority to support such position.

extraterritorial use of force is always governed by IHL because of its nexus to a pre-existing NIAC, regardless of geographical location.[69] Meanwhile, others have mitigated this position and asserted, for example, that IHL pursues activities, instead of individuals. 'Fighters' and civilians directly participating in hostilities would hence only remain targetable if they continued to engage in an NIAC from their location.[70] While the distinction between a 'status' versus 'activities'-based approach does not matter for civilians directly participating in hostilities (whose direct participation is dependent on specific acts/omissions in any case), 'fighters' would hereby only be targetable based on their continued engagement in the armed conflict and not on their status alone.[71] However, the ICRC has taken the position that a person does not carry an NIAC to the territory of a non-belligerent state under any circumstances. It argues that, 'based on reasons of law and policy',[72] the application of a law enforcement-paradigm to the use of force against individuals on the territory of a non-neighbouring, non-belligerent state is preferable. The ICRC asserts that the application of IHL to such cases (1) would signify the recognition of the concept of a 'global battlefield', which (2) has not been endorsed by state practice and *opinio juris*, which (3) would entail 'disturbing'[73] consequences if invoked by all states involved in an NIAC, and which (4) would be less protective for the general population, as the application of the rules on the conduct of hostilities (including the principle of proportionality) would put civilians and civilian objects in non-belligerent states at risk.[74]

Whether the application of IHL to the territory of non-neighbouring, non-belligerent states, either based on status or activity, necessarily signifies the recognition of a 'global battlefield' may be challenged. It would certainly not imply the automatic endorsement of a 'global armed conflict'-doctrine,[75] even though

[69] See especially N Melzer, 'Human Rights Implications of the Usage of Drones and Unmanned Robots in Warfare' (European Parliament, Directorate-General for External Policies Policy Department EXPO/B/DROI/2012/12 May 2013) 21 <http://www.europarl.europa.eu/RegData/etudes/etudes/join/2013/410220/EXPO-DROI_ET(2013)410220_EN.pdf>.

[70] See eg N Lubell, 'The War Against Al-Qaeda' in E Wilmshurst (ed), *International Law and the Classification of Conflicts* (OUP 2012) 421, 449.

[71] It has also been suggested that while IHL should apply without territorial constraints, a distinction should be made between 'zones of active hostilities', 'peacetime zones' and 'lawless zones' with enhanced substantive and procedural standards applying in the latter two. Accordingly, an individualized threat finding, a least harmful means-test as well as meaningful *ex ante* and *ex post* procedural safeguards, should limit targeting and detention operations outside 'zones of active hostilities', see J Daskal, 'The Geography of the Battlefield: A Framework for Detention and Targeting Outside the "Hot" Conflict Zone' (2013) 161 University of Pennsylvania Law Review 1165, 1192.

[72] ICRC (n 40) 14.

[73] Ibid, 15.

[74] Ibid, 16. For an earlier expression of the same position, see Pejic (n 30) 36. Also note that civilians sitting at an outdoor café in Paris unaware that they may be affected by a strike as 'collateral damage' had been chosen as a case depicting the consequences of the application of IHL to non-neighbouring, non-belligerent countries; see Daskal (n 71).

[75] See similarly G Rona, 'The Start, End, and Territorial Scope of Armed Conflict' (*Just Security Blog* 11 November 2015) <https://www.justsecurity.org/27543/start-end-territorial-scope-armed-conflict> who notes, in discussing the ICRC's Challenges Report 2015 (n 40), that '[o]ne can conclude that there

references to both notions have frequently been lacking clarity and distinction. What distinguishes such NIACs from a 'global armed conflict' is the occurrence of both required criteria (ie threshold of violence and degree of organization of conflict parties)[76] in at least one territory.[77] The US Government, however, while having abandoned the term 'Global War on Terror' (GWOT) in 2009,[78] indeed continues to consider itself engaged in a 'global armed conflict' against Al-Qaeda, the Taliban, and associated forces. It seems ready to accept that hostilities across the globe with different non-state organized armed groups linked to each other may be added up to reach the required threshold of violence. In its view, this 'global armed conflict' consequently provides authority for the use of lethal force outside of 'hot battlefields',[79] that is on a 'global battlefield'. The United States' construction of a 'global armed conflict' has provoked extensive criticism—which, however, currently seems to focus on factual rather than legal arguments. While some commentators have expressed concern over the United States' legal approach in 'connecting the dots',[80] most restrict their remarks to noting that Al-Qaeda (and more

is no global war against terrorism, or for that matter, against al-Qaeda, but still concede that hostilities between States and a non-State armed group could "carry" IHL to wherever the players go'.

[76] *Tadić* (n 5) para 70.

[77] See generally S Radin, 'Global Armed Conflict? The Threshold of Extraterritorial Non-International Armed Conflicts' (2013) 89 US Naval War College International Law Studies 696.

[78] See J Brennan, 'Remarks' (Center for Strategic and International Studies 6 August 2009) <https://www.csis.org/events/john-brennan-assistant-president-homeland-security-and-counterterrorism> in which he argued that President Obama's Administration would not refer to a 'war on terrorism' because '"terrorism" is but a tactic' which 'can never fully [be] defeat[ed] ... any more than ... the tactic of war itself'. He further asserted that it would not describe its counter-terrorism efforts as a 'global war' because '[i]t plays into the misleading and dangerous notion that the U.S. is somehow in conflict with the rest of the world' and 'risks reinforcing the very [inaccurate] image that al Qaeda seeks to project of itself—that it is a highly organized, global entity capable of replacing sovereign nations with a global caliphate'. Also note that following President Obama's inauguration for his second term as POTUS in 2013, he announced that 'this war [against Al-Qaeda], like all wars, must end'; B Obama, 'Remarks' (National Defense University 23 May 2013) <https://www.whitehouse.gov/the-press-office/2013/05/23/remarks-president-national-defense-university>.

[79] US Department of Justice, 'White Paper on the Lawfulness of a Lethal Operation Directed Against a US Citizen who is a Senior Operational Leader of Al-Qa'ida or an Associated Force' (leaked to the press) < https://casebook.icrc.org/case-study/us-lethal-operations-against-al-qaida-leaders>. For an overview of the development of the US Government's legal position, see also various public statements by senior officials, such as H Koh, 'Keynote Speech: The Obama Administration and International Law' (Annual Meeting of the American Society of International Law, 25 March 2010) < https://2009-2017.state.gov/s/l/releases/remarks/139119.htm >; J Brennan, 'Remarks: Strengthening our Security by Adhering to our Values and Laws' (Harvard Law School, 16 September 2011) <https://obamawhitehouse.archives.gov/the-press-office/2011/09/16/remarks-john-o-brennan-strengthening-our-security-adhering-our-values-an>; JC Johnson, 'National Security Law, Lawyers and Lawyering in the Obama Administration—Dean's Lecture at Yale Law School February 22, 2012' (2012) 31 Yale Law & Policy Review 141; E Holder, 'Remarks' (Northwestern University School of Law, 5 March 2012) <https://www.justice.gov/opa/speech/attorney-general-eric-holder-speaks-northwestern-university-school-law>.

[80] See especially UNCHR, 'Report of the Special Rapporteur on the Promotion and Protection of Human Rights and Fundamental Freedoms while Countering Terrorism—Interim Report to the General Assembly on the Use of Remotely Piloted Aircraft in Counter-Terrorism Operations' (18 September 2013) UN Doc A/68/389, 18, para 63. See *contra* Crawford and Pert (n 63) 84 who argue that '[i]f the U.S. is correct and there is one global armed conflict between the U.S. (primarily) and

recently the group known interchangeably as the 'Islamic State' (IS) of Iraq and Syria (ISIS)/of Iraq and the Levant (ISIL)/Daesh)[81] factually does not possess the degree of organization necessary for considering it a single party to a 'global armed conflict'[82]—thus preserving a future possibility and legal avenue.

The debate on the spilling-over of IHL to the territories of (non-neighbouring) non-belligerent states in an NIAC and/or 'global armed conflict' is likely to continue given, inter alia, the increase in capabilities of non-state armed groups to geographically expand hostilities and states' determination to engage them wherever considered appropriate. At the same time, different legal views persist about the proper classification of hostilities between a state and a non-state armed group exclusively on the territory of another state and without any nexus to a pre-existing NIAC or 'global armed conflict'.[83] So-called 'transnational' armed conflicts have been classified as (1) NIACs between the intervening state and a non-state armed group, (2) IACs between the intervening state and territorial state, (3) IACs between the intervening state and a non-state armed group, or (4) a new category of armed conflicts in need of further regulation regarding both scope of application and substantive content.[84] Recently, commentators seem to be less reluctant to classify such hostilities as NIACs where the threshold of violence and degree of organization is fulfilled within the territorial state's boundaries. One could argue that, in light of the evolving legal discourse on the 'global battlefield' described above, armed hostilities of a sufficient threshold of violence between a state and an

Al-Qaeda, the various attacks and hostile responses in different locations could be aggregated to determine if the intensity requirement for an armed conflict is satisfied'.

[81] For a recent expression of this position, see ICRC (n 40) 18 which argues that '[w]ith respect to the phenomenon of armed groups that are perceived as having a global reach, such as al-Qaeda or the Islamic State group, the ICRC does not share the view that an armed conflict of global dimensions is, or has been, taking place. This would require, in the first place, the existence of a "unitary" non-State party opposing one or more States. Based on available facts, there are not sufficient elements to consider the al-Qaeda "core" and its associated groups in other parts of the world as one and the same party within the meaning of IHL. The same reasoning also applies, for the time being, to the Islamic State group and affiliated groups.' For an overview of the organizational structure and strategy of 'IS' (in comparison to Al-Qaeda), see R Goodman, 'Associated Forces: Why the Differences between ISIL and al-Qaeda Matter' (*Just Security Blog* 30 March 2015) <https://www.justsecurity.org/21621/forces-differences-isil-al-qaeda-matter> and R Chesney, 'ISIL's "Associated Forces" and the Scope of the Conflict' (*Lawfare Blog* 10 December 2015) <https://www.lawfareblog.com/isils-associated-forces-and-scope-conflict>.

[82] Sassòli (n 47) 10.

[83] See eg Israel's fight against Hezbollah on Lebanese territory in 2006 and the ensuing legal debate; A Yuile, 'At the Fault-Lines of Armed Conflict: The 2006 Israel-Hezbollah Conflict and the Framework of International Humanitarian Law' (2009) 16 Australian International Law Journal 189 or Y Ronen, 'Israel, Hizbollah, and the Second Lebanon War' (2006) 9 Yearbook of International Humanitarian Law 362.

[84] See M Milanovic, 'The Applicability of the Conventions to "Transnational" and "Mixed" Conflicts' in A Clapham, P Gaeta, and M Sassòli (eds), *The 1949 Geneva Conventions: A Commentary* (OUP 2015) 27; C Kreß, 'Some Reflections on the International Legal Framework Governing Transnational Armed Conflicts' (2010) 15 Journal of Conflict and Security Law 245; and RS Schöndorf, 'Extra-State Armed Conflicts: Is There a Need for a New Legal Regime?' (2004) 37 New York University Journal of International Law and Politics 1.

organized non-state armed group on the territory of a third state today would more readily be classified as an NIAC (alongside a separate IAC) than a decade ago.

4. Geographical Scope of NIACs Involving Multinational Military Operations

Common Article 3's application to 'multinational armed conflicts' has increasingly found support regardless of geographical proximity. While it was once argued that relations between states intervening in an NIAC in support of a territorial state and the opposing non-state armed group should be governed by the laws of IACs, this theory is no longer supported by most.[85] Recent cases have shown that states seem to be willing to accept being bound by Common Article 3 outside their national borders in these instances.[86] Some even reconsider the possibility of an extra-territorial application of AP II in case of 'multinational armed conflicts'.[87] It had commonly been rejected because of the wording of Article 1 AP II which refers to armed conflicts taking place in the territory of a High Contracting Party between *its* armed forces and a non-state armed group.[88] In cases in which multinational forces support a High Contracting Party in an NIAC fulfilling the criteria of AP II, it indeed seems worth reviewing whether AP II should apply not only to the territorial state, but also to the multinational forces (at least to those having ratified AP II) within the territorial state's boundaries.[89]

However, questions remain about the applicability of the laws of NIACs to (1) the intervening (or assisting) states' own territories as well as (2) the territories of non-belligerent states from which multinational forces might operate. While 'at present official pronouncements by States on this specific issue [ie (1)]

[85] Note that cases in which a state intervenes on behalf of an NSA (ie in which an NSA is under the 'effective' or 'overall' control of another state) are commonly classified as IACs. See *contra* A Clapham, 'The Concept of International Armed Conflict' in Clapham, Gaeta, and Sassòli (ibid) 25 who argues for a parallel application of the law of IAC and NIAC in 'proxy wars'. Recognizing that '[t]his [...] does not seem to be the conventional way of looking at this', he puts forward that '[t]he better solution seems to be that when states are fighting non-state armed groups who are the proxies of another state, the law of NIAC applies between the state and the non-state armed group; while the law of IAC ... applies to the conflict between the two states.'

[86] See, for instance, the various statements by the International Security Assistance Forces (ISAF) Troop Contributing Nations (TCN) on the application of Common Article 3 to TCN in Afghanistan, such as G Westerwelle, 'Paving the Way for a Responsible Handover: Germany's Engagement in Afghanistan after the London Conference' (German Parliament, 10 February 2010) <http://www.auswaertiges-amt.de/DE/Infoservice/Presse/Reden/2010/100210-BM-BT-Afghanistan.html>.

[87] For an argument regarding the case of Afghanistan, see A Bellal, G Giacca and S Casey-Maslen, 'International Law and Armed Non-State Actors in Afghanistan' (2011) 93 International Review of the Red Cross 47, 59.

[88] For a summary of the traditional argument, see Crawford and Pert (n 63) 83.

[89] An analysis of the rules of AP II (n 6) shows that most of them could quite easily be applied in an extraterritorial context, eg the fundamental guarantees of Arts 4, 5 and 13 AP II (n 6). Some clarification is necessary where the rules refer to a domestic authority or domestic law, especially regarding penal prosecutions provided for in Art 6 AP II (n 6).

are scarce',[90] commentators have argued both that the application of IHL is limited to the territory of the state within whose borders the conflict is taking place, and that IHL extends to the territories of the intervening states. For example, the 2013 attack against the Westgate Centre in Nairobi, for which Al-Shabaab claimed responsibility as 'retributive justice for crimes committed by Kenyan armed forces in Somalia' as part of their support to Somalian armed forces, may be deemed to be part of this armed conflict or not. If yes, the use of tear gas and expanding bullets by Kenyan security forces in Nairobi may be found to be not in compliance with international humanitarian law.[91] For the time being, the ICRC has concluded that '[t]here are cogent legal reasons to consider that IHL applies to the territories of the assisting States' as they 'should not be able to shield themselves from the operation of the principle of equality of belligerents under IHL'.[92] Consequently, acts by non-state armed groups (such as direct attacks against military objectives) on the intervening state's own territory would be governed by and potentially be lawful under IHL (even if penalized under domestic law). Concerning the application of IHL to state's acts or omissions, the ICRC has specified with respect to the use of force against non-state armed groups on the assisting state's territory that—in its view—'it would be governed by the standard included in Recommendation IX of the ICRC's Guidance ... as well as by the State's domestic law and its international and/or regional human rights obligations'.[93]

The applicability of the laws of NIACs to (2) the territories of non-belligerent states from which multinational forces might operate primarily depends on whether they can truly be considered 'non-belligerent'. The question of which state has become a party to an armed conflict has been a matter of controversy for some time as assistance to a conflict party not only takes the form of kinetic operations, but also of intelligence activities, participation in the planning and coordination of military operations, as well as logistical support.[94] It has been suggested that—in line with a 'support-based approach'—if (a) there is a pre-existing NIAC taking place on the territory in which multinational forces are called to intervene; (b) actions related to the conduct of hostilities are undertaken by multinational forces in the context of the pre-existing conflict; (c) the military operations of multinational forces are carried out in support of a party to the pre-existing conflict; and (d) the action in question is undertaken pursuant to an official decision by the troop-contributing country or the relevant organization to support a party involved in the pre-existing conflict, a state must be considered a party to a pre-existing NIAC.[95]

[90] ICRC (n 40) 14.
[91] Casey-Maslen (n 39) 186.
[92] ICRC (n 40) 14.
[93] Ibid.
[94] See generally T Ferraro, 'The Applicability and Application of International Humanitarian Law to Multinational Forces' (2013) 95 International Review of the Red Cross 561 and ICRC, 'Challenges Report 2015' (n 40) 21.
[95] See Ferraro (n 94) 584.

Where the use of a state's territory by conflict parties fulfils these cumulative conditions, a state can be considered party to the pre-existing NIAC and its territory to be subject to the application of the rules of IHL.[96] Should the state not have become a conflict party, the applicability of IHL depends on one's views about IHL's application to the territory of non-belligerent states as outlined above.

5. Conclusion

The political and legal issues that multinational military operations raise are diverse. This chapter has focused on the legal challenges associated with the classification of armed conflicts involving multinational military operations, in particular with the definition of the geographical scope of NIAC.

An examination of the debate on the 'boundaries of the battlefield' reveals that whereas its focus has recently been on the external geographical scope of NIACs, a need for clarification persists with respect to IHL's application within the borders of a High Contracting Party. In accordance with Article 29 VCLT, which can be considered applicable in interpreting both Common Article 3 and Additional Protocol II, states and non-state armed groups that are party to an NIAC should be considered bound by IHL within a High Contracting Party's entire territory (comprising land, sea, and airspace) with respect to all acts and omissions having a nexus to the armed conflict. Possible limitations, such as the creation of 'localized' armed conflicts within the vicinity of hostilities, are factually and legally not convincing. The possible (re)introduction of a distinction in the geographical scopes of permissive and protective rules of IHL seems especially problematic.

While a certain reluctance in asserting a comprehensive geographical scope (as evidenced in the ICRC's statements on the scope of the Syrian armed conflict) may be understandable, it seems to be based primarily on concerns about the appropriateness of applying IHL in specific scenarios, such as the use of force against individuals outside the battlefield (in the Syrian case: initially against civil protesters). An honest evaluation of the geographical scope of IHL should not only be wider in scope but also defer to other legal regimes and their interplay with IHL where applicable—most importantly to international human rights law. If one

[96] See, for example, the debate on the legal consequences of the use of Ramstein Air Base in Germany for US drone operations triggered through news reports in 2013 (C Fuchs, J Goetz, and H Leyendecker, 'US-Streitkräfte steuern Drohnen von Deutschland aus' (*Süddeutsche Zeitung* 30 May 2013) <http://www.sueddeutsche.de/politik/luftangriffe-in-afrika-us-streitkraefte-steuern-drohnen-von-deutschland-aus-1.1684414>) and leading to court proceedings between three Yemeni nationals and the Federal Republic of Germany in 2014 (Administrative Court Cologne, Court File No 3 K 5625/14, 27 May 2015) which is, however, currently focused on Germany's responsibility to prevent the use of German territory for US drone operations rather than a possible application of IHL within Germany. For more on this see: <https://www.justiz.nrw.de/nrwe/ovgs/vg_koeln/j2015/3_K_5625_14_Urteil_20150527.html>.

attempts to establish IHL's scope of application by addressing, for example, the distinction between a conduct of hostilities and law enforcement-paradigm, one risks overburdening and consequently threatening IHL's acceptance.

Contrary to its traditional interpretation, Common Article 3 (and partly Additional Protocol II) may be interpreted (based on its wording, context, as well as object and purpose) to generally allow for its extraterritorial application. At least with respect to 'transnational', 'multinational', and 'spill-over' armed conflicts, this possibility now seems to be well accepted—even though certain issues remain controversial. In case of 'transnational' armed conflicts, the existence of an NIAC should be accepted (alongside an IAC) where the threshold of violence and degree of organization of non-state armed groups are sufficient even though hostilities do not take place within the state's own territory. Where a state is involved in a 'multinational' armed conflict, the geographical scope of the NIAC should be considered to extend not only to the territory of the High Contracting Party fighting the non-state armed group on its own territory, but also to the intervening state's territory. If an NIAC (either between a High Contracting Party and a non-state armed group or between non-state armed groups) spills over into the territory of a neighbouring state, the application of IHL should not be limited to certain 'spill-over' areas but extend to the neighbouring state's entire territory. In each of these cases, the application of IHL should be restrained by functional considerations, such as a nexus test, and cover all acts or omissions having a sufficient link to an existing NIAC.

Given that geographical proximity (so far) is not a determining factor in IHL, the same should apply where the territory of a non-neighbouring, non-belligerent state is affected. While it is certainly good humanitarian policy to express a preference for a law enforcement-paradigm to the use of force against individuals on the territory of a non-neighbouring, non-belligerent state, the exclusion of such territory from the geographical scope of IHL is not legally compelling. It ignores (or at least trivializes) the interdependence of different branches of international law in regulating behaviour, such as the use of force on foreign territory. Whereas it is certainly opportune to note that, most importantly, the *jus ad bellum* is 'increasingly being interpreted by some States and experts in ways that make it easier for third States to use force extraterritorially, particularly against non-State actors',[97] it may be debated whether a restrictive interpretation of the geographical scope of IHL is the appropriate legal avenue to prevent the spreading of armed conflict.

In any case, future state practice and *opinio juris* will have to provide further guidance. The fight against the 'Islamic State' and its legal classification is an important case in point as it raises various issues regarding the extraterritorial use of force. Whereas there are indications that the United States considers its fight against 'IS' as a continuation of its 'global armed conflict' with Al-Qaeda,[98] its legal

[97] ICRC (n 40) 16.

[98] See A Deeks, 'U.S. Airstrikes Against ISIS in Syria? Possible International Legal Theories' (*Lawfare Blog* 23 August 2014) <https://www.lawfareblog.com/us-airstrikes-against-isis-syria-

position has not been comprehensively set out (at least publicly).[99] Official pronouncements by allied partners on the legal basis of their own involvement are of crucial importance for the future definition of the 'boundaries of the battlefield'. So far, they seem to have continued to adopt a case-by-case approach to classifying military operations against 'IS' in Iraq, Syria, and elsewhere.[100] For example, the UK Government argued with respect to the killing of three individuals (two of which were British nationals) in Syria on 21 August 2015, that the drone strike leading to their death was lawful under the United Kingdom's right to self-defence.[101] While some have claimed that the United Kingdom's position represents 'a further step towards U.S. practice' in a 'broader trend',[102] others have rightly stressed the differences in the United States' and United Kingdom's position given that the United Kingdom, unlike the United States, relied on self-defence arguments rather than

possible-international-legal-theories> and A Deeks, 'Narrowing Down the U.S. International Legal Theory for ISIS Strikes in Syria' (*Lawfare Blog* 12 September 2014) <https://www.lawfareblog.com/narrowing-down-us-international-legal-theory-isis-strikes-syria>, concluding that 'the Administration seems to suggest that ISIS *is* [emphasis in original] al Qaeda' and not 'just' an associated force and that therefore 'the idea that ISIS is AQ certainly invites the United States to use the argument that the use of force in this context is simply a continuation of an armed conflict that has been underway for years'. See also R Chesney, 'The Global War on ISIL and its Associated Forces' (*Lawfare Blog* 14 November 2015) <https://www.lawfareblog.com/global-war-isil-and-its-associated-forces>, who argues that 'some observers have not appreciated till now that the United States would take the same position [as regards Al-Qaeda] vis-à-vis ISL' and that 'with the passage of time, the use of force against ISIL in locations outside of Syria and Iraq eventually will engender the same sorts of legal friction that strikes on al Qaeda targets in Yemen, Somalia, and Pakistan have generated'. For an early comment on the (*jus ad bellum*) legality of the use of force against 'IS' fighters in Libya, see J Rylatt, 'The Use of Force against ISIL in Libya and the Sounds of Silence' (*EJIL: Talk Blog* 6 January 2016) <http://www.ejiltalk.org/the-use-of-force-against-isil-in-libya-and-the-sounds-of-silence>.

[99] See J Bellinger, 'The Administration Should Explain its International Legal Basis to Attack ISIL in Syria' (*Lawfare Blog* 13 September 2014) <https://www.lawfareblog.com/administration-should-explain-its-international-legal-basis-attack-isil-syria> where he urges government officials to explain the United States' domestic and international legal basis for the use of force against ISIL in Iraq and Syria and concludes that 'although there is not an obvious international law basis, the Administration has legally available options to defend its actions'.

[100] For an overview of the different legal approaches regarding Syria, see J Horowitz, 'A Legal Map of Airstrikes in Syria (Part 1)' (*Just Security Blog* 7 December 2015) <https://www.justsecurity.org/28167/legal-map-airstrikes-syria-part-1> and J Horowitz, 'A Legal Map of Airstrikes in Syria (Part 2)' (*Just Security Blog* 8 December 2015) <https://www.justsecurity.org/28199/legal-map-airstrikes-syria-part-2>.

[101] For an analysis of the United Kingdom's legal position, see N Lubell, 'The Legal Questions About the UK's Drone Strike in Syria' (*Just Security Blog* 10 September 2015) <https://www.justsecurity.org/25951/legal-questions-uks-targeted-killing-syria> and N Lubell, 'The UK's Letter to the UN Security Council Leaves Plenty of Unanswered Questions About Last Month's RAF Drone Strike' (*Just Security Blog* 11 September 2015) <https://www.justsecurity.org/26006/uks-letter-security-council-leaves-open-questions-drone-strike>. See also the different submissions made to the Joint Committee on Human Rights (JCHR) tasked to investigate the United Kingdom's policy on the use of armed drones for targeted killings, especially UK Government, 'Memorandum to the JCHR' (3 December 2015) <http://www.parliament.uk/documents/joint-committees/human-rights/Government_Memorandum_on_Drones.pdf> and D Akande, 'UK Parliamentary Inquiry into UK Policy on the Use of Drones for Targeted Killing' (*EJIL: Talk Blog* 23 December 2015) <http://www.ejiltalk.org/uk-parliamentary-inquiry-into-uk-policy-on-the-use-of-drones-for-targeted-killing>.

[102] A Dworkin, 'European Countries are Edging Toward their Own War on Terror' (*Just Security Blog* 11 September 2015) <https://www.justsecurity.org/26010/european-countries-edging-war-terror>.

asserting that the strike was carried out as part of an armed conflict.[103] Similarly, France does not seem to consider itself engaged in a 'global armed conflict' against 'IS' on French or foreign territory. Apart from certain statements in the aftermath of the 13 November 2015 Paris attacks (which may be considered rhetorically important),[104] French officials have not expressed a legal position according to which France's fight against 'IS' is seen as being part of a 'global armed conflict'.[105]

Time will tell which legal position states will adopt in confronting 'IS' or similar opponents in the future. The debate will hopefully also serve to inform the debate on the geographical scope of IHL, and of NIACs in particular.

[103] See K Martin, 'UK's Legal Rationale for Drone Strikes Differs Fundamentally from U.S. Rationale' (*Just Security Blog* 25 September 2015) <https://www.justsecurity.org/26343/uk-rationale-drone-strikes-differs>.

[104] See especially F Hollande, 'Speech Before Joint Session of Parliament' (Versailles, 16 November 2015) <http://www.diplomatie.gouv.fr/en/french-foreign-policy/defence-security/parisattacks-paris-terror-attacks-november-2015/article/speech-by-the-president-of-the-republic-before-a-joint-session-of-parliament>, in which he noted that 'France is at war' and that the 'acts of war' were carried out by 'a jihadist army, by Daesh'.

[105] See A Dworkin, 'France Maps Out its War Against the Islamic State' (*European Council on Foreign Relations Website* 19 November 2015) <http://www.ecfr.eu/article/commentary_france_maps_out_its_war_against_the_islamic_state5021>, who notes that France distinguishes its military campaigns in the Middle East and North Africa as separate armed conflicts with territorial limitations in legal terms (eg regarding its legal powers to target or capture and hold enemy fighters). Furthermore, he recalls that France was already engaged in an armed conflict with 'IS' prior to the Paris attacks since French armed forces began military operations in Iraq and extended them to Syria in September 2015. The new wave of French airstrikes against 'IS' in Syria and Iraq starting 23 November 2015 consequently did not alter France's legal classification.

2

The Temporal Scope of the Laws of Armed Conflict in Multinational Military Operations

Christian Schaller

1. Introduction

International humanitarian law (IHL) is generally applicable to multinational military operations conducted in an international or non-international armed conflict, regardless of the mandate or classification of the operation.[1] The focus of the present chapter is on the temporal scope of application of IHL in such situations. This aspect may be especially relevant where troop-contributing countries send and withdraw their contingents of armed forces at different stages during an operation.

Some provisions contained in the four Geneva Conventions of 1949 (GC I–IV) and the two Additional Protocols of 1977 (AP I and II) have to be observed at all times;[2] and some individual protections continue to apply for a certain period of time even after the end of an armed conflict.[3] Most rules of IHL, however, apply only as long as the conflict actually lasts. Hence, two issues arise in this context: at what point in time does a confrontation turn into an armed conflict; and when does an armed conflict cease to exist? As there is already plenty of literature on how armed conflicts come into existence, this chapter will mainly concentrate on the

[1] T Ferraro, 'The Applicability and Application of International Humanitarian Law to Multinational Forces' (2014) 95 International Review of the Red Cross 561, 565; L Cameron and others, 'Article 3: Conflicts Not of an International Character' in K Dörmann and others (eds), *Commentary on the Second Geneva Convention: Convention (II) for the Amelioration of the Condition of Wounded, Sick and Shipwrecked Members of Armed Forces at Sea* (ICRC 2017) para 434.

[2] See, eg, the obligation to respect and ensure respect for the Geneva Conventions and Protocols in all circumstances (Common Article 1 GC I–IV; Article 1(1) AP I), to disseminate the text of the Conventions and Protocols as well as to train armed forces and civil authorities in IHL (Article 47 GC I; Article 48 GC II; Article 127 GC III; Article 144 GC IV; Articles 82, 83, 87(2) AP I; Article 19 AP II), to review the lawfulness of new weapons, means, and methods of warfare (Article 36 AP I), and to enact legislation for the prosecution of grave breaches of the Conventions and Additional Protocol I (Article 49 GC I; Article 50 GC II; Article 129 GC III; Article 146 GC IV; Article 85 AP I).

[3] See Article 5 GC I, Article 5(1) GC III, Article 6(4) GC IV, Article 3(b) AP I, Article 2(2) AP II. These provisions shall guarantee that persons who have fallen into the power of the enemy during an international armed conflict or whose liberty has been restricted for reasons related to a non-international armed conflict are protected by the Conventions and Protocols until their final release.

Christian Schaller, *The Temporal Scope of the Laws of Armed Conflict in Multinational Military Operations* In *The 'Legal Pluriverse' Surrounding Multinational Military Operations*. Edited by Robin Geiß and Heike Krieger, Oxford University Press (2020).
DOI: 10.1093/oso/9780198842965.003.0003

second question. The end of an international armed conflict is commonly associated with the 'general close of military operations'—a notion explicitly used in GC IV and AP I. As far as non-international armed conflicts are concerned, there is no consensus on the conditions under which such conflicts terminate as a matter of law. Common Article 3 GC I–IV and AP II are silent in this regard. Therefore, a test based on the traditional threshold criteria—organization of the parties and intensity of the hostilities—might be useful to determine the end of a non-international armed conflict. Irrespective of the legal character of the conflict, it remains a critical question after what period of time it can be reasonably concluded that a certain turn of events, for example the withdrawal or defeat of one party or a decrease in the intensity of violence, really marks the end of the conflict.

2. The Law of International Armed Conflict

An international armed conflict exists whenever there is a resort to armed force between two or more states.[4] In order to trigger an international armed conflict, an act must be hostile in nature.[5] It is not required, however, that the resort to armed force by one party is answered with force by the other party or that there is an incursion of armed forces into enemy territory.

2.1 The threshold question

The International Committee of the Red Cross (ICRC) holds the view that the confrontation does not need to reach a certain level of intensity or be of a certain duration.[6] Strictly speaking, IHL has to be applied to the fullest extent as soon as the first protected person is affected by the actions of a party to the conflict. This understanding has occasionally been called into question. Christopher

[4] *Prosecutor v Tadić* (Decision on the Defence Motion for Interlocutory Appeal on Jurisdiction) (1995) IT-94-1-AR72 (*Tadić* Decision on Jurisdiction) para 70. See also ICRC, *How is the Term 'Armed Conflict' Defined in International Humanitarian Law?* (Opinion Paper, March 2008) available at <https://www.icrc.org/eng/assets/files/other/opinion-paper-armed-conflict.pdf>. All URLs accessed 27 December 2018.

[5] The action must be directed against the other state, its armed forces, territory, infrastructure or population; and it must be carried out by state agents acting in an official capacity and under instructions or by other persons specifically instructed by state agents or organs to carry out such hostilities (T Ferraro and L Cameron, 'Article 2: Application of the Convention' in Dörmann and others, *Commentary on the Second Geneva Convention* (n 1) para 263).

[6] See, eg, JS Pictet (ed), *Commentary on Geneva Convention IV Relative to the Protection of Civilian Persons in Time of War* (ICRC 1958) 20; JS Pictet (ed), *Commentary on Geneva Convention III Relative to the Treatment of Prisoners of War* (ICRC 1960) 23; B Zimmermann, 'Protocol I, Article 1—General Principles and Scope of Application' in Y Sandoz, C Swinarski, and B Zimmermann (eds), *Commentary on the Additional Protocols of 8 June 1977 to the Geneva Conventions of 12 August 1949* (ICRC 1987) 62; Ferraro and Cameron (n 5) para 258.

Greenwood observed that states sometimes refrained from treating isolated incidents involving the use of interstate force as armed conflicts.[7] His observation received support by the International Law Association's Committee on Use of Force (2005–10). In its *Final Report on the Meaning of Armed Conflict in International Law* of 2010, the Committee listed a number of cases in which states drew a distinction between, on the one hand, hostile actions that they considered as 'naval incidents', 'border clashes', 'skirmishes', or 'armed provocations' and, on the other hand, situations they classified as armed conflicts.[8] These cases seem to indicate a trend in state practice that interstate uses of force are regarded as international armed conflicts only to the extent that the fighting reaches a certain intensity. The question is, however, in which cases a government's decision to abstain from characterizing a particular incident as an armed conflict was based on a legal judgment reflecting *opinio juris*, and in which instances the decision was motivated by political opportunism. A more detailed analysis would be necessary to examine whether there really is sufficient state practice and *opinio juris* to warrant the assumption that the existence of an international armed conflict presupposes a certain level of violence. From a humanitarian perspective it is advisable to stick to the traditional view advanced by the ICRC to preserve a minimum amount of legal certainty and to avoid situations in which governments and military administrations become entrapped in lengthy debates about whether an armed confrontation has already reached a certain threshold. As Gabriella Venturini noted, the functional approach followed by the ICRC 'has the merit of gradually bringing the humanitarian machinery into operation in order to ensure the best protection to individuals'.[9]

In any case, it is important to recall that the existence of an armed conflict is a matter of fact and that a state cannot evade its obligation to respect and ensure respect for IHL by simply avoiding the terminology of armed conflict. Multinational military operations must not be treated any differently. It has been suggested that multinational forces—UN forces and national units operating in association with these forces under national command—which are deployed in a peacekeeping or humanitarian mission should be regarded as parties to an armed conflict only when they become engaged in hostilities on a scale considerably higher than that defining the state of armed conflict in other contexts.[10] On the one hand, it is

[7] C Greenwood, 'Scope of Application of Humanitarian Law' in D Fleck (ed), *The Handbook of International Humanitarian Law* (2nd edn, OUP 2008) 45, 202.

[8] ILA, Committee on Use of Force (2005–10), *Final Report on the Meaning of Armed Conflict in International Law* (2010) 9–28. See also ME O'Connell, 'Defining Armed Conflict' (2009) 13 Journal of Conflict and Security Law 393, 397.

[9] G Venturini, 'The Temporal Scope of Application of the Conventions' in A Clapham, P Gaeta, and M Sassòli (eds), *The 1949 Geneva Conventions: A Commentary* (OUP 2015) 51, 55.

[10] C Greenwood, 'International Humanitarian Law and United Nations Military Operations' (1998) 1 Yearbook of International Humanitarian Law 3, 23–25. See also D Shraga, 'The Applicability of International Humanitarian Law to Peace Operations, from Rejection to Acceptance' in GL Beruto (ed), *International Humanitarian Law, Human Rights and Peace Operations* (International Institute of Humanitarian Law, 31st Round Table, Sanremo 2008) 90, 94, available at <http://www.icrc.org/eng/assets/files/other/sanremo-2008_peace_ops.pdf>.

understandable that a country which contributes armed forces to a peacekeeping or humanitarian mission might be reluctant to admit it has become party to an armed conflict.[11] One consequence for a state becoming a conflict party is that its troops qualify as legitimate targets in the sense of the principle of distinction under IHL. On the other hand, however, there is no rule in IHL that would require or justify a distinction between different types of military forces depending on the character of their mission. Even to the extent that multinational forces operate on the basis of a UN Security Council authorization and under UN command and control, the criteria for determining whether these forces are involved in armed conflict (international or non-international) are strictly the same as those applying to any other situation of armed conflict. There is no special threshold for applying IHL to multinational military operations.[12]

2.2 End of application of the law of armed conflict

The end of application of the law of international armed conflict in a particular case will be fairly easy to determine where the conflict was triggered, for instance, by the capture of soldiers or by a limited military incursion. In these cases, the release of the soldiers or the withdrawal of the intruding forces would normally put an end to the conflict.[13] The more complex and prolonged the conflict gets, the more difficult it will be to precisely identify the point in time when it actually terminates.

In the Geneva Conventions and AP I, the temporal dimension of IHL is addressed in only two provisions: Article 6 GC IV regulates the temporal scope of application of this particular Convention; and Article 3(b) AP I defines the end of application of all four Geneva Conventions as well as of the Protocol itself.[14] Both provisions differentiate between the routine application of the Conventions and Protocol on the territory of the conflict parties, situations of occupation, and cases in which individual persons remain in custody of a conflict party after the general close of military operations or after the occupation.

[11] See Greenwood, 'IHL and UN Military Operations' (n 10) 24 (referring to the operations in the former Yugoslavia and Somalia).

[12] O Engdahl, 'The Status of Peace Operation Personnel under International Humanitarian Law' (2008) 11 Yearbook of International Humanitarian Law 109, 118; Ferraro (n 1) 582.

[13] Ferraro and Cameron (n 5) para 303. See also ICRC, *International Humanitarian Law and the Challenges of Contemporary Armed Conflicts* (32nd International Conference of the Red Cross and Red Crescent, Geneva 2015) available at <http://www.icrc.org/en/document/international-humanitarian-law-and-challenges-contemporary-armed-conflicts> 9.

[14] Article 3(b) AP I stipulates that the application of the Conventions and of this Protocol shall cease, in the territory of Parties to the conflict, on the general close of military operations and, in the case of occupied territories, on the termination of the occupation, except, in either circumstance, for those persons whose final release, repatriation, or re-establishment takes place thereafter. These persons shall continue to benefit from the relevant provisions of the Conventions and of this Protocol until their final release, repatriation, or re-establishment.

2.2.1 General close of military operations

Pursuant to Article 3(b) AP I, the application of the Geneva Conventions and AP I shall cease, in the territory of the conflict parties, 'on the general close of military operations'. This notion, which is also used in Article 6(2) GC IV, has been identified by some authors as being part of customary IHL.[15] Military operations are defined by the ICRC as 'the movements, manoeuvres, and actions of any sort, carried out by the armed forces with a view to combat'.[16] Such movements, manoeuvres, and actions may also include maintaining troops on alert, deploying or redeploying troops, or mobilizing reservists.[17] Military operations in the sense of Article 6(2) GC IV and Article 3(b) AP I do not necessarily imply the use of armed force. They can continue even though hostilities have already ceased.[18] It is therefore important to draw a distinction between the general close of military operations and the cessation of active hostilities. The latter concept is used in Article 118(1) GC III, which stipulates that prisoners of war shall be released and repatriated without delay 'after the cessation of active hostilities'.[19] Julia Grignon described the difference as follows: 'While the term "hostilities", in essence, refers to the use of force as such, "military operations" refers to everything that contributes to the use of force.'[20] Consequently, an international armed conflict within the meaning of IHL might persist even beyond the cessation of hostilities.[21]

2.2.2 General conclusion of peace?

Some confusion has been caused by the Appeals Chamber of the International Criminal Tribunal for the Former Yugoslavia (ICTY) in the 1995 *Tadić* decision on jurisdiction, in which it stated that IHL in the case of an international armed conflict applied 'beyond the cessation of hostilities until a general conclusion of peace is reached'.[22] It was the understanding of the Appeals Chamber that, until

[15] R Kolb and R Hyde, *An Introduction to the International Law of Armed Conflicts* (Hart Publishing 2008) 102.
[16] B Zimmermann, 'Protocol I, Article 3—Beginning and End of Application' in Sandoz, Swinarski, and Zimmermann, *Commentary on the Additional Protocols* (n 6) 152.
[17] Ferraro and Cameron (n 5) paras 301–02.
[18] ibid 300.
[19] Other provisions of the Geneva Conventions and Additional Protocol I simply refer to the 'end of hostilities' (Article 17(4) GC I), 'end of active hostilities' (Article 33(1) AP I), or 'close of hostilities' (Articles 67, 111 GC III, Articles 46, 130(3), 133(1), 134 GC IV). These terms are considered to have the same meaning as 'cessation of active hostilities' (Y Sandoz, 'Protocol I, Article 33—Missing Persons' in Sandoz, Swinarski, and Zimmermann, *Commentary on the Additional Protocols* (n 6) 1235–38).
[20] J Grignon, 'The Geneva Conventions and the End of Occupation' in Clapham, Gaeta, and Sassòli, *The 1949 Geneva Conventions* (n 9) 1575, 1580.
[21] D Jinks, *The Temporal Scope of Application of International Humanitarian Law in Contemporary Conflicts* (Harvard Program on Humanitarian Policy and Conflict Research 2004) available at <https://hhi.harvard.edu/publications/temporal-scope-application-international-humanitarian-law-contemporary-conflicts>, 3. See also ICRC, *Challenges of Contemporary Armed Conflicts* (2015) (n 13) 9.
[22] *Tadić* Decision on Jurisdiction (n 4) para 70. See also ibid para 67. The relatively high standard formulated by the ICTY in the *Tadić* case may be owed to a certain disposition of the Appeals Chamber to construe the temporal and geographical scope of application of IHL within the purview of the Tribunal's jurisdiction as broad as possible.

such a general conclusion of peace, IHL continued to apply in the whole territory of the warring states, whether or not actual combat took place there. In 2011, the ICTY Trial Chamber in the *Gotovina* case had to assess whether the international armed conflict between Croatia and Serbia (having overall control over the Serbian Army of Krajina) had ended during the indictment period. In particular, the Trial Chamber referred to the *Tadić* formula and examined 'whether there was a general close of military operations and a general conclusion of peace'.[23] Neither the Appeals Chamber in *Tadić* nor the Trial Chamber in *Gotovina* defined what was meant by a 'general conclusion of peace'. The wording suggests that there must be some kind of formal settlement between the conflict parties.

Historically, the conclusion of a peace treaty was regarded as the standard mode to terminate a state of war.[24] Later state practice, however, has led to an understanding according to which a war may also be terminated by an armistice agreement if the parties intend that it should have this effect (as opposed to a ceasefire or truce, which is supposed to merely suspend the hostilities).[25] Since the end of the Second World War, there have not been many instances in which states concluded an actual peace treaty.[26] One example is the 1979 Treaty of Peace between Egypt and Israel;[27] another is the Peace Treaty between Israel and Jordan of 1994.[28] Jann Kleffner pointed out that belligerent states at times used instruments resembling by substance and form classical peace treaties for the purpose of ending armed conflicts that did not amount to a declared war.[29] It must be emphasized, however, that peace treaties or armistice agreements as such are neither necessary nor sufficient to terminate the application of IHL in a situation of international armed conflict.[30] On the one hand, it is very well conceivable that an armed conflict simply runs out without any legal settlement. The Falkland Islands War between Argentina and the United Kingdom, for example, ended after 10 weeks of hostilities with a de facto ceasefire in June 1982 (while it took the parties several years to restore their relations afterwards).[31] On the other hand, even a peace treaty is by far

[23] *Prosecutor v Gotovina et al* (Judgment) (2011) ICTY-06-90-T, para 1694.

[24] Greenwood, 'Scope of Application' (n 7) 222.

[25] ibid 233; W Heintschel von Heinegg, 'Factors in War to Peace Transitions' (2004) 27 Harvard Journal of Law & Public Policy 843, 849–50 (referring, in particular, to the 1949 General Armistice Agreements between Israel and Egypt, Israel and Lebanon, Israel and Jordan, and Israel and Syria, as well as to the 1953 Panmunjom Agreement concerning a military armistice in Korea). Until the World Wars, armistice agreements were considered to merely suspend a war. See Articles 36–41 of the Hague Regulations.

[26] For an overview of peace treaties linked to the Second World War, see Y Dinstein, *War, Aggression and Self-Defence* (5th edn, CUP 2011) 35.

[27] Treaty of Peace between the Arab Republic of Egypt and the State of Israel (26 March 1979) 1136 UNTS 100. See also registration effected in the name of Israel on 14 June 1979, 1138 UNTS 59.

[28] Treaty of Peace between the State of Israel and the Hashemite Kingdom of Jordan (26 October 1994) 2042 UNTS 351.

[29] JK Kleffner, 'Peace Treaties' in R Wolfrum (ed), *Max Planck Encyclopedia of Public International Law* (Online Edn, OUP 2017) available at <http://opil.ouplaw.com/home/epil> 8.

[30] Zimmermann, 'Protocol I, Article 3' (n 16) s 152; Venturini (n 9) 57.

[31] See M Waibel, 'Falkland Islands/Islas Malvinas' in Wolfrum, *Max Planck Encyclopedia* (n 29) 14–16.

no guarantee that the hostilities effectively stop. In 1973, the parties to the Vietnam War concluded an *Agreement on Ending the War and Restoring Peace in Vietnam*.[32] This Agreement contained provisions on an immediate and unlimited ceasefire, the withdrawal of troops, and the return of captured and detained persons; and it also provided for national reconciliation, the settlement of disputed questions, the reunification of Vietnam, and the re-establishing of normal relations in various fields. Despite this agreement, the fighting continued for over two years. Only in April 1975, the Vietnam War finally ended with the unconditional surrender of the government of South Vietnam following a major military offensive by North Vietnam and the capture of Saigon.[33]

Marko Milanovic thus noted that agreements or unilateral statements by the conflict parties, as well as resolutions of international organizations, may provide important evidence that the conflict is over. At the same time, he cautioned that a formal peace treaty 'might not be worth the paper it is written on if hostilities continue unabated'.[34] In his view, it ultimately mattered whether the hostilities had in fact stopped with a degree of stability and permanence.[35] Even a ceasefire agreement may have the effect that the hostilities come to a permanent close. Given the factual nature of the concept of armed conflict introduced by the Geneva Conventions, it is consequential to focus on the effectiveness of the termination rather than on any formal criteria.[36]

2.2.3 End of application in cases of occupied territory

In the case of occupied territory, the application of GC IV shall cease one year after the general close of military operations (Article 6(3) GC IV). For the duration of the occupation, however, the occupying power shall still be bound by certain core provisions to the extent that it exercises the functions of government in the territory. Article 3(b) AP I provides for a different solution by stating that, in the case of occupied territories, the Conventions and AP I shall cease to apply on the termination of the occupation. According to Article 3(b) AP I, the law of occupation contained in GC IV and the Protocol is thus applicable in its entirety for as long as the occupation lasts. While some authors argue that Article 3(b) AP I now reflects customary international law and that the limitation contained in Article 6(3) GC IV has become largely obsolete,[37] others doubt that the concept embodied in

[32] Agreement on Ending the War and Restoring Peace in Viet-Nam (27 January 1973) 935 UNTS 2; Protocol to the Agreement on Ending the War and Restoring Peace in Viet-Nam Concerning the Return of Captured Military Personnel and Foreign Civilians and Captured and Detained Vietnamese Civilian Personnel (27 January 1973) 935 UNTS 202.

[33] See ND Hopt-Nguyen, 'Vietnam' in Wolfrum, *Max Planck Encyclopedia* (n 29) 32–35.

[34] M Milanovic, 'The End of Application of International Humanitarian Law' (2014) 96 International Review of the Red Cross 163, 172.

[35] ibid 171–72. See also Kolb and Hyde (n 15) 102.

[36] See Greenwood, 'Scope of Application' (n 7) 250.

[37] Kolb and Hyde (n 15) 104.

Article 3(b) AP I really has a binding effect on the United States, Israel, and other states that are not parties to AP I.[38]

Occupation generally comes to an end when the occupying power loses effective territorial control and the ability to exercise governmental authority in that territory (eg when it withdraws or is driven out of the occupied territory), or when the local government in the occupied territory validly consents to the occupant's presence.[39] The fact that an occupation has been terminated does not necessarily mean that the international armed conflict is over. This would be the case only if there was a general close of military operations. It is, however, beyond the purview of this chapter to examine the temporal scope of the law of belligerent occupation in greater detail.

2.2.4 Individual protection against continued detention

Some protective provisions in the Geneva Conventions and AP I survive the end of the armed conflict. For wounded and sick persons who enjoy protection under GC I and who have fallen into the hands of the enemy, the Convention shall apply 'until their final repatriation' (Article 5 GC I). Geneva Convention III applies to prisoners of war from the time they fall into the power of the enemy 'until their final release and repatriation' (Article 5(1) GC III). Persons protected under GC IV as well as under AP I shall continue to benefit from such protection even if their final release, repatriation, or re-establishment takes place after the general close of military operations or after the end of an occupation (Article 6(4) GC IV and Article 3(b) AP I). Likewise, persons specifically protected by Article 75 AP I who are arrested, detained, or interned for reasons related to the armed conflict shall enjoy that protection 'until their final release, repatriation or re-establishment, even after the end of the armed conflict' (Article 75(6) AP I).

'Final release' within the meaning of these provisions denotes the end of any form of deprivation or restriction of a person's liberty in the context of an armed conflict or occupation; 'repatriation' means that a person returns to his or her home country; and 're-establishment' refers to the transfer of a person to a third country where he or she is permitted to settle.[40]

These provisions are of vital practical importance because the process of release, repatriation, and re-establishment may take some time. Robert Kolb and Richard Hyde mentioned in particular the armed conflict between India and Pakistan (1971) as well as the Iran-Iraq War (1980–88), where it took several years to release and repatriate prisoners.[41] Other examples are the 1990/91 Gulf War and the

[38] For an overview, see Grignon (n 20) 1578–79 and 1581–85; Venturini (n 9) 59.

[39] On the temporal scope of the law of belligerent occupation see A Roberts, 'Occupation, Military, Termination of' in Wolfrum, *Max Planck Encyclopedia* (n 29); E Benvenisti, *The International Law of Occupation* (2nd edn, OUP 2012) 55–58.

[40] Zimmermann, 'Protocol I, Article 3' (n 16) s 158.

[41] Kolb and Hyde (n 15) 103.

war between Eritrea and Ethiopia (1998–2000).[42] In multinational military operations and situations of multinational occupation as in the 2003 Iraq War (but also in non-international armed conflict scenarios such as Afghanistan), the issue of detention and internment is particularly critical. In such contexts, each troop-contributing country is individually bound by the relevant provisions for as long as it exercises power over protected persons, irrespective of whether the armed conflict still exists in a legal sense.

3. The Law of Non-international Armed Conflict

Multinational military operations that are conducted against non-state organized armed groups are governed by the law of non-international armed conflict. Such a conflict involving multinational forces begins and ends as a matter of IHL under conditions no different from those applying to non-international armed conflicts in which a single state fights against an organized armed group.[43]

As far as the temporal dimension of the law of non-international armed conflict is concerned, one provision deserves particular attention: according to Article 2(2) AP II, all persons who have been deprived of their liberty or whose liberty has been restricted for reasons related to the conflict (as well as persons who were arrested after the end of the conflict for the same reasons) shall enjoy protection under Articles 5 and 6 of the Protocol until the end of such deprivation or restriction.[44] This guarantee covers all possible situations from police supervision to imprisonment. It is an equivalent to those Articles in the Geneva Conventions and AP I that guarantee protection of combatants and civilians who have fallen into the hands of the enemy during an international armed conflict until their final release, repatriation, or re-establishment.

The bulk of the law of non-international armed conflict (whether customary IHL or codified in AP II), however, is applicable only as long as the conflict actually lasts. While it is generally accepted that a non-international armed conflict comes into existence when the hostilities between a state and sufficiently organized armed groups or between such groups reach a certain level of intensity, it is less clear under which conditions such a conflict terminates as a matter of law.[45]

[42] See Venturini (n 9) 57.

[43] It is debatable, though, whether a troop-contributing country that has not joined the operation from the beginning will become a conflict party by merely providing technical support to other troop-contributing countries already active in a pre-existing conflict or whether it will acquire this status only when its forces actually get involved in protracted armed violence with the enemy. For an in-depth discussion see Ferraro (n 1) 583–87.

[44] Article 25(1) AP II contains a corresponding guarantee in case a High Contracting Party denounces the Protocol.

[45] Transformation from international to non-international armed conflict and vice versa is not subject to examination in this chapter, although such a process also implies the end of one type of armed conflict and the beginning of another. See D Akande, 'Classification of Armed Conflicts: Relevant Legal

3.1 Recalling the threshold criteria

Common Article 3 GC I–IV covers all armed conflicts not of an international character. This provision is supplemented by AP II of 1977 regulating non-international armed conflicts that take place in the territory of a High Contracting Party between its armed forces and dissident armed forces or other organized armed groups which, under responsible command, exercise such territorial control as to enable them to carry out sustained and concerted military operations and to implement the Protocol (Article 1(1) AP II). The Protocol does not apply to situations of internal disturbances and tensions, such as riots, isolated and sporadic acts of violence, and other acts of a similar nature (Article 1(2) AP II). Such situations are generally not regarded as armed conflicts under IHL.

The standard definition of a non-international armed conflict within the meaning of Common Article 3 GC I–IV and corresponding customary IHL originates from the ICTY Appeals Chamber's 1995 *Tadić* decision on jurisdiction. According to that definition, a non-international armed conflict exists whenever there is 'protracted armed violence between governmental authorities and organized armed groups or between such groups within a State'.[46] The *Tadić* definition has since been widely recited in national and international jurisprudence, military manuals, and a variety of other legal and interpretive documents.[47] It is now fairly well established that the existence of a non-international armed conflict requires a certain intensity of violence and a certain degree of organization of the parties.[48] These criteria help to distinguish armed conflicts from banditry, unorganized and short-lived insurrections, or terrorist activities not falling under IHL.[49]

The use of the word 'protracted' by the ICTY Appeals Chamber in the 1995 *Tadić* decision on jurisdiction seems to add a temporal element to the definition of non-international armed conflict. The majority view, however, does not consider 'protractedness' to be a separate constitutive criterion of armed conflict. Mostly, this element is treated as an integral component of the intensity test.[50] As Derek Jinks noted, the 'protracted' armed violence requirement is best understood as little more than a restatement of the general rule excluding isolated and sporadic acts of violence from the scope of IHL.[51] Sandesh Sivakumaran illustrated that a

Concepts' in E Wilmshurst (ed), *International Law and the Classification of Conflicts* (OUP 2012) 32, 57–63; Milanovic (n 34) 181–83.

46 *Tadić* Decision on Jurisdiction (n 4) para 70.

47 See S Sivakumaran, *The Law of Non-international Armed Conflict* (OUP 2012) 166. See also ICRC, *How is the Term 'Armed Conflict' Defined in International Humanitarian Law?* (n 4).

48 For a detailed discussion of the threshold criteria, see A Cullen, *The Concept of Non-International Armed Conflict in International Humanitarian Law* (CUP 2010) 117–58.

49 *Prosecutor v Tadić* (Opinion and Judgment) (1997) ICTY-94-1-T, para 562.

50 See, eg, Cameron and others (n 1) para 462.

51 Jinks (n 21) 6.

relatively brief period of violence could also cross the threshold of an armed conflict as far as there are other significant factors indicating a certain degree of intensity.[52] In the *La Tablada* case, dealing with an attack on a military base in Argentina in 1989, the Inter-American Commission on Human Rights even classified a situation that lasted only about 30 hours as a non-international armed conflict within the meaning of Common Article 3 GC I–IV.[53] In particular, the Commission referred to the concerted nature of the hostile acts undertaken by the attackers, the direct involvement of governmental armed forces, and the level of violence.[54]

Because there is no general consensus on the exact degree of intensity and organization necessary to turn a situation into a non-international armed conflict, the ICTY identified a number of indicative factors that may provide some guidance.[55] Indicative factors relating to the intensity criterion include the number, gravity, duration, and geographic spread of individual confrontations, the number of forces, the extent of material destruction, the number of casualties, and the number of civilians fleeing combat zones. Another important aspect is whether a state uses means and methods of warfare or whether it confines itself to policing and law enforcement. Relevant factors indicating the necessary degree of organization include the existence of disciplinary mechanisms and of an infrastructure enabling the group to recruit fighters and provide them with arms and training; also the ability to develop a unified military strategy, to use military tactics, and to plan, coordinate, and carry out concerted military operations, as well as the ability to speak with one voice, negotiate and conclude agreements, and to apply IHL. The control of a certain territory may also be regarded as evidence for an effective organizational structure of an armed group. It is important to note, however, that these factors were mainly developed with a view to larger-scale civil wars like the one in the former Yugoslavia. Different characteristics may therefore be relevant in other conflict scenarios, especially in the context of military counterterrorism operations.[56] Hence, the assessment will always have to be made on a case-by-case basis with due regard to the specifics of the particular conflict.

The evolution of a relatively high threshold for non-international armed conflicts (which presupposes a level of violence higher than that required for the existence of an international armed conflict) results from general concerns shared by many states that IHL could restrict their freedom of action when dealing with rebellions, insurgencies, and civil war. More and more, however, the law of non-international armed conflict has become an important concept for governments to legitimize

52 Sivakumaran (n 47) 168. See also Cullen (n 48) 145.

53 *Juan Carlos Abella v Argentina*, Case No 11.137, Report No 55/97, Inter-American Court of Human Rights (1997) paras 154–56.

54 ibid para 155.

55 See, eg, *Prosecutor v Limaj et al* (Judgment) (2005) ICTY-03-66-T, paras 84–173; *Prosecutor v Haradinaj et al* (Judgment) (2008) ICTY-04-84-T, paras 37–100; *Prosecutor v Boškoski and Tarčulovski* (Judgment) (2008) ICTY-04-82-T, paras 175–206.

56 Sivakumaran (n 47) 167–68, 170.

certain measures that would otherwise be prohibited under international human rights law. This tendency is particularly apparent in the fight against terrorism.[57] Claus Kreß observed that states seemed to be more interested in availing themselves of the wider powers they could derive from the application of the law of non-international armed conflict (compared to international human rights law) than they were concerned by the restraining effect of the ensuing obligations.[58]

3.2 Determining the end of a non-international armed conflict

Additional Protocol II does not contain any provision that defines the Protocol's temporal scope of application. The 1987 ICRC Commentary on Article 2 AP II notes that a proposed amendment to the Protocol according to which its application should have ceased 'upon the general cessation of military operations' could not be adopted during the Diplomatic Conference in Geneva. [59] It can be argued that AP II becomes inapplicable already when the territorial control exercised by the non-state party falls below the level necessary for carrying out sustained and concerted military operations and for implementing the Protocol. In such a case of significant loss of territorial control, the requirements established by Article 1 AP II would not be fulfilled anymore.[60] A different question is when an armed conflict falling under Common Article 3 GC I–IV and corresponding customary IHL ceases to exist.

3.2.1 Peaceful settlement?

In the 1995 *Tadić* decision on jurisdiction, the ICTY Appeals Chamber held that, in the case of a non-international armed conflict, IHL applies beyond the cessation of hostilities 'until a peaceful settlement is achieved'.[61] This statement corresponds to the Appeals Chamber's position that IHL in international armed conflicts continues to apply 'until a general conclusion of peace is reached'.[62] The *Haradinaj* judgment of 2008 contains a passage in which the Trial Chamber also employed the 'peaceful settlement' standard.[63] Here, the Trial Chamber deemed it

[57] See, eg, C Schaller, 'Using Force Against Terrorists "Outside Areas of Active Hostilities"—The Obama Approach and the Bin Laden Raid Revisited' (2015) 20 Journal of Conflict and Security Law 195.

[58] C Kreß, 'Some Reflections on the International Legal Framework Governing Transnational Armed Conflicts' (2010) 15 Journal of Conflict and Security Law 245, 260.

[59] SS Junod, 'Protocol II, Article 2—Personal Field of Application' in Sandoz, Swinarski, and Zimmermann, *Commentary on the Additional Protocols* (n 6) s 4492.

[60] On Additional Protocol II conflicts turning into conflicts under Common Article 3 GC I–IV see *Proceedings of the 13th Bruges Colloquium, Scope of Application of International Humanitarian Law* (College of Europe and ICRC 2013) available at <http://www.coleurope.eu/news/publication-proceedings-13th-bruges-colloquium>, 102–03.

[61] *Tadić* Decision on Jurisdiction (n 4) para 70.

[62] ibid.

[63] *Prosecutor v Haradinaj et al* (n 55) para 100.

unnecessary to explore the 'oscillating intensity' of the armed conflict in question because it found that there was no evidence of a peaceful settlement. In the view of the Trial Chamber, even a possible decrease in the intensity of the hostilities would have been of no relevance as long as a peaceful settlement was not achieved. The 'peaceful settlement' standard created by the ICTY has since been affirmed in several other decisions and legal documents[64] and has found some support in the literature. Lindsay Moir, for example, is convinced that once the threshold of intensity had been crossed, it could undulate without affecting the existence of the armed conflict and the application of IHL.[65]

But what did both Chambers of the ICTY mean by using the notion of a peaceful settlement? The term 'settlement' points to some kind of agreement. It is not uncommon that parties to a non-international armed conflict conclude a formal peace agreement to resolve their differences.[66] Sometimes, specific aspects of the settlement are regulated in separate agreements, and sometimes even ceasefire agreements might pave the way for a permanent resolution of the conflict.[67] These kinds of instruments have to be distinguished from peace treaties *strictu sensu*, which can be concluded between state parties only.[68] Peace agreements that involve non-state actors are not subject to the 1969 and 1986 Vienna Conventions on the Law of Treaties. This does not exclude that such agreements could have legal force.[69] Their status under international law, however, is controversial.[70]

The ICRC considers the *Tadić* reference to 'peaceful settlement' as insufficient to provide practical guidance on the temporal scope of application of IHL because it could be interpreted as 'introducing a measure of formalism in a determination that should, first and foremost, be driven by facts on the ground'.[71] Again, it has to be underlined that the conclusion of a formal agreement is neither necessary nor sufficient to end application of IHL.[72] On the one hand, a non-international armed conflict, which is a state of fact, can terminate very well without any kind of cooperative settlement. Rogier Bartels illustrated that non-international armed conflicts may 'just taper until they have withered away until no warring parties exist anymore'.[73] On the other hand, just like in situations of international armed

[64] For further references see Cameron and others (n 1) para 508.

[65] L Moir, 'The Concept of Non-International Armed Conflict' in Clapham, Gaeta, and Sassòli, *The 1949 Geneva Conventions* (n 9) 391, 413.

[66] See C Bell, 'Peace Agreements: Their Nature and Legal Status' (2006) 100 AJIL 373; Venturini (n 9) 62.

[67] C Bell, 'Ceasefire' in Wolfrum, *Max Planck Encyclopedia* (n 29) 14–15.

[68] Kleffner (n 29) 1.

[69] See Article 3 of the Vienna Convention on the Law of Treaties and Article 3 of the Vienna Convention on the Law of Treaties between States and International Organizations or between International Organizations.

[70] Kleffner (n 29) 21–24.

[71] ICRC, *Challenges of Contemporary Armed Conflicts* (2015) (n 13) 10.

[72] Cameron and others (n 1) para 512.

[73] R Bartels, 'From *Jus In Bello* to *Jus Post Bellum*: When do Non-International Armed Conflicts End?' in C Stahn, JS Easterday, and J Iverson (eds), *Jus Post Bellum: Mapping the Normative Foundations* (OUP 2014) 297, 303.

conflict, a formal peace agreement does not necessarily have an impact on the actual conduct of hostilities.

To be clear, a formal act intended to reach a peaceful settlement may very well constitute the end of the conflict—but only if it is effectively implemented by the parties.[74] Jann Kleffner rightly noted that the statement made by the ICTY Appeals Chamber in *Tadić* holds true to the extent that the settlement would not be a matter of mere agreement but is also an accurate description of the factual situation on the ground.[75]

3.2.2 Towards a threshold criteria test

The International Law Association's Committee on Use of Force (2005–10) suggested that if an armed conflict exists when organized armed groups are engaged in intense fighting, then, logically, the conflict ends when these criteria are no longer present.[76] According to this approach, it must be assessed whether the degree of organization of the parties or the intensity of violence has dropped below a certain threshold separating non-international armed conflicts from lower-intensity post-conflict violence.

First of all, it is important to recall that a non-international armed conflict exists only as far and as long as there are at least two opposing factions sufficiently organized to qualify as conflict parties in terms of IHL. Non-state armed groups cease to fulfil the conditions for being a conflict party when they become so disorganized that they are not capable anymore of participating in protracted collective hostilities of a certain intensity. As far as states are concerned, there seems to be a presumption that their armed forces generally meet the requisite level of organization.

Obviously, an armed conflict ends when one side is completely defeated.[77] It is more likely, however, that a conflict drags on for a long time—perhaps with new parties entering the stage while others fall apart—without any clear signs of who might be victorious at the end. The *Conflict Data Program* established by the Department of Peace and Conflict Research at Uppsala University in Sweden (UCDP) shows that most conflicts do not end with the clear victory of one side or with the conclusion of a peace agreement but more often terminate under unclear circumstances where fighting simply ceases.[78] UCDP reveals that the majority of intra-state armed conflicts since 1956 ended without any decisive outcome.[79]

In the logic of a threshold test, a non-international armed conflict can also end with a decrease in the intensity of violence. Application of the law of

[74] Y Dinstein, *Non-international Armed Conflicts in International Law* (CUP 2014) 48.

[75] Kleffner (n 29) 10.

[76] ILA, *Final Report on the Meaning of Armed Conflict* (n 8) 30. See also Milanovic (n 34) 170; Bartels (n 73) 303; Dinstein, *Non-international Armed Conflicts* (n 74) 48.

[77] Cameron and others (n 1) para 511.

[78] J Kreutz, 'How and When Armed Conflicts End: Introducing the UCDP Conflict Termination Dataset' (2010) 47 Journal of Peace Research 243.

[79] ibid 246.

non-international armed conflict is triggered only where acts of violence are sufficiently protracted and not just isolated and sporadic. It is plausible to argue that the very same threshold should apply to the end of application of IHL in situations of non-international armed conflict. This means that the dividing line between the armed conflict and post-conflict violence would be crossed when the violence falls below a certain level of intensity. Accordingly, the end of a non-international armed conflict would not require a total absence of armed violence on the territory in question. If such a total absence of violence was required it could happen that a situation will continuously be treated as a non-international armed conflict even though the fighting has already lost the quality that originally turned the situation into an armed conflict. Terrorists, sectarian groups, and organized criminals often benefit from the failure of the state to maintain law and order during and after an armed conflict. Thus, there may still be a general atmosphere of insecurity. The decisive question is whether violent acts committed in this environment are merely isolated and sporadic or whether they are sufficiently protracted to constitute a non-international armed conflict.[80] To the extent that the old conflict between the original parties flares up (or additional parties emerge and start a new conflict), IHL will of course start to apply again. The situation in Afghanistan, Iraq, Libya, and Syria illustrates how difficult it is to draw a line between, on the one hand, hostilities that are directly related to one or more existing armed conflicts and, on the other hand, incidental acts of unorganized non-state violence that are more or less a by-product of those conflicts.

4. When is an Armed Conflict Really Over? The Question of Evidence

While it may be possible to formulate abstract criteria for determining the end of an armed conflict, it is completely unclear after what period of time it can be reasonably presumed in a specific case that these criteria are definitely fulfilled (that a certain turn of events in the course of the conflict actually marks the end of that conflict). In other words: for how long must the phase during which military operations have come to a general close continue to last before it can be concluded that an international armed conflict is definitely over as a matter of IHL? And for how long does the intensity of the fighting have to fall below a certain level in order to warrant the assumption that the end of a non-international armed conflict is actually reached?

It is not unusual for both international and non-international armed conflicts that the intensity of the hostilities decreases gradually and slowly. The *UCDP*

[80] See Cameron and others (n 1) paras 511, 516.

Conflict Termination Dataset demonstrates that many conflicts are in fact 'on-and-off' affairs where periods of relative calm alternate with heavy clashes.[81] Sometimes conflicts are interrupted by an unstable ceasefire or become frozen in the aftermath of an outside intervention. It is therefore important to clarify in each case whether a decline in hostile action already indicates the end of the conflict, or whether it is merely an interlude.

4.1 International armed conflicts—waiting for a general, definitive, and effective termination

In the *Gotovina* judgment of 2011, the ICTY Trial Chamber stressed that '[o]nce the law of armed conflict has become applicable, one should not lightly conclude that its applicability ceases'.[82] Otherwise, the participants in the conflict could find themselves in a 'revolving door between applicability and non-applicability, leading to a considerable degree of legal uncertainty and confusion'.[83] Therefore, the Trial Chamber examined whether the armed conflict in question had found 'a sufficiently general, definitive and effective termination'.[84] According to Marko Milanovic, a certain degree of stability and permanence should be required for the termination of an international armed conflict due to the fact that the threshold of such conflicts is relatively easy to satisfy and 'because it would be both impractical and would open the door to abuse to treat every lull in the fighting as an end to [the conflict] and each resumption of combat as the start of a new one'.[85]

A similar approach is followed by the ICRC, which assumes that an international armed conflict continues to exist as long as there are ongoing military movements by the belligerents and as far as it can be reasonably expected that the hostilities are likely to resume in the near future.[86] This standard implies that it is not sufficient to monitor the actual movements on the ground. Rather, in order to evaluate whether there is a risk of resumption of hostilities, one would also have to take into account, as far as possible, the intentions and expectations of the conflict parties. Wolff Heintschel von Heinegg asserted that every termination of war necessarily comprised a consensual element and that states never relied upon objective criteria alone.[87] Consequently, there should be clear evidence of a genuine intent of all parties to terminate the conflict. Such consent does not need to be demonstrated by an explicit agreement. Yoram Dinstein expounded that a war might also end if the

[81] Kreutz (n 78) 244.
[82] *Prosecutor v Gotovina et al* (n 23) para 1694.
[83] ibid.
[84] ibid.
[85] Milanovic (n 34) 171. See also ICRC, *Challenges of Contemporary Armed Conflicts* (2015) (n 13) 9.
[86] Ferraro and Cameron (n 5) para 300. See also ICRC, *Challenges of Contemporary Armed Conflicts* (2015) (n 13) 9.
[87] Heintschel von Heinegg (n 25) 853.

belligerent parties implicitly consented to terminate the hostilities or if one party unilaterally declared such termination and the other party was willing to abide by that declaration.[88] At the same time, he cautioned that tacit consent should not be presumed too easily and that some supplementary evidence was necessary to unequivocally demonstrate that none of the parties intended to resume fighting.[89] The withdrawal of troops could be strong evidence, especially if monitored by the United Nations or a regional organization. The fact that refugees and internally displaced persons start to return to their home regions is also reflective of a general expectation that the conflict is about to be overcome. Similarly, the beginning of reconstruction efforts or declarations and decisions by external actors often reflect such an expectation. A clear sign would be the start of a process towards establishing a state of positive peace through the settlement of disputed questions and the resumption of diplomatic or economic relations between the former belligerents.[90] The more convincing such evidence, the sooner it may be established that the conflict has found a sufficiently general, definitive, and effective termination. The less clear the signs, the more time should have passed before it ought to be assumed that military operations have not only been suspended temporarily but indeed have come to a general close.

4.2 Applying a similar standard to non-international armed conflicts—the 'risk of resumption' test

The rationale of the standard developed by the ICTY in *Gotovina*—to avoid 'revolving door' classifications which might lead to legal uncertainty and confusion—also applies to non-international armed conflicts.[91] As Marko Milanovic notes, it would be undesirable as a matter of policy to have a non-international armed conflict 'which peters in and out of existence on a daily basis'.[92] This consideration has to be taken into account when employing a threshold criteria test to determine the end of a non-international armed conflict.

A closer look at the conflict parties may provide some evidence. If an armed group is deprived of its leadership, suffers from internal anarchy and decay, or loses its combat infrastructure due to arrests, killing, or defection of fighters, there are good reasons to assume that its level of organization is about to fall below the threshold relevant for the existence of a non-international armed conflict. The effective and complete disarmament and demobilization of the military arm of a non-state party would certainly constitute the end of the given conflict

[88] Dinstein, *War, Aggression and Self-Defence* (n 26) 48–51.
[89] ibid.
[90] ibid.
[91] Cameron and others (n 1) paras 515, 518.
[92] Milanovic (n 34) 180.

(as far as there are no other organized armed groups involved).[93] In many cases, the United Nations plays an important role in the supervision and implementation of such processes. Rogier Bartels referred to the armed conflict in Sierra Leone during the 1990s, which had survived a ceasefire and a peace agreement before the Revolutionary United Front (RUF) was finally defeated and dissolved.[94] In January 2002, the civil war was officially declared over by the government following the disarmament and demobilization of more than 75,000 former fighters under the supervision of the UN Mission in Sierra Leone. Another case that displays how a non-international armed conflict may terminate with a clear defeat of one side is the conflict between the Government of Sri Lanka and the Liberation Tigers of Tamil Eelam (LTTE), which came to an end in May 2009 after many years of intense fighting.[95] An important turn in the course of the conflict had been the break-away from the LTTE of an influential commander and some 5,000 troops in 2004. Ultimately, it was the killing of nearly the entire LTTE leadership that set the seal on the organization's defeat in May 2009.

An armed group that has suffered merely a minor defeat, however, may regroup and, after a certain period of time, carry on with its operations, especially if it still controls a part of the territory and continues to recruit, train, and arm new fighters.[96] In such cases, it should not be assumed too quickly that the armed conflict has already come to an end.[97] Concentrating on temporary lulls in violence might also lead to a premature conclusion that the conflict has been terminated. Marko Milanovic therefore suggests that the hostilities must fall—with a certain degree of permanence and stability—below the threshold of protracted armed violence.[98] As with determining the beginning of an armed conflict, identifying its end requires an assessment based on the specific facts of the case. Attention should be paid to a possible decline in the gravity, frequency, duration, and geographic spread of individual confrontations between the parties. Especially, a noticeable decrease in material destruction and in the number of casualties may warrant the assumption that the fighting has lost its original intensity. A particularly strong signal would be the disengagement of state armed forces from combat zones following an official proclamation by the government that military operations have been concluded. Where the parties used to resort to hit-and-run attacks, pinprick assaults, or sporadic drone strikes, however, it may be particularly difficult to interpret the ups and downs in the intensity of hostilities. The ICRC therefore advocates a standard similar to that employed for determining the end of an international

93 Cameron and others (n 1) para 511.
94 Bartels (n 73) 303.
95 See Report of the Secretary-General's Panel of Experts on Accountability in Sri Lanka (31 March 2011) available at <http://www.un.org/News/dh/infocus/Sri_Lanka/POE_Report_Full.pdf>. See also SR Ratner, 'Accountability and the Sri Lankan Civil War' (2012) 106 AJIL 795.
96 Cameron and others (n 1) para 511.
97 ibid.
98 Milanovic (n 34) 180.

armed conflict: 'a lasting cessation of armed confrontations without real risk of resumption'.[99] Accordingly, the ICRC waits for the complete cessation of hostilities between the parties to a non-international armed conflict before assessing, based on the surrounding factual circumstances, whether there is a real risk of resumption of hostilities.[100] But the focus of the 'risk of resumption' test is not only on the cessation of hostilities. The test also includes an evaluation of whether related military operations of a hostile nature have ended.[101]

To sum up, in the words of Tristan Ferraro, a non-international armed conflict involving multinational forces can be considered to have terminated when either the non-state armed group has disappeared or otherwise no longer meets the requisite level of organization, or when the hostilities have ceased and there is no risk of their resumption.[102] Where the conflict continues to exist between the territorial state and the non-state armed group, troop-contributing countries that definitely and effectively disengage from the conduct of hostilities will no longer be parties to that conflict.[103]

5. Concluding Remarks: Coping with Uncertainty

Ex post, in court trial or in an academic exercise, it may be possible to trace the decisive episodes and tipping points of an armed conflict and to identify a single date that marks its termination (although this sometimes seems somewhat arbitrary). In the midst of action, however, a reliable assessment is almost impossible.[104] In particular, it is difficult to imagine how it could be ascertained that an apparent decrease in the intensity of violence or even a complete cessation of hostilities is not only temporary and that there is no real risk of resumption. Such determinations involve a considerable degree of subjectivity, projection, and uncertainty. Using standards based on duration—as explained by Marco Sassòli—is always problematic not only for the conflict parties, their commanders, and soldiers, but also for the civilian population and humanitarian actors because they would be required to foresee how the situation develops before they could know whether they have to comply with the pertinent rules of IHL, are protected by them, or could invoke them at all.[105] The facts pertaining to a situation under consideration are mostly

[99] Cameron and others (n 1) para 513. See also ICRC, *Challenges of Contemporary Armed Conflicts* (2015) (n 13) 10–11.
[100] ICRC, *Challenges of Contemporary Armed Conflicts* (2015) (n 13) 11.
[101] ibid.
[102] Ferraro (n 1) 607.
[103] ibid.
[104] See AJ Carswell, 'Classifying the Conflict: A Soldier's Dilemma' (2009) 91 International Review of the Red Cross 143.
[105] M Sassòli, 'The Concept and the Beginning of Occupation' in Clapham, Gaeta, and Sassòli, *The 1949 Geneva Conventions* (n 9) 1389, 1398.

unclear or disputed. Collating the necessary evidence is thus often impeded by conflicting narratives and, as Louise Arimatsu described it, by the 'volatile chaos that is the very nature of armed conflict'.[106]

The ICRC noted that it is impossible to state in the abstract how much time needs to pass without armed confrontations before it can be concluded with an acceptable degree of certainty that a situation has stabilized.[107] Therefore, a longer period of observation might be necessary while, in the meantime, IHL will continue to apply.[108] In the view of the ICRC, it would be 'preferable not to be too hasty and thereby risk a "revolving door" classification' switching between applicability and non-applicability of IHL.[109] It could be argued that, as a general guideline, the longer the period of hostilities has lasted, the more time should elapse during the cool-down phase before the armed conflict as such should be considered over.

Finally, two other issues that are closely linked to the subject of this chapter should be highlighted. First, it is hardly feasible to determine the end of an armed conflict without having precisely identified the geographic dimension of the conflict. Possible trends in the quality and quantity of hostilities can only be tracked and interpreted if it is clear where exactly the conflict takes place. For example, if a non-international armed conflict exists across state borders or spreads to different regions, it is unlikely that the hostilities in these different places occur synchronously. In some locations the hostilities may be finished whereas in other locations the fighting may have just begun. The rolling US 'war' against Al-Qaeda and associated forces in Afghanistan, Pakistan, Yemen, Somalia, Iraq, Libya, and other places is a particularly instructive example as it raises a variety of issues relating to the geographic scope of application of the law of armed conflict.[110]

Secondly, it needs to be taken into account that in many cases, transformation from conflict to post-conflict is a gradual process. Therefore, the question arises whether and to what extent IHL, which is *lex specialis* to the continuously applicable body of international human rights law in situations of armed conflict, should be complemented by an even more tailor-made framework of legal norms during such cool-down periods. The most pragmatic approach would be a functional application of different overlapping branches of international law. The role of and interplay between the relevant branches of law is dealt with under the concept of *jus post bellum*. In the words of Jann Kleffner, the applicability *ratione temporis* of the *jus post bellum* would 'not be an abrupt "all or nothing" exercise, but a fluid and flexible gradual phasing in and out'.[111] According to Kleffner, constant monitoring

[106] L Arimatsu, 'The Democratic Republic of the Congo [1993–2010]' in Wilmshurst, *Classification of Conflicts* (n 45) 146, 197.
[107] Cameron and others (n 1) para 514.
[108] ibid.
[109] ibid para 518.
[110] See, eg, N Lubell and N Derejko, 'A Global Battlefield? Drones and the Geographical Scope of Armed Conflict' (2013) 11 Journal of International Criminal Justice 65.
[111] JK Kleffner, 'Towards a Functional Conceptualization of the Temporal Scope of the Jus Post Bellum' in Stahn, Easterday, and Iverson, *Jus Post Bellum* (n 73) 287, 296.

of the situation would be necessary to see which parts of the *jus post bellum* should be phased in or out. This position is based on a progressive understanding of the relationship between *jus post bellum* and *jus in bello*, one that is 'characterized not by mutual exclusivity but by at least partial simultaneous application' of the two concepts.[112] With regard to the use of force during the final stages of a non-international armed conflict, it has been suggested by other authors that the state parties concerned should gradually shift from an armed conflict mode to a law enforcement mode with international human rights law becoming the relevant standard for action.[113] While such an approach may be desirable for humanitarian reasons and could even have a de-escalating effect, it is difficult to imagine that states would voluntarily adhere to a more restrictive normative framework when they are not fully convinced that the armed conflict is really over.

112 ibid.
113 See, eg, Bartels (n 73) 311.

3
The Legal Interoperability of the Laws of Armed Conflict

Michael Newton

1. Introduction

This chapter considers the pragmatic aspects of fielding effective multinational coalitions insofar as they necessitate cooperation amongst various sovereign states with differing treaty obligations, diverging interpretations of shared norms, and different command structures. Coalition partners deployed to pursue such larger goals must manage operational friction in order to achieve the necessary cohesion that should be the *sine quibus non* for sending citizens into conflict. Allied components of multinational forces have different domestic legal systems and varying legal obligations in the midst of almost any armed conflict. State practice demonstrates discrepancies between allies over what international law obligations apply to forces in the field which in turn produces disagreements about the conditions those duties entail.

At the same time, the modern law of armed conflict provides a sort of centripetal force providing essential cohesion to modern multinational coalitions. It provides normative regularity constraining the class of persons against whom violence may be lawfully applied. For Grotius, the realization that justice is best described as pursuit of 'the common good' anticipated an interconnected but legally independent set of corollary doctrines.[1] The quest for legal interoperability instantiates the insight that Grotius articulated within the context of multinational military missions. Though it provides affirmative authority for waging war in accordance with accepted legal restraints, modern international law strives to protect non-combatants from the onset of unlawful conflicts (*jus ad bellum*) and from the effects of armed conflicts irrespective of their legality (*jus in bello*). Thus, international law norms become the load bearing pillar for minimizing the 'scourge of war' (to echo the preambular language of the UN Charter).

[1] H Grotius, *De Jure Belli Ac Pacis [The Law of War and Peace]*, vol 1 (first published 1625, FW Kelsey (trs), Oxford Clarendon Press 1925) ch 1, sec VIII. Modern translation available online at <http://oll.libertyfund.org/titles/grotius-the-rights-of-war-and-peace-2005-ed-vol-1-book-i>. All URLs accessed 27 December 2018.

Michael Newton, *The Legal Interoperability of the Laws of Armed Conflict* In *The 'Legal Pluriverse' Surrounding Multinational Military Operations*. Edited by Robin Geiß and Heike Krieger, Oxford University Press (2020).

DOI: 10.1093/oso/9780198842965.003.0004

Interoperability in the legal context refers to the need for sovereign states to work together in a variety of contexts despite differing legal frameworks applicable to (or shared obligations interpreted differently by) each nation.[2] This notion of legal interoperability mirrors the broader concept of force interoperability, which NATO defines as '[t]he ability of the forces of two or more nations to train, exercise and operate effectively together in the execution of assigned missions and tasks'.[3] As one close observer of NATO defined it, '"[l]egal interoperability" is understood here as the ability of the forces of two or more nations to operate effectively together in the execution of assigned missions and tasks and with full respect for their legal obligations, notwithstanding the fact that nations concerned have varying legal obligations and varying interpretations of these obligations'.[4] As but one example, NATO Heads of State and Government referred to the need for interoperability to accomplish Alliance objectives in the Warsaw Summit Communiqué:

> through training and exercises, the development of NATO standards and common technical solutions, the NATO Response Force, Assurance Measures, forward presence in the eastern part of the Alliance, and joint operations in Afghanistan, Kosovo and the Mediterranean. [...] This enables [our] armed forces to work together successfully, be it in NATO operations or in national, coalition, EU or UN formats.[5]

Another adviser with NATO legal experience echoed this definition and emphasized 'the ability to have a generally shared single common body of law—as it allows for a critical analysis to focus, compare and identify potential areas of legal divergences and strains and, in turn, assess, for the operational commander, the impact these divergences may have on operational interoperability'.[6] Legal interoperability seeks to minimize or eliminate actual operational effects of disparate national obligations.

Legal interoperability can also counterbalance the inherently shifting political dynamics of coalition decision-making. Armed conflict as an act of state is, by definition, designed to achieve the political purposes of the state. Military structures

[2] See ICRC, 'International Humanitarian Law and the challenges of contemporary armed conflicts' Report 2011, highlighting that '[a]n important practical challenge is to ensure that peace operations are conducted taking into consideration the different levels of ratification of international humanitarian law (IHL) instruments and the different interpretations of those treaties and of customary IHL by troop contributing states', p 32.

[3] NATO Standardisation Office, NATO Glossary of Terms and Definitions, AAP-06(2014), available at <http://wcnjk.wp.mil.pl/plik/file/N_20130808_AAP6EN.pdf>.

[4] M Zwanenburg, 'International Humanitarian Law Interoperability in Multinational Operations' (2013) 95 International Review of the Red Cross (IRRC) 681–684.

[5] ibid para 49.

[6] K Abbott, 'A Brief Overview of Legal Interoperability Challenges for NATO Arising from the Interrelationship between IHL and IHRL in Light of the European Convention on Human Rights' (2014) 96 IRRC 107.

around the world are accordingly premised on order and the achievement of organized authority orchestrated to accomplish the goals of conflict. Central tenets of the legal regime regulating armed conflicts such as command responsibility, civilian control over military actors, and the imposition of discipline by virtue of binding criminal codes reinforce centralized military efforts towards defined military (and by necessary implication, political) goals. Overarching warfighting goals provide the template for evaluating military and legal efficacy as well as the very modalities for justifying and waging the conflict. For this reason, the classic and universally recognized Principles of War begin with the cornerstone concept of Objective.[7]

However, multinational coalitions inevitably face political headwinds that can inhibit swift and effective military planning and operations. Absence of legal homogeneity between coalition partners often requires such *ad hoc* solutions and improvisation. Agreement on the organizing principles of each operation requires coordination between political branches which can adversely impact ongoing operations. For example, during the 1999 NATO operations against the Federal Republic of Yugoslavia, NATO planners modified established military doctrines in order to maintain alliance cohesion. NATO planners and political leaders 'initially adopted an operation of limited scope and duration with vague objectives' which 'emphasized avoiding collateral damage and alliance force casualties'.[8] US military experts later concluded that 'these departures resulted in a longer campaign, more damage to Yugoslavia, and greater risk to alliance forces than likely would have occurred if doctrine had been followed'. Similar concerns arising from the sensitivities of NATO political officials during operations in Afghanistan resulted in overly rigorous review of operational plans submitted by General McChrystal.[9] In particular, the role of Special Forces and the procedures for night raids were problematic elements that resulted in the refusal of some nations to approve planning until oversight mechanisms could be developed.[10] To counter these challenges, the law of war itself should be a fulcrum to balance competing goals and ameliorate strains within multinational forces.

Legal interoperability should reinforce relationships between professionalized military forces while simultaneously strengthening *jus in bello* norms. This chapter

[7] The Principles of War crystallized as military doctrine around the world around 1800. The accepted principles are: Objective, Offensive, Mass, Economy of Forces, Manoeuvre, Unity of Command, Security, Surprise, and Simplicity. John Whiteclay Chambers II (ed), *The Oxford Companion to American Military History* (OUP 1999) 557.

[8] 'KOSOVO AIR OPERATIONS: Need to Maintain Alliance Cohesion Resulted in Doctrinal Departures' GAO-01-784 (US General Accounting Office, 27 July 2001) 1, available at <http://www.gpo.gov/fdsys/pkg/GAOREPORTS-GAO-01-784/pdf/GAOREPORTS-GAO-01-784.pdf>.

[9] In NATO parlance, EXOPLAN exercise operational plan (d'opération d'exercice). NATO Standardisation Office, NATO Glossary of Terms and Definitions, AAP-06(2014), available at <http://wcnjk.wp.mil.pl/plik/file/N_20130808_AAP6EN.pdf>.

[10] O Schmitt, 'International Organization at War: NATO Practices in the Afghan Campaign' (2017) 52 Cooperation and Conflict 502.

seeks to offer pragmatic suggestions in light of the legal lessons extrapolated from recent state practice. Section 2 of this chapter frames the nature of the core problem, while section 3 considers the challenges to legal interoperability posed by the conflicting normative perspectives within multinational forces. Commanders must be careful to shape appropriate expectations that balance the *lex lata* of the laws of armed conflict against the overarching objectives of the coalition. Section 4 summarizes the emerging practice of the International Criminal Court (ICC), with particular focus on the implementation of the proportionality principle within coalitions. Given the reality of differing interpretations of the law, *jus in bello* embeds within its normative framework the necessary latitude for commanders to operate in effective multinational operations. Section 4 also highlights the beneficial effects of the ICC Elements of Crimes on legal interoperability due to their consensus adoption. Section 5 concludes by noting that the noncontroversial duty to investigate allegations of war crimes can morph depending on national perspectives.

2. Framing the Legal Dilemma Faced by Deployed Forces

Tenets of the laws of armed conflict represent the common property of all professionalized military forces. By extension, units that operate in good faith to implement the laws and customs of warfare do so on behalf of the civilized societies that foot their costs and fill their ranks. Compliance with the law of war is thus a primary focus of the forces in the field as well as the nations whose interests they serve. At the same time, responsible commanders 'consider the broader imperatives of winning the war as quickly and efficiently as possible' which inevitably requires consideration of many competing factors because '*military necessity* justifies those measures necessary to achieve the object of war, and the object of war is not simply to prevail, but to prevail as quickly and efficiently as possible'.[11]

The variability of human rights-based limitations in national guidance is the primary obstacle in this context. Actions that may be discretionary policy to some forces may well be viewed as legally obligatory by others within a multinational coalition. By contrast to the restrictive nature of human rights norms, the *lex lata* applicable to armed conflict embeds principles of military necessity, discretion, and concepts of reasonableness at the precise points of friction within the law where they are relevant to the actual conduct of military operations. Perpetrators charged with war crimes cannot subjectively inject those concepts at their own convenience because they are baked into the extant structure of the laws and customs where relevant. These subjective strands represent fault-lines for debate amongst coalition partners because the permissive nature of the laws of armed conflict are

[11] DoD Law of War Manual, para 2.2.3.1.

suffused with discretionary latitude to balance competing objectives. Preparing consolidated force rules of engagement requires multinational force commanders to map a consolidated matrix depicting the overlaps and interrelationships posed by national caveats as a predicate to combat operations. This is particularly important in combined forces operating under uniform rules of engagement and with consolidated reporting mechanisms.

In the ideal world, political officials and the professionalized forces they deploy would confront these dilemmas directly in order to synergize military operations. Experienced practitioners recognize that the 'law of war and international human rights law occupy the same normative space, are deeply intertwined and appear to be locked into a process of gradual convergence'.[12] A nuanced understanding of international human rights law is an essential element of legal interoperability. As noted above, human rights obligations of multinational forces are among the key drivers of national caveats. To address the challenges that such caveats present to mission accomplishment, US commanders must fully understand the legal position and sensitivities of coalition partners. There is at least one example where a domestic court has accepted that a sending state must respect the international human rights obligations of a territorial state as a consequence of private international law.[13] The US Department of Defense (DoD) Law of War Manual avoids analysis of this interrelationship by noting the US 'view that the International Covenant on Civil and Political Rights (ICCPR) does not create obligations for an Occupying Power with respect to occupied territory because a contracting State's obligations under the ICCPR only extend to persons within its territory and subject to its jurisdiction'.[14] Though conceding that 'some coalition partners, may interpret their human rights treaty obligations to create obligations for their military operations outside their home territory in the context of belligerent occupation'[15] there is no acknowledgment that the US perspective is an increasingly minority view.

DoD notes with an unwarranted tone of finality that because the law of war constitutes the *lex specialis*, it serves as the 'controlling body of law' during all armed conflicts.[16] In addressing the wrinkles inherent during modern armed conflicts, the Manual appears to distinguish between 'an internal non-international armed conflict' during which states 'continue to be bound by applicable human rights treaty obligations' and other contexts in which

[12] R Provost, *International Human Rights and Humanitarian Law* (CUP 2002); R Kolb and G Gaggioli (eds), *Research Handbook on Human Rights and Humanitarian Law* (Edward Elgar 2013) and G Oberleitner, *Human Rights in Armed Conflict: Law, Practice, Policy* (CUP 2015) paras 3.01–3.71.

[13] *Nuhanović v The Netherlands*, Judgment, 200.020.174/01 (Court of Appeal in The Hague, 5 July 2011) paras 6.3, 6.4, and 6.8.

[14] DoD Law of War Manual, para 11.1.2.6.

[15] ibid. See also D Murray and others, *Practitioners' Guide to Human Rights Law in Armed Conflict* (OUP 2016).

[16] DoD Law of War Manual, para 11.3.2.

> applicability of human rights treaty obligations during non-international armed conflict may depend on a variety of factors. Such applicability depends on the terms of the particular treaty in question, and whether the State has exercised an authorized derogation from its provisions due to an emergency situation. The applicability of a human rights treaty obligation with respect to an individual, such as an obligation under the International Covenant on Civil and Political Rights, for example, may depend on whether the person is located outside the territory of the State Party. In addition, law of war rules constitute the *lex specialis* during situations of armed conflict, and as such, serve as the controlling body of law with regard to the conduct of hostilities and the protection of war victims.[17]

The literature on the relationship between human rights norms and the broader field of international humanitarian law is vast; but the forces of many allied nations deployed alongside US forces and often under the overall command of US leaders will export their own treaty-based human rights obligations over any area or persons where they exercise 'effective control'.[18] As a result, they will tend to import the human rights-based restraints that mandate that military personnel must apply force only as a 'last resort' measure and even in dire circumstances in a restrictive manner that is most narrowly tailored to eliminate an immediate threat. The human rights regime requires a statement of affirmative authority while *jus in bello* operates on a permissive basis subject to express limitations. As an additive requirement, lethal force under the human rights paradigm must be proportionate to the immediate context, meaning that the force used is directly proportionate to the risk posed by the individual at the moment force is employed. This mindset is worlds removed from the normative framework of *jus in bello* normally applicable to war-fighters. Lethal force in armed conflicts is permissible whenever reasonably necessary to achieve a military objective absent evidence of some prohibited purpose or unlawful tactic.[19] As early as 1863, this permissiveness was expressed in Article 14 of the Lieber Code as follows:

[17] ibid para 17.2.1.3.

[18] R Wilde, 'Triggering State Obligations Extraterritorially: The Spatial Test in Certain Human Rights Treaties' in R Arnold and NNR Quénivet (eds), *International Humanitarian Law and Human Rights Law: Towards a New Merger in International Law* (Martinus Nijhoff 2008) 133.

[19] N Melzer, 'Targeted Killing or Less Harmful Means?—Israel's High Court Judgment on Targeted Killing and the Restrictive Function of Military Necessity' (2006) 9 Yearbook of International Humanitarian Law 109 (TMC Asser Press 2006).

> Military necessity, as understood by modern civilized nations, consists of the necessity of those measure which are indispensable for securing the ends of the war, and which are lawful according to the modern law and usages of war.[20]

Coalition commanders should be as precise as possible in recognizing that military operations will generally entail operational components whose overall operational posture should be disaggregated. Law enforcement missions (along with indigenous personnel) for which the human rights framework is solely appropriate will often be intertwined with combat operations. Well organized and armed criminal organizations may also be commingled with non-state parties to an ongoing armed conflict. Hence, commanders should strive for clarity of guidance and legal expectations to various force contingents depending on the intent of each disaggregated operation within an overall operational plan.

Similarly, while the expectation of full compliance with applicable legal norms is non-negotiable, commanders and politicians should be alert to quash any expectation that armed conflict can be conducted with no expectation of civilian casualties. President Obama's Executive Order prescribing policies related to civilian casualties in US operations obliquely echoed the same concerns (emphasis added):[21]

> *The protection of civilians is fundamentally consistent with the effective, efficient, and decisive use of force in pursuit of U.S. national interests. Minimizing civilian casualties can further mission objectives;* help maintain the support of partner governments and vulnerable populations, especially in the conduct of counterterrorism and counterinsurgency operations; and enhance the legitimacy and sustainability of U.S. operations critical to our national security. *As a matter of policy, the United States therefore routinely imposes certain heightened policy standards that are more protective than the requirements of the law of armed conflict that relate to the protection of civilians.*

Any effective commander issues plans and guidance prior to the onset of operations, and sets a command climate of professionalism in which he or she empowers subordinates.[22] General David Petraeus wrote to 'Soldiers, Sailors, Airmen, Marines, and Coast Guardsmen serving in Multi-National Force-Iraq':

[20] Lieber Code, Article 14.

[21] DoD Law of War Manual, para 5.1.2.1 (citing Executive Order 13732, *United States Policy on Pre- and Post-Strike Measures to Address Civilian Casualties in U.S. Operations Involving the Use of Force* (1 July 2016) 81 Federal Register 44485, § 1).

[22] ICRC, *Commentary to Protocol I*, Article 87, para 3550, available at <http://www.icrc.org/ihl.nsf/COM/470-750001?OpenDocument> ('Undoubtedly the development of a battle may not permit a commander to exercise control over his troops all the time; but in this case he must impose discipline to a sufficient degree, to enforce compliance with the rules of the Conventions and the Protocol, even when he may momentarily lose sight of his troops').

> Our values and the laws governing warfare teach us to respect human dignity, maintain our integrity, and do what is right. Adherence to our values distinguishes us from our enemy. This fight depends on securing the population, which must understand that we—not our enemies—occupy the moral high ground. This strategy has shown results in recent months. Al Qa'ida's indiscriminate attacks, for example, have finally started to turn a substantial proportion of the Iraqi population against it.[23]

The core *jus in bello* imperative that the 'right of belligerents to adopt means of injuring the enemy is not unlimited' forms the backbone of the connected set of war-making principles. It follows that Michael Walzer is entirely correct that forces are 'not entitled to do anything that is or seems to them necessary to win wars. They are subject to a set of restrictions that rest in part on the agreements of states but that also have an independent foundation in moral principle'.[24]

To accomplish the larger strategic mission, which necessarily includes sustaining a strong sense of legitimacy within the civilian population of coalition states as well as within the zone of conflict, a commander could decide to impose greater restrictions on attacks in areas where civilians are known to be present. Commanders have full discretion to impose Rules of Engagement that exceed 'even beyond the requirements of the law of war'.[25]

Thus, COMISAF guidance required coalition forces in Afghanistan to

> continue—indeed, redouble—our efforts to reduce the loss of innocent civilian life to an absolute minimum. Every Afghan civilian death diminishes our cause. If we use excessive force or operate contrary to our counterinsurgency principles, tactical victories may prove to be strategic setbacks. We must never forget that the center of gravity in this struggle is the Afghan people; it is they who will ultimately determine the future of Afghanistan ... Prior to the use of fires, the commander approving the strike must determine that no civilians are present.[26]

Commanders seeking legal interoperability must be keen to ascertain the precise line between legal obligation and discretionary policy. There is ample evidence that states did not intend to undermine the core principles of the law of war through the adoption of human rights treaties.[27] Expectations that armed conflict does not

[23] See, eg, Letter from General DH Petraeus, Commanding Officer of Multi-National Force-Iraq, to Multi-National Force-Iraq (10 May 2007) (copy on file with the author).

[24] M Walzer, *Just and Unjust Wars* (Basic Books 1977) 131.

[25] DoD Law of War Manual, paras 5.11.2 and 17.5.1.3 (citing General Petraeus, *Unclassified Excerpts from Tactical Directive*, 1 August 2010).

[26] ibid para 17.5.1.3, fn 95.

[27] Commission on Human Rights, Draft International Covenant on Human Rights, Summary Record of the 97th Meeting, E/CN.4/SR.97 (3 June 1949) at 8 (Philippines: '[t]he Commission, however, could not, either directly or indirectly, alter the laws of war in any way whatsoever'); ibid at 6–7 (United Kingdom); Commission on Human Rights, Draft International Covenant on Human Rights, Summary

entail significant loss of human life or destruction of property within the bounds of the law are false and should not be reinforced.

3. Legal Interoperability and the Challenge of Conflicting Perspectives

Legal interoperability requires keen sensitivity to varying national perspectives and articulation of the precise legal rationale for decision-making. NATO allies do not have the benefit of one consolidated chart listing the provisions of Protocols I and II that the United States accepts as binding customary international law notwithstanding the unexpected (at the time) failure to obtain the advice and consent of the Senate on the underlying treaties. The burden of fielding a disciplined force that strives for legal interoperability as a facet of mission accomplishment falls to multinational force commanders. As a logical corollary, commanders frequently develop ad hoc innovations to address otherwise complex legal barriers. The Israeli Supreme Court summarized this notion by noting that the authority of commanders 'must be properly balanced against the rights, needs, and interests of the local population: the law of war usually creates a delicate balance between two poles: military necessity on one hand, and humanitarian considerations on the other'.[28]

The scope and feasibility of the commander's duty to implement certain precautionary measures to protect civilians represents one of the primary obstacles to legal interoperability. Article 57(1) of Additional Protocol I (AP I) states: 'In the conduct of military operations, constant care shall be taken to spare the civilian population, civilians and civilian objects.'[29] As an additive duty, parties must take all feasible precautions in launching attacks that may affect the civilian population. This includes taking all feasible measures to ensure that targets are military objectives,[30] as well as selecting the means and methods of attack expected to provide the greatest protection against loss of civilian life and damage to civilian property.[31]

Record of the 194th Meeting, E/CN.4/SR.194 (25 May 1950) para 34 (France: the 'purpose was to ensure protection of human rights, but not to endeavour to change or amend international law as it was practiced'); Commission on Human Rights, Summary Record of the 330th Meeting E/CN.4/SR.330 (1 July 1952) at 7 (Belgium: suggesting that the ICCPR would be suspended between belligerents).

[28] *Beit Sourak Village Council v the Government of Israel* [2004] HCJ 2056/04, para 34, available at <https://www.refworld.org/cases,ISR_SC,4374ac594.html> (quoting Y Dinstein, 'Legislative Authority in the Administered Territories' (1973) 2 Iyunei Mishpat 505, 509).

[29] ICRC, *Protocol Additional to the Geneva Conventions of 12 August 1949, and relating to the Protection of Victims of International Armed Conflicts (Protocol I)* (adopted 8 June 1977, entered into force 7 December 1978) 1125 UNTS 3, Article 57(1).

[30] DoD Law of War Manual, para 5.2.3.2.

[31] For example, one common method of taking precautions is to launch attacks on particular targets at night when the civilian population is not on the streets or at work, thus minimizing potential casualties. The NATO attacks on the Radio Televizije Srbije building in the territory of the Federal Republic of Yugoslavia took place at a time when civilian employees were not expected to be present. Decision

State practice has included many of the following measures based on the accepted definition that:

> Feasible precautions are those that are practicable or practically possible, taking into account all circumstances ruling at the time, including humanitarian and military considerations. These circumstances may include:
>
> - the effect of taking the precaution on mission accomplishment;
> - whether taking the precaution poses a risk to one's own forces or presents other security risks;
> - the likelihood and degree of humanitarian benefit from taking the precaution;
> - the cost of taking the precaution, in terms of time, money, or other resources; or
> - whether taking the precaution forecloses alternative courses of action.
>
> For example, a commander may determine that a precaution would not be feasible because it would result in increased operational risk (i.e., a risk of failing to accomplish the mission) or an increased risk of harm to his or her forces.[32]

Wanton disregard for civilian casualties or harm to other protected persons and objects is clearly prohibited but that provides an utterly unhelpful lowest common denominator that fails to advance actual legal integration. In practice, there is disagreement within multinational forces over the precise nature of obligatory precautions, particularly in light of the differing perspectives on the applicability of human rights-based limitations regarding the use of force noted above. There is also dispute whether the precautionary principle as reflected in multinational rules of engagement applies to *both* analysis of the duty to distinguish civilian from military targets and in applying the proportionality principles.

Recent struggles by coalition commanders to implement uniform standards for implementing the requirement to seek affirmative personal identification (termed 'PID' and defined as 'reasonable certainty that the proposed target is a legitimate military target') provide another potent impediment to legal interoperability.[33] For some nations, the PID requirement represents an example of the commander's authority to 'impose greater restrictions than the requirements of the law of war' by 'applying heightened standards of identification'.[34] For others, such

as to the admissibility of Application no 52207/99 of 12 December 2001 (Grand Chamber) in the case ECtHR, *Bankovic and Others v Belgium and 16 Other Contracting States* App no 52207/99 (Judgment, 12 December 2001) 890, 123 International Law Reporter 94.

[32] DoD Law of War Manual, para 5.2.3.2.

[33] ibid para 5.4.3.1, fn 87.

[34] ibid para 5.4.3.1 (the text describes the 'PID' Rule of Engagement as 'a policy choice to reduce the risk of incidental harm in conducting an attack').

'higher thresholds' represent legal mandates rather than policy-based pragmatism. Multinational forces are handicapped by differing perspectives on the relationship between lawful prerogatives in self-defence, deemed to be an inherent right in the plain language of rules of engagement, and the limitations imposed by human rights norms.

In reality, experience in Iraq and Afghanistan has repeatedly shown that 'PID' is an essential safeguard for lawful operations. Consider the case of the US Marines that killed 24 unarmed Iraqi civilians in the village of Haditha by entering their homes following the death of one Marine from an improvised explosive device. What should have been a swift arc of investigative efficiency became bogged down with rationalizations and red tape that shifted only after the shock of public revelation and recrimination. The official investigation documented a command culture that devalued the lives of Iraqi civilians, which contributed to the incident and made follow-up a low priority. In the official terminology of the investigation conducted by General Bargewell: 'All levels of command tended to view civilian casualties, even in significant numbers, as routine and as a natural and intended result of insurgent tactics.'[35]

The pervasive attitude that all Iraqis were either the enemy or supporters of the enemy removed the incentive for individual Marines to follow applicable rules of engagement mandating ceaseless efforts to distinguish between combatants and non-combatants. One US Marine, SSgt Frank Wuterich (who entered a plea of guilty at his court-martial) remarked that '[a]s for the PID (Positive Identification of civilians versus combatants as required in the Rules of Engagement), we didn't want my Marines to check if they had weapons first. We told them to shoot first and deal with it later'.[36] His conviction resulted from the issuance of the unlawful order, which violated the rules of engagement and in legal terms violated the principle of distinction.

On the other hand, multinational forces acting under immediate unit or personal self-defence do not violate international norms by returning suppressive fire. No conscientious commander should permit deployed personnel to believe that either human rights law or *jus in bello* prohibit actions designed to protect their own right to life. There are nevertheless many documented examples in recent years whereby forces under fire could not obtain indirect artillery support from another coalition partner even after suffering casualties from enemy contact. No commander should sustain conditions that generate the all too frequently encountered frustration expressed by one British soldier speaking of his experience in Afghanistan, who said, 'I agree with [the restrictions imposed by commanders on the basis of their understandings of proportionality and necessity during

[35] US Department of the Army, Major General EA Bargewell, Investigation, 'Simple Failures' and 'Disastrous Results' (15 June 2006) 18.

[36] Sworn Statement of SSgt FD Wuterich (taken 21 February 2001).

counterinsurgency operations] to the extent that previously too many civilians were killed but we have got people shooting at us and we are not allowed to shoot back'.[37] Coalition commanders should explicitly acknowledge that those under attack are legally entitled to a certain latitude when they reasonably believe their own lives to be at great risk.[38]

4. The Impact of the International Criminal Court (ICC)

The Rome Statute was designed to largely align criminal norms with actual state practice based in the realities of warfare. Its war crimes provisions represent neither a rejection of prior practice nor an evisceration of the core precepts that were widely accepted prior to the treaty's completion in 1998. The range of substantive war crimes embodied in Article 8 reflects a complex commingling of *lex lata* hard law and established state practice, as informed by the much more diffuse expectations and assessments of expert practitioners. The intentional integration of hard and soft law within the structure of Article 8 is ubiquitous. There are dozens of instances whereby Article 8 incorporates terminology drawn from the larger framework of established *jus in bello* without amplification; commonly encountered law of war terms such as, inter alia, 'military necessity', '*hors de combat*', 'direct participation in hostilities', 'combatant', 'civilian', 'protected persons', and 'military objective' appear throughout.

With respect to legal integration, *jus in bello* permits significant discretion, which accords with the precepts of the Rome Statute when they are properly applied. The proportionality principle provides a frequent flashpoint for disrupting the quest for legal integration because of the misperception that its normative content relies upon whether a state has ratified the Rome Statute. In fact, the proportionality principle facilitates legal interoperability because it is designed to create a certain normative flexibility that permits multinational force commanders to create the optimal balance of operational coherence. In this vein, proportionality operates in the shadow of Article 51 AP I, which itself implements the categorical admonition that the 'civilian population and individual civilians shall enjoy general protection against dangers arising from military operations. To give effect to this protection, the following rules, which are additional to other applicable rules of international law, shall be observed in all circumstances'.

Indeed, the principle of distinction represents one of the 'intransgressible principles of customary international law' which must accordingly 'be observed by all States whether or not they have ratified the conventions that contain them'.[39] The

[37] T Harding, 'Curbs on Firing at Taliban are Putting Us at Risk, Troops Warn' *The Telegraph* (London, 7 July 2010) 14.

[38] MA Newton and L May, *Proportionality in International Law* (OUP 2014) 290–92.

[39] *Legality of the Threat or Use of Nuclear Weapons* (Advisory Opinion) [1996] ICJ 226, 257.

overarching prohibition is followed by the more specific and pointed application in Article 51(4) that 'indiscriminate attacks are prohibited'. Article 51(5)(b) then provides the classic AP I articulation of the proportionality principle by defining indiscriminate attacks as, inter alia, 'an attack which may be expected to cause incidental loss of civilian life, injury to civilians, damage to civilian objects, or a combination thereof, which would be excessive in relation to the concrete and direct military advantage anticipated'.

This balancing test is the core of the modern *jus in bello* proportionality conversation. Article 57(2)(a)(iii) echoes the proportionality limitation by obligating an attacker to 'refrain from deciding to launch any attack which may be expected to cause incidental loss of civilian life, injury to civilians, damage to civilian objects, or a combination thereof, which would be excessive in relation to the concrete and direct military advantage anticipated'. These provisions must be understood in light of subsequent state practice. The governments of the United Kingdom, the Netherlands, Spain, Italy, Australia, Belgium, New Zealand, Germany, and Canada each published a virtually identical reservation with respect to Articles 51 and 57 as they acceded to AP I. The overwhelming body of reservations makes plain that ratifying states intended that the proportionality principle would provide war fighters with a broad, but not unbounded, latitude dependent on the facts and contextual application. The New Zealand reservation, for example (virtually identical to those of other states listed above), reads as follows:

> In relation to paragraph 5 (b) of Article 51 and to paragraph 2 (a) (iii) of Article 57, the Government of New Zealand understands that the military advantage anticipated from an attack is intended to refer to the advantage anticipated from the attack considered as a whole and not only from isolated or particular parts of that attack and that the term 'military advantage' involves a variety of considerations, including the security of attacking forces. It is further the understanding of the Government of New Zealand that the term 'concrete and direct military advantage anticipated', used in Articles 51 and 57, means a bona fide expectation that the attack will make a relevant and proportional contribution to the objective of the military attack involved.

Modern incantations are often informed by the undercurrent of human rights-derived restrictiveness to attempt to squeeze proportionality into a binding straitjacket deduced from *post hoc* assessments. This is a serious error that undermines legal integration. Larger 'objectives' are clearly relevant as well to the considerations of the anticipated 'contribution to the objective of the military attack involved'. This latitude is in turn anchored by the textual limitation that the desired benefit to appropriate coalition ends must be 'concrete and direct'.

By way of facilitating legal integration, the Elements of Crimes to the Rome Statute specify, for the first time in world history, the *actus reus, mens rea*, and circumstantial elements for every offence. The consensus adoption of the Elements on 30 June 2000 included delegations from major non-state parties to include the United States, China, and Russia. At the time of this writing, 123 states parties adopted the statute as a binding treaty. Article 8(2)(b)(iv) describes proportionality in a manner consistent with modern state practice following the adoption of AP I as:

> *Intentionally launching an attack in the knowledge that such attack will cause incidental loss of life or injury to civilians or damage to civilian objects or widespread, long-term severe damage to the natural environment which would be clearly excessive in relation to the concrete and direct overall military advantage anticipated* [emphasis added to show contrast to Protocol I text].

Furthermore, the Elements of Crimes (adopted by consensus of all states as mentioned above) included a key explanatory footnote that reads as follows:

> The expression 'concrete and direct overall military advantage' refers to a military advantage that is foreseeable by the perpetrator at the relevant time. Such advantage may or may not be temporally or geographically related to the object of the attack. The fact that this crime admits the possibility of lawful incidental injury and collateral damage does not in any way justify any violation of the law applicable in armed conflict. It does not address justifications for war or other rules related to *jus ad bellum*. It reflects the proportionality requirement inherent in determining the legality of any military activity undertaken in the context of an armed conflict.

The Rome Statute offence thus widens the scope of the military advantage that can be considered in the proportionality analysis (through inclusion of the word 'overall') and narrows what level of collateral damage is considered excessive (by specifying that the damage needs to be clearly excessive to generate criminal liability). These textual improvements comfortably accommodate *jus post bellum* imperatives. This accordingly means that larger coalition objectives need not be static at the strategic, operational, or even tactical levels of war.

Furthermore, revisions to the treaty terminology employed by the drafters of AP I reflect the broadly accepted view of state practice. The language of the UK Law of War Manual summarizes the state of the law that was captured in the prohibition of Article 8(2)(b)(iv) as it should be understood in light of the Elements of Crimes:

> The military advantage anticipated from the attack refers to the advantage anticipated from the attack considered as a whole and not only from isolated or particular parts of the attack. The point of this is that an attack may involve a number of co-ordinated actions, some of which might cause more incidental

> damage than others. In assessing whether the proportionality rule has been violated, the effect of the whole attack must be considered. That does not, however, mean that an entirely gratuitous and unnecessary action within the attack as a whole would be condoned. Generally speaking, when considering the responsibility of a commander at any level, it is necessary to look at the part of the attack for which he was responsible in the context of the attack as a whole and in the light of the circumstances prevailing at the time the decision to attack was made.[40]

From this perspective, articulation of proportionality in the Rome Statute provides the maypole around which commanders from all nations can coordinate. Considering these developments as a synergistic whole means that policymakers and war fighters must be aware that their actions affect the larger quest for just and sustainable peace. Coalition commanders should recognize that the Rome Statute simply cannot be implemented as a self-standing island of international law principles isolated from the larger definitional underpinnings of *jus in bello*. In the express language of Article 8(b)(2)(b)(iv), *jus in bello* proportionality by definition and accepted state practice will very likely depend upon the broader contextual set of aggregate circumstances, which in turn inform the commander's assessment of the 'overall military advantage anticipated'. This should in turn be implemented in a manner that reinforces rather than degrades legal integration. The Elements of Crimes provide a consensus-based cornerstone that generates momentum towards truly integrated legal interoperability, despite the normative difficulties arising from human rights law.

5. Defining the Modern Duty to Investigate

Military commanders 'have a duty to investigate reports of alleged law of war violations committed by persons under their command or against persons to whom they have a legal duty to protect'.[41] Recognition of this overarching duty is reinforced by the reminder that 'duties to implement and enforce the law of war also imply duties to investigate reports of alleged violations of the law of war'.[42] Commanders of all nations have wide discretion to order actions or take such precautionary measures as they deem appropriate to ensure efficient and viable investigations into alleged atrocities. At the same time, they should remain mindful that there is no per se hierarchy of investigative norms. With respect to 'appropriate' investigations, the conjunction of human rights law and law of armed conflict in the

[40] UK Ministry of Defence, *The Manual of the Law of Armed Conflict* (OUP 2004) para 5.33.4.
[41] DoD Law of War Manual, para 18.4.3.
[42] ibid para 18.13.

same operational time and space requires careful consideration, and all the more in light of the reality that allegations of impropriety within a coalition have the power to disintegrate all other efforts at legal integration.

Applying the *lex specialis* doctrine favoured by the United States, both human rights law and *jus in bello* require investigations into alleged improprieties, hence the duty is not contradictory. At best, the duty to investigate might represent what scholars call 'an opposing norm' in the sense that there is no conflict as both legal regimes include the duty to investigate, but depending on the context would 'require actions that cannot be fulfilled at the same time'.[43]

The sweeping conclusion that *lex specialis* law of war duties displace human rights standards with respect to investigations obviously offers little aid to coalition commanders. There are at present competing models for the form and function of field investigations, such as the Fact Finding Assessments used by Israeli forces, the Joint Investigative Assessment Teams used by the International Security Assistance Force (ISAF) in Afghanistan,[44] modern American administrative inquiries such as the Taguba Report into the crimes committed at Abu Ghraib, or the published CENTCOM report analysing the Kunduz bombing.[45] The investigative chasm between best practices during armed conflicts and normal peacetime investigations envisioned by the human rights regime remains vast, yet application of the norms might not be automatically incompatible.

Absolute uniformity of investigative standards across all contexts is impossible, but commanders should know that the human rights standard provides a template for the minimum level of protection that should be unassailable in any human rights-based forum, domestic or international. The line of European Court of Human Rights (ECtHR) cases that culminated in the *Jaloud* case in November 2014 illustrates the litmus test for an 'effective investigation' in human rights terms.[46] To be sure, there are questionable aspects of the ECtHR analysis in *Jaloud* as applied to the actions of a Dutch officer whose troops were taking fire at a roadblock during operations in Iraq, but the discussion of what constitutes an effective investigation for the purposes of European human rights law is illustrative to coalition commanders:

> For an investigation into alleged unlawful killing by State agents to be effective, it is necessary for the persons responsible for and carrying out the investigation to

[43] DM Banaszewska, 'Lex Specialis' in F Lachenmann and R Wolfrum (eds), *The Law of Armed Conflict and the Use of Force, The Max Planck Encyclopedia of Public International Law* (OUP 2017) 659, 660.

[44] Center for Civilians in Conflict, *Civilian Harm Tracking: Analysis of ISAF Efforts in Afghanistan* (2014).

[45] Doctors Without Borders, 'Investigation Report of the Airstrike on the Médecins Sans Frontières/Doctors Without Borders Trauma Centre in Kunduz, Afghanistan' (3 October 2015) <http://fpp.cc/wp-content/uploads/01.-AR-15-6-Inv-Rpt-Doctors-Without-Borders-3-Oct-15_CLEAR.pdf>.

[46] *Jaloud v The Netherlands* App No 47708/08 (ECtHR, Judgment, 20 November 2014).

> be independent from those implicated in the events. This means not only a lack of hierarchical or institutional connection but also a practical independence (see, for example, Shanaghan, cited above, § 104). A requirement of promptness and reasonable expedition is implicit in this context. While there may be obstacles or difficulties which prevent progress in an investigation in a particular situation, a prompt response by the authorities in investigating a use of lethal force may generally be regarded as essential in maintaining public confidence in their adherence to the rule of law and in preventing any appearance of collusion in or tolerance of unlawful acts. For the same reasons, there must be a sufficient element of public scrutiny of the investigation or its results to secure accountability in practice as well as in theory. The degree of public scrutiny required may well vary from case to case. In all cases, however, the victim's next-of-kin must be involved in the procedure to the extent necessary to safeguard his or her legitimate interests (see *Ahmet Özkan and Others*, cited above, §§ 311–314; *Isayeva*, cited above, §§ 211–214 and the cases cited therein).[47]

As *Jaloud* stressed, the duty to conduct an effective investigation is 'not an obligation of result, but of means'.[48] For coalition commanders, the hallmarks of investigative independence paired with a fully informed and neutral prosecutorial determination mark the pathway to satisfying the duty to investigate under both human rights law and the law of armed conflict. The goal is to ensure that any investigation includes appropriate follow-up and authoritative oversight.

Processes for securing key evidence and the potential sharing of that evidence with either a criminal investigation or an international tribunal remain necessary cornerstones. *Jaloud* provides an overall template of considerations, though a full autopsy of every civilian death is obviously impossible under all circumstances. In the middle of ongoing conflicts, however, procedural differences between normal domestic criminal investigations and those conducted in a combat zone may well be overcome by the commander's clear explication of the investigation's legal sufficiency in a particular context. Careful explication of the contextual goal of an 'appropriate investigation' may well allow harmonization of the law of war within a specific human rights analysis.[49] NATO has made halting progress towards such objectives but much greater clarity of both process and procedure along with invocation of the factors mitigating against normal law enforcement applications remains highly desirable.

[47] ibid para 167.

[48] ibid para 166.

[49] *Hassan v United Kingdom* App No 29750/09 (ECtHR, Judgment, 16 September 2014) para 104 ('accommodating', as far as possible, the power to detain in international armed conflict with the right to liberty, but expressly declining to extend that right broadly into all armed conflict scenarios).

6. Conclusion

Coalition commanders should seek legal integration as an affirmative vehicle for augmenting the moral and military power of available forces. *Jus in bello* seeks to facilitate lawful military operations, while hindering those who would co-opt the field and divorce it from state practice. Humanitarian imperatives form the essence of legal integration, yet carry the seeds that could corrode compliance with the law itself.[50] Michael Walzer brilliantly observed the nexus between competing legal precepts in his classic work *Just and Unjust Wars* by noting that proportionality

> is a matter of adjusting means to ends, but as the Israeli philosopher Yehuda Melzer has pointed out, there is an overwhelming tendency in wartime to adjust ends to means instead, that is to redefine initially narrow goals in order to fit the available military forces and technologies . . . It is necessary in such arguments to hold ends constant, but how does one do that? In practice, the inflation of ends is probably inevitable unless it is barred by considerations of justice itself.[51]

In contrast, coalition commanders have an operational imperative to manage competing national visions and priorities as a necessary precondition for victory. The new US Department of Defense Law of War Manual expresses that reality as follows (emphasis added):

> *implementation and enforcement of the law of war are also supported by the fact that violations of the law of war are counterproductive to the political goals sought to be achieved by military operations. For example, violations of the law of war in counter-insurgency operations may diminish the support of the local population.* Violations of the law of war may also diminish the support of the populace in democratic States, including the United States and other States that would otherwise support or participate in coalition operations.[52]

Coalition adversaries who exploit legal ambiguities to advance their own military objectives should find no solace in the legal crevices amongst coalition partners. Illegitimate exploitation of *jus in bello* norms could permit the legal structure to be portrayed as a mass of indeterminate subjectivity that is nothing more than another weapon in the moral domain of conflict at the behest of the side with the best cameras, biggest microphones, and most compliant media accomplices. The quest for legal integration is founded on the powerful impulse to cement military

[50] NK Modirzadeh, 'The Dark Sides of Convergence: A Pro-Civilian Critique of the Extraterritorial Application of Human Rights Law in Armed Conflict' (2010) 86 International Law Studies 349–410.
[51] M Walzer, *Just and Unjust Wars* (Basic Books 1977) 119–20.
[52] DoD Law of War Manual, para 18.2.3.

alliances around the notion that the law of armed conflict cannot be permitted to atrophy. Misrepresentations of the law and manipulation of the media to mask genuine war crimes could lead to a cycle of cynicism and second-guessing that weakens the overall commitment of some military members to remain bound by the law.

PART II

LAWS OF ARMED CONFLICT AND INTERNATIONAL HUMAN RIGHTS LAW IN THE CONTEXT OF MULTINATIONAL MILITARY OPERATIONS

A Matter of Perspective?

4
An Operational Perspective

Hans Boddens Hosang

1. Introduction

International humanitarian law (IHL) and international human rights law (IHRL) are the two principal bodies of international law governing the use of force in international military operations. While national (criminal) law also plays a relevant role, and national law may provide the primary grounds for national military operations including military support to civilian authorities, the international legal framework for the use of force *in bello*[1] consists of either IHRL or IHL, or a combination of both. These observations may appear rather obvious from a legal point of view, but the operational significance of the differences between the legal paradigms is considerable. Moreover, given divergent national views on some issues within each of the two legal frameworks, both paradigms lead to interoperability challenges in the actual conduct of multinational operations.

As the principal body of international law directly designed and intended to regulate the conduct of hostilities and the use of (military) force, IHL has a significant influence on the conduct of military operations. That impact will be discussed further below 93–100, on the basis of a selection of elements of IHL and illustrations of how those elements influence and direct the conduct of current and recent military operations in practice, as well as how they can (and often do) have an impact on multinational interoperability. Although IHL is clearly uniform, contrary to the combination of international and regional approaches to IHRL and their concomitant instruments, the interpretation of IHL and the ratification of certain instruments of IHL is neither uniform nor universal. This leads to divergences as regards operational options and decisions, especially in the context of (pre-planned) targeting.

Due to the expansive approach adopted by a number of human rights bodies as regards the concept of 'jurisdiction' in terms of its role as a threshold criterion for the applicability of the various IHRL instruments,[2] the same level of self-evident

[1] The term '*in bello*' is used loosely here, to denote the legal framework that applies to the actual conduct of the operation, regardless of whether the operation is part of an armed conflict and thus regardless of the *ad bellum* basis for the operation.

[2] The exception to this observation is the African Charter on Human and Peoples' Rights, whose scope (in Article 1 of the Charter) makes no reference to 'jurisdiction' (African Charter on Human and Peoples' Rights (adopted 27 June 1981, entered into force 21 October 1986) 1520 UNTS). The

Hans Boddens Hosang, *An Operational Perspective* In *The 'Legal Pluriverse' Surrounding Multinational Military Operations*. Edited by Robin Geiß and Heike Krieger, Oxford University Press (2020). © The Several Contributors.
DOI: 10.1093/oso/9780198842965.003.0005

influence on the conduct of international military operations can be said to hold true for IHRL. This observation will likewise be demonstrated below. As regards multinational military operations, the observation just made leads to operational challenges *ipso facto* in a number of situations, but also leads to interoperability challenges. The latter effect is due in part to differences between the regional systems, although that aspect is becoming increasingly less relevant, as will be discussed below 92–93. The interoperability challenges also arise, however, as a result of different national views as regards the applicability of IHRL to extraterritorial action[3] as well as the simple observation that adherence to and observance of IHRL obligations are not quite universal.

But in discussing the law from the operational perspective, there are two additional observations which need to be discussed. First, as has been dealt with at length in other academic writing and in case law, the two bodies of law under examination are not mutually exclusive.[4] While international humanitarian law applies only during armed conflicts,[5] human rights law applies not only in all other situations but also during armed conflicts. Given some of the significant differences as regards permissible use of force and the constraints or conditions imposed on the use of force by each of the two bodies of law, the simultaneous applicability of the law requires careful consideration in terms of military operational rules and instructions on the use of force. Additionally, the methods of resolving the rare instances of true conflict between rules of the two bodies of law must be understood and carefully applied to those same rules on the use of force, as well as during their implementation in operational practice.

Secondly, and as already implied by the observation earlier that human rights law applies 'in all other situations', there is no 'gap' between the two bodies of law.

other instruments relevant to the present discussion, that is the International Covenant on Civil and Political Rights (adopted 16 December 1966, entered into force 23 March 1976) 999 UNTS 171 (hereafter ICCPR), the American Convention on Human Rights (adopted 22 November 1969, entered into force 18 July 1978) 1144 UNTS 123 (hereafter ACHR) and the Convention for the Protection of Human Rights and Fundamental Freedoms (adopted 4 November 1950, entered into force 3 September 1953) ETS 5 (hereafter ECHR), all refer to 'jurisdiction' in the respective articles defining the scope of each of those instruments.

[3] See, eg, UNCHR, 'Consideration of reports submitted by states parties under article 40 of the Covenant: International Covenant on Civil and Political Rights: 4th Periodic Report: United States of America' (22 May 2012) UN Doc CCPR/C/USA/4; UNCHR, 'Consideration of reports submitted by states parties under article 40 of the Covenant pursuant to the optional reporting procedure: Fourth periodic reports of states parties due in 2013, Israel' (12 December 2013) UN Doc CCPR/C/ISR/4.

[4] See, eg, E Pouw, *International Human Rights Law and the Law of Armed Conflict in the Context of Counterinsurgency—With a Particular Focus on Targeting and Operational Detention* (NLDA 2013); E De Wet and J Kleffner (eds), *Convergence and Conflicts of Human Rights and International Humanitarian Law in Military Operations* (PULP 2014); *The Legality of the Threat or Use of Nuclear Weapons* (Advisory Opinion) [1996] ICJ Rep 226, para 25 (hereafter *Nuclear Weapons*).

[5] Many states, including the Netherlands, apply the restrictions and limitations derived from international humanitarian law as a matter of policy in all operations, regardless of whether the operation is an armed conflict. What is meant here, however, is the *de jure* applicability of the law.

While Aristotle used the concept of *horror vacui*[6] to describe elements of early physics, it may be said that the modern rule of (international) law similarly 'abhors a (legal) vacuum', at any rate as regards the applicability of at least one of the two bodies of law in question to the use of force by government agents, including military personnel engaged in military operations. Although states are understandably reluctant to accept, essentially, the universal applicability of human rights law to their actions, including extraterritorial operations, both the case law of regional human rights bodies and the current draft General Comment on the right to life that is being drafted by the Human Rights Committee under the International Covenant on Civil and Political Rights make it clear that extraterritorial applicability of human rights law is rapidly becoming an inescapable standard.[7]

Given these preliminary observations, and especially given the understanding which may be derived from them that at least one, and sometimes both, of the bodies of law are applicable at all times to the use of force, an examination of their impact on the conduct of operations and the interoperability aspects in multinational operations becomes even more relevant. Finally, this examination also needs to address the differences between conceptual, abstract analysis of the law, and the actual practice from an operational perspective.

2. Operational Aspects of Multinational Operations under International Humanitarian Law

As was stated in the introduction, and as clearly stated in common Article 2 of the Geneva Conventions, IHL applies to all armed conflicts. While much can be said about the differences in the volume of IHL rules applicable to international armed conflicts (IACs) and those applicable to non-international armed conflicts (NIACs), the difference is becoming increasingly irrelevant as a result of the recognition of many (or perhaps even most) of the rules of IHL applicable to IACs as being part of customary law also applicable during NIACs.[8]

However, apart from this rather obvious statement on the *in bello* aspects of IHL, it should additionally be noted that the clear intent behind the adoption of the factual concept of 'armed conflict' to eliminate political debate as to the *ad bellum* aspects of applicability of the law has not been as successful as initially hoped. The difficulties relating to the recognition of an NIAC, as opposed to

[6] 'Nature abhors a vacuum'; D Bostok, *Aristotle: Physics* (Robin Waterfield (trs), OUP 1996) 78.

[7] See, eg, *Jaloud v Netherlands* App no 47708/08 (ECtHR, Grand Chamber Judgment, 20 November 2014); *Armando Alejandre Jr, Carlos Costa, Mario De La Peña, and Pablo Morales v Cuba*, Inter-American Commission on Human Rights, Case 11.589, Report No 86/99 (29 September 1999); UNCHR, 'Draft General Comment No. 36—Article 6: Right to Life' (2 September 2015) UN Doc CCPR/C/GC/R.36/Rev.2 (hereafter Draft General Comment No 36).

[8] See, eg, JM Henckaerts and L Doswald-Beck (eds), *Customary International Humanitarian Law—Volume I: Rules* (ICRC/CUP 2005).

'internal disturbances' and similar concepts, are well-known and lie at the heart of the threshold criteria set forth in Article 1 of Additional Protocol II (AP II) to the Geneva Conventions, as well as leading to the various questions regarding the scope of applicability of Common Article 3 of the Geneva Conventions.[9] But such threshold discussions also exist as regards the political recognition of the existence of an IAC, and are similarly related to a reluctance on the part of states to acknowledge that their armed forces are engaged in an armed conflict.[10] While a full examination of these issues falls well outside of the scope of the present discussion,[11] it is important to realize that for operational military personnel the question is more than academic, given the significant legal consequences as to whether a criminal act is prosecuted as a 'simple' crime or as a war crime.[12] Consequently, and notwithstanding the political realities which cause the reluctance referred to above, a greater willingness on the part of governments to adopt the initially intended factual approach to the applicability of the law would not only serve the interests of the law, but also of their military personnel.

A final introductory comment regarding the application of IHL to a given military operation concerns the concept of military necessity. As will be discussed below 104, the concept of 'necessity' as part of IHRL and its role in that context as a threshold criterion for the use force differs considerably from the meaning of 'necessity' in the context of IHL. During armed conflict, after all, the use of force is generally understood to be an expected part of the overall context and the necessity to use force is consequently more principally an element in the *ad bellum* considerations. Given this observation, the concept of 'military necessity' is generally understood as 'the necessity of those measures which are indispensable for securing the ends of the war, and which are lawful according to the modern law and usages of war'.[13] In other words, the concept of military necessity is an underlying

[9] Y Sandoz, C Swinarski, and B Zimmerman (eds), *Commentary on the Additional Protocols of 8 June 1977 to the Geneva Conventions of 12 August 1949* (ICRC/Martinus Nijhoff 1987) 1348–56; Committee on Use of Force, 'Final Report on the Meaning of Armed Conflict in International Law' in *International Law Association Report of the Seventy-Fourth Conference* (The Hague 2010) 12–13.

[10] A Gioia, 'The Role of the European Court of Human Rights in Monitoring Compliance with Humanitarian Law in Armed Conflict' in O Ben-Naftali (ed), *International Humanitarian Law and International Human Rights Law* (OUP 2011) 220; MC Zwanenburg, 'Accountability under International Humanitarian Law for United Nations and North Atlantic Treaty Organization Peace Support Operations' (doctoral thesis, University of Leiden 2004) 197; C Greenwood, 'Scope of Application of Humanitarian Law' in D Fleck (ed), *Handbook of International Humanitarian Law in Armed Conflict* (2nd edn, OUP 2008) 48.

[11] For a detailed discussion of these issues, see JFR Boddens Hosang, 'Rules of Engagement: Rules on the Use of Force as Linchpin for the International Law of Military Operations' (doctoral thesis, University of Amsterdam 2016) 153–63.

[12] An observation shared by P Ducheine, 'ISAF en oorlogsrecht: Door het juiste te doen, vreest gij niemand' (2009) Militair Rechtelijk Tijdschrift 287–88.

[13] Article 14 of General Orders No 100 (The Lieber Code, 1863) 'Instructions for the Government of Armies of the United States in the Field'. See also the definition given in the UK Manual of the Law of Armed Conflict, amendment 3, September 2010: 'The principle whereby a belligerent has the right to apply any measures which are required to bring about the successful conclusion of a military operation and which are not forbidden by the laws of war.'

principle of the conduct of hostilities, but its application in practice is regulated by the rules of IHL, not as a separate legal requirement or consideration.[14] Given this role of the principle, it will not be discussed in greater detail here.

2.1 The principle of distinction and multinational targeting

The term 'targeting' seems linguistically simple, but in a military operational context refers to a complex and extensive process. While the term readily invites a focus on the kinetic use of force and the actual application of force against a target, targeting in modern operations not only covers a process including policy and legal considerations, technological aspects, and economy of force concerns,[15] but also includes activities such as 'key leader engagement' and similar more diplomatically oriented operations.[16] However, as such non-kinetic activities are not readily relevant for the application of IHL, the present discussion will give in to the ready invitation mentioned above and focus on kinetic use of force in military operations.

The targeting process includes legal evaluations at two stages (at least) of the process: (1) selected or intended targets are 'vetted' against applicable law before being approved and placed on the Joint (Prioritized) Target List; and (2) an assessment is made prior to any weapon release whether the use of that particular force against that particular target is lawful under the real-time circumstances ruling at the time. Both of these legal evaluations can give rise to interoperability challenges in practice during multinational operations in terms of differences in interpretation of IHL as regards who and what constitute lawful targets under the law and, consequently, differences in application of the principle of distinction.

In terms of targeting persons, IHL makes a clear distinction between combatants and civilians in IACs, with combatants being members of the armed forces of a party to the conflict and civilians being all those who are not such members.[17] With

[14] J Kleffner, 'Section IX of the ICRC Interpretative Guidance on Direct Participation in Hostilities: the end of *jus in bello* proportionality as we know it?' (2012) 45 Israel Law Review 36, 41; MN Schmitt, 'The Interpretive Guidance on the Notion of Direct Participation in Hostilities: A Critical Analysis' (2010) 1 Harvard National Security Journal 39–41.

[15] For a discussion and explanation of the modern targeting process, see, eg, PR Pratzner, 'The Current Targeting Process' in PAL Ducheine, MN Schmitt, and FPB Osinga (eds), *Targeting: The Challenges of Modern Warfare* (TMC Asser Press 2016); NATO Standardization Office, 'Allied Joint Doctrine for Joint Targeting—Edition A Version 1' (Allied Joint Publication 3.9, 8 April 2016) <https://assets.publishing.service.gov.uk/government/uploads/system/uploads/attachment_data/file/628215/20160505-nato_targeting_ajp_3_9.pdf>. All URLs accessed 27 December 2018.

[16] United States Department of the Army, 'Field Manual Counterinsurgency FM 3-24 MCWP 3-33.5' (Headquarters of the Department of the Army, December 2006) <https://www.hsdl.org/?abstract&did=468442>; JF Hull, *Iraq: Strategic Reconciliation, Targeting, and Key Leader Engagement* (US Army War College Strategic Studies Institute 2009).

[17] This is intended as a simplified statement of the law and is obviously without prejudice to the non-combatant status of certain members of the armed forces, including medical personnel, as well as other exceptions such as civilians who become combatants as part of a *levée en masse* and as evidenced by the more careful wording of Protocol Additional to the Geneva Conventions of 12 August 1949 and relating

the exception of civilians taking a direct part in hostilities, as will be discussed below 96–97, only combatants may be legally targeted during an IAC.[18] As regards the rules of IHL governing NIACs, the term 'combatant' and the concomitant 'combatant privilege' are notably absent. This means that targeting in NIACs focuses instead on the definitions of the terms used to describe the non-governmental parties to an NIAC.

Since all of the current multinational operations constituting an armed conflict are to be qualified as NIACs,[19] the issue of defining 'the enemy' in an NIAC is of great current interest. Agreeing on who is 'the enemy' becomes complicated, however, in conflicts in which one or more parties in a multinational force apply a different scope to the conflict itself. This is the case, for example, in the conflict in Iraq and Syria against ISIS, in which some of the participating states, including the Netherlands, consider the legal basis to be the request by Iraq for assistance, and the enemy to be those members of ISIS who either have a continuous combat function or who lose protection as civilians for such time as they directly participate in hostilities.[20] Other participating states, most notably the United States, consider the conflict to be part of a larger ongoing conflict against Al-Qaeda and all its derivative and associated organizations (including ISIS), and the enemy to be all those who are part of those groups, applying a wider range of criteria to determine that status.[21] This leads to complications in the event that persons are to be targeted

to the Protection of Victims of International Armed Conflicts (adopted 8 June 1977, entered into force 7 December 1978) 1125 UNTS 3, Article 43, 50, para 1 (AP I).

[18] Another possible exception would the use of force in self-defence against a civilian or (other) non-combatant. It may be argued, however, that the use of force in self-defence during an IAC is not regulated by IHL as such, but rather by the (national, usually criminal law) rules governing lawful self-defence.

[19] The term 'transnational NIAC' is used here to describe situations in which the government of a state engaged in an NIAC is assisted by other states in defeating the enemy. Obviously, if states were to assist the non-state forces in an NIAC, the conflict would become an IAC. See, eg, TD Gill, 'Classifying the Conflict in Syria' (2016) 92 US Naval War College International Law Studies 353.

[20] The legal basis for participation in the conflict was explained, inter alia, in the most recent letter from the government to parliament of 11 September 2017 (parliamentary document no 27 925 nr P). The reference to direct participation in hostilities was made, inter alia, in the answers by the government to questions from parliament, submitted on 18 December 2012 (parliamentary document no 29 521 nr 200). Attacking civilians who do not directly participate in hostilities is punishable in the Netherlands as a war crime under the International Crimes Act (*Wet internationale misdrijven*) Article 5 para 5(m).

[21] For the legal basis of the fight against ISIS, see, eg, S Preston, 'Speech on the Legal Framework for the United States Use of Military Force Since 9/11' (Annual Meeting of the American Society of International Law, Washington, 10 April 2015) <https://www.defense.gov/News/Speeches/Speech-View/Article/606662/>; E Holder, 'Speech' (Northwestern University School of Law, Chicago, 5 March 2012) <https://www.justice.gov/opa/speech/attorney-general-eric-holder-speaks-northwestern-university-school-law>; S Preston, 'Statement on the Framework Under U.S. Law for Current Military Operations' (United States Senate Committee on Foreign Relations, 21 May 2014) <https://www.foreign.senate.gov/imo/media/doc/Preston_Testimony.pdf>. As regards the range of criteria or scope as to who may be targeted, see, in addition to the references above, the United States Judge Advocate General's Legal Center and School, 'Operational Law Handbook' (International and Operational Law Department 2015) 17 <http://www.loc.gov/rr/frd/Military_Law/pdf/operational-law-handbook_2015.pdf>; Office of General Counsel Department of Defense, 'Law of War Manual' (United States Department of Defense June 2015, updated December 2016) 103–04, 160–62 < https://dod.defense.

based on their status instead of on the basis of their conduct, an issue which primarily arises in pre-planned targeting. In operations in which a Joint (Prioritized) Target List is applied, states which apply views on IHL similar to the ICRC[22] can only engage persons who are placed on that list on the basis of their status if those persons can be considered to have a continuous combat function,[23] leaving the other persons on that list for other states to engage.

Similar challenges, albeit related more to the interpretation of IHL than to the scope of the armed conflict, can arise as regards the targeting of objects. While Article 52 AP I sets forth the criteria for determining whether an object is a valid military objective, and those criteria can be considered part of customary law in both IACs and NIACs,[24] the United States has consistently expressed its views that objects which make an effective contribution to the enemy's ability to sustain the war also fall under the definition of a valid military objective.[25] Since that view is not widely supported,[26] and given the relevance of sources of income such as oil for organizations like ISIS and its dependency on certain infrastructure in the area of conflict, the divergence of legal opinion on this issue can cause challenges if such more economical rather than clearly military objects are placed on the target list. Here, too, the states will have to determine which targets on the list are valid objectives on the basis of their national views on the interpretation of IHL, leaving the other objects for other states.[27]

While the 'pick and choose' approach to pre-planned target engagement may appear to be a viable (and in any case valid and unavoidable) approach to such

gov/Portals/1/Documents/pubs/DoD%20Law%20of%20War%20Manual%20-%20June%202015%20Updated%20Dec%202016.pdf?ver=2016-12-13-172036-190>.

[22] N Melzer, *Interpretative Guidance on the Notion of Direct Participation in Hostilities Under International Humanitarian Law* (ICRC 2009).

[23] This also supposes that sufficient intelligence is available to make such a determination. The challenges in exchanging intelligence in multinational operations falls outside of the scope of this chapter, however.

[24] Henckaerts and Doswald-Beck (n 8) 29–32.

[25] ibid. See also B Egan, 'Speech on International Law, Legal Diplomacy and the Counter-ISIL Campaign' (American Society of International Law, 4 April 2016) <https://www.justsecurity.org/wp-content/uploads/2016/04/Egan-ASIL-speech.pdf>; Office of General Counsel Department of Defense (n 21) 208–10, esp paras 5.7–6.2.

[26] For example, Y Dinstein, 'Legitimate Military Objectives under the Current *Jus in Bello*' (2002) 78 US Naval War College International Law Studies 145–46.

[27] While this may lead to discussions as regards the obligation 'to ensure respect' for IHL as set forth in Common Article 1 of the Geneva Conventions, there is as yet no clear consensus as to the positive external dimension of that obligation (Geneva Convention (I) for the Amelioration of the Condition of the Wounded and Sick in Armed Forces in the Field (entered into force 21 October 1950) 75 UNTS 31; Convention (II) for the Amelioration of the Wounded, Sick and Shipwrecked Members of Armed Forces at Sea (entered into force 21 October 1950) 75 UNTS 85; Geneva Convention (III) Relative to the Treatments of Prisoners of War (entered into force 21 October 1950) 75 UNTS 135; Geneva Convention (IV) Relative to the Protection of Civilian Persons in Time of War (entered into force 21 October 1950) 75 UNTS 287). For a recent evaluation of the obligation, see M Zwanenburg, 'The Obligation to "Ensure Respect" for IHL: The Debate Continues' (*ICRC Intercross Blog*, 26 September 2017) <http://intercrossblog.icrc.org/blog/the-obligation-to-ensure-respect-for-ihl-the-debate-continues>.

differences in the interpretation and application of IHL, the effect on operational personnel should not be dismissed. In multinational operations, especially those which take place in armed conflicts or other situations of high risks and high tensions, the cohesion of the force and the 'group effort' nature of the deployment are not only of high importance but also distinctly felt by the units actually participating in the operation. When viewed from that perspective, it may become clear that having one part of the force engaging targets which are off-limits to the other part of the force does not support or enhance the cohesion of the force as a whole.

The desired unity of effort and necessary unity of response is most prevalent in the case of close air support, in which ground units from one state may require the assistance of combat aircraft from another state, often including situations in which the lives of the ground unit are at stake. Fortunately, the different views on aspects of IHL are less of a hindrance in such situations. First, in the case of close air support for a unit actually under attack, the status of the attackers to be targeted by the combat aircraft as valid targets would appear clear and it is irrelevant whether they are fighters with a continuous combat function or directly participating in hostilities at the time of the engagement. Secondly, in cases which do not involve a unit under direct attack, a 'work-around' has been implemented in practice. This approach, which can be applied by aircraft from states bound by less lenient views on IHL when delivering close air support to units from states with more lenient views, consists of applying a set of control questions to be asked by the pilot to the controller on the ground (preferably a trained and qualified Joint Terminal Attack Controller (JTAC)), designed to provide the pilot with sufficient information to make a determination as to the legality of engaging the target in question. In other words, even when the pilot cannot gather sufficient visual or other information about the target directly, the pilot can use the JTAC to provide that necessary information.[28]

2.2. The principle of proportionality

The IHL principle of proportionality requires, simply stated, that the incidental loss of, or injury to, civilians or the incidental destruction of, or damage to, civilian objects to be anticipated from an attack is not excessive in relation to 'the concrete and direct military advantage anticipated' from that attack.[29] In other words, the proportionality evaluation is essentially a consideration of the military advantage

[28] For a more detailed discussion of this approach, see Boddens Hosang (n 11) 180–82. The observations in this part of the discussion, as well as the described solution, also apply to differences in legal interpretation or differences of opinion as regards application of the principle of proportionality in cases of close air support and will not be discussed further in the discussion on proportionality below.

[29] Paraphrased from AP I (n 17) Article 57, para 2(a)(iii).

in relation to the expected collateral damage in order to ensure a reasonable balance between operational interests and humanitarian concerns. This aspect will be discussed below 104–105 in the context of the rather different definition of proportionality under IHRL. In practice, the principle of proportionality rarely leads to interoperability challenges in multinational operations on the basis of interpretation or application of the law as such, although other concerns and interests can give rise to different procedures in this context.

The procedural aspects of the proportionality requirement are evidenced by the approach taken by the Netherlands, which leaves the proportionality determination up to the unit in question (and, where necessary, supported by either a deployed military legal adviser or a 24/7 reach-back system), as opposed to the approach taken by the United States, which applies a Collateral Damage Estimation (CDE) approach requiring increasingly higher ranks to approve target engagement as the CDE level increases.[30] It may be argued, however, that concerns over collateral damage in modern operations are less driven by legal restraints and more related to public opinion and the desire to avoid collateral damage in general, far beyond the requirements of IHL; in fact, they may have been for some time now.[31]

2.3 Prisoners of war

A final aspect of IHL which can give rise to challenges in interoperability is one that is partly related to the observations above regarding defining the enemy, and partly related to issues of extraterritorial applicability of IHRL in (multinational) military operations, to be discussed in the next section. This aspect concerns prisoners of war (POW) and other forms of detention in the context of an armed conflict.

The categories of persons entitled to POW status in the context of an IAC are set forth in Article 4 of Geneva Convention III (GC III) and Articles 43 and 44(1) AP I. In modern military operations, however, application of these provisions is rare, and detained persons more commonly fall under different provisions of IHL, as well as IHRL. Leaving the IHRL aspects for the next section, IHL requires that persons deprived of their liberty in the context of an IAC following participation in hostilities and who are not entitled to POW status, shall at least be accorded

[30] D Le Clercq and J Velzeboer, 'Air Task Force—Middle East. Een juridische terugblik op luchtoperaties in het Midden Oosten' (2017) 110 Militair Rechtelijk Tijdschrift, https://puc.overheid.nl/mrt/doc/PUC_85829_11/1/. See also the Chairman of the Joint Chiefs of Staff Instruction, 'No-Strike and the Collateral Damage Estimation Methodology' (CJCSI 3160.01, 13 February 2009) <https://www.aclu.org/files/dronefoia/dod/drone_dod_3160_01.pdf>.

[31] See inter alia D Porch, 'No Bad Stories: The American Media—Military Relationship' (2002) 55 Naval War College Review 85; United Kingdom Ministry of Defence, 'The Future Strategic Context for Defence' (2001); EV Larson and B Savych, *Misfortunes of War: Press and Public Reactions to Civilian Deaths in Wartime* (RAND Project Air Force 2006).

certain fundamental guarantees.[32] In the context of NIAC, in which the concept of POW does not exist, persons deprived of their liberty are to be accorded, as a minimum, the guarantees and provisions set forth in Common Article 3 of the Geneva Conventions as well as those set forth in Articles 4 and 5 AP II.

While IHL thus appears to make a clear distinction between two categories of persons as regards their status following capture and detention, the concept of 'illegal combatants' as an additional category identified by some states raises difficulties. At the operational level,[33] the transfer of detainees may become problematic if the receiving state cannot guarantee the same status or level of protection for the detainee to be transferred. Although written guarantees are usually sought wherever possible,[34] it is clearly not always possible to reach agreement on such matters. On the other hand, the detaining unit may not be able to apply all of the requirements of IHL itself, given the various logistical and infrastructural aspects of those requirements. Such a situation may then very well lead to an avoidance of capturing persons, regardless of the threat they pose, with all concomitant risks to the force. This aspect will be discussed further below 100, in the section on IHRL.

3. Operational Aspects of Multinational Operations under Human Rights Law

A full discussion on the extraterritorial applicability of IHRL goes well beyond the scope of the present discussion, as would certainly be the case for a full discussion of the interaction between IHRL and IHL. Consequently, a few introductory remarks on these topics will need to suffice as a stepping stone to the operational aspects of IHRL and the interoperability issues IHRL can cause in multinational operations.

While it is undeniable that the European Court of Human Rights (ECtHR) has been the most prolific as regards its case law on the criteria and scope of the extraterritorial applicability of IHRL, including its application to military operations, it is certainly not alone in expressing those views. While in this discussion, reference will be made to several decisions of the ECtHR, it may be pointed out that such

32 AP I (n 17) Article 45, para 3, Article 75. As the present discussion is related to the previous discussion of the principle of distinction, the application of the Fourth Geneva Convention (n 27) and the concept of internment will not be discussed here.

33 Obviously, this issue can raise difficulties at the political level as well, such as regarding the transfer of such persons to other states in the attempts by the Obama administration to close the controversial detention facility in Guantánamo Bay. See, eg, the answers by the Minister of Foreign Affairs of the Netherlands to questions from parliament regarding the refusal to take over detainees from the United States (Annex to the Parliamentary Records, Volume 2015–2016, no 2387, no 1004).

34 A practice applied by, inter alia, the Netherlands in the context of the ISAF mission in Afghanistan and the previous mission in Iraq (SFIR). See the answers by the government to questions from parliament regarding the transfer of detainees in these missions (Parliamentary Document 23 432 no 216 (2006) and Annex to the Parliamentary Records, Volume 2010–2011, no 1075).

views are not only shared by other human rights bodies but that some of those bodies appear to be adopting the views of the ECtHR in making their own decisions and formulating their own views on such issues.[35] As regards the applicability of IHRL during armed conflicts, the human rights bodies are joined by the International Court of Justice (ICJ), which has similarly expressed this view in some of its cases.[36] Finally, the Human Rights Committee has made it clear that the International Covenant on Civil and Political Rights (ICCPR) also applies to peacekeeping operations,[37] although the ECtHR has appeared reluctant to render decisions on operations under direct command and control of the United Nations.[38]

As regards the interaction between IHRL and IHL during an armed conflict, it has been observed that true conflicts are rare and that the two bodies of law often share a similar goal or purpose.[39] However, when conflicts do arise, the *lex specialis* rule is the commonly accepted norm for resolving such conflicts and during armed conflicts, the *lex specialis* will normally be IHL.[40] In applying the *lex specialis* rule, two approaches are possible. The first approach resolves an apparent conflict that is not really a conflict by using the more specific applicable rule as an interpretative tool for also adhering to the more general norm (*lex specialis complementa*).[41] An example of such application is provided by Kleffner, who points to the requirement in Common Article 3 to the Geneva Conventions that sentences may only be passed after 'previous judgment pronounced by a regularly constituted court' and the detailed requirements in IHRL as regards the composition, functioning, etc, of such courts.[42] The second approach to the *lex specialis* rule is, of course, the *lex specialis derogat* principle in which the more specific norm takes precedence over the more general norm, if necessary even excluding application of the more general norm. This approach is ultimately the only resolution for the rare instances of true conflicts of obligations under the two bodies of law.

35 See, eg, Draft General Comment No 36 (n 7).

36 *Nuclear Weapons* (n 4) para 25; *Legal Consequences of the Construction of a Wall in the Occupied Palestinian Territory* (Advisory Opinion) [2004] ICJ Rep 136, para 106.

37 UNCHR, 'General Comment No. 31. The Nature of the General Legal Obligation Imposed on States Parties to the Covenant' (2004) UN Doc CCPR/C/21/Rev.1/Add.13, para 10.

38 *Behrami and Behrami v France* and *Saramati v France, Germany and Norway* App no 71412/01 and 78166/01 (ECtHR, Grand Chamber Decision as to Admissibility, 2 May 2007); in combination with *Al Jedda v United Kingdom* App no 27021/08 (ECtHR, Grand Chamber Judgment, 7 July 2011).

39 L Doswald-Beck and S Vité, 'International Humanitarian Law and Human Rights Law' (1993) 33 International Review of the Red Cross 94.

40 *Nuclear Weapons* (n 4) para 25. See also TD Gill, 'Some Thoughts on the Relationship Between International Humanitarian Law and International Human Rights Law: A Plea for Mutual Respect and a Common Sense Approach' (2013) 16 Yearbook of International Humanitarian Law 251 who not only points out that the *lex specialis* approach is 'prevailing opinion and practice' but also illustrates that conflicts between the two bodies of law are not as prevalent as the extent of the debate on this issue might indicate.

41 J Kleffner, 'Human Rights and International Humanitarian Law: General Issues' in TD Gill and D Fleck (eds), *The Handbook of the International Law of Military Operations* (2nd edn, OUP 2015) 57–58; Pouw (n 4) 133.

42 Kleffner (ibid) 57–58.

Finally, applying a different use of the *derogat* principle in law, states may derogate from their obligations under IHRL instruments, although this is rare in practice. It should also be pointed out that the formal requirements for derogation are considerable,[43] and some rights are quite simply non-derogable. One of those rights, and perhaps the most relevant to military operations, is the right to life to be discussed in section 3.1. Since derogations are rare in the context of international, multinational military operations, they will not be discussed any further.

3.1 The right to life

The right to life as a non-derogable right under IHRL is protected by Article 6 ICCPR and Article 4 of the American Convention on Human Rights (ACHR), both of which ban 'arbitrary' deprivation of life, and by Article 2 of the European Convention on Human Rights (ECHR), which lists, in paragraph 2, the only legitimate exceptions to the right to life. It is possible, however, to argue whether the exception to the right to life under Article 15(2), regarding 'lawful acts of war', requires a prior derogation, or whether it is simply an exception to the right to life itself. Although the phrasing of the provision in question appears to indicate that invoking 'lawful acts of war' would require a derogation, the Guide issued by the Court seems to indicate that lawful acts of war are an exception to the right to life similar to the exceptions set forth in Article 2(2) ECHR.[44] The significant difference between the European approach and the international and American approach is, of course, the absence of any room for interpretation as to whether a death was 'arbitrary'; if the use of force leading to the death in question does not fall under the legitimate exceptions set forth in the ECHR itself, the death will be considered a breach of Article 2. Finally, a distinction should be made between intentional death and incidental death. Based on a thorough analysis of the case law of the ECtHR, Hessbruegge concludes that self-defence is the only legitimate basis for intentional lethal use of force under Article 2 ECHR, leaving the other exceptions

[43] For an overview of these requirements, see ibid 53. Note, however, that the formal requirement of prior notification appears to have been reduced somewhat by the ECtHR, who appears to accept derogation at the start of a case before the Court even without prior formal derogation before the operation itself. See *Hassan v United Kingdom* App no 29750/09 (ECtHR, Grand Chamber Judgment, 16 September 2014) para 107. The present author uses the word 'appears' in this context, since it remains to be seen whether the Court will accept this approach in practice. In the same case, the Court also points out, in para 40, that states have never derogated from the Convention for extraterritorial (military) operations. This is interesting, since many of those operations qualify as an (transboundary) NIAC in which HRL is far more likely to be the *lex specialis*, as also clearly indicated by a number of cases before the ECtHR. See also W Abresch, 'A Human Rights Law of Internal Armed Conflict: The European Court of Human Rights in Chechnya' (2005) 16 European Journal of International Law 741.

[44] ECtHR, 'Guide on Article 15 of the European Convention on Human Rights' (30 April 2017) 10 <http://www.echr.coe.int/Documents/Guide_Art_15_ENG.pdf>.

in the second paragraph as only justifying incidental loss of life.[45] The present author submits that the exception, assuming it to be such, set forth in Article 15(2) regarding 'lawful acts of war', similarly justifies intentional loss of life (as well as incidental loss of life) in the same way that deaths resulting from such lawful acts would not be considered 'arbitrary'.

If self-defence is considered the sole justification for intentional deprivation of life in military operations subject to IHRL, challenges can arise in multinational operations in which the views of the participating states differ as regards the criteria and scope of the concept of self-defence. Even when limiting the concept to unit and personal self-defence, as opposed to national self-defence, and leaving aside the rather unique approach to self-defence adopted by the United Nations,[46] national views diverge as regards at what point force may be used in self-defence as well as who and what may be defended.[47] Variances include aspects such as defence of others and defence of property, both of which can give rise to critical situations during military operations.[48] Quite obviously, diverging views will lead to divergence in the use of force by the units from the various nations, thus rendering unity of effort and unity of command impossible.

However, even absent any divergence of national views, the concept of self-defence as the sole basis for the use of force can raise challenges in the conduct of the operation as a result of common limitations regarding self-defence. If defence of others is restricted in general or is limited to only certain categories, as it is in some national views, this will clearly have profound influences on the ability to incorporate the notion of 'protection of civilians' in operations mandated by, but not under the command and control of, the United Nations.[49] Similarly, as many—especially European—national views limit or even rule out the use of force in

[45] JA Hessbruegge, *Human Rights and Personal Self-Defense in International Law* (OUP 2017) 103–17.

[46] For a discussion of the UN approach to self-defence, see KE Cox, 'Beyond Self-Defense: United Nations Peacekeeping Operations & The Use of Force' (1999) 27 Denver Journal of International Law and Policy 239; S Chesterman, 'The Use of Force in UN Peace Operations' (External Study for the UN Department of Peacekeeping Operations, August 2004) <http://www.operationspaix.net/DATA/DOCUMENT/5808~v~The_Use_of_Force_in_UN_Peace_Operations.pdf>; M Bothe, 'Peace-Keeping' in B Simma (ed), *The Charter of the United Nations: A Commentary* (Clarendon Press 1994).

[47] Boddens Hosang (n 11) 117–25; Hessbruegge (n 45).

[48] The observations on national views on self-defence are based on the answers provided by states to the questionnaire by the International Society for Military Law and the Law of War: see JFR Boddens Hosang and others, 'Report on the Role of Self-Defence in Multinational Operations' in S Horvat and M Benatar (eds), *Legal Interoperability and Ensuring Observance of the Law Applicable in Multinational Deployments—Recueil XIX* (Recueils of the International Society for Military Law and the Law of War 2013).

[49] Although conversely an unrestricted right to defend others could jeopardize force unity of effort and unity of command, given the inherent nature of self-defence, it seems very unlikely that national views on self-defence would authorize the use of force in defence of others without any restrictions. Such an approach would, after all, change the exceptional nature of self-defence as a justification for otherwise unlawful use of force into a *carte blanche* for vigilantism. The present author is not familiar with any national position allowing such latitude, without at the very least requiring some proximity to the victim to be defended as well as other criteria.

defence of property under self-defence, defending or guarding critical force property, such as weapon depots, combat vehicles and aircraft, and cryptographic communication systems, becomes a significant challenge. Essentially, this approach leaves such guards little choice other than to put themselves in harm's way in order to then justify the use of force as personal self-defence (that is, defence of life) instead of defence of property.[50]

Regardless of whether the national views on the use of force in self-defence are lenient or restrictive as regards the subject to be defended, IHRL and the case law of the various human rights bodies are clear and unequivocal as regards two aspects of the use of force. The first aspect is that under IHRL, the necessity to use force must be an absolute necessity, essentially meaning that it is a measure of last resort.[51] This is, of course, a rather different meaning of 'necessity' than the concept of 'military necessity' discussed earlier and raises the threshold for the use of force significantly. It may also be considered obvious that the different views as discussed earlier regarding the legal basis for certain military operations can cause distinct challenges in interoperability between units from states adhering to a human rights basis for the use of force, and consequently the absolute necessity standard, and units from states considering the use of force to be governed by IHL and its military necessity standard.

The second aspect concerns the principle of proportionality. Under IHRL, any use of force must be reasonably proportionate to the countered threat, meaning no more force and no more destructive means may be applied than objectively reasonable in comparison to the threat in question.[52] In other words, while proportionality under IHL focuses on the collateral effects of the use of force and arguably ignores the threat posed by the actual target of the use of force, proportionality under IHRL focuses specifically on the threat posed by the actual target. Apart

[50] In the present author's professional experience, this approach is not uncommon. The only exception often considered valid would arise if the property being guarded is inherently dangerous and its loss would pose a direct threat to life, thus authorizing the use of force in defence of such property as 'defence of life'.

[51] Apart from the observation that the phrase 'absolutely necessary' is included literally in the ECHR (n 2) Article 2, para 2; see, inter alia, ICRC, 'Report on the Expert Meeting on the Use of Force in Armed Conflicts: Interplay between the Conduct of Hostilities and Law Enforcement Paradigms' (ICRC November 2013) 8 <https://www.icrc.org/eng/assets/files/publications/icrc-002-4171.pdf>; *McCann and Others v United Kingdom* App no 18984/91 (ECtHR, Grand Chamber Judgment, 27 September 1995) para 149; *Jaloud v The Netherlands* (n 7) para 199. Note that while the ECtHR accepts that in exceptional circumstances the use of military forces and heavy combat weapons may be necessary, it still applies the absolute necessity test for the actual use of force if no derogation has been lodged. *Isayeva v Russia* App no 57950/00 (ECtHR, Judgment, 24 February 2005) paras 180–81. Invoking self-defence in such situations is similarly evaluated against the absolute necessity requirement, including the requirement of a prior (imminent) attack. *Isayeva v Russia, Yusupova v Russia and Bazayeva v Russia* App no 57947/00, 57948/00 and 57949/00 (ECtHR, Judgment, 24 February 2005) paras 178, 182.

[52] See, inter alia, N Lubell, 'Challenges in Applying Human Rights Law to Armed Conflict' (2005) 87 International Review of the Red Cross 737, 745–46; ICRC. (n 51) 8–9; *Jaloud v The Netherlands* (n 7) paras 199, 202; *McCann and Others v United Kingdom* (n 51) para 149. Note that the ECtHR generally combines the principles of necessity and proportionality as aspects of the same requirement.

from the self-evident observation that this can raise similar challenges in interoperability as just discussed in connection with the principle of necessity, the definition and role of the requirement of proportionality under IHRL also distinctly influences choices made in planning and equipping a military operation. That influence extends to decisions as to whether the deployment of military forces is even the most appropriate option in the given circumstances or in countering specific threats such as terrorists.[53]

3.2 Capture and detention

The protection against unlawful or arbitrary deprivation of liberty is set forth in Article 9 ICCPR, Article 7 ACHR, and Article 5 ECHR. Although derogations from these obligations are possible, it was already observed earlier that derogations in the context of international military operations are rare.[54] In the absence of such derogations, the articles just mentioned have significant influence on the conduct of military operations and can yield interoperability challenges as well.

While the rules of IHL governing prisoners of war and the internment of civilians who pose a security risk in the context of an IAC are clear, and are the *lex specialis* in such contexts,[55] such clarity is lacking in the context of NIACs. The law governing NIACs simply does not contain specific rules on the issue of who may be detained (and why), but merely sets forth minimum guarantees for those who are detained. It is not surprising, therefore, that the ECtHR appears to consider security detention, as well as most likely all other forms of detention, in the context of an NIAC to be governed by Article 5 ECHR.[56] It is also quite clear, on the basis of the case law of the human rights bodies, that detention outside the context of an armed conflict in any case gives rise to application of IHRL and constitutes one of the clearest grounds for (extraterritorial) applicability of IHRL on the basis of 'authority and control' and 'jurisdiction'—and the variations on those wordings—as used in the case law of those bodies.[57]

[53] *McCann and others v United Kingdom* (n 51). Note that this case concerns the deployment of special units in the context of national counter-terrorist operations and that many of the factors considered in the case are not necessarily translatable to international (multinational) operations. The views expressed by the court as regards necessity and proportionality are, however, applicable beyond the national context, as evidenced by later ECtHR case law.

[54] See *Hassan v United Kingdom* (n 43) paras 40–42.

[55] ibid para 104.

[56] ibid.

[57] See, eg, *Öcalan v Turkey* App no 46221/99 (ECtHR, Judgment, 12 May 2005); *Al-Skeini and Others v United Kingdom* App no 55721/07 (ECtHR, Grand Chamber Judgment, 7 July 2011); *Rafael Ferrer-Mazorra et al v United States*, Inter-American Commission on Human Rights, Case 9903, Report No 51/01 (4 April 2001). Jurisdiction (in the HRL sense of the word) can also arise if the person was effectively deprived of his or liberty by being on board a ship at sea, once the state in question takes control of the vessel (*Medvedyev and others v France* App no 3394/03 (ECtHR, Grand Chamber Judgment, 29 March 2010), as well as if the state intended to bring a person under its control by imposing a road block (*Jaloud v The Netherlands* (n 7)).

Applying IHRL to detainees in the context of a military operation raises three clear difficulties from the outset. First, the ECHR system as regards deprivation of liberty limits the grounds for detention to those set forth in the treaty and case law of the ECtHR. Security detention is not one of those grounds. That means that if a person poses a threat to the force, but there is not enough probable cause to warrant an arrest under criminal law, detention is not legally possible.[58] Assuming that states are not willing to intentionally violate IHRL requirements, this only leaves the options of letting the person move about freely, or derogating from the Convention for the duration of the military operation in question. Neither option would appear entirely satisfactory, whether from an operational or a legal perspective.[59]

The second difficulty arising from the applicability of IHRL to detainees in the context of military operations concerns the requirement of due process. Even if, in spite of the difficulties discussed, sufficient evidence exists to warrant an arrest under criminal charges or criminal suspicions, that subsequently means that the arrested individual must be brought before a judge or in any case handed over to duly authorized officials in the context of law enforcement. Clearly, military forces are not equipped to carry out judicial review themselves, but the reality of military operations is that they commonly take place in environments where the local law enforcement and judicial authorities and institutions are either not functional at all or raise serious concerns as to their functioning. Satisfying the due process requirement can therefore oftentimes be practically impossible, once again leaving only the options of releasing the person in question or derogating from the IHRL obligations.

The third and final difficulty to be considered in this context is closely related to the previous one and concerns the IHRL requirements governing the transfer of persons from one jurisdiction to another. Such transfers are most definitely governed by IHRL and require that the transferring state must be sure, or obtain guarantees, that the person's rights will not be negatively affected by the transfer.[60]

[58] While in some cases a threat to the force *ipso facto* provides suspicion of criminal behaviour, that is not always the case. In states allowing the (open) carrying of weapons, for example, mere possession or carrying of a firearm would not constitute probable cause, while intelligence indicating a threat often either cannot be shared with third parties (such as local law enforcement or local judges) or cannot meet the requirements for criminal law prosecutorial evidence.

[59] Note that the ICCPR (n 2) does not contain such a restriction and refers to 'arbitrary arrest or detention' in Article 9. Although the Human Rights Committee has expressed considerable concerns regarding security detention, it does not consider such detention to be a violation of the Covenant, provided a number of strict conditions and requirements are met: UNCHR, 'General Comment No. 35—Article 9 Liberty and Security of Person' (16 December 2014) UN Doc CCPR/C/GC/35, para 15. This leaves states parties to the ECHR the option of derogating from their obligations under Article 5 ECHR (n 2) while implementing their human rights obligations under Article 9 ICCPR (n 2). However, as was pointed out above (n 43), states have so far chosen not to derogate from the ECHR (n 2) in the context of international military operations, meaning this option is, to date, only relevant in domestic operations.

[60] See, eg, Human Rights Committee, *Mohammad Munaf v Romania*, Communication No 1539/2006, UN Doc CCPR/C/96/D/1539/2006 (2009); *Al-Saadoon and Mufdhi v United Kingdom* App no 61498/08 (ECtHR, Judgment, 2 March 2010).

In situations such as described above, this leads to a conflict of obligations under IHRL itself: the requirement of due process requires speedy transfer to (local) judicial authorities, while the prohibition of transfers which negatively affect a person's human rights prevents such transfers to local authorities. In operations which take place at the request of, or at least by permission of, the local government, this raises even greater difficulties, as the local authorities can simply, and lawfully, demand the force to hand over the detained person. Refusing such a transfer not only negatively affects the interoperability with the local authorities[61] but can even undermine the mandate for the mission in question. Conversely, complying with such a demand can result in a breach of IHRL obligations, thus leaving release of the detainee as the only recourse.

4. Conclusion

This discussion has pointed out that, not surprisingly, IHL provides fewer difficulties as regards multinational operations and interoperability within such operations than IHRL. Given the object and purpose of IHL, it would be worrying if that were otherwise. Furthermore, the few interoperability challenges in the context of IHL can also be addressed and overcome more easily, and 'work-arounds' have been established in practice to deal with such issues. That is far less often the case as regards IHRL.

While it should be stressed that the observations presented in this discussion are not in any way meant as criticism or, even less, as suggestions that IHRL is flawed or in need of amendment, it should equally be stressed that the (original) object and purpose of IHRL are less amenable to full application in the context of a military operation. Put simply, the IHRL obligations and especially the interpretation given to those obligations by the various human rights bodies presuppose a level of authority and control over the situation, apart from the use of those terms in regard to subjects of the law in the context of jurisdiction in the case law of those same bodies. While control of the overall situation or area is not considered necessary for activation of IHRL obligations,[62] the operational realities of military operations create considerable challenges as regards fulfilling those obligations.

However, rather than ending this discussion on such a dour tone, solutions are possible. As regards IHL, continued dialogue aimed at mutual understanding of the law as well as universal compliance needs to be encouraged and pursued, not only in the context of actual military operations but especially before interoperability

[61] In a similar way, demands by a partner in the coalition to hand over a detainee can also affect interoperability if the detaining state has human rights concerns regarding the partner demanding the transfer.

[62] For example, *Hassan v United Kingdom* (n 43) para 75.

issues arise. This requires constant commitment from all states. As regards IHRL, the difficulties and challenges appear to be less related to the law itself than with the interpretation and application of the law by the human rights bodies. A greater understanding, or perhaps willingness to acknowledge, the practical realities of military operations in difficult circumstances as well as the local conditions in such operations might lend an element of realism to the application of IHRL in the cases evaluated or judged by the human rights bodies.[63]

While neither of the solutions presented above can serve to remove interoperability issues entirely, they can perhaps contribute to an even more important goal: interoperability between practitioners of the law and the units tasked with carrying out military operations.

[63] See, eg, the Joint Concurring Opinion of Judges Casadevall, Berro-Lefevre, Šikuta, Hirvelä, López Guerra, Sajó and Silvis in *Jaloud v The Netherlands* (n 7).

5

A North American Perspective

The Overlap of the Laws of Armed Conflict and International Human Rights Law

Kenneth Watkin

1. Introduction

The requirement to consider the application of human rights arises in a number of ways during contemporary multinational military operations, such as those that have occurred in the post 9/11 period including in Afghanistan, Iraq, and Syria. It occurs frequently in the context of the use of force, particularly when military forces encounter civilians who are not engaged in hostilities. For example, this was evident in June 2017 as US-backed Syrian groups prepared to enter Raqqa, which was estimated to have 'tens of thousands of civilians believed to be trapped within the city'.[1] However, this issue is not limited to the conduct of hostilities. Multinational military operations may involve the detention of persons providing indirect support to organized armed groups, the quelling of civil disorder and unrest, as well as the arrest of members of criminal organizations taking advantage of the general disorder often associated with armed conflict. The post-2003 invasion hostilities within Iraq demonstrated that these situations can arise during inter-state conflict (ie occupation).[2] It is furthermore evident in other situations—such as in Nigeria, where the non-governmental armed group Boko Haram is dealt with under national terrorism legislation—that human rights compliance also comprises a significant component of counterinsurgency and counterterrorism operations occurring around the world.[3] During the course of many

[1] L Loveluck and Z Zakaria, 'U.S.-backed forces battle ISIS around the edges of Raqqa's Old City' *The Washington Post* (13 June 2017) <https://www.washingtonpost.com/world/on-syria-fronts-us-backed-forces-probe-raqqa-defenses-as-iran-allied-fighters-gain-key-foothold/2017/06/13/dc9f7cdc-4fa1-11e7-b74e-0d2785d3083d_story.html?utm_term=.eea435ba9764>, all URLs accessed 27 December 2018.

[2] P Williams, *Criminals, Militia, and Insurgents: Organized Crime in Iraq* (Book Express Publishing 2009) 109–24 setting out the insurgent groups and criminal gang relationship in Iraq.

[3] S Olukoya, 'Nigerian court convicts 45 in Boko Haram mass trial' *The Globe and Mail* (13 October 2017) <https://www.theglobeandmail.com/news/world/nigerian-court-convicts-45-in-boko-haram-mass-trial/article36593374/>.

Kenneth Watkin, *A North American Perspective* In *The 'Legal Pluriverse' Surrounding Multinational Military Operations*. Edited by Robin Geiß and Heike Krieger, Oxford University Press (2020). © The Several Contributors.
DOI: 10.1093/oso/9780198842965.003.0006

operations, questions may be raised regarding the authority to detain persons in non-international armed conflict and the standards of detention to be applied.[4]

Human rights law is most directly associated with law enforcement. The involvement of military forces in law enforcement-style operations frequently occurs during insurgencies where an approach which emphasizes policing (ie 'police primacy') has proven to be particularly effective.[5] Where there is an overlap of international humanitarian law (IHL) and international human rights law (IHRL), the result is often the favouring of the latter legal regime as a matter of policy. Importantly, human rights-based law enforcement is normally the default position for the United States, Canada, Europe, and other states when dealing internally with the threat of transnational violence posed by non-state actors. As was demonstrated in President Obama's 2013 'Drone Speech', human rights-based norms may also be applied as a matter of policy during armed conflict when there is a goal of providing additional control over the use of force.[6] Such action is reflected not only in the context of drone strikes, but also concerning the use of special forces to carry out the arrest of persons in third countries who might be considered direct participants in an ongoing armed conflict with jihadist organized armed groups.[7] Reflective of both the evolving nature of transnational threats, and the emphasis that is being placed on law enforcement when combating insurgencies, military missions have changed over the course of the last decade from 'kill or capture' to 'capture or kill', and, finally, to 'arrest or kill'.[8] In view of such a complex interaction of law and policy, it is clear that it is necessary to examine the overlap of the international humanitarian and human rights legal frameworks.

In seeking to address this overlap, it is helpful to look at the issue from a number of different perspectives. First, there is the strategic, theoretical conflict that continues between the advocates of exclusionary applications of IHL or IHRL. This is a conflict that appears to be firmly grounded in different views emanating from each side of the Atlantic. Secondly, there are the different perspectives brought to

[4] S Aughey and A Sari, 'Targeting and Detention in Non-International Armed Conflict: Serdar Mohammed and the Limits of Human Rights Convergence' (2015) 91 US Naval War College International Law Studies 60, 117; R Goodman, 'Authorization versus Regulation of Detention in Non-International Armed Conflicts' (2015) US Naval War College International Law Studies 91, 155.

[5] K Watkin, *Fighting at the Legal Boundaries: Controlling the Use of Force in Contemporary Conflict* (OUP 2016) 223–28 and The US Army and Marine Corps, *Counterinsurgency Field Manual* (University of Chicago Press 2007) 229, 6-90 ('The primary frontline COIN force is often the police—not the military').

[6] B Obama, 'Speech on Drone Policy' *New York Times* (23 May 2013) <http://www.nytimes.com/2013/05/24/us/politics/transcript-of-obamas-speech-on-drone-policy.html>.

[7] P Baker and DE Sanger, 'Raids Show the Limits of U.S. Military Strikes' *New York Times* (6 October 2013) <http://www.nytimes.com/2013/10/07/world/africa/raids-show-the-limits-of-us-military-strikes.html> (outlining raids in Libya and Somalia to arrest Al-Qaeda linked terrorists. The Libyan raid was successful, while US Navy seals withdrew from Somalia after an intense firefight).

[8] S McCrystal, *My Share of the Task: A Memoire* (Penguin 2013) 149 (where it is noted that the 2006 airstrike that killed the Al-Qaeda leader in Iraq, al Zaqwari, was followed up with a helicopter borne team tasked to 'secure the site and *arrest* anyone who escaped the blast') (emphasis added).

this issue based on the unique North American and European legal systems, as well as differing geographic and experiential factors.[9] Thirdly, there is the ongoing reliance on customary international law, domestic law, and policy to assist in resolving what appears on its surface to be an intractable theoretical impasse. Finally, notwithstanding the exclusionary debate, the reality is that military forces are applying both IHL and IHRL norms during contemporary military operations, although approaches that seek to uniquely apply one legal framework over the other will continue to present operational challenges.

2. Exclusionary Approaches

Little has occurred in the past few years to suggest that there has been a reconciliation of the 'hard' positions adopted by those who favour exclusionary approaches towards the application of IHR and IHRL.[10] At times almost verging on an ideological debate, the impasse is perhaps most vividly reflected in different approaches applied on the European and North American continents, respectively. The fault line between these opposing takes is represented in two areas of dispute: the principle of *lex specialis derogat legi generali*, and the issue of the extraterritorial application of IHRL treaty law. Efforts by those seeking to apply alternative interpretations of what *lex specialis* means in order to challenge the plain reading of the *Nuclear Weapons* decision,[11] which favours the application of IHL, have not been successful to date.[12] It is unlikely that over the short term, this *lex specialis* debate, which appears designed to insert a greater role for IHRL, will have significant impact on positions firmly grounded in IHL displacing IHRL. For example, this dialogue does not seem to have convinced the United States to fundamentally change its traditional view that IHL operates during armed conflict, excluding the application of human rights law.[13] Although it has been indicated that the United

[9] While North America includes Canada, the United States, Mexico, and Caribbean countries the reference to this continent is limited to the first two states in the context of this chapter.

[10] MJ Dennis, 'Application of Human Rights Treaties Extraterritorially in Times of Armed Conflict and Military Occupation' (2005) 99 American Journal of International Law 119, 139 (for an approach favouring the exclusion of human rights treaty law) and W Abresch, 'A Human Rights Law of Internal Armed Conflict: The European Court of Human Rights in Chechnya' (2005) 16 European Journal of International Law 741, 743–7 (arguing that human rights is the special law applicable to non-international armed conflict).

[11] *Legality of the Threat or Use of Nuclear Weapons* (Advisory Opinion) [1996] ICJ Rep 226.

[12] K Watkin, 'Use of Force During Occupation: Law Enforcement and Conduct of Hostilities' (2012) 94 International Review of the Red Cross 267, 301–10 (for a discussion of various interpretations of the principle of *lex specialis derogate lex generali*).

[13] Office of General Counsel Department of Defense, 'Law of War Manual' (US Department of Defense, June 2015, updated December 2016) 22–3 [1.6.3.1] https://dod.defense.gov/Portals/1/Documents/pubs/DoD%20Law%20of%20War%20Manual%20-%20June%202015%20Updated%20Dec%202016.pdf?ver=2016-12-13-172036-190<https://www.defense.gov/Portals/1/Documents/pubs/DoD%20Law%20of%20War%20Manual%20-%20June%202015%20Updated%20Dec%202016.pdf?ver=2016-12-13-172036-190> (DoD Law of War Manual). See also the US Judge Advocate General's Legal Center and School, 'Operational Law Handbook' (International and Operational Law

States has recently moved away from a 'displacement' theory towards one applying a more 'complementary' approach,[14] the 2015 *Department of Defense Law of War Manual* notes that '[a]lthough there are different approaches and although the ultimate resolution may depend on the specific rules and context, the law of war, as the *lex specialis* of armed conflict, is the controlling body of law with regard to the conduct of hostilities and the protection of war victims'.[15] That said, it has been acknowledged that there is an emerging view that '[w]here LOAC is silent or its guidance inadequate, specific provisions of applicable human rights law may supplement, or possibly even displace, at least to a limited degree, the LOAC in a particular situation'.[16]

The United States and Canada appear to look at the extraterritorial application of human rights obligations very differently than European states. While the issue of the intersection between IHRL and IHL arises from the case law of the International Court of Justice (ICJ),[17] it is the extraterritorial application of the European Convention on Human Rights (ECHR) that has particularly drawn international attention to the question of extending human rights law protection during contemporary international operations.[18] The United States has been consistently clear in its rejection of a broad extraterritorial application of human rights treaty law,[19] even though it was acknowledged in late 2014 that the Convention Against Torture and Other Cruel, Inhuman or Degrading Treatment or Punishment[20] has limited extraterritorial application.[21] The Canadian position

Department 2015) 49 Sec V, Part A.(1). <http://www.loc.gov/rr/frd/Military_Law/pdf/operational-law-handbook_2015.pdf>.

[14] Operational Law Handbook (n 13) 49–50 Part V.A. (1&2).

[15] DoD Law of War Manual (n 13) 9 (1.3.2).

[16] Operational Law Handbook (n 13) 49–51, Part IV.A.

[17] *Nuclear Weapons* (n 11) para 25; *Legal Consequences of the Construction of a Wall in the Occupied Palestinian Territory* (Advisory Opinion) [2004] ICJ Rep 136; and *Case Concerning Armed Activities on the Territory of the Congo (Democratic Republic of the Congo v Uganda)* (Judgment) [2005] ICJ Rep 168, 231 177.

[18] See, eg, *Al-Skeini and Others v The United Kingdom* App no 55721/07 (ECtHR, Grand Chamber Judgment, 7 July 2011).

[19] UNCHR, 'Concluding Observations on the Fourth Periodic Report of the United States of America' (23 April 2014) UN Doc CCPR/C/USA/CO/4, 4 (where it is noted '[t]he Committee regrets that the State party [the United States] continues to maintain the position that the Covenant does not apply with respect to individuals under its jurisdiction, but outside its territory, despite the interpretation to the contrary of article 2, paragraph 1, supported by the Committee's established jurisprudence, the jurisprudence of the International Court of Justice and State practice'). See also ICRC, 'Report on the Expert Meeting on the Use of Force in Armed Conflicts: Interplay between the Conduct of Hostilities and Law Enforcement Paradigms' (ICRC November 2013) 8 <https://www.icrc.org/eng/assets/files/publications/icrc-002-4171.pdf> (for an outline of the position of the United States regarding the extraterritorial application of human rights law) and Dennis (n 10) 141.

[20] Convention Against Torture and Other Cruel, Inhuman or Degrading Treatment or Punishment (adopted 10 December 1984, entered into force 26 June 1987) 1465 UNTS 85, 113.

[21] ME McLeod 'Opening Statement' (Committee Against Torture, Geneva, 12–13 November 2014) <https://geneva.usmission.gov/2014/11/12/acting-legal-adviser-mcleod-u-s-affirms-torture-is-prohibited-at-all-times-in-all-places/>.

regarding the extraterritorial application of human rights treaties also reflects a restricted application of human rights treaty law. In October 2017, the Canadian Government stated that an expansive Human Rights Committee interpretation of Article 6 supporting an extraterritorial application of the International Covenant on Civil and Political Rights (eg to occupied territory, territory under effective control of the state, on registered aircraft and marine vessels) 'attempts to expand the scope of the Covenant beyond the territory under the jurisdiction of the State. Such an interpretation would impinge on well-established principles of sovereignty'.[22] Significantly, in 2008, the Canadian Federal Court of Appeal also ruled in litigation involving the transfer of detainees in Afghanistan that the domestic Charter of Rights and Freedoms did not extraterritorially apply to that conflict, and that '[t]here is no legal vacuum, considering that the applicable law is international humanitarian law'.[23] The lower court in the same case also rejected the idea that there is broad application of IHRL based on the United Nations commentaries.[24] While the question of the extension of domestic human rights law in situations where there is no functioning territorial government is left to another day, it is clear there is judicial reluctance to extend the operation of domestic human rights law. This is particularly evident where IHL is available to fill any perceived void.

Conversely, from a European perspective the exclusionary nature of the IHL/IHRL debate is grounded in the fact that the European Court of Human Rights (ECtHR) has, until relatively recently, looked at international conflicts exclusively through a human rights lens. The 2014 *Hassan* judgment did little to clarify the basis for extending extraterritorial jurisdiction of the ECHR,[25] discussed in terms of 'effective control over an area' and 'state agent control' tests as established in

[22] 'Comments by the Government of Canada, Human Rights Committee, Draft General Comment No. 36 on Article 6 of the International Covenant on Civil and Political Rights—Right to life', para 7 (23 October 2017) <http://www.ohchr.org/EN/HRBodies/CCPR/Pages/GC36-Article6Righttolife.aspx>; see also 'General comment No. 36 on article 6 of the International Covenant on Civil and Political Rights, on the right to life', Human Rights Committee, paras 22 and 26 <http://www.ohchr.org/Documents/HRBodies/CCPR/GCArticle6/GCArticle6_EN.pdf>.

[23] See *Amnesty International Canada v Canada (Chief of the Defence Staff)* [2009] 4 FCR 149, 2008 FCA 401 (CanLII). See M Milanovic, *Extraterritorial Application of Human Rights Treaties: Law, Principles, and Policy* (OUP 2011) 62–65 (for a critique of the Canadian case law concerning the extraterritorial application of domestic law).

[24] *Amnesty International Canada v Canada (Chief of the Defence Staff)* [2008] 4 FCR 546, 2008 FC 336 (CanLII), paras 239–40 (in referring to the Human Rights Committee, *General Commentary 31: Nature of the General Legal Obligation Imposed on State Parties to the Covenant* (26/05/2004 CCPR/C/21/Rev./1/Add.13) and the United Nations Committee on Torture, *General Commentary No. 2: Implementation of Article 2 by State Parties* (23/11/2007 CAT/CGC/2/CRP.1/Rev.3) the court noted '[i]nsofar as the commentaries of the United Nations Committees are concerned, as the respondents [the Government] observed, these are recommendations made by groups with advocacy responsibilities. While they clearly reflect the views of knowledgeable individuals, they do not reflect the current state of international law, but more the direction that those groups believe the law should take in the future'. Further, it was noted the commentaries related to the operation of the ICCPR and not Canadian domestic law).

[25] *Hassan v The United Kingdom* App no 29750/09 (ECtHR, Grand Chamber Judgment, 16 September 2014).

Al-Skeini.[26] However, notably, the Court finally accepted that IHL could be applied to interpret the Convention.[27] In doing so, the Court acted in a manner that is consistent with the ICJ approach first adopted in the 1996 *Nuclear Weapons* Advisory Opinion.[28]

However, numerous issues remain unresolved, including whether this approach will be limited to international armed conflicts involving occupied territory, or even apply at all to internal conflicts occurring within member states' territory.[29] Further, the option of relying on IHL is left entirely in the discretion of states, which in the past have been reluctant to acknowledge any armed conflict as occurring on their territory.[30] In addition, the more limited IHL applicable to internal armed conflicts may prompt the Court to rely more heavily on the provisions of the ECHR when assessing internal conflicts even when they occur outside of the territory of member states. The decision appears to continue an 'incremental' approach towards the extension of ECHR-based human rights law. In line with such an approach, the 2014 *Jaloud* decision extended the jurisdiction of that body of law to persons passing through a checkpoint.[31] What remains to be determined is how the European human rights tribunal system will deal with other cases, such as those involving force where the degree of 'control' over territory is linked to the alleged unique nature of the weapons used (eg drones), offering a relatively persistent aerial presence rather than exerting physical control.[32]

It is also uncertain to what extent humanitarian law will have an impact on the assessment of the human rights treaty provisions, since the ruling indicates that Article 5 of the ECHR 'should be accommodated as far as possible' with the applicable IHL treaty law.[33] Like the Inter-American court system, which has demonstrated a greater willingness to at least address the application of IHL norms, the

[26] *Al-Skeini v UK* (n 18) paras 131–40. See also N Lubell, 'Human Rights Obligations in Military Occupation' (2012) 94 International Review of the Red Cross 317, 320.

[27] *Hassan v UK* (n 25) para 103. This possibility appears to have been first addressed in *Varnava and Others v Turkey* App no 16064/90, 16065/90, 16066/90, 16068/90, 16069/90, 16070/90, 16071/90, 16072/90 and 16073/90 (ECtHR, Grand Chamber Judgment, 18 September 2009) para 185 (where the court held 'Article 2 must be interpreted in so far as possible in light of the general principles of international law, including the rules of international humanitarian law which play an indispensable and universally accepted role in mitigating the savagery and inhumanity of armed conflict').

[28] *Nuclear Weapons* (n 11) para 25 (the Court ruled that the deprivation of life under Article 6 ICCPR, 'can only be decided by reference to the law applicable in armed conflict and not deduced from the terms of the Covenant itself').

[29] Aughey and Sari (n 4) 113–15 (for a discussion of the *Hassan* decision).

[30] *Hassan v UK* (n 25) para 107.

[31] *Jaloud v The Netherlands* App no 47708/08 (ECtHR, Grand Chamber Judgment, 20 November 2014) para 152.

[32] Public Interest Lawyers, 'Written evidence on behalf of Peacerights' (UK Parliament, Defence Committee HC 772, 3 June 2013) 5.14 <http://www.publications.parliament.uk/pa/cm201314/cmselect/cmdfence/772/772vw17.htm>. But see *Sadoon & Ors v Secretary of State for Defence* [2016] EWCA Civ 811, paras 69–72 (where a UK appellate court held that using physical force alone was insufficient to extend the jurisdiction of the ECHR).

[33] *Hassan v UK* (n 25) para 104.

ECtHR is likely to remain firmly grounded in a human rights framework.[34] As a result, the strategic struggle between IHL and IHRL advocates battling for the jurisdictional high ground is likely to continue.

3. Different Worlds/Different Perspectives

In assessing the Canadian and American approaches towards the application of IHL and IHRL, it is helpful to look at a number of factors that distinguish those states from Europe. The courts of these North American countries, as is the case with a significant number of the world's states, are not subject to the oversight of regional human rights tribunals.[35] For example, 'the Asia-Pacific region has no unique regional human rights instrument nor any regional human rights court or commission', and 'as a practical matter, not all States are parties to international human rights instruments' although many international rights law provisions can be considered to be customary law.[36] While both Canada and the United States are members of the Organization of American States, they are not subject to the binding jurisdiction of either the Inter-American Commission on Human Rights, or the Inter-American Court of Human Rights.[37] The decisions of those bodies may influence Canadian and American courts but they do not act in the capacity of an external supervisory body. The courts of Canada and the United States apply their own domestic constitutional and human rights frameworks, and interpret the decisions of other legal jurisdictions (including European Court decisions) as is appropriate to their national legal systems. ECtHR decisions are not binding, and Canadian and American courts are unlikely to adopt Europe's exclusionary model that is the only one to date which has applied human rights law even in situations of bombing by aircraft.[38]

[34] S Sivakumaran, *The Law of Non-International Armed Conflict* (OUP 2012) 501–3 (for a discussion of the American human rights tribunal system case law) and J Römer, *Killing in a Gray Area Between Humanitarian Law and Human Rights* (Springer 2010) 35.

[35] A Cassese, *International Law* (2nd edn, OUP 2004) 389 who notes that regional supervisory mechanisms include judicial bodies such as the ECtHR, the Inter-American Commission, and the Inter-American Court of Human Rights. There is also the African Court on Human and People's Rights, as well as a monitoring body lacking judicial functions, the African Commission on Human Rights and the Rights of Peoples. However, not all countries are subject to these human rights bodies.

[36] E Crawford, *The Treatment of Combatants and Insurgents under the Law of Armed Conflict* (OUP 2010) 120.

[37] A Huneeus, 'International Criminal Law by Other Means: The Quasi-Criminal Jurisdiction of the Human Rights Courts' (2013) 107 The American Journal of International Law 1, 7 n 25 (where it is noted that twenty-two of the twenty-four countries that signed the American Convention accepted the binding jurisdiction of the Convention, although Trinidad and Tobago, and Venezuela have denounced the Convention and withdrawn from the jurisdiction of the Court).

[38] See, eg, *Isayeva v Russia and Bazayeva v Russia* App nos 57947/00, 57948/00, 57949/00 (ECtHR, Former First Section Judgment, 24 February 2005).

Furthermore, the influence exerted by the European or Inter-American human rights tribunals can also be affected by their judgments being the product of particular regional treaty language. In this respect, the International Covenant on Civil and Political Rights (ICCPR), which has a broader scope of application, may be more influential in a Canadian or US legal context than the regionally based ECHR. What is more, the Canadian and American domestic legal frameworks address human rights differently.[39] As a result, the analyses of human rights obligations by Canadian and US courts can proceed along different paths within each country, as well as in relation to Europe. Significantly, the lack of an external, European-style supervisory tribunal mechanism that looks primarily through a human rights lens provides space within which the North American courts may more readily consider the application of IHL.[40]

These are not the only systemic differences between Europe and North America. While there appears to be little discussion of the issue, it seems inevitable that the predominantly civil code-based European legal system, which incorporates a different analytical approach than the primarily common law-based analysis applied in Canada and the United States, will influence how human rights law is interpreted from a European perspective. For example, 'common law statutes have to be read against a case law background, while civil law codes and statutes are the primary source of law'.[41] The result may be a greater willingness in the North American context to consider the customary international law basis for the conduct of operations, rather than searching for a textual authority (in either treaty law or domestic law) to justify military action.

European and North American approaches toward the application of international law may also differ because of geographic and experiential factors, or as a result of different perceptions of the nature of the threat. In 1951, Richard Baxter noted that the United States, the United Kingdom, Canada, and Australia prosecuted war crimes at the end of the Second World War as violations of international law,[42] while France, Norway, and initially the Netherlands, tried war criminals for offences against municipal law.[43] In his view it was not unnatural in respect to the latter states (having had the experience of enemy occupation) that recourse would be made to 'the convenient instrument of local law rather that to the long arm of the law of nations'.[44] Conversely, the United States and Canada have a long history

[39] *Canadian Charter of Rights and Freedoms*, Constitution Act (1982), Article 1 (where rights are specifically referred to as being 'subject to ... reasonable limits prescribed by law as can be demonstrably justified in a free and democratic society').

[40] See, eg, US Supreme Court, *Hamdan v Rumsfeld*, No 05-184 (29 June 2006) 1155 and the Canadian case, *Amnesty International Canada v Canada* (n 23).

[41] W Tetley, 'Mixed Jurisdictions: Common Law vs Civil Law (Codified and Uncodified)' (2000) 60 Louisiana Law Review 677.

[42] DF Vagts and T Meron, 'The Municipal and International Law Basis of Jurisdiction Over War Crimes' in R Baxter, DF Vagts, T Meron, SM Schwebel, and C Keever (eds), *Humanizing the Laws of War* (OUP 2013) 60.

[43] ibid 62.

[44] ibid.

of expeditionary military deployments, which appears to influence their greater reliance on IHL. The different approach can also be seen in their more ready acceptance of the extraterritorial operation of military justice systems superintended by military officers as compared to other jurisdictions.[45]

It is not uncommon for the United States, Canada, and other like-minded states to enter into Status of Forces Agreements with host nations (assuming there is a functioning state) in order to exclude the military forces from the jurisdiction, and therefore domestic law, of the territorial state where they are operating. Historically, this has meant that IHL and the domestic military law of the intervening states are viewed as being the primary bodies of law to regulate participation in armed conflict. Different perspectives regarding the nature of the transnational terrorist threat can also be seen in the approaches adopted on each continent towards hijacked aircraft in the aftermath of the 9/11 terrorist attacks. In North America, reliance is placed on the United States/Canada defence arrangement, NORAD, to intercept aircraft,[46] while Germany, for example, chose to deal with the threat as one amenable to a policing response.[47]

4. Available Options

The widely, and often loudly, debated differing approaches do not actually represent how the law (IHL or IHRL) is being applied—at least in the way it is functionally implemented into operational and tactical directives—particularly in the North American context. Rather than exclusively apply norms stemming from either IHL or IHRL, the reality of contemporary conflict is that both normative frameworks often need to be, and in fact are, applied concurrently. The application of human rights-based norms occurs less often by way of considering IHRL treaty law obligations than by operation of customary law obligations (both from IHRL and IHL), the application of domestic law, or as a matter of policy.

An example for the customary law application of human rights norms can be found in the *Amnesty International Canada* cases, where the Canadian

[45] The Turkel Commission, 'Israel's Mechanisms for Examining and Investigating Complaints and Claims of Violations of the Laws of Armed Conflict According to International Law' (Public Commission to Examine the Maritime Incident of 31 May 2010, Second Report February 2013) Part 2 Chap B <http://www.humanrightsvoices.org/assets/attachments/documents/turkel.report.2.pdf> (for an overview of the military and civilian justice systems applied for the investigation and prosecution of war crimes by the United States, Canada, Australia, the United Kingdom, Germany, and the Netherlands. The United States, Canada, and Israel have military justice systems staffed by military judges, prosecutors, and defence counsel).

[46] EC Sloan, *Security and Defence in the Terrorist Era* (McGill-Queens University Press 2005) 85–89.

[47] *Dr H et al v s 14.3 of the Aviation Security Act of 11 January 2005* (2006), Case No 1 BvR 357/05. 115 BVerfGE 118; N Naske and G Nolte, 'Aerial Security Law' (2007) 101 American Journal of International Law 466. See Watkin (n 5) 559–64 (for a discussion of the different approaches taken by Canada and the United States, Germany, and Australia towards the shoot down of hijacked aircraft).

Government argued that 'where an individual detained in the context of armed conflict is charged with criminal offences, Common Article 3 and Article 75 of Protocol I Additional to the Geneva Conventions (AP I) apply, either directly or as a matter of customary international law, to guarantee a number of due process rights'.[48] Article 75 was clearly influenced by the 1948 Universal Declaration on Human Rights and the ICCPR. In this regard, Christopher Greenwood noted that the relationship between IHL and IHRL 'is expressed in the adoption of major human rights principles in Article 75 AP I'.[49] Importantly, the human rights norms reflected in IHL treaty and customary law must be applied regardless of the geographic location of the armed conflict, which then avoids the debate regarding the extraterritorial application of IHRL treaty law.

In 2011, the United States indicated that out of a sense of legal obligation it would apply the norms of Article 75 AP I in international armed conflicts in relation to the treatment of detainees.[50] It has been suggested that this was not a recognition of that provision's customary law status.[51] However, the language of 'obligation' raises the issue of *opinio juris*. US Department of State legal adviser Harold Koh subsequently acknowledged not only that the *opinio juris* issue is indeed raised[52] but that the Department of Defense Law of War Manual furthermore indicates that such an acknowledgement 'was intended to contribute to the crystallization of the principles contained in Article 75 as rules of customary international law applicable in international armed conflict'.[53] This approach towards Article 75 AP I is in fact not new. Lawyers who served with previous administrations had also made references to the safeguards provided in Article 75.[54]

[48] *Amnesty International Canada and British Columbia Civil Liberties Association v Chief of the Defence Staff for the Canadian Forces, Minister of National Defence and Attorney General of Canada* (Court File No T-324-07) Respondent's Factum (18 January 2008) [83] (Afghanistan was considered to be a non-international armed conflict for the purposes of the litigation).

[49] C Greenwood, 'Scope of Application of Humanitarian Law' in D Fleck (ed), *The Handbook of International Humanitarian Law* (2nd edn, OUP 2008) 45, 74, Rule 254.

[50] HR Clinton, 'Reaffirming America's Commitment to Humane Treatment of Detainees' (Press Statement, Washington, 7 March 2011) <https://2009-2017.state.gov/secretary/20092013clinton/rm/2011/03/157827.htm>.

[51] JB Bellinger and VM Padmanabhan, 'Detention Operations in Contemporary Conflicts: Four Challenges for The Geneva Conventions and Other Existing Law' (2001) 105 American Journal of International Law 201, 207 (the authors note 'the administration neither stated that Article 75 is customary international law nor agreed to apply Article 75 in non-international armed conflicts, such as the conflict with Al Qaeda').

[52] H Koh, 'Libya and War Powers, Responses to Questions Submitted by Senator Richard G. Lugar' (Testimony Before the Committee on Foreign Relations US Senate, 112th Congress, First Session, 28 June 2011) 57 <https://fas.org/irp/congress/2011_hr/libya.pdf> ('The U.S. statement, coupled with a sufficient density of State practice and *opinio juris*, would contribute to creation of the principles reflected in Article 75 as rules of customary international law, which all States would be obligated to apply in international armed conflict. (The 168 States that are party to Protocol I are of course already required to comply with Article 75 as a matter of treaty law)' (Protocol Additional to the Geneva Conventions of 12 August 1949, and relating to the Protection of Victims of International Armed Conflicts (Protocol I) (opened for signature 8 June 1977, entered into force 7 December 1978) 1125 UNTS 3 (AP I).

[53] DoD Law of War Manual (n 13) 490, 8.1.4.2.

[54] WH Taft IV, 'The Law of Armed Conflict After 9/11: Some Salient Features' (2003) 28 Yale Journal of International Law 319, 322 (where it was suggested the United States did 'regard the provisions of

When combined with the *Hamdan* decision, in which a plurality of the US Supreme Court Justices ruled that Article 75 AP I applied to the non-international armed conflict with Al-Qaeda as a matter of customary international law, there is considerable evidence that the United States' position is moving towards an application of human rights norms as part of customary humanitarian law.[55] This was further demonstrated by the issuance in August 2014 of a directive on the treatment of detainees, the DoD Detainee Program, which references, albeit merely as matter of policy, Common Article 3 of the Geneva Conventions, Articles 4– 6 AP II, and Article 75 AP I, which together form the minimum standards regarding treatment of detainees. International humanitarian law remains the governing *lex specialis*, but there is a greater recognition of human rights norms within that body of law in both the United States and Canada.

Unfortunately, the public dialogue regarding the extraterritorial application of human rights law has been almost entirely limited to reference to IHRL in a treaty law context. However, in *Restatement of the Law: The Foreign Relations Law of the United States*, the United States have indicated that customary human rights law includes protection from murder, torture, or other cruel, inhuman, or degrading treatment or punishment, or prolonged arbitrary detention.[56] While not all commentators embrace the idea that customary human rights law solves the extraterritoriality challenge,[57] others more readily accept its universal application.[58] Importantly, from a practical perspective, the 2017 US Army *Operational Law Handbook* makes reference to this customary law extension of human rights norms, noting that 'fundamental customary IHRL binds a State's forces during all operations, both inside and outside the State's territory'.[59] Such extraterritorial application sets the scene for the previously mentioned interpretation that views the *lex specialis* debate as not precluding the use of IHRL to guide the interpretation of IHL, or being applied whether or not there are gaps in the law governing the conduct of hostilities.

article 75 as an articulation of the safeguards to which all persons in the hands of the enemy are entitled'). See also MJ Matheson, 'Session One: The United States Position on the Relation of Customary International Law to the 1977 Protocols Additional to the 1949 Geneva Conventions' (1987) 2 American University Journal of International Law and Policy 416, 427; MJ Matheson, 'Continuity and Change in the Law of War: 1975 to 2005: Detainees and POWs' (2006) 38 George Washington International Law Review 547–48.

---

55 *Hamdan v Rumsfeld* (n 40).

56 Restatement of the Law Third, The Foreign Relations Law of the United States, Vol 2 (1987) 161–75.

57 Milanovic (n 23) 3.

58 Y Dinstein, *The International Law of Belligerent Occupation* (CUP 2009) 71, 166; N Lubell, *Extraterritorial Use of Force Against Non-State Actors* (OUP 2010) 232–35.

59 Operational Law Handbook (n 13) 49 Sect IV, Part B.1 (it is also stated '[t]he prohibition against genocide, slavery, murder/causing disappearance of individuals, torture/cruel, inhuman degrading treatment, prolonged arbitrary detention, and systematic racial discrimination are considered to be *jus cogens*').

What is often missed in the theoretical debate surrounding the relationship of IHL and IHRL is the degree to which domestic courts undertake human rights analysis regarding armed conflict-related issues. It has been noted that they 'substitute themselves for international enforcement agencies that either do not exist or have proved extremely ineffectual'.[60] In the United States, the courts have been used to challenge a variety of issues related to contemporary armed conflict, including targeted killings through the use of drones,[61] and the detention of 'enemy unprivileged belligerents' at Guantánamo Bay.[62] The influence exerted by domestic human rights law cannot be overstated. The 2013 change in the US policy on drone use was prompted by the discussion and controversy surrounding the targeting of American citizens. There appears to have been ready acceptance that American citizens enjoyed extraterritorial constitutional protection. The extraordinary policy decision was to extend the protection being offered 'to all potential terrorist targets regardless of whether they are American citizens'.[63] The reference to this step being one that 'respects the inherent dignity of every human life' has a particular resonance with a universal application of human rights norms.[64]

Questions can be asked about how realistic the drone policy standard is that 'before any strike is taken, there must be a near-certainty that no civilians will be killed or injured'.[65] The acknowledgement in September 2014 that this standard had been abolished in favour of one that is more broadly grounded in IHL for governing airstrikes against ISIS in Syria and Iraq suggests that the 2013 drone policy may be quite limited in terms of its application to armed conflicts.[66] However, this more 'human rights-like' approach can also be seen in the frequent use of capture, or 'arrest', rather than kill operations that were conducted in the final phase of the Coalition operations in Iraq.[67] The application of human rights 'norms' often arises in situations of governance (ie occupation, insurgency) where there is considerable strategic interest in avoiding the alienation of the local population. Capture missions not only usually facilitate that goal, they can also lead to more effective

[60] Cassese (n 35) 391. See also ibid 392 ('The country where national courts have taken the most vigorous action against crimes involving serious violations of human rights committed abroad is the USA').

[61] For example, see US District Court of Columbia, *Al-Aulaqi v Panetta*, Civil Action No 12-1192 (RMC) (4 April 2014). See <http://ccrjustice.org/targetedkillings> (for an outline of the challenge to the US targeted killing policy).

[62] See, eg, D Lamothe, 'U.S. judge permits Pentagon to force-feed Guantanamo prisoner but issues rebuke' *The Washington Post* (23 May 2014) <http://www.washingtonpost.com/world/national-security/us-judge-permits-pentagon-to-force-feed-guantanamo-prisoner-says-pain-possible/2014/05/23/a385cf72-e290-11e3-8dcc-d6b7fede081a_story.html>.

[63] Obama Speech on Drone Policy (n 6).

[64] ibid.

[65] ibid.

[66] K Dilanian, 'U.S.-led Airstrikes Launched Amid Significant Intelligence Gaps' *CTV News* (1 October 2014) <http://www.ctvnews.ca/world/u-s-led-airstrikes-launched-amid-significant-intelligence- gaps-1.2033338#>.

[67] M Urban, *Task Force Black: The Explosive True Story of the SAS and the Secret War in Iraq* (St Martin Griffin's 2010) 257 (where it is noted that A Squadron, SAS, operating in Iraq from May to November 2007 'mounted raids almost nightly, during which it arrested 335 people and killed 88').

intelligence-led operations. One of the problems with a policy approach is that it may not fully embrace human rights standards, and is subject to rapid change. However, what is clear is that human rights-based norms have an impact on the conduct of contemporary operations, whether introduced as a matter of law or policy.

As can be seen in the UK case of *Serdar Mohammed*,[68] domestic human rights standards of the territorial state within which an armed conflict is occurring can also form a basis for legal challenges filed by human rights advocates. That case raises a number of interesting issues related to the operational feasibility of relying on the domestic human rights law of a failed or failing state to set standards for the actions of intervening military forces. In terms of a potentially broader applicability, a distinction can be drawn between that case and the Canadian *Amnesty International Case*. Ultimately, in the *Serdar* case a majority of the court found that 'the existence of a legal right in international law to detain members of opposing armed forces in a non-international armed conflict must depend on (i) customary international law, and/or (ii) the authority of the Security Council of United Nations'.[69] While the court was not prepared to state that a customary right to detain had been recognized by states, it argued that 'the authorisation given to troop-contributing states in Afghanistan by Resolution 1386 (2001) to use "all necessary measures" included the detention of members of the opposing armed forces when this was required for imperative reasons of security'.[70]

A critical analysis of the lower court judgment in the *Serdar* case[71] had noted that the decision, which had held that detention authority had to be found in the host state's domestic law or in UN Security Council (UNSC) resolutions

> reflects an overly positivist approach which fails to appreciate the true reason for the paucity of treaty law applicable in NIAC, and leaves insufficient room for the possibility of a legal basis either implicit in CA3 [Common Article 3 to the 1949 Geneva Conventions] and AP II or under customary law.[72]

In contrast, the American and Canadian legal systems have already demonstrated a greater willingness to accept the application of customary IHL, and generally are less likely to adopt such a positivist approach in dealing with issues related to the regulation of armed conflict.[73] Ironically, the recognition of the extraterritorial

68 *Serdar Mohammed and Others v Ministry of National Defence* [2017] UKSC 2.
69 ibid 7 (13) (Lord Sumption's Judgment).
70 ibid 16 (28).
71 *Serdar Mohammed v Ministry of National Defence* [2014] EWHC 1369 (QB).
72 Aughey and Sari (n 4) 117.
73 *Amnesty International Canada v Canada* (n 24) (where after noting that 'international humanitarian law is a highly developed branch of international law comprised of both customary international law and treaties', the court at the trial division went on to state that '[t]he application of international humanitarian law to the situation of detainees in Afghanistan would not only give certainty to the situation, but would also provide a coherent legal regime governing the actions of the international

application of customary international human rights law by countries such as the United States and Canada avoids the struggle that the ECtHR continues to have regarding the incremental extension of human rights law that is almost obsessively focused on treaty application.

5. Dealing with Overlap

The reality is that military forces regularly apply both IHL and IHRL during the conduct of hostilities. Human rights may be applied as a matter of law through treaty and customary law norms reflected in IHL (ie Geneva Convention IV, AP I, Article 75, Common Article 3), or similarly as part of the extraterritorial application of IHRL. Clearly, states and their military commanders may make a policy decision to apply a human rights-based normative framework in lieu of IHL depending upon the threat being faced, or mission being accomplished. In terms of the use of force, what are basically human rights norms have long been incorporated in Rules of Engagement (RoE).[74] In this respect, the RoE issued to the US Marines who were engaged in the 2004 assault on Al-Qaeda forces in Fallujah included direction to only use self-defence against non-combatant civilians, and to 'consider escalation of force procedures and limit force to that amount necessary to terminate the threat'.[75]

This does not mean that the separation of what might be considered law enforcement levels of force from those associated with conduct of hostilities will not be challenging. For example, the manner in which self-defence is exercised can depend on unique national views regarding its scope. The distinctions can lead to interpretations that rely on doctrinal concepts such as 'extended self-defence', 'defence of the mandate', 'mission accomplishment', 'force protection', 'unit self-defence', 'hostile intent', and 'hostile act' to put theory into practice in a manner that permits the successful conduct of multinational operations.[76] It is also sometimes not clear how well the concept of imminence associated with national self-defence

community in Afghanistan'). See also *Hamdan v Rumsfeld* (n 40) (for reference to customary international law trial protections found in AP I (n 51) Article 75 being incorporated into customary IHL).

[74] GS Corn and E Talbot Jensen 'Untying the Gordian Knot: A Proposal for Determining Applicability of the Laws of War to the War on Terror' (2008) 81 Temple Law Review 787, 814 (in discussing the American SRoE notes that 'the engagement authorization provided by the self-defense prong of the RoE essentially extends traditional criminal law enforcement self-defense and defense of others principles to the operational environment').

[75] D Camp, *Operation Phantom Fury: The Assault and Capture of Fallujah, Iraq* (Zenith Press 2009) 151.

[76] Watkin (n 5) 458–64; JFR Boddens Hosang, 'Force Protection, Unit Self-Defence, and Extended Self-Defence' in TD Gill and D Fleck (eds), *The Handbook of The International Law of Operations* (OUP 2010) Rule 22.04, 413 (for a discussion of the self-defence and doctrinal approaches found in RoE).

is differentiated from its human rights-based counterpart.[77] However, that is not usually the case regarding the maintenance of civil law and order. There are situations occurring during armed conflict that 'closely resemble those for which human rights standards have been developed'.[78] Examples include maintaining public order during occupation, 'or in areas under the firm control of State authorities in times of non-international armed conflicts'.[79]

The degree to which there is an overlap between IHL and IHRL will ultimately depend on the interpretation of the scope of each body of law. As states continue to be threatened by small cell and lone wolf attacks, both integral parts of Salafi jihadist doctrine, the debate will probably increasingly focus on 'one off' exercises of self-defence.[80] These operations will likely prompt a deeper analysis of the *Prosecutor v Tadić*[81] threshold for the existence of an armed conflict, which was not developed in the context of the exercise of self-defence. An overreliance on the 'duration' criterion, which is fundamentally retrospective in nature, is of little practical value to security forces that must look prospectively toward threats as they develop, and attacks as they occur. Those threats may only be successfully addressed by engaging in hostilities governed by IHL. However, its application requires the existence of an armed conflict.[82] Consideration of the *Abella* threshold[83] and treaty-based standards (Common Article 3 and Article 1(2) AP II, which excludes application to 'situations of internal disturbance and tensions'), a more informed discussion of how insurgent and terrorist groups organize,[84] and the application of other context-specific criteria, may lead to a broader application of IHL norms.[85] What may be more challenging are interpretations of the law that view the exercise of self-defence against non-state actors as falling under a unique

[77] 'Chairman of The Joint Chiefs of Staff Instr. 3121.01b, Standing Rules Of Engagement (SRoE)/ Standing Rules For The Use of Force (SRUF) For U.S. Forces, 13 June 2005' in *Operational Law Handbook* (n 13) 88–108 Annex A (where in contrast to a human rights law approach the SRoE states '[i]mminent does not necessarily mean immediate or instantaneous').

[78] J Kleffner, 'Human Rights and International Humanitarian Law: General Issues' in Gill and Fleck (n 75) 75.

[79] ibid.

[80] B Lia, *Architect of Global Jihad: The Life of Al-Qaeda Strategist Abu Mus'ab al-Suri* (Columbia University Press 2008) 382–407 (for an outline of a doctrinal approach towards individual and small cell jihad).

[81] *Prosecutor v Duško Tadić a/k/a 'Dule'* (Appeals Chamber Decision on The Defence Motion for Interlocutory Appeal on Jurisdiction) ICTY–94–1–A (2 October 1995) para 70.

[82] ibid para 67.

[83] *Juan Carlos Abella v Argentina*, Inter-America Commission on Human Rights, Case 11.137, Report No 55/97 (18 November 197) 1.

[84] Sivakumaran (n 34) 170–80 (for a discussion of group organization).

[85] For example, the types of forces/number of persons involved (organized armed group-leader, specialists-bomb makers in a hierarchal or cellular organization taking central direction, etc); the purpose of the attack (not criminal—ie for profit motive like with transnational criminal organizations); the intended target (Embassy, warship-representative of state power), an attack for a political purpose; the nature of the threat (and in particular the potential use of explosives—VBIEDs, IEDs, suicide bombers, etc); the type of forces, weapons, tactics, etc reasonably required to defeat the threat (missiles, mortars, heavy weapons, airpower—will state armed forces have to engage in 'combat'); and the potential for collateral damage resulting that exceeds that ordinarily expected from a law enforcement situation.

legal framework, one within which rules concerning the conduct of hostilities are applied exclusively.[86]

The broad application of IHRL to situations that are clearly armed conflicts makes a greater consideration of the interaction between that body of law and IHL necessary. Reflecting the reality facing soldiers on the ground, the European human rights tribunal system has faced increasing pressure to incorporate IHL standards into its analysis of human rights. A similar requirement to recognize the existence of an armed conflict was experienced in the 1990s in respect to the United Nations peacekeeping operations that had begun to apply a very narrow interpretation of 'self-defence'. This ultimately led to the development of 'robust peacekeeping',[87] with a broader authority to use force in defence of the mission, as well as the adoption of a Secretary-General's Bulletin that included guidance on the application of IHL to peacekeeping operations.[88]

Unfortunately, to date little analysis has been undertaken on the full impact of applying a human rights regime to situations involving levels of violence not ordinarily experienced in the peacetime environment for which that body of law was developed. As is evident from the UK experience in Northern Ireland, human rights-based law enforcement is capable of being applied in security environments involving considerable violence and disorder. However, there are limits in its ability to do so without fundamentally changing its character. This was particularly evident in that context in respect to the 'shoot to kill' controversy, and the question as to whether hostilities-type norms were being applied in a law enforcement context.[89] Inevitably, there will be a requirement to accept the likelihood of greater collateral damage under the human rights framework if it is to be applied to situations of hostilities. As was seen in *Finogenov*, the ECtHR has been prepared to do just that in what it saw as the exceptional circumstances of terrorism.[90] What is less evident is the point at which a reliance on human rights law will be viewed as having been overextended. This issue may have particular relevance as consideration is

[86] JJ Paust, 'Self-Defense Targetings of Non-state Actors and Permissibility of U.S. Use of Drones in Pakistan' (2010) 19 Journal of Transnational Law & Policy 237, 260 ('[a]rticle 51 self-defense actions provide a paradigm that is potentially different than either a *mere* law enforcement or war paradigm').

[87] United Nations, 'United Nations Peacekeeping Operations: Principles and Guidelines' (Department of Peacekeeping Operations, Department of Field Support, 2008) 34 https://peacekeeping.un.org/sites/default/files/capstone_eng_0.pdf <http://www.un.org/en/peacekeeping/documents/capstone_eng.pdf> (where the Security Council has 'given United Nations peacekeeping operations "robust" mandates authorizing them to "use all necessary means" to deter forceful attempts to disrupt the political process, protect civilians under imminent threat of physical attack, and/or assist the national authorities in maintaining law and order').

[88] B Oswald, H Durham, and A Bates, *Documents on the Law of UN Peace Operations* (OUP 2010) 201–05 (where the 1999 Secretary General's Bulletin: Observance by United Nations Forces of International Humanitarian Law is reproduced).

[89] N Melzer, *Targeted Killing in International Law* (OUP 2008) 22–24.

[90] *Finogenov and Others v Russia* App no 18299/03, 27311/03 (ECtHR, First Section Judgment, 20 December 2011) para 236 (where the European Court accepted the infliction of collateral deaths during a hostage rescue operation on a level that is not ordinarily associated with a law enforcement response).

given to using military forces to counter the 'business model' of immigrant smuggling across the Mediterranean.[91] The use of airpower by the European Union to destroy Somali pirate infrastructure in 2011 suggests that human rights law may now be used in circumstances for which it was never designed, or intended to be applied.[92]

Finally, the participation within a coalition of military forces, which are subject to a regional human rights supervisory regime that primarily applies human rights law, will undoubtedly have some influence on operations as accommodations are being made to address their unique legal requirements. Military commanders are experienced in making those types of adjustments, which can occur for a variety of reasons including nation-specific interpretations of the law and policy-based caveats. However, in situations where national or regional legal obligations limit the participation of military forces during operations requiring the application of both IHL and IHRL, that may ultimately have an impact on the missions or roles to which those forces can be assigned. This in turn can limit the protection they can provide to the civilian population.

6. Conclusion

It is evident that military forces, regardless of whether they are deployed by European or North American states, must apply human rights law as they confront the contemporary insurgent and terrorist threats. This inevitably leads to a requirement to address the overlap of that legal framework with IHL. In doing so, states must reconcile the strategic legal conflict that has developed between advocates of exclusionary application of those bodies of law, and resolve the different perspectives brought to this issue by North American and European approaches to the law. The ability to do so inevitably involves relying on customary international law, domestic law, and policy decisions focused on eliminating the theoretical impasse that has developed on the strategic level. While operational challenges will continue to be presented, the reality for military forces is that IHL and IHRL will frequently have to be applied concurrently on the complex battlefields of the twenty-first century.

[91] N Squires and P Sherwell, 'UN could give the green light to EU plans for Libya military action' *The Telegraph* (15 May 2015) <http://www.telegraph.co.uk/news/worldnews/europe/eu/11609210/UN-could-give-the-green-light-to-EU-plans-for-Libya-military-action.html>.

[92] E Lieblich, 'Quasi-Hostile Acts: The Limits on Forcible Disruption Operations under International Law' (2014) 32 Boston University International Law Journal 101 (for an analysis of this operation).

6

A European Perspective on the International Human Rights and Humanitarian Law Relationship in the Context of Multinational Military Operations

Gentian Zyberi and Anna Andersson

1. Introduction

The nature of the relationship between international human rights law (IHRL) and international humanitarian law (IHL) has drawn significant interest in different professional circles, including academia, military, governments, international and regional organizations and agencies, and humanitarian organizations and their workers.[1] This chapter will analyse, from a European perspective, this complex

[1] For academic commentary see inter alia R Provost, *International Human Rights and Humanitarian Law* (CUP 2002); H Krieger, 'A Conflict of Norms: The Relationship Between Humanitarian Law and Human Rights Law in the ICRC Customary Law Study' (2006) 11 Journal of Conflict and Security Law 265; R Arnold and N Quénivet (eds), *International Humanitarian Law and Human Rights Law: Towards a New Merger in International Law* (Brill, Nijhoff 2008); A Orakhelashvili, 'The Interaction Between Human Rights and Humanitarian Law: Fragmentation, Conflict, Parallelism, or Convergence?' (2008) 19 European Journal of International Law 161–82; F Hampson, 'The Relationship Between International Humanitarian Law and Human Rights Law from the Perspective of a Human Rights Treaty Body' (2008) 90 International Review of the Red Cross (IRRC) 549–72; O Ben-Naftali (ed), *International Humanitarian Law and International Human Rights Law: Pas de Deux* (OUP 2011); Sir D Bethlehem QC, 'The Relationship Between International Humanitarian Law and International Human Rights Law in Situations of Armed Conflict' (2013) 2(2) Cambridge Journal of International and Comparative Law 180–95; T Ferraro, 'The Applicability and Application of International Humanitarian Law to Multinational Forces' (2013 95 IRRC 561–612; L Zhu, 'International Humanitarian Law in the Universal Periodic Review of the UN Human Rights Council: An Empirical Survey' (2014) 5 Journal of International Humanitarian Legal Studies 186–212; TD Gill and D Fleck (eds), *The Handbook of the International Law of Military Operations* (2nd edn, OUP 2015); TD Gill and others (eds), *Leuven Manual on the International Law Applicable to Peace Operations* (CUP 2017). For the inclusion of human rights in military manuals, see among others L Doswald-Beck and S Krähenmann, 'Incorporating International Human Rights Law' in N Hayashi (ed), *National Military Manuals on the Law of Armed Conflict* (2nd edn, Torkel Opsahl Academic EPublisher 2010) 157–71. See also the ICRC, *Handbook on International Rules Governing Military Operations* (ICRC 2016); 'IHL and Human Rights' at <http://www.icrc.org/en/war-and-law/ihl-other-legal-regmies/ihl-human-rights>; UN Office of the High Commissioner for Human Rights, 'International legal protection of human rights in armed conflict'

Gentian Zyberi and Anna Andersson, *A European Perspective on the International Human Rights and Humanitarian Law Relationship in the Context of Multinational Military Operations* In *The 'Legal Pluriverse' Surrounding Multinational Military Operations*. Edited by Robin Geiß and Heike Krieger, Oxford University Press (2020).
DOI: 10.1093/oso/9780198842965.003.0007

relationship in the context of multinational military operations. This is quite important, since many European states have participated in such operations in different parts of the world in the context of operations led by the UN,[2] the EU,[3] as part of North-Atlantic Treaty Organization (NATO),[4] or by the United States. In construing a European perspective, the case law of the European Court of Human Rights (ECtHR) is given specific attention, since all European states are bound by the European Convention on Human Rights (ECHR), and the EU is in the process of becoming a party to this Convention. Our analysis also takes into account relevant legal documents by organs of the Council of Europe (CoE) and of the EU, as well as practice by European states involved in multinational military operations. While our focus remains on the European perspective at a regional level,[5] due attention is paid to the international level, especially positions taken by UN organs or the International Committee of the Red Cross (ICRC). This chapter takes an instrumental approach, inquiring whether and to what extent the convergence between human rights and humanitarian law helps to ensure a higher level of protection for civilians and civilian objects from the effects of armed conflicts, both international (IAC) and non-international (NIAC).

After discussing the shared foundational value of both these branches of international law, namely protecting human dignity (section 2), the degree of convergence between IHRL and IHL is assessed in three main areas which are of significant relevance to the conduct of such operations: the protection of civilians (section 3), the right to humanitarian assistance (section 4), and the right to reparations for victims of armed conflicts (section 5).[6] This substantive convergence is driven by several shared core concerns, specifically safeguarding human dignity, ensuring the protection of life and bodily integrity, and reducing, as much as possible, material damage to private and public property and to cultural heritage objects. The progressive trend towards the so-called 'humanization' of international legal obligations,[7] consisting of using basic concepts and human rights instruments

(New York and Geneva 2011) 7 at <http://www.ohchr.org/Documents/Publications/HR_in_armed_conflict.pdf>; all URLs accessed 27 December 2018.

[2] For more information see <https://peacekeeping.un.org/en>.

[3] For more information see <https://eeas.europa.eu/topics/military-and-civilian-missions-and-operations_en>.

[4] For more information see <https://www.nato.int/cps/en/natohq/topics_52060.htm>.

[5] See among others K Oellers-Frahm, 'A Regional Perspective on the Convergence and Conflicts of Human Rights and International Humanitarian Law in Military Operations: The European Court of Human Rights' in E de Wet and J Kleffner (eds), *Convergence and Conflicts of Human Rights and International Humanitarian Law in Military Operations* (Pretoria University Law Press 2014) 333–63; A Gioia, 'The Role of the European Court of Human Rights in Monitoring Compliance with Humanitarian Law in Armed Conflict' in O Ben-Naftali (ed), *International Humanitarian Law and International Human Rights Law: Pas de Deux* (OUP 2011) 201–50.

[6] For a detailed discussion of these issues see, inter alia, D Murray (ed), *Practitioners' Guide to Human Rights Law in Armed Conflict* (OUP 2016) esp chs 9, 12, and 17.

[7] ICTY, *Prosecutor v Kupreškić et al* (Judgment) IT-95-16-T (14 January 2000) paras 518 and 525.

and practices as subsidiary means of interpretation for filling in legal gaps, contributes to the substantive convergence between IHL and IHRL.

2. Substantive Convergence between Human Rights and Humanitarian Law: Human Dignity

The increasing interaction between IHRL and IHL and their substantive convergence are the result of a gradual process, which has been taking place both at a conceptual and at an institutional level. Conceptually, such convergence rests on shared core values, including the protection of human life, human dignity, and bodily integrity, as well as avoiding or reducing material damage to public and private property. At an institutional level, this convergence is driven by the concurrent use of both human rights and humanitarian law in the practice of international and regional organizations and judicial and quasi-judicial bodies.[8] Although admittedly such application does not occur in a systematic manner, Article 31(3)(c) of the 1969 Vienna Convention on the Law of Treaties (VCLT), requiring for a treaty to be interpreted in harmony with other applicable rules of international law provides a legal basis for such an effort. Arguably, then, the concurrent use of IHRL and IHL should be more prominent and visible in the work of international fact-finding commissions and the UN Human Rights Council. Simultaneously, the difficulties of such systemic integration are more pronounced in the case law of international courts and regional human rights courts, largely due to jurisdictional gaps, but also because of differences between these branches of public international law.

The International Court of Justice (ICJ) has identified three possible situations concerning the relationship between international human rights and humanitarian law, namely some rights may exclusively be matters of IHL; others may exclusively be matters of IHRL; yet others may be matters of both these branches of international law.[9] The International Criminal Tribunal for the Former Yugoslavia (ICTY) has noted that '[t]he laws of war do not necessarily displace the laws regulating a peacetime situation; the former may add elements requisite to the protection which needs to be afforded to victims in a wartime situation'.[10] Moreover, the

[8] See among others UNGA Res 2444 (XXIII) of 1968, 3500 (XXX) of 1975; UNSC Res (1995) UN Doc S/RES/1034, (2004) UN Doc S/RES/1565, (2006) UN Doc S/RES/1738, (2015) S/RES/2225; Human Rights Council Res 5/1 (2007), Human Rights Council Res 9/9 (2008); CCPR General Comment 29 ('States of Emergency: Article 4', paras 3, 9, 11, and 16) and General Comment 31 ('Nature of the General Legal Obligation Imposed on States Parties to the Covenant', para 11); Parliamentary Assembly of the Council of Europe Recommendation 1427 (1999) and Res 2133 (2016), see also <http://www.coe.int/en/web/cahdi/humanitarian-international-law-theme>; Updated European Union Guidelines on promoting compliance with international humanitarian law (IHL), 2009/C 303/06.

[9] *Legal consequences of the construction of a wall in the occupied Palestinian territory* (Advisory Opinion) [2004] ICJ Rep 178, para 106. See also *Armed activities on the territory of the Congo (Democratic Republic of the Congo v Uganda)* (Judgment) [2005] ICJ Rep 242–43, para 216.

[10] See ICTY, *Prosecutor v Dragoljub Kunarac, Radomir Kovač and Zoran Vuković* (Appeals Chamber Judgement) IT-96-23 & IT-96-23/1 A (12 June 2002) para 60.

ICTY has emphasized that with regard to certain of its aspects, IHL can be said to have fused with IHRL.[11] The ECtHR has found that even in situations of international armed conflict, the safeguards under the ECHR continue to apply, albeit interpreted against the background of the provisions of IHL.[12] These broad legal findings support a model of interaction between IHRL and IHL that can be applied to multinational military operations, those with 'active hostilities' where IHL provides the primary legal framework, and the 'security operations' where IHRL provides the primary legal framework.[13] Looking at this relationship from a holistic perspective, Bethlehem has argued that the interaction between human rights and humanitarian law could take six different forms, including: (1) IHRL acting as a gateway for the application of IHL by way of *renvoi*; (2) IHRL giving effect to a relevant but otherwise inapplicable provision of IHL; (3) IHRL informing the interpretation of IHL, including possibly by supplementing or completing the IHL rule; (4) IHRL prevailing over inconsistent IHL; (5) IHRL filling in the gaps in circumstances in which there is no relevant IHL provision; and (6) IHRL augmenting IHL through IHRL procedural and accountability mechanisms.[14] These six different scenarios highlight the complex interaction between these bodies of law and the difficult choices that the ECtHR has to make when deciding cases.

The concept of human dignity occupies an important place in both international human rights law and international humanitarian law, centring on the inherent worth of respecting and protecting every human being.[15] As the ICTY has stated:

> The essence of the whole corpus of international humanitarian law as well as human rights law lies in the protection of the human dignity of every person, whatever his or her gender. The general principle of respect for human dignity is the basic underpinning and indeed the very *raison d'être* of international humanitarian law and human rights law; indeed in modern times it has become of such paramount importance as to permeate the whole body of international law. This principle is intended to shield human beings from outrages upon their personal dignity, whether such outrages are carried out by unlawfully attacking

[11] *Prosecutor v Kunarac et al.* (Trial Judgment) IT-96-23-T & IT-96/23/1-T (22 February 2001) (*Kunarac* Trial Judgment) para 467.

[12] *Hassan v United Kingdom* App no 29750/09 (ECtHR, Grand Chamber Judgment, 16 September 2014) para 104.

[13] D Murray (ed), *Practitioners' Guide to Human Rights Law in Armed Conflict* (OUP 2016) 88–108, esp 90–92.

[14] Bethlehem, 'The relationship between international humanitarian law and international human rights law' (n 1) 195.

[15] See, eg, C McCrudden, 'Human Dignity and Judicial Interpretation of Human Rights' (2008) 19(4) European Journal of International Law 655–724; A Barak, *Human Dignity: The Constitutional Value and the Constitutional Right* (CUP 2015) esp at 34–48.

the body or by humiliating and debasing the honour, the self-respect or the mental well being of a person.[16]

Several international human rights treaties and other relevant instruments make reference to human dignity.[17] The same goes for IHL treaties.[18] First, at a general level, this concept covers the protection of persons against acts which go against their personal dignity, both in peacetime and in times of armed conflict. Secondly, the commission of crimes against humanity and the most serious violations of the laws and customs of war is considered a serious infraction of human dignity.[19]

[16] *Prosecutor v Furundžija* (Judgment) IT-95-17/1-T (10 December 1998) para 183. See also para 162 of this judgment where the ICTY states that the primary purpose of this body of law (IHL) is to safeguard human dignity.

[17] See among others preamble, Articles 1, 22, and 23, of the 1948 Universal Declaration on Human Rights, UNGA Res 217 A (III), UN Doc A/810 at 71; preamble to the 1965 International Convention on the Elimination of All Forms of Racial Discrimination (adopted 21 December 1965, entered into force 4 January 1969) 660 UNTS 195; preamble, Article 10 of the 1966 International Covenant on Civil and Political Rights (adopted 16 December 1966, entered into force 23 March 1976) 999 UNTS 171 (ICCPR); preamble, Article 13 of the 1966 International Covenant on Economic, Social and Cultural Rights (adopted 16 December 1966, entered into force 3 January 1976) 993 UNTS 3; preamble to the 1979 Convention on the Elimination of All Forms of Discrimination against Women (adopted 18 December 1979, entered into force 3 September 1981) 1249 UNTS 13; preamble to the 1984 Convention against Torture and Other Cruel, Inhuman or Degrading Treatment or Punishment (adopted 10 December 1984, entered into force 26 June 1987) 1465 UNTS 85; preamble, Articles 23(1), 28(2), 37(c), 39, and 40(1) of the 1989 Convention on the Rights of the Child (adopted 20 November 1989, entered into force 2 September 1990) 1577 UNTS 3; Articles 17(1) and 70 of the 1990 International Convention on the Protection of the Rights of All Migrant Workers and Members of Their Families (adopted 18 December 1990, entered into force 1 July 2003) 2220 UNTS 3; preamble, Articles 1, 3, 8(1)(a), 16(4), 24(1)(a), and 25(d) of the 2006 Convention on the Rights of Persons with Disabilities (adopted 13 December 2006, entered into force 3 May 2008) 2515 UNTS 3; Articles 19(2) and 24(5)(c) of the 2006 International Convention for the Protection of all Persons from Enforced Disappearance (adopted 20 December 2006, entered into force 23 December 2010) 2716 UNTS 3. See also the preamble to Protocol 13 to the ECHR (adopted 3 May 2002, entered into force 1 July 2003) ETS No 187, concerning the abolition of the death penalty in all circumstances.

[18] See Article 3(1)(c) Common to the Four Geneva Conventions of 1949, namely the Geneva Convention for the Amelioration of the Condition of the Wounded and Sick in Armed Forces in the Field (First Geneva Convention, GC I) (adopted 12 August 1949, entered into force 21 October 1950) 75 UNTS 31, the Geneva Convention for the Amelioration of the Condition of Wounded, Sick and Shipwrecked Members of Armed Forces at Sea (Second Geneva Convention, GC II) (adopted 12 August 1949, entered into force 21 October 1950), the Geneva Convention Relative to the Treatment of Prisoners of War (Third Geneva Convention, GC III) (adopted 12 August 1949, entered into force 21 October 1950) 75 UNTS 135, the Geneva Convention Relative to the Protection of Civilian Persons in Time of War (Fourth Geneva Convention, GC IV) (adopted 12 August 1949, entered into force 21 October 1950) 75 UNTS 287; Articles 75(2)(b) and 85(4)(c) of the Protocol Additional to the Geneva Conventions of 12 August 1949, and Relating to the Protection of Victims of International Armed Conflicts (Protocol I, AP I) (adopted 8 June 1977, entered into force 7 December 1978) 1125 UNTS 3; Article 4(2)(e) of the Protocol Additional to the Geneva Conventions of 12 August 1949, and relating to the Protection of Victims of Non-International Armed Conflicts (Protocol II, AP II) (adopted 8 June 1977, entered into force 7 December 1978) 1125 UNTS 609; preamble to European Convention on the Non-Applicability of Statutory Limitations to Crimes against Humanity and War Crimes (adopted 25 January 1974, entered into force 27 June 2003) ETS No 082; preamble to the Convention on Cluster Munitions (adopted 30 May 2008, entered into force 1 August 2010) 2688 UNTS 39.

[19] See inter alia Article 3 of the Statute of the Special Court for Sierra Leone (SCSLSt), adopted by UNSC Res 1315 (2000) UN Doc S/RES/1315, Article 4(e) of the Statute of the International Criminal Tribunal for the Prosecution of Persons Responsible for Genocide and Other Serious Violations of International Humanitarian Law Committed in the Territory of Rwanda and Rwandan Citizens

Thirdly, the dignity of victims and witnesses is also safeguarded during the criminal legal process.[20] And fourthly, particular attention has also been paid to child soldiers between 15 and 18 years of age, with a view to their rehabilitation.[21] Together, these different aspects of the concept of dignity lay down broad standards of conduct relevant for both states and non-state actors in situations of armed conflict.

3. Substantive Convergence Concerning Protection of Civilians in Armed Conflict

Article 15 ECHR allows for derogations 'in time of war or other public emergency threatening the life of the nation'. No derogations can be made to Article 2 on the right to life though, 'except in respect of deaths resulting from lawful acts of war'. Many cases relating to armed conflicts have been brought before the ECtHR, including the Turkey-Cyprus and Turkey-PKK conflict, Armenian-Azerbaijani conflict over Nagorno-Karabakh, the 1990s armed conflicts in the Balkans, Chechnya, Georgia, and Ukraine.[22] Challenges remain in reconciling the rules of IHL with the rules of European human rights law.[23] The EU's involvement in armed conflicts is closer to the 'security operations', where IHRL provides the primary framework.[24] This section addresses two issues, namely protection of the right to life under Article 2, and detention and the protection of personal liberty under Article 5 ECHR.

Responsible for Genocide and Other Such Violations Committed in the Territory of Neighbouring States, between 1 January 1994 and 31 December 1994 (ICTRSt), adopted by UNSC Res 955 (1994) UN Doc S/RES/955, amended by UNSC Res 1165 (1998) UN Doc S/RES/1165, 1329 (2000) UN Doc S/RES/1329, 1411 (2002) UN Doc S/RES/1411 and 1431 (2002) UN Doc S/RES/1431, Article 8 of the Rome Statute of the International Criminal Court (ICCSt) (adopted 17 July 1989, entered into force 1 July 2002) 2187 UNTS 3. These articles criminalize outrages upon personal dignity, in particular humiliating and degrading treatment, rape, enforced prostitution, and any form of indecent assault.

[20] Article 68 ICCSt, 'Protection of the victims and witnesses and their participation in the proceedings'.

[21] Article 7(1) SCSLSt, 'Jurisdiction over Persons of 15 Years of Age'.

[22] For a general overview of relevant cases see the ECtHR factsheet on 'Armed Conflicts', at <http://www.echr.coe.int/Documents/FS_Armed_conflicts_ENG.pdf>.

[23] See among others C Landais and L Bass, 'Reconciling the Rules of International Humanitarian Law with the Rules of European Human Rights Law' (2015) 97 IRRC 1295–311.

[24] See among others F Naert, *The Application of International Humanitarian Law and Human Rights Law in CSDP Operations* (Brill 2011); G Zyberi, 'The Applicability of General Principles and Instruments of International Law to Peace Missions of the European Union' in A Sari and RA Wessel (eds), *Human Rights in EU Crisis Management Operations: A Duty to Respect and to Protect?* (CLEER Working Paper Series 2012/6) 21–37; F Naert, 'Observance of International Humanitarian Law by Forces under the Command of the European Union' (2013) 95 IRRC 637–43.

3.1 Protection of the right to life in armed conflict

The approach to the right to life is where the difference between human rights and humanitarian law, and 'security operations' and 'active hostilities' paradigms, respectively, comes most to the fore. The arbitrary taking of life is prohibited under both human rights[25] and humanitarian law.[26] When it comes to active hostilities, what is *arbitrary* is specifically regulated under international humanitarian law, as the ICJ has emphasized.[27] Following a similar line of reasoning, in its November 2015 General Comment 3 on the right to life, the African Commission on Human and Peoples' Rights (African Commission) has stated:

> [t]he right to life continues to apply during armed conflict. During the conduct of hostilities, the right to life needs to be interpreted with reference to the rules of international humanitarian law. In all other situations the intentional deprivation of life is prohibited unless strictly unavoidable to protect another life or other lives.[28]

Doswald-Beck has argued that the human rights law relating to the right to life is suitable to supplement and interpret IHL rules relating to the use of force for non-international conflicts and occupation, as well as the law relating to civilians taking a 'direct part in hostilities'.[29] Tomuschat goes one step further by arguing that cases of the use of force outside active hostilities should all be reviewed on the basis of human rights—exclusively according to human rights.[30] Oberleitner seems to provide a more nuanced approach to the 'capture or kill' debate, by arguing that the

[25] Article 6(1) ICCPR; Article 2(2) of the European Convention for the Protection of Human Rights and Fundamental Freedoms (ECHR) (adopted 4 November 1950, entered into force 3 September 1953) ETS No 5; Article 4(1) of the American Convention on Human Rights (ACHR) (adopted 22 November 1969, entered into force 18 July 1978) available at <http://www.refworld.org/docid/3ae6b36510.html>; Article 4 of the African Charter on Human and Peoples' Rights (ACHPR) (adopted 27 June 1981, entered into force 21 October 1986) CAB/LEG/67/3 rev 5, 21 ILM 58. See also Principles on the Effective Prevention and Investigation of Extra-Legal, Arbitrary and Summary Executions, UN ESCOC Res 1989/65 (1989) UN Doc E/RES/1989/65, annex; Supp (No 1) (1989) UN Doc E/1989/89, at 52.

[26] Common Article 3 to the four Geneva Conventions. The prohibition on killing civilians and persons *hors de combat* is also included in many military manuals. See also Rule 89 of the CIHL Study on 'Violence to Life' at <https://ihl-databases.icrc.org/customary-ihl/eng/docs/v1_rul_rule89>.

[27] *Legality of the threat or use of nuclear weapons* (Advisory Opinion) [1996] ICJ Reports 240, para 25.

[28] African Commission on Human and Peoples' Rights, 'General Comment No. 3 on the African Charter on Human and Peoples' Rights: The Right to Life (Article 4)' (November 2015) para 13; at <http://www.achpr.org/instruments/general-comments-right-to-life>.

[29] L Doswald-Beck, 'The Right to Life in Armed Conflict: Does International Humanitarian Law Provide All the Answers?' (2006) 88 IRRC 903–04; V Gowlland-Debbas, 'Harmonising the Individual Protection Regime: Some Reflections on the Relationship between Human Rights and International Humanitarian Law in the Light of the Right to Life' in A Constantinides and N Zaikos (eds), *The Diversity of International Law: Essays in Honour of Professor Kalliopi K. Koufa* (Brill 2009) 399–418.

[30] C Tomuschat, 'Human Rights and International Humanitarian Law' (2010) 21(1) European Journal of International Law 22.

idea of a human rights-based approach to the use of force should not be ruled out as a matter of principle, but that it is rather about analysing its feasibility under operational, tactical, and resource constraints in order to find out when it is legally sound and realistically applicable.[31] Schabas has added another important if controversial element to this discussion by arguing that killing that results from resort to illegal war and acts of aggression is *prima facie* a violation of the human right to life.[32] It is doubtful whether the ECtHR will explicitly address the issue of lawfulness of resorting to armed force.

The issue of respect for the right to life in multinational operations has been raised in several cases, involving military operations under UN mandate in Kosovo (UNMIK)[33] and in Afghanistan (ISAF),[34] as well as multinational military operations in Iraq.[35] For alleged violations of the right to life in situations where military personnel were operating under a UN mandate, the ECtHR has invoked the immunity of the UN before domestic courts and has dismissed the cases.[36] A similar reasoning was adopted for cases relating to NATO operations in the former Yugoslavia.[37] Such immunity does not seem to be a problem in multinational military operations not undertaken under the umbrella of an international or regional organization. Thus, in deciding whether the transfer by the British authorities into Iraqi custody put two Iraqi nationals at real risk of execution by hanging, in violation of Article 2 or Article 1 of Protocol No 13, as regards the latter the ECtHR took the view that 'in respect of those States which [were] bound by it, the right under Article 1 of Protocol No. 13 not to be subjected to the death penalty, which admit[ted] of no derogation and applie[d] in all circumstances, rank[ed] along with the rights in Articles 2 and 3 as a fundamental right, enshrining one of the basic values of the democratic societies making up the Council of Europe'.[38] This would mean that unless guarantees are given that the person will not be subjected to the death penalty, European states that are a party to Protocol 13 cannot transfer a person to the custody of another state that applies the death penalty. While the

[31] G Oberleitner, *Human Rights in Armed Conflict: Law, Practice, Policy* (CUP 2015) 131–43 at 140.

[32] W Schabas, 'Right to Life' in A Clapham and P Gaeta (eds), *The Oxford Handbook of International Law in Armed Conflict* (OUP 2014) 385.

[33] *Behrami and Behrami v France* App no 71412/01 (ECtHR, Grand Chamber Decision on Admissibility, 2 May 2007).

[34] *Hanan v Germany* App no 4871/16 (pending application).

[35] See *Al-Saadoon and Mufdhi v the United Kingdom* App no 61498/08 (ECtHR, Judgment, 2 March 2010); *Al-Skeini and Others v UK* App no 55721/07 (ECtHR, Grand Chamber Judgment, 7 July 2011); *Hassan v The UK* App no 29750/09 (ECtHR, Grand Chamber Judgment, 16 September 2014); *Jaloud v Netherlands* App no 47708/08 (ECtHR, Grand Chamber Judgment, 20 November 2014).

[36] *Behrami and Behrami v France* (n 33); see also *Stichting Mothers of Srebrenica and Others v the Netherlands* App no 65542/12 (ECtHR, Judgment, 11 June 2013).

[37] See *Banković and Others v Belgium and 16 Other Contracting States* App no 52207/99 (ECtHR, Grand Chamber Decision on Admissibility, 12 December 2001); *Markovic and Others v Italy* App no 1398/03 (ECtHR, Grand Chamber Judgment, 14 December 2016).

[38] *Al-Saadoon and Mufdhi v the United Kingdom* App no 61498/08 (ECtHR, Judgment, 2 March 2010) para 118.

ECtHR still has to develop its case law on Article 2 in relation to multinational military operations, it is foreseeable that its use of IHL vocabulary such as 'incidental loss of human life', 'choice of means and methods', 'disproportionality in the weapons used', and resort to the fundamental principles of IHL, namely distinction, proportionality, and precautions in attack,[39] could potentially bridge the gap between IHL and IHRL.

3.2 Detention and the protection of the right to liberty

Perhaps the clearest shift and trend towards convergence between IHL and human rights in the European legal context relates to substantive and procedural norms governing detention. For European states, the treaty text of the ECHR on the right to liberty and security of person appeared for a long time to be hard to reconcile with the rules on internment in the Geneva Conventions (GC) III and IV, resulting in ambiguity concerning the lawfulness of detention connected to armed conflicts. Recent years have brought about a significant change in this regard, with substantive convergence of the ECHR and IHL relating to IACs. Yet questions remain as to whether this tendency is equally relevant for detention in NIACs. This part will examine the developments concerning the fundamental issue of lawfulness of detention in IAC and NIAC.[40]

Detention is a severe control measure, which involves a serious restriction of a person's liberty but also constitutes an important tool in military operations authorized to use force, whether as part of counter-terrorism, counter-insurgency, an armed conflict or occupation, or in the context of a peace operation mandated to employ forceful measures.[41] The legal issues related to security internment or administrative detention constitute some of the most complex legal challenges in multinational military operations.[42] Both IHL and IHRL prohibit arbitrary detention.[43] Yet there is controversy as to how to assess what is arbitrary in situations where both areas of law apply. The ambiguity involves the overall relationship

[39] Oellers-Frahm (n 5) 350.

[40] Other detention-related challenges include treatment, conditions of detention facilities, transfer and hand-over of detainees (eg between troop-contributing states and to the host state) but these will not be dealt with in this chapter.

[41] B Oswald, 'Interplay as Regards Dealing with Detainees in International Military Operations' in E de Wet and J Kleffner (eds), *Convergence and Conflicts of Human Rights and International Humanitarian Law in Military Operations* (Pretoria University Law Press 2014) 69. See also (iii) in the preamble of the Copenhagen Principles and Guidelines on the Handling of Detainees in International Military Operations, welcomed 19 October 2012, available via <http://um.dk/>.

[42] B Oswald, 'Some Controversies of Detention in Multinational Operations and the Contributions of the Copenhagen Principles' (2013) 95 IRRC 707, 711.

[43] Article 9 ICCPR, Article 5 ECHR, and Rule 99 ICRC, *Customary International Humanitarian Law Database on Rules and Practice* (ICRC based on the 2005 CUP publication, continuously updated) (ICRC CIHL Study) stating that arbitrary detention is prohibited in both IAC and NIAC. See also Copenhagen Principles.

between IHL and IHRL and is further complicated by differences in treaty provisions concerning IACs and NIACs, and that IHRL instruments provide different texts on the right to liberty. As Oswald has held, the failure to 'settle on the precise relationship between IHL and IHRL means that states will continue to determine their interpretation of applicable law on a case-by-case basis'.[44]

As regards internment in IACs, IHL contains specific rules on basis, treatment, and procedures. GC III authorizes and regulates the internment of prisoners of war (POW); here, necessity for internment is implied based on the function of a combatant.[45] GC IV authorizes the internment of civilians (protected persons) when it is 'absolutely necessary' (on own territory) or warranted for 'reasons of imperative security' (on occupied territory), coupled with rules on procedures and the end of such internment.[46] This stands in contrast to the more narrow regulation for NIACs. While IHL regulates treatment of persons deprived of liberty, conditions of detention, and criminal procedure and punishment in NIACs, it provides no explicit authorization or ground for security internment in NIACs, or procedural requirements that are comparable to those in GC III and IV applicable in IACs.[47] States and the ICRC generally consider that IHL, with the regime briefly described above, provides a sufficient legal basis for detention in IACs, even in the absence of relevant domestic law.[48] The issue is less clear concerning NIACs. Some scholars argue that IHL applicable in NIACs contains an implicit legal basis for detention.[49] The ICRC has formulated it as IHL contains an 'inherent power to intern' which is sufficient to serve as a legal basis for detention in NIACs.[50] Others argue that a basis for detention must not be implicit but explicit, and that therefore detention in NIACs has no legal basis in IHL, but must be established in domestic law (or, possibly, UNSC resolutions).[51]

[44] Oswald (n 42), 723.

[45] Articles 4 (definition of a POW), 5 (procedure in case of doubt), 21 (basis for internment), and 118–19 (repatriation) GC III.

[46] Articles 4 (defines protected persons), 27.4 (basis for internment of civilians when grounds are met), 41–42 (basis for internment in own territory), 43 (procedure), 78 (basis for internment in occupied territory), and 132 (end of internment) GC IV; see also Article 75 AP I.

[47] See Article 3 GC I–IV and Articles 5–6 AP II.

[48] This view was, eg, expressed by several states in the initial phases of the Copenhagen Process, see Oswald (n 42) 721; see also ICRC, 'Internment in Armed Conflict: Basic Rules and Challenges, Opinion Paper' (November 2014) avilable at <https://www.icrc.org/en/document/internment-armed-conflict-basic-rules-and-challenges> 4–6. Note that ICRC mentions that this position has sometimes been challenged concerning internment of civilians, at 5.

[49] For example, S Sivakumaran, *The Law of Non-International Armed Conflict* (OUP 2012) 301, S Aughey and A Sari, 'Targeting and Detention in Non-International Armed Conflict: Serdar Mohammed and the Limits of Human Rights Convergence' (2015) 91 International Law Studies 60, 116. See also D Murray, *Examining Detention Authority in NIAC: A Response to Heller* (Opinio Juris 2017).

[50] ICRC, 'Internment in Armed Conflict: Basic Rules and Challenges, Opinion Paper' (November 2014) available at <https://www.icrc.org/en/document/internment-armed-conflict-basic-rules-and-challenges> 7.

[51] For example, L Hill-Cawthorne, *Detention in Non-International Armed Conflict* (OUP 2016) 75. See also KJ Heller, *IHL Does Not Authorise Detention in NIAC: A Response to Murray* (Opinio Juris 2017).

The ECtHR has found that restriction of the right to liberty must be established by law, the ground for detention must be legitimate, and adequate procedures must be in place and respected in order to be lawful under Article 5 ECHR.[52] The Court has provided that while the requirement for 'law' in the meaning of providing a legal basis for deprivation of liberty most commonly refers to domestic legislation,[53] international law may constitute 'law' in this sense if it is clearly defined and foreseeable.[54] Multinational military operations may of course detain under domestic law, but there may also be reason to base detention on international law—especially IHL. The issue is particularly complex in NIACs as it is questionable if IHL in NIACs would be considered as providing (sufficiently clear) authorization and regulation of detention. While IHL in IACs contains clearly defined rules for internment and should be deemed foreseeable, it does give rise to challenges concerning grounds and procedure as required under Article 5 ECHR.

As regards 'grounds', the ECHR is special in comparison to Article 9(1) ICCPR, since Article 5(1)(a)–(f) ECHR set out an exhaustive list of legitimate grounds for detention—none of which mentions internment or administrative detention. The ECtHR has continuously held that Article 5 only allows for a narrow interpretation,[55] and that Article 5(1)(c) ECHR does not allow for detention if there is no intent to bring criminal charges within a reasonable time frame.[56] Detention not based on one of the grounds in Article 5(1)(a)–(f) is in violation of the ECHR, which in effect means that security internment or administrative detention is unlawful in normal circumstances.

Article 5 ECHR is derogable, however, and based on a valid derogation under Article 15, a state party could take measures that would otherwise depart from the Convention, for example to establish a temporary ground for administrative detention.[57] Derogating measures must be restricted to what is strictly required by the exigencies of the situation and must not be unjustifiably discriminatory.[58] Whether derogations related to situations outside the state party's territory (which

[52] L Doswald-Beck, *Human Rights in Times of Conflict and Terrorism* (OUP 2011) 253.

[53] *Saadi v the United Kindgom* App no 13229/03 (ECtHR, Grand Chamber Judgment, 29 January 2008) para 67.

[54] *Medvedyev and others v France* App no 3394/03 (ECtHR, Grand Chamber Judgment, 29 March 2010) paras 80 and 99–100 (in this case a diplomatic note authorizing certain measures was seen as legally binding between the two relevant states but did not meet the criteria of clarity and foreseeability to suffice as law restricting the right to liberty and security of person).

[55] *Engel and Others v the Netherlands* App no 5100/71; 5101/71; 5102/71; 5354/72; 5370/72 (ECtHR, 8 June 1976) para 58; *Medvedyev v France* (n 54).

[56] *Lawless v Ireland (no. 3)* App no 332/57 (ECtHR, 1 July 1961) paras 13–14; *Ireland v United Kingdom* App no 5310/71 (ECtHR, 18 January 1978) para 196; *Guzzardi v Italy* App no 7367/76 (ECtHR, 6 November 1980) para 102; *Jėčius v Lithuania* App no 34578/97 (ECtHR, 31 July 2000) paras 47–52; *Al Jedda v the United Kingdom* App no 27021/08 (ECtHR, Grand Chamber Judgment, 7 July 2011) paras 100 and 110. Note also *Hassan v The UK* App no 29750/09 (ECtHR, Grand Chamber Judgment, 16 September 2014).

[57] See Article 15 ECHR and *Al Jedda v the United Kingdom* (n 56).

[58] Article 15.1.

is relevant in multinational military operations) are permitted under the ECHR is still unclear.[59] Based on the ECtHR's findings in *Hassan v the United Kingdom* (see below), this is unnecessary for internment under IHL in IACs, and thus likely only to be relevant in NIACs and emergency situations falling short of an armed conflict.

The issue of security internment based on UNSC resolution and its relation to ECHR was raised in *Al Jedda v the United Kingdom. Al Jedda v UK* concerned internment for imperative reasons of security (partly) during an occupation, but the case was primarily focused on the relationship between a UNSC resolution and the ECHR. The primary reason for such focus was that the United Kingdom had argued that the internment was based on UNSC resolution 1546 (2004),[60] which the United Kingdom claimed 'created an obligation on the United Kingdom to detain the applicant which, pursuant to Article 103 of the Charter of the United Nations, overrode obligations under the Convention'.[61] The Court found that the broad authorization (to use all necessary means) in resolution 1546 did not create an 'obligation' upon the United Kingdom to subject *Al Jedda* to indefinite security internment.[62] Further, the ECtHR held that internment under IHL in occupation 'is to be viewed not as an obligation on the Occupying Power but as a measure of last resort'.[63] Accordingly, the Court concluded that there was no obligation under the Charter of the United Nations[64] that was in conflict with (and could have replaced) the obligations under Article 5 ECHR. Thus, the internment—which did not comply with Article 5—was deemed unlawful.[65]

The issue of whether security internment based on GC III and IV may be compatible with Article 5 ECHR was raised in *Hassan v UK*. This case, decided in 2014, was the first where a responding government argued that the Court should displace or interpret Article 5 ECHR in light of IHL. Given previous case law, the point of departure in *Hassan* was that Article 5 ECHR—normally—excludes internment and administrative detention. The Court also held that the internment regime of GC III and IV is prima facie inconsistent with the grounds set out in Article 5(1)(a)–(f).[66] However, the Court then turned to the particularities of armed

[59] The Court avoided the issue in *Hassan v UK*, which concerned a situation in Iraq, but pointed out that no derogation was made, which could be read as an indication that it is possible, see *Hassan v The UK* (n 56). For a detailed analysis of the issues pertaining to of extraterritorial derogations, see M Milanovic, 'Extraterritorial Derogations from Human Rights Treaties in Armed Conflict' in N Bhuta (ed), *The Frontiers of Human Rights* (OUP 2016).

[60] UNSC Res 1546 (8 June 2004) UN Doc S/RES/1546, adopted by the Security Council at its 4987th meeting.

[61] *Al Jedda v the United Kingdom* (n 56).

[62] ibid.

[63] ibid.

[64] Charter of the United Nations (adopted 26 June 1945, entered into force 24 October 1945) 1 UNTS XVI (UN Charter).

[65] *Al Jedda v the United Kingdom* (n 56).

[66] *Hassan v The UK* (n 56).

conflicts and IHL and recognized the significant differences in context and purpose between detention in peacetime and internment under IHL during an armed conflict.[67] Further, the Court held that it was to take into account, for instance, subsequent practice and IHL when interpreting the ECHR. Notably, the Court also held that subsequent practice could not only inform the interpretation, but also modify the provisions of the ECHR.[68] Importantly, it also emphasized that Article 5 ECHR (as Article 2) should be interpreted in light of IHL as far as is possible.[69] It accordingly applied Article 5 ECHR in light of the regulation in GC III and IV and effectively added to Article 5 ECHR the additional grounds and modified the procedures as provided for in GC III and IV in IACs—concluding that there had been no violation. Hence, security internment of POW and civilians is acceptable under Article 5 during IACs, when it conforms to the relevant rules of IHL.[70] The extent to which the Court included IHL into its interpretation of Article 5 ECHR in *Hassan* constitutes a novelty. While the Court did not develop a general theory on the relationship of IHL and the ECHR, it emphasized its role in interpreting the ECHR in line with other relevant rules of international law in a manner which potentially contributes to a better working relationship between IHL and the ECHR. The result of this pragmatic interpretation is substantive convergence which fits with the general understanding of states and the ICRC of detention under IHL in IACs.

After *Hassan*, much of the remaining controversies regarding the relationship between IHL and IHRL in regard to detention concerns NIAC; here, the trend of convergence may meet other difficulties—the ambiguity over whether IHL provides a basis for detention at all. The relationship between IHL and IHRL concerning detention in multinational military operations in NIACs (and peace operations) was subject to discussions during the Copenhagen Process.[71] Ultimately, IHRL was merely mentioned in the preamble of the non-legally binding Copenhagen Principles, and not given a prevalent role in the principles.[72] Oswald has noted that 'it would therefore seem that those participating in the Process had no difficulties in accepting the application of both IHL and IHRL—the problem rested on agreeing on the precise interaction between the two bodies of law'.[73] The ECtHR

[67] ibid.

[68] ibid. Note also the dissenting opinion criticizing the majority's finding in this regard.

[69] ibid para 102.

[70] ibid paras 104–06.

[71] The Danish Government initiated the so-called Copenhagen Process in 2007. It consisted of a series of meetings for (some) states, international organizations, and representatives of civil society on the topic of detention in multinational military operations and resulted in the Copenhagen Principles, 'welcomed' in 2012.

[72] Preamble. This is one of the reasons why the process was criticized, for example Amnesty International expressed fear that the Principles may be used by states to reinterpret their obligations under international law in a manner which risk undermining IHL and IHRL and the protection of the human person. Amnesty International, 'Outcome of Copenhagen Process on detainees in international military operations undermines respect for human rights' (23 October 2012) at <http://www.amnesty.org/en/documents/IOR50/003/2012/en/>.

[73] B Oswald, 'Some Controversies of Detention in Multinational Operations and the Contributions of the Copenhagen Principles' (2013) 95 IRRC 707, 723.

has accepted customary international law as legal basis for serving a prison sentence under Article 5(1)(a) ECHR. However, this customary rule was supported by related domestic regulation—and, notably, the ground was clearly within Article 5.[74] Given how the Court has emphasized the context of an IAC and the particularities of the detailed regulation of internment IHL in IACs (which exist in treaty and customary international humanitarian law (CIHL)) in *Hassan* while simultaneously upholding the prohibition on such detention in peacetime, and taking into account the difference in regard to the practice of detention, the Court might find it more challenging to modify Article 5(1) and 5(4) ECHR in NIACs in a similar way as it did in *Hassan*.

In conclusion, with the *Hassan* judgment, the ECtHR provided clarification to important aspects of the legal challenges relating to detention in IACs and took the convergence of the relevant norms in IHL and ECHR a significant step further. The clear focus on IACs though means that questions relating to detention in NIACs remain and the controversies over IHL in NIACs implicate that a similar approach to that in *Hassan* is unlikely. Thus, in relation to detention in IACs there is clear substantive convergence in the European perspective, but there are seemingly obstacles to a similar convergence in NIACs. As regards UNSC resolutions as a basis for detention, the normal formulation of authorizing 'all means necessary' does not absolve a state party of its obligations under Article 5 ECHR—but a clearly expressed obligation to detain likely would, based on Article 103 UN Charter. Hence, ECHR state parties in multinational military operations engaged in NIACs or situations falling short of armed conflicts would need to derogate in order to use a detention regime based on other grounds or procedures than those provided for in Article 5(1)–(4) ECHR.

4. The Right to Humanitarian Assistance

The number of persons fleeing from conflicts and in need of humanitarian assistance and protection has increased considerably over the last decade. Amongst the most severe, large-scale humanitarian crises are those occurring in Iraq, Syria, and Yemen.[75] The EU—member states and EU institutions collectively—is among the leading donors of humanitarian aid in the world.[76] Providing humanitarian assistance for persons in need has a strong basis on international humanitarian law, human rights law, refugee law, and international emergency law.[77] The core

[74] *Drozd and Janousek v France and Spain* App no 12747/87 (ECtHR, 22 June 1992) para 107.

[75] For more information, see <http://www.unocha.org/where-we-work/current-emergencies>. See also P Orchard, *A Right to Flee: Refugees, States and the Construction of International Cooperation* (OUP 2014).

[76] For more information, see <https://ec.europa.eu/echo/what/humanitarian-aid_en>.

[77] The main sources of refugee law are treaty law, notably the 1951 Convention relating to the status of refugees (adopted 28 July 1951, entered into force 22 April 1954) (Refugee Convention) 189 UNTS

principles of neutrality (not taking sides) and impartiality (provision of assistance with no regard to ethnicity, religion, race, or any other consideration, and proportional to need), plus the operational imperative (rather than a formal principle) to seek the consent of the belligerent parties have guided the provision of humanitarian assistance to persons in situations of armed conflict or humanitarian or other emergencies.[78] As the ICJ put it in the *Nicaragua* case:

> [i]f the provision of 'humanitarian assistance' is to escape condemnation as an intervention in the internal affairs of Nicaragua, not only must it be limited to the purposes hallowed in the practice of the Red Cross, namely 'to prevent and alleviate human suffering' and 'to protect life and health and to ensure respect for the human being'; it must also, and above all be given without discrimination to all in need[79]

This finding of the ICJ emphasizes the basic requirements concerning the provision of humanitarian assistance, namely fulfilling basic human needs and non-adverse discrimination. These fundamental principles have been endorsed by the EU.[80] First, humanitarian assistance is a right of the civilian population that is guaranteed under both IHL and human rights; secondly, states and humanitarian aid agencies have a legal basis for acting to ensure compliance with obligations stemming from this right; and thirdly, humanitarian actors can offer humanitarian aid, with or without the consent of the parties to a conflict.[81] Importantly, humanitarian workers are entitled to protection under IHL.

137 and its 1967 Protocol (adopted 31 January 1967, entered into force 4 October 1967) 606 UNTS 267, and customary international law. Internally displaced persons (IDPs) are defined in the 1998 Guiding Principles on Internal Displacement as 'persons or groups of persons who have been forced or obliged to flee or to leave their homes or places of habitual residence, in particular as a result of or in order to avoid the effects of armed conflict, situations of generalized violence, violations of human rights or natural or human-made disasters, and who have not crossed an internationally recognized State border'.

[78] See inter alia ICRC, 'Principles Guiding Humanitarian Action' (2015) 97 IRRC 987–88.

[79] *Military and Paramilitary Activities in and against Nicaragua (Nicaragua v United States of America)* (Merits) [1986] ICJ Rep 4, 125, para 243.

[80] See inter alia European Commission, 'The European Consensus on Humanitarian Aid' (26 January 2018) <http://ec.europa.eu/echo/who/humanitarian-aid-and-civil-protection/european-consensus_en>. Paragraph 16 of this document emphasizes that 'The EU will advocate strongly and consistently for the respect of International Law, including International Humanitarian Law, Human Rights Law and Refugee Law'.

[81] See inter alia RA Stoffels, 'Legal Regulation of Humanitarian Assistance in Armed Conflict: Achievements and Gaps' (2004) 86 IRRC 515, 515–45; R Barber, 'Facilitating Humanitarian Assistance in International Humanitarian and Human Rights Law' (2009) 91 IRRC 371, 371–97; HJ Heintze and A Zwitter (eds), *International Law and Humanitarian Assistance: A Crosscut Through Legal Issues Pertaining to Humanitarianism* (Springer 2011); A Müller, *The Relationship between Economic, Social and Cultural Rights and International Humanitarian Law: An Analysis of Health-Related Issues in Non-International Armed Conflicts* (Martinus Nijhoff Publishers 2013) 239–70.

In his 2014 Report on the Responsibility to Protect, the UN Secretary-General has addressed the *protection of refugees and the internally displaced*, as well as on the *protection of civilians in humanitarian emergencies*. The Report notes that in situations of crisis, the Office of the United Nations High Commissioner for Refugees (UNHCR), sometimes working in collaboration with non-governmental organizations such as the Norwegian Refugee Council, can offer concrete forms of protection by supporting requests for asylum or protecting refugees in safe facilities.[82] With regard to *protection of civilians in humanitarian emergencies*, the Report notes that both on the field and global levels, humanitarian actors undertake coordination and protection efforts under the framework of the humanitarian protection clusters. This assistance not only enhances national efforts to protect populations at risk, but also contributes to mitigating conditions conducive to the commission of atrocity crimes.[83]

In more recent years, national governments, humanitarian agencies, and other actors have had serious difficulties in carrying out the legal obligations incumbent upon them. Despite their legal obligations, parties to armed conflicts often have denied access to humanitarian aid agencies. Access for humanitarian relief to civilians in need is a rule of customary IHL, applicable to both types of armed conflict.[84] Parties to an armed conflict, that is both states and non-state armed groups, must allow and facilitate rapid and unimpeded passage of humanitarian relief for civilians in need, which is impartial in character and conducted without any adverse distinction.[85] However, this broad legal protection is affected in practice by problems with getting access, as well as certain shortcomings of standard practices of aid agencies. The denial of humanitarian assistance as a crime under international law covers both the right to access and provision of humanitarian assistance, as well as protection for humanitarian workers and their equipment.[86] Such denial of access in certain cases could amount to the war crime of starvation.

[82] Report of the Secretary General, 'Fulfilling our collective responsibility: international assistance and the responsibility to protect' (11 July 2014) UN Doc A/68/947–S/2014/449, para 65.

[83] Fulfilling our collective responsibility: international assistance and the responsibility to protect, para 66.

[84] See Rule 55 of the 2005 ICRC CIHL Study 'Access for Humanitarian Relief to Civilians in Need', available at <http://www.icrc.org/customary-ihl/eng/docs/v1_cha_chapter17_rule55>.

[85] ibid.

[86] See inter alia C Rottensteiner, 'The Denial of Humanitarian Assistance as a Crime under International Law' (1999) 835 IRRC, at 555 <http://www.icrc.org/eng/resources/documents/article/other/57jq32.htm>; P Wynn-Pope, 'Humanitarian Access in International Humanitarian Law: The Case of Syria and Security Council Resolution 2139 (2014)' in J Petrovic (ed), *Accountability for Violations of International Humanitarian Law: Essays in Honour of Tim McCormack* (Routledge 2015) 117–35.

5. Reparations for Serious Violations of Human Rights and Humanitarian Law

The past decades have demonstrated a trend of claims for reparations and remedies related to harm resulting from conduct undertaken in armed conflicts and other military operations. In several cases discussed above, the ECtHR has found violations of the ECHR and ordered the responsible state to pay compensation. This part will describe the ECHR regulation on just satisfaction and examine the practice of the ECtHR in determining monetary compensation for non-pecuniary damage in selected cases related to multinational military operations.

State responsibility under international law entails that a state is obliged to remedy violations of international law by reparation when the act or omission is attributable to that state and there are no reasons precluding wrongfulness.[87] Specific IHL obligations under treaty and customary law provide that states are to make reparations in the form of compensation for violations of IHL.[88] The IHL obligation involves an underlying presumption of inter-state claims.[89] Over time, arguments have been advanced that a customary right of individuals to reparations for damage by violations of IHL has emerged, or is about to do so.[90] This development is heavily influenced by IHRL, where the right to remedies is essential, and may also be seen as a sign of convergence between the two areas of law. This is further illustrated by the UN Basic Principles and Guidelines on the Right to a Remedy and Reparation for Victims of Gross Violations of International Human Rights Law

[87] Article 1 UNGA Res 56/83 (12 December 2001) Articles on Responsibility of States for Internationally Wrongful Acts (ARSIWA). The Permanent Court of International Justice (PCIJ) famously held in the *Chorzow Factory-case* that '[i]t is a principle of international law, and even a general conception of law, that any breach of an engagement involves an obligation to make reparation': *The Chorzow Factory Case (Germany v Poland)* PCIJ Rep Series A No 9, 29.

[88] Article 3 Hague Convention IV Respecting the Laws and Customs of War on Land and its Annex: Regulations concerning the Laws and customs of War on Land (adopted 18 October 1907, entered into force 26 January 1910) 36 Stat 2277, TS No 539. Article 91 AP I. The obligation to make reparations is also implied in the Grave Breaches regime of the Geneva Conventions, according to which states cannot absolve themselves or another High Contracting Party of any liability incurred in respect of grave breaches; Article 51 GC I, Article 52 GC II, Article 131 GC III, Article 148 GC IV. It is widely held that these rules have developed in scope and now form part of customary international law. See ICRC and others (eds), *Commentary on the Additional Protocols of 8 June 1977 to the Geneva Conventions of 12 August 1949* (ICRC, Martinus Nijhoff Publishers 1987) para 3645; L Zegveld and F Kalshoven, *Constraints on the Waging of War* (ICRC 2001) 147; M Sassòli in C Bassouni (eds), *International Protection of Victims* (Éres 1988) 1165; C Evans, *The Right to Reparation in International Law for Victims of Armed Conflict* (CUP 2012) 33. The treaty law of NIAC lacks a similar provision on reparations, which has been criticized as constituting a 'major lacuna' in IHL. ibid, 31. According to the ICRC, *Customary International Humanitarian Law Database on Rules and Practice*, however, the customary international law rule on reparations is applicable both in IAC and NIAC, see Rule 150.

[89] ICRC and others (eds), *Commentary on the Additional Protocols of 8 June 1977 to the Geneva Conventions of 12 August 1949* (n 87) commentary to Article 91, paras 3645–61.

[90] See Evans (n 88) and P Gaeta, 'Are Victims of Serious Violations of International Humanitarian Law Entitled to Compensation?' in O Ben-Naftali (ed), *International Humanitarian Law and International Human Rights Law: Pas de Deux* (OUP 2011).

and Serious Violations of International Humanitarian Law (Basic Principles).[91] The Basic Principles is a non-legally binding instrument of soft law which was intended to guide reparations to victims of armed conflicts who had suffered harm by violations of IHL and IHRL, but not to create new obligations. In effect, they do demonstrate the trend towards convergence of IHL and IHRL in this regard.[92] The principal difference between the two areas of law in this respect is their institutional mechanisms. The evident lack of IHL bodies to which individuals have standing has led them to turn to human rights bodies to seek remedies for injury resulting from armed conflicts. This tendency is perhaps particularly evident in the European legal context.

The ECHR provides a right to remedies[93] and possibilities for individual complaints of human rights violations with claims of just satisfaction.[94] These provisions form an integral part of the protection of the rights and freedoms in the Convention, but the ECtHR is not intended to function as a tort mechanism and has been careful in how it decides on damages. The ECtHR has emphasized the obligation of the wrongdoing states to cease ongoing violations and remedy harm. In the case of *Akdivar and others v Turkey*, it stated that 'a judgment in which it finds a breach imposes on the respondent State a legal obligation to put an end to such breach and make reparation for its consequences in such a way as to restore as far as possible the situation existing before the breach (*restitutio in integrum*)'.[95] However, the ECtHR has continuously rejected ordering punitive damages aimed at forcing states to comply with their ECHR obligations.[96] Instead it has relied on the Committee of Ministers to act in accordance with Article 46 ECHR and supervise compliance with its judgments.[97] The regular practice of the ECtHR is to review claims of just satisfaction in connection to its findings of violations and order pecuniary and non-pecuniary damages. Article 41 ECHR provides that the Court shall, if necessary, award just satisfaction to the injured party when it has found a

[91] Basic Principles and Guidelines on the Right to a Remedy and Reparation for Victims of Gross Violations of International Human Rights Law and Serious Violations of International Humanitarian Law, adopted by UNGA Res 60/147 (16 December 2005) UN Doc A/RES/60/147.

[92] Evans (n 88) 5.

[93] Article 13 ECHR set out the right to an effective remedy and Article 3 Protocol 7 to ECHR set out a right to remedies for arbitrary detention and miscarriage of justice. Comparable rights exist in several other rights treaties, eg Article 2.3 ICCPR (right to an effective remedy).

[94] Article 34 and 41 ECHR.

[95] *Akdivar and Others v Turkey (Article 50)* App no 21893/93 (ECtHR, Grand Chamber Judgment, 1 April 1998) para 47.

[96] *Cable and Others v the United Kingdom* App nos 24436/94, 24582/94, 24583/94, 24584/94, 24895/94, 25937/94, 25939/94, 25940/94, 25941/94, 26271/95, 26525/95, 27341/95, 27342/95, 27346/95, 27357/95, 27389/95, 27409/95, 27760/95, 27762/95, 27772/95, 28009/95, 28790/95, 30236/96, 30239/96, 30276/96, 30277/96, 30460/96, 30461/96, 30462/96, 31399/96, 31400/96, 31434/96, 31899/96, 32024/96 and 32944/96 (ECtHR, Grand Chamber Judgment, 18 February 1999) para 30; *Orhan v Turkey* App no 25656/94 (ECtHR, Judgment, 18 June 2002) paras 447–49; *Varnava and Others v Turkey* App nos 16064/90 16065/90, 16066/90, 16068/90, 16069/90, 16070/90, 16071/90, 16072/90 and 16073/90 (ECtHR, Grand Chamber Judgment, 18 September 2009) para 223.

[97] *Akdivar v Turkey* (n 95) and *Varnava v Turkey* (n 96) para 222.

violation of the Convention (or its Protocols), but only if the domestic law of the responsible state merely allows for partial reparation.[98] Thus, an order of just satisfaction depends on the Court's decision that it is necessary in the specific case and that it is not possible to get full reparation within the domestic system. As this indicates, and as the ECtHR has pointed out, it is not a tort mechanism but serves a different purpose and therefore has a different function. [99] The Court therefore decides damages upon what is fair in the overall context.[100]

Applicants shall, according to the Rules of Court, establish whether their application includes a claim of just satisfaction.[101] If no such claim is properly made, including when an application merely indicates a wish for reparations, the ECtHR normally does not examine damages under Article 41 ECHR.[102] However, this practice may be sidestepped in exceptional circumstances. In *Nagmetov v Russia*, the Court held that Article 41 ECHR is hierarchical to the Rules of Court and Practice Directions on just satisfaction, and found that it had the discretion to award compensation also in the absence of a properly made claim.[103] The prerequisites would be that the applicant had indicated a wish for reparations, that there was a causal link between violation and the non-material harm, and that there were compelling reasons.[104] Compelling reasons involve two elements: (i) 'particular gravity and impact of the violation, and overall context of the case', determined, for example, by its degree or nature based on the circumstances of the case; reflecting the overall objective of the Convention to protect fundamental human rights;[105] and (ii) 'unavailability or partial availability of adequate reparation at domestic level'; reflecting the (subsidiary) nature of Article 41.[106]

Just satisfaction under Article 41 ECHR may be limited to the judicial finding of a violation of the ECHR but may also include pecuniary damage, non-pecuniary damage, and compensation for costs and expenses. The Court has largely distinguished between two types of situations in examining whether damages should be awarded or not: (i) where the applicants' suffering and/or trauma is manifest, in which case damages are warranted; and (ii) where the judgment with a finding of a violation by the state (and the injury caused to the applicant) in itself is sufficient as just satisfaction, thus no damages are awarded.[107] The first type of situations

[98] Previously Article 50.
[99] *Varnava v Turkey* (n 96); *Al-Skeini v UK* (n 35) para 114. For in-depth analyses of the ECtHR's overall practice on just satisfaction see O Ichim, *Just Satisfaction under the European Convention on Human Rights* (CUP 2015) and A Fenyves and W Berka, *Tort Law in the Jurisprudence of the European Court of Human Rights* (De Gruyter 2011).
[100] *Varnava v Turkey* (n 96); *Al-Skeini v UK* (n 35) para 114.
[101] Rule 60, Rules of Court, as amended by the Registry of the Court (ECtHR), 19 September 2016, Strasbourg.
[102] *Nagmetov v Russia* App no 35589/08 (ECtHR, Grand Chamber Judgment, 30 March 2017) para 59.
[103] ibid para 74.
[104] ibid paras 79–80.
[105] ibid para 81.
[106] ibid para 82.
[107] *Varnava v Turkey* (n 96) para 224.

typically involves 'physical or psychological, pain and suffering, distress, anxiety, frustration, feelings of injustice or humiliation, prolonged uncertainty, disruption to life, or real loss of opportunity' caused by the violation.[108] The other category typically involves less individual suffering and often concerns legislation, procedures, or practices that do not comply with ECHR obligations. In judgments concerning the latter type of situations, the Court often makes a statement that the responsible state is to take measures to amend the situation so that it complies with obligations under the ECHR.[109]

The ECtHR's guiding principle in determining specific sums of damages is equity. The Court has held that equity 'involves flexibility and an objective consideration of what is just, fair and reasonable in all the circumstances of the case, including not only the position of the applicant but the overall context in which the breach occurred'.[110] All circumstances should be assessed, for example it has implications if the applicant contributed to the situation or could have eased the situation or reduced the harm.[111] Assessment of moral damages pose special challenges as it cannot easily be quantified or calculated based on concrete facts, which is usually done in assessment of other damages. In the words of the Court, non-pecuniary damages aim to 'give recognition to the fact that moral damage occurred as a result of a breach of a fundamental human right and reflect in the broadest of terms the severity of the damage'.[112] Also, if the parties to a case have reached an agreement before the Court has decided on just satisfaction, the Court shall verify

[108] ibid. See, eg, *Elsholz v Germany* App no 25735/94 (ECtHR, Grand Chamber Judgment, 13 July 2000) paras 68–71 (distress and anxiety); *Selmouni v France* App no 25803/94 (ECtHR, Grand Chamber Judgment, 28 July 1999) paras 120–23 (pain and suffering); *Smith and Grady v the United Kingdom* App nos 33985/96 and 33986/96 (ECtHR, 25 July 2000) paras 10–13 (devastation, distress, and humiliation). In *Elsholz* and *Selmouni*, the Court stated that it could not establish a causal link between the violation and parts of the claimed injuries/sufferings of the applicant, but that the applicant had indeed suffered personal injury by the violations and thus was entitled to non-pecuniary damages for that part.

[109] *Varnava v Turkey* (n 96) para 224. Further, see, eg, *Cable v UK* (n 96) paras 27–28; *Christine Goodwin v the United Kingdom* App no 28957/95 (ECtHR, Grand Chamber Judgment, 11 July 2002) paras 116–20; and *S and Marper v the United Kingdom* App nos 30562/04 and 30566/04 (ECtHR, Grand Chamber Judgment, 4 December 2008) paras 132–34. In both *Goodwin* and *Marper*, the Court pronounced that it would be for the states in question to implement adequate measures to the effect that the rights of the applicants in the respective cases, as well as other affected individuals, be respected (eg in *Goodwin* (para 120): 'It will be for the United Kingdom Government in due course to implement such measures as it considers appropriate to fulfil its obligations to secure the applicant's, and other transsexuals', right to respect for private life and right to marry in compliance with this judgment'); thereafter, the Court found that the finding of a violation of the ECHR and its consequences for the future were considered sufficient just satisfaction. See also *Chahal v the United Kingdom* App no 22414/93 (ECtHR, Grand Chamber Judgment, 15 November 1996) paras 157–58; and *Saadi v Italy* App no 37201/06 (ECtHR, Grand Chamber Judgment, 28 February 2008) paras 182–88, where the Court found that its finding that the deportation of the applicant would be in violation of Article 3 ECHR and that this finding was sufficient as just satisfaction.

[110] *Al-Skeini v UK* (n 35) para 182; *Al Jedda v the United Kingdom* (n 56); *Varnava v Turkey* (n 96) para 224; *Nagmetov v Russia* (n 102) para 73.

[111] See, eg, *The Estate of Nitschke v Sweden* App no 6301/05 (ECtHR, Judgment, 27 September 2007) paras 68–70. See also *Elsholz v Germany* (n 108).

[112] *Al-Skeini v UK* (n 35) para 182; *Al Jedda v the United Kingdom* (n 56) para 114; *Varnava v Turkey* (n 96) para 224; *Nagmetov v Russia* (n 102) para 73.

that the agreement is indeed equitable.[113] The principle of equity is also used by the ICJ when it determines this kind of reparations. The ICJ has also referred to human right bodies' case law, including the *Al Jedda* case, when examining non-pecuniary damage for human rights violations which had caused harm to individuals. A notable difference is that in the *Diallo* case, the ICJ awarded a higher sum than that generally ordered by the ECtHR.[114]

We turn now to how the ECtHR has assessed the specific sums of damages in two cases involving situations with a connection to a multinational military operation: *Al Skeini* and *Jaloud*. The applicants in both *Al Skeini* and *Jaloud* had asked the ECtHR to remedy the violation by ordering the respective states to undertake an(other) investigation, compliant to the standards of Article 2 ECHR, into the respective relatives' deaths, and—in the case of *Jaloud*—to the extent possible, prosecute responsible persons while keeping the applicant informed.[115] Further, the applicants in *Al Skeini* and *Jaloud* claimed non-pecuniary damage, and in both cases, the ECtHR found it equitable to award the respective amount which the applicants had claimed for the distress they had suffered because of the lack of an independent investigation into the deaths of their relatives. In *Al Skeini* this meant that the (first five) applicants were awarded €17,000 plus tax in non-pecuniary damage.[116] In *Jaloud*, this meant €25,000 plus tax.[117] As per usual, the Court ordered in both cases that the damage and compensation for costs and expenses was to be payed within three months, and, had it not been paid within this time frame, simple interest would be payable in addition plus three percentage points.[118] It is notable that the Court did not assess further what was an equitable amount in *Jaloud*, since it, similarly to *Al Skeini*, concerned the procedural obligations under

[113] Rule 75.4 Rules of Court.

[114] See *Case Concerning Ahmadou Sadio Diallo (Guinea v Democratic Republic of the Congo)* (Compensation) [2012] ICJ Rep 324, para 24 citing *Al Jedda v the United Kingdom* on the flexible and objective elements of equity in determining a reasonable amount in the overall context of the violation. The ICJ ultimately awarded an amount in *Diallo* which was notably higher than most human rights bodies have awarded for similar violations (including in cases cited by the Court). See Declaration by Judge Christopher Greenwood, paras 9 and 11, to *Case Concerning Ahmadou Sadio Diallo (Guinea v DRC)*, but much lower than what was claimed by Guinea. See a summary of Guinea's claim of US$250,000 for non-material damage in ibid para 10.

[115] *Al-Skeini v UK* (n 35) para 179 and *Jaloud v the Netherlands* App no 47708/08 (ECtHR, Grand Chamber Judgment, 20 November 2014) para 232.

[116] *Al-Skeini v UK* (n 35) para 182. (Whereas the sixth applicant was no longer considered a victim of the relevant violation.) The applicants had also claimed a total cost of £119,928 for cost and expenses related to legal aid, which the United Kingdom claimed was excessive while agreeing that it was a complex case. Based on the documentation available and what the Court was deemed reasonable it set the sum to cover costs and expenses for legal aid to €50,000 plus tax (paras 183–85).

[117] *Jaloud v the Netherlands* (n 115). The applicant had initially claimed compensation for costs for his lawyers, while maintaining that this was only relevant in case he would not receive domestic legal aid. In addition, a claim was made in regard to other expenses. The sum to cover expenses of his lawyers was set to €1,372.06 plus tax, as the ECtHR assumed the applicant had received the domestic legal aid he had sought for the costs of his lawyers (paras 236–40).

[118] *Al-Skeini v UK* (n 35) para 186 and *Jaloud v the Netherlands* (n 115) para 241. See also Rule 75.3 of the Rules of Court (ECtHR).

Article 2 ECHR within an extraterritorial armed conflict context but the applicant's claims for non-pecuniary damage differed. The Netherlands opposed the claim by emphasizing that this was higher than what the Court had awarded in *Al Skeini*,[119] but the Court merely stated that—as in *Al Skeini*—it considered 'it equitable to award to the applicant the sum which he claims'.[120]

The ECtHR has developed its case law on just satisfaction on a case-by-case basis rather than thematically or systematically.[121] This is also apparent from the cases of *Al Skeini* and *Jaloud*—which had contextual similarities, but the Court did not compare the sum for non-pecuniary damages—that the fact that the violation was committed in the course of or related to an extraterritorial military operation had no particular impact as such on the decision on the specific sum of damages. The decisions on just satisfaction in the cases of *Al Skeini* and *Jaloud* demonstrate that the sum claimed by the applicant has a significant impact on the sum the Court settles on. The Court takes the claim as a starting point and assesses if it is reasonable based on the principle of equity in the overall context of the case. The non-pecuniary damages in these cases, plus what is awarded for costs and expenses, constitute a significant total sum for the state, but may not be seen as punitive damages—and are still lower than what the ICJ has awarded for reparations in a case of diplomatic protection of human rights.

6. Concluding Remarks

The substantive convergence between human rights and humanitarian law has been largely driven by shared core concerns, namely protecting human life and human dignity, providing humanitarian assistance, and reducing to the maximum extent possible the negative effects of armed conflicts. This ongoing process has become more prominent after the 1990s, due to an increased use of IHRL and IHL norms by judicial and non-judicial mechanisms at national, regional, and international levels. Given the paucity of enforcement mechanisms under IHL, individuals are likely to bring claims relating to military operations to human rights bodies, especially the ECtHR. European states have been involved in different multinational military operations, and issues concerning the right to life and detention have been raised in several cases. The fact that the ECHR applies extraterritorially when states exercise jurisdiction in the sense of Article 1 ECHR involves a need to carefully address regional human rights obligations in multinational military operations. That

[119] *Jaloud v the Netherlands* (n 115) para 233.
[120] *Al-Skeini v UK* (n 35) para 179 and *Jaloud v the Netherlands* (n 115) para 235.
[121] See, eg, *Varnava v Turkey* (n 96). The applicants had based their claim of just satisfaction on other disappearances cases, but the Court held that there are no 'specific scales of damages' for certain type of cases.

is why the precise scope of substantive convergence between IHL and IHRL, in particular the ECHR, is important.

When humanitarian law safeguards are applied as their content requires, human rights and humanitarian law norms reveal a similar content.[122] While the 'capture or kill' debate and the issue of the use of force in armed conflicts will continue to be prone to debate, it must be emphasized that the principles of distinction and proportionality and the prohibition of arbitrary killings are useful in safeguarding the right to life in armed conflicts. The ECtHR's approach to interpret, at least Articles 2 and 5 ECHR, in line with IHL as far as possible opens up for further convergence. Recent ECtHR case law has contributed to significant substantive convergence between the ECHR and IHL concerning the lawfulness of detention. Internment based on GC III and IV is considered lawful deprivation of liberty under the ECHR during IACs, with no need to derogate. ECtHR's findings in *Hassan* are, however, clearly focused on the particularities of IHL in IACs, meaning that there remains ambiguity as to whether detention in NIACs may be based on IHL. Given the lack of a treaty authorization and regulation of internment in IHL applicable in NIACs and the controversy as to whether CIHL in NIACs authorizes internment, it is likely to be a very different issue than in *Hassan*. In *Hassan*, the ECtHR confirmed its continuous practice that detention outside armed conflict is to be determined by the normal standards of Article 5 ECHR, which, in the absence of a derogation, means that administrative detention is not allowed.

The issue of reparations for victims of armed conflicts has received significant international attention and lip service, although that has not necessarily translated into more victims receiving reparations for injuries suffered. New rules and principles have emerged in human rights law and international criminal law, as applied by international courts. In addition, there have been significant developments under the human rights regime to address reparations to situations of armed conflicts, and there is a clear tendency to recognize the right of the individual to reparations for violations of international humanitarian law. The decisions on specific damages are made with the claim of the applicant as a starting point and assessed based on the principle of equity, a flexible concept involving a determination of what is fair and just in the specific case and with regard to the overall context. While the nature and context of a situation of armed conflict may have an impact on what is equitable in a particular case, the practice of the ECtHR concerning reparations for serious violations in the context of multinational military operations remains underdeveloped.

[122] Orakhelashvili (n 1) 182.

PART III

LAWS OF ARMED CONFLICT AND INTERNATIONAL HUMAN RIGHTS LAW IN THE CONTEXT OF MULTINATIONAL MILITARY OPERATIONS

Law Enforcement, Detention, Hostilities, and Precautions in Attack as Relevant Cases in Point

7

Law Enforcement Activities in Peacekeeping and Multinational Military Operations

The Cases of Haiti and Afghanistan

Héctor Olásolo, Felipe Tenorio-Obando, Sergio Andrés Díaz, and Antonio Varón

1. Introduction

In the twenty-first century, the number of multinational military interventions has increased significantly.[1] The deployment of military force has been increasingly entwined with law enforcement activities (LEAs), normally carried out by both local and foreign agents.[2] As a result, UN peacekeeping operations (PKOs) and multinational military operations (MMOs) now often include LEAs as part of their mandates.

PKOs consist of capacity-building efforts to strengthen aptitudes, resources, relationships and facilitating individual, institutional, and environmental conditions.[3] As part of them, LEAs are defined as those functions exercised by law enforcement officers appointed or elected by internationally recognized authorities, with no further specification apart from a general reference to arrest and detain as an example of the said functions.[4] Despite this general definition, LEAs are

[1] D Fleck, 'Legal Issues of Multinational Military Units—Tasks and Missions, Stationing Law, Command and Control' (2005) 75 International Law Studies 161, 161–62.

[2] US Army Joint Staff, 'Multinational Operations' [2013] Joint Publication 3-16, available at <http://www.jcs.mil/Portals/36/Documents/Doctrine/pubs/jp3_16.pdf>. All URLs accessed 27 December 2018, I-1; Defence and Security Committee (NATO) 'Afghanistan, Draft Special Report' (7 October 2017) 164 DSC 17 E, available at <https://www.nato-pa.int/download-file?filename=sites/default/files/2017-11/2017%20-%20164%20DSC%2017%20E%20bis-%20%20AFGHANISTAN.pdf>, para 9, fn 3. See also NATO, 'Warsaw Summit Declaration on Afghanistan' (9 July 2016) Press Release 121, available at <https://www.nato.int/cps/en/natohq/official_texts_133171.htm?selectedLocale=en>; ND White, 'The Use of Weapons in Peace Operations' in S Casey-Maslen (ed), *Weapons Under International Human Rights Law* (CUP 2014) 197–239.

[3] Department of Peacekeeping Operations, Department of Field Support (UN), 'Guidelines on Police Capacity-Building and Development' (2015) Ref 2015.08, 37; C Kimber, 'Enforcing the Peace: Multinational Forces and the UN' (1993) 3 Irish Student Law Review 48.

[4] UN, Guidelines: Police Capacity-Building and Development 2015 (n 3); Department of Peacekeeping Operations, Department of Field Support (UN), 'Guidelines on Police Command in

Héctor Olásolo, Felipe Tenorio-Obando, Sergio Andrés Díaz, and Antonio Varón, *Law Enforcement Activities in Peacekeeping and Multinational Military Operations* In *The 'Legal Pluriverse' Surrounding Multinational Military Operations*. Edited by Robin Geiß and Heike Krieger, Oxford University Press (2020). © The Several Contributors.
DOI: 10.1093/oso/9780198842965.003.0008

regulated by several UN guidelines and policy documents which are only applicable to UN personnel.[5]

MMOs are operations characterized by military-to-military coordination among several states.[6] They can be led by the United Nations, a regional or subregional organization (ie the North Atlantic Treaty Organization (NATO) or the Organization for the Security and Cooperation in Europe (OSCE)), or an ad hoc coalition of states.[7] They can be carried out in collective self-defence pursuant to Article 51 UN Charter or, with the authorization of the UN Security Council (UNSC) acting under Chapter VII of the UN Charter, to further collective security.[8]

MMOs rely on status of forces agreements (SOFAs) as foundational legal instruments.[9] SOFAs are usually formal international treaties and contain most of the legal framework applicable to MMOs on the ground.[10] The issues most commonly addressed by SOFAs are related to administrative matters and privileges and immunities of those participating in MMOs. Due to the complexity of the functions carried out by MMOs, their applicable law also includes norms of public international law, international humanitarian law (IHL), international human rights law (IHRL), and national law.[11] In particular, neither the legal basis for the use of armed force nor the rules of engagement are usually contained in SOFAs. The same holds true for LEAs and other non-military functions carried out by MMOs.[12]

International organizations are usually not subject to the clear-cut type of obligations imposed on states. For instance, as the UN, NATO, and the OSCE are not parties to most IHL and IHRL instruments,[13] the question arises as to whether military units acting under their command must abide by the international standards contained therein. Although a negative answer to this question would lead to the counter-intuitive conclusion that MMOs are, to an important extent, carried out outside the legal framework of international law, this situation shows the need to rely on non-conventional law to regulate MMOs.

United Nations Peacekeeping Operations and Special Political Mission' (2016) Ref 2015.14; Department of Peacekeeping Operations, Department of Field Support (UN), 'Policy on United Nations Police in Peacekeeping Operations and Special Political Missions' (2014) Ref 2014.01.

---

[5] ibid.

[6] Fleck (n 1) 161–62.

[7] BF Klappe, 'The Law of International Peace Operations' in D Fleck (ed), *The Handbook of International Humanitarian Law* (OUP 2013) 611.

[8] G Wilson, *The United Nations and Collective Security* (Routledge 2014) 38.

[9] PI Labuda, 'Peacekeeping and Peace Enforcement' in *The Max Planck Encyclopedia of Public International Law* (OUP 2015) 2.

[10] ibid 38.

[11] Klappe (n 7) 618.

[12] ibid 1, 8–12.

[13] C Stahn, '"Jus ad Bellum", "Jus in Bello" ... "Jus Post Bellum"?—Rethinking the Conception of the Law of Armed Force' (2006) 17 European Journal International Law 928.

As a result, the legal regime concerning MMOs is rather complex and lacks clarity.[14] As shown by the cases of Haiti and Afghanistan, this also affects the regulation of LEAs carried out as part of MMOs, which usually aim at the following two goals: (i) providing operational support for the effective prevention, detection, and investigation of crime, the protection of life and property, and the maintenance of public order;[15] and (ii) furthering the rebuilding, reorganization, and/or reform of the host state's law enforcement institutions and policies.[16]

Practice shows that multilateral interventions sometimes combine PKOs and MMOs. For instance, in Haiti a PKO and several MMOs authorized by the UNSC were jointly deployed and simultaneously regulated. In turn, in Afghanistan, an MMO conducted by a foreign military coalition was initially deployed and subsequently authorized by the UNSC. Over time, LEAs in support of the Afghan Government became also part of the MMO. The diversity of PKOs and MMOs has an impact on the role LEAs play in them.

Since LEAs are taking place in PKOs, MMOs, and mixed scenarios, there are national and international legal frameworks that interact in order to regulate them. This increases the complexity and degree of legal pluralism of their applicable legal regime. In light of the cases of Haiti and Afghanistan, this chapter analyses this legal pluriverse and the way in which it is interpreted to take law enforcement decisions.

In contrast to PKOs and MMOs, special political missions (SPMs), which have recently regained international attention[17] due to the Colombian peace process,[18] 'can be broadly defined as UN civilian missions that are deployed for a limited duration to support the member states in good offices, conflict prevention, peacemaking, and peace-building'.[19] The foundational instruments of SPMs are the status of mission agreements (SOMAs) which regulate administrative matters, privileges, and immunities of those participating in SPMs.[20] Although the law applicable to SPMs also includes other sources of law, such as national law, IHRL, and UN policy directives and internal regulations, the legal regime is altogether rather simple and clear, mainly when, as shown by the Colombian case, their mandate is concrete and specific.[21] Nevertheless, as SPMs do not include LEAs because law

[14] ILC, 'Draft Articles on the Responsibility of International Organizations, with Commentaries' (2011) 2(2) Yearbook of the International Law Commission 40, General Commentary 7.

[15] UN, Guidelines: Police Capacity-Building and Development 2015 (n 3) para 14.

[16] ibid para 53.

[17] A Boutellis, *Driving the System Apart? A Study of United Nations Integration and Integrated Strategic Planning* (International Peace Institute 2013) 8.

[18] UN Secretary-General, 'Report of the Secretary-General: United Nations Political Missions' (2014) available at <http://www.unis.unvienna.org/pdf/0_Regular_Updates/Political_Missions_Report.pdf>, paras 4, 34.

[19] UN, Report of the Secretary-General (n 18) para 34.

[20] Department of Political Affairs (UN), 'Special Political Missions Start-Up Guide' (2012) available at <https://peacemaker.un.org/sites/peacemaker.un.org/files/SPMStartupGuide_UNDPA2012.pdf>.

[21] UN, Guidelines: Police Command in United Nations Peacekeeping Operations and Special Political Mission (n 4) para 48.

enforcement remains in the hands of the state concerned, they will not be analysed in the present chapter.

2. Legal Regimen of Law Enforcement Activities in PKOs: The Guidelines of the UN Department of PKOs

As an effort to regulate LEAs in PKOs, the UN Department of PKOs (DPKO), which is entrusted with the planning, execution,[22] and establishment of the legal regime of UN PKOs,[23] issued its first policy document for law enforcement in UN PKOs in 2014.[24] DPKO's guidelines are applicable to UN law enforcement units, which are comprised of 'experts on missions' (that is to say, individual police officers hired and trained by specialized police teams).[25] Although they have been used in situations like Haiti, Kosovo, and Bosnia–Herzegovina,[26] the general rule appears to be that contributing states conduct MMOs with their own law enforcement agents following their own legal framework. The case of Afghanistan is an excellent example for such a situation.

According to the DPKO, LEAs should be, in principle, entrusted with police agencies of national, regional, or local governments—as long as there is a domestic legal order based, to some extent, on the rule of law, comprised of representative, responsive, and accountable institutions.[27] This requires a framework that (i) offers human rights protection without any unjustified distinction; (ii) is responsive to existing and emerging public needs and expectations; and (iii) is accountable to all individuals and state institutions. Nevertheless, according to the DPKO, these conditions are usually not met in those situations that justify the establishment of PKOs.[28]

For the DPKO, UN law enforcement agents must maintain a civilian profile, which is distinguishable from official and unofficial parties to the violence. Only when the threats exceed the operational limitations of law enforcement, the responsibility to deal with them must be handed over to UN military forces.[29]

[22] R Sismanidis, 'Police Functions in Peace Operations' (1997) 14 Peaceworks 5, 5–6.

[23] M Bothe, 'Peacekeeping' in B Simma and others (eds), *The Charter of the United Nations: A Commentary* vol I (3rd edn, OUP 2012) 1183.

[24] UN, Policy: United Nations Police in Peacekeeping Operations and Special Political Missions (n 4) para 4.

[25] ibid para 5.

[26] UNSC, 'Report of the Secretary-General: The rule of law and transitional justice in conflict and post-conflict societies' (23 August 2004) UN Doc S/2004/616.

[27] UN, Policy: United Nations Police in Peacekeeping Operations and Special Political Missions (n 4) para 15.

[28] ibid paras 15–19.

[29] UN, Guidelines: Police Capacity-Building and Development 2015 (n 3) paras 94–95; UN, Guidelines: Police Command in United Nations Peacekeeping Operations and Special Political Mission (n 4) para 48.

Furthermore, in carrying out LEAs, the DPKO requires the observance of national law, UN standards, norms of crime prevention and criminal justice, and IHL and IHRL (in particular, the Universal Declaration of Human Rights (UDHR) and the International Covenant on Civil and Political Rights (ICCPR)).[30]

Since 2014, the DPKO has issued four additional documents developing policies on specific law enforcement matters. Nevertheless, the 2015 General Guidelines,[31] the 2016 Guidelines on Police Command,[32] and the 2016 Guidelines on Police Operations[33] use equally extensive references to national law, UN standards, IHL, and IHRL as regulatory sources of UN law enforcement activities. In turn, the 2017 Guidelines on Police Administration provide for some functional divisions among UN law enforcement units, including the establishment of a 'Police Internal Investigations Unit' to address allegations of misconduct against those participating in UN-led peacekeeping missions.[34]

In light of the aforementioned, it can be concluded that the distribution of functions among UN law enforcement units, local police agencies, and national and international police forces remains unclear. Moreover, since the core regulation of every UN operation is dependent on its specific mandate, the DPKO's regulations simply restate the core functional differences between law enforcement and military operations, without further elaboration on its practical implications.

On the ground, military and police units taking part in PKOs consist of many institutional layers with cultural and legal diversity. As a result, every decision concerning LEAs is taken in a scenario of legal plurality. Although the DPKO's guidelines acknowledge this reality, they lack clarity as they refer to a number of regulatory sources without providing specific interpretative criteria on how to jointly apply them. Consequently, the existence of a *legal pluriverse* is acknowledged without addressing its complexity. As there is no competent authority to decide on these grey areas, practical solutions are usually taken by mission commanders in their executive directives, undermining the coherence of the mission and blurring the regulatory limits of the use of force.

[30] UN, Guidelines: Police Capacity-Building and Development 2015 (n 3) para 53.

[31] ibid para 34.

[32] UN, Guidelines: Police Command in United Nations Peacekeeping Operations and Special Political Mission (n 4) para 18.

[33] Department of Peacekeeping Operations, Department of Field Support (UN), 'Guidelines on Police Operations in United Nations Peacekeeping Operations and Special Political Mission' (2016) Ref 2015.15, para 11.

[34] Department of Peacekeeping Operations, Department of Field Support (UN), 'Guidelines on Police Administration in United Nations Peacekeeping Operations and Special Political Mission' (2017) Ref 2016.26, para 110.

3. Legal Pluriverse and Complexity in the Regulation of Law Enforcement Activities Undertaken in the Context of Multinational Military Operations: The Cases of Haiti and Afghanistan

3.1 The case of Haiti

In 1993, the UNSC approved the first UN peacekeeping mission in Haiti to support the modernization of its army and the establishment of a police force. Its mandate did not include the use of force.[35] Nevertheless, UN personnel assigned to the mission were unable to enter Haiti during its first year, due to violence and institutional instability. As a result, the mission could not fulfil its mandate.[36]

In light of this situation, the UNSC, in its resolution 940 (1994), authorized member states to assemble a multinational military force to secure and stabilize the country in order to allow UN personnel to carry out their mandate.[37] As a result, the primary role in Haiti was given to an MMO, leaving the UN peacekeeping mission with a minor and secondary role. This situation continued for several years.

In 2004, the UNSC authorized, with resolution 1529 (2004), a new deployment of a multinational military force with the same mandate as the 1994 MMO.[38] Moreover, the UNSC declared 'its readiness to establish a follow-on UN stabilization force to support the continuation of a peaceful and constitutional political process and the maintenance of a secure and stable environment'.[39]

UNSC resolutions 940 (1994) and 1529 (2004) were followed by two MMOs led by the United States.[40] Only after the country was secured and stabilized by the application of *decisive* force, the command was shifted back to the UN peacekeeping mission in Haiti. As a result, whenever the use of military coercion was needed on the ground, the responsibility for applying it was given to an MMO.

Each transfer of command entailed profound rearrangements in the units involved in the missions and significant changes in the nationalities, backgrounds, and legal training of the members of such units. The understanding of the missions also varied notably among the different commanders.[41] This situation, along with

[35] UNSC Res 867 (23 September 1993) UN Doc S/RES/867.

[36] UNSC Res 905 (23 March 1994) UN Doc S/RES/905; J Leininger, 'Democracy and UN Peace-Keeping-Conflict Resolution through State-Building and democracy Promotion in Haiti' in A von Bogdandy and R Wolfrum (eds), *Max Planck Yearbook of United Nations Law* vol 10 (Koninkljke Brill NV 2006) 465–530.

[37] Leininger (n 36) 465–530; D Malone, *Decision-Making in the UN Security Council: The Case of Haiti 1990–1997* (Clarendon Press 1998) 110.

[38] UNSC Res 1529 (29 February 2004) UN Doc S/RES/1529.

[39] ibid.

[40] Leininger (n 36) 506–17; J Dobbins and others, *America's Role in Nation-Building: from Germany to Iraq* (Rand 2003) 71–86.

[41] ED McGrady and JS Ivancovich, *Operation Uphold Democracy: Conflict and Culture* (Center for Naval Analyses 1998) 19–21.

the inadequate legal training of the units involved in the national law of Haiti and the UN law enforcement standards, led to the result that the main law enforcement standards under which the two MMOs operated in Haiti were those included in the executive directives of the MMOs' military commanders.[42]

The mandates of later UN peacekeeping missions in Haiti,[43] which have followed an advisory-support-approach, have continued to provide for the regulation of LEAs by Haitian national legislation, IHL, IHRL, general and specific UN guidelines, and executive directives from mission commanders.[44] Nevertheless, in light of the existing obstacles to implementation and institutional weaknesses, the DPKO has continued issuing specific rules of engagement for UN civilian police units in Haiti, which remain confidential to date.[45] This has increased the complexity and lack of clarity of the already intricate legal framework under which LEAs have been carried out in Haiti.

In conclusion, the case of Haiti shows the lack of consistency in the legal regime of LEAs in UN-led missions[46] as a result of amendments to the missions' mandates, transfers of command, different backgrounds and poor legal training of the units involved, and broad diversity of the applicable sources of law.[47]

3.2 The case of Afghanistan

The UN is not the only scenario where MMOs are conceived, negotiated, and executed. On the contrary, MMOs are rather common in current international society, yet mainly through regional or sub-regional organizations (ie NATO or OSCE)[48] or ad hoc coalitions of states, like the Combined Joint Task Force—Operation

[42] 'Port-au-Prince Agreement' (signed 18 September 1994) available at <https://www.cartercenter.org/documents/642.pdf>; T Kidder, 'The Siege of Mirebalais' *The New Yorker* (New York, 17 April 1995); L Rohter, 'Legal Vacuum in Haiti is Testing U.S. Policy' *The New York Times* (New York, 4 November 1994); McGrady and Ivancovich (n 41) 19–21.

[43] Leininger (n 36) 465–530; Malone (n 37) 110.

[44] S Sheeran (director), 'Peacekeeping and the Model Status of Forces Agreement: Experts' Workshop' (University of Essex 2011).

[45] Department of Peacekeeping Operations (UN), 'United Nations Civilian Police Mission in Haiti (MIPONUH)—Rules of Engagement (ROE)' (1997) S-1840-0005-0004.

[46] Six UN peacekeeping missions have operated in Haiti since 1993: United Nations Mission in Haiti (September 1993–June 1996); United Nations Support Mission in Haiti (July 1996–June 1997); United Nations Transition Mission in Haiti (August 1997–November 1997); United Nations Civilian Police Mission in Haiti (December 1997–March 2000); United Nations Stabilization Mission in Haiti (June 2004–October 2017); United Nations Mission for Justice Support in Haiti (since October 2017).

[47] Leininger (n 36) 465–530.

[48] US Army Joint Staff, Multinational Operations 2013 (n 2) I-1; GW Casey and JE Morrow, 'The Army in Multinational Operations' (Department of the Army, Field Manual, 2010) 100-8, No 3–16, 2–10; R Clayton and I Henderson, 'Legal Issues in Multinational Military Operations' in GS Corn, RE van Landingham, and SR Reeves (eds), *US Military Operations: Law, Policy and Practice* (OUP 2016).

Inherent Resolve, led by the United States,[49] and the Russian-led '4+1' Alliance (both acting in Syria).[50] MMOs built outside the UN regulatory framework follow a more complex and diverse regulation. This section focuses on the legal regime of the International Security Assistance Force (ISAF) and the Resolute Support Mission (RSM) in Afghanistan.

The ISAF coalition commenced in December 2001 during the UN conference in Bonn that was held to negotiate a plan to rebuild the Afghan institutional framework.[51] The participating states signed the Bonn Agreement with an annex on the creation of an international security force.[52] Subsequently, the UNSC authorized ISAF to assist the Afghan Interim Authority to maintain security in Kabul and its surrounding areas. The UNSC also called upon ISAF-contributing states 'to take all necessary measures to fulfil its mandate', which aimed at rooting terrorism out of Afghanistan.[53] ISAF's initial mandate covered a six-month period.[54] It was annually renewed during the following years,[55] covering all Afghan territory.[56] An 'all measures are allowed' approach was taken in the regulation of the execution of the mission, with no legal limitations specifically provided for.[57]

Despite the UNSC support, ISAF was not as a UN force, but acted as an MMO of a coalition of forty states. Upon request of the UN and Afghan authorities, NATO took command of ISAF in August 2003 to inter alia conduct stability and security operations, assist in the development of the Afghan National Security Forces, identify areas to be reconstructed, and support the Afghan Government to disarm illegally armed groups.[58]

ISAF's military goals were formally withdrawn in 2016 during the Warsaw Summit, turning ISAF into the RSM.[59] Its new mandate focused on furthering electoral reforms,

[49] Operation Inherent Resolve, 'CJTF-OIR' <http://www.inherentresolve.mil/About-Us/>; see also Lead Inspector General for Overseas Contingency Operations, 'Quarterly Report Operation Inherent Resolve (October 1st–December 31st· 2016)' available at <https://oig.usaid.gov/sites/default/files/other-reports/quarterly_oir_102016.pdf>, 3.

[50] News Sources, 'Hezbollah joins Russia, Iran, Syria and Iraq in "4+1 Alliance"' (*War in* Context, 15 September 2015) <http://warincontext.org/2015/09/27/hezbollah-joins-russia-iran-syria-and-iraq-in-41-alliance/>.

[51] D Muhopadhyay, *Warlords, Strongman Governors, and the State in Afghanistan* (CUP 2014) 26; Public Diplomacy Division (NATO), 'Afghanistan Report 2009' available at <http://www.nato.int/nato_static/assets/pdf/pdf_2009_03/20090331_090331_afghanistan_report_2009.pdf>, 4.

[52] UNSC, 'Letter dated 5 December 2001 from the Secretary-General addressed to the President of the Security Council' (5 December 2001) UN Doc S/2001/1154, 9.

[53] UNSC Res 1386 (20 December 2001) UN Doc S/RES/1381.

[54] UNSC Res 1413 (23 May 2002) UN Doc S/RES/1413.

[55] UNSC Res 1444 (23 May 2002) UN Doc S/RES/1444; UNSC Res 1510 (13 October 2003) UN Doc S/RES/1510; UNSC Res 1563 (17 September 2004) UN Doc S/RES/1563; UNSC Res 1623 (13 September 2005) UN Doc S/RES/1623; UNSC Res 1707 (12 September 2006) UN Doc S/RES/1707; UNSC Res 1776 (19 September 2007) UN Doc S/RES/1776; UNSC Res 1833 (22 September 2008) UN Doc S/RES/1833.

[56] UNSC Res 1510 (13 October 2003) UN Doc S/RES/1510.

[57] ibid.

[58] International Security Assistance Force, 'ISAF Mandate' (*NATO*, 29 April 2009) <http://www.nato.int/isaf/topics/mandate/>.

[59] NATO, *Afghanistan Report 2009* (n 51) 4.

empowerment of women, economic opportunities, and job creation. Moreover, it had a broad law enforcement mandate to ensure a stable security environment, combat corruption, and fight drugs trafficking.[60] Nevertheless, in September 2017, the RSM was given again the mandate to support Afghan forces to prevent a new terrorist crisis.[61] As a result, the RSM mandate is currently defined as a 'non-combat, train, advise and assist mission',[62] legitimized by the Afghan Government's invitation to assist local and international law enforcement institutions.[63]

As a result of the amendments to the mission mandate, several police agencies have been involved in ISAF and the RSM. This has increased institutional complexity and has demanded multilevel cooperation among them.[64] Key cultural, linguistic, and religious differences and significant gaps between command structures and ground forces have generated high levels of operational uncertainty.[65] Furthermore, an ethnocentric approach developed through several stereotypes on the 'technologically challenged people of the Third World'[66] has also undermined the operational capacities of the mission.[67]

In order to address some of these institutional issues, Afghan authorities have launched the National Development Strategy,[68] which included the Joint-Coordination and Monitoring Board and the International Police Coordination Board, to strengthen the dialogue between the Afghan National Police and international police organizations, such as the European Union Police Mission (EUPOL) and the Combined Security Transition Command for Afghanistan (CSTC-A).[69]

The discussion regarding the applicable legal framework was initially linked to the military component of ISAF. ISAF-contributing states formally recognized that IHL and IHRL were binding for their troops.[70] Nevertheless, the practice has

[60] NATO, Warsaw Summit Declaration on Afghanistan 2016 (n 2).
[61] NATO, Afghanistan, Draft Special Report 2017 (n 2) para 9.
[62] ibid n 3.
[63] ibid para 81.
[64] T Ferraro, 'The Applicability and Application of International Humanitarian Law to Multinational Forces' (2013) 95(891/892) IRRC 561–612.
[65] B McKee, AR Febbraro, and SL Riedel (eds), *Multinational Military Operations and Intercultural Factors* (NATO/Research and Technology Organization 2008) ch 9; NATO, 'NATO's Counterterrorism and Counterinsurgency Experience in Afghanistan' (Ankara, 18–20 November 2014) available at <http://www.coedat.nato.int/publication/workshop_reports/05-CounterterrorismCounterinsurgencyExperience.pdf>, 31–33; Ferraro (n 64) 475–83.
[66] AJ van Vliet and D van Amelsfort, 'Multinational Military Teams' in B McKee, AR Febbraro, and SL Riedel, *Multinational Military Operations and Intercultural Factors* (NATO/Research and Technology Organization 2008).
[67] United States Forces-Afghanistan, 'Memorandum for Record: Findings and Recommendations (AR 15-6 Investigation)—Credibility Assessment of Allegations of Human Rights Violations Appearing in a Human Rights Watch Report', Doc No USFOR-A-DJ2 (December 2011) 11.
[68] Islamic Republic of Afghanistan, 'National Police Plan' (April 2011) 6; NATO, *Afghanistan Report 2009* (n 51) 16.
[69] NATO, *Afghanistan Report 2009* (n 51) 16.
[70] US Army Joint Staff, Multinational Operations 2013 (n 2) xiii; J Fussnecker, 'The Effects of International Human Rights Law on the Legal Interoperability of Multinational Military Operations' (2014) The Army Lawyer 7, 20.

shown that mission commanders have regulated through confidential directives numerous practical matters without taking into account IHL and IHRL.[71] A good example of this situation is the ISAF directive banning access to religious or historical sites, which included a general self-defence exception without elaborating on the specific criteria for its application.[72]

Since the transformation of ISAF into the RSM, both local and international authorities are bound by the Afghan constitution, human rights, and the national reconciliation process, without any interpretative clause to articulate these bodies.[73] Furthermore, all contributing states have issued exceptions for military and non-military activities, reflecting more than fifty different domestic legal orders. Exceptions often result from disagreements among the contributing states on the military or non-military nature of some activities and the applicability of IHRL.[74] Disagreements on the military or civilian status of particular individuals are also common due to different interpretations of international law among foreigners and locals, as a consequence of cultural and axiological diversity.[75]

Detention and treatment of detainees are paramount examples of the significant operational impact of these exceptions. Despite efforts to provide some degree of consistency in the understanding of the applicable law,[76] as shown by the adoption in 2012 of the *Copenhagen Process Principles and Guidelines on the Handling of Detainees in International Military Operations*,[77] no concrete agreement could be reached[78] between major troop-contributing states on the legal characterization of detention operations and the applicability of IHRL.[79] As a result, as the Danish

[71] CD Amore, 'Rules of Engagement: Balancing the (Inherent) Right and Obligation of Self-Defense with the Prevention of Civilian Casualties' (2013) 1 National Security Law Journal 39, 59–70; International Security Assistance Force, 'Tactical Directive' (*NATO*, 6 July 2009) <http://www.nato.int/isaf/docu/official_texts/Tactical_Directive_090706.pdf>; Clayton and Henderson (n 51).

[72] NATO, Tactical Directive 2009 (n 71).

[73] US Army Joint Staff, Multinational Operations 2013 (n 2) xiii; NATO, Afghanistan, Draft Special Report 2017 (n 2) fn 3. See also, NATO, Warsaw Summit Declaration on Afghanistan 2016 (n 2); ND White, 'The Use of Weapons in Peace Operations' in S Casey-Maslen (ed), *Weapons Under International Human Rights Law* (CUP 2014) 197–239.

[74] LR Blank, 'Rules of Engagement and Legal Frameworks for Multinational Counter-Piracy Operations' (2013) 46 Case Western Reserve Journal of International Law 397, 397–407; Fussnecker (n 73); O Engdahl, 'Compliance with International Humanitarian Law in Multinational Peace Operations' (2009) 78 Nordic Journal of International Law 513, 513–26.

[75] Fleck (n 1) 161–78.

[76] See for instance US Army Joint Staff, Multinational Operations 2013 (n 2) III-9; J Hartmann, 'Detention in International Military Operations' (2013) 52 Military Law and the Law of War Review 303, 304–49; Ferraro (n 64) 475–83.

[77] B Oswald and T Winkler, 'Copenhagen Process Principles and Guidelines on the Handling of Detainees in International Military Operations, Insights' (2012) 39(16) American Society of International Law 12; C Brannagan, 'The Copenhagen Process on the Handling of Detainees in International Military Operations: A Canadian Perspective on the Challenges and Goals of Humane Warfare' (2010) 15 Journal of Conflict and Security Law 501, 501–05; T Winkler, 'The Copenhagen Process on Detainees: A Necessity' (2009) 78(4) Nordic Journal of International Law 489.

[78] Hartmann (n 76) 304–49.

[79] Fussnecker (n 70); Hartmann (n 76) 304–49.

Legal Adviser to the Ministry of Foreign Affairs has stated, in Afghanistan 'nobody thought about the implications of what was taking place on the ground'.[80] Indeed, in the midst of the uncertainty, troops of states that did not have the mandate to participate in offensive combat operations were involved at times in such operations (ie *Operation Medusa*).[81]

This legal uncertainty, along with the absence of clear interpretative criteria, has led to improvised ways of dealing with practical law enforcement decisions. As a result, for the most part, it has been up to the MMOs' commanders to try to make sense of the unclear legal framework regulating LEAs as part of ISAF and the RSM.

Consequently, the case of Afghanistan serves as a paradigmatic example of the high level of complexity of the institutional settings of law enforcement in MMOs and the legal pluriverse that regulates their LEAs. Moreover, it also shows that, although references to national and international law are often contained in MMOs' mandates, such references often appear to be a pure formality, as rules of engagement are issued by contributing states' commanders with different approaches to the extent of legal constraints. As in PKOs, this type of multilateral intervention is also bound to a wide catalogue of legal sources with no interpretative criteria to jointly apply them.

4. Conclusion

Due to the plurality of functions carried out by PKOs and MMOs, their LEAs are regulated by a *legal pluriverse* comprised of PKO/MMO mandates, SOFAs, IHL, IHRL, national laws, and internal institutional law (including rules of engagement, executive directives of mission commanders, and UN standards and norms for crime prevention and criminal justice). Although the DPKO guidelines acknowledge the existence of this *legal pluriverse*, they do not provide interpretative criteria to jointly apply the several applicable sources of law.

The cases of Haiti and Afghanistan show the complexity of the institutional settings of law enforcement in UN-led and other MMOs. As a result of the multiple sources of applicable law, the absence of specific interpretative criteria to jointly apply them and the lack of competent authorities to decide on the grey areas, practical solutions are usually taken by mission commanders in their executive directives and rules of engagement, undermining the coherence of the missions and blurring the regulatory limits of the use of force.

[80] Hartmann (n 76) 304–49.

[81] WS Williams, 'Multinational Rules of Engagement: Caveats and Friction' [2013] (reference number DA PAM 27-50-476) Army Lawyer 24, 24–25.

In light of this situation, the first step towards providing more clarity in the application of the *legal pluriverse* that regulates LEAs in PKOs and MMOs is to analyse each law enforcement operation on a case-by-case basis with a functional approach. The purpose of this analysis is to have at the outset more clarity about the applicable sources of law by determining whether the relevant law enforcement operation could be also considered as a hostile act.

8

Detention in the Context of Multinational Military Operations

Jacques Hartmann

1. Introduction

Detention is, and has always been, a regular occurrence in armed conflict.[1] Often, detention of an enemy fighter is a direct alternative to using lethal force, and may even be an obligation, for example when a fighter surrenders.[2] Individuals may be detained for a variety of other reasons, most commonly as part of law enforcement operations or for reasons of security. Accordingly, individuals may be detained because they are suspected of a crime or because they are believed to pose a threat to the armed forces of a multinational military operation, to local authorities or the civilian population of a host country.

The legal basis for detention, procedural safeguards, and the treatment of detainees are of critical importance, not only from a legal and policy perspective, but also in terms of the legitimacy of any military operation. Despite its importance, and despite being a regular occurrence, there is little agreement on the rules that authorize and regulate detention in many multinational military operations, especially in non-international armed conflicts.[3]

Summarizing the findings of a study on strengthening legal protection for victims of armed conflicts, former president of the International Committee of the Red Cross (ICRC), Jakob Kellenberger, noted numerous 'gaps or weaknesses in the existing legal framework' and emphasized detention as an area where there is 'an urgent need to explore new legal ways for dealing exhaustively with the subject of protection for persons deprived of liberty during non-international armed conflict'.[4]

[1] The first recorded use of the term 'prisonnier de guerre' (prisoner of war) was used in the fourteenth century. cf R Ambühl, 'Joan of Arc as Prisonnière de Guerre' (2017) 132 The English Historical Review 1045.

[2] The prohibition on declaring that no quarter will be given is a long-standing rule of customary international law, which was already recognized in the Lieber Code of 1863. See JM Henckaerts and L Doswald-Beck (eds), *Customary International Humanitarian Law* (CUP 2005) Rule 46.

[3] On this topic, see especially L Hill-Cawthorne, *Detention in Non-International Armed Conflict* (OUP 2016).

[4] J Kellenberger, 'Strengthening Legal Protection for Victims of Armed Conflicts' (2010) 92 International Review of the Red Cross 799, 799–800.

Jacques Hartmann, *Detention in the Context of Multinational Military Operations* In *The 'Legal Pluriverse' Surrounding Multinational Military Operations*. Edited by Robin Geiß and Heike Krieger, Oxford University Press (2020).

DOI: 10.1093/oso/9780198842965.003.0009

The gaps or weaknesses can largely be explained by the changing nature of multinational military operations. As detailed later, the 1949 Geneva Conventions contain numerous rules on detention in international armed conflicts.[5] Modern military operations are, however, fundamentally different from the armed conflicts that the Geneva Conventions were established to regulate. The Geneva Conventions are premised on a world in which inter-state conflicts are the predominant type of conflict, where most fighting occurs between privileged combatants and civilians do not regularly engage in hostilities. Most importantly, with regard to detention, the Geneva Conventions are made for a world in which people are detained on the battlefield wearing a uniform during the course of a belligerent act. Nowadays, this type of conflict is rare.

Today, the predominant type of conflict is no longer between states, but between governmental armed forces and armed groups, or between armed groups themselves. Also, the status of those fighting is not always clear and often depends on an assessment of an individual's involvement in hostilities and not on membership of the belligerents' armed forces.[6] It is, furthermore, important to remember that not all multinational military operations necessarily involve fighting of an intensity that automatically implies the application of international humanitarian law.

The past decades have, moreover, seen a significant change in the character of multinational military operations, which, as described in a 2007 report, have

> developed from traditional peacekeeping operations ... through peacemaking operations ... to a new type of operation in which military forces are acting in support of governments that need assistance to stabilise their countries or in support of the international administration of territory.[7]

The report was the first step in the 'Copenhagen Process on the Handling of Detainees in International Military Operations': a five-year multistakeholder effort to develop principles and good practices on detention in international military operations. The Copenhagen Process concluded in 2012 when eighteen states

[5] Geneva Convention (I) for the Amelioration of the Condition of the Wounded and Sick in Armed Forces in the Field (entered into force 21 October 1950) 75 UNTS 31; Geneva Convention (II) for the Amelioration of the Wounded, Sick and Shipwrecked Members of Armed Forces at Sea (entered into force 21 October 1950) 75 UNTS 85; Geneva Convention (III) Relative to the Treatments of Prisoners of War (entered into force 21 October 1950) 75 UNTS 135; Geneva Convention (IV) Relative to the Protection of Civilian Persons in Time of War (entered into force 21 October 1950) 75 UNTS 287; Protocol Additional to the Geneva Conventions of 12 August 1949 and relating to the Protection of Victims of International Armed Conflicts (Protocol I) (opened for signature 8 June 1977, entered into force 7 December 1978) 1125 UNTS 3 (AP I).

[6] The presence on the battlefield of individuals who are not formally members of the belligerents' armed forces is not a new phenomenon, but it has received increasing attention in light of modern military operations. cf MN Schmitt, 'The Interpretive Guidance on the Notion of Direct Participation in Hostilities: A Critical Analysis' in *Essays on Law and War at the Fault Lines* (Springer 2011) 513–46.

[7] Ministry of Foreign Affairs of Denmark, 'The Copenhagen Process on the Handling of Detainees in International Military Operations' (2007) 46 Military Law and the Law of War Review 363.

'welcomed' a set of non-binding 'Principles and Guidelines'. The Principles and Guidelines address uncertainties surrounding the legal basis for the detention, treatment, and transfer of detainees during multinational military operations, drawing on both human rights and international humanitarian law.[8] Crucially, however, they did not develop the law.[9]

The ICRC has long been focused on detention. In 2011, it adopted Resolution 1 on Strengthening Legal Protection for Victims of Armed Conflict.[10] In this resolution, the ICRC invited states and other actors to work together to strengthen international humanitarian law in two areas, namely the protection for persons deprived of their liberty in relation to armed conflict, and mechanisms of compliance with international humanitarian law. Since then, the ICRC has conducted research and facilitated consultations with and among states and other relevant actors on how to address the identified gaps, and it has adopted a set of non-binding guidelines.[11]

Despite efforts to develop the legal framework, gaps or weaknesses persist. These predominantly relate to non-international armed conflicts. The four Geneva Conventions from 1949, and Additional Protocol I (AP I) from 1977, which all apply to international armed conflicts, contain more than 175 provisions regulating numerous aspects of detention, such as the legal basis, the conditions in which detainees are held, and procedural safeguards.[12] Today, however, the vast majority of armed conflicts are non-international in character, and most multinational military operations are conducted in circumstances in which the Geneva Conventions do not apply. Instead, such operations are commonly regulated by the lesser developed rules in Common Article 3 of the Geneva Conventions and, where applicable, Additional Protocol II (AP II) from 1977.

[8] Available at <http://um.dk/en/~/media/UM/English-site/Documents/Politics-and-diplomacy/Copenhangen%20Process%20Principles%20and%20Guidelines.pdf>. All URLs accessed 27 December 2018. Reproduced in Ministry of Foreign Affairs of Denmark, 'The Copenhagen Process on the Handling of Detainees in International Military Operations: Introductory Comments by the Chair, Principles and Guidelines with Chairman's Commentary, and Minutes of the Third Copenhagen Conference' (2012) 51 Military Law and the Law of War Review 187.

[9] cf J Hartmann, 'Detention in International Military Operations: Problems and Process' (2013) 52 The Military Law and the Law of War Review 303.

[10] ICRC, 'Resolution 1—Strengthening legal protection for victims of armed conflicts' (31st International Conference, 1 December 2011). The Resolution was adopted in response to a report by the ICRC, based on a three-year internal study. The resolution is available at <https://www.icrc.org/eng/resources/documents/resolution/31-international-conference-resolution-1-2011.htm>.

[11] J Pejic, 'Procedural Principles and Safeguards for Internment/Administrative Detention in Armed Conflict and Other Situations of Violence' (2005) 87 International Review of the Red Cross 375. While the author produced the article in her personal capacity, the ICRC has adopted it as an official ICRC paper. For an overview of ICRC activity on detention, see ICRC, 'Strengthening IHL protecting persons deprived of their liberty in relation to armed conflict' (1 April 2017) <http://www.icrc.org/en/document/detention-non-international-armed-conflict-icrcs-work-strengthening-legal-protection-0>.

[12] ICRC, 'Strengthening Legal Protection for Persons deprived of their Liberty in relation to Non-International Armed Conflict - Background Paper' (Regional Consultations 2012–13) <https://www.icrc.org/eng/assets/files/2013/strengthening-legal-protection-detention-consultations-2012-2013-icrc.pdf>.

The limited number of provisions that are directly related to detention in non-international armed conflicts only expressly concern the treatment of detainees, and it is disputed whether they implicitly provide a legal basis for detention. The controversy, among others, is evident in the disagreement surrounding the rules that authorize and regulate detention in multinational military operations. The intervention in Iraq (2003–09) has, for example, resulted in the initiation of several hundred claims proceedings by Iraqi nationals who allege that they were unlawfully imprisoned and ill-treated by British armed forces.[13] Detention in other parts of the world has created similar controversy.[14]

Disagreement not only affects the legal protection of individual detainees, but also the capability and willingness of states to participate in, and cooperate with other states during, multinational military operations.

The following provides an overview of the rules that authorize and regulate detention in international as well as non-international armed conflicts. The focus is on international humanitarian law, although comments are also made about human rights law, which is increasingly encroaching upon the traditional remit of international humanitarian law, and which will continue to encroach as long as states are unable to agree on an adequate legal framework applicable for detention in non-international armed conflicts.

2. Detention in International Armed Conflicts

Detention in international armed conflicts is predominantly regulated by the four Geneva Conventions and AP I. The Conventions distinguish between combatants and civilians, one of the cardinal principles of international humanitarian law. In addition to the general distinction, the Conventions define various categories of participants in armed conflicts. The various groups enjoy different levels of protection.[15] In relation to detention, the main categories are: prisoners of war, spies and mercenaries, interned civilians, and criminals.

The status of an individual is critical as it determines the lawfulness of that person's conduct during hostilities, and the rights and protections afforded in case of detention. The status of a person may itself be sufficient reason for depriving a person of his or her liberty, such as in the case of prisoners of war.

[13] The proceedings are known as the 'Iraqi Civilian litigation' in which several hundred Iraqi civilians have sought damages for allegedly unlawful detention and ill-treatment by British armed forces. See *Alseran and Others v Ministry of Defence* [2017] EWHC 3289 (QB).

[14] For case studies, see, eg, E Wilmshurst (ed), *International Law and the Classification of Conflicts* (OUP 2012) Part III.

[15] See GD Solis, *The Law of Armed Conflict: International Humanitarian Law in War* (2nd edn, CUP 2016) 200–67.

2.1 Prisoners of war and other special status individuals

The treatment of prisoners of war has long been regulated in international law and is part of customary law.[16] Importantly, the status of prisoners of war is only applicable in international armed conflicts. By contrast, this status is not recognized in a non-international armed conflict.

Most rules concerning prisoners of war are found in the third Geneva Convention (GC III) Relative to the Treatment of Prisoners of War, which, like all the Geneva Conventions, only applies to international armed conflicts, as well as cases of partial or total occupation of the territory of a party to a conflict.[17] It provides a right to intern individuals and comprehensively regulates the conditions of internment. The authority to intern is confirmed in Article 21:

> The Detaining Power may subject prisoners of war to internment. It may impose on them the obligation of not leaving, beyond certain limits, the camp where they are interned, or if the said camp is fenced in, of not going outside its perimeter.

The right to intern continues until the cessation of active hostilities, after which prisoners must be released without delay.[18] The European Court of Human Rights (ECtHR) has accepted that GC III may provide a lawful ground for detention in international armed conflicts, emphasizing that human rights safeguards continue to apply, albeit interpreted against the background of the provisions of international humanitarian law.[19] Detention based on Article 21 also seems in compliance with other human rights instruments, such as the International Covenant on Civil and Political Rights (ICCPR).[20]

The question remains: Who may be detained? Generally, combatants may be detained because of their status whereas civilians may only, as will be discussed in more detail later, be detained in exceptional circumstances, namely where it is either 'absolutely necessary' or 'imperative' for reasons of security.

16 The 1874 Brussels Declaration contained rules on prisoners of war and although the Declaration never entered into force, its provisions influenced later international agreements. Project of an International Declaration concerning the Laws and Customs of War (Brussels, 27 August 1874) <https://ihl-databases.icrc.org/ihl/INTRO/135>.

17 Geneva Conventions (n 5) Common Article 2.

18 Geneva Convention III (n 5) Article 118.

19 *Hassan and Others v France* App no 29750/09 (ECtHR, Grand Chamber Judgment, 16 September 2014) paras 104–06. See also *Abd Ali Hameed Al-Waheed v Ministry of Defence* [2017] UKSC 2 and *Serdar Mohammed v Ministry of Defence* [2017] UKSC 2.

20 See UNCHR, 'General Comment 35—Article 9 (Liberty and Security of Persons)' (2014) UN Doc CCPR/C/GC/35, 15 and 64. See also HRC, 'Report of the Working Group on Arbitrary Detention' (24 December 2012) UN Doc A/HRC/22/44.

Civilians are defined negatively as all individuals that are not combatants or do not have some other special status.[21] Special status includes spies and mercenaries. Spies are combatants that lose their protection and their right to be treated as prisoners of war because of their involvement in espionage.[22] Mercenaries are not combatants and consequently are never entitled to prisoner of war status.[23]

The definition of combatants goes back to the 1907 Hague Regulations. Traditionally, Articles 1 and 2 of the Hague Regulations contained standards for combatants. These standards are incorporated into Article 4(A) GC III, which defined various categories of individuals that are entitled to prisoner of war status when they have fallen into the power of the enemy. The principal categories are:

(1) Members of the armed forces of a Party to the conflict as well as members of militias or volunteer corps forming part of such armed forces.
(2) Members of other militias and members of other volunteer corps, including those in organised resistance movements, belonging to a Party to the conflict and operating in or outside their own territory, even if this territory is occupied, provided that such militias or volunteer corps, including such organized resistance movements, fulfil the following conditions:
   (a) that of being commanded by a person responsible for his subordinates;
   (b) that of having a fixed distinctive sign recognizable at a distance;
   (c) that of carrying arms openly;
   (d) that of conducting their operations in accordance with the laws and customs of war.
(3) Members of regular armed forces who profess allegiance to a government or an authority not recognized by the detaining power.

Article 4(A) distinguishes between members of regular armed forces and irregular combatants, who must satisfy four conditions in order to be accorded equivalent status as regular armed forces. Although not explicitly stated, it is well established that regular combatants must also meet the four conditions outlined in Article 4(A)(2). Thus, all combatants must be under responsible command, wear a fixed distinctive sign, carry arms openly, and observe the laws and customs of war.[24]

[21] Additional Protocol I (n 5) Article 50(1) defines civilians as all those who are not referred to in Geneva Convention III (n 5) Article 4(A)(1), (2), (3), and (6) and in Additional Protocol I (n 5) Article 43.
[22] Additional Protocol I (n 5) Article 46.
[23] Additional Protocol I (n 5) Article 47.
[24] See further Y Dinstein, *The Conduct of Hostilities under the Law of International Armed Conflict* (CUP 2010) 92.

There is a presumption that, by their very nature, members of regular armed forces would meet these conditions.[25] But the presumption can be rebutted.[26] In practice, it is often difficult for irregular combatants to satisfy the requirements. AP I attempts to alter this situation and largely assimilates regular and irregular combatants.[27] It also lowers the standard by which combatants must distinguish themselves from the civilian population.[28]

The adoption of Article 44 AP I proved highly controversial and is one of the main reasons that several states, including the United States, decided not to ratify AP I. The fact that not all states have ratified AP I has the unfortunate consequence that states participating in multinational military operations may apply different standards for lawful combatant status; this, again, will affect who can be detained as a prisoner of war. The multinational military operation in Afghanistan, waged by the United States and its allies against the Taliban regime and their Al-Qaeda associates, has raised multiple problems pertinent to the understanding of lawful/unlawful combatant status, which again affected the legal basis for detention.[29]

Those who satisfy the conditions, either in GC III or AP I, may be interned as prisoners of war, with all the rights and privileges this entails. A combatant who fails to distinguish himself from the civilian population commits the war crime of perfidy and forfeits his entitlement to prisoner of war status. He may nonetheless still be detained and is entitled to the same protection as a prisoner of war convicted of his crime.[30]

While the loss of prisoner of war status will not immediately affect the right to protection, it will affect combat immunity. This means that individuals who have lost their prisoner of war status may be prosecuted for hostile acts, which would not otherwise be punishable. Such prisoners can therefore be prosecuted under the ordinary penal code of the party to the conflict which has captured them.

In addition to combatants, other groups of individuals are entitled to the same rights and privileges as prisoners of war. This includes individuals who accompany the armed forces without being a member thereof, such as war correspondents or contractors.[31] In addition, medical and religious personnel may be deprived of their liberty. Unlike combatants, so-called 'retained personnel' may not be interned for the duration of hostilities, but only as long as their services are needed.[32]

[25] ibid.

[26] The Privy Council held that Indonesian soldiers who were wearing civilian clothes when captured were not entitled to be treated as prisoners of war under Geneva Convention III. *Mohamed Ali and Others v Public Prosecutor* [1969] AC 430, 449–50.

[27] Additional Protocol I (n 5) Article 44.

[28] C Greenwood, 'The Law of War (International Humanitarian Law)' in M Evans (ed), *International law* (2nd edn, OUP 2006) 788.

[29] See, eg, Dinstein (n 24) 107–09; F Hampson, 'Afghanistan 2001–2010' in Wilmshurst (n 14) 255–58.

[30] Additional Protocol I (n 5) Article 44(4).

[31] Geneva Convention III (n 5) Article 4(4).

[32] Geneva Convention III (n 5) Article 33. See also Dinstein (n 24) 233–39.

There is some controversy concerning individuals who participate in hostilities without being entitled to do so and therefore cannot be classified as lawful combatants. This group is sometimes referred to as 'unlawful' combatants, or other similar terms.[33] While the discussion of unlawful combatants is not new, it became subject of an intensive debate following the multinational military operations in Afghanistan in 2001. Some states, notably the United States, assert that unlawful combatants fall outside the protection of the Geneva Conventions. They are supported by scholars such as Yoram Dinstein, who argues that a 'person who engages in military raids by night, while purporting to be an innocent civilian by day, is neither a civilian nor a lawful combatant. He is an unlawful combatant'.[34]

Most states have rejected the suggestion that the Geneva Conventions allow for categories other than the binary distinction between combatants and civilians. In this regard, Emily Crawford writes that, given 'the almost uniform resistance to US attempts to proclaim a "Geneva" status of "unlawful enemy combatant", it is doubtful such a legal category exists'.[35] The latter interpretation is not only supported by the vast majority of state practice, but is also better reconcilable with the text of the Geneva Conventions and AP I.[36]

Uncertainty concerning an individual's combat status was foreseen during the drafting of the Geneva Conventions. Article 5 GC III therefore requires that a tribunal be established in the case that an individual's status is not immediately obvious. Any person detained on this basis shall, moreover, enjoy prisoner of war status until the tribunal has determined his status.[37]

Finally, it should be noted that the detaining power is responsible for the treatment of prisoners of war; such prisoners may only be transferred to other parties to GC III, and only after the detaining power has satisfied itself of the willingness and ability of the receiving state to apply the protection of the Convention.[38]

2.2 Civilians and protected persons

Unlike the detention of prisoners of war, the detention of civilians is less well-regulated in international law. Most rules are found in the fourth Geneva Convention (GC IV) Relative to the Protection of Civilian Persons in Time of

[33] On this topic, see especially K Dörmann, 'The Legal Situation of "Unlawful/Unprivileged Combatants"' (2003) 85 International Review of the Red Cross 45; Solis (n 15) 212 et seq.

[34] Dinstein (n 24) 83.

[35] E Crawford, *The Treatment of Combatants and Insurgents Under the Law of Armed Conflict* (OUP 2010) 60.

[36] Dörmann (n 33).

[37] See Geneva Convention III (n 5) Article 5 and Additional Protocol I (n 5) Article 45(1).

[38] Geneva Convention III (n 5) Article 12. The United Kingdom violated this provision when it transferred a Pakistani citizen who was apprehended in Iraq in 2004 to US custody. *Secretary of State for Foreign and Commonwealth Affairs and another v Yunus Rahmatullah* [2012] UKSC 48.

War, as well as in customary international law.[39] GC IV applies to all international armed conflicts, as well as cases of partial or total occupation.

All civilians are entitled to general protection against the dangers arising from hostilities and may not be made the object of an attack. Correspondingly, civilians do not have the right to participate directly in hostilities.[40] If they nonetheless take direct part, they remain civilians but become lawful targets of attacks.[41] They may also be subject to criminal prosecution.

In regard to internment, GC IV distinguishes between civilians in the territory of a party to the conflict and those in occupied territory. The basic norm governing all civilian internment is, however, found in Article 27(4), which also provides the authority to intern:

> the Parties to the conflict may take such measures of control and security in regard to protected persons as may be necessary as a result of the war.

The authority to intern only applies to 'protected persons', these are civilians who find themselves in the hands of a party to the conflict of which they are not nationals.[42] Nationals of co-belligerents or neutral states may also be excluded from the category of protected persons.[43]

A protected person coming under the power of the enemy—if he did not directly participate in the hostilities—is guaranteed not only his life, health, and dignity, but also his personal liberty.[44] Individuals therefore cannot be detained without proper cause, and then only in accordance with relevant procedures.

In the territory of a party to the conflict, the relevant procedures are contained in Articles 41–43 GC IV, which also provide substantial limitations. Thus, Article 42(1) only allows internment or assigned residence of protected persons if the security of the detaining power makes it 'absolutely necessary'. The ICRC Commentary states that it did not seem possible to define the expression 'security of the State'.[45] It was therefore left largely to states themselves to decide on the measure of activity prejudicial to their security which consequently justifies internment or assigned residence. The Commentary, however, offers examples, such as subversive activity, sabotage, or espionage.[46]

[39] Henckaerts and Doswald-Beck (n 2) Rules 99 and 118–28.

[40] Except for the relatively rare case of civilians spontaneously taking up arms in response to an invasion (*levée en masse*).

[41] Direct participation in hostilities is a vexed issue in international humanitarian law. See, eg, Dinstein (n 24) 233–39; Solis (n 15) 217–22.

[42] Geneva Convention IV (n 5) Article 4.

[43] ibid.

[44] Dinstein (n 24) 83–84.

[45] J Pictet (ed), *Commentary to Geneva Convention IV Relative to the Protection of Civilian Persons in Time of War* (ICRC 1958) 257.

[46] ibid 258.

In occupied territory, the relevant procedures are contained in Article 78(1) GC IV. This provision also contains substantial limitations: assigned residence or internment is only permitted where the 'Occupying Power considers it necessary, for imperative reasons of security'. According to the ICRC Commentary, the phrase 'imperative reasons of security' indicates that internment in occupied territory 'should be even more exceptional than it is inside the territory of the Parties to the conflict'.[47] This reading has, however, been questioned.[48]

Notwithstanding the difference in language, both Articles 42 and 78 stress the exceptional character of measures of internment and assigned residence. The exceptional character has been confirmed by the ICTY:

> internment and assigned residence, whether in the occupying power's national territory or in the occupied territory, are exceptional measures to be taken only after careful consideration of each individual case.[49]

The authority to detain under Article 78 only applies in occupied territory. According to the 1907 Hague Convention, territory is considered occupied when it is 'actually placed under the authority of the hostile army' and the occupation extends only to the territory 'where such authority has been established and can be exercised'.[50]

For a territory to be considered occupied, foreign armed forces must have established effective control over the territory.[51] The threshold for occupation is therefore high, and Article 78 does not provide a legal basis for internment in territory which has been invaded but not placed under effective control.[52]

Strict procedural rules apply both in the territory of a party to the conflict as well as in an occupied territory. The procedural rules are designed to ensure that parties to an armed conflict, which resort to measures of internment, respect the basic rights of the persons interned. For internment in territory of a party to the conflict, Article 43 provides that any

[47] ibid 367.

[48] Hill-Cawthorne (n 3) 68.

[49] ICTY, *Prosecutor v Zejnil Delalić et al* (Trial Chamber Judgment) IT-96-21-T (16 November 1998) 574 and *Prosecutor v Dario Kordić and Mario Čerkez* (Trial Chamber Judgment) IT-95-14/2-T (26 February 2001) 285.

[50] Annex to Convention (IV) respecting the Laws and Customs of War on Land: Regulations Respecting the Laws and Customs of War on Land (adopted 18 October 1907, entered into force 26 January 1910) Article 42.

[51] E Benvenisti, *The International Law of Occupation* (2nd edn, OUP 2012) 43–51.

[52] It is sometimes suggested that invasion and occupation are not distinct phases of an international armed conflict and that the rules of GC IV which relate to occupation apply as soon as troops invade foreign territory; commonly known as the Pictet theory. For a debate hereof, see *Alseran and Others v Ministry of Defence* (n 13) 253–62.

> protected person who has been interned or placed in assigned residence shall be entitled to have such action reconsidered as soon as possible by an appropriate court or administrative board designated by the Detaining Power for that purpose.

The ICRC Commentary to Article 43 states that decisions to intern people or place them in assigned residence 'are not reconsidered automatically, but only at the request of the person concerned'. But once an application has been put forward, the court or administrative board must examine it at the 'earliest possible moment'. There is an inherent flexibility in determining what 'as soon as possible' means, but the ICRC Commentary emphasizes that the detaining authority must never forget that internment or assigned residence are exceptional measures which may be applied only if they are absolutely necessary for the security of the state.[53]

For internment in occupied territory the rules are less detailed. Article 78 provides that decisions regarding 'assigned residence or internment shall be made according to a regular procedure to be prescribed by the Occupying Power in accordance with the provisions of the present Convention'. The ICRC Commentary states that it is for the occupying power to decide on the procedure to be adopted but specifies that 'it is not entirely free to do as it likes; it must observe the stipulations in Article 43'.[54]

The ICRC Commentary implies that both forms of detention require the same procedural rules.[55] The decision to detain an individual must therefore be 'reconsidered as soon as possible by an appropriate court or administrative board', although only at the request of the detainee. Hereafter, continued detention must be reviewed at least once every six months, whether or not the detainee requests the review.[56]

During occupation, Article 68 GC IV also grants an occupying power the authority to enact penal legislation to maintain the orderly government of the territory, and to ensure the security of the occupying power. This provision also provides a legal basis for enacting criminal law, which may also authorize detention.

The rules in GC IV are strict and explicitly require the release of interned individuals 'as soon as the reasons which necessitated his internment no longer exist'.[57] Article 79 GC IV further states that:

[53] Y Sandoz, C Swinarski, and B Zimmermann (eds), *Commentary on the Additional Protocols of 8 June 1977 to the Geneva Conventions of 12 August 1949: Protocol I* (Martinus Nijhoff Publishers 1987) 260.

[54] ibid 368.

[55] This was confirmed in *R (on the application of Al-Jedda) v Secretary of State for Defence* [2005] EWHC 1809 (Admin) [139].

[56] ICTY, *Prosecutor v Zejnil Delalić et al* (Appeal) IT-96-21-A (20 February 2001) 582.

[57] Geneva Convention IV (n 5) Article 132(1).

> The parties to the conflict shall not intern protected persons, except in accordance with the provisions of article 41, 42, 43, 68 and 78.

It follows that these provisions provide the only legal bases for internment of protected persons in international armed conflict and occupation, and that internment on any other basis is contrary to international humanitarian law.[58]

Involuntary confinement of a civilian where the security of the detaining power does not make this absolutely necessary, or in disregard of the relevant procedural rules, will be unlawful and may give rise to individual criminal liability.[59]

3. Detention in Non-international Armed Conflicts

As most conventional law applies to international armed conflicts, it is not surprising that there are fewer rules in relation to detention in non-international armed conflicts. The few rules that do exist concern only the treatment of detainees, and there is neither explicit legal basis for the deprivation of liberty nor any procedural safeguards. The relevant rules are found in Common Article 3 to the Geneva Conventions and Articles 2, 4–6 AP II.

Common Article 3, which applies in 'armed conflict not of an international character' occurring in the territory of one of the parties to the conventions, establishes minimum rules for this specific type of conflict. It states, inter alia, that:

> Persons taking no active part in the hostilities, including members of armed forces who have laid down their arms and those placed 'hors de combat' by sickness, wounds, detention, or any other cause, shall in all circumstances be treated humanely, without any adverse distinction founded on race, colour, religion or faith, sex, birth or wealth, or any other similar criteria. (emphasis added)

Thus, Common Article 3 provides for the humane and non-discriminatory treatment of persons taking no active part in hostilities. While it explicitly makes reference to 'detention' it does not provide an explicit legal basis for the deprivation of liberty.[60]

AP II extends the rules applicable to non-international armed conflicts.[61] While providing more detailed rules, however, it is less widely ratified than the Geneva Conventions. The scope of application of AP II is also far more restricted than the

[58] *Alseran and Others v Ministry of Defence* (n 13) 248.
[59] *Prosecutor v Zejnil Delalić et al* (Appeal) (n 56) 379.
[60] Hill-Cawthorne (n 3) 101 et seq.
[61] Protocol Additional to the Geneva Conventions of 12 August 1949 and Relating to the Protection of Victims of Non-International Armed Conflicts (opened for signature 8 June 1977, entered into force 7 December 1978) 1125 UNTS 609 (AP II).

Geneva Conventions, limited in effect to armed conflicts where both parties control territory.[62] The lack of ratification and restricted scope of application mean that AP II is not always applicable to multinational military operations, or that it may only apply to conduct by some of the contributing states.

Like Common Article 3, AP II also anticipates but does not authorize detention. Article 2 states:

> At the end of the armed conflict, all the persons who have been deprived of their liberty or whose liberty has been restricted for reasons related to such conflict, as well as those deprived of their liberty or whose liberty is restricted after the conflict for the same reasons, shall enjoy the protection of Articles 5 and 6 until the end of such deprivation or restriction of liberty.

The ICRC Commentary states that the article uses the terms 'deprived of . . . liberty' and 'whose liberty has been restricted' to ensure that there is no gap in protection,[63] emphasizing that it covers 'all possible situations, from release subject to police supervision (e.g. house arrest or assigned residence), to imprisonment'.[64]

While there is no gap in its scope of application, AP II provides no explicit authority to detain, nor any procedural safeguards. The same is true for Articles 5 and 6. Article 5 explicitly concerns 'persons whose liberty has been restricted' and contains minimum rules which are an additional protection to the 'fundamental guarantees' contained in Article 4 AP II. According to the ICRC Commentary, the purpose of Article 5 is to ensure 'that conditions of detention for persons whose liberty has been restricted for reasons related to the conflict will be reasonable', and it contains an obligation to provide food, drinking water, and other necessities.[65] Article 6 concerns penal prosecution, and mostly contains rules related to fair trial, similar to those found in most human rights treaties.[66]

The fact that neither Common Article 3 nor AP II expressly authorizes internment, or contains any procedural safeguards, has become a source of contention.[67] Some argue that any legal basis for internment would have to be explicit. Another view, held by many states, and shared by the ICRC, is that international humanitarian law contains an inherent power to intern.[68] The latter position is based on the

[62] ibid Article 1.

[63] Sandoz, Swinarski, and Zimmermann (n 53) 1360.

[64] ibid.

[65] ibid 1384.

[66] See eg, International Covenant on Civil and Political Rights (adopted 16 December 1966, entered into force 23 March 1976) 999 UNTS 171, Article 14.

[67] For a more detailed discussion, see Hill-Cawthorne (n 3) 100–06.

[68] At the 32nd international conference (Geneva, 8–10 December 2015), the constituent associations of the Red Cross and Red Crescent approved a resolution by consensus according to which states have, in all forms of armed conflict, the power to detain. Strengthening international humanitarian law protecting persons deprived of their liberty (32IC/15/R1). See also J Pejic, 'Conflict Classification and the Law Applicable to Detention and the Use of Force' in Wilmshurst (n 14) 94.

fact that both Common Article 3 and AP II explicitly refer to detention or internment and that internment is a form of deprivation of liberty which is a common occurrence in armed conflict. Emphasis is further put on the fact that deprivation of liberty is not explicitly prohibited by international humanitarian law. Some also argue that since there is a legal basis to kill in non-international armed conflicts, there must also exist the lesser power to detain.[69]

The UK Government relied, inter alia, on the inherent power argument in the *Serdar Mohammed* case, concerning the detention by British forces of an Afghan national in Afghanistan in 2010. The inherent power claim was rejected at first instance and on appeal.[70] The majority of the Supreme Court likewise rejected the argument that either Common Article 3 or AP II provided an implicit legal basis for detention.[71] Whereas the majority did not find it necessary to express a comprehensive opinion on whether customary international law sanctions the detention of combatants in a non-international armed conflict, Lord Sumption, who gave the lead judgment, stated that the existence of a legal right in international law to detain must be found elsewhere.[72] Lord Reed, furthermore, thoroughly dealt with customary international law and concluded that:

> There appears to be a paucity of state practice which is supportive of the contention ... In those circumstances, I have not been persuaded that there exists at present either sufficient opinio juris or a sufficiently extensive and uniform practice to establish the suggested rule of customary international law.[73]

The fact that neither treaty nor customary international law authorize detention does not necessarily imply that detention in non-international armed conflicts is unlawful. Authority to detain must simply be found elsewhere. Often, this authority will be found in domestic law, either that of the detaining state or of the state on whose territory the detention occurs. But the authority cannot simply be assumed. In relation to the United Kingdom's military intervention in Iraq, for example, the High Court found that after the end of the occupation on 28 June 2004, the UK Government could not rely on Iraqi law as it provided no legal basis for the detention of Iraqi civilians by invading or occupying armed forces.[74]

[69] For an overview of the arguments, see Hill-Cawthorne (n 3) 104–05.
[70] Both the High Court of England and Wales and the Court of Appeal found that neither treaty nor customary law applicable to non-international armed conflict provide a legal basis for detention.
[71] *Secretary of State for Foreign and Commonwealth Affairs and another v Yunus Rahmatullah* (n 38).
[72] Lord Sumption, ibid 12–13.
[73] Lord Reed, ibid 12–13. 275. See also Lord Sumption 14.
[74] *Alseran and Others v Ministry of Defence* (n 13) 116.

The authorization to detain may also be contained in a United Nations Security Council resolution. The authorization does not have to be explicit but may be inferred from the common expression of 'all necessary measures'.[75] Importantly, human rights safeguards continue to apply. Thus, while a Security Council resolution may provide the necessary legal basis for the deprivation of liberty, it will not displace human rights law, unless explicitly stated. For European states, this means that the six permitted grounds for detention, set out in the European Convention of Human Rights, continue to apply.[76] The permitted grounds were formulated in relation to peacetime conditions and cannot be regarded as exhaustive in conditions for armed conflict. Even so, their main objective—to protect individuals from arbitrary detention—must be preserved. This objective may be preserved where the legal basis for detention, and the power to detain, are not exercisable on grounds which are unduly broad, opaque, or discretionary.[77] This requires that similar standards of protection are applied to those imposed by Articles 43 and 78 GC IV in international armed conflicts. Thus, in addition to the legal basis for detention, there needs to be an impartial body carrying out initial, and regular subsequent, reviews in accordance with a fair procedure.

4. Conclusion

While there is a clear legal basis, and fairly robust procedural rules, for detention in international armed conflict, only a very limited set of treaty rules regulates detention in non-international armed conflicts. Neither Common Article 3, AP II, or customary international law provide a legal basis for detention. The legal basis, procedural safeguards, and the rules concerning the treatment of detainees must therefore be found elsewhere. Often, the legal basis can be found in either domestic law or in an authorization by the Security Council. In both cases, international human rights law will play an important role in ensuring that the legal framework secures the basic rights of the persons deprived of their liberty. This state of affairs is largely the result of states' reluctance to develop the legal framework applicable to non-international armed conflicts. Notwithstanding the persistent advocacy of the ICRC and many scholars in favour of applying the same rules in both international and non-international armed conflicts, states have been reluctant to accept this

[75] See *Behrami and Behrami v France* and *Saramati v France, Germany and Norway* App no 71412/01 and 78166/01 (ECtHR, Grand Chamber Decision as to Admissibility, 2 May 2007) 124, 127; [2017] UKSC 2. See also D Fleck, *The Handbook of International Humanitarian Law* (2nd edn, OUP 2008) 25.03.

[76] Sub-paragraphs (a)–(f) of Article 5. On this issue, [2017] UKSC 2 (n 19), 60, 134–36, 164, 224 and *Al Jedda v United Kingdom* App no 27021/08 (ECtHR, Grand Chamber Judgment, 7 July 2011) 109–10.

[77] [2017] UKSC 2 (n 19) 63, 93, 164–67, 224.

conclusion. Their concern is that unless a special regime is devised for the latter, it would imply legal equality of the participants and the immunity of non-state actors in non-international armed conflicts. Regardless of the soundness of this concern, the consequence of states' reluctance to abolish the traditional distinction, as well as their unwillingness to develop new rules, has meant that human rights play an ever more important role in many multinational military operations.

9

An Exercise in Defragmentation

The Grand Chamber Judgment in *Hassan v UK*

Andreas von Arnauld

1. Exposition of the Case: Facts and Pertinent Legal Questions

On 20 March 2003, an international coalition, led by the United States, invaded Iraq. Major combat operations were declared complete on 1 May 2003. A week before that date, on 23 April, British soldiers searching for the applicant, Khadim Hassan, a general of the Al-Quds Army and official of the ruling Ba'ath Party, had entered his house in the City of Umm Qasr in South-eastern Iraq. There, they encountered the applicant's 22-year-old brother, Tarek Hassan, who was reported to have stood on the roof of the house with an AK-47 machine gun. Aware that British forces were searching for high-ranking party members, the applicant had gone into hiding together with his family and asked his brother and cousin to protect the house. Inside the house, the British soldiers seized a number of firearms and documents on the Ba'ath Party and the Al-Quds Army.

Tarek Hassan was arrested at 6.30 am and taken to Camp Bucca, jointly managed by British and US-American forces. According to the Memorandum of Arrangement (MoA), the British army was in control of detention and interrogation of all prisoners held in the Joint Forward Interrogation Team (JFIT). In other parts of the camp, guarding and escorting detainees fell within the authority of the US army. Every detainee was registered as a prisoner of war of either British or US forces. Tarek Hassan was assigned the registration number UK107276, designating him as having been captured by the British army.

Shortly after his arrival at Camp Bucca and again on 25 April, Tarek Hassan underwent the regular 'screening process'. As usual, British and US interrogation teams shared the work, Hassan being interviewed at first by US agents. The records show that he was neither seen as a security risk nor as a possible source of any intelligence value. Consequently, he was transferred to the civilian holding area at Camp Bucca. According to the United Kingdom's military database ('AP3-Ryan'), Hassan was released 'by coach' in Umm Qasr on 2 May 2003, though there is another entry recording 12 May as the date of his release. Having not been in contact with any family member since his arrest, Tarek Hassan was found dead on 1 September 2003 north of Baghdad, in the US-controlled part of Iraq. He had

Andreas von Arnauld, *An Exercise in Defragmentation* In *The 'Legal Pluriverse' Surrounding Multinational Military Operations*. Edited by Robin Geiß and Heike Krieger, Oxford University Press (2020).
DOI: 10.1093/oso/9780198842965.003.0010

eight bullet wounds from an AK-47 machine gun in his chest. According to his brother, his hands were tied with plastic wire as was usual practice with new arrivals at Camp Bucca.

Having ended his hiding, Khadim Hassan filed a suit before the High Court of England and Wales on 19 July 2007, seeking declarations in respect of breaches of his brother's rights under Articles 2, 3, and 5 of the European Convention on Human Rights (ECHR), financial compensation, and an order requiring the government to initiate an independent and public investigation into Tarek Hassan's fate. The claim was rejected on 25 February 2009[1] as the judge held that, according to the House of Lords' recent *Al-Skeini* judgment,[2] Tarek Hassan had not been within the United Kingdom's jurisdiction under Article 1 ECHR at any time. The applicant was advised that an appeal would have no prospect of success.

On 5 June 2009, Khaled Hassan filed a complaint against the United Kingdom before the European Court of Human Rights (ECtHR) (no 29750/09) under Article 34 ECHR. The applicant complained that his brother's arrest and detention were arbitrary and unlawful and lacking in procedural safeguards (Article 5(1), (2), (3), (4)), and that the UK authorities had failed to carry out an investigation into the circumstances of Tarek Hassan's detention, ill-treatment, and death (Articles 2, 3, and 5). The Fourth Section of the ECtHR decided to adjourn the examination of the application pending the *Al-Skeini v UK* case. After the decision of that case,[3] the Chamber communicated the application to the Government on 30 August 2011. On 4 June 2013, it decided to relinquish jurisdiction to the Grand Chamber which delivered its judgment on 16 September 2014.

The Grand Chamber summarily dismissed the complaint with respect to an alleged breach of a duty to investigate based on Articles 2 and 3 ECHR.[4] There had been no evidence to suggest any ill-treatment of Tarek Hassan during his stay in Camp Bucca nor had there been evidence that the UK authorities were in any way involved in his death which occurred four months after his detention and in a distant part of the country not controlled by British forces. Since it is up to the applicant to make a 'credible assertion'[5] of any such violation, there could hardly have been another decision at that point. The crucial legal questions therefore related to the alleged violation of Article 5 ECHR. Before being able to address that question (see section 4), however, the ECtHR had to deal with two preliminary objections raised by the government: whether the Convention applied extraterritorially in the

1 *Hassan v Secretary of State for Defence* [2009] EWHC 309 (Admin).

2 *Al-Skeini and Others v Secretary of State for Defence* [2007] UKHL 26.

3 *Al-Skeini and Others v UK* App no 55721/07 (ECtHR, Grand Chamber Judgment, 7 July 2011).

4 *Hassan v UK* App no 29750/09 (ECtHR, Grand Chamber Judgment, 16 September 2014).

5 The Court here cites *Labita v Italy* App no 26772/95 (ECtHR, Grand Chamber Judgement, 6 April 2000) para 131; *Members of the Gldani Congregation of Jehovah's Witnesses v Georgia* App no 71156/01 (ECtHR, Judgement, 3 May 2007) para 97.

case at hand (see section 2), and whether the ECHR is in general superseded by international humanitarian law (IHL) in times of armed conflict (see section 3).

2. Extraterritorial Application of the ECHR?

2.1 Affirmation of the *Al-Skeini v UK* principles

Given the fact that the proceedings had been adjourned to await the decision in the *Al-Skeini* case, it comes as no surprise that, in *Hassan*, the Grand Chamber affirmed the principles set out in its own 2011 judgment by incorporating a *verbatim* quotation of paragraphs 130 to 142 of *Al-Skeini*.[6] The starting point is the rule according to which a contracting state's 'jurisdiction' giving rise to its obligations under Article 1 ECHR is primarily territorial. Thus, only in exceptional cases are states bound to respect the ECHR extraterritorially.[7] These cases, as enumerated in *Al-Skeini* and upheld in *Hassan*, are:

(1) State agent authority and control, namely in the following cases: (1.1) acts of diplomatic and consular agents; (1.2) performance of executive or judicial functions on the territory of another state with the consent of that state; (1.3) exercise of physical power and control over a person (custody and detention cases).
(2) Effective control over an area: When, as a consequence of military action, a contracting state effectively controls an area outside its own territory it assumes responsibility to secure within that area the entire range of ECHR rights; it is not necessary to determine whether the contracting state exercises detailed control over acts of the subordinate local administration (thus, the Court refers to a standard of an effective overall control). Whether effective control exists is said to be a matter of fact.
(3) The Convention legal space ('espace juridique'): In case of a military occupation of the territory of one contracting state by the armed forces of another, 'the occupying State should in principle be held accountable under the Convention for breaches of human rights within the occupied territory, because to hold otherwise would be to deprive the population of that territory of the rights and freedoms hitherto enjoyed and would result in a "vacuum" of protection within the "Convention legal space"'.[8] This criterion adds nothing

[6] *Hassan v UK* (n 4) para 74.
[7] *Banković and Others v Belgium and Others* App no 52207/99 (ECtHR, Grand Chamber Judgment, 12 December 2001) paras 61, 66, 67.
[8] *Al-Skeini v UK* (n 3) para 142.

> to the previous one and actually is only a thinly disguised attempt to correct the problematic use of the 'espace juridique' trope in *Banković*.[9]

While *Al-Skeini* certainly meant an improvement over the flawed *Banković* decision, the Court should preferably have adopted a functional approach,[10] differentiating instead between negative, positive, and procedural obligations: concerning negative obligations (the prohibition of arbitrary killing), these are easy to apply in an extraterritorial context as well; concerning positive obligations (eg the obligation to protect life), these are, first, limited by the factual possibilities and, secondly, have to be harmonized under international law with the sovereign rights of the territorial state; concerning procedural guarantees (eg in the case of deprivation of liberty), these have to have a legal basis and must in essence confirm to the exigencies of the respective ECHR right.[11]

2.2 Effective control over an area?

The ECtHR first dealt with the question whether the United Kingdom had effective control over South East Iraq during the period of Tarek Hassan's detention.[12] In *Al-Skeini*, the Grand Chamber had caused some irritation when it based jurisdiction on the fact that the British Government had formally accepted the status of an occupying power—which did not fit under any of those cases just listed.[13] If only by a mere *dictum*, the *Hassan* judgment might shed some light on that issue. Referring to *Al-Skeini*, the ECtHR here states that the United Kingdom's role as an occupying power made it unnecessary then to determine 'whether jurisdiction also arose on the ground that the United Kingdom was in effective military control of South East Iraq during that period'.[14] This clearly points to an additional criterion for an extraterritorial reach of the Convention which might be dubbed as *de jure* control (as opposed to the *de facto* effective control criterion). If this really is a separate criterion (as the 'also' suggests) or if it only leads to shifting the standard of proof whether the control has to be seen as effective, might still not have been decided yet. In the case of Tarek Hassan, the ECtHR noted that he was detained

[9] M Milanovic, '*Al-Skeini* and *Al-Jedda* in Strasbourg' (2012) 23 European Journal of International Law 121, 129.

[10] *Al-Skeini v UK* (n 3) concurring opinion of J Bonello, paras 4–20.

[11] For a closer analysis A von Arnauld, 'Das (Menschen-)Recht im Auslandseinsatz: Rechtsgrundlagen zum Schutz von Grund- und Menschenrechten' in D Weingärtner (ed), *Streitkräfte und Menschenrechte* (Nomos 2008) 61; A von Arnauld, 'Rechtsbindungen im Auslandseinsatz: Elemente einer Kollisionsrechtsordnung für militärische und polizeiliche Auslandseinsätze' (2010–11) 2 Jahrbuch Öffentliche Sicherheit 77; M Milanovic, *Extraterritorial Application of Human Rights Treaties: Law, Principles, and Policy* (OUP 2011) 209–22.

[12] *Hassan v UK* (n 4) para 75.

[13] cf only Milanovic (n 9) 129–31.

[14] *Hassan v UK* (n 4) para 75.

before 1 May 2003 when combat operations had been declared complete and the United Kingdom had assumed authority for the maintenance of security in the area. Instead of determining, however, whether the United Kingdom had in fact effective control over the area around Umm Qasr (already) by that time, it left the question open in favour of another basis for British jurisdiction over Tarek Hassan.

2.3 Exercise of physical power and control?

The *Hassan* case also bears some interest for further specifying the 'physical power and control' criterion in the context of multinational operations. Little needs to be said about Tarek Hassan being within the physical power and control of the United Kingdom during the time from his arrest by British soldiers until his arrival at Camp Bucca.[15] The question of jurisdiction gets more complex, however, concerning the proceedings inside the camp. Here, the British Government argued with a transferral of custody to the United States. According to Article 12(2) and (3) of the Third Geneva Convention (GC III), in such a case the primary responsibility shifts from the detaining power to the accepting power. The ECtHR rejected that line of reasoning, chiefly based on the fact that Tarek Hassan had been admitted to the camp as a United Kingdom prisoner.[16] According to the MoA, the United Kingdom bore the responsibility for the classification of its detainees under GC III and IV and for deciding whether they should be released. Since the decision to keep Hassan in or release him from detention remained with the United Kingdom alone, the Court discounted 'certain operational aspects relating to Tarek Hassan's detention at Camp Bucca [. . .] transferred to United States forces, in particular the tasks of escorting him to and from the JFIT compound and guarding him elsewhere in the Camp'. Given that US authority over those other parts of the camp were not seen as sufficient reason for a shift of responsibility from the United Kingdom to the United States, the additional reference to the JFIT compound having been entirely controlled by United Kingdom forces does not seem to carry decisive weight for assigning jurisdiction to the United Kingdom. That the ECtHR mentioned it nevertheless might open up a future path leading to a shared responsibility[17] for prisoners of war in a detention facility run jointly by several partner nations.

[15] ibid paras 76–77.

[16] ibid para 78.

[17] See in general A Nollkaemper and I Plakokefalos (eds), *Principles of Shared Responsibility in International Law: An Appraisal of the State of the Art* (CUP 2014). Specifically, on the problem of plurinational forces, see C Ahlborn, 'To Share or Not to Share? The Allocation of Responsibility between International Organizations and their Member States' (2014) 88(3–4) Journal of International Peace and Organization: Friedens-Warte 45.

3. Does International Humanitarian Law Supersede the ECHR?

A general line of argument proposed by the British Government was that the ECHR did not apply in times of armed conflict, at least not in the active hostilities phase of an international armed conflict, referring to the notion of *lex specialis*.[18] Since Article 15 ECHR allows for limited derogations in times of 'war or other public emergency threatening the life of the nation', the Court decided to deal with the derogation issue first (see section 3.1) before entering into a discussion of the general relationship between the ECHR and IHL (see section 3.2).

3.1 The role of derogations: Article 15 ECHR

Concerning Article 15 ECHR, neither the United Kingdom nor any other contracting state has ever lodged a declaration of derogation regarding the deployment of forces abroad. The dissenters on the bench, favouring a strict reading of the Convention, concluded therefore that the United Kingdom should be held accountable by the standards of the ECHR alone and to the full extent:[19] Article 15 ECHR gives the state parties a right to derogate to a certain extent from their treaty obligations during armed conflict; if a state does not make use of that option it remains fully bound by the Convention. The Court's majority, however, intended to take into account the context of armed conflict nevertheless. To arrive at a more flexible solution, it chose to deconstruct Article 15 ECHR.

For this, the judges turned to general international law, namely to Article 31(3)(b) of the Vienna Convention on the Law of Treaties (VCLT). According to this provision, in interpreting a treaty clause it shall be taken into account 'any subsequent practice in the application of the treaty which establishes the agreement of the parties regarding its interpretation'. At first, the Court emphasizes that 'a consistent practice on the part of the High Contracting Parties, subsequent to their ratification of the Convention, could be taken as establishing their agreement not only as regards interpretation but even to modify the text of the Convention'.[20] It then goes on noting that none of the contracting states has ever derogated from its obligations under Article 5 in order to detain persons on the basis of GC III and IV during international armed conflicts. Derogations relating to Article 5 have so far only concerned situations of internal conflicts or terrorist threats.[21] After having

[18] See, eg, *Hassan v UK* (n 4) para 76.

[19] *Hassan v UK* (n 4) partly dissenting opinion of J Spano, joined by Nicolaou, Bianku, and Kalaydjieva.

[20] *Hassan v UK* (n 4) para 101.

[21] See, eg, *Brannigan and McBride v UK* App nos 14553/89 and 14554/89 (ECtHR, Judgment, 25 May 1993); *Aksoy v Turkey* App no 21987/93 (ECtHR, Judgment, 18 December 1996); *A and Others v UK* App no 3455/05 (ECtHR, Grand Chamber Judgment, 19 February 2009).

reassured itself that state practice under the derogation clause in the International Covenant on Civil and Political Rights (ICCPR) (Article 4) is the same, the Grand Chamber finds a general agreement between the contracting parties that it is not necessary to formally derogate from a state's ECHR obligations in situations of international armed conflict for 'taking account of the context and the provisions of international humanitarian law'.[22]

Subsequent practice of the state parties to a treaty and its relationship to the interpretation of that treaty is a tricky issue. It is one of the leftovers from the ILC's work in preparation of the 1969 VCLT and it has been taken up since by the Commission.[23] Though one should not expect of a court that has to decide a case the same degree of diligence as the ILC brings to the matter, one might have expected the ECtHR to refer to the most recent Commission reports and opinions—especially when the judgment is based expressly on Article 31(3)(b) VCLT.[24] Without going into detail, there seems to be some agreement that 'subsequent practice' in the sense of that provision should fulfil three conditions:[25] 'it should be a i) practice of the member states, ii) in the application of the treaty, iii) which establishes the agreement of the parties'.[26] The first questions that turn up might still be solved without need for extravagance: depending on the circumstances, omissions can also be seen as relevant state practice, and state practice under Article 31(3)(b) VCLT does not have to include all parties to the treaty, as long as 'it is "accepted" by those parties not engaged in the practice'.[27]

More taxing, however, is to determine that the practice reflects an application of the treaty and establishes a tacit agreement of the parties. Without discussing other possible interpretations, the Court assumed that the practice of not lodging declarations under Article 15 generated a tacit agreement that no formal derogation was necessary for introducing IHL into the language game of the ECHR for external military operations. This, however, is far from obvious: as the Grand Chamber's dissenters point out, the United Kingdom—relying on the ECtHR's own *Banković* decision—used to deny the extraterritorial applicability of the ECHR altogether. Under these premises, it would have been nothing less than contradictory

[22] *Hassan v UK* (n 4) para 103.

[23] See ILC, Draft conclusions on subsequent agreements and subsequent practice in relation to the interpretation of treaties, with commentaries (20 December 2018, A/RES/73/202, Annex). At the time of the ECtHR's decision, the ILC's rapporteur had already presented two reports: G Nolte, 'First report on subsequent agreements and subsequent practice in relation to treaty interpretation' (19 March 2013) UN Doc A/CN.4/660; 'Second report on subsequent agreements and subsequent practice in relation to the interpretation of treaties' (26 March 2014) UN Doc A/CN.4/671.

[24] L Hill-Cawthorne, 'The Grand Chamber Judgment in Hassan v UK' (*EJIL: Talk!*, 16 September 2014) <http://www.ejiltalk.org/the-grand-chamber-judgment-in-hassan-v-uk/>; all URLs accessed 27 December 2018; L Crema, 'Subsequent Practice in Hassan v United Kingdom: When Things Seem to go Wrong in the Life of a Living Instrument' (2015) 15 Questions of International Law Zoom-in 3, 7–8.

[25] Nolte, 'First report' (n 23) paras 91–118; in greater detail Nolte, 'Second report' (n 23).

[26] Crema (n 24) 9 with further references.

[27] Nolte, 'Second report' (n 23) para 60; ILC, 'Draft conclusions' (n 23) Conclusion 10(2) with comment 12.

to declare derogation from any ECHR obligation regarding the deployment of forces abroad. It would therefore not have seemed far-fetched to assume that the British Government (as well as other governments) did not declare derogation because it held that extraterritorial military operations were outside the scope of the ECHR.[28] The Grand Chamber's majority was certainly well aware of this possible (and indeed more realistic) interpretation. This is probably why they included the irksome[29] reference to state practice under Article 4 ICCPR. While the ECtHR itself, by issuing *Banković*, had caused irritation about the territorial scope of the ECHR, the extraterritorial reach of the ICCPR had been made quite clear by the ICJ before.[30] Thus, by assuming the same motives for the lack of derogation under both human rights treaties,[31] the Grand Chamber felt entitled to infer from that practice the common consensus they were looking for. Even if one were prepared to accept this construction, the problem remains that neither ICCPR nor ECHR *oblige* contracting states to derogate. So not lodging a derogation might express a political choice and not a principled position on whether or not a derogation has to be declared.[32]

Another critical point is the modification of treaties by way of subsequent practice. Again, this is a tricky issue under Article 31(3)(b) VCLT. In his second report on the subject, available to the ECtHR when deciding *Hassan*, ILC rapporteur Nolte stated that such a tacit modification by subsequent practice 'is not to be presumed'.[33] But this, it seems, is exactly what the Grand Chamber did here. Furthermore, in the context of human rights law, such an argument is not without danger when it comes to lowering the standards of human rights protection.[34] The precedent cited by the Grand Chamber in this respect—*Soehring, Öcalan,*

[28] *Hassan v UK* (n 4) dissenting opinion of J Spano and others (n 19) para 12. See also E Bjorge, 'What is Living and What is Dead in the European Convention on Human Rights? A Comment on *Hassan v United Kingdom*' (2015) 15 QIL Zoom-in 23, 35.

[29] Critical Crema, 'Subsequent Practice' (n 24) 10, as that practice does not relate to the parties of the ECHR, cf Article 31(3) VCLT.

[30] *Legal Consequences of the Construction of a Wall in the Occupied Palestinian Territory* (Advisory Opinion) [2004] ICJ Rep 178, para 106; *Armed Activities on the Territory of the Congo (Democratic Republic of the Congo v Uganda)* (Judgment) [2005] ICJ Rep 168, paras 215–16.

[31] Though this seems plausible enough at first sight one must not disregard procedural context: actions brought against a contracting state are much more likely under the ECHR (individual complaint procedure, enforcement of ECHR through the national judiciary) than under the ICCPR which could afford a different explanation for the lack of practice under Article 4 ICCPR.

[32] Crema, 'Subsequent Practice' (n 24) 9–10; C De Koker, '*Hassan v United Kingdom*: The Interaction of Human Rights Law and International Humanitarian Law with Regard to the Deprivation of Liberty in Armed Conflicts' (2015) 31(81) Utrecht Journal of International and European Law 90, 94.

[33] Nolte, 'Second report' (n 23) para 142. cf also ILC, 'Draft conclusions' (n 23), Conclusion 7(3): 'It is presumed that the parties to a treaty, by ... a practice in the application of the treaty, intend to interpret the treaty, not to amend or to modify it. The possibility of amending or modifying a treaty by subsequent practice of the parties has not been generally recognized.'

[34] For a closer analysis Crema, 'Subsequent Practice' (n 24) 19–21. See in general JE Alvarez, 'Limits of Change by Way of Subsequent Agreements and Practice' in G Nolte (ed), *Treaties and Subsequent Practice* (OUP 2013) 123, 126: 'where a treaty creates a third party beneficiary ... as in the case of human rights treaties ... the capacity for the states parties to modify their treaty through practice faces additional constraints'.

Al-Sadoon[35]—all related to an extension of human rights obligations.[36] While there might be no fundamental principle pressing for an ever expanding human rights jurisprudence, it is still not without danger to take the opposite direction: a consensus-based derogation from express human rights obligations. As long as this line of argument can be confined to the quite special case of Article 15 ECHR, however, Pandora's box might yet be closed again.

3.2 Reconstructing ECHR obligations in international armed conflict

In line with its reasoning on the derogation issue, the Court also rejects any 'either/ or' solution regarding the applicable substantive standards. '[C]onsistently with the case-law of the International Court of Justice, the Court considers that, even in situations of international armed conflict, the safeguards under the Convention continue to apply, albeit interpreted against the background of the provisions of international humanitarian law'.[37] As point of reference, the ECtHR chooses the VCLT's 'de-fragmentation clause',[38] Article 31(3)(c), according to which account shall be taken of 'any relevant rules of international law applicable in the relations between the parties'.[39] The passage[40] which is central to the Court's reasoning deserves to be quoted at length since it refers to the very essence of the relationship of IHL and human rights law as conceived by the Grand Chamber:

> The four Geneva Conventions of 1949, intended to mitigate the horrors of war, were drafted in parallel to the European Convention on Human Rights and enjoy universal ratification. The provisions in the Third and Fourth Geneva Conventions relating to internment, at issue in the present application, were designed to protect captured combatants and civilians who pose a security threat. The Court has already held that Article 2 of the Convention should 'be interpreted in so far as

[35] *Soering v UK* App no 14038/88 (ECtHR, Judgement, 7 July 1989) paras 102–03; *Öcalan v Turkey* App no 46221/99 (ECtHR, Grand Chamber Judgment, 12 May 2005) paras 162–65; *Al-Saadoon and Mufdhi v UK* App no 61498/08 (ECtHR, Judgment, 2 March 2010) para 120.

[36] *Hassan v UK* (n 4) dissenting opinion of J Spano and others (n 19) para 13. See also Crema, 'Subsequent Practice' (n 24) 15–16; Bjorge (n 28) 25–26, points, however, to *Mangouras v Spain* App no 12050/04 (ECtHR, Judgment, 28 September 2010) paras 86–89 as precedent.

[37] *Hassan v UK* (n 4) para 104.

[38] See M Koskenniemi, 'Fragmentation of International. Law: Difficulties Arising from the Diversification and Expansion of International Law: Report of the Study Group of the International Law Commission' (13 April 2006) UN Doc A/CN.4/L.682, paras 410–80.

[39] For recourse to that provision in the previous case law of the ECtHR, see J d'Aspremont, 'Articulating International Human Rights and International Humanitarian Law: Conciliatory Interpretation Under the Guise of Conflict of Norms-Resolution' in M Fitzmaurice and P Merkouris (eds), *The Interpretation and Application of the European Convention of Human Rights* (Martinus Nijhoff 2013) 3, 12–14.

[40] *Hassan v UK* (n 4) para 102.

> possible in light of the general principles of international law, including the rules of international humanitarian law which play an indispensable and universally-accepted role in mitigating the savagery and inhumanity of armed conflict' (see *Varnava and Others v. Turkey* [GC], nos. 16064/90, 16065/90, 16066/90, 16068/90, 16069/90, 16070/90, 16071/90, 16072/90 and 16073/90, § 185, ECHR 2009), and it considers that these observations apply equally in relation to Article 5. Moreover, the International Court of Justice has held that the protection offered by human rights conventions and that offered by international humanitarian law co-exist in situations of armed conflict [...]. [...] The Court must endeavour to interpret and apply the Convention in a manner which is consistent with the framework under international law delineated by the International Court of Justice.

The ECtHR especially rejects the idea proposed by the British Government that the ECHR should be generally inapplicable in international armed conflict as long as the active hostilities have not come to an end.[41] This is especially convincing since any such differentiation according to the phases of a conflict would negate the continued relevance of human rights in armed conflict in general. That its 'defragmentation approach' serves in a way as a substitute for the derogation according to Article 15 ECHR becomes palpable when the Grand Chamber declares that it will only interpret provisions of the ECHR in the light of applicable IHL rules if this is specifically pleaded by the respondent state: 'It is not for the Court to assume that a State intends to modify the commitments which it has undertaken by ratifying the Convention in the absence of a clear indication to that effect.'[42]

4. Violation of Article 5(1), (2), (3), and (4) ECHR?

Having established in principle that Article 5 ECHR has to be applied in light of the context and legal framework of international armed conflict, the ECtHR addresses the specific legal questions raised by the application: whether Tarek Hassan's detention was in conformity with the grounds for deprivation of liberty spelled out in Article 5(1) (see section 4.1) and whether the procedural safeguards as set out in Article 5(2)–(4) were met (see section 4.2).

4.1 IHL detention and Article 5(1) ECHR

The Grand Chamber wisely chose not to squeeze deprivations of liberty according to IHL (detention, prisoner of war) into the list of grounds of permissible detention

41 ibid para 77.
42 ibid para 107.

in Article 5(1) ECHR. It briefly touches upon covering these cases by Article 5(1)(c) (pretrial and preventive detention), but convincingly rejects that line of reasoning: security internment under Article 42, 78 GC IV does not need to have any correlation to the suspicion of having committed an offence or risk of the commission of a criminal offence; and in the case of prisoners of war, such an interpretation would even disregard the combatant privilege.[43]

With the interim result that Tarek Hassan's detention could not be based on any of the grounds listed in Article 5(1) ECHR, the Grand Chamber had two possibilities: either to declare his detention illegal for that reason or to admit further grounds for the deprivation of liberty on the basis of IHL. The majority chose the latter path, probably because it foresaw some irritation should detentions firmly established under GC III and GC IV be declared as a violation of Article 5 ECHR for lack of an express mention alone.[44] While it had previously held that the grounds listed in Article 5(1) ECHR are exhaustive,[45] the ECtHR now openly states that '[b]y reason of the co-existence of the safeguards provided by international humanitarian law and by the Convention in time of armed conflict, the grounds of permitted deprivation of liberty set out in subparagraphs (a) to (f) of that provision should be accommodated, as far as possible, with the taking of prisoners of war and the detention of civilians who pose a risk to security under the Third and Fourth Geneva Conventions',[46] thus actually admitting further grounds on the basis of IHL.

The Court expressly limits its acceptance of additional grounds for the deprivation of liberty to those contained in GC III and IV for international armed conflicts.[47] There was no need in this case to address the thorny issue of detention in non-international armed conflict.[48] The Court did, however, recall its established jurisprudence that in peacetime—a declaration of derogation under Article 15 notwithstanding—internment or preventive detention without an intention to bring criminal charges within a reasonable time are prohibited.[49] While one might

[43] ibid para 97.

[44] cf the telling reference to 'accepted features of international humanitarian law' in *Hassan v UK* (n 4) para 104.

[45] *Ireland v UK* App no 5310/71 (ECtHR, Judgment, 18 January 1978) para 194; *Saadi v UK* App no 13229/03 (ECtHR, Judgment, 29 January 2008) para 43; *A and Others v UK* (n 21) paras 162–63. Concerning detention by the military abroad during armed conflict, see *Al-Jedda v UK* App no 27021/08 (ECtHR, Grand Chamber Judgment, 7 July 2011) paras 99–100.

[46] *Hassan v UK* (n 4) para 104.

[47] ibid.

[48] For an in-depth study on this topic see E Crawford, *The Treatment of Combatants and Insurgents under the Law of Armed Conflict* (OUP 2010). See also M Sassòli, 'Legal Framework for Detention by States in Non-International Armed Conflict' in S Kolanowski (ed), *Detention in Armed Conflicts: Proceedings of the Bruges Colloquium, 16–17 October 2014* (College of Europe/ICRC 2015) 51. G Rose (ed), *Detention of Non-State Actors Engaged in Hostilities: The Future Law* (Brill 2016).

[49] *Hassan v UK* (n 4) paras 97, 104. Citing, among others, *Lawless v Ireland (no 3)* App no 332/57 (ECtHR, Judgment, 1 July 1961) paras 13–14; *Ireland v UK* (n 45) para 196; *Al-Jedda v UK* (n 45) para 100.

read this reference to Article 15 as a preference to cover non-international armed conflicts via a formal derogation,[50] this might only refer to internal conflicts, whether they pass the threshold of Article 1(2) of the Second Additional Protocol of 1977 (AP II) or not. How to deal with the involvement of contracting states in non-international armed conflicts in third states remains an open question.

Admitting these further grounds for deprivation of liberty to the list in Article 5(1) ECHR is probably the most controversial part of the judgment. The dissenters clearly oppose such a deviation from a wording that strongly suggests an exhaustive character ('No one shall be deprived of his liberty save in the following cases').[51] They criticize the majority for their 'method of "accommodation"' whose 'scope is ambiguous and its content wholly uncertain, at least as a legitimate method of interpretation of a legal text'.[52] They advocate instead for a formal derogation as the only way to allow for detentions on the basis of GC IV under the regime of the ECHR. For obvious reasons, the approach chosen by the majority of the Grand Chamber has been called 'an exercise in *contra legem* interpretation'.[53]

Less controversial are the other 'accommodations' made by the Grand Chamber: in order to be 'lawful' in the sense of Article 5(1) ECHR, the detention must comply with the rules of IHL and has to be 'in keeping with the fundamental purpose of [Article 5(1)], which is to protect the individual from arbitrariness'.[54] Through this, the Court claims for itself to review detention cases according to IHL rules, but also reserves a right to interpret those rules in light of the principle object and purpose of Article 5(1) ECHR.[55] Applying these standards to the case, the Court judged Tarek Hassan's detention as lawful. Having stood with a machine gun on the roof of a house, in which weapons and documents of value for military intelligence were found, gave the United Kingdom authorities sufficient 'reason to believe that he might be either a person who could be detained as a prisoner of war or whose internment was necessary for imperative reasons of security, both of which provided a legitimate ground for capture and detention (see Articles 4A and 21 of the Third Geneva Convention and Articles 42 and 78 of the Fourth Geneva Convention . . .)'.[56]

[50] Insofar in line with J Leggatt in *Serdar Mohammed and Others v Secretary of State for Defence* [2014] EWHC 1369 (QB) paras 155–57, 284. This judgment was unconvincingly overturned by *Mohammed and Others v Secretary of State for Defence and Others* [2015] EWCA Civ 843, paras 123, 162 on the basis of extending the ECtHR's *Hassan* judgment to non-international armed conflicts and UN-mandated operations.

[51] *Hassan v UK* (n 4) dissenting opinion of J Spano and others (n 19) paras 5, 16, 18.

[52] ibid para 18.

[53] S Borelli, '*Jaloud v Netherlands* and *Hassan v United Kingdom*: Time for a Principled Approach in the Application of the ECHR to Military Action Abroad' (2015) 16 QIL Zoom-in 25, 39.

[54] *Hassan v UK* (n 4) para 105.

[55] Concurring Crema, 'Subsequent practice' (n 24) 21–22.

[56] *Hassan v UK* (n 4) para 109.

4.2 Procedural safeguards

Concerning procedural safeguards, the Grand Chamber uses Article 5(2) and (4) ECHR for raising the standards of protection as laid down in Articles 43 and 78 GC IV.[57] While admitting that—as different from peacetime[58]—in an international armed conflict the 'competent body' (Articles 43, 78 GC IV) for reviewing the lawfulness of a detention does not need to be a 'court' in the strict sense of Article 5(4) ECHR, the Grand Chamber nevertheless demands that this body 'should provide sufficient guarantees of impartiality and fair procedure to protect against arbitrariness'.[59] It further complements the IHL duty to subject a detainee 'to periodical review, if possible every six months' by a requirement taken from Article 5(2) ECHR that 'the first review should take place shortly after the person is taken into detention, with subsequent reviews at frequent intervals, to ensure that any person who does not fall into one of the categories subject to internment under international humanitarian law is released without undue delay'.[60]

In the case of Tarek Hassan, the ECtHR saw no violation of these procedural safeguards:[61] he had been subjected to a first interview on the day of his arrival at Camp Bucca, and since the screening had led to his being cleared for release the Court took the outcome as an indication for the fairness of that process. The Court also found that Hassan had been released 'shortly thereafter', that is, after his clearance. Since at least a week passed between those two dates (the second interview on 25 April, the release probably on 2 May), one might have some doubts about Hassan having been released without undue delay; but clearly the Court did not want to bother with an arguably only minor infraction, especially given the somewhat unreliable dates as recorded in AP3-Ryan. Interestingly, the Grand Chamber did not apply Article 5(3) ECHR to the case 'since Tarek Hassan was not detained in accordance with the provisions of paragraph 1(c) of Article 5'.[62] Mentioning it, however, shows that the Court would probably apply that provision insofar as a deprivation of liberty under IHL should be based on charges of a criminal offence (see especially Chapter III GC III, Article 68 GC IV).

Unsurprisingly, the dissenters could not support the 'reading down'[63] of Article 5(4) ECHR from a 'court' to a 'competent body' without express derogation. Furthermore, they emphasized the difference in conception between deprivations of liberty according to Article 5(1) ECHR on the one hand and IHL detention and prisoner of war status on the other.[64] While a review by a 'competent tribunal' is

[57] Hill-Cawthorne (n 24): 'symbiotic' approach.

[58] See, in this context, *Reinprecht v Austria* App no 67175/01 (ECtHR, Judgment, 15 November 2005) para 31.

[59] *Hassan v UK* (n 4) para 106.

[60] ibid.

[61] ibid para 109.

[62] ibid para 106.

[63] Hill-Cawthorne (n 24).

[64] *Hassan v UK* (n 4) dissenting opinion of J Spano and others (n 19) para 5.

only demanded according to Article 5(3) GC III for determining the status, a prisoner of war will be regularly deprived of liberty until the end of hostilities without any further review of his detention. And though in the case of civilians interned for security reasons there is a right to periodic review, they might still remain interned indefinitely as long as their detention remains and is considered 'imperative' for the security of the detaining power (Articles 42, 78 GC IV). For reasons of conceptual clarity, it might have been welcome had the Grand Chamber taken the pain to address these questions;[65] the *Hassan* case, however, did not beg them. Furthermore, had a derogation been formally declared these questions would also have posed themselves to the dissenters. How far human rights obligations derived from Article 5 ECHR can modify the traditional institutions of prisoner of war status and of internment in armed conflict is still open to further development and discussion.

5. Too Bold a Step Forward: Attempting a Final Assessment

The Grand Chamber's *Hassan* judgment is a landmark decision with flaws. It is certainly not the first case in which the ECtHR dealt with situations of armed conflict. However, in previous cases the Court decided exclusively on the basis of the substantive ECHR law without dealing with its relation to IHL.[66] One could even see *Banković* as an attempt to avoid the pitfalls of that complex relationship, especially when it comes to military targeting and collateral damage. There, instead of dealing with how to reconcile the different rationales of IHL and human rights law with respect to the right to life, the Court instead opted for restricting the territorial scope of the ECHR altogether. Bearing this overcautious track-record concerning extraterritorial military action of the contracting states in mind, *Hassan* certainly is a bold step forward.[67]

[65] Hill-Cawthorne (n 24).

[66] Borelli (n 53) 28, calls this a 'self-contained approach'. For a closer analysis, see C Droege and L Arimatsu, 'The European Convention on Human Rights and International Humanitarian Law: Conference Report' (2009) 12 Yearbook of International Humanitarian Law 435; A Gioia, 'The Role of the European Court of Human Rights in Monitoring Compliance with Humanitarian Law in Armed Conflict' in O Ben-Naftali (ed), *International Humanitarian Law and International Human Rights Law: Pas de Deux* (OUP 2011) 201; L Moir, 'The European Court of Human Rights and International Humanitarian Law' in R Kolb and G Gaggioli (eds), *Research Handbook on Human Rights and Humanitarian Law* (Edward Elgar 2013) 480.

[67] De Koker (n 32) 93.

5.1 Making it explicit: a plea for derogation

However, the majority did make some rather unfortunate choices. As has been discussed in some detail earlier, the deconstruction of Article 15 ECHR on the basis of subsequent practice does not meet the required standards under Article 31(3)(b) VCLT. Ironically, an easier way to get around the missing derogation could have been to stick to the letter of Article 15. According to that provision, derogations can be declared in the case of 'war or other public emergency threatening the life of the nation'. As the words 'or other' make clear, the *ratio* behind the derogation rule is therefore a threat to the life of the nation, a situation in which public order in a contracting state cannot be upheld without recourse to more robust measures. While such a threat can certainly exist in times of armed conflicts on the territory of a contracting state, the life of the British nation at least was hardly threatened in Southeast Iraq in 2003.[68]

Still, there are some general doubts about any solution circumventing a declaration of derogation. Such a narrow reading might observe the letter of the clause, but perhaps not its spirit. When the Convention was drafted, the extent and variety of external military action of the contracting states could not have been foreseen—neither could the extent to which the ECHR would apply to situations abroad. Thus, it seems reasonable also to extend the possibility to derogate from ECHR obligations extraterritorially.[69] Especially when a Convention state exercises *de facto* control over a territory and its inhabitants, the same situation might appear which Article 15 ECHR describes.[70] That the 'nation' in this case is another state's population should not make any difference: Article 15 relates to the actual Convention obligations. Such an extraterritorial extension of Article 15 ECHR must not be regarded as a means to reduce respect for human rights. Derogation presupposes a state of public emergency also in the case of external military action, and it is limited to the exigencies of the situation. What is more, by opening up a way to further reconcile ECHR obligations with the situational constraints in extraterritorial military operations, it could promote the acceptance of and respect for human rights in such situations.[71] Another advantage of the dissenters' approach is that it

[68] cf *Al-Jedda v Secretary of State for Defence* [2007] UKHL 58 [38] (Lord Bingham): '[i]t is hard to think that these conditions could ever be met when a state had chosen to conduct an overseas peace-keeping operation, however dangerous the conditions, from which it could withdraw'. Also doubtful J Pejic, 'The European Court of Human Rights' *Al-Jedda* Judgment: The Oversight of International Humanitarian Law' (2011) 93 International Review of the Red Cross 837, 850.

[69] M Sassòli, 'The Role of Human Rights and International Humanitarian Law in New Types of Armed Conflicts' in O Ben-Naftali (ed), *International Humanitarian Law and International Human Rights Law* (OUP 2011) 66; K Mujezinovic Larsen, *The Human Rights Treaty Obligations of Peacekeepers* (CUP 2012) 308–09; Crema, 'Subsequent Practice' (n 24) 21–22; Bjorge (n 28) 26–27; M Milanovic, 'Extraterritorial Derogations from Human Rights Treaties in Armed Conflict' in N Butha (ed), *The Frontiers of Human Rights: Extraterritoriality and its Challenges* (OUP 2016) 55, 71.

[70] Z Bohrer, 'Human Rights vs Humanitarian Law or Rights vs Obligations: Reflections Following the Rulings in *Hassan* and *Jaloud*' (2015) 16 QIL Zoom-in 5, 13–14.

[71] For a more detailed analysis, cf Milanovic (n 69).

is not necessary to distinguish between international and non-international armed conflicts in order to decide whether a derogation is needed or not.[72]

Thus, the approach favoured by the dissenters on the bench seems to be preferable.[73] It has the advantage of greater transparency and clarity—and it fits more smoothly into the previous jurisprudence of the ECtHR.[74] As long as no derogation has been declared, external military action of the contracting states will be reviewed against the guarantees of the ECHR alone; the existence of an armed conflict as such is of no relevance, though in assessing the necessity and proportionality of measures taken, the factual situation will certainly have to be taken into account as usual.[75] Only when a formal derogation has been lodged, the ECtHR will have regard to relevant provisions of IHL and accordingly modify the conventional obligations, since according to Article 15 ECHR derogations are only allowed 'to the extent strictly required by the exigencies of the situation, provided that such measures are not inconsistent with its other obligations under international law'. 'No accommodation without derogation', one might summarize the dissenters' position. According to this view, the Court would have had to find a violation of Tarek Hassan's rights enshrined in Article 5 ECHR as his detention was neither based on one of the grounds listed in paragraph 1 nor had it been under review by a proper court in accordance with paragraph 4 of that provision. The judgment would thus have served as a wake-up call to the contracting states to formally declare derogation for military operations abroad crossing the threshold of armed conflict.[76]

5.2 Defragmentation needed: harmonizing human rights and humanitarian law

While concurring with the majority of the Grand Chamber as to the parallel applicability of IHL and ECHR in times of armed conflict, the dissenters criticized the reference to Article 31(3)(c) VCLT as a catch-all solution. By stressing that '[i]nternational human rights law and international humanitarian law exhibit quite extensive differences both methodologically and structurally', they argue against an 'automatic assimilation of these distinct regimes of international law, at least where the relevant provision of the Convention is not legally amenable to such an

[72] For the danger of eroding Article 15 ECHR entailed by the majority's approach, cf *Mohammed and Others v Secretary of State for Defence and Others* [2015] EWCA Civ 843, paras 123, 162.

[73] Crema (n 24) 6; Borelli (n 53) 27, passim.

[74] cf Borelli (n 53) 35: *Hassan* as a 'radical departure from the traditional approach of the Court'.

[75] cf *Al-Skeini v UK* (n 3) paras 163–67; *Jaloud v Netherlands* App no 47708/08 (ECtHR, Judgment, 20 November 2014) para 186.

[76] To avoid stigmatizing a state which actually acted in conformity with its IHL obligations, Crema (n 24) 6, suggests that the ECtHR should have 'opted simply to contest the UK's lack of notification and sanctioned the violation of Article 5, but without awarding pecuniary damages, leaving the decision itself as satisfaction'.

approach'.[77] The latter qualification levels criticism against the Grand Chamber's way of specifically 'harmonizing' Article 5 ECHR with GC III and IV and does not concern the general approach of the majority. In fact, in stating that other relevant rules on international law 'shall be taken into account' as a means of treaty interpretation, Article 31(3)(c) VCLT takes the respective treaty as the point of reference and does not advocate a rough-and-ready amalgam of provisions taken from different sources. Even if it is true that '[j]ust as reliance on the lex specialis maxim cannot determine finally which rule prevails, so pointing to Article 31(3)(c) is not the end of the matter',[78] pointing to Article 31(3)(c) VCLT may well serve as a point of entry.[79] As the dissenters themselves point out, Article 15 expressly demands that '[i]n reviewing the legality of a declaration lodged by a Member State to the Convention within the context of an international armed conflict, the domestic courts, and, if need be, this Court, must … examine whether the measures in question are in conformity with the State's obligations under international humanitarian law'.[80] The respective phrase in Article 15 can thus be seen as an expression of the general rule enshrined in Article 31(3)(c) VCLT.

Contrary to the first impression, therefore, the 'no accommodation without derogation' model does eventually lead to very much the same lines of reasoning the majority of the bench followed. It should be kept in mind that in cases under Article 15 ECHR, the ECtHR is not only reviewing the derogation as such, in general, but remains competent to deal with individual complaints. Here, it will have to assess the conformity of the contentious measure with IHL as much as the necessity under the given circumstances.[81] What certainly is remarkable is the unanimity with which the members of the Grand Chamber accept the task to include IHL in their reasoning—be it with or without a formal declaration of derogation. By demanding that IHL standards must be pleaded in order to be taken into account,[82] the majority of the bench tried to keep the floodgates closed. The future will have to show how much IHL rules and arguments will figure in the Court's jurisprudence. That the ECtHR has given up its self-imposed isolation from IHL should be greeted without reserve. That it made a serious—and in general convincing—attempt to overcome the usual commonplaces of '*lex specialis*' or of 'parallel' or 'partly overlapping' applicability of IHL and human rights law should also be acknowledged.[83]

[77] *Hassan v UK* (n 4) dissenting opinion of J Spano and others (n 19) para 17.

[78] Hill-Cawthorne (n 24). Similarly sceptical Borelli (n 53) 27.

[79] cf d'Aspremont (n 39) 16: 'a useful and handy interpretative tool, especially when it comes to articulate HRL and IHL'.

[80] *Hassan v UK* (n 4) dissenting opinion of J Spano and others (n 19) para 9.

[81] For a useful overview, see ECtHR (Press Unit), 'Factsheet—Derogation in Time of Emergency' (*ECtHR*, July 2019) <http://www.echr.coe.int/Documents/FS_Derogation_ENG.pdf>.

[82] *Hassan v UK* (n 4) para 107.

[83] Concurring Hill-Cawthorne (n 24); M Milanovic, 'A Few Thoughts on Hassan v. United Kingdom' (*EJIL Talk!*, 22 October 2014) <http://www.ejiltalk.org/a-few-thoughts-on-hassan-v-united-kingdom/>; De Koker (n 32) 93–94.

5.3 *Quis judicabit*, or: is a human rights court fit for the job?

For all that, one might pause to think whether the Court's previous reluctance to engage with questions of IHL might not have had its merits.[84] At the end of the day, the ECtHR is and will remain a specialized human rights court, no IHL agency. Especially when it comes to questions of the right to life under Article 2 ECHR, assessing the legality of combat action in armed conflict by recourse to the fine-tuned instruments of human rights law will prove difficult;[85] for situations *en combat*, the rules of IHL (eg on military targets or collateral damage) will often prove more adequate, relegating human rights considerations to procedural or other corollary obligations or to the function of an interpretive guidance.[86] But ought this to be a reason not to deal with such questions should they turn up before the ECtHR? That in fact the Court is entitled and expected to judge even on matters of life and death in armed conflict can actually be seen from Article 15(2) ECHR, which reads: 'No derogation from Article 2, except in respect of deaths resulting from lawful acts of war ... shall be made under this provision.' Since according to paragraph 1 of that provision it is the ECtHR's task to control whether any such act of a contracting state was 'strictly required by the exigencies of the situation' and 'not inconsistent with its other obligations under international law', the Court cannot eschew dealing with essential questions and concepts of humanitarian law.

To somewhat reduce the concerns, it might help to remember the actual task of the ECtHR. Regardless whether one takes Article 15(1) ECHR or Article 31(3)(c) VCLT as the starting point, its task is to interpret the Convention. It is only asked to 'take into account' the relevant rules of IHL in situations of armed conflict. This does not necessarily mean that they have to be *applied* in each and every case. In the past, the Court often came to results on the basis of the ECHR alone which also conformed to the relevant IHL rules.[87] The need to get deeper into the matter arises only in situations in which the rules of IHL either conflict with human rights law or where human rights law is needed to fill in certain gaps of IHL.[88] The *Hassan* case can serve as a good illustration for this.[89] Of course, the ECtHR will have to

[84] Emphatically Bohrer (n 70) 15–19, passim.
[85] Borelli (n 53) 40–41.
[86] cf as a rule of thumb A von Arnauld, *Völkerrecht* (4th edn, CF Müller 2019) para 1174. In greater detail M Sassòli and LM Olson, 'The Relationship between International Humanitarian and Human Rights Law Where it Matters: Admissible Killing and Internment of Fighters in Non-International Armed Conflicts' (2008) 90 International Review of the Red Cross 599.
[87] Borelli (n 53) 30.
[88] See Milanovic (n 69) 76–85, for the different options to deal with those conflicts.
[89] For an analysis of the divergent standards of human rights law and IHL with regard to procedural guarantees in detention cases, see J Pejic, 'Procedural Principles and Safeguards for Internment/Administrative Detention in Armed Conflict and Other Situations of Violence' (2005) 87 International Review of the Red Cross 375.

further develop its case law on such questions, step by step, as usual.[90] It should not be expected to turn into a specialized court for IHL. However, taking into account the contracting states' obligations from IHL will avoid a divergence between an assessment based on IHL and one based on the ECHR, thus giving guidance to the actors involved instead of leaving them with the risk of conflicting legal obligations. With *Hassan*, the Grand Chamber has finally assumed that role and responsibility. That such a bold exercise in defragmentation does not come without the occasional rough edge and that some loose ends will still have to be resolved should be hardly surprising.

[90] Milanovic (n 83) comments laconically: 'In Hassan we thus have yet another incremental decision, with the Court deciding only what it absolutely needed to on the facts of the case, but providing only limited guidance for the future. This caution makes perfect sense from the standpoint of the Court itself, but it is of course of little help to those who have to deal with operational questions on a daily basis.'

10
International Human Rights Law and Extraterritorial Hostilities

Yaël Ronen

1. Introduction

Prevalent orthodoxy holds that international human rights treatylaw (IHRL) applies in situations of extraterritorial armed conflict, in which states engage in hostilities outside their sovereign territory. This orthodoxy is reflected in the often-cited *Nuclear Weapons* Advisory Opinion, where the International Court of Justice (ICJ) stated that 'the protection offered by human rights conventions does not cease in case of armed conflict';[1] and is supported by subsequent international decisions and in the work of numerous academics.[2] The full implications of this statement have not yet been fully explored despite its potential consequences, including in the context of multinational military operations which take place extraterritorially, namely in the territory of third states.

This chapter argues that the above statement is overly sweeping. 'Armed conflict' is an umbrella term for a variety of phenomena, which should not all be treated uniformly. The use of a single term obscures the differences between these phenomena. Further obfuscation is caused by the fact that the literature on issues which impact on the applicability of IHRL in armed conflict is concerned almost exclusively with the rights to life and liberty from detention. This has resulted in the development of doctrines which were then generalized, despite the particularities of the rights which underlay them originally. Analysis of these doctrines with respect to human rights other than life and liberty reveals the difficulties with the sweeping proposition.

[1] *Legality of the Threat or Use of Nuclear Weapons* (Advisory Opinion) [1996] ICJ Rep 226, para 25.

[2] See, eg, *Legal Consequences of the Construction of a Wall in the Occupied Palestinian Territory* (Advisory Opinion) [2004] ICJ Rep 136, para 105; *Hassan v The UK* App no 29750/09 (ECtHR, Grand Chamber Judgment, 16 September 2014) para 35; L Doswald-Beck, 'International Humanitarian Law and the Advisory Opinion of the International Court of Justice on the Legality of the Threat or Use of Nuclear Weapons' (1997) 316 International Review of the Red Cross 35; the various articles in O Ben-Naftali (ed), *International Humanitarian Law and International Human Rights Law* (OUP 2011); F Coomans and MT Kamminga (eds), *Extraterritorial Application of Human Rights Treaties* (Intersentia nv 2004); (2008) 40 Israel Law Review (an issue dedicated to the relationship between IHRL and IHL); H Krieger, 'A Conflict of Norms: The Relationship Between Humanitarian Law and Human Rights Law in the ICRC Customary Law Study' (2006) 11 Journal of Conflict and Security Law 265.

Yaël Ronen, *International Human Rights Law and Extraterritorial Hostilities* In *The 'Legal Pluriverse' Surrounding Multinational Military Operations*. Edited by Robin Geiß and Heike Krieger, Oxford University Press (2020).

DOI: 10.1093/oso/9780198842965.003.0011

Consider the following scenarios, which involve limitations on human rights other than life and liberty:

- Coalition forces operating in Syria are preparing for an attack on an ammunition depot in a state where it is involved in hostilities. In the immediate vicinity of the depot a group of local civilians have gathered to protest against their government's involvement in the conflict. The troops can inform the civilians that they should disperse so as not to be harmed by the impending attack, thereby satisfying the requirement of taking precautions to avoid injury to civilians. Do they also need to calculate into their course of action the harm that they would cause to the civilians' right to assemble and to voice their opinions?
- The same troops also prevent the population from moving through the immediate area so as not to impede the quick access of the military to its destination. Do they need to take into account the consequences of their action on freedom of movement of the civilian population (and on related rights)?
- The West African Force in the Gambia, which is preparing for an attack, wishes to block electronic communications over a certain area in order to prevent the local military from coordinating its movements. In doing so, it would also interfere with the transmission of reports by journalists operating in the area. Does it need to take into account the effect of its operation on freedom of the media and freedom of information of civilian listeners?
- Coalition forces in Iraq are using surveillance drones to locate and target enemy combatants. In the course of doing so, they also collect information about the entire population. Do the operators of the drones need to take into account their infringement on civilians' privacy?

In the scenarios described above, neither the applicability of international humanitarian law (IHL) nor the forces' compliance with it are at issue. What *is* at issue is the applicability of IHRL and the standards by which compliance with this legal framework should be evaluated. Such compliance cannot be generally deduced from compliance with IHL, since IHL and IHRL are structured to protect different interests. The permissibility of targeting a military object depends, under IHL, on the incidental *physical* injury that might be caused to civilians and civilian objects. In contrast, under IHRL, human interests are protected beyond life and limb. Even interests which are protected by both regimes, such as life and bodily integrity, are regulated differently under each of them. Accordingly, conduct that is compliant with IHL is not necessarily compliant with IHRL.[3]

[3] Krieger (n 2) 276–89; unless the standard of IHRL is modified in light of the existence of extraterritorial hostilities, an issue considered below.

This contribution holds that in all the scenarios above, IHRL as such should not be considered for application. This view rests on grounds from the realms of both the laws of armed conflict and IHRL itself. First, as is often argued, a state engaged in military activity cannot realistically be expected to constrain itself solely for the benefit of the social and political interests described in the examples above. It is difficult enough to demand from parties to conflict that they respect the fundamental rights to life, physical integrity, and liberty; imposing additional obligations to respect rights that are not directly related to physical well-being may be overly ambitious. This line of argument could arguably be faulted for allowing expediency to dictate law rather than use law to shape state behaviour. Without delving into the general question of the social role of law, it bears to recall that the very existence of IHL is a compromise between humanitarianism—an attempt to spare lives and bodies which would ideally be achieved by prohibiting warfare altogether—and realism—the knowledge that states will in reality sacrifice lives and bodies in the pursuit of military goals. Extending this methodology to IHRL[4] merely extends the reach of the compromise.

Secondly, and more centrally, this chapter holds that IHRL is unsuitable for, and unworkable in, situations of extraterritorial hostilities. IHRL is premised on, and geared to regulate, a political relationship which does not normally exist in situations of extraterritorial hostilities. Even if it could be applied mechanically (which, as argued below, is not the case), its rationale would be abused. This would both undermine the regime's integrity and detract from its effectiveness in other contexts.[5] The challenge to the applicability of IHRL in situations of extraterritorial hostilities therefore rests not only on utilitarian grounds but also on deontological ones.

The questions of principle underlying the issue addressed here, namely the applicability of IHRL extraterritorially and in situations of armed conflict, have been explored at length in the last decade. However, the exploration of these questions, particularly when they overlap, should be carried out in a more nuanced fashion which better acknowledges the differences between types of armed conflict. This contribution does not purport to discuss all such types but rather to focus on extraterritorial hostilities. This term refers to situations in which states are carrying out military operations, individually or jointly, outside their sovereign territories. I will focus on the relationship between the state or states carrying out an attack[6] and

[4] M Milanovic, 'The Lost Origins of Lex Specialis: Rethinking the Relationship between Human Rights and International Humanitarian Law' in JD Ohlin (ed), *Theoretical Boundaries of Armed Conflict and Human Rights* (CUP 2016) 78, 116–17.

[5] For an articulation of this position as human rights 'purism' see D Kretzmer, 'Human Rights: Their Place on the Battlefield' in *The Law of Armed Conflict: Problems and Prospects, Chatham House, 18-19 April 2005, Transcripts and Summaries of Presentations and Discussions* 52, 55, <https://www.chathamhouse.org/sites/files/chathamhouse/public/Research/International%20Law/ilparmedconflict.pdf>. All URLs accessed 27 December 2018.

[6] The term 'attack' is used in this article in its *jus in bello* sense, by loose reference to the definition of the term under Protocol Additional to the Geneva Conventions of 12 August 1949 and relating to

the population residing in the territory. Furthermore, I hold that some of the difficulties in applying IHRL in extraterritorial hostilities have been glossed over by the almost exclusive reference to the rights to life and liberty, which have special characteristics and unique regulation that make them the exception rather than a reflection of the rule. The chapter focuses on rights other than life or liberty in order to highlight and challenge some of the un- or less-articulated premises of the doctrines of IHRL applicability in armed conflict which create the gaps in analysis.

The analysis takes the following path: it begins by putting forward the argument that the inapplicability of IHRL in situations of extraterritorial hostilities is grounded both in the exclusivity of IHL, and in the IHRL mechanism. This inapplicability is reflected in the requirement of jurisdiction in the sense of prior control, which is not fulfiled in situations of extraterritorial hostilities. The contribution identifies the prevalent trend of minimizing to oblivion the requirement of prior control, thereby expanding the recognition of state jurisdiction for IHRL purposes, including over situations of extraterritorial hostilities. It is contended that this trend should and can be contained or reversed. A second line of analysis examines the view that IHRL does apply in extraterritorial hostilities subject to the *lex specialis* doctrine. It is first noted that the use of the doctrine as an interpretative tool in the *Nuclear Weapons* Advisory Opinion does not provide an adequate framework with respect to rights other than the right to life as articulated under the International Covenant on Civil and Political Rights (ICCPR).[7] The chapter then considers the use of *lex specialis* as pronounced in the *Wall* Advisory Opinion, namely as a tool for resolving conflicts between norms. The analysis demonstrates that the doctrine leads to unacceptable results when applied to rights not regulated under IHL.

2. Exclusivity of IHL in Situations of Extraterritorial Hostilities

IHL regulates only a limited range of interests recognized as human rights under IHRL, those that are directly endangered by hostilities (life, physical integrity, and liberty).[8] It is maintained that this is an exhaustive arrangement, which on the

the Protection of Victims of International Armed Conflicts (entered into force 7 December 1978) 1125 UNTS 3 (AP I) Article 49(1), and not in its *jus ad bellum* sense under Article 51 UN Charter.

[7] International Covenant on Civil and Political Rights (adopted 16 December 1966, entered into force 23 March 1976) 999 UNTS 171 (ICCPR).

[8] M Sassòli, AA Bouvier, and A Quintin, *How Does Law Protect in War?* (3rd edn, ICRC 2011) vol I 452, citing specifically freedom of opinion as a matter on which IHL has less rules than on physical integrity, since the former is less affected by armed conflict.

basis of *expressio unius est exclusio alterius* excludes other alleged rights,[9] such as freedom of expression or assembly, or the rights to movement or privacy.[10]

Undoubtedly, at the time of the drafting of existing IHL instruments, human rights law had hardly begun to develop, and accordingly the question arises whether the absence of reference to the entire gamut of rights should not be viewed as a lacuna.[11] However, IHL instruments are not entirely silent on entitlement later codified as human rights law. First, the Fourth Geneva Convention (GC IV),[12] drafted at the time when IHRL was indeed at its inception, provides a general guarantee of various rights in Article 27, in situations in which states exercise effective control over territory, either their own or that of an adversary. No parallel provision exists with respect to situations of extraterritorial hostilities, which are therefore covered only by Common Article 3. This article enumerates only a limited set of rights. Arguably, the drafters of the two articles were not oblivious to human rights concerns but intended to distinguish between different types of situations; even where they intended to guarantee rights, those were handpicked.

Secondly, any lacunae created by post-1949 development of IHRL could have been filled in the First Protocol Additional to the Geneva Conventions (AP I), adopted in 1977, by which time the ICCPR and the International Covenant on Economics, Social and Cultural Rights[13] had already entered into force. Yet AP I also contains only a very limited reference to IHRL, in Articles 75 and 72. Article 75 essentially reiterates Article 27 GC IV, and thus does not cover extraterritorial hostilities. Article 72 provides: 'The provisions of this Section are additional to . . . other applicable rules of international law relating to the protection of fundamental human rights *during international armed conflict*' (emphasis added). Had this provision terminated after 'fundamental human rights', it would have been pertinent to debate which are the 'fundamental' rights which may fill the lacunae in IHL. However, the final words of the sentence refer only to rules relating *specifically to international armed conflict* rather than to IHRL in general. There is therefore

[9] But see High Court of Justice, *Serdar Mohammed v Ministry of Defence and Others* [2014] EWHC 1369 (QB), para 293, in which the Court held that absence of regulation under IHL of the right to detain in extraterritorial NIAC is not intended to displace and is not capable of displacing human rights law. For discussion whether the rejection of the *a contrario* interpretation is encapsulated in the Martens clause see T Meron, 'The Martens Clause, Principles of Humanity, and Dictates of Public Conscience' (2000) 94 American Journal of International Law 78, 81; but also A Cassese, 'The Martens Clause: Half a Loaf or Simply Pie in the Sky?' (2000) 11 European Journal of International Law 187, 192–93, 207.

[10] OA Hathaway and others, 'Which Law Governs During Armed Conflict—The Relationship between International Humanitarian Law and Human Rights Law' (2011) 96 Minnesota Law Review 1883, find that these rights are governed also by IHL, but that is the case either under the law of occupation, or through provisions that may impact on these rights but only indirectly, such as limitations on expression if damage is caused to property used for communication.

[11] T Meron, 'On the Inadequate Reach of Humanitarian and Human Rights Law and the Need for a New Instrument' (1983) 77 American Journal of International Law 589, 603.

[12] Geneva Convention (IV) Relative to the Protection of Civilian Persons in Time of War (entered into force 21 October 1950) 75 UNTS 287.

[13] International Covenant on Economic, Social and Cultural Rights, 993 UNTS 3 (entered into force 3 January 1976).

nothing to support an argument that IHRL may be sweepingly applied when IHL is silent.[14]

The view that in extraterritorial hostilities IHL applies exclusively can find support in the ICJ's *Wall* Advisory Opinion. Following up on (and expanding) the *Nuclear Weapons* Advisory Opinion's statement that the protection offered by human rights conventions does not cease in case of armed conflict save through derogation, the Court held that there are three possible situations in the relationship between international humanitarian law and human rights law: 'some rights may be exclusively matters of international humanitarian law; others may be exclusively matters of human rights law; yet others may be matters of both these branches of international law', in which case IHL is the *lex specialis*.[15] Arguably, the ICJ's statement should be read as distinguishing situations[16]—those governed exclusively by IHL, those governed exclusively by IHRL, and those governed by both. The first category, rights that are 'exclusively matters of international humanitarian law', indicates that there is some situation of armed conflict in which IHRL does not apply. Occupation certainly is not such a situation, as the Advisory Opinion proceeds to demonstrate. Nor could IHRL be said to be inapplicable in armed conflicts within states' own territories. In contrast, extraterritorial hostilities appear to be precisely that situation. Admittedly, the *Nuclear Weapons* Advisory Opinion contained no qualification regarding the applicability of the ICCPR in hostilities. Moreover, in *Congo v Uganda*, the Court further hinted that IHRL applies specifically in hostilities, when it noted that 'international human rights instruments are applicable "in respect of acts done by a State in the exercise of its jurisdiction outside its own territory", *particularly* in occupied territories'.[17] The argument here, that IHRL does not apply in extraterritorial hostilities, is certainly against the grain of the ICJ's jurisprudence. However, insofar as the *Nuclear Weapons* Advisory Opinion and its legacy are concerned, it only joins at the heels of already voluminous critique.

[14] MJ Dennis, 'Application of Human Rights Treaties Extraterritorially in Times of Armed Conflict and Military Occupation' (2005) 99 American Journal of International Law 119, 138.

[15] *Wall* (n 2) para 106; *Armed Activities on the Territory of the Congo (Democratic Republic of the Congo v Uganda)* (Judgment) [2005] ICJ Rep 168, para 216.

[16] The terminology is also used in the chapeau of its proposition. For an analysis in this vein see A Orakhelashvili, 'The Interaction between Human Rights and Humanitarian Law: Fragmentation, Conflict, Parallelism, or Convergence?' (2008) 19 European Journal of International Law 161, esp at 168.

[17] *Congo v Uganda* (n 15) (emphasis added). In the absence of implementation in the circumstances, Cerone cautions against overstating this statement. See J Cerone, 'Jurisdiction and Power: The Intersection of Human Rights Law & the Law of Non-International Armed Conflict in an Extraterritorial Context' (2007) 40 Israel Law Review 396, 424.

3. Unsuitability of IHRL to Situations of Extraterritorial Hostilities

The moral foundation of human rights is recognition of the inherent value of the human person. Human rights derive from the order of nature and not from society or history, and are thus universal, not relative to any particular social or historical culture.[18] However, rights exist *within a* society. As an international legal concept, human rights are grounded in a relationship between government and individual, in which the government is bound to follow the directions given by the rights concerned[19] as well as according to other imperatives.[20] For this purpose, it may exercise certain powers, including the power to impose limitations on rights. Indeed, few rights protected by IHRL are absolute. The majority may be limited for purposes enumerated under the respective instruments. Accordingly, human rights law concerns the regulation of rights against competing interests through a balancing formula. In situations of extraterritorial hostilities such as in the scenarios presented at the outset, national security and the maintenance of public order[21] appear particularly pertinent as grounds for limiting rights. However, before a mechanical application of the limitation formula is embarked upon, its rationale should be recalled and tested against the circumstances underlying extraterritorial hostilities.

The moral justification for limiting rights is that those who suffer from the limitation are also its beneficiaries, directly or indirectly. When individuals' rights are limited in pursuit of a public (communal) interest,[22] these individuals, being members of the same community, also benefit, together with the community at large, from the realization of the interest that the limitations pursue. Similarly, when individuals' rights are limited in order to ensure respect of the rights or reputations of other individuals, they benefit from a guarantee that if need be, their own rights or reputations would be similarly protected from harm by others.[23]

However, in situations of extraterritorial hostilities, the conditions underlying this moral justification for limiting rights do not exist. The attacking states are acting in the interest of their own populations, or of the international community when operating under a Chapter VII UN Charter mandate, and not of

[18] D Sidorsky, 'Contemporary Reinterpretations of the Concept of Human Rights' in D Sidorsky (ed), *Essays on Human Rights: Contemporary Issues and Jewish Perspectives* (Jewish Publication Society of America 1979) 89.

[19] C Tomuschat, *Human Rights: Between Idealism and Realism* (OUP 2014) 74.

[20] NK Modirzadeh, 'The Dark Sides of Convergence: A Pro-Civilian Critique of the Extraterritorial Application of Human Rights Law in Armed Conflict' [2010] 86 US Naval War College International Law Studies (Blue Book) Series 349, 357.

[21] See, eg, ICCPR (n 7) Articles 19(3), 21, 22; European Convention on Human Rights and Fundamental Freedoms (entered into force 3 September 1953) 213 UNTS 222 (ECHR) Articles 10(2), 11(2).

[22] ICCPR (n 7) Article 19(3)(b).

[23] ICCPR (n 7) Article 19(3)(a).

the population under attack or of individuals within it. The members of the latter community are therefore deprived of their rights for the benefit of a different community. This is particularly evident if the deprivation purports to rest on justifications such as national security, when the national security interest of the attacking state is almost by definition inimical to that of individuals in the attacked territory (otherwise there would be no need for hostilities).

Notably, a choice by an attacking force to employ a less injurious limitation on the population instead of a more injurious one should not be misconstrued as that force pursuing the population's interests. For example, in the first scenario above, if the enemy civilians are not removed from the area where they have assembled, they would be harmed. By imposing limitations on their freedom of speech and assembly the attacking force could ostensibly be said to be securing other rights that are under jeopardy (life and bodily integrity), of the very same individuals. However, this presentation of the matter is misleading. The choice of depriving individuals of their freedom of speech rather than of life is obviously a choice of a less injurious measure to achieve the military goal; but it is still a measure taken in pursuit of the interests of a community—that of the attacking state—that is different from the one being limited. In other words, the fundamental flaw, that of limiting the rights of one community for the benefit of another, persists.

Notwithstanding the above, the existence of extraterritorial hostilities cannot be regarded as a *categorical* proxy for the absence of a community joining the attacking state and the affected population. The existence of extraterritorial hostilities creates a *presumption* that the requisite relationship is absent, but this presumption may be rebutted depending on the particular circumstances. For example, the military forces of European Council member states bound by the European Convention of Human Rights (ECHR) and operating in Iraq or Afghanistan with the consent of the territorial states against insurgents are not acting in the interests of their own populations but of the local one.[24] In that case, limitations that those forces impose on the local population do serve that population's interests. This is because the European forces are essentially acting as an arm of the territorial government, which is part of the local political community and therefore should be (and is) without doubt bound by IHRL.[25]

The question whether the needs of one community may justify limitation on rights of the members of another community has not yet been addressed directly in international practice. It arose by implication in the *Wall* Advisory Opinion, when the ICJ stated that the construction by Israel of the separation barrier interfered with (and violated) the Palestinian population's freedom of movement.[26] The

[24] *Mohammed and Others v Secretary of State for Defence, Rahmatullah v MoD*, Case Nos A2/2014/1862; A2/2014/4084; A2/2014/4086, [2015] EWCA Civ 843, para 127.

[25] That the European forces legally bear obligations under IHRL independently does not detract from this political role.

[26] *Wall* (n 2) paras 128 and 134.

Court cited necessity and proportionality as criteria for evaluating whether a limitation on movements was lawful under the IHRL paradigm.[27] It then stated that it was not convinced that the specific course which Israel has chosen for the wall 'was necessary to attain its security objectives',[28] and that the infringement on rights could therefore not be justified by 'the requirements of national security or public order'.[29] The reference to necessity and proportionality suggests that in the view of the Court, protection of the occupying power's own national security was, in principle, a legitimate purpose which justifies imposing limitations on the human rights of residents in occupied territory (because if the purpose were illegitimate, there would be no sense in examining its necessity or proportionality). However, it is unclear whether by Israel's 'security objectives' (as a presumably legitimate aim to pursue) the Court was referring to the security of Israeli forces within the West Bank, who do, together with the local population, constitute the political community of 'occupation' sanctioned by international law, or rather the security of Israel's sovereign territory.[30] Reference to the latter might have constituted confirmation by the Court that the national security of one community (residents of sovereign Israeli territory) is a legitimate purpose for which to limit the rights of another (the rights of Palestinian residents of the West Bank).[31] But since the Court did not address the effect of the separation barrier on national security or public order in either region in any substantive manner,[32] it would be imprudent to view the Advisory Opinion as an implicit admission of such a principled proposition.[33] There is every reason to reject such an interpretation because under the law of occupation, an occupying power is categorically prohibited from taking measures which adversely affect the population in the occupied territory if their goal is to promote the welfare of its own population exclusively.[34]

If the court was referring to the security of Israeli forces within the West Bank, then its statement does not inform the question at hand at all, because it does not

[27] ibid para 136.

[28] ibid para 137.

[29] ibid.

[30] To the extent that those can be distinguished from each other, given that the separation barrier was built in order to prevent terrorist infiltration into Israel from the West Bank.

[31] What national security obviously did not include was the security of Israeli residents of the West Bank (which, with the Palestinian residents of the West Bank could be said to form a single unit of population living in occupied territory), given the ICJ's holding that the construction of settlements was unlawful.

[32] For criticism of this see *Wall* (n 2) Judge Buergenthal's declaration, para 7.

[33] See Judge Higgins' statement that combined treatment of IHL and IHRL makes it 'extremely difficult to see what exactly has been decided by the court'. ibid separate Opinion of Judge Higgins, para 24. The ICJ also held that the restrictions on economic, social, and cultural rights resulting from the construction of the wall were not 'solely for the purpose of promoting the general welfare in a democratic society', without indicating to which 'society' it was referring, see ibid para 136.

[34] But see Justice Witkon, who held that the military needs of the occupation forces include the protection of the security of their own state, HCJ 302/72 *Abu Hilu and Others v Government of Israel* (1973) 27(2) PD 169, 182, and HCJ 606/78 *Ayyub and Others v Minister of Defence and Others* (1979) 33(2) PD 113.

involve two different communities. A community may take various forms and is not limited to sovereign statehood. Its constituent element is the exercise of control—whether legal or factual—which engenders obligations and consequently the authority to discharge them. A military occupation is such a situation. That there is a conflict of interests between the government and the population is reflected in specific provisions of the law of occupation; but that does not detract from the applicability of the human rights paradigm.

The requisite of the existence of a joint political community to which both the government and population belong is not explicit in the international instruments.[35] However, without it, the balancing mechanism is unworkable. This is demonstrable, for example, in the unavailability of a law under which limitations may be imposed. Under IHRL, restrictions on rights are permitted if they are 'under law' or 'prescribed by law' (which are interchangeable terms), or at least 'in conformity' with the law (permitting administrative action based on general authorization in law[36]). 'Law' refers primarily to domestic law, but may also refer to international law, provided that the latter is explicit and sufficiently clear and accessible.[37]

There is no law governing different communities which allows one to limit the human right of the other. The domestic law of the attacking states cannot be relied upon, because the reach of domestic law is limited to sovereign territory. The attacking state may exercise extraterritorial personal jurisdiction over its nationals under its domestic law and require its agents to abide by its law even when acting outside its territory in a manner which benefits non-nationals there.[38] In other words, it can rely on its own law extraterritorially to impose obligations on itself. But it cannot rely on the law to impose limitations on persons that are neither its citizens nor on its territory. As for the domestic law of the state in which the hostilities are taking place, it might contain provisions which allow the government to limit rights. However, the attacking force is not a government.[39] Even if it is subject to this law,[40] surely it cannot invoke the law as a source of authority to limit the rights of the local population.[41]

[35] Other than by implication from the references to 'society', eg ICCPR (n 7) Articles 14, 21, 22, 23, 24.

[36] M Nowak, *U.N. Covenant on Civil and Political Rights: CCPR Commentary* (NP Engel 2005) 489 m 17.

[37] *Groppera Radio AG and Others v Switzerland*, App no 10890/84, 12 EHRR 321 (28 March 1990) para 68.

[38] See, eg, Israel's Basic Law: Human Dignity and Freedom, Article 11.

[39] Unless it exercised effective control, in which the situation is one of occupation, and the present analysis becomes redundant.

[40] This is a difficult proposition in itself, see A Sari's contribution, Chapter 18 in this book.

[41] Nor would the attacking state's interests be viewed as legitimate purposes under that law. In *Mohammed* (n 24) para 127, the Court of Appeal was willing to regard Afghan law as a source of authority for limiting rights, but there the attacking force was acting, as noted, by consent of the local government.

Nor does public international law—which is the body of law regulating the relationship between different communities which may have conflicting interests—provide a general authority to limit rights in extraterritorial hostilities. IHL contains certain injunctions to respect rights, and explicitly regulates certain rights (eg rights to life and liberty). Otherwise, it is silent.[42] It does not prohibit limitations on rights, but the absence of a prohibition is not tantamount to an authorization to limit rights. Even if it were, it could not qualify as sufficiently clear and precise.[43]

To conclude, the limitation mechanism of IHRL is unworkable in situations of extraterritorial hostilities because there is no political community joining the attacking force and the affected population. The implication is not, however, that such a state is bound to respect human rights without being permitted to limit them. Such a conclusion would render the entire gamut of human rights absolute in situations of extraterritorial hostilities. This would be absurd and is even less acceptable than holding that military commanders of an attacking state must consider human rights of individuals in the area under attack in the first place. Rather, the implication is that when there is a disparity between the community whose rights are being limited and the one who benefits from the limitations, the IHRL paradigm is simply unworkable and should therefore be presumed inapplicable.[44] Such a disparity is almost inherent to situations of extraterritorial hostilities.

4. The Requirement of Jurisdiction under IHRL

4.1 Jurisdiction as prior control

The previous section argued that IHRL is premised on the existence of a community connecting the military force and the affected population, namely a situation in which the force exercises control over the population. As noted, this requisite

[42] The closest to authorization is Article 27 GC IV. However, this article does not apply to extraterritorial hostilities, and it is doubtful whether it is sufficiently precise and its consequences foreseeable so as to constitute a lawful limitation in terms of IHRL. See *Medvedyev and Others v France* App no 3394/03 (ECtHR, Grand Chamber Judgment, 29 March 2010) para 80.

[43] L Hill-Cawthorne and D Akande, 'Does IHL Provide a Legal Basis for Detention in Non-International Armed Conflicts?' (*EJIL: Talk!*, 7 May 2014) <http://www.ejiltalk.org/does-ihl-provide-a-legal-basis-for-detention-in-non-international-armed-conflicts/>. See *Mohammed* (n 24) para 197 on the general proposition in international law, and confirming the High Court of Justice's analysis of IHL specifically in *Mohammed* (n 9) paras 239–68; A Conte, 'The UK Court of Appeal in Serdar Mohammed: Treaty and Customary IHL Provides No Authority for Detention in Non-International Armed Conflicts' (*EJIL: Talk!*, 6 August 2015) <http://www.ejiltalk.org/the-uk-court-of-appeal-in-serdar-mohammed-treaty-and-customary-ihl-provides-no-authority-for-detention-in-non-international-armed-conflicts/>.

[44] One might further query that even if the formula is applied mechanically, it cannot be *a priori* assumed that the limiting ground would also take precedence over the rights, given the requirements of necessity and proportionality.

is not explicit in international instruments. However, it is reflected in the requirement of 'jurisdiction' under various frameworks. The question is what level of control is required to create jurisdiction. There seems to be a consensus that when a state exerts effective control, whether over territory or over a person, it exercises jurisdiction, which gives rise to human rights obligations. What is less clear is the circumstances under which a state should be deemed to be exercising such control. Much of the discourse on this issue revolves around extraterritorial situations, since within a state there is a presumption of effective control over territory.

Two approaches to the matter can be identified in international practice. Under the first, jurisdiction is understood as nothing more than the exercise of state power; under the other, jurisdiction depends on a relationship of control which pre-dates the conduct which allegedly constitutes the human right violation. The first approach is the one ostensibly governing the universal system, while the second was adopted by the European Court of Human Rights (ECtHR).[45] The present section briefly recaps the relevant jurisprudence, in order to highlight its significance in the context of extraterritorial hostilities.

4.2 International practice

According to the jurisprudence and practice of the Human Rights Committee (HRC), states must respect and ensure the rights laid down in the ICCPR to 'anyone within the power or effective control of that State Party, even if not situated within the territory of the State Party'.[46] The rationale leading to this doctrine was that 'it would be unconscionable to so interpret the responsibility under article 2 of the Covenant as to permit a State party to perpetrate violations of the Covenant on the territory of another State, which violations it could not perpetrate on its own territory'.[47] Some of the cases through which this doctrine has developed concerned the abduction and detention of individuals abroad. In those cases, the HRC held that the government could be held accountable for 'violations of rights under the Covenant which its agents commit upon the territory of another State'.[48] Other cases concerned the refusal of diplomatic agents situated abroad to renew passports of the state's nationals, also situated abroad. The HRC found that the state in

[45] M den Heijer and R Lawson, 'Extraterritorial Human Rights and the Concept of "Jurisdiction"' in M Langford (ed), *Global Justice, State Duties: The Extraterritorial Scope of Economic, Social, and Cultural Rights in International Law* (CUP 2013) 173.

[46] General Comment 31/80 on the Nature of States' General Legal Obligation under Article 2 of the Covenant, of 29 March 2004, para 10, which consolidated earlier work of the Committee.

[47] Human Rights Committee, *Lilian Celiberti de Casariego v Uruguay*, Communication No 56/1979, UN Doc CCPR/C/OP/1 92 (1984) para 10.3; Human Rights Committee, *Sergio Euben Lopez Burgos v Uruguay*, Communication no R.12/52, UN Doc Supp No 40 (A/36/40) 176 (1981) para 12.3.

[48] *Celiberty de Casariego* and *Lopez Burgos*, ibid.

question had exercised jurisdiction under the Covenant and thus was answerable under it for limiting the complainants' freedom of movement.[49]

The HRC's rationale was that the distinction between sovereign and non-sovereign territory is immaterial. Indeed, where a state exercises control, the legal status of the territory is immaterial to its obligation. However, while with respect to the territory sovereign states the existence of control by the state is presumed, with respect to extraterritorial conduct, control cannot be presumed. Its existence has to be established, hence the reference to 'jurisdiction'. By doing away with sovereignty as a requisite for jurisdiction, the HRC removed the element which embodied the existence of control. It therefore did more than eliminate formalities; it obviated pre-existing control as necessary for human rights obligations.

This approach is reflected in the *Nuclear Weapons* Advisory Opinion, in which the ICJ held that 'the protection of the International Covenant for the Protection of Civil and Political Rights does not cease in times of war [except by derogation under Article 4]'.[50] Although this statement is usually cited in the context of the relationship between IHRL and IHL, it also addresses the question of jurisdiction. The scenario underlying the *Nuclear Weapons* Advisory Opinion is necessarily one in which prior control over person or territory does not exist. If there had been such prior exercise of control, the rules on targeting during hostilities, on which the ICJ relied to interpret the right to life, would not have applied, since these rules do not apply when a state holds a person in custody; nor can they be presumed to apply when the state exercises effective control over territory, namely in a situation of occupation, since the use of force would then be based on a policing paradigm, which does not allow predictable incidental damage on the basis of proportionality. The Advisory Opinion thus appears to follow the HRC's expansive interpretation, according to which jurisdiction generating human rights obligations does not depend on any prior control. This becomes explicit in the *Wall* Advisory Opinion, where one of the HRC's passport cases is mentioned in order to demonstrate that the Covenant is 'applicable in respect of acts done by a State in the exercise of its jurisdiction outside its own territory'.[51] This can also be seen in *Congo v Uganda*. If the ruling is read as acknowledging the applicability of IHRL not only in occupation, then within the statement that 'international human rights instruments are applicable "in respect of acts done by a State in the exercise of its *jurisdiction* outside its own territory"',[52] the term 'jurisdiction' does not denote prior control since Congo did not exercise such control.[53] The doctrine appears to be that that jurisdiction,

[49] Human Rights Committee, *Sophie Vidal Martins v Uruguay*, Communication No R.13/57, UN Doc Supp No 40 (A/37/40) 157 (1982); *Mabel Pereira Montero v Uruguay*, Communication no 106/1981, UN Doc CCPR/C/OP/2 136 (1990).

[50] *Nuclear Weapons* (n 1) para 25.

[51] *Wall* (n 2) para 111.

[52] *Congo v Uganda* (n 15) para 2016 (emphasis added).

[53] Other than with respect to conduct that constituted torture or forcible conscription of children, *Congo v Uganda* (n 15) paras 201, 211, 217.

at this point already pertaining to IHRL generally and not only to the right to life under the ICCPR, can emanate from the very act which constitutes the alleged violation.[54] This renders the requirement of jurisdiction virtually superfluous.

The Inter-American Commission for Human Rights appears to share the view that jurisdiction does not constitute a substantive prerequisite to human right obligations, both in a situation of armed conflict and otherwise. In *Salas v US*, for example, the Commission held that rights were implicated when 'use of military force [during the takeover of Panama City by US forces] has resulted in noncombatant deaths, personal injury, and property loss' as violations of rights guaranteed under the American Declaration.[55] In *Alejandre v Cuba*, the Commission considered an incident in which Cuba's airplanes had fired on another airplane flying in international airspace. The Commission held that Cuban responsibility was engaged because 'when agents of a state, whether military or civilian, exercise power and authority over persons outside national territory, the state's obligation to respect human rights continues' even though 'the events took place outside Cuban jurisdiction'.[56] In this case, it is not that control was not required for jurisdiction, but that jurisdiction was not required for obligations to exist. As in the case of abductions examined by the HRC, the 'power and authority' which gave rise to the obligation to respect the rights were the same act that was capable of infringing on those rights, and not any prior control.[57]

A different approach to jurisdiction was adopted by the ECtHR, which has expressly refused to accept that jurisdiction could be established by the conduct which constitutes the alleged violation, or entirely forgone.[58] Instead, the Court held that jurisdiction requires the exercise of effective control prior to the alleged violation of the ECHR.[59] According to ECtHR jurisprudence, jurisdiction hinges

[54] M Scheinin, 'Extraterritorial Effect of the International Covenant on Civil and Political Rights' in Coomans and Kamminga (n 2) 73.

[55] *Salas et al.*, Decision on Admissibility, (United States) Inter-American Commission on Human Rights Case no 10.573, Report No 31/93 (14 October 1993) para 6 of the Analysis. Note that the Commission referred only to those human rights violations that might also have constituted violations of IHL, despite the fact that the petition alleged violations of other rights, para 9.

[56] *Armando Alejandre Jr, Carlos Costa, Mario de la Peña, and Pablo Morales* (Cuba) Inter-American Commission on Human Rights, Case No 11.589, Report no 86/99 para 25, Annual Report, OEA/Ser.L/V/II.106 Doc 3 rev. 586 (1999) (29 September 1999).

[57] For additional case law see den Heijer and Lawson (n 45) 175–76. The Inter-American Commission has addressed the restrictions which Chile included in passports issued by its consular officers abroad, thereby violating the prohibition on expulsion and entry into the county. Report on Chile, IACHR, OAS/Ser.1/V/II.66 Doc 17, September 1985 paras 25, 34, <http://www.cidh.oas.org/countryrep/Chile85sp/indice.htm>.

[58] Most vehemently in *Bankovic and Others v Belgium and Others* App no 52207/99 (ECtHR, Grand Chamber Decision as to the admissibility,12 December 2001) para 75, a decision that has been severely criticized.

[59] For a regional court's institutional motives for limiting its jurisdiction see VP Tzevelekos, 'Reconstructing the Effective Control Criterion in Extraterritorial Human Rights Breaches: Direct Attribution of Wrongfulness, Due Diligence, and Concurrent Responsibility' (2014) 36 Michigan Journal of International Law 129, 146–47; CM Cerna, 'Out of Bounds? The Approach of the Inter-American System for the Promotion and Protection of Human Rights to the Extraterritorial Application of Human Rights Law' Center for Human Rights and Global Justice Working Paper Number 6 (2006)

primarily on effective territorial control, in national territory or beyond it,[60] as well as in certain enumerated circumstances when state agents exercise authority and control over individuals, such as when state agents are acting in accordance with provisions of international law; when they exercise, by invitation, public powers normally exercised by a host government; or when they have custody of a person.[61] Even the ECtHR, however, has not been entirely consistent in its practice, and appears to be gradually distancing itself from its original doctrine.[62] It does so either by expanding the notion of control,[63] at times inexplicably,[64] or, in some cases, by altogether disregarding the issue and holding that states have jurisdiction despite the absence of any pre-existing control, relying solely on the conduct which constituted the alleged violation.[65] In *Issa*, the ECtHR went so far as to adopt the HRC's rationale, which, as explained above, has seemingly served for dispensing altogether with the requirement of pre-existing control.[66]

4.3 Revisiting the universal approach

Notably, the universal case law which developed the view that prior control was entirely or almost completely superfluous concerned the rights to life and liberty.[67] The regional human rights bodies' decisions to that effect all concerned the right to

170–73 <http://chrgj.org/wp-content/uploads/2012/07/WPS_NYU_CHRGJ_Cerna_Final.pdf>; A Nußberger, 'The Concept of "Jurisdiction" in the Jurisprudence of the European Court of Human Rights' (2012) 65 Current Legal Problems 241.

[60] In the case of intrastate situations, territorial control is presumed to exist unless otherwise shown, although the case law on this is not entirely consistent. See discussion in O De Schutter, *International Human Rights Law* (2nd edn, CUP 2014) 133–35.

[61] *Al Skeini and Others v UK* App no 55721/07 (ECtHR, 7 July 2011) paras 131–37; *Hassan* (n 2) para 74.

[62] Heijer and Lawson (n 45) 177. They note that the European Commission on Human Rights held a view close to that of the HRC, 173; A Sari, 'Jaloud v Netherlands: New Directions in Extra-Territorial Military Operations' (*EJIL: Talk!*, 24 November 2014) <http://www.ejiltalk.org/jaloud-v-netherlands-new-directions-in-extra-territorial-military-operations/>; R Lawson, 'Across the Universe? The Extra-Territorial Application of the European Convention on Human Rights' in *European Yearbook on Human Rights 2011* (European Academic Press 2012) 427.

[63] In *Al Skeini* (n 61) the United Kingdom exercised jurisdiction because it 'assumed authority and responsibility for the maintenance of security in South East Iraq', para 149.

[64] In *Jaloud v The Netherlands* App No 47708/08 (ECtHR, Grand Chamber Judgment, 20 November 2014) para 152. Sari argues that the jurisdiction of the Netherlands stemmed from it maintaining a road block; see Sari (n 62). Lawson argues that jurisdiction emanated from 'state agents open[ing] fire at a fairly close range', R Lawson, 'Si Vis Pacem, Para Bellum: Application of the European Convention on Human Rights in Situations of Armed Conflict' in L Early and A Austin (eds), *The Right to Life under Article 2 of the European Convention on Human Rights: in honour of Michael O'Boyle* (Wolf Legal Publishers 2016) 213.

[65] See, eg, *Pad and Others v Turkey* App no 60167/00 (ECtHR, 28 June 2007) para 54; Heijer and Lawson (n 45) 182.

[66] *Issa and Others v Turkey* App no 31821/96 (ECtHR, 30 March 2005) para 71.

[67] In the passport cases, refusal to renew the passports would have entailed return to Uruguay where at least the physical liberty of the authors of the communication would have been at risk.

life.[68] The question arises whether the adoption by the various human right bodies of a liberal view of the applicability of IHRL is related to the character of this right. The right to life is the only truly inherent human right, which necessarily underlies any society, irrespective of its values and mores; it is non-derogable and, some would say, peremptory. It is already interpreted differently from other rights, for example in that it includes obligations which do not exist for other rights, such as the obligations of investigation and enforcement in cases of alleged violations.[69] It might therefore not be the appropriate benchmark by which the standard treatment should be set for all rights.

Thus, although the view is gaining popularity that the ability to infringe on rights engenders the obligation to respect them,[70] even existing jurisprudence is susceptible to other readings, which support the view that prior control has not necessarily been abandoned as a requisite for jurisdiction. The following are examples of such alternative readings.

In the *Celiberti de Casariego* abduction case, the complainant had been arrested and detained by Uruguayan forces in Brazil, with the connivance of two Brazilian police officials. She was subsequently forcibly abducted into Uruguayan territory, where she was detained and held incommunicado. The HRC found that Uruguay had violated the complainant's rights 'because *the act of abduction into Uruguayan territory* constituted an arbitrary arrest and detention' and on the basis of treatment to which she was subsequently subjected.[71] In other words, jurisdiction emerged only *after* the detention in Brazil, that is once the Uruguayan authorities had established physical control over her person.

Similarly, in the passport cases the HRC reasoned that '[t]he issue of a passport to a Uruguayan citizen is clearly a matter within the jurisdiction of the Uruguayan authorities and [the author of the communication] is "subject to the jurisdiction" of Uruguay for that purpose'.[72] The HRC can be regarded as having relied on the fact that Uruguay had internationally sanctioned legal power over the person (jurisdiction) in a context relevant to the communication. It is in this context that the HRC relied on the 'very nature of the right' to leave one's country to hold that the ICCPR imposes extraterritorial obligations on the state of nationality.[73] In other

[68] See, eg, *Issa and Others v Turkey* App no 31821/96 (ECtHR, Merits, 16 November 2004); *Jaloud v The Netherlands* App no 47708/08 (ECtHR, 20 November 2014); *Salas* (n 55); *Alejandre* (n 56); Separate Opinion of Judge Bonello in *Al Skeini* (n 61) para 11.

[69] *Velasquez Rodriguez* Case, Judgment, 29 July 1988, Inter-AmCtHR (Ser C) No 4 (1988).

[70] M Milanovic, *Extraterritorial Application of Human Rights Treaties, Law, Principles and Policy* (OUP 2011) 207 (with respect to negative obligations); Separate Opinion of Judge Bonnello in *Al Skeini* (n 61) para 11.

[71] *Celiberti de Casariego* (n 47) paras 9, 11 (emphasis added). See also *Lopez Burgos* (n 47) para 13. Their doing so in collusion with Brazilian authorities, namely with the consent of the territorial state, suggest that they may also be regarded as having some measure of territorial control, since they benefitted from and drew on the effective control exercised by the territorial state.

[72] *Vidal Martins* (n 49) para 7; *Montero v Uruguay* (n 49) para 5.

[73] *Vidal Martins* and *Montero v Uruguay*, ibid.

words, the applicability of the ICCPR did hinge on prior control, albeit of a legal nature.[74] Moreover, the HRC implied that jurisdiction can be tailored to rights, calling for different levels or types of control. A similar notion appears in the abduction cases, where the HRC stated that '[t]he reference ... to "individuals subject to its jurisdiction" is ... to *the relationship between the individual and the State in relation to* a violation of any of the rights set forth in the Covenant, wherever they occurred'.[75] These words imply that there needs to be a 'relationship', namely control, between the state and the individual, that is separate from the violation (and therefore can be 'in relation' to it); and also that the particular level of control that is required to create obligations is contingent upon the right at issue.

Similarly, the ICJ's statement in the *Nuclear Weapons* Advisory Opinion might not necessarily mean that IHRL applies to *any* conduct of the state, regardless of circumstances.[76] The ICJ did state that '[i]n *principle*, the right not arbitrarily to be deprived of one's life applies also in hostilities'.[77] But by noting that IHRL does not *cease* to apply because of the armed conflict, the ICJ arguably did not take an express position on whether IHRL applies in armed conflict *to begin with*. The words 'in principle' may further suggest that the ICJ was not inclined to consider the question of the trigger for applicability; it thus left the question what particular circumstances would trigger this applicability outside the scope of analysis, stipulating only that where IHRL does (already) apply (eg in a non-international armed conflict (NIAC) within a state's territory), obligations under it would not be extinguished merely because of the occurrence of extraterritorial hostilities.

If human rights obligations hinge on jurisdiction as prior control, it follows that any situation, including of armed conflict, must be distinguished depending on the level or prior control that is involved before the scope of obligation can be ascertained. Occupation is defined by the existence of control over territory. In an NIAC within a state's territory there is also a presumption of effective territorial control. Once a person is taken into custody, whether as a prisoner of war (POW) or otherwise, again jurisdiction exists and human rights obligations are triggered.[78] In

[74] See also Heijer and Lawson (n 45) 181. The ECtHR maintains a similar category of jurisdiction based on 'acts of diplomatic and consular agents, who are present on foreign territory in accordance with provisions of international law ... when these agents exert authority and control over others, *Al Skeini* (n 61) para 134.

[75] *Celiberti de Casariego v Uruguay* (n 47) para 10.2; *Lopez Burgos v Uruguay* (n 47) para 12.2 (emphasis added); and later in *Al Skeini* (n 61) para 137.

[76] Specifically, in *Wall* (n 2) para 112, the Court's reference to the HRC was in the context of the applicability of IHRL in occupied territory. In that debate, the existence of effective control over territory was not disputed and may have underlain the Court's analysis as the source of jurisdiction, ibid para 110, citing CCPR/C/79/Add.93 para 10. See also ibid para 112: 'it is not to be excluded that [the ICESCR] applies both to territories over which a State party has sovereignty and to those over which that State exercises territorial jurisdiction'.

[77] *Nuclear Weapons* (n 1) para 25 (emphasis added).

[78] Kretzmer distinguishes these situations by the distance from the battlefield, and by the fact that in the former cases, the individuals are *hors de combat*. D Kretzmer, 'Human Rights: Their Place on the Battlefield in *'The Law of Armed Conflict: Problems and Prospects', Chatham House, 18–19 April 2005,*

contrast, in situations of extraterritorial hostilities, which are not defined by control over territory or persons, a state cannot *a priori* be assumed to have jurisdiction.[79] An evaluation of the situation would need to take into account the extent of control both factually, that is, how much control is exercised and of what type, and normatively, that is, what level of control is required for the state to become obligated to secure rights, and, if necessary, to be authorized also to limit them. The latter question calls for differentiation between rights. This is not an unprecedented notion. The notion that jurisdiction is not monolithic has been proposed before, with differentiating factors including the distinction between positive and negative obligations[80] and among different types of rights.[81] The obligation to respect the right to life, for example, might be triggered by a lower level of prior control than obligations regarding other rights (perhaps, exceptionally, none at all).

5. The ICJ's Doctrine: IHL as *Lex Specialis* in Extraterritorial Hostilities

As noted at the outset, the first port of call in current international practice for engaging with the applicability of IHRL norms in armed conflict seems to be the ICJ's jurisprudence, primarily the *Nuclear Weapons* Advisory Opinion. So far, the chapter has proposed a non-traditional reading of jurisprudence with respect to the applicability of IHRL. It now turns to examining its import on the relationship between IHL and IHRL.

In the *Nuclear Weapons* Advisory Opinion, the Court used the term *lex specialis* as an interpretative tool. Later, in the *Wall* Advisory Opinion, it proposed *lex specialis* as a means of resolving conflict between norms and regarded IHL as the substantive *lex specialis*.[82] Needless to say that if, as the analysis in the previous sections concludes, IHRL is inapplicable in extraterritorial hostilities, the question of *how* it is interpreted or *how* it is pitted against conflicting IHL norms becomes redundant. However, it could be argued that since both variants of the *lex specialis* doctrine give precedence to substantive content of IHL over that of IHRL,

Transcripts and Summaries of Presentations and Discussions, 52, 55, <https://www.chathamhouse.org/sites/files/chathamhouse/public/Research/International%20Law/ilparmedconflict.pdf>.

[79] Classifying a situation in which significant hostilities are occurring in occupied territory is controversial. N Lubell, 'Challenges in Applying Human Rights Law to Armed Conflict' (2005) 87 International Review of the Red Cross 737, 740–41, inter alia citing *Al Skeini* (n 61) paras 284–85; Kretzmer (n 77) 48.

[80] Milanovic (n 69); see also Cerone (n 52) 440–49. For judicial practice see *Al Skeini* (n 61) para 137; *Hirsi Jamaa and Others v Italy* App No 27765/09 (ECtHR, 23 February 2012) para 74.

[81] Cerone (n 52) 436–40; N Lubell, 'Parallel Application of International Humanitarian Law and International Human Rights Law: An Examination of the Debate' (2007) 40 Israel Law Review 648, 653–54 and references therein.

[82] *Wall* (n 2) para 106.

resort to the doctrine is preferable to holding that IHRL is inapplicable, because it achieves the result sought in the present analysis—namely that in situations of extraterritorial hostilities states would not be bound by IHRL norms that are not also regulated by IHL—without compromising the universality of IHRL. This section examines the feasibility of this proposition. It holds that in addition to the conceptual arguments against the validity and utility in international law of the *lex specialis* doctrine,[83] each of its variants corresponds only to a particular formulation of rights and is therefore no panacea for regulating the relationship between IHRL and IHL.

5.1 *Lex specialis* as an interpretative tool

In the *Nuclear Weapons* Advisory Opinion, the ICJ interpreted the scope of the right to life under Article 6 ICCPR in light of the IHL norm pertaining to the same right. Both norms have exceptional features that permit this construction. First, the right to life under the ICCPR may be limited so long as the limitation is not 'arbitrary', and so long as it is—as all limitations on human rights must be—necessary and proportionate to the aim it pursues. The term 'non-arbitrary' excludes unlawfulness, injustice, capriciousness and unreasonableness.[84] IHRL therefore provides a wide berth for limiting the right, and can easily accommodate IHL norms, which, being norms of international law, are obviously non-arbitrary. As for the IHL norm on the right to life, it provides not only the grounds for deprivation of life (military necessity), but also speaks to the requirement of necessity and proportionality (through the principle of distinction and permissibility of incidental injury to civilians[85]), which are fundamental in IHRL. The combination of the flexibility of IHRL which can incorporate a norm as such from a different body of law, with the comprehensiveness of the IHL provision which incorporates not only the grounds for limitation but a balancing standard, is unique. Even under the ICCPR, the open-ended 'non-arbitrary' formula appears only with respect to the rights to personal liberty from arrest or detention, to enter one's own country, and to non-interference with privacy, family, home, or correspondence.[86] Of these rights, only the right to liberty is also regulated under IHL pertaining to extraterritorial hostilities.[87] However, under IHL it is not subject to a balancing formula but is simply a permissive provision. The ICJ's formula would therefore be applicable at most

[83] N Prud'homme, 'Lex Specialis: Oversimplifying a More Complex and Multifaceted Relationship?' (2007) 40 Israel Law Review 355; C Dröge, 'The Interplay between International Humanitarian Law and International Human Rights Law in Situations of Armed Conflict' (2007) 40 Israel Law Review 310, 339–40; M Milanovic (n 4); Third Party Submission, referred to in *Hassan* (n 2) para 93.
[84] Nowak (n 36) 128.
[85] AP I (n 6) Articles 51(5)(b), 57(2)(a)(iii).
[86] ICCPR (n 7) Articles 9(1), 12(4) and 17(1).
[87] Through the norms regarding POWs. In NIAC, even that provision does not apply.

to that right. With respect to the others, the open-endedness under the ICCPR is not matched by any IHL provision.[88] Moreover, even importing the content of the IHL norm into the IHRL one does not necessarily exhaust the IHRL analysis. This is demonstrable in *Hassan*, where after somehow squaring the authority to detain prisoners of war under IHL with the exhaustive list of purposes allowing for detention under the ECHR on the basis of the *Nuclear Weapons* Advisory Opinion formula,[89] the majority proceeded to apply IHRL directly, and not merely as an interpretation of IHL, because there are no IHL provisions to interpret. It applied it to aspects of detention other than its grounds, namely the procedural guarantees stipulated in the ECHR.[90] In short, the notion that the IHRL norm can be interpreted in light of IHL is workable only in the exceptional case of the right to life under the ICCPR.

Looking further afield, to rights on which limitations cannot be merely 'non-arbitrary' but must fall within enumerated purposes, the ICJ formula becomes entirely unworkable.[91] Freedom of speech or movement, for example, may be limited only for respect of the rights or reputations of others, for the protection of national security or of public order, or of public health or morals.[92] This structure does not provide space for incorporating IHL as *lex specialis* à la *Nuclear Weapons* Advisory Opinion (leaving aside, for the time being, what the content of that *lex* might be). It allows for taking account of the existence of extraterritorial hostilities only as a *factual* factor, following which the *normative* consequences would be determined by IHRL. Not only is this not what the *Nuclear Weapons* Advisory Opinion formula calls for, but also, as explained above, an IHRL analysis is unworkable because there is no express authorization under IHL law to limit these rights which can be incorporated in the interpretation of the enumerated purposes.

Various scholars (and now the ECtHR in *Hassan*) have advocated for the use of derogations to avoid or resolve the inability of IHRL provisions to accommodate corresponding IHL ones.[93] Leaving aside the general question whether derogations are appropriate for extraterritorial hostilities,[94] derogations cannot overcome the limitations of the *Nuclear Weapons* Advisory Opinion formula with respect to

[88] Unless their absence under IHL is interpreted as their rejection, but that would effectively be applying *lex specialis* as a conflict resolving tool (addressed below) rather than an interpretative one.
[89] *Hassan* (n 2) para 107.
[90] ibid para 106.
[91] For a similar critique see Krieger (n 2) 282.
[92] ICCPR (n 7) Articles 12(3), 19(2).
[93] See, eg, M Milanovic, 'Extraterritorial Derogations from Human Rights Treaties in Armed Conflict' in N Bhuta (ed), *The Frontiers of Human Rights: Extraterritoriality and its Challenges, Collected Courses of the Academy of European Law* (OUP 2016) 55; but see Dennis (n 14) 134–39.
[94] See, eg, D Kretzmer, 'Targeted Killing of Suspected Terrorists: Extra-Judicial Executions or Legitimate Means of Defence?' [2005] 16 European Journal of International Law 171, 185, and responses by Milanovic, ibid. One shortcoming of the latter's analysis is that it assumes that as a matter of *fact*, states control the timing of their entry into conflict and can therefore be required to follow the necessary constitutional process of derogation.

rights not regulated under IHL.[95] Derogations may not nullify a right.[96] Insofar as the rights to life and liberty from detention are concerned, deference to IHL does not nullify the rights, since they are also protected under IHL, albeit to a lesser extent. But if a different right were at issue, not regulated under IHL, the effect of derogation based on IHL's silence would be to nullify it, making the derogation impermissible and therefore invalid. Alternatively, if the silence of IHL is viewed as a lacuna which can be filled by IHRL, the derogation becomes altogether meaningless, because IHL would then absorb the IHRL norm as it is. Either way, then, a derogation does not resolve the general issue of the relationship between the two regimes but is operational only with respect to the rights to life and to liberty from detention under the ECHR.

5.2 *Lex specialis* as a tool for resolving norm conflict

In the *Wall* Advisory Opinion, the ICJ declared a second *lex specialis* doctrine, one of 'partial displacement'.[97] This doctrine provides that in case of a genuine conflict between rules of IHL and IHLR that cannot be avoided through interpretation alone, the 'special' IHL rule would displace or prevail over the IHRL rule.[98] The question is therefore whether the absence of regulation under IHL of certain rights, such as freedom of expression or movement, should be viewed as contradictory to the regulation of these rights under IHRL and thus as displacing it.

IHL prohibits certain conduct. Conduct that is not prohibited is permitted, but, needless to say, is not obligatory. Thus, IHL might not prohibit a state from imposing limitations on movement, but it does not obligate it to impose them. Accordingly, with respect to rights not regulated under IHL, a state engaged in extraterritorial hostilities is not simultaneously subject to contradictory prescriptions. Although it is obligated to respect them, it is not prohibited from doing so under IHL. There is actually is no conflict between the two bodies of law, and the IHRL provision can apply unencumbered.[99] This, however, leads to an absurd result: the fundamental rights to life and liberty, which are regulated under

[95] The substantive flaws of reading an automatic derogation into the application of IHL are analysed in detail in *Hassan* (n 2), Partly Dissenting Opinion of Judge Spano joined by Judges Nicolaou, Bianku, and Kalaydjieva; Milanovic (n 93) in anticipation of the judgment; Z Bohrer, 'Human Rights vs Humanitarian Law or Rights vs Obligations: Reflections Following the Rulings in Hassan and Jaloud' (2016) 16 Questions of International Law 5, 11.

[96] L Doswald-Beck, 'Human Rights: Their Place on the Battlefield' in *'The Law of Armed Conflict: Problems and Prospects', Chatham House, 18-19 April 2005, Transcripts and Summaries of Presentations and Discussions*, 49, <https://www.chathamhouse.org/sites/files/chathamhouse/public/Research/International%20Law/ilparmedconflict.pdf>.

[97] Milanovic (n 4) section 3.

[98] M Sassòli, 'The Role of Human Rights and International Humanitarian Law in New Types of Armed conflicts' in Ben-Naftali (n 2) 34.

[99] Dröge (n 82) 336.

IHL, are more limited in situations of extraterritorial hostilities than they are in a non-armed conflict situation, while the scope of other, less fundamental rights remains the same under IHL. The implementation of these rights would admittedly be evaluated in light of the existence of hostilities as a factual circumstance, but as argued above, this implementation fails from within since there is no 'law' which would allow limitations, and it is unreasonable to hold that the rights are absolute. Again, the *lex specialis* doctrine as applied in a specific type of armed conflict (occupation) fails to operate when applied more widely, to other rights or situations.

6. Conclusion: Challenging the Applicability of IHRL in Extraterritorial Hostilities

This contribution argues that the IHRL paradigm is ill-suited to situations of extraterritorial hostilities. Not only does IHL exclude it, but the mechanism of IHRL was not designed for situations in which a government, or a coalition of governments, exercises powers over persons who do not in any way form a part of the society which it governs. Secondly, and relatedly, while this contribution accepts that extraterritorial conduct does not necessarily *negate* jurisdiction under IHRL, it does hold that extraterritorial conduct does not *ipso facto create* jurisdiction. Rather, human rights obligations only arise from the exercise of some measure of prior control; in extraterritorial hostilities, in which the government does not exercise such prior control, jurisdiction should be presumed absent. Otherwise, it would appear that the conduct of hostilities triggers the applicability of international human rights obligations that otherwise would not exist.

A separate line of enquiry pursued in the chapter acknowledges that present international jurisprudence marginalizes the jurisdictional constraint on the applicability of IHRL in extraterritorial hostilities. This line of enquiry examines whether, if IHRL is nonetheless deemed applicable, the solution to its inoperability lies in the *lex specialis* doctrines. The chapter first considers the notion of interpreting IHRL in light of IHL, as laid down by the ICJ in the *Nuclear Weapons* Advisory Opinion. It demonstrates the shortcomings of this construct when an attempt is made to apply it to rights other than life or liberty from detention under the ICCPR. The analysis then turns to the doctrine of *lex specialis* as laid down by the ICJ in the *Wall* Advisory Opinion, according to which IHL should replace IHRL in case of a conflict of norms. It shows that with respect to human rights not regulated under IHL, this leads to absurd and unacceptable outcomes.

As this contribution indicates, some of the difficulties in applying prevailing orthodoxy stem from the fact that it was developed by reference to the right to life, without adequate attention to its implications in other contexts. Once this is acknowledged, the appeal of the orthodoxy might diminish, in favour of a more nuanced approach.

A potential critique of the view put forward in this chapter may be that parsing armed conflict into separate situations runs counter to the prevalent trend of adopting uniform rules across the board, playing down differences rather than highlighting them. This is particularly discernible with respect to the distinction between NIACs and international ones;[100] it can also be important for normalizing multinational military operations. For example, Milanovic rejects arguments regarding jurisdiction which attach significance to the convergence of extraterritoriality and armed conflict, on the ground that the development of the law of NIACs has rendered this approach obsolete.[101] Indeed, international law has rejected the extraterritorial conflict/internal peace dichotomy. Extraterritoriality is no longer a bar to the applicability of IHRL, while intra-territoriality is no bar to the applicability of IHL. But neither does either of these designations dictate the applicability of the respective bodies of law. Just as not every intra-territorial situation is governed by IHL (because there might be no armed conflict), not every extraterritorial situation should necessarily be governed by IHRL (in the relationship between the attacking state and the enemy population). The question essentially boils down to whether the very existence of extraterritorial hostilities should trigger the applicability of IHRL. To respond positively would undermine the very notion of IHL as the body of international law governing armed conflict. More generally, uniformity between the regulation of international armed conflict and intra-state armed conflict, while convenient, should not be an overriding goal where substantive arguments pull in a different direction.

It might seem that the difference between holding IHRL inapplicable in extraterritorial hostilities and holding that it applies but defers to the precedence of IHL is merely conceptual and of no practical consequence. The ICJ's *Nuclear Weapons* Advisory Opinion, for example, interpreted the right to life in light of IHL. In *Hassan*, the ECtHR effectively allowed the detention of POWs under IHL despite the stricter standard of the ECHR. In both cases, this was achieved without formally compromising the applicability of IHRL. This view has both factual and normative weaknesses.

It is true that in decisions given to date the applicability of IHRL has not resulted in outcomes that differ from those which would have obtained under IHL. Indeed, when practical differences between the two bodies of law appeared inevitable, the applicability of IHRL was resisted (in *Bankovic*), or its content was oddly interpreted as to constrain its practical consequences (in *Hassan*).[102] But these instances

[100] On the relationship between classification of conflicts as an IAC or an NIAC by reference to assumptions on the applicability of IHRL and its relationship with IHL see Y Shereshvsky, 'Politics by Other Means: The Battle over the Classification of Asymmetrical Conflicts' (2016) 19 Vanderbilt Journal of Transnational Law 455.

[101] Milanovic (n 92).

[102] *Hassan* (n 2); but see *Mohammed* (n 24).

do not belie the question of principle.[103] Practical differences are inevitable and cannot be circumvented when rights other than life or liberty from detention are at issue. The matter has simply not been explored, possibly because other rights have not been invoked before international human rights bodies.[104] This absence of invocation may reflect a choice of priorities. But as judicial review of armed conflict expands, the possibility that additional rights would be invoked cannot be ruled out.

Normatively, if concrete rulings under IHRL do not differ from those that would obtain under IHL,[105] this is in part a result of the dilution of the IHRL norms. This is demonstrable in the ECtHR's *Isayeva* judgment. When examining whether the human right to life has been violated by Russian forces operating in Chechnya, the Court adopted an IHL-like, watered-down interpretation of the right.[106] The formal applicability of IHRL (given that the conflict was domestic) therefore did not enhance protection; but the adoption of a diluted interpretation may have repercussions when the right is invoked in situations not involving hostilities. This is hardly beneficial to IHRL, which is a body of law that applies primarily outside of conflict.[107] It is therefore preferable to declare the inapplicability of IHRL rather than gloss over the obstacles to its application during hostilities and weaken both the contents of specific norms and the standing of the regime as a whole.

Maintaining the integrity of IHRL in the manner proposed in this chapter does come at an institutional price. Accepting the non-applicability of IHRL in situations of extraterritorial hostilities may deprive judicial and quasi-judicial human rights monitoring bodies such as the HRC or the ECtHR of the competence to hear complaints, whereas if IHRL applies (but is somehow interpreted in light of IHL), complaints to these bodies would be admissible, albeit addressed largely in terms of IHL. In other words, the insistence on the applicability of IHRL is significant

[103] Bohrer (n 94) relies on the factual convergence of outcomes to support a normative conclusion. His reliance is an example of the generalization from the specific right. Bohrer argues that the IHRL standard for the obligation to investigate instances of civilian loss of life in hostilities is not more demanding than the IHL standard, rendering the resort to IHRL in *Jaloud* redundant. He also holds that in *Hassan* (n 2), the ECtHR ended up applying the IHL standard, again rendering IHRL redundant. However, the similarity between the obligation under IHL and IHRL with respect to the obligation to investigate is not coincidental, but rather the consequence of IHL having been interpreted in light of IHRL standards. With respect to *Hassan*, Bohrer's argument begs the issue. The Court has made the effort to circumvent IHRL (in a legal construct which Bohrer himself criticizes) precisely because IHRL is more protective.

[104] Although see *Salas* (n 55) para 9, where petitioners invoked, in addition to the right to life, liberty, and security, also the right to protection of mothers and children, to inviolability of the home, to work, and to property under the American Declaration of the Rights and duties of Man.

[105] Doswald-Beck (n 2) 51 considers that this is an imperative of the *Nuclear Weapons* Advisory Opinion.

[106] *Isayeva v Russia* App no 57950/00 (ECtHR, 24 February 2005) para 176; Dröge (n 82) 346–47.

[107] Report of the Study Group of the International Law Commission on the topic 'Fragmentation of International Law: Difficulties Arising from Diversification and Expansion of International Law', adopted by the International Law Commission at its fifty-eighth session in 2006. The Analytical Study of the Study Group on the same topic, 13 April 2006 (A/CN.4/L.682) para 104.

because IHRL has at its disposal monitoring or enforcement mechanisms which IHL does not.[108] However, this is not a sufficient reason to force the applicability of IHRL where it does not fit. The preservation of international law as a relevant constraint on parties involved in hostilities depends on maintaining a delicate balance between idealism and pragmatism. IHL is geared to provide this balance but is already struggling against the weight of contemporary challenges. IHRL alleviates some of the strains in situations which have not been in the core of IHL, such as occupation and NIAC. But imposition of IHRL on the core of IHL, namely the conduct of hostilities, carries the risk of weakening the regime rather than strengthening it.

[108] But see *Juan Carlos Abella v Argentina*, Inter-American Commission on Human Rights, Case no 11.137, Report No. 55/97 (18 November 1997) paras 157–71, in which the Inter-American Commission on Human Rights held itself competent to apply humanitarian law directly even though its competence is normally limited to the American Convention on Human Rights.

11

The Invaluable Civilian Risk Mitigation Contribution of Recognizing the Value of Precautionary Measures

Geoffrey Corn

1. Introduction

Protecting civilians from the risks resulting from hostilities during armed conflict is an enduring challenge for armed forces and other organized armed groups genuinely committed to the humanitarian objectives of international law. Few interests protected by this critically important branch of international law are more important; and few aspects of international legal regulation of armed conflict are more challenging to implement effectively. This has led to a continuous effort to clarify 'targeting' rules in international humanitarian law (IHL),[1] efforts that focus primarily on applicability, content, and implementation methodology for these rules.[2] Such efforts remain essential to ensure the most effective alignment between the humanitarian objectives of IHL, targeting law on the one hand, and the realities of operational implementation on the other, which unfortunately often expose the substantial gap between the law's goals and the actual reality of warfare.

[1] For a discussion of the relationship between military targeting doctrine and IHL rules applicable to targeting law, see WH Boothby, *The Law of Targeting* (OUP 2012); see also GS Corn and GP Corn, 'The Law of Operational Targeting: Viewing the LOAC through an Operational Lens' (2012) 47 Texas International Law Journal 337.

[2] This was an important feature of the International Law Association's (ILA's) 2017 Report by The Study Group on the Conduct of Hostilities in the 21st Century (SG). This focus is reflected in the SG's mandate, as explained in the Report: 'Thus, the central question is the extent to which the rules governing the conduct of hostilities need to be clarified, both in terms of their scope of application and their substantive aspects. Although some sub-aspects of this issue have been examined before, what is still missing is a coherent and more principled approach to the challenges of 21st century warfare. The central focus of the SG lies on the actual rules governing the conduct of hostilities ... it was not the aim of the SG to comprehensively deal with all of the various issues arising in relation to the conduct of hostilities, but to focus on selected issues where the SG felt that there is a need and/or potential for further clarification', see International Law Association Study Group on the Conduct of Hostilities in the 21st Century, 'The Conduct of Hostilities and International Humanitarian Law: Challenges of 21st Century Warfare' (2017) 93 US Naval War College International Law Studies 322, 325.

Geoffrey Corn, *The Invaluable Civilian Risk Mitigation Contribution of Recognizing the Value of Precautionary Measures*
In *The 'Legal Pluriverse' Surrounding Multinational Military Operations*. Edited by Robin Geiß and Heike Krieger,
Oxford University Press (2020).
DOI: 10.1093/oso/9780198842965.003.0012

More specifically, these efforts tend to focus on three principal IHL targeting rules: military objectives,[3] precautions in attack,[4] and proportionality.[5] This focus is reflected in both academic and civil discourse, and in military doctrine. Indeed, it is almost common knowledge among those familiar with these sources that strong consensus exists that these three rules, all enumerated in the text of the 1977 Protocol I Additional to the Geneva Conventions of 1949 (AP I) provide the essential regulatory framework for implementing the animating objective of IHL: reconciling military necessity and interests of humanity. For example, a report issued by the International Law Association Study Group on the Conduct of Hostilities in the 21st Century noted that 'these three topics were unanimously determined to be core issues within IHL in relation to the conduct of hostilities in modern warfare and each topic contained a number of sub-topics set out in the three working papers'.[6]

Few would question that the military objective and proportionality rules provide the foundation for lawful targeting decisions. However, precautions in the attack, while vital in the civilian risk mitigation equation, have only recently gained the attention they deserve as a 'co-equal' pillar of this foundation.[7] Ideally, this attention will continue to increase as IHL experts, scholars focused on IHL, and armed forces themselves recognize the value of precautionary measures as an imperative component of the civilian risk mitigation equation. Indeed, raising the proverbial profile of precautions was the principal goal of a 2014 law review article by the author of the present contribution,[8] fortunately at a time when other experts also began to focus on the fact that precautionary measures had been undervalued in this civilian protection equation in IHL.

This chapter summarizes the reasons for this, and why the author believes that continued emphasis on precautions in the attack, both 'active' and 'passive', is essential not only to mitigate civilian risk during armed conflict, but also to enhance the professionalism of armed forces. Importantly, as will be explained, precautions should not be viewed in isolation, but instead as part of a symbiotic relationship

[3] Protocol Additional to the Geneva Conventions of 12 August 1949, and Relating to the Protection of Victims of International Armed Conflicts (Protocol I) (adopted 8 June 1977, entered into force 7 December 1978) 1125 UNTS 3 (AP I) (signed by the United States 12 December 1977, not transmitted to US Senate, see US Senate, '100th Congress 1st Session' [1987] Treaty Doc No 100-2).

[4] AP I (n 3) Article 57.

[5] ibid.

[6] 'The Report' (n 2) 322–24.

[7] See GS Corn, 'Targeting, Distinction, and the Long War: Guarding against Conflation of Cause and Responsibility' (2016) 46 Israel Yearbook on Human Rights 135; see also GS Corn and JA Schoettler, Jr, 'Targeting and Civilian Risk Mitigation: The Essential Role of Precautionary Measures' (2015) 223 Military Law Review 785; see also ET Jensen, 'Precautions Against the Effects of Attacks in Urban Areas' (2016) 98 (901) International Review of the Red Cross 147, writing on the advantages of precautions in a densely populated area; see also I Henderson, *The Contemporary Law of Targeting: Military Objectives, Proportionality and Precautions in Attack under Additional Protocol I* (Martinus Nijhoff 2009), writing about the location of civilian objects relative to military objects; WH Boothby, *The Law of Targeting* (OUP 2012).

[8] GS Corn, 'The Future of National Security Law: War, Law, and the Oft Overlooked Value of Process as a Precautionary Measure' (2014) 42 Pepperdine Law Review 419.

with the more substantive proportionality rule. To that end, the chapter will address how implementation of precautionary measures contributes to more effective proportionality judgments.[9] The chapter will also explain why prioritization of precautions as a critical targeting principle will often be better aligned with instinctive military logic than the more amorphous proportionality rule, and why this alignment—and beneficial effect—is especially important in the context of the type of decentralized and dynamic attack decisions that define combined arms manoeuvre operations.[10] Finally, the chapter will address why more work is needed to better align the importance of precautionary measures with criminal responsibility for subjecting civilians to unjustifiable risk, and how the relative commitment to implementation of precautionary measures can contribute substantially to the assessment of overall attack judgment reasonableness.

2. Precautions in the Attack: An Undervalued Civilian Risk Mitigation Tool

From 1997 to 2000, I taught at the US Army Judge Advocate's School as a member of the uniformed International and Operational Law Department faculty. Our centrepiece course was the Law of War Workshop where military legal advisers, uniformed and civilian, US and foreign, devoted a full week to a pragmatically oriented treatment of IHL. Like so many published authorities on this law, including military manuals, three key 'principles' dominated our coverage of targeting law: military objective, proportionality, and the prohibition against unnecessary suffering. Both in the classroom and during scenario-based exercises, emphasis was placed on assessing what qualified as a lawful military objective and implementation of the proportionality rule when risk to civilians was inherent in a planned attack.

This approach was probably indicative of those followed in other military education and training venues, with the focus on military objective and proportionality reflective of the general emphasis in published sources of the law. While there was always some discussion of the 'precautions in the attack' rule enumerated in Article 57 AP I, the significance of that rule, and its relationship to implementation of the other two targeting rules, was arguably never sufficiently addressed. In retrospect, this was probably an unfortunate manifestation of a broader failure to recognize the tremendous value of the rule of precautions as a civilian risk mitigation tool.

As I have addressed in greater detail elsewhere,[11] I believe there are several explanations for why precautions always seemed to exist in the shadow of the military

[9] 'The Report' (n 2) provides a more detailed look at the issues brought forth in this chapter.

[10] Corn and Schoettler, Jr (n 7) citing to and analysing US Army Doctrine implementing civilian risk mitigation strategies into their tactical land operation objectives.

[11] Corn (n 8).

objective and proportionality rule. First, when the destructive consequence of war is subjected to public scrutiny, the focus logically gravitates towards questions of whether a target was in fact legitimate, and why it was necessary to inflict collateral damage.[12] This focus is a consequence of a broader phenomenon of what I have called 'effects-based' critiques of military operations: the almost exclusive reliance on evidence of attack effects to infer non-compliance with IHL. This methodology is of course inconsistent with the *ex ante* focus of targeting law, which turns on the objective reasonableness of attack *judgments*, not attack *effects*.[13] But tendency to gravitate towards the much easier process of treating effects as dispositive indicators of IHL non-compliance instead of one aspect of the totality of information that must be considered in assessing compliance has impacted which IHL targeting rules dominate public and international legal discourse.

Secondly, unlike the precautions rule, violations of the military objective and proportionality rules have been incorporated into international criminal law, and are today among the enumerated offences within the jurisdiction of the International Criminal Court.[14] While this inclusion should not *ipso facto* necessitate an elevated *regulatory* status for these rules, there is little doubt that it has had this outcome.[15] Further, it is not illogical for military legal advisers and those who critique the conduct of hostilities to gravitate towards the targeting rules that provide a basis for international criminal responsibility.

Thirdly, the proportionality rule is simply a more attractive topic of legal discourse than the precautions rule.[16] No one can seriously contest the significance of legal scholarship as the primary source of IHL discourse, and that scholarship has reflected a far more extensive focus on proportionality than it has on precautions. This in turn reinforces the perception of what might best be understood as a kind of prioritization of importance: because proportionality is such a dominant focus of legal scholarship, it must be the most important rule in practice. However, as I argue in my prior publications,[17] this subtle message distorts the reality of *operational* significance. Proportionality is appealing from a scholarly perspective because of the elusive nature of the balance of substantive interests central to the

[12] P Bump, 'War is Ugly: Kerry Defends Israel's Incursion into Gaza' *The Washington Post* (Washington DC, 30 July 2014) <http://www.washingtonpost.com/news/post-politics/wp/2014/07/20/war-is-ugly-kerry-defends-israels-incursion-into-gaza/?utm_term=.d4397d1e98dc>. All URLs accessed 27 December 2018.

[13] See generally Corn (n 7).

[14] See Corn (n 8) 422.

[15] Jensen (n 7), writing that 'when the defending forces intentionally commingle military headquarters or other installations with civilians and civilian objects, or by their own actions intentionally put civilians at increased risk of attack and fail to warn or take other protective actions, particularly after the onset of hostilities, the international community ought to find a violation of the defending force's obligations and prosecute responsible individuals for a war crime'.

[16] Corn (n 8), stating that the attractiveness of the rule comes from the 'inherent uncertainty' associated with the rule.

[17] ibid 461.

rule: what qualifies as a 'concrete and direct' military advantage? Does the civilian risk aspect of the equation need to be equally concrete, or do 'reverberating' effects factor into the equation? What qualifies as 'excessive'? How should actual effects play into the compliance assessment? These are the types of questions that understandably attract scholarly inquiry; inquiry that has contributed to a better appreciation of the rule's complexity.

However, the scholarly imbalance between the focus on proportionality compared to precautions is not indicative of the *operational* significance of these two critical IHL targeting rules. Indeed, the elusive nature of the proportionality rule that leads to its scholarly appeal actually undermines its operational significance.[18] In practice, within the margins of the extreme, the proportionality rule provides very little practical guidance to commanders deciding on when, where, and how to conduct an attack. This is not to suggest the rule has no value; to suggest that would be absurd. Commanders must understand that at some point, incidental injury and collateral damage become unacceptable even when they are not an intended effect. But balancing anticipated military advantage against anticipated civilian risk is so highly contextual that in most situations the margin of reasonable judgment makes it unlikely that the rule will have a substantial limiting impact on combat action.

In fact, it is almost certainly true that precautionary measures are far more operationally effective in mitigating civilian risk than is proportionality. Why is this so? First and foremost, precautionary measures are simply better aligned with operational practice than the proportionality rule.[19] Military operations at every level are rarely ad hoc adventures, but instead are planned and prepared for as extensively as the time and situation will allow. Even dynamic attack decisions undergo a time-sensitive deliberation process. Precautions in attack are aligned with the type of decision-making process that commanders instinctively utilize when making tactical use of force decisions.[20] Considerations such as timing of attack, weapon selection, and alternate attack options are inherent in the military decision-making

[18] ibid 423, stating that '[t]his uncertainty associated with the balance between military advantage and civilian risk central to implementing the proportionality rule is, in practice, an inherent limitation on the rule's efficacy in all but extreme situations. As the recent hostilities between the Israel Defence Forces and Hamas in Gaza so dramatically illustrated, this limitation results in wildly conflicting assessments of legal compliance in the execution of combat operations. This should come as no surprise, but instead serve as a reminder that the operational implementation of this very general concept is so intensely fact dependent that it has limited utility in providing a predictable and tactically logical framework for mitigating civilian risk during the execution of combat operations'.

[19] Corn and Schoettler, Jr (n 7) 810, stating that 'the objectives of Article 57 are completely aligned with operational and tactical logic: develop attack options that maximize the disabling effect on the enemy while mitigating risk to friendly forces and civilians alike. Failing to consider civilian risk mitigation in selecting among courses of action in the attack planning process is, therefore, inconsistent with both the LOAC's humanitarian objectives and U.S. military doctrine'.

[20] ibid 799, writing that the precautionary obligations are 'directed towards those who plan or decide upon attacks' and that 'every soldier who engages a target is planning and deciding upon an attack' thus placing the precautionary measures taken during an attack squarely within the soldier's responsibility and training.

process. Accordingly, these types of *precautionary* measures may be integrated into the decision-making process with relative ease, and military operations need not rely on a legal adviser to be effective.

Secondly, precautionary measures are inherently more objective in nature than the more subjective assessments necessary to implement the proportionality rule. Commanders rely on expertise in weapons and tactics to identify the most effective synchronization of combat power to achieve intended objectives. This requires that commanders, and the subordinates they rely on, develop tactical and technical proficiency: understanding the dynamics of the weapon systems they control and how to best employ those systems for maximum effect. These considerations are generally objective in nature: the blast effect of a munition; the maximum effective range of a rifle; the doctrinally established method for manoeuvre; and the list goes on. These objective considerations provide the foundation upon which courses of action are assessed and adopted. Because precautionary measures implicate similar objective considerations related to the means and methods of warfare, they are more readily assessed and integrated into course of action development than the much more amorphous notion of proportionality.

Thirdly, precautionary measures are better suited to implementation at *all* levels of tactical execution than the proportionality rule. The inherent complexity associated with the proportionality balance almost certainly explains the increasingly significant role played by legal advisers in the deliberate targeting process. These military legal experts assist commanders facing the challenge of implementing the rule. However, even in the deliberate targeting process, where the contribution of legal advice, along with the opportunity to consider substantial information—related to both the anticipated civilian risk and the value of the target—facilitate proportionality assessments, they remain highly complex and rarely clear-cut.

Expecting an analogous level of deliberation and decision-making sophistication at the tactical level of operations, especially in relation to dynamic targeting judgments, is unrealistic. Rarely will those responsible for making attack decisions benefit from the time, information, and legal advice that can be expected at deliberate targeting decisions on higher levels. Instead, junior combat leaders will be expected to exercise tactical initiative in the employment of their assets, which means in most situations that they will be making time-sensitive attack decisions in situations that are often chaotic and confusing. It is almost axiomatic that in such situations, the precautions rule can bear more weight than its proportionality counterpart. Expecting combat leaders to pause during operations to engage in the complex proportionality assessment may be aspirational, but that expectation probably rarely aligns with reality.

Conversely, expecting these same combat leaders to rapidly assess pragmatic options for mitigating civilian risk *is* much more realistic. These combat leaders constantly engage in such time-sensitive assessments for tactical advantage. Implementation of precautions merely involves shifting the focus of the objective, not the method of analysis. Even at the lowest tactical level, soldiers are capable of rapidly assessing the choice of methods and means of attack in order to mitigate civilian risk, and they are equally capable of making rapid judgments about whether adjusting an attack option is tactically feasible in the way they would all other tactical decisions.

In this regard, it is important to remember that while the relatively high-level deliberate targeting process has dominated public interest and scholarly discourse during the era of 'drone' warfare and counter-terror military operations,[21] IHL must function in all operational scenarios. While the proportionality rule may play a significant role in this context, such attack decisions are better understood as the exception and not the rule. Most combat operations involve decentralized attack decisions by combat leaders at every level of command. This decentralized model of military decision-making is the central feature of US military doctrine,[22] and likely that of many other armed forces. Known as 'mission command',[23] subordinates execute operations pursuant to broadly defined commander's intent and are expected to exploit opportunities that arise during the inevitable chaos and shifting situation of manoeuvre warfare. In this context, it is even more illogical to expect the proportionality rule to play the dominant civilian risk mitigation role. In contrast, so long as this risk mitigation is emphasized as an important command objective—which ideally it will be—the precautions rule can genuinely be expected to do the heavy lifting.

Precautionary measures are also more amenable to the combat leader training and professional development process. For the same reasons that precautions are more naturally integrated into the military decision-making process, they are more naturally integrated into training than the proportionality rule. Emphasizing the relevance of precautionary measures during combat training will also contribute to an overall civilian risk mitigation mindset, and in so doing advance the IHL mandate to take 'constant care' to avoid unnecessary harm to civilians and civilian property. Training will ideally lead to a tactical instinct to constantly endeavour to mitigate civilian risk. And, as such measures are primarily objective in nature, training assessments will be more informative than critiquing proportionality judgments.

[21] See M Bowden, 'The Killing Machines' *The Atlantic* (September 2013) <http://www.theatlantic.com/magazine/archive/2013/09/the-killing-machines-how-to-think-about-drones/309434/>; I Henderson and B Cavanagh, 'Unmanned Aerial Vehicles: Do They Pose Legal Challenges?' in H Nasu and R McLaughlin (eds), *New Technologies and the Law of Armed Conflict* (Springer 2014) 203–04; these operations have also been the focus of American Civil Liberties Union (ACLU) litigation, eg *ACLU v CIA*, 109 F. Supp. 3d 220 (2015); *ACLU v. Department of Justice*, 808 F. Supp. 2d 280 (2011).

[22] US Army, *Doctrine Reference Publication 6-0, Mission Command* (17 May 2012) paras 1-2, 1-3; see also US Army, *Field Manual 3-60, Targeting* (7 May 2015) viii.

[23] US Army, *Doctrine Reference Publication 6-0, Mission Command* (17 May 2012) paras 1-2, 1-3.

Precautions in the attack are not, of course, limited to 'active' measures like those enumerated in Article 57 AP I.[24] Civilian risk will also be mitigated by implementation of what may be understood as 'passive' precautions as enumerated in Article 58 AP I. These precautions are concededly more amorphous in nature than the more active measures included in Article 57. Unlike active precautions that focus on measures implemented by the *attacking* force to mitigate civilian risk, passive precautions involve protecting civilians by endeavouring to avoid creating situations where they will fall victim to an opponent's attack. However, because it is unrealistic, indeed probably impossible, to expect armed forces to completely avoid co-mingling their personnel and assets among the civilian population, these passive precautions are more aspirational in nature than their active counterparts.[25] Nonetheless, it is reasonable to expect combat leaders at every level to understand and embrace the basic notion of endeavouring to consider civilian risk mitigation in decisions related to the placement of assets and manoeuvre of forces. Like their active counterparts, such considerations can be readily integrated into combat training and assessments and will rarely necessitate legal advice to be effectively implemented.

All of these considerations indicate that while the proportionality rule may be the dominant focus of public and scholarly discourse, the precautions rule is capable of bearing far more operational weight. It is for this reason that I have argued the rule has been unfortunately undervalued in IHL discourse. Increased attention to precautions will ideally make a positive contribution to the recognition that, in practice, emphasizing precautions will likely enhance the effectiveness of civilian risk mitigation measures. Furthermore, instead of being viewed in isolation, understanding the symbiotic relationship between precautionary measures and proportionality will ultimately enhance the effectiveness of the proportionality rule itself.

3. Understanding the Integrated Nature of IHL Targeting Rules

The positive effect of IHL's substantive targeting rules, principally the military objective and proportionality rule, depend on process to ensure effective implementation.[26] This implementation process is in itself a precautionary measure, although not one specifically enumerated in Article 57 AP I. When attack decisions

[24] Y Sandoz and others, *Commentary on the Additional Protocols of 8 June 1977 to the Geneva Conventions of 12 August 1949* (ICRC 1987) para 2241, stating that the ICRC has felt the need to lay down provisions for 'passive' precautions.

[25] Corn (n 7) 21, stating that '[m]ilitary forces will always seek tactical and operational advantages in the conduct of hostilities, and such advantage will often be derived from tactics that rely on the use of civilian property or exploit proximity to civilian population centers'.

[26] US Department of Defense, *Law of War Manual* (June 2015, updated December 2016) 56, citing the remarks of MJ Matheson (Deputy Legal Adviser, Department of State) on 'the United States Position on the Relation of Customary International Law to the 1977 Protocols Additional to the 1949 Geneva Conventions' at 'The Sixth Annual American Red Cross-Washington College of Law Conference on

are made pursuant to a systemic analytical process—implemented in relation to both deliberate and dynamic attacks—the effect of these substantive rules will almost always be enhanced. Accordingly, precautions can also be understood as part of an overall process of civilian risk mitigation.

This process involves three critical legal analytical steps. First, application of the military objective rule to determine who or what qualifies as a lawful object of deliberate attack. The accuracy of this assessment is obviously dependent on the quality of information available to a commander. The collection and analysis of combat information is therefore a critical precaution because it informs the implementation of the military objective rule. This precautionary measure also informs the assessment of collateral risk to civilians and civilian property if an attack is launched. In this regard, it provides the information needed to determine whether implementation of other precautions and a proportionality assessment are required. If the assessment indicates that the attack may be conducted without creating such risk, these rules are not implicated. However, when an attack is expected to create such risk, the next step in the legality assessment should be to implement, where feasible, the active precautions enumerated in Article 57 AP I. This step will ideally reduce the potential civilian risk *before* the third step in the analysis, the proportionality assessment, is made. Ideally, integrating precautionary measures into this decision-making process will simplify the ultimate proportionality assessment by reducing the risk of incidental injury and/or collateral damage.

Emphasizing precautions during training and integrating a coherent target legality assessment process into the military decision-making process will ultimately contribute to accurate military objective determinations and proportionate uses of force when civilian risk cannot be avoided. Even in the decentralized time-sensitive attack context, developing a 'precautions process' instinct among combat leaders at all levels will contribute substantially to protecting civilians and civilian property from unnecessary risk. In short, precautions must not be viewed as an afterthought to military objective and proportionality assessments, but instead a critical facilitator for those assessments, embedded within the overall targeting process. The following two charts (see Figure 11.1), reproduced from a co-authored text titled *The Law of Armed Conflict: An Operational Approach*,[27] illustrate how precautions can be effectively integrated into this process.

International Humanitarian Law' (22 January 1987) 2(2) American University International Law Review 415, 419, 426–27 ('We support the principle that all practicable precautions, taking into account military and humanitarian considerations, be taken in the conduct of military operations to minimize incidental death, injury, and damage to civilians and civilian objects, and that effective advance warning be given of attacks which may affect the civilian population, unless circumstances do not permit'); United Nations General Assembly Res 2675 'Basic Principles for the Protection of Civilian Populations in Armed Conflict' (9 December 1970) UN Doc A/8028 ('In the conduct of military operations, every effort should be made to spare the civilian populations from the ravages of war, and all necessary precautions should be taken to avoid injury, loss or damage to civilian populations').

[27] GS Corn and others, *The Law of Armed Conflict: An Operational Approach* (Kluwer 2012) 175 and 185.

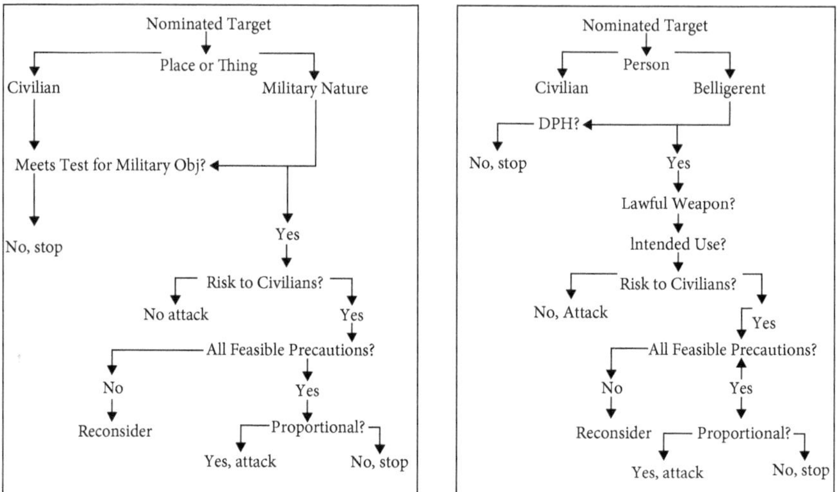

Originally Published in Corn, et. at., The Law of Armed Conflict: An Operational Approach, Wolters Kluwer (2012)

Originally Published in Corn, et. al., The Law of Armed Conflict: An Operational Approach, Wolters Kluwer (2012).

Fig. 11.1

None of this is intended to suggest that implementing precautions in the attack is easy or that the rule is purely objective. Because the obligation to implement these precautions is qualified by feasibility assessments, implementation of precautionary obligations is never purely objective, but rather involves considerations of the same tactical and operational variables associated with implementing the precautions rule. This obviously injects an element of subjectivity into the precautions equation and requires assessing the same totality of tactical considerations that usually renders the proportionality assessment so complex. But the nature of the feasibility assessment vis-à-vis precautions is arguably less amorphous and more aligned with tactical decision-making than the assessment of values associated with the proportionality rule. In the precautions context, feasibility almost always involves assessing whether implementing a precaution will result in tactical compromise. This type of assessment is made constantly by combat leaders on every level of command as they develop and implement tactical courses of action. For example, assessing whether delaying an attack, or issuing a warning to civilians that will degrade the effect of an attack, is an assessment combat leaders should be competent to make. In contrast, assessing whether the number of potential civilian casualties is excessive in comparison to the concrete and direct military advantage anticipated from an attack is far more attenuated from normal tactical instincts. Thus, even the more subjective component of precautions aligns more logically with the competence of combat leaders than the proportionality rule.

Concededly, assessing when, where, and how to implement 'passive' precautions in the sense of Article 58 AP I is more complex. As noted earlier, a primary reason for this increased complexity is that this aspect of precautionary measures is framed in terms of 'endeavour', which necessarily creates a wider margin of appreciation. The complexity of assessing when and how the use of a place or object in support of military operations means that it is extremely difficult to conclude that such a use indicates a violation of this obligation.[28] What is certainly invalid is to simply presume that this obligation is violated whenever military personnel or assets are arrayed in a way that exposes civilians or civilian property to risk that results from an opponent attacking those personnel or assets. Nonetheless, in certain situations it would be possible to identify a prima facie violation of this obligation. For instance, when a military asset is located amongst the civilian population, the nature of the location in comparison to alternate proximate locations will often indicate an effort to exploit the civilian object to shield the asset. Similar inferences may arise when military personnel fail to wear uniforms or other indicia of a status distinct from the civilian population.

Emphasizing the importance of passive precautions may not ultimately produce the same civilian risk mitigation payoff as emphasizing active precautions in the attack, but it nonetheless deserves greater attention. Hostilities have been, and almost certainly will continue to be, conducted in densely populated civilian areas. Encouraging armed forces and other organized armed groups to constantly seek to avoid creating unnecessary risk to civilians as the result of manoeuvre and placement of forces and assets is perhaps more essential today than ever before. Emphasis on this aspect of precaution is also critically important for ensuring credible assessment of responsibility for civilian casualties and damage to civilian property. Such assessments must focus not only on the party to the conflict that launched the attack that causes such harm, but also on the conduct of the party subjected to attack.

This latter consideration highlights how the tendency to overlook the passive precautions obligation contributes to a primarily effects-based approach to

[28] Jensen (n 7) 159, writing that '[a]lthough the [precautions] rule is fairly easy to articulate, complying with it has proven to be more difficult. A number of issues quickly present themselves. For example ... moving the civilian population may not always be the most humane alternative, such as during times of severe weather ... segregation in urban areas [recognizes] "the attainment of this goal is difficult in a densely populated place or one in which war industry is closely integrated in with the civilian population" ... avoiding locating military objectives in populated areas may simply not be feasible ... Additionally ... by moving its military forces out of populated areas, a defender may "make them more readily identifiable by the enemy" '; see also Henderson (n 7) 187–88, writing about Iraqi actions during Operation Desert Storm and Operation Southern Watch, and the proximity of targets to civilian objects, vis-à-vis the application of the precautions requirements.

assessing responsibility for harm to civilians and civilian property.[29] This obligation is especially important in the post-attack assessment phase of IHL implementation. It is far too easy, and increasingly common, to automatically equate direct cause with legal responsibility for civilian casualties. However, failing to consider whether blatant or obvious violations of the passive precautions obligation created the foreseeable—if not intended—likelihood of civilian casualties not only contributes to a distorted accountability conclusion, but actually incentivizes tactics that increase civilian risk.[30] This latter effect, while especially perverse, is all too common in contemporary armed conflicts involving tactically mismatched opponents. In this context, the militarily weaker party to the conflict is almost encouraged to deliberately embed assets amongst the civilian population in an effort to offset the opponent's superior combat capability.

When the passive precautionary obligations of a party are minimized or ignored when assessing responsibility for civilian harm, the risk to civilians will almost inevitably be increased.[31] Such a phenomenon virtually eliminates any disincentive for deliberate co-mingling. Instead, civilians and civilian property will likely be viewed as both a tactical and strategic force-multiplier. At the tactical level, the party exploiting the presence of civilians will often reap the benefit of attack hesitation or forbearance by the militarily superior opponent, especially when the opponent is committed to good-faith compliance with IHL. This is an inevitable consequence of the critical IHL axiom that an enemy's violation of the law in no way releases the opponent from its civilian risk mitigation obligations.[32] In fact, it is probably true that in the context of contemporary 'asymmetric' conflicts, illicit tactics intended to exploit the presence of civilians by one party to a conflict will almost always lead to *increased* efforts by the other party to mitigate that risk.[33] Conversely, where the law-abiding party is compelled to launch attacks that endanger civilians, the illicit enemy often reaps a strategic windfall in the broader 'information war', based on the often false assumption that the party that directly caused civilian harm is ultimately responsible for that harm.

This latter consideration leads to the final point of discussion in this chapter: accountability—or lack thereof—for precautions violations. The overall

[29] Corn (n 7) 4, writing that '[a]n enemy's pattern of ignoring or deliberately violating these obligations—most notably the "passive distinction" obligation—would, according to this interpretation [that an important factor in the implementation equation is the relative compliance or non-compliance by an enemy with its own LOAC obligations], be a legitimate consideration in assessing the reasonableness of an attack judgment and the accordant compliance with the "active distinction" obligation'.

[30] Jensen (n 7).

[31] Corn and Schoettler, Jr (n 7), writing that the 'constant care' requirement of the precautionary measures rules and their respective implementation, decrease the risk of harm to civilians.

[32] DoD Law of War Manual (n 26) 1083; see also AP I (n 3) Article 51.

[33] Corn and Schoettler, Jr (n 7), writing that '[e]ven if a failure to implement passive precautions is attributed to a deliberate attempt to use civilians or civilian property to gain an illicit tactical and/or strategic advantage, the attacking force remains obligated to do everything inherent in the constant care rule to minimize civilian risk'.

lack of accountability is the result of a general failure to recognize both the importance of these IHL rules on civilian risk mitigation and the complementary nature of active and passive precautions. Equally unfortunate is the fact that the precautions rule to date does not figure prominently, if at all, in the international criminal law equation on accountability.

4. Elevating the Status of Precautions through Enhanced Accountability

IHL targeting rules function primarily as a regulatory framework: they regulate the conduct of hostilities.[34] These rules were not developed as criminal proscriptions, although AP I does include violation of the distinction and proportionality rules within the scope of the 'grave breaches'. This is indicative of a broader relationship between IHL targeting rules and international criminal law (ICL). Today, there is widespread agreement that violations of the distinction or proportionality rules may qualify as violations of ICL. The most obvious indication of this consensus is the inclusion of crimes based on such violations within the jurisdiction of the International Criminal Court (ICC). In the context of an international armed conflict, both distinction and proportionality violations are included within the court's jurisdiction;[35] in the context of a non-international armed conflict, violating the rule of distinction by directing an attack against a civilian (not directly participating in hostilities) or the civilian population is within the court's jurisdiction.[36]

While the ICC statute does not include proportionality violations during a non-international armed conflict within the court's jurisdiction, this does not undermine the conclusion that proportionality violations during international armed conflicts are considered ICL violations. While this does raise questions about the applicability of a proportionality-based war crime to the context of non-international armed conflicts, it must also be noted that the International Criminal Tribunal for the Former Yugoslavia (ICTY) has considered such violations to fall within its war crimes jurisdiction.[37]

[34] *AP Commentary* (n 24) para 2207, stating that '[t]he principle of proportionality merely contributes to the clarification of matters' and is not 'quite at the same level as the fundamental principles governing [the Protection of Civilians]'.

[35] Rome Statute of the International Criminal Court (adopted 17 July 1998, entered into force 1 July 2002) 2187 UNTS 90, Article 8, Sec 2(b). Specifically, the ICC Statute (ICCSt) prohibits directing an attack against civilians or civilian property during an international armed conflict; launching an attack when the 'perpetrator knew that the attack would cause incidental death or injury to civilians or damage to civilian objects ... and that such death, injury or damage would be of such an extent as to be clearly excessive in relation to the concrete and direct overall military advantage anticipated' during an international armed conflict; directing an attack against a civilian or the civilian population during a non-international armed conflict; see ICCSt, Article 8, Sec 2(b)(iv)(3).

[36] ICCSt (n 35) Article 8, Sec 2(c).

[37] ICTY, *Prosecutor v Tadić* (Decision on Defence Motion for Interlocutory Appeal on Jurisdiction) IT-94-1-AR72 (2 October 1995).

Unlike the distinction and proportionality rules, there is no indication that a violation of the precautions rule is considered a war crime. Unlike its proportionality and distinction counterparts, violation of the precautions rule was not included in AP I's expansion of 'grave breaches'. Consistent with this omission, precautions violations are not included within the enumerated ICC offences, nor has a precautions violation been tried as a war crime before any of the ad hoc war crimes tribunals. Even the US Military Commission Act,[38] enacted by Congress to, inter alia, enumerate war crimes within the jurisdiction of the military commission established to prosecute unprivileged belligerents captured in the context of the ongoing non-international armed conflict between the United States and Al-Qaeda and associated groups, does not include precautions violations as a basis for criminal responsibility.

To be sure, the general failure to recognize a violation of the precautions obligation as a war crime does not have any legal effect on the importance of the obligation. However, it almost certainly contributes to the general perception that the rule of precautions is 'second rate' or 'second tier' to the more important rules concerning distinction and proportionality. As noted already, this is not only an unjustified and unfortunate perception, but in many operational situations actually inconsistent with the practical significance of the rule. If, as it appears to be increasingly recognized, the precautions rule—both active and passive—is an equally and at times even more significant civilian risk mitigation rule than proportionality, it seems that like its counterparts, it should provide the basis for criminal responsibility when violated.

Like the crimes based on violations of distinction or proportionality, defining a crime based on a violation of the precautions obligation will certainly pose challenges. Ultimately, whether a certain precautionary measure should have been implemented, or whether manoeuvre of forces or location of military assets violated the passive precautions obligation, turns on an assessment of objective reasonableness. Like proportionality assessments, this would require the finder of fact to assess the situation that confronted a commander at the time of the attack decision and determine whether the conduct deviated from a reasonable standard of care in terms of active or passive precautionary measures. In order to limit *criminal* responsibility to only the most obvious violations of the obligation, the offence could include a qualification analogous to the 'clearly excessive' qualification to the proportionality offence included in the ICC statute. For example, criminal responsibility could be conditioned on a finding that the failure to implement a certain precautionary measure was *clearly* unreasonable under the circumstances; or that under the circumstances, there is no *plausible* military justification for the placement of personnel or assets.

[38] Military Commissions Act of 2006, Public Law 109-366, 120 Stat 2600.

Because of the wide margin of appreciation associated with precautions judgments, it is concededly unlikely that incorporating offences based on precautions violations into the fabric of international criminal law will result in a substantial number of prosecutions or convictions. However, the same can be said of proportionality and distinction offences, and therefore does not undermine the value of aligning the importance of precautions in the operational context with war crimes liability. Such an alignment will almost certainly result in increased attention to the implementation of feasible active and passive precautions. It will also provide a mechanism to impose accountability on commanders and subordinate tactical decision-makers in extreme cases where the failure to implement feasible precautions contributes to unnecessary civilian suffering.

5. Conclusion

The ILA Report's emphasis on precautionary measures as a critical civilian risk mitigation component of the IHL targeting equation is a welcome and important development. These measures, both active and passive, must not be viewed in isolation, but instead as part of an integrated assessment equation concerning the legality of a target. Indeed, good-faith implementation of precautions will almost always enhance the risk mitigation effect of the distinction and proportionality rules. Furthermore, in many operational situations, most notably in the context of ground manoeuvre operations conducted pursuant to 'mission type' orders, precautions will often do the proverbial 'heavy lifting' of civilian risk mitigation. This is because of the inherent compatibility between IHL precautions, the military decision-making process, and the overall notion of tactical instinct. When attack decisions are decentralized and based on the exercise of initiative by junior-level combat leaders, emphasizing implementation of feasible precautions is far more likely to produce a positive civilian risk mitigation effect than emphasizing the proportionality rule. As in any attack decision-making context, implementation of precautions will ultimately enhance the quality of distinction and proportionality judgments.

However, more should be done to elevate the stature of precautions. First, more attention is needed on how to implement the passive component of the precautions obligation and how to assess violations of this obligation. Of equal if not more urgency is to identify when and how such violations influence assessment of responsibility of civilian harm. In the context of the type of asymmetric conflicts that dominate today's strategic environment, where armed forces committed to IHL compliance confront non-state organized armed groups who not only routinely disregard IHL, but often deliberately ignore passive precautionary obligations in an effort to reap tactical and strategic advantage, addressing this issue is critical. While such violations certainly do not release an attacking force from its IHL civilian risk mitigation obligations, they will almost inevitably impact the efficacy of those efforts. Greater attention to this aspect of civilian risk creation will lead to a more credible alignment of assertions of responsibility with the reality of military operations.

Finally, it seems that the operational significance of precautions justifies considering their inclusion within the scope of war crimes jurisdiction. Developing offences derived from an objectively unreasonable failure to implement feasible precautions in the attack, or an operationally inexplicable decision to co-mingle military assets amongst the civilian population will ideally enhance the overall commitment to precautions. While prosecuting such offences will certainly pose challenges, the current absence of any precaution-based offence in the war crimes equation undermines the imposition of criminal responsibility on those whose unreasonable attack decisions exacerbate civilian suffering.

12

European Partners in Multinational Military Operations—Extended Legal Restraints

The ECtHR's Rights-based Conception of Precautions in and against the Effects of Attacks

Tilmann Altwicker

1. Introduction

Partners in multinational military operations will usually share some legal restraints—for example, those imposed by the United Nations Charter and the Geneva Conventions—but some legal obligations will only be binding upon a limited number of participating forces. This is evident in the case of legal restraints following from domestic law but also for those restraints coming from regional human rights law.

The resulting imbalance between multinational partners in their respective sets of legal restraints is likely to augment in the future given two trends in regional human rights law: the growing recognition of extraterritorial application of regional human rights law and its co-applicability, together with international humanitarian law (IHL), to cases of armed conflict. Situations of varying legal obligations in multinational military operations pose a key operability challenge.[1]

One example in which regional human rights law can potentially lead to serious imbalances regarding the degree and scope of legal obligations in multinational military operations relates to 'precautions in and against the effects of attacks'. Naturally, the IHL concept of precautions in and against the effects of attacks is a field with close affinities to human rights.[2] It is, therefore, not surprising that the

[1] See, for a general discussion, M Zwanenburg, 'International Humanitarian Law Interoperability in Multinational Operations' (2013) 95 International Review of the Red Cross 681.

[2] On the IHL-conception of precautions see I Henderson, *The Contemporary Law of Targeting* (Martinus Nijhoff 2009) 157–96; JF Quéguiner, 'Precautions under the Law Governing the Conduct of Hostilities' (2006) 88 International Review of the Red Cross 793; R Geiß, 'The Conduct of Hostilities in Asymmetric Conflicts—Reciprocity, Distinction, Proportionality, Precautions' (2010) 23 Humanitäres Völkerrecht: Informationsschriften 122–32.

Tilmann Altwicker, *European Partners in Multinational Military Operations—Extended Legal Restraints* In *The 'Legal Pluriverse' Surrounding Multinational Military Operations*. Edited by Robin Geiß and Heike Krieger, Oxford University Press (2020). © The Several Contributors.
DOI: 10.1093/oso/9780198842965.003.0013

European Court of Human Rights (ECtHR) has embarked on developing its own case law on 'precautions', starting in 1998 with a case concerning the conflict of Turkish security forces with the Kurdistan Workers' Party (PKK).[3] The leading case on rights-based precautions is *Isayeva v Russia* dealing with casualties in an air attack on a convoy of civilians trying to flee from a village in Chechnya.[4]

The ECtHR either explicitly refers to 'precautions' or to the 'standard of care prerequisite to an operation involving use of lethal force by State agents'.[5] Rights-based precautions bear a strong 'family resemblance' with their counterpart in IHL. In IHL, precautions refer to the principle that 'no attack shall be launched without a careful preparation with a view to sparing civilians and civilian objects from the adverse effects of the attacks as much as feasible'.[6] According to the rights-based conception under the European Convention on Human Rights (ECHR), 'precautions' can be defined as measures relating to the planning, conduct, and control of a law enforcement or military operation taken with a view to avoiding and, in any event, minimizing incidental loss of (civilian) life.[7] Whereas the scope of rights-based precautions is broader, encompassing both law enforcement and military operations, the content and even the wording of individual precautions—that is the obligation to verify the objective—are partially overlapping with their IHL counterparts. The regime of rights-based precautions remains, however, a body of law to be distinguished from IHL due to its legal source, and it is accordingly to be interpreted and applied within a human rights framework.

So far, the rights-based conception of precautions in situations involving the use of (lethal) force has not received the scholarly attention it deserves. This contribution takes up three major questions: How can the obligation to take precautions be integrated into the general framework of Convention rights? What are the standards required by a rights-based conception of precautions? Is a human rights-based obligation to take precautions a desirable development? The main argument of this contribution is that the rights-based conception of precautions is still in its infancy and needs to be further developed both within the framework of positive obligations under the ECHR and in close alignment with IHL. The structure of the chapter is as follows: section 2 deals with the doctrinal integration of precautions

[3] *Ergi v Turkey* App no 23818/94 (ECtHR, Judgment, 28 July 1998) para 79.

[4] *Isayeva v Russia* App no 57950/00 (ECtHR, Former First Section Judgment, 24 February 2005).

[5] In one case the ECtHR also used the formulation of a 'duty to take all necessary measures to prevent lives from being unnecessarily exposed to danger and, ultimately, from being lost', *Özalp and Others v Turkey* App no 32457/96 (ECtHR, First Section Judgment, 8 April 2004) para 36.

[6] R Kolb, *Advanced Introduction to International Humanitarian Law* (Edward Elgar Publishing 2014) 81.

[7] *Özalp v Turkey* (n 5) 34; *Kerimova and Others v Russia* App nos 17170/04, 20792/04, 22448/04, 23360/04, 5681/05, 5684/05 (ECtHR, First Section Judgment, 3 May 2011) para 238 (the Court assesses 'not only the actions of State agents who actually administer the force but also all the surrounding circumstances including such matters as the planning and control of the actions under examination'). Convention for the Protection of Human Rights and Fundamental Freedoms (adopted 4 November 1950, entered into force 3 September 1953) ETS 5 (ECHR).

into the Convention system of rights; section 3 elucidates the present state of rights-based precautions under the ECHR and the content of the obligations and compares them with their IHL counterpart; section 4 concludes by discussing the advantages and disadvantages of a rights-based conception of precautions.

2. A Human Rights-Based Conception of Precautions

This section addresses the doctrinal foundations of the rights-based conception of precautions in and against the effects of attacks under the ECHR. The obligation to take precautions in military operations is not easily read into the Convention text. A starting point is the right to life contained in Article 2 ECHR.[8] In order for the right to life to serve as a legal basis for precautions, the Court had to make the following argumentative steps: first, the right to life is a human right of a fundamental character. It does not only deal with the intentional deprivation of life attributable to the state but it also regulates the *legitimate use of lethal force* in a comprehensive way, encompassing both law enforcement and military operations.[9] Secondly, adherence to a set of precautions is a condition for the legitimacy of any use of lethal force by the state, including the use of force by the military.

2.1 The human right to life as foundation

2.1.1 Comprehensive regulation of the use of (lethal) force

The right to life in Article 2 ECHR constitutes 'one of the most fundamental provisions in the Convention' and 'enshrines one of the basic values of the democratic societies making up the Council of Europe'.[10] The fundamental status of the human right to life flows from its character as a 'prerequisite for the enjoyment of all other human rights'.[11] Some commentators even count the right to life among customary

[8] Most ECtHR cases dealing with precautions concern Article 2 ECHR (right to life) (n 7). This study will therefore concentrate on the right to life. Other potentially affected Convention rights, such as the right to property are not taken into account here (Article 1 Protocol No 1 to the Convention for the Protection of Human Rights and Fundamental Freedoms (adopted 20 March 1952, entered into force 18 May 1954) ETS 9 (Prot No 1 ECHR)).

[9] Note that—in order for a case to be considered under Article 2 ECHR (n 7)—the force used must (at least potentially) be lethal, see *Khamzayev and Others v Russia* App no 1503/02 (ECtHR, First Section Judgment, 3 May 2011) para 174. Otherwise, Article 3 ECHR (n 7) (prohibition of torture, inhuman, or degrading treatment) or even Article 8 (right to private life) are *leges speciales*. See A Peters and T Altwicker, *Europäische Menschenrechtskonvention* (2nd edn, CH Beck 2012) 49, 59–60, 193.

[10] *Lambert and Others v France* App no 46043/14 (ECtHR, Grand Chamber Judgment, 5 June 2015) para 117. The right to life is often regarded as the least controversial of all rights, see J Griffin, *On Human Rights* (OUP 2008) 212.

[11] *Montero-Aranguren et al (Detention Center of Catia) v Venezuela*, Judgment, Inter-American Court of Human Rights, Series C No 150 (5 July 2006) para 63.

jus cogens.[12] Under the Convention, the fundamental character of the right to life manifests itself in its non-derogability.[13] In principle, therefore, the state may not cease to respect the right to life, not even in times of war or public emergency.

What is the scope of the right to life? At its core, Article 2 ECHR contains a negative right, namely the right not to die a violent death.[14] There are two different formulations of the core of the right to life in international human rights law: as it is formulated in the second sentence of Article 2(1) ECHR, the state must not 'intentionally' deprive anyone of his life.[15] Other human rights instruments formulate the core as the right not to be *arbitrarily* deprived of one's life by an act attributable to the state (the International Covenant on Civil and Political Rights, the American Convention on Human, and the African Charter on Human and Peoples' Rights).[16] The *intentionality* solution chosen by the ECHR is unfortunate for two reasons: first, the ECtHR has long accepted that not only intentional killing but also negligence attributable to the state can lead to a violation of Article 2 ECHR.[17] The state must do all that can be required of it 'to prevent the applicant's life from being avoidably put at risk'.[18] Secondly, the *intentionality* solution in the Convention is problematic as it complicates the relationship between the ECHR and IHL. The conduct of armed hostilities by nature involves 'intentional' killing by state forces. If Article 2 ECHR were non-derogable in an absolute way, no member state to the Council of Europe would be allowed to engage in armed hostilities. Thus, the Convention states in Article 15(2) ECHR—in what must be considered a doctrinally unfortunate 'exception to the exception'—that the right to life

[12] JJ Paust, 'The Right to Life in Human Rights Law and the Law of War' (2002) 65 Saskatchewan Law Review 411, 412. For criticism see T Weatherall, *Jus Cogens: International Law and Social Contract* (CUP 2015) 264–65 (objecting that the right to life is not an absolute right but one that may be restricted under certain circumstances).

[13] Article 15(2) ECHR (n 7); *Özalp v Turkey* (n 5) para 32.

[14] See Peters and Altwicker (n 9) 49–50.

[15] The restriction originally provided for in the text of Article 2(1) concerning the death penalty is no longer of relevance with the entering into force of Protocol No 6 to the Convention for the Protection of Human Rights and Fundamental Freedoms Concerning the Abolition of the Death Penalty, as amended by Protocol 11 (adopted 28 April 1983) ETS 114 (Prot No 6 ECHR) and Protocol No 13 to the Convention for the Protection of Human Rights and Fundamental Freedoms Concerning the Abolition of the Death Penalty in All Circumstances (adopted 3 May 2002, entered into force 1 July 2003) ETS 187 (Prot No 13 ECHR) to the ECHR (n 7).

[16] Article 6(1) of the International Covenant on Civil and Political Rights (opened for signature 16 December 1966, entered into force 23 March 1976) 999 UNTS 171 (ICCPR); Article 4(1) of the American Convention on Human Rights (entered into force 18 July 1978) 1144 UNTS 123 (ACHR); Article 4 of the African Charter on Human and Peoples' Rights (opened for signature 27 June 1981, entered into force 21 October 1986) 1520 UNTS (AfrChHPR).

[17] *McCann and Others v the United Kingdom* App no 18984/91 (ECtHR, Grand Chamber Judgment, 27 September 1995) para 148.

[18] *LCB v the United Kingdom* App no 23413/94 (ECtHR, Judgment, 9 July 1998) para 36 (concerning the complaint that the state failed to take measures in respect of the child of a serviceman taking part in nuclear tests); *Panaitescu v Romania* App no 30909/06 (ECtHR, Third Section Judgment, 10 April 2012) para 30 (concerning the complaint that the state failed to prevent the applicant's life from being avoidably put at risk by not providing him with appropriate health-care as ordered by the national courts).

is derogable regarding 'deaths resulting from lawful acts of war'. Importantly, the armed conflict exception in Article 15(2) ECHR needs to be read into the list of legitimate restrictions of the right to life, contained in Article 2(2) ECHR. This solution chosen in the ECHR appears unnecessarily complicated.

The scope of the right to life under the Convention is, therefore, far broader than a textual reading of Article 2 ECHR suggests. Together with Article 15 ECHR and Protocol No 6 and Protocol No 13 ECHR,[19] the right to life in Article 2 ECHR provides for a set of norms *comprehensively* regulating the legitimate use of (lethal) force by the state. There are several reasons for this broad interpretation of the right to life. To begin with a textual argument: Article 2(2) ECHR explicitly speaks of the 'use of force which is no more than absolutely necessary'. There is clearly a connection between 'force which is no more than absolutely necessary' and 'legitimate force'. Furthermore, while the second sentence of Article 2(1) ECHR provides for the core content of the right to life (ie not having to die a violent death), the extensive interpretation of the scope by the ECtHR must be taken into account: according to the ECtHR, the right to life captures the intentional as well as the unintentional deprivation of life; furthermore, there is an obligation to protect individual life.[20] Finally, a systematic interpretation of Article 2 ECHR must take the content and regulatory design of Article 15, Protocol No 6 and Protocol No 13 ECHR into account. As the right to life must be considered foundational for the enjoyment of all other rights, the Convention aims for the highest level of protection possible in this regard. In sum, the ECtHR interprets the right to life as a comprehensive norm on the conditions of the legitimate use of (lethal) force.

2.1.2 Conditions of legitimate use of (lethal) force by the state

The Convention accepts—in Article 2(2) and the exception in Article 15(2) ECHR—that the state may (and sometimes must) resort to the use of (lethal) force. More specifically, the Convention accepts not only the state monopoly on the use of force but also the fact that the deprivation of life may be legitimate under certain circumstances. The conditions under which a deprivation of life is legitimate are only partially spelled out in the Convention norms themselves. The legitimacy requirements can be classified as follows: adherence to absolute prohibitions, use of (lethal) force in only a limited number of permissible situations of interference,

[19] Prot No 6 ECHR (n 15) Article 1 abolishes the death penalty in times of peace; Prot No 13 ECHR (n 15) Article 1 abolishes the death penalty—without the possibility of derogations or reservations (Prot No 13 (n 15) Articles 2 and 3)—at all times.

[20] *Pisari v the Republic of Moldova and Russia* App no 42139/12 (ECtHR, Third Section Judgment, 21 April 2015) para 47 ('The exceptions contained in paragraph 2 of Article 2 indicate that this provision extends to, but is not concerned exclusively with, intentional killing. The text of Article 2, read as a whole, demonstrates that paragraph 2 does not primarily define instances where it is permitted intentionally to kill an individual, but describes the situations where it is permitted to "use force" which may result, as an unintended outcome, in the deprivation of life').

respect for the principles of legality and proportionality, and—finally—compliance with precautions.

First, starting with the requirement of adherence to absolute prohibitions, Protocol No 6 and Protocol No 13 ECHR ban the death penalty at all times. In addition, the ECtHR has called the contracting states of the Council of Europe a 'zone free of capital punishment'.[21] Secondly, the deprivation of life is only legitimate in six situations of interference, five of which are listed in Article 2(2) ECHR: for the 'defence of any person from unlawful violence', 'to effect a lawful arrest', 'to prevent the escape of a person lawfully detained', and 'in action lawfully taken for the purpose of quelling a riot or insurrection'. A last situation of legitimate interference—as argued above—is contained in Article 15(2) ECHR, namely the deprivation of life 'resulting from lawful acts of war'. Thirdly, the principle of legality is another condition of legitimacy, as indicated both by the reference to the 'lawfulness' of the interference in Articles 2(2) and 15(2) ECHR, and by the reference in Article 2(1) ECHR that everyone's right to life shall be protected *by law*. As with other Convention rights (eg Article 5(1) ECHR and Article 2 Protocol No 4 ECHR), the requirement of lawfulness essentially relates to all laws applicable domestically in the respondent state—encompassing both rules of domestic and international origin. Therefore, in Article 2(2) ECHR the requirement of lawfulness can be equated primarily with domestic law (eg the law of criminal procedure or the law of policing), whereas the 'lawfulness' in Article 15(2) ECHR primarily relates to IHL.[22] Furthermore, the Court does not only require the existence of a domestic legal framework on the use of force (and the conformity of the authorities' conduct with such framework), it also makes concrete claims regarding the substance of the domestic regulatory framework on the use of force. This has sometimes led to in-depth examinations by the Court of state security legislation (eg criminal procedure or policing laws).[23] Fourthly, any deprivation of life attributable to an act by the state has to be in conformity with the (human rights) principle of proportionality. This requirement can be found in Article 2(2) ECHR stipulating that the deprivation of life is only acceptable if the use of (lethal) force was 'absolutely necessary'. Proportionality, here, functions as a limit on lawful interference with a Convention right by state action (eg demanding a legitimate aim and a certain quality of the means-end relationship of the measure), thereby further limiting the

[21] *Koktysh v Ukraine* App no 43707/07 (ECtHR, Fifth Section Judgment, 10 December 2009) para 55. See also the Parliamentary Assembly of the Council of Europe's (PACE), Resolution 1560—Promotion by Council of Europe member states of an international moratorium on the death penalty (26 June 2007) stating that the 'member states of the Council of Europe [are] a de facto death penalty-free zone'.

[22] A Gioia, 'The Role of the European Court of Human Rights in Monitoring Compliance with Humanitarian Law in Armed Conflict' in O Ben-Naftali (ed), *International Humanitarian Law and International Human Rights Law* (OUP 2011) 201–16.

[23] Regarding the use of lethal force by military personnel see *Esmukhambetov and Others v Russia* App no 23445/03 (ECtHR, First Section Judgment, 29 March 2011) para 143. See L Lavrysen, 'Protection by the Law: The Positive Obligation to Develop a Legal Framework to Adequately Protect ECHR Rights' in Y Haeck and E Brems (eds), *Human Rights and Civil Liberties in the 21st Century* (Springer 2014) 69.

recourse to the use of (lethal) force in law enforcement or conduct of armed hostilities.[24] Fifthly, most important for the purposes of this contribution, a final requirement of the legitimacy of the use of (lethal) force relates to the compliance with a set of 'precautions' or—as the ECtHR sometimes formulates it—'standards of care'. In the following, compliance with precautions as a condition of the legitimate use of (lethal) force shall be analysed in detail.

2.1.3 Precautions as a requirement of proportionality or as positive obligations?

How is the obligation to take precautions best classified doctrinally? It is argued here that precautions to avoid or minimize the incidental loss of life should be classified doctrinally as 'positive obligations'. 'Positive obligations' require the state to take *positive* action to preserve or otherwise further a protected legal interest (in contrast to 'negative obligations' which merely demand non-interference with a protected legal interest).[25] This is the approach taken by the Court in the leading case of *Isayeva v Russia*.[26] Here, the Court found that—since the operation was not planned and executed with the required care for the lives of the civilian population—the respondent state had violated a positive obligation under Article 2 ECHR.[27]

Unfortunately, in some cases the ECtHR misleadingly omits treating precautions as positive obligations and instead reads them into the principle of (strict) proportionality in Article 2(2) ECHR.[28] The Court deduces from the stricter test of proportionality envisaged in Article 2(2) ECHR ('absolutely necessary') that it is not only the actual use of force which must be assessed but also 'the surrounding circumstances including such matters as the planning and control of the actions under examination.'[29] This route of developing specific obligations concerning the

[24] On the functions and functioning of the principle of proportionality see M Newton and L May, *Proportionality in International Law* (OUP 2014).

[25] On positive obligations under the ECHR see A Mowbray, *The Development of Positive Obligations under the European Convention on Human Rights by the European Court of Human Rights* (Hart Publishing 2004); M Klatt, 'Positive Obligations under the European Convention on Human Rights' (2011) 71 ZaöRV 691; D Xenos, *The Positive Obligations of the State under the European Convention of Human Rights* (Routledge 2012); L Lavrysen, 'The Scope of Rights and the Scope of Obligations: Positive Obligations' in E Brems and J Gerards (eds), *Shaping Rights in the ECHR: The Role of the European Court of Human Rights in Determining the Scope of Human Rights* (CUP 2013) 162.

[26] *Isayeva v Russia* (n 4).

[27] *Isayeva v Russia* (n 4) paras 200–01 (since the civilians were killed as a result of the respondent state's fire-power, it would be more correct to classify it as a violation of the positive obligation relating to organization and procedure).

[28] See, eg, the case of *Khatsiyeva and Others v Russia* App no 5108/02 (ECtHR, Fifth Section Judgment, 17 January 2008). While the case essentially dealt with the obligation to verify the objectives, the Court examined the shortcomings in planning the attack under the issue of proportionality. See also *Esmukhambetov and Others v Russia* (n 23) where the Court blends considerations relating to the obligation to minimize collateral damage with considerations of proportionality. More problematic still, the ECtHR mingles proportionality concerns with both, issues of the positive obligation to protect and positive obligations relating to organization and procedure, see *Kerimova and Others v Russia* (n 7) para 257. All of these cases are discussed below.

[29] *Khamzayev and Others v Russia* (n 9) para 172.

planning and conducting of an operation based on the principle of proportionality is problematic: most of the precautions clearly require the state to take positive action, for example deploying military intelligence resources to verify the objective of an attack or issuing effective advance warnings. Admittedly, there are other precautions where the aspect of positive action is less visible, for instance in the case of the obligation to refrain from launching an attack if the expected collateral damage is excessive in relation to the military advantage.

Nevertheless, all rights-based precautions should be constructed doctrinally as positive obligations for three reasons: first, as the Court has repeatedly held, it can be difficult to distinguish between positive and negative obligations.[30] Thus, it often seems artificial to clearly classify an obligation. Secondly, if one—like this contribution and arguably today also the ECtHR—subscribes to the view that the test for positive obligations should be similar to that of negative obligations, the differences in the doctrinal assessment are not significant.[31] Thirdly, the alternative—deriving substantive rules of general application from the principle of proportionality—is less appealing: The human rights principle of proportionality is designed for balancing conflicting interests in concrete cases, not for generating generalizable rules as needed with regard to precautions.

2.2 Precautions as positive obligations under the ECHR

In the following, a general typology of positive obligations is provided which can be used for the further analysis of the rights-based conception of precautions. Mowbray's finding in 2004 that the Court has not yet articulated a 'general theory' of positive obligations still holds.[32] Nevertheless, after being in use for more than forty years now, the Convention conception of 'positive obligations' is not only widely accepted, but has reached a mature state of development.

2.2.1 Classifying precautions on the basis of content

Precautions can best be located in the framework of positive obligations under the ECHR. On the basis of their content, one may distinguish three broad categories of positive obligations in the Convention: obligations to protect, obligations to

[30] With respect to Article 8 ECHR (n 7) (right to private life) and Prot No 1 ECHR (n 8) Article 1 (right to property), the ECtHR has held that 'the boundaries between the State's positive and negative obligations under this provision do not lend themselves to precise definition', see, eg, *Uçar v Turkey* App no 52392/99 (ECtHR, Second Section Judgment, 11 April 2006) (regarding Article 8 ECHR (n 7)).

[31] *Oliari and Others v Italy* App nos 18766/11 and 36030/11 (ECtHR, Fourth Section Judgment, 21 July 2015) para 160 (stating that '[t]he principles applicable to assessing a State's positive and negative obligations under the Convention are similar').

[32] Mowbray (n 25) 221. The Court itself has denied the need to develop a 'general theory of the positive obligations', *Plattform 'Ärzte für das Leben' v Austria* App no 10126/82 (ECtHR, Judgment, 21 June 1988) para 31.

provide certain social goods,[33] and obligations relating to organization and procedure.[34] While it is by now clear that positive obligations may arise from virtually any Convention right, for the present purposes it is sufficient to focus exclusively on positive obligations in the context of Article 2 ECHR.

In the context of precautions, the relevant categories are the obligation to protect and the obligations relating to organization and procedure. The *obligation to protect* requires the authorities to take preventive action against criminal acts by a third party threatening the life of an individual,[35] life-threatening natural disasters[36], or in life-threatening factual situations where the state has a special responsibility towards the individual (eg in state schools, hospitals, or prisons).[37] The obligation to protect thus serves to shield the individual against acts adversely impacting the enjoyment of a Convention right (ie 'interferences' with a Convention right in a non-technical sense) by non-state actors, foreign public authorities, and against the effects of natural disasters.[38] Structurally, it is of crucial importance that the obligation to protect is directed at the prevention of acts adversely impacting the enjoyment of a Convention right (or the materialization of life-threatening risks) stemming from non-state actors or sources outside the effective control of the state.[39]

Apart from the obligation to protect, the Court derives *obligations relating to organization and procedure* from Article 2 ECHR. One important manifestation of a positive obligation relating to organization and procedure is the duty of authorities to carry out an (effective) investigation in cases of violent death.[40] Structurally, it should be emphasized that—other than the obligation to protect—the positive obligation relating to organization and procedure is directed against risks to the right to life originating from the use of force *by the state* itself.

[33] The ECHR (n 7) does not generally contain obligations to provide social goods (such as access to health care or housing). In the words of the Court: 'Although many of the rights it contains have implications of a social or economic nature, the Convention is essentially directed at the protection of civil and political rights', *A.S. v Switzerland* App no 39350/13 (ECtHR, Second Section Judgment, 30 June 2015) para 31. However, the Court recognizes some exceptional circumstances under which an obligation to provide certain social goods may arise, see H Krieger, 'Funktionen von Grund- und Menschenrechten' in O Dörr, R Grote, and T Marauhn (eds), *EMRK/GG. Konkordanzkommentar zum europäischen und deutschen Grundrechtsschutz* (2nd edn, Mohr Siebeck 2013) 344–49.

[34] For an overview see Peters and Altwicker (n 9) 21–24. For more details see Krieger (n 33) 298–364.

[35] *Osman v the United Kingdom* App no 23452/94 (ECtHR, Judgment, 28 October 1998).

[36] *Budayeva and Others v Russia* App nos 15339/02, 21160/02, 20058/02, 11673/02, 15343/02 (ECtHR, First Section Judgment, 20 March 2008).

[37] See *Özalp v Turkey* (n 5) para 33 (Article 2 may also imply in certain well-defined circumstances a positive obligation for the authorities to take preventive operational measures to protect an individual for whom they are responsible).

[38] Peters and Altwicker (n 9) 21.

[39] See also Krieger (n 33) 287, 318 (for the obligation to protect to arise '[t]he state must be excluded as the origin of the threat', (my translation)).

[40] *McShane v UK* App no 43290/98 (ECtHR, Fourth Section Judgment, 28 May 2002) para 94 ('effective official investigation when individuals have been killed as a result of the use of force').

On this basis, precautions can be classified based on their content as follows: in human rights terminology, *precautions in attack* fall into the group of positive obligations relating to organization and procedure. The reason is that they regulate risks to the right to life stemming from the use of force by the state itself (and not by a third party). This is different with—thus far underdeveloped in the case law of the ECtHR—*precautions against the effects of attack* where the risk to the right to life stems from an attack of a foreign public authority or an act of a third party. If a state has to protect its population from the effects of an attack by a foreign state or an attack by a third party, this set of precautions should be constructed as a positive obligation to protect.

2.2.2 Classifying precautions on the basis of the nature of the obligation

For a formal distinction of the nature of obligation following from the duty to take precautions, the classification of 'obligations of result' and 'obligations of conduct' (or 'obligations of means') is useful.[41] Obligations of result are those—as their name suggests—which require the attainment of a particular product or outcome (eg the architect's legally binding promise to construct a house) or which clearly define the permissible course of action or omission (eg the prohibition to smoke in public places, the obligation to prosecute or extradite).[42] In contrast, obligations of conduct prescribe the progressive realization of a particular goal (eg the obligation to protect the environment) or a course of conduct (eg the physician who promises to undertake all reasonable steps to heal the sick).[43] Obligations of conduct are often couched in terms of an obligation to take 'all measures', 'all appropriate measures to protect', or to 'do everything possible'.[44] Obligations of conduct are essentially due diligence obligations. In contrast, obligations of result further restrict the options to act (often reducing them to exactly one permissible course of conduct). It should be kept in mind that—when contained in legal norms—both types of obligations constitute binding standards against which the conduct of an actor can be assessed. Whether a norm contains an obligation of conduct or an obligation of result is to some degree a matter of interpretation.

The distinction can be gainfully applied to precautions. Under IHL, *precautions in attack* are obligations of conduct or due diligence obligations. As a textual interpretation reveals, the obligation to verify the military nature of the target and

[41] See on this distinction PM Dupuy, 'Reviewing the Difficulties of Codification: On Ago's Classification of Obligations of Means and Obligations of Result in Relation to State Responsibility' (1999) 10 European Journal of International Law 371.

[42] Dupuy (n 41) 375. See also CP Economides, 'Content of the Obligation: Obligations of Means and Obligations of Result' in J Crawford, A Pellet, and S Olleson (eds), *The Law of International Responsibility* (OUP 2010) 371, 374–81 and R Wolfrum, 'Obligation of Result Versus Obligation of Conduct: Some Thoughts About the Implementation of International Obligations' in MH Arsanjani, J Cogan, R Sloane, and S Wiessner (eds), *Looking to the Future: Essays on International Law in Honor of W. Michael Reisman* (Brill 2010) 363–83.

[43] ibid.

[44] See the list in Economides (n 42) 378.

the obligation regarding the choice of means of attack (Article 57(2)(a)(i) and (ii) AP I) are obligations of conduct, requiring the belligerents to 'do everything feasible' to attain that end.[45] The nature as obligations of conduct is less evident in the case of other precautions. This is true, for example, for the obligation to refrain from deciding to launch an attack, to cancel or to suspend an attack in cases where the expected collateral damage would be excessive in relation to the anticipated military advantage (Article 57(2)(a)(iii) and (b) AP I). Once a commander of an attack determines that the expected collateral damage would be excessive, his or her choices to act lawfully are reduced to refraining from, to cancelling, or to suspending the attack. The practical implications of this obligation, however, entail an 'obligation of conduct': in practice, it follows from the obligations in Article 57(2)(a)(iii) and (b) AP I that the commander of an attack must ensure constantly updated military intelligence regarding the target and its surroundings.[46] This obligation, evidently, can only be one of conduct, not of result.[47] Not even the obligation to issue an effective advance warning of the attacks is an obligation of result, but of conduct: While every reasonable effort has to be made to issue a warning, its effectiveness cannot be guaranteed. *Precautions against the effects of attack* are already textually formulated as 'obligations of conduct'. They contain phrases such as 'endeavour to' and 'avoid', not mandating the achievement of a result, but demanding to actively work towards the realization of a goal. It is, therefore, possible to generalize the 'feasibility' element as a constitutive element of all precautions. Similarly, in its rights-based conception of precautions, the ECtHR includes the obligation 'to take all feasible precautions'.[48] This formula, too, indicates an obligation of conduct.

2.2.3 Classifying precautions on the basis of the mode of implementation

The mode of implementation (in the form of legislation, executive action, or adjudication) depends largely on the content of the positive obligation. For example, the obligation to protect is foremost an obligation to legislate. The primary status as an obligation to legislate already follows from the text of the first sentence of Article 2(1) ECHR. Nowhere else does the Convention text explicitly set up legislative obligations.[49] Accordingly, the ECtHR held on numerous occasions that the

[45] Protocol Additional to the Geneva Conventions of 12 August 1949, and relating to the Protection of Victims of International Armed Conflicts (Protocol I) (opened for signature 8 June 1977, entered into force 7 December 1978) 1125 UNTS 3 (AP I).

[46] Kolb (n 6) 169.

[47] ibid.

[48] Standard formula, see *Damayev v Russia* App no 36150/04 (ECtHR, First Section Judgment, 29 May 2012) para 60.

[49] In line with general international law, the Convention generally does not prescribe to the contracting states *how* they implement the positive obligations incurred. See *Kolyadenko and Others v Russia*, App nos 17423/05, 20534/05, 20678/05, 23263/05, 24283/05 35673/05 28 (ECtHR, First Section Judgment, February 2012) para 160 ('As to the choice of particular practical measures, the Court has consistently held that where the state is required to take positive measures, the choice of means is in principle a matter that falls within the Contracting State's margin of appreciation. There are different

obligation to protect 'entails above all a primary duty on the state to put in place a legislative and administrative framework designed to provide effective deterrence against threats to the right to life'.[50] In various cases, the Court further specified this obligation to enact appropriate legislation catering to the protection of the right to life.[51] Today, the obligation has been transformed into a comprehensive obligation of risk prevention by legislation, applying to all sorts of 'dangerous activities' and requiring rules on 'licensing, setting up, operation, security and supervision of the activity'.[52] The omission to enact adequate legislation on life-threatening activities can lead to a violation of Article 2 ECHR. The Court found violations of the obligation to enact adequate legislation, for example in connection with the risk of asbestos-related activities,[53] and concerning the prevention of risks by flash floods.[54] Often, however, executive action will be called for as the proper mode of implementing positive obligations (eg to start a police search when a person is reported missing).[55]

Under the rights-based conception, the primary mode of implementation of precautions in and against effects is that of executive action. Precautions require the authorities to engage in military or police intelligence gathering, to issue warnings of attacks, and to incorporate certain humanitarian considerations when deciding upon an attack. All precautions, both under IHL and under the ECHR, relate to the planning, conducting, and control of a law enforcement or military operation, that is fields of executive action. The obligation to take precautions is therefore addressed to military or police commanders and to the soldier or—in the case of rights-based precautions also—the police officer carrying out the operation.[56] In contrast to IHL, the rights-based conception of precautions in addition requires a legislative approach to precautions. Especially with regard to precautions in law enforcement operations, the ECtHR has recognized the obligation to legislate on the conditions of the use of firearms, for example.[57] There are indications

avenues to ensure Convention rights, and even if the state has failed to apply one particular measure provided by domestic law, it may still fulfil its positive duty by other means').

[50] See only *Öneryildiz v Turkey* App no 48939/99 (ECtHR, Grand Chamber Judgment, 30 November 2004) para 89.

[51] *Makaratzis v Greece* App no 50385/99 (ECtHR, Grand Chamber Judgment, 20 December 2004) para 57; *Ciorcan and Others v Romania* App nos 29414/09, 44841/09 (ECtHR, Third Section Judgment, 27 January 2015) para 105.

[52] *Prilutskiy v Ukraine* App no 40429/08 (ECtHR, Judgment, 26 February 2015) para 31.

[53] *Brincat and Others v Malta* App nos 60908/11, 62110/11, 62129/11, 62312/11, 62338/11 (ECtHR, Fifth Section Judgment, 24 July 2014) paras 107–11.

[54] *Kolyadenko and Others v Russia* (n 49) para 185.

[55] *Deyanov v Bulgaria* App no 2930/04 (ECtHR, Fifth Section Judgment, 30 September 2010) paras 52–60.

[56] For IHL see, *mutatis mutandis*, Kolb (n 6) 167.

[57] *Makaratzis v Greece* (n 51) para 59 ('[P]olice officers should not be left in a vacuum when performing their duties, whether in the context of a prepared operation or a spontaneous chase of a person perceived to be dangerous: a legal and administrative framework should define the limited circumstances in which law-enforcement officials may use force and firearms, in the light of the international standards which have been developed in this respect'). Similarly, the Inter-American Court of

that the ECtHR may also consider the appropriateness of the legal framework with regard to military operations.[58] For example, in the case of *Esmukhambetov and others v Russia*, the Court examined whether an 'appropriate legal framework concerning the use of lethal force by military personnel was in place and, if so, whether it contained clear safeguards to prevent arbitrary deprivation of life and to satisfy the requirement of protection "by law" of the right to life secured by Article 2 of the Convention'.[59] In other words, compared to the IHL conception, the required mode of implementation is broader in the case of the rights-based conception of precautions: it encompasses both obligations for the executive regarding the planning, conducting and controlling, and operation, and an obligation for the legislative to establish a legal framework for operations involving the use of (lethal) force.

2.3 Structure of precautions under the ECHR

How does the rights-based conception of precautions translate into a doctrinal scheme to assess concrete cases? The appropriate test for positive obligations—providing a doctrinal super-structure for precautions—under the ECHR is far from settled. The Court usually only examines whether the state complied with the relevant positive obligations without distinguishing different steps of analysis.[60]

This single-tier test is unsatisfactory, especially in cases involving precautions. As some commentators have argued, the Court should approximate the examination of positive and negative obligations under the Convention as far as possible.[61] This would result in a two-stage model, requiring—as a first step—a determination by the Court of whether inaction or inadequate action (omission) by the state constitutes an encroachment on a protected legal interest falling within the ambit of Article 2 ECHR, and—as the second step—the inquiry by the Court whether the omission of the authorities can be justified.[62] As this contribution shows, the two-stage model better integrates IHL considerations into the examination of rights-based precautions, and is to be favoured over the single-tier test.

Human Rights has used the 'UN Principles on the Use of Force and Firearms by the Law Enforcement Officials' as benchmarks for the minimum content of domestic regulation on the lethal use of force, see *Montero-Aranguren et al v Venezuela* (n 11) para 75.

[58] *Kerimova and Others v Russia* (n 7) paras 243, 256.

[59] *Esmukhambetov and Others v Russia* (n 23) para 143.

[60] *Prilutskiy v Ukraine* (n 52) para 33 (mixing the scope of a positive obligation and the disproportionality analysis and stating that the scope of the positive obligation must be interpreted in a way that does not impose an unrealistic or disproportionate burden on the authorities).

[61] One reason is that there is rationality to each step in a differentiated test that gets lost in the one-step model applied by the Court. See recently Lavrysen (n 25) 181.

[62] For a similar model see ibid.

2.3.1 Omission by the authorities falling within the ambit of Article 2 ECHR

The first stage of the analysis requires that it be established that a protected legal interest was infringed upon by an omission attributable to the respondent state. Therefore, first, the legal interest to be protected by means of precautions must be identified. What is the legal interest protected by precautions? Under the IHL-conception, precautions aim to 'spare' and 'protect' the civilian population, individual civilians, and civilian objects.[63] The obligation to take precautions is a practical and operational consequence of the general principle of distinction in Article 48 AP I (requiring the belligerents to differentiate between legitimate military targets and illegitimate civilian targets).[64] For the rights conception, the Court has formulated the protected legal interest as follows: precautions are to be taken 'with a view to avoiding and, in any event, to minimising, incidental loss of civilian life'.[65] The formulations of the legal interest are strikingly similar. The rights-based conception uses a literal adoption of a formulation used in Article 57(2)(a)(ii) AP I. Importantly, both aim at averting similar risks and are directed at the protection of individuals.

Secondly, in order for the legal interest to be implicated, there must be some active involvement of the respondent state in a law enforcement operation or in the conduct of armed hostilities, involving the (lethal) use of force. In the leading case of *Isayeva v Russia*, the Court rightly examined whether the facts of the case fell 'within the ambit of Article 2'.[66] The ECtHR has applied its Convention-based conception of precautions to a wide array of situations: to an ambush operation by the security forces leading to an armed clash with the PKK in the vicinity of a village,[67] to an armed operation at a site belonging to a mining company allegedly used as a shelter for terrorists,[68] to the dropping of an aviation bomb near a minivan in the context of armed hostilities in Chechnya,[69] or to the bombing of residential buildings by Russian military jets during the Chechen war.[70] There is no particular degree of force required in order to trigger the Convention-based obligation to take precautions. It can be a single shot from a rifle by a member of the state security forces that makes precautions necessary.[71]

Thirdly, there is a requirement of positive awareness or knowledge to be fulfilled. For an omission to count as an encroachment upon a protected legal interest, it must be established that the authorities 'knew or ought to have known at the time of the existence of a real and immediate risk to the life of an individual or

[63] See AP I (n 45) Articles 57, 58.
[64] See Quéguiner (n 2) 793, 796 (quoting the Commentary to AP I (n 45)).
[65] *Ergi v Turkey* (n 3) para 79; *Damayev v Russia* (n 48) para 60.
[66] *Isayeva v Russia* (n 4) para 179.
[67] *Ergi v Turkey* (n 3).
[68] *Oğur v Turkey* App no 21594/93 (ECtHR, Grand Chamber Judgment, 20 May 1999).
[69] *Isayeva v Russia* (n 4).
[70] *Khamzayev and Others v Russia* (n 9).
[71] *Abdurashidova v Russia* App no 32968/05 (ECtHR, First Section Judgment, 8 April 2010).

individuals'.[72] The common standard used here is that of 'proof beyond reasonable doubt'; however, the case law allows for alleviations of that rule.[73] For example, in the case *Özalp and others*, a PKK captive died in an explosion when he showed a terrorist shelter to the security forces.[74] The soldiers had asked the PKK captive to open the shelter while they had kept a safe distance. From this fact, the Court inferred that the authorities knew about the risk to life involved in the breaking into the shelter.[75] In *Finogenov v Russia*, the Court added a control element: the authorities must have 'retained a certain degree of control over the situation'.[76] It is too early to say how this new element will influence the rights-based conception of precautions.

2.3.2 Failure to comply with the positive obligation to take (adequate) precautions?

The next step in the analysis requires establishing that the state failed to comply with the positive obligation to take (adequate) precautions. To this end, several considerations must be taken into account. First, the general obligation to take precautions must be specified with a view to the particular situation. The obligation to take precautions in order to avoid or minimize incidental loss of civilian life must be turned into a 'definitive' positive obligation by using the feasibility test.[77] The test applied by the Court is again strikingly similar to the one applied under IHL: the state is required to take 'all feasible' precautions.[78] Under the IHL conception, 'feasible precautions' are those 'which are practicable or practically possible, taking into account all circumstances ruling at the time, including humanitarian and military considerations'.[79] A crucial factor of feasibility under the IHL conception are available resources and technical capabilities.[80] While these considerations also play a role under the rights-based conception, 'feasibility' is further determined by the following factors: the Court has indicated that it determines the required standard of precautions with a view to the concrete security situation, that is whether a situation of martial law or a state of emergency had been declared at the time and whether a derogation under Article 15 ECHR had been made.[81]

[72] *Özalp v Turkey* (n 5) para 34. The *Osman-test* was originally formulated in the context of the positive obligation to protect the life of individuals in the case of *Osman v the United Kingdom* (n 35) para 116.

[73] *Özalp v Turkey* (n 5) para 35 ('proof may follow from the coexistence of sufficiently strong, clear and concordant inferences or of similar unrebutted presumptions of fact'); *Ergi v Turkey* (n 3) para 81.

[74] *Özalp v Turkey* (n 5) para 37.

[75] ibid.

[76] *Finogenov and Others v Russia* App nos 18299/03, 27311/03 (ECtHR, First Section Judgment, 20 December 2011) para 209.

[77] Lavrysen (n 25) 162, 167–69.

[78] *Dimitrov and Others v Bulgaria* App no 77938/11 (ECtHR, Judgment, 1 July 2014) para 131 (standing case law).

[79] JM Henckaerts and L Doswald-Beck, *Customary International Humanitarian Law* (ICRC/CUP 2009) 54; Henderson (n 2) 161 (with references to the *travaux préparatoires*).

[80] Kolb (n 6) 167.

[81] *Isayeva v Russia* (n 4) para 191.

The Court is, thus, apparently willing to make adjustments regarding the required standard of precautions. Usually, the required standard will be higher in times of peace and for ordinary law enforcement operations. For example, the 'massive use of indiscriminate weapons' in a law enforcement operation was found to be irreconcilable with the positive obligation to take precautions.[82]

Secondly, the Court developed general requirements to be fulfilled in cases of positive obligations which also apply to the special case of precautions. Among these general requirements are 'the domestic legality of the authorities' acts or omissions, the domestic decision-making process, including the appropriate investigations and studies, and the complexity of the issue, especially where conflicting Convention interests are involved'.[83] It is at this point that the Court will assess the appropriateness of the domestic legal framework governing the (lethal) use of force. As stated above, the rights-based conception of precautions requires the domestic legislation to have in place an appropriate legal framework on the (lethal) use of force.[84] Furthermore, in cases concerning precautions, the Court usually undertakes a thorough analysis of the military decision-making process, having due regard to the planning, execution, and control of the operation. In addition, the decision not to take precautions may not be based on manifestly illegitimate reasons (eg for the purpose of punishing the local population).[85]

Thirdly, the obligation to take precautions 'must be interpreted in a way which does not impose an impossible or disproportionate burden on the authorities'.[86] This indicates that the question whether the positive obligation to take precautions has been complied with is ultimately a question of balancing. For example, the Court has recognized that although the deployment of ground troops would likely have a minimizing effect on the number of civilian casualties, there are circumstances in which the state may have resort to aerial strikes despite their greater destructive potential.[87]

2.3.3 A role for the margin of appreciation in situations requiring the adoption of precautions?

Cases on precautions are exceptional with regard to the margin of appreciation. Usually, the Court acknowledges a wide margin of appreciation in the fulfilment of positive obligations.[88] In particular, the specific means chosen to fulfil a positive

[82] *Abuyeva and Others v Russia* App no 27065/05 (ECtHR, First Section Judgment, 2 December 2010) para 200.

[83] *Kolyadenko and Others v Russia* (n 49) para 161.

[84] See above.

[85] Similarly, *mutatis mutandis*, Lavrysen (n 25) 162, 181.

[86] *Suleymanova v Russia* App no 9191/06 (ECtHR, First Section Judgment, 12 May 2010) para 81; *Khamzayev and Others v Russia* (n 9) para 178.

[87] *Kerimova and Others v Russia* (n 7) paras 246, 248.

[88] *Kolyadenko and Others v Russia* (n 49).

obligation, fall—in principle—within the margin of appreciation.[89] This is different in the case of precautions. Given that precautions are required in situations where there is a real, immediate, and high risk that lives will be endangered, the Court rarely, if ever, concedes to the respondent state a margin of appreciation. Recently, the Court held that—once the knowledge- and control-requirements (see above) are fulfilled—a 'duty to take specific measures arises'.[90]

3. Comparison of the Human Rights-Based Conception with the IHL Conception of Precautions

In this section, the two conceptions on precautions—that provided under IHL in Articles 57, 58 AP I, Article 13 AP II, and the human rights-based under Article 2 ECHR—shall be compared.[91]

3.1 Scope

Under IHL, the scope of precautions is limited to attacks in 'armed conflict', that is the conduct of armed hostilities.[92] The scope of precautions under the human rights-based conception is broader than its IHL counterpart as the obligation to take precautions relates to both law enforcement and military operations.[93] The formulation used for precautions in both cases of application is similar, but not identical: in cases of law enforcement, there is an obligation to 'minimise *to the greatest extent possible* recourse to lethal force or incidental loss of life' (emphasis added).[94] In the context of military operations, the obligation seems slightly weaker, as precautions have to be taken with a view to 'avoiding and, in any event, to minimizing, incidental loss of civilian life'.[95]

Under both conceptions of precautions, the personal scope of application is comprehensive. For the IHL conception, Robert Kolb stated that the obligation

[89] See, *mutatis mutandis*, *Prilutskiy v Ukraine* (n 52) para 35 (stating that 'the choice of means for ensuring the positive obligations under Article 2 is in principle a matter that falls within the state's margin of appreciation').

[90] *Finogenov and Others v Russia* (n 76) para 209.

[91] Protocol Additional to the Geneva Conventions of 12 August 1949, and relating to the Protection of Victims of Non-International Armed Conflicts (Protocol II) (opened for signature 8 June 1977, entered into force 7 December 1978) 1125 UNTS 609 (AP II).

[92] On the application of IHL see Kolb (n 6) 93–123.

[93] On the distinction between law enforcement and military operations see N Melzer, 'Conceptual Distinction and Overlaps between Law Enforcement and the Conduct of Hostilities' in TD Gill and D Fleck (eds), *The Handbook of the International Law of Military Operations* (OUP 2010) 33–49.

[94] For precautions in the case of law enforcement see *Wasilewska and Kalucka v Poland* App nos 28975/04, 33406/04 (ECtHR, Fourth Section, 23 February 2010) para 46.

[95] *Ergi v Turkey* (n 3) para 79; *Damayev v Russia* (n 48) para 60.

to take precautions 'is geared towards all military personnel effectively having the power to influence the decisions or the execution of an attack'.[96] The obligation is not limited to military commanders, but is also addressed to the individual soldier carrying out an attack. This is similar under the rights-based conception, where the Court has repeatedly held that both the 'actions of State agents who actually administer the force' and the 'planning and control of the actions' are under scrutiny.[97]

As to the beneficiaries of precautions, a significant difference between the two conceptions must be noted. Precautions under IHL are designed to 'spare the civilian population, civilians and civilian objects' (Article 57(1) and Article 58 AP I; similarly, Article 13 AP II). IHL precautions are conceptually not directed at protecting legitimate military objectives. In contrast, due to the absence of a distinction between civilians and combatants under human rights law, the scope of human rights-based precautions regarding their beneficiaries is much wider. Even in situations of armed hostilities, such as in Chechnya, the Court has extended the obligation to 'avoid or minimise, to the greatest extent possible, the risk of a loss of life, *both for the persons at whom the measures [are] directed and for civilians*'.[98]

3.2 Precautions in attack

The content of the obligation to take precautions is more explicitly spelled out in the case of IHL. Articles 57 and 58 AP I mention the following obligations: the obligation to verify objectives, to avoid/minimize collateral damage, to refrain from launching, to cancel or suspend an attack in cases of expected excessive collateral damage, to give effective advance warning of an attack, and to select the military objective expected to cause the least collateral damage.[99] In contrast, the human rights-based conception appears far less specific. Rather, it is phrased as a general clause from which specific obligations may be deduced (to be developed in the case law by the ECtHR): the human rights-based conception obliges contracting states to 'take all feasible precautions in the choice of means and methods of a security operation with a view to avoiding and, in any event, to minimising incidental loss of civilian life'.[100] The wording (which bears a striking resemblance to Article 57(2)(a)(ii) AP I) is evocative of—what Jean-Marie Henckaerts and Louise Doswald-Beck

[96] Kolb (n 6) 167 (claiming that the wording of Article 57(2)(a) AP I is too narrow).
[97] *Khatsiyeva v Russia* (n 28) para 129.
[98] *Esmukhambetov and Others v Russia* (n 23) para 146 (emphasis added); *Khamzayev and Others v Russia* (n 9) para 180; *Kerimova and Others v Russia* (n 7) para 248.
[99] Based on the list by Kolb (n 6) 167–71. See also M Bothe, KJ Partsch, and WA Solf, *New Rules for Victims of Armed Conflicts: Commentary on the Two 1977 Protocols Additional to the Geneva Conventions of 1949* (2nd edn, Martinus Nijhoff 2013) 400, 402.
[100] *Özalp v Turkey* (n 5) para 34.

have framed as—Rule 15 of Customary International Humanitarian Law.[101] This may be no coincidence. It can be argued that the ECtHR merely draws the consequences of a pre-existing customary rule.[102] Nevertheless, the ECtHR has fleshed out the general clause to take precautions in attack in its case law, as the following survey will show.

The IHL obligation to verify that the targets of attack are military targets is a direct practical consequence of the principle of distinction and is recognized in both conceptions. This obligation requires the 'collection, collation, evaluation and dissemination of timely target intelligence'.[103] Regarding the obligation to verify, the human rights-based and the IHL conception of precautions also bear similarities. In *Khamzayev and others v Russia*, the Court stated—in words reminiscent of the IHL counterpart—that it is up to the 'authorities to verify, to the extent possible, whether any civilians were present in buildings presumably selected as targets for an aerial strike'.[104] The general approach of the rights-based obligation to verify the objective is outlined in the case of *Kerimova and others v Russia*.[105] Here, the ECtHR required 'clear and reliable' information that the objectives were in fact military targets.[106] In the case of *Khatsiyeva and others v Russia*, the ECtHR found that the military commanders directing an attack on persons working in a field in an area bordering Chechnya had not exercised sufficient care in identifying the targets and found Russia responsible for a violation of Article 2 ECHR.[107] This conclusion is compatible with IHL: as the International Committee of the Red Cross (ICRC) Commentary states, in cases of doubt regarding the military nature of a target, those in command of an attack must make further inquiries.[108] The standard under IHL, at least with regard to international armed conflict (IAC), may even be stricter than the rights-based standard: under the IHL conception of precautions, an attack without prior verification of the objectives leads to an 'automatic' violation of Article 57(2)(a)(i) AP I.[109] The ECtHR, in contrast, has accepted

[101] 'Rule 15: … All feasible precautions must be taken to avoid, and in any event to minimise, incidental loss of civilian life, injury to civilians and damage to civilian objects', Henckaerts and Doswald-Beck (n 79) 51.

[102] See similarly the *Kupreškić et al* case ICTY (Trial Chamber Judgment) IT-95-16-T (14 January 2000) para 524 (claiming that the rules contained in Articles 57 and 58 AP I (n 45) constitute customary international law).

[103] Bothe, Partsch, and Solf (n 99) 405.

[104] *Khamzayev and Others v Russia* (n 9) para 183.

[105] *Kerimova and Others v Russia* (n 7) paras 250–52.

[106] ibid.

[107] *Khatsiyeva v Russia* (n 28) para 136 (in particular, the Court held that the attacking pilots had not been requested by the military commanders to provide further information regarding local visibility, whether the area was populated or whether there had been an attack on the pilots themselves).

[108] Y Sandoz, C Swinarski, and B Zimmermann (eds), *Commentary on the Additional Protocol of 8 June 1977 to the Geneva Conventions of 12 August 1949* (Martinus Nijhoff Publishers 1987) 680.

[109] Kolb (n 6) 168 (with reference to the *Central Front Award* by the Eritrea/Ethiopia Claims Commission).

the fact that 'an armed conflict, such as that in Chechnya, may entail developments to which State agents are called upon to react without prior preparation'.[110]

The obligation to minimize collateral damage relates to the planning of the circumstances of the attack, in particular with regard to the choice of weapons, the time, place, and angle of attack.[111] Typical problems discussed in IHL concern the questions whether there is an obligation to use precision weapons or which altitude of the aircraft is required when carrying out an aerial attack.[112] The ECtHR, too, requires documentary evidence for the careful planning of the attack (eg a plan of the operation, copies of orders, log-book entries, photos, records); mere allegations that there was 'reliable and sufficient' information about the objectives of an attack are insufficient.[113] In the leading case of *Isayeva v Russia*, the Court assessed the effectiveness of the measures taken by the authorities to minimize the collateral damage (in particular the establishment of a humanitarian corridor).[114] In the case of *Ergi v Turkey*, the Court found the planning of the attack by the state security services to be deficient: no precautions had been taken to protect the villagers from being affected by the ambush against members of the PKK.[115] The choice of means was criticized in *Esmukhambetov and others v Russia*.[116] The case concerned an air strike on a village in Chechnya, killing five civilians.[117] The Court argued that the respondent state should have considered employing ground troops instead of indiscriminate bombing.[118] The Court found that the respondent state had not taken 'any measures in order to avoid, or at least to minimize, the risk to the lives of the residents'.[119] In *Kerimova and others v Russia*, the Court heavily criticized the use of high-explosive fragmentation bombs of calibre 250–270 kg in air strikes on residential quarters.[120]

Under IHL, '[e]ffective warning shall be given of attacks which may affect the civilian population, unless circumstances do not permit' (Article 57(2)(c) AP I). An 'effective warning' requires that every effort is undertaken that the warning actually reaches the civilian population affected by the attack.[121] However, as the saving clause indicates, the obligation to warn is not absolute, and allows attacks by surprise.[122] Until today, the ECtHR

[110] *Suleymanova v Russia* (n 86) para 81.
[111] See Kolb (n 6) 168.
[112] See MN Schmitt, 'Precision Attack and International Humanitarian Law' (2005) 87 International Review of the Red Cross 445.
[113] *Esmukhambetov and Others v Russia* (n 23) paras 144–46.
[114] *Isayeva v Russia* (n 4) para 193–99.
[115] *Ergi v Turkey* (n 3) 80.
[116] *Esmukhambetov and Others v Russia* (n 23).
[117] ibid.
[118] ibid para 148.
[119] ibid para 149.
[120] *Kerimova and Others v Russia* (n 7) para 253.
[121] See Kolb (n 6) 170–71.
[122] See ibid 170.

has only implicitly recognized the obligation to warn civilians of a planned attack.[123]

There are two specific obligations arising from the IHL precautions regime that have until now not found their counterparts in the rights-based conception of precautions. The first relates to the detailed obligations in IHL to refrain from launching an attack, or—if already launched—to cancel or suspend the attack under certain circumstances (Article 57(2)(a)(iii) and(b) AP I). This IHL obligation textually requires a proportionality analysis using the humanitarian law principle of proportionality, prohibiting a disproportionality between civilian losses and military advantage.[124] The other IHL precaution that has until now not played a role in the case law of the ECtHR concerns the choice of the military objective causing the least collateral damage (Article 57(3) AP I). It may be a wise exercise of judicial restraint that keeps the ECtHR from embarking deeply on the evaluation of military strategy which would be necessary if it started to adjudicate upon these two precautions.

3.3 Precautions against the effects of attacks

Particularly with regard to precautions against the effects of attacks in non-international armed conflict (NIAC), a human rights-based conception can have an important complementary function in relation to IHL. In this field, the IHL conception is underdeveloped. Under the human rights-based conception of precautions, the state is obliged to not only take precautions against the incidental loss of civilian life through fire of its own forces but also through that of its adversary.[125] Accordingly, the ECtHR has developed quite far-reaching obligations in the case of *Kerimova and others v Russia*.[126] The case concerned a situation where the inhabitants were held hostage by fighters which were later attacked by the respondent state in an air strike.[127] In that difficult (human shield) situation, the Court criticized the respondent state for not having 'attempted to organise a safe exit for civilians, to negotiate their evacuation with the fighters, or the like'.[128] In the case of *Albekov and others v Russia*, concerning civilian casualties through anti-personnel mines, the authorities had a positive obligation to protect the civilians against the effects of

[123] *Kerimova and Others v Russia* (n 7) para 252 (finding that the authorities had not taken 'any meaningful steps to inform the civilian inhabitants of Urus-Martan of the attacks beforehand or to secure their evacuation'). See also *Isayeva v Russia* (n 4) para 189.

[124] See the formulation which would be excessive in relation to the concrete and direct military advantage anticipated, AP I (n 45) Article 57(2)(a)(iii) and (b). On proportionality in the context of IHL see Kolb (n 6) 172–75.

[125] *Ergi v Turkey* (n 3) para 79.

[126] *Kerimova and Others v Russia* (n 7) paras 250–52.

[127] ibid.

[128] ibid para 252. For the IHL perspective see MN Schmitt, 'Human Shields in International Humanitarian Law' (2008) 47 Columbia Journal of Transnational Law 292.

land mines.[129] In a situation like that, the Court requires the authorities to seal off the area; abstract verbal warnings are not sufficient.[130]

4. Conclusion: Establishing a Human Right to Precautions in Armed Conflict?

The doctrine of human rights-based precautions in and against the effects of attack under the ECHR is still in its infancy. There are a number of inherent problems with a Convention-based conception of precautions. A first set of objections concerns the problem of institutional legitimacy.[131] Some commentators point to—what they consider—'ivory tower' solutions taken by the ECtHR in relation to situations of armed hostilities.[132] More concretely, the objection is that the law governing precautions in and against the effects of attack is of a technical character that requires special (military) expertise which the Court lacks. This objection may be rebutted as follows: once one accepts that Convention rights are applicable to situations of armed conflict, the Court is competent to exercise its jurisdiction 'to ensure the observance of the engagements undertaken by the High Contracting Parties in the Convention'.[133] Absent a valid derogation under Article 15 ECHR, the Court will and must apply the Convention rights to *any* act constituting an interference with these rights (given that the case is admissible). When assessing the facts, the ECtHR will apply human rights doctrine, as its task is the interpretation of *rights* (not of IHL).[134] The substantive legitimacy (ie the correctness) of the findings by the Court will be enhanced if the Court manages to show that under both conceptions of precautions—though their foundations and sources are different—similar

[129] *Albekov and Others v Russia* App no 68216/01 (ECtHR, First Section Judgment, 9 October 2008) paras 86–90.

[130] ibid.

[131] 'Institutional legitimacy' means—in a normative sense—the 'right to rule', see A Buchanan, 'The Legitimacy of International Law' in S Besson and J Tasioulas (eds), *The Philosophy of International Law* (OUP 2010) 79. There are several factors that may give an institution the right to rule. While domestically, institutional legitimacy is strongly associated with 'democratic accountability', international governance institutions derive their institutional legitimacy commonly from state consent, respect for human rights and expertise, see D Bodansky, 'Legitimacy in International Law and International Relations' in JL Dunoff and MA Pollack (eds), *Interdisciplinary Perspectives on International Law and International Relations: The State of the Art* (CUP 2013) 321.

[132] See V Gowlland-Debbas and G Gaggioli, 'The Relationship between International Human Rights and Humanitarian Law: An Overview' in R Kolb and G Gaggioli (eds), *Research Handbook on Human Rights and Humanitarian Law* (Edward Elgar Publishing 2013) 77, 89–93 (commenting on the '"Ivory Tower" Approach of the European Court of Human Rights').

[133] Article 19 ECHR (n 7).

[134] Convention rights, as all human rights, belong to a special class of law: they formulate legitimacy conditions, ie they function as rules and limits for other rules, and they are usually endowed with special normative force, ie the domestic legal order may make the legality of a governmental act dependent on its conformity with Convention rights. These are the normative consequences of understanding rights as 'trumps', to use the famous formulation coined by R Dworkin, *Taking Rights Seriously* (Harvard University Press 1977) xi.

conclusions may be reached in a given case.[135] Finally, there are indications in the case law of the ECtHR that the Court is willing to accommodate the differences between the obligations flowing from human rights in peacetime and those in times of armed conflict.[136]

A second objection is the lack of clarity of a rights-based conception of precautions. If precautions are constructed as positive obligations, the balancing test used by the Court for assessing the justification of non-compliance with positive obligations applies. The bottom line of the test is whether the compliance with a positive obligation would have constituted an 'impossible or disproportionate burden'.[137] This can hardly be regarded as a clear yardstick. However, the clarity of an obligation is especially important if it concerns the use of military force. To this it may be responded that the more the ECtHR decides cases concerning situations of armed conflict, the more clearly it will have to elaborate on the concrete nature of the obligations. Furthermore, it is not the case that IHL norms are always precise on what is required of the state conducting an attack: Articles 57 and 58 AP I contain general clauses (do 'everything feasible', 'take all feasible precautions', or 'take the other necessary precautions'); Article 13 AP II in very broad terms declares that civilians 'enjoy general protection against the dangers arising from military operations', without specifying how the obligation to protect civilians or civilian objects translates into concrete precautionary measures.[138]

A third objection is that the further the ECtHR pushes its own human rights-based conception of precautions, the more relevant it becomes as a legal restraint binding upon European partners in multinational military operations, too. The emerging (regional) human right to precautions in armed conflict under the ECHR is one example for the growing imbalance in the set of legal obligations faced by participants in multinational military operations. Ultimately, the progressive approach by the ECtHR to precautions could lead to a situation in which military judgment becomes answerable to human rights claims and also amenable to claims for compensation by individuals.[139] From this perspective, the ECtHR's progressive stance towards precautions can potentially hamper the willingness of European states to engage in multinational military operations abroad.

[135] In practice, this often seems to be the case, see Gowlland-Debbas and Gaggioli (n 132) 91 (citing cases in which the ECtHR reached conclusions that were deemed compatible with IHL by the authors).

[136] See *Hassan v the United Kingdom* App no 29750/09 (ECtHR, Grand Chamber Judgment, 16 September 2014) (the Court is of the opinion that there are important differences of context and purpose between an arrest carried out during peacetime and an arrest of a combatant in the course of an armed conflict).

[137] *Abdurashidova v Russia* (n 71) para 74.

[138] AP II (n 91) Articles 14–16 contain prohibitions relating to targeting.

[139] In contrast, eg, to the German Federal Court which denied that individuals could claim damages in cases of a violation of IHL, Bundesgerichtshof, Judgment of 6 October 2016, III ZR 140/15, para 17. Similarly, Anne Peters argued that individuals neither have a general treaty-based, nor a customary law-based claim right concerning damages for violations of IHL, A Peters, *Beyond Human Rights: The Legal Status of the Individual in Public International Law* (CUP 2016) 210.

On the whole, however, the benefits of the evolution of a human rights-based conception of precautions outweigh the downsides. First, in a very general sense, there is reason to believe that the 'duplication' of precautions contributes to their practical effectiveness. The Convention mechanism is a powerful and—according to many observers—effective tool to influence the behaviour of states.[140] Consequently, some commentators have welcomed the Court's venture into the territory of IHL because they expect the standard of protection especially for civilians and civilian objects to rise.[141] For example, regarding the training of security forces, the Convention establishes a concrete obligation that the personnel 'must be trained to assess whether or not there is an absolute necessity to use firearms, not only on the basis of the letter of the relevant regulations, but also with due regard to the pre-eminence of respect for human life as a fundamental value'.[142] In contrast, specific training of the security forces regarding the respect for the right to life is neither mentioned in Article 57 or 58 AP I, nor in Article 13 AP II.[143] Secondly, the Convention conception of precautions may fill gaps in the protection offered by IHL by complementing existing IHL rules on precautions. The IHL norms governing precautions in NIACs are underdeveloped; a general treaty-based legal regime on precautions in NIAC is currently lacking.[144] Here, a human rights-based conception may be helpful. Also, it may fill a gap in protection resulting from a state's refusal to acknowledge the existence of an NIAC on its territory.[145] Thirdly, the case law of the European Court of Human Rights may help to clarify general clauses used in IHL. For example, Article 57(2)(a)(i) and (ii) AP I contain the obligation to 'do everything feasible to verify that the objectives to be attacked are neither civilians nor civilian objects' or to 'take all feasible precautions in the choice

[140] LR Helfer, 'Redesigning the European Court of Human Rights: Embeddedness as a Deep Structural Principle of the European Human Rights Regime' (2008) 19 European Journal of International Law 125 ('the world's most effective international human rights tribunal'). See also S Dothan, *Reputation and Judicial Tactics: A Theory of National and International Courts* (CUP 2015) 218 note 9 ('most of the sources that dealt with this issue claim that compliance rates [with ECHR judgments, TA] are very high').

[141] For example, William Abresch has argued: '[T]he ECtHR has begun to develop an approach that may prove more protective of victims and more politically viable than that of humanitarian law', W Abresch, 'A Human Rights Law of International Armed Conflict: The European Court of Human Rights in Chechnya' (2005) 16 European Journal of International Law 741, 767.

[142] *Wasilewska and Kalucka v Poland* (n 94) para 47; *Kakoulli v Turkey* App no 38595/97 (ECtHR, Fourth Section Judgment, 22 November 2005) para 114 (law enforcement officials 'are required to have the ability to assess all parameters and to organise their actions carefully with a view to minimising a risk of deprivation of life or bodily harm. In this connection, the Contracting States have a duty to provide effective training to law-enforcement officials operating in border areas and to give them clear and precise instructions as to the manner and circumstances in which they should make use of firearms, with the objective of complying with international standards on human rights and policing').

[143] The obligation to train soldiers in international humanitarian law is usually contained in domestic legal sources, see, eg, Article 33(2) of the German Law on the Legal Status of Military Personnel (30 May 2005, BGBl. I 1482): 'Soldiers are to be instructed with regard to their duties and rights under . . . public international law in times of peace and in times of war' (trans. by ICRC, <https://www.icrc.org/customary-ihl/eng/docs/v2_cou_de_rule142> accessed 27 December 2018).

[144] See Henckaerts and Doswald-Beck (n 79) 52.

[145] See Gowlland-Debbas and Gaggioli (n 132) 91.

of means and methods of attack'. The case law of the ECtHR can contribute to a further clarification of what may legitimately be considered as 'feasible' precautions both in law enforcement and military operations.[146]

Given the at least partially overlapping legal interests protected by IHL and human rights law, the gradual development of a Convention human rights-based regime on precautions must generally be considered a welcome step. Ideally, both legal regimes should inform and complement each other, so that eventually the right to life—one of the most essential legal interests—is better protected, both in times of peace and in times of armed conflict. In any case, however, the ECtHR is well-advised to approach the sensitive topic of precautions in situations of armed conflict with care and in close alignment with IHL.

[146] In the recent case of *Tagayeva and Others v Russia* App no 26562/07 et al (ECtHR, Judgment, 13 April 2017) para 595, the ECtHR seems to distinguish law-enforcement operations even further by differentiating between 'routine police operations' (governed by the rules of 'absolute necessity' in the meaning of Article 2 ECHR (n 7) and 'situations of large-scale anti-terrorist operations' (requiring 'tailor-made' responses).

PART IV

THE ROLE OF PERTINENT SUBFIELDS OF PUBLIC INTERNATIONAL LAW IN RELATION TO MULTINATIONAL MILITARY OPERATIONS

13

UN Security Council Resolutions as a Legal Framework for Multinational Military Operations

Pia Hesse

1. Introduction

Multinational military operations are in many cases established on the basis of a United Nations Security Council mandate. As the Council continues to expand its purview by classifying more and more situations and phenomena as threats to the peace within the meaning of Article 39 UN Charter,[1] the diversity of possible and actual theatres of operation for multinational military operations grows, too. The spectrum of military deployments authorized by the UN Security Council is wide. It covers robust operations with a strong military focus[2] as well as more defensive operations mandated to oversee a ceasefire agreement.[3] Whereas some operations are designed to address specific security issues such as maritime piracy[4] or migrant trafficking,[5] others have a mandate encompassing a variety of different tasks,[6] even including the administration of entire territories.[7] For some operations, the UN retains the command and control, for others it delegates its powers to member states or regional organizations.

[1] M Koskenniemi, 'The Police in the Temple. Order, Justice and the UN: A Dialectical View' (1995) 6 European Journal of International Law 325, 341; see also the Note by the President of the Security Council stating that '[t]he absence of war and military conflicts amongst States does not in itself ensure international peace and security' UNSC, 'Note by the President of the Security Council' (31 January 1992) UN Doc S/23500, 3.

[2] International Security Assistance Force (ISAF), authorized by UNSC Res 1386 (20 December 2001) UN Doc S/RES/1386.

[3] United Nations Observer Mission in Georgia (UNOMIG), authorized by UNSC Res 858 (24 August 1993) UN Doc S/RES/858.

[4] European Naval Force Somalia (Operation Atalanta), authorized by UNSC Res 1816 (2 June 2008) UN Doc S/RES/1816.

[5] European Union Naval Force Mediterranean (Operation Sophia), authorized by UNSC Res 2240 (9 October 2015) UN Doc S/RES/2240.

[6] This is the case for most UN peacekeeping operations. Their mandated tasks range from the protection of civilians, over the provision of security across conflict lines, to military training.

[7] United Nations Interim Administration Mission in Kosovo (UNMIK), authorized by UNSC Res 1244 (10 June 1999) UN Doc S/RES/1244 and United Nations Transitional Administration in East Timor (UNTAET), authorized by UNSC Res 1272 (25 October 1999) UN Doc S/RES/1272.

Pia Hesse, *UN Security Council Resolutions as a Legal Framework for Multinational Military Operations* In *The 'Legal Pluriverse' Surrounding Multinational Military Operations*. Edited by Robin Geiß and Heike Krieger, Oxford University Press (2020).
DOI: 10.1093/oso/9780198842965.003.0014

All these operations follow a UN Security Council resolution as their constitutive instrument. The texts of these resolutions are just as diverse as the situations the UN Security Council decides to engage in. Mandates do not only differ from operation to operation as they are tailored to meet the specific circumstances of each area of deployment, they may also change over the course of one operation. UN Security Council resolutions authorizing the use of force have evolved from terse texts comprising only few paragraphs that give the go ahead for a military mission to comprehensive legal instruments characterized by an increasing specification. While generally a higher degree of regulation on the part of the Security Council is likely to create more clarity of what the operation is expected to do, the risk of legal inconsistencies with other rules applying simultaneously increases, too.

Since resolution 678 (1990), which was referred to as a 'carte blanche authorization',[8] the Security Council has refined its practice under Chapter VII UN Charter. Rather than confining itself to deciding *whether* measures are to be taken, it can be observed that the Council increasingly tends to determine *how* these measures are to be adopted. The Council's practice shifting from the announcement of general political guidelines towards an ever more specific prescription of how States, as the principal addressees of Security Council resolutions, shall implement the Council's efforts to maintain or restore international peace and security is the focus of this chapter. With this practice, the Security Council answers to states' wishes for clear mandates which make operation planning and fulfilment easier. However, another demand often articulated by force commanders is to retain the mandate flexible in order to be able to react to changing circumstances on the ground. The following analysis will demonstrate how UN Security Council resolutions add to the 'legal pluriverse' of multinational military operations.

2. UN Security Council Resolutions and the Operationalization of the Mission

Practitioners involved in the planning and the implementation of a military operation are aware of the fragmented nature of the applicable law. A multitude of legal sources are relevant for such operations. However, military legal advisers would usually as a first step identify the legal basis for the initial military intervention in order to confirm the legality of the operation itself. A second and distinct task is the operationalization of the mission. Here, military lawyers generally turn to the laws of armed conflict in order to establish the legal framework within which

[8] BH Weston, 'Security Council Resolution 678 and Persian Gulf Decision Making: Precarious Legitimacy' (1991) 85 American Journal of International Law 516; similar, see J Quigley, 'The Privatization of Security Council Enforcement Action: A Threat to Multilateralism' (1996) 17 Michigan Journal of International Law 249.

they could move. But depending on the actual wording of the mission mandate, Security Council resolutions might become, beyond their function as a legal requirement for the deployment of forces onto a state's territory, a legal instrument also with respect to the measures and methods used during a mission.

On occasions, the Council has made incursions into the branch of the *jus in bello*. This can have both legal and practical implications. A more precisely formulated mission mandate reduces the risk of abuse by those who carry it out and makes excesses visible. However, where political objectives of a mission by means of an ever more detailed description turn into specific instructions, compatibility with the *jus in bello* can become an issue.

2.1 Resolutions authorizing the use of force and the *jus in bello*

In the absence of agreements concluded within the meaning of Article 43 UN Charter, the Security Council, pursuant to Article 42 UN Charter, authorizes the use of military force. The use of armed force, regardless of whether it is deployed in a UN-authorized or a UN-led mission, is generally subject to a number of different rules. The most relevant sets of rules for military operations are the *jus ad bellum* and the *jus in bello*. International law clearly distinguishes between the legality to resort to force in the international relations, regulated by the *jus ad bellum*, and the lawful means and methods of the use of force within an armed conflict, governed by the rules of the *jus in bello*, otherwise known as international humanitarian law (IHL) and the law of armed conflict or war. Both branches of law apply separately and concurrently.[9] This means that the legality of the recourse to force under the *jus ad bellum* has no effect on the applicability of IHL, nor does it render conduct that is in violation of the rules of IHL lawful.[10] In reverse, it means that compliance with IHL does not cure a breach of the *jus ad bellum* which is also expressed in preambular paragraph four of the First Additional Protocol to the 1949 Geneva Conventions (AP I). The concurrent application of the *jus ad bellum* and the *jus in bello* during a conflict is a corollary of that separation. Now, the legal pluriverse unfolds where instruments typically belonging to one of the two sets regulate matters of the other.

As recognized exception to the general prohibition of the use of force as laid down in Article 4(2) UN Charter and touching upon the sovereignty of the targeted state, Security Council resolutions authorizing the use of armed force generally fall within the ambit of the *jus ad bellum*, regulating the *if* of a military engagement. Pursuant to Articles 25, 48 UN Charter, member states are bound to carry out the

[9] *Legality of the Threat or Use of Nuclear Weapons* (Advisory Opinion) [1996] ICJ Rep 226.

[10] K Okimoto, *The Distinction and Relationship between Jus ad Bellum and Jus in Bello* (Hart Publishing 2011) 14.

decisions taken by the Security Council. Thus, military operations must be carried out in line with the prescriptions made in Security Council resolutions. Following the aforementioned principle of concurrent application, *jus in bello* also needs to be complied with.[11] Where the Security Council, in the formulation of its missions mandates, becomes involved in IHL-related matters, this clear-cut distinction between the two branches of law is difficult to sustain. A resolution text contradicting IHL norms would raise questions of competences, validity, and overriding application. Above all, it would undermine the confidence of commanders and soldiers that their decisions are lawful, which is essential for any military mission to be effective. Whereas many IHL norms themselves are already subject to doctrinal discussions, a resolution text spelling out additional orders would enhance the adverse effects of legal uncertainty on armed forces. This is even more true as the interpretation of Security Council resolutions following the recognized rules for treaty interpretation without restriction is not always an easy task.[12]

While not going that far as to contradict IHL, the Council at times makes reference to the *jus in bello*. The more involved the Security Council becomes in IHL-related matters, the more likely it is that the Council's practice has an impact on the normative development of this branch of law. The question being looked into here is whether a Security Council that increasingly deals with questions of *how* force is to be used, runs the risk of blurring the distinction between the *jus ad bellum* and the *jus in bello*. This theoretical distinction, however, is important for very practical reasons. It ensures protection during armed conflict by guaranteeing the application of IHL regardless of the cause of the conflict.[13]

[11] Once subject to debate, it is now widely accepted that IHL generally applies to UN peacekeeping missions, see C Greenwood, 'International Humanitarian Law and United Nations Military Operations' (1998) 1 Yearbook of International Humanitarian Law 3; K Okimoto, 'Violations of International Humanitarian Law by United Nations Forces and Their Legal Consequences' (2003) 6 Yearbook of International Humanitarian Law 199; the former UN Secretary-General Kofi Annan promulgated in its bulletin Observance by United Nations Forces of International Humanitarian Law that, by custom, IHL is applicable to 'United Nations forces when in situations of armed conflict they are actively engaged therein as combatants', UN Secretary-General, 'Bulletin: Observance by United Nations Forces of International Humanitarian Law' (6 August 1999) UN Doc ST/SGB/1999/13, Article 1.1.

[12] See MC Wood, 'The Interpretation of Security Council Resolutions' (1998) Max Planck Yearbook of United Nations Law 73; E Papastavridis, 'Interpretation of Security Council Resolutions under Chapter VII in the Aftermath of the Iraqi Crisis' (2007) 56 International & Comparative Law Quarterly 83.

[13] M Sassòli, 'Ius ad Bellum and Ius in Bello, The Separation between the Legality of the Use of Force and Humanitarian Rules to Be Respected in Warfare: Crucial or Outdated' in MN Schmitt and J Pejic (eds) *International Law and Armed Conflict: Exploring the Faultlines. Essays in Honour of Yoram Dinstein* (Brill 2007) 241, 244 et seq; H Lauterpacht, 'The Limits of the Operation of the Law of War' (1953) 30 British Yearbook of International Law 212; J Gardam, 'Proportionality and Force in International Law' (1993) 87 American Journal of International Law 39; J Moussa, 'Can Jus ad Bellum Override Jus in Bello? Reaffirming the Separation of the Two Bodies of Law' (2008) 90 International Review of the Red Cross 963, 967.

2.1.1 Reference to IHL by the UN Security Council

Before turning to the question on which occasions the UN Security Council deals with IHL-specific matters, it needs to be mentioned that the UN Charter does not contain any reference to IHL. The authors of the Charter deliberately avoided mentioning the laws of armed conflict as this was perceived to undermine the credibility with regard to the Charter's main purpose to outlaw the use of force in international relations.[14] In the same vein, the resolutions adopted by the Security Council during its first twenty years of existence are characterized by little interest in IHL.

It was in 1967 that the Security Council for the first time made reference to issues of humanitarian concern. It recommended to the government of Israel to respect the principles laid down in the Geneva Conventions of 1949 (GC) during the Six-Day War fought by Israel, Egypt, Jordan, and Syria.[15] Ever since, the Security Council has included statements on IHL in its resolutions—isolated at first, more frequently later. Today, any resolution that is adopted in connection with situations of armed violence contains a reference to IHL. The mention of IHL takes on different forms.

The most frequent form of reference is found in resolutions that recall the actors involved in a conflict situation to act 'in compliance with applicable IHL'[16] or 'to carry out operations in accordance with IHL, as applicable'.[17] In these cases, the Council either assumes the existence of an armed conflict and thus the application of IHL, or it stresses the observance of IHL whenever the requirements for it to apply are met. It does so without determining the conditions for the scope of application of IHL in general or certain rules of that legal branch in particular. Some resolutions focus on specific parties to the conflict,[18] on violations of IHL in a particular region,[19] during a certain period of time, or with regard to specific sub-branches of IHL[20] or even specific rules of IHL.[21] Whereas the statements that deal

[14] ILC, 'Report to the General Assembly' (1949) Yearbook of the International Law Commission 281.

[15] UNSC Res 237 (14 June 1967) UN Doc S/RES/237.

[16] To mention only one recent example of many, UNSC Res 2217 (28 April 2015) UN Doc S/RES/2217, para 45.

[17] UNSC Res 2211 (26 March 2015) UN Doc S/RES/2211, para 24.

[18] See, eg, UNSC Res 2147 (28 March 2014) UN Doc S/RES/2147 on the situation in the DRC, demanding that the FDLR, the ADF, the LRA, the Bakata-Katanga and various Mayi-Mayi groups demobilize children from their ranks.

[19] See, eg, UNSC Res 1778 (25 September 2007) UN Doc S/RES/1778 on attacks in 'Eastern Chad, the north-eastern Central African Republic and western Sudan (...), which result in serious violations of IHL'.

[20] See, eg, UNSC Res 2198 (29 January 2015) UN Doc S/RES/2198, para 10 condemning violations of IHL in the DRC and focusing on 'attacks on the civilian population, MONUSCO peacekeepers and humanitarian actors, summary executions, sexual gender-based violence and large-scale recruitment and use of children'.

[21] UNSC Res 1472 (28 March 2003) UN Doc S/RES/1472 outlining the duty of the Occupying Power under Article 55 of the Fourth GC in the situation between Iraq and Kuwait; UNSC Res 2139 (22 February 2014) UN Doc S/RES/2139 deals with the principle of distinction. By demanding all parties to 'cease the indiscriminate employment of weapons in populated areas, (...), such as the use of barrel

with the implementation of IHL in general, regardless of a particular situation, are more prevalent, the frequency of more focused calls to comply with IHL appears to be on the increase.

In other instances, the Security Council characterized a situation and identified the corresponding legal rules. Such was the case in resolution 672 (1990)[22] and 1472 (2003),[23] in which the Council determined Israel and the coalition forces in Iraq, respectively, as the occupying powers. As a consequence, it held the provisions of GC IV to be applicable. Thus, the UN Security Council, similar to a judicial body, applies existing legal rules to a concrete situation. It, thereby, exerts influence on the interpretation of a contested legal issue of IHL.[24]

The Security Council makes reference to IHL on many occasions and in different ways. However, in most cases, it contents itself with reaffirming the legal framework of IHL as it exists. Against this background, the obligations for military forces that derive from Security Council resolutions rarely deviate from the general obligations IHL imposes on them. Where Security Council resolutions contain decisions that are not identical with the substantive framework of IHL—either because they go beyond what is provided for by IHL or because they restrict the room for manoeuvre envisaged by IHL, questions relating to their relationship to the *jus in bello* arise.

2.1.2 The relationship between Security Council resolutions and IHL

Former Secretary-General Kofi Annan regarded the Security Council as the appropriate body to 'help forge consensus over when and *how* resort to force is appropriate'[25] (emphasis added). Without indulging in the question of the Council's competence to follow this proposal at this point,[26] a few paragraphs in Security Council resolutions that are prone to narrow the gap between the *jus ad bellum* and the *jus in bello* will be looked at in more detail.

2.1.2.1 Strategic goals of military operations determining the military advantage

With respect to *Operation Unified Protector*, the NATO operation in Libya in 2011 based on resolution 1973,[27] the view was expressed that a determination of the

bombs' the Council makes clear that it is not the bomb as such that contravenes IHL, but the way it is employed by Syrian forces that is in violation of IHL.

---

[22] UNSC Res 672 (12 October 1990) UN Doc S/RES/672.

[23] UNSC Res 1472 (n 21).

[24] G Nolte, 'Practice of the UN Security Council with Respect to Humanitarian Law' in K Dicke and others (eds), *Weltinnenrecht: liber amicorum Jost Delbrück* (Duncker & Humblot 2005) 495 et seq.

[25] K Annan, '"In larger freedom": Decision Time at the UN' (*Foreign Affairs*, May/June 2005) <https://www.foreignaffairs.com/articles/2005-05-01/larger-freedom-decision-time-un>. All URLs accessed 27 December 2018.

[26] On this question, see M Roscini, 'The United Nations Security Council and the Enforcement of International Humanitarian Law' (2010) 43 Israel Law Review 330, 332.

[27] UNSC Res 1973 (17 March 2011) UN Doc S/RES/1973.

military advantage within the meaning of IHL must take into account the humanitarian purpose of the Security Council mandate.[28]

UN Security Council resolutions authorizing the use of force determine the purposes for which force may be used. Recent resolutions invoke, among others, the protection of civilians, the facilitation of humanitarian assistance, the protection of the United Nations, the enforcement of compliance with a ban on flights, the monitoring of arms embargoes, the creation of a secure environment, and the disarmament of armed groups as purposes for which military force was authorized. The development of identifying precise mission goals is laudable from a rule-of-law perspective and has been endorsed by the Institut de Droit International.[29] However, the interpretation of IHL rules in the light of these political goals may conflate the *jus ad bellum* and the *jus in bello*. Proportionality, a concept common to both branches of law but following different logics in each of the two regimes, is at stake here.

In IHL, the military advantage is one factor of reference in the assessment of the proportionality of an attack. The fundamental principle of proportionality is codified in Article 51(5)(b) AP I. Thus, 'an attack which may be expected to cause incidental loss of civilian life, injury to civilians, damage to civilian objects, or a combination thereof, which would be excessive in relation to the concrete and direct military advantage anticipated' is considered disproportionate.[30] Hence, humanitarian considerations, the expected civilian loss and damage, are to be balanced against the military advantage anticipated. According to the Commentary on AP I, the military advantage under IHL 'consist(s) in ground gained and in annihilating or weakening the enemy armed forces'.[31] If, in the case of Libya, one regards the protection of 'civilians and civilian populated areas under threat of attack'[32] to be the military advantage, the balancing test would presumably reach a different conclusion as to when the military advantage was to be seen to exclusively capture military needs. Military troops could, depending on the reading, be either more or less restrained in their choice of means and methods. If the explicit military goal is to protect civilians, an attack carried out for that purpose that results in suffering and loss of civilian lives seems to have missed the target. Whereas some

[28] J Lehmann, 'All Necessary Means to Protect Civilians: What the Intervention in Libya Says About the Relationship Between the *Jus in Bello* and the *Jus Ad Bellum*' (2012) 17 Journal of Conflict and Security Law 117, 134; C Greenwood, 'Historical Development and Legal Basis' in D Fleck (ed), *The Handbook of International Humanitarian Law* (2nd edn, OUP 2008) 36–37.

[29] Institut de Droit International, 'Tenth Commission: Present Problems of the Use of Force in International Law—Resolution on Authorization of the Use of Force by the United Nations' (Session de Rhodes, 9 September 2011) Article 2. <http://www.idi-iil.org/app/uploads/2017/06/2011_rhodes_10_-D_en.pdf>.

[30] See also JM Henckaerts and L Doswald-Beck (eds), *Customary International Humanitarian Law* (CUP 2005) Rule 14.

[31] Y Sandoz, C Swinarski, and B Zimmermann (eds), *Commentary on the Additional Protocols of 8 June 1977 to the Geneva Conventions of 12 August 1949* (Martinus Nijhoff Publishers 1987) para 2218.

[32] UNSC Res 1973 (n 27) para 4.

collateral damage would even be acceptable under these circumstances, the restrictions to the means and methods of warfare that are required to satisfy the principle of proportionality would be greater for attacks enforcing humanitarian goals than for those carried out for purely military needs *strictu sensu*. Here, the *jus ad bellum* would have a limiting effect on the *jus in bello*. The humanitarian purpose would translate into more obligations on the part of the authorized party, and, in turn, touch upon the principle of equal applicability.[33]

On the other hand, one could consider the declared military advantage to protect civilians as a particularly aspirational objective, given the concept's origin in the purposes and principles of the UN Charter.[34] Its special value would legitimize a strong military action and would tip the balance in favour of the military advantage allowing for greater collateral damage which, in turn, would influence the choice of means or methods of warfare. As is demonstrated by this comparison, taking the strategic objectives into account during the proportionality assessment changes the outcome. It adds another layer of subjective judgement, and, hence, impreciseness to the proportionality test. It is therefore preferable to have constant—though themselves also prone to subjective evaluation—variables on both sides of the scale. Without considering its moral value, it is therefore indispensable to agree that the military advantage lies in the submission of the enemy, accepting it as the 'sad necessit[y] of war'.[35]

A reading that considers the overall political goal for the determination of the military advantage resembles the concept of proportionality in the *jus ad bellum*. If questions of the *jus in bello* are subordinated to considerations of *jus ad bellum*, the principle of separation of these two bodies is challenged. In the context of the right to self-defence, the principle of proportionality has been used in two senses. Some follow the 'tit for tat' approach, under which the forcible act of state A must be proportionate to the amount of force used by state B which provoked the response of A.[36] There is strong support for the view, referred to as the 'means-ends' test, which maintains that the means, that is the amount of force used, must be proportionate to the legitimate ends of the use of force.[37] The legitimate end of the right to self-defence is to halt and repel the ongoing armed attack. Factors that need

[33] F Mégret, 'Missions autorisées par le Conseil de sécurité à l'heure de la R2P: au-delà du jus in bello?' (2013) 52 Military Law and the Law of War Review 205, 235, stating that 'Il se peut en effet que la logique humanitaire classique (d'égalité entre parties) aille à l'encontre d'une réelle plus-value humanitaire consistant en un surcroit d'obligations à la charge de certains acteurs'.

[34] H Willmot and S Sheeran, 'The Protection of Civilians Mandate in UN Peacekeeping Operations: Reconciling Protection Concepts and Practices' (2013) 95 International Review of the Red Cross 517, 529.

[35] Sandoz, Swinarski, and Zimmermann (n 31) para 2219.

[36] *Military and Paramilitary Activities in and against Nicaragua (Nicaragua v USA)* (Merits) [1986] ICJ Rep 14, para 176; *Oil Platforms (Iran v USA)* (Merits) [2003] ICJ Rep 161, para 77; *Nuclear Weapons* (n 9), para 41.

[37] J Gardam, *Necessity, Proportionality and the Use of Force by States* (CUP 2004) 11; R Ago, 'Eighth Report on State Responsibility' (1980) II Yearbook of the International Law Commission 69–70.

to be taken into account to assess proportionality are the nature of the target, the effects on civilians, and both the geographical and the temporal scope of the right to self-defence.[38]

Whereas the necessity/proportionality test has obtained the status of custom in the law of self-defence, it is not clear whether this standard applies analogously to resolutions adopted by the Security Council under Chapter VII.[39] The wording of Article 42 UN Charter, allowing for 'such action (...) *as* may be necessary' (emphasis added), support the supposition that necessity concerns not only the question of whether there are alternatives to the use of force, but also the choice of forcible means.[40] The latter meaning of necessity is equivalent to proportionality. The Charter's emphasis on pacific settlement of international disputes,[41] with the prohibition on the use of force in Article 2(4) as the cornerstone, justifies the conclusion that any exception thereto is to be construed narrowly.[42] Against this background, the *ad bellum* proportionality for military enforcement requires a use of force that does not exceed the scale, duration, and intensity of what is necessary to maintain or restore international peace and security.

When the Security Council decides to authorize coercive military action pursuant to Article 42 UN Charter, it generally expresses that decision by the authorization to use or take 'all necessary means'.[43] Whereas this phrase is generally recognized to be the Council's terminology authorizing the use of force, it has been doubted that the term 'necessary' had a meaning extending beyond the *if* of the use of force. Rather, the phrase has become common practice as a euphemistic alternative to the explicit mentioning of 'force' on the initiative of the Soviet Union in connection with the adoption of resolution 678 (1990).[44] However, in line with the aforementioned considerations regarding the *ad bellum* proportionality, this phrase may also express a requirement of necessity limiting the actions taken to what would be proportionate to achieving the actual objective.[45] This view is supported by a UN report that commended to the Security Council to apply a proportionality test when authorizing military options.[46]

[38] K Okimoto, 'The Relationship Between *Jus ad bellum* and *Jus in bello*' in M Weller (ed), *The Oxford Handbook of the Use of Force in International Law* (OUP 2015) 1216.

[39] Lehmann (n 28) 132.

[40] N Krisch, 'Article 42' in B Simma and others (eds), *The Charter of the United Nations: A Commentary* (3rd edn, OUP 2012) para 19.

[41] Charter of the United Nations (adopted 26 June 1945, entry into force 24 October 1945) Article 1(1).

[42] Lehmann (n 28) 133.

[43] The alternative phrase frequently used is 'all necessary measures'.

[44] S Chesterman, *Just War or Just Peace?: Humanitarian Intervention and International Law* (OUP 2001) 163–64, citing MR Beschloss and S Talbott, *At the Highest Levels: The Inside Story of the End of the Cold War* (Little Brown 1993) 284.

[45] Lehmann (n 28) 130; *contra*, see R McLaughlin, 'The Legal Regime Applicable to Use of Lethal Force When Operating under a United Nations Security Council Chapter VII Mandate Authorising "All Necessary Means"' (2008) 12 Journal of Conflict and Security Law 389, 412–13.

[46] UNGA, 'Report of the Secretary-General: In larger freedom: towards development, security and human rights for all' (21 March 2005) UN Doc A/59/2005, para 126.

A reading of 'military advantage' that allows to accommodate the goal to protect civilians would bring the IHL proportionality standard extremely close to the understanding of proportionality within the context of Chapter VII resolutions.[47] It is against this background that an interpretation of *jus in bello* rules in accordance with Security Council mandates was rejected by many authors.[48] It would lead to a conflation of *jus ad bellum* and *jus in bello* elements.[49] Getting back to the example of Libya, any use of force that had the sole aim of weakening forces loyal to Gaddafi without being able to demonstrate that these forces were at the time of the attack threatening 'civilians [or] civilian populated areas' would not be covered by the Security Council mandate. Even though the attack would be in accordance with IHL insofar as only military objects were targeted, it would have to be discontinued as the *jus ad bellum* was violated. Thus, the more stringent requirements for the military operation are not imposed by the IHL proportionality analysis but by the overall proportionality standard under the *jus ad bellum*. Such parallel application is the essence of the concurrent application of the *jus ad bellum* and the *jus in bello*. The idea behind the concurrent application of the *jus ad bellum* and the *jus in bello* is that branches of international law regulating two distinct aspects of the use of force should not be mutually dependent in their application or interpretation in order to prevent that either aspect is left unregulated or affected by an unsuitable set of rules.

Whereas the foregoing example demonstrates how military operation mandates formulated in UN Security Council resolutions can converge with other legal norms by way of interpretation, convergence can also occur through overlapping regulation of the same matter. In cases where the Security Council, by stating how force is to be used, deviates from IHL norms, questions of relationship may arise.

2.1.2.2 Overlapping regulation

Article 48 AP I formulates the basic rule that 'the parties to the conflict shall at all times distinguish between the civilian population and combatants and between civilian objects and military objectives and accordingly shall direct their operations only against military objectives' (meaning persons and objects). The rationale of this 'cardinal principle'[50] of IHL, which aims to protect civilians from the effects of

[47] Lehmann (n 28) 134.

[48] G Bartolini, 'Air Targeting in Operation Unified Protector in Libya, Jus ad Bellum and IHL Issues: An External Perspective' in S Horvat and M Benatar (eds), *L'interopérabilité juridique et la garantie du respect du droit applicable dans le cadre des déploiements multinationaux* (Société internationale de Droit militaire et Droit de la Guerre 2013) 269; MH Hoffman, 'Peace-Enforcement Actions and Humanitarian Law: Emerging Rules for Interventional Armed Conflict' (2000) 82 International Review of the Red Cross 193.

[49] M Bothe, 'The Protection of the Civilian Population and NATO Bombing on Yugoslavia: Comments on a Report to the Prosecutor of the ICTY' (2001) 12 European Journal of International Law 531, 535.

[50] *Nuclear Weapons* (n 9).

hostilities, is found in many resolutions of the Security Council dealing with conflict situations.

In 1999, acting under Chapter VII, the Security Council for the first time authorized a UN peacekeeping force to 'take the necessary action (...) to afford protection to civilians under imminent threat of physical violence'.[51] Nowadays, the inclusion of such protection mandates based on Chapter VII UN Charter is standard in UN peacekeeping missions.[52] They generally regulate only the purpose for which resort to force is authorized and thereby limit the scope of the robust mandate. However, their concrete content has been developed since. The resolution creating the Intervention Brigade within MONUSCO, the UN peacekeeping mission established in the Democratic Republic of the Congo, mandates the mission through its regular forces and its Intervention Brigade to take all necessary measures to 'mitigate the risk to civilians before, during and after any military operation'.[53] Here, the Security Council gives guidance as to how force is used at the tactical level. The question is how this instruction relates to IHL rules with overlapping content.

AP I comprises a section entitled 'General protection against effects of hostilities' within Part IV that is concerned with the civilian population. Provisions that deal with risk mitigation are primarily Articles 57 and 58, enumerating precautionary measures both in attack and against the effects of attack. These obligations derive from the principle of distinction insofar as they aim to avoid or to minimize the collateral effects of hostilities on civilian persons, the civilian population, and civilian objects.[54] The principle of precautions in attack, inter alia, is reflected in Article 57(1) AP I which stipulates that 'in the conduct of military operations, constant care shall be taken to spare the civilian population, civilians and civilian objects'.

However, a comparison between the obligation spelled out in Security Council resolution 2098 and the duty under general IHL to take precautions in attack and against the effects of attack reveals that the temporal scope of the former obligation is broader than that of the latter. Whereas the protection mandate binds the UN forces 'before, during and after any military operation', IHL rather focuses on protective measures during ('in the conduct of') a military operation. The term 'military operation', however, should be understood to include troop movements, manoeuvres, and other activities carried out by armed forces before actual combat,[55] and thereby including preventive action. The paragraphs following paragraph 1 of Article 57 list more concrete precautions that are to be taken. The

[51] UNSC Res 1270 (22 October 1999) UN Doc S/RES/1270 establishing UNAMSIL.
[52] Roscini (n 26) 350.
[53] UNSC Res 2098 (28 March 2013) UN Doc S/RES/2098, para 12(a)(i) and (b); UNSC Res 2147 (n 18).
[54] JF Quéguiner, 'Precautions under the Law Governing the Conduct of Hostilities' (2006) 88 International Review of the Red Cross 793, 794.
[55] Sandoz, Swinarski, and Zimmermann (n 31) para 2191.

wording clearly indicates that these measures are to be taken either before ('those who *plan* or *decide upon* an attack shall: (...)',[56] '*advance* warning shall be given'[57]) or during ('an attack shall be *cancelled* or *suspended* if (...)'[58]) an attack and thus in the early stages of and amidst a military operation, respectively. In the same vein, Article 58 focuses on *pre*cautions. Whereas the aim of this provision is to tackle the effects of attacks and thus the aftermath of a military operation, the actual measures to achieve this aim are to be taken in advance. Measures to mitigate the risk after such operation, on the other hand, are not demanded of the warring parties.

One could well argue that the obligation spelled out in Security Council resolution 2098 is to be understood in exactly the same way. If one reads the qualification 'before, during and after any military operation' to apply to 'risk' and not to 'mitigate' within the meaning of 'the risk to the civilians *arising* before, during and after any military operation', it would not necessarily include an obligation to act after the military operation has taken place. The wording allows for both interpretations. The invocation of the French version, stating 'atténuer les risques auxquels sont exposés les civils avant, pendant et après toute opération militaire' does not help in this regard, either. However, the Spanish translation that mentions the qualifications 'before' and 'after' at the end of the sentence and thereby somehow detached from the 'risk' suggests that the temporal indication rather relates to 'mitigate' ('mitigar el riesgo para los civiles durante cualquier operación militar, así como antes y después'). According to this reading, the mandate requires the forces, in their strive to protect civilians, to become active before, during, *and after* any military operation.

In the specific context, the Secretary-General, however, does not specify what such responsive measures could look like. One could imagine steps that target those risks associated with possible countermeasures by the opposing party and their implications for the civilian population. Other measures could aim at victim assistance, clearance of remnants of war, risk education, repairing damage to the environment, or target other threats that the legacy of military operations poses to the civilian population. Whereas AP I in its chapter on civil defence envisages the performance of some tasks to help the civilian population to recover from the immediate effects of hostilities which, by definition, take place after a military operation, the relevant provisions (Articles 61–71 AP I) do not create an obligation but rather grant civil defence organizations a status ensuring them protection in the performance of their task.[59] Measures addressing the post-hostilities threats are found in some weapons treaties. For instance, the Fifth Protocol to the 1980

[56] Protocol Additional to the Geneva Conventions of 12 August 1949 and relating to the Protection of Victims of International Armed Conflicts (Protocol I) (opened for signature 8 June 1977, entered into force 7 December 1978) 1125 UNTS 3, Article 57(2)(a) (AP I).

[57] AP I (n 56) Article 57(2)(c).

[58] AP I (n 56) Article 57(2)(b).

[59] Sandoz, Swinarski, and Zimmermann (n 31) para 2321.

Convention on Certain Conventional Weapons (CCW) on Explosive Remnants of War and the Convention on Cluster Munitions spell out the responsibility of the belligerent parties to clear contaminated areas[60] and to ensure care and rehabilitation to survivors and their communities.[61] However, the focus in IHL with respect to the protection of civilians lies on preventive considerations. This prioritization is wise as it is always better to prevent risks for the civilian population from arising in the first place. Nevertheless, considering that the relevant IHL provisions formulate obligations 'of due diligence and acting in good faith',[62] hence obligations of conduct, further risks might continue to exist. Adding obligations that are remedial in nature do not release the forces from their duty to take precautions before and in the course of hostilities but rather aim to reduce civilian casualties whenever they occur, including afterwards.

This example demonstrates how the Security Council comments on how force is to be used, while creating obligations that go beyond what is required by IHL. The principal responsibility of the UN Security Council is to maintain and restore international peace and security and, hence, to do everything within its power to prevent or reverse a situation of violence which needs to be regulated. However, where the very way in which armed violence is carried out qualifies as a threat to the peace,[63] decisions may be taken by the Security Council to ensure humanitarian protection during the conflict.

Violations of IHL were qualified as a threat to the peace for the first time in 1993 with respect to the conflict in Bosnia–Herzegovina.[64] The practice of the Security Council shows that for an IHL violation to amount to a threat to the peace, it needs to be 'systematic, widespread and flagrant'. Moreover, the determination has always been made in connection with a particular conflict.[65] Once the Security Council has opened the door to Chapter VII by determining the existence of a threat to

[60] Protocol on Explosive Remnants of War to the Convention on Prohibitions or Restrictions on the Use of Certain Conventional Weapons which may be deemed to be Excessively Injurious or to have Indiscriminate Effects (Protocol V) (adopted 28 November 2003, entered into force 12 November 2006) 2399 UNTS 100, Article 3.

[61] Convention on Cluster Munitions (adopted 30 May 2008, entered into force 1 August 2010) 2688 UNTS 39, Article 5.

[62] Y Dinstein, *The Conduct of Hostilities under the Law of International Armed Conflict* (CUP 2004) 126.

[63] Within the meaning of Article 39 UN Charter (n 41).

[64] UNSC Res 808 (22 February 1993) UN Doc S/RES/808.

[65] ibid; UNSC Res 955 (8 November 1994) UN Doc S/RES/955; UNSC Res 941 (23 September 1994) UN Doc S/RES/941, stating that the practice of ethnic cleansing in some areas in Bosnia–Herzegovina constitutes a violation of IHL and poses a threat to the peace; in resolutions on the thematic issue on 'protection of civilians in armed conflict', the Council reiterated that the commission of systematic, flagrant, and widespread violations of IHL in situations of armed conflict might constitute a threat to international peace and security, UNSC Res 1296 (19 April 2000) UN Doc S/RES/1296; UNSC Res 1674 (28 April 2006) UN Doc S/RES/1674; UNSC Res 1778 (25 September 2007) UN Doc S/RES/1778; UNSC Res 1894 (11 November 2009) UN Doc S/RES/1894.

the peace, a breach of the peace, or an act of aggression, it enjoys wide latitude regarding how to maintain and restore peace and security.[66]

Nevertheless, many maintain that its discretion ends where it would result in derogation from IHL. This debate, so far, is mainly taking place detached from examples drawn from Security Council practice, since there are very few instances in which derogation has been claimed. This was, for example, the case in the context of resolution 1483 (2003) and resolution 1511 (2003) concerning the occupation of Iraq. Here, concerns have been raised whether the Council had gone beyond what was permitted by the law of occupation.[67] Whereas some argue that an effective exercise of the Council's responsibility for the maintenance of international peace and security requires it to be able to take any measure it deems necessary for that purpose, others see its powers restricted by the purposes and principles of the UN Charter. According to Article 1(3), one purpose is to promote and encourage respect for human rights. Taking subsequent practice of the UN into account, it is said that the term 'human rights' in this context is to be construed broadly, including IHL.[68] Hence, the Security Council would act *ultra vires* authorizing military enforcement measures that would be in conflict with IHL. No obligations can derive out of such resolutions.[69] In contrast, Council resolutions deviating from IHL insofar as it imposes stricter standards do not contradict the humanitarian purpose of IHL.[70] The Security Council resolution and IHL place cumulative requirements on the deployment of military operations.

2.2 Clarity and flexibility

A frequently voiced request by UN member states is that mission mandates need to be both clear and flexible. Clarity of the mandate is crucial during the planning, the training, and the implementation phase. An ambiguous mandate is particularly difficult to handle for a diverse multinational mission. Troops coming from different cultures, speaking different languages, following different legal obligations and maybe different political objectives will come to different interpretations of a mission's role if the mandate allows. At the same time, however, multinational

[66] E López-Jacoiste, 'The UN Collective Security System and its Relationship with Economic Sanctions and Human Rights' (2010) 14 Max Planck Yearbook of United Nations Law 273, 284 et seq.

[67] R Kolb, 'Occupation in Iraq since 2003 and the Powers of the UN Security Council' (2008) 90 International Review of the Red Cross 29; D Scheffer, 'Beyond Occupation Law' (2003) 97 American Journal of International Law 842.

[68] M Zwanenburg, 'United Nations and International Humanitarian Law' (2013) Max Planck Encyclopedia of Public International Law 44; Okimoto (n 38) 1220.

[69] ILC, 'Report of the Study Group of the International Law Commission on its Fifty-eight Session: Fragmentation of International Law: Difficulties Arising from the Diversification and Expansion of International Law' (1 May–9 June and 3 July–11 August 2006) UN Doc A/CN.4/L.682, para 331.

[70] Lehmann (n 28) 130.

military operations are often deployed in unstable areas characterized by unpredictable dynamics. The deployment in such an unsteady environment requires the ability to swiftly react to changing circumstances. A mandate staying abreast of such developments leaves room for a mission to evolve according to the needs on the ground.

The range of objectives pursued by a multinational military operation is wide. However, the same issues are of relevance to many missions. In the course of the Council's drafting practice, some concepts have evolved and have been refined that are implemented in many mission mandates. One such example is the mandate to protect the civilian population. Featuring in almost any resolution that authorizes military operations, the protection of civilians (PoC) mandate has undergone a normative development. While this has helped to clarify what measures may be taken by a mission tasked to protect the civilian population, the wide range of possible activities maintains a high degree of flexibility.

The UN Security Council started to include the task to protect the civilian population into mission mandates in 1999[71] and has continued to do so for many ensuing operations.[72] Whereas the PoC mandate of the United Nations Mission in Sierra Leone (UNAMSIL) in 1999 was confined to simply determining that the protection of the civilian population was one task falling to the peacekeepers, the assignment of the PoC task within UN mandates has been substantiated with ever more instruction of how the task is to be performed. For instance, the resolutions authorizing MONUSCO and United Nations Mission in the Republic of South Sudan (UNMISS) devote up to six subparagraphs, filling a half page, to their PoC mandate.[73] Even though UN Security Council resolutions do not have legal effects beyond the particular mission authorized by it, many ideas of what peacekeepers are asked to do as part of their PoC responsibility are found in more than one mission mandate, and identical wording is used. The concrete activity called for within a resolution under the heading 'protection of civilians' is illustrative of the type of action the Council subsumes under the rather broad concept of PoC. In addition to specific instructions within mission mandates, the UN has also by now developed a comprehensive PoC policy. The Department of Peacekeeping Operations (DPKO) and the Department of Field Support (DFS) have published a policy document on the *Protection of Civilians in United Nations Peacekeeping*.[74] It supersedes other UN doctrine produced lately on specific aspects of UN peacekeeping

[71] United Nations Mission in Sierra Leone (UNAMSIL), UNSC Res 1270 (n 51) para 14.

[72] The UNSC, to date, has issued mandates embodying the demand to protect civilians into thirteen peacekeeping missions.

[73] United Nations Organization Stabilization Mission in the Democratic Republic of the Congo (MONUSCO), UNSC Res 2147 (n 18) para 4(i)–(iii); United Nations Mission in the Republic of South Sudan (UNMISS), UNSC 2155 (27 May 2014) UN Doc S/RES/2155, para 4(i)–(iv).

[74] UN DPKO and DFS, 'Policy: The Protection of Civilians in United Nations Peacekeeping' (1 April 2015) <http://providingforpeacekeeping.org/wp-content/uploads/2017/08/2015-07-Policy-on-PoC-in-Peacekeeping-Operations.pdf>.

related to the PoC mandate,[75] and it refers to many Security Council resolutions on the thematic issue of the protection of civilians. The aim of this publication is to channel the many positions on the meaning of the PoC mandate and to support its coherent implementation. Such guidance is not only valuable for multinational operations, but also for multidimensional operations, meaning operations using a mix of civilian, police, and military capabilities, because protection concepts are understood differently in the humanitarian and the human rights community.[76] The policy reconciles different points of view and, thus, reduces the risk that conceptual misunderstandings result in inefficient mission implementation. Although this internal policy of the UN is not a legally binding definition of the PoC mandate, it proclaims the UN's understanding of what action could be taken under it. As such, it will nonetheless shape the interpretation and evolution of UN peacekeeping and the conduct of those actors involved in UN missions.

2.3 Robust peacekeeping

Although UN guidance on PoC mandates provides a framework for the fulfilment of the mandate and thus adds precision to the overly broad notion, the range of actions subsumable under it still remains wide. Since the multinational operation in Libya, the issue of protection of civilians, and particularly the military side of it, has gathered further momentum. The Council authorized a Force Intervention Brigade (FIB) in the DRC in 2013 and a Regional Protection Force (RPF) in South Sudan in 2016. These are attempts to utilize the military aspect of peace enforcement for the protection of civilians.[77] Both deployments are part of the respective UN mission and operate alongside their regular military components. Both are tasked to, inter alia, protect the civilian population through military means.[78]

After intense fighting in the region of North Kivu in the DRC, in March 2013, the UN Security Council passed resolution 2098 which mandated the FIB to address the main threat to the civilian population, Congolese and foreign armed groups, by 'neutralizing' them.[79] The term 'neutralize' in the military context means to render

[75] UN DPKO and DFS, 'Operational Concept on the Protection of Civilians in United Nations Peacekeeping Operations' (2010) <http://www.peacekeeping.org.uk/wp-content/uploads/2013/02/100129-DPKO-DFS-POC-Operational-Concept.pdf>; UN DPKO and DFS, 'Framework for Drafting Comprehensive Protection of Civilians Strategies in UN Peacekeeping Operations' (2011) <http://www.refworld.org/docid/523998464.html>.

[76] Willmot and Sheeran (n 34) 535.

[77] J Benson, 'The UN Intervention Brigade: Extinguishing Conflict or Adding Fuel to the Flames?' (A One Earth Future Discussion Paper, June 2016), 2 <http://oefresearch.org/sites/default/files/documents/publications/uninterventionbrigade.pdf>.

[78] UNSC Res 2098 (n 53) authorized MONUSCO and the FIB to '[e]nsure [...] effective protection of civilians under imminent threat of physical violence' and UNSC Res 2304 (12 August 2016) UN Doc S/RES/2304 authorized the RPF to 'Promptly and effectively engage any actor that is credibly found to be preparing attacks, or engages in attacks, against [...] civilians'.

[79] UNSC Res 2098 (n 53) para 12(b).

enemy personnel incapable of interfering which can amount to targeting with lethal force. Whereas the practice of deploying supporting military missions parallel to UN peacekeeping missions is not new,[80] the integration of such offensive force under UN command gives the entire peacekeeping mission a much more robust character. This robust posture, however, has legal and political ramifications. It may conflict with fundamental principles of UN Peacekeeping. A UN force established to neutralize non-state armed groups will, taking on its responsibility,[81] find itself engaged in an armed conflict with opposing forces—a departure from the principle of mission impartiality and limited use of force.[82]

The offensive mandate and the advanced military capabilities of the FIB raised questions about the status of the MONUSCO under IHL. As a party to the conflict, the FIB would be required to abide by IHL and become a legitimate target itself.[83] Whether this leads to the loss of the protected status of the entire mission or whether the status of the FIB must be assessed isolated from the rest of MONUSCO has been subject to legal debates.[84] Even though the law might be able to draw a straight line, the robust character of FIB is likely to alter the image of MONUSCO as a whole. As the Capstone Doctrine highlights, a particularly valuable asset of the UN is to act as an impartial arbiter.[85] Fighting armed groups alongside government forces risks losing credibility as a mediator between conflict parties, even for future missions.

The RPF in South Sudan has similarly robust elements and is charged with using all means to enforce peace in Juba. Its actual deployment was opposed by the government of South Sudan despite initially having agreed to it.[86] Before the UN, the representative of South Sudan declared that the adoption of the resolution establishing the RPF went against the basic principle of UN peacekeeping

[80] French forces have been mandated to support the United Nations Operation in Côte d'Ivoire (UNOCI), UNSC Res 1528 (27 February 2004) UN Doc S/Res/1528, para 16; in June 2003 a French-led EU force (Operation Artemis) was deployed to the Bunia region in the DRC to support MONUC in its endeavour to protect civilians from the horrific violence, UNSC Res 1484 (30 May 2003) UN Doc S/RES/1484; deployed in 1999, NATO-led KFOR and Australian-led INTERFET were charged to take the military role alongside the UN mission in Kosovo and in East Timor, respectively, UNSC Res 1244 (n 7) and UNSC 1264 (15 September 1999) UN Doc S/RES/1264.

[81] Which the FIB did right from the start, see Kenny Katombe, 'UN Intervention Brigade Fires on Congo Rebel Positions' (*Reuters*, 23 August 2013) <htp://www.reuters.com/artcle/us-congo-democratc-fghtng-idUSBRE97M0WA20130823>.

[82] N Tsagourias, 'Consent, Neutrality, Impartiality and the Use of Force in Peacekeeping: Their Constitutional Dimension' (2006) 11 Journal of Conflict and Security Law 465.

[83] Secretary-General's Bulletin (n 11).

[84] B Oswald, 'The Force Intervention Brigade and UN Peace Operations: Some Legal Issues' in J Farrall and H Charlesworth (eds), *Strengthening the Rule of Law through the UN Security Council* 2016 (Routledge 2016) 245; S Sheeran and S Case, *The Intervention Brigade: Legal Issues for the UN in the Democratic Republic of the Congo* (International Peace Institute November 2014) 9.

[85] UN DPKO, 'United Nations Peacekeeping Operations Principles and Guidelines' (2008) 36 <http://www.un.org/en/peacekeeping/documents/capstone_eng.pdf>.

[86] R Gladstone, 'UN Bolsters Peacekeeping in South Sudan Despite Government's Objections' *The New York Times* (New York, 12 August 2016) <https://www.nytimes.com/2016/08/13/world/africa/united-nations-mission-south-sudan.html>.

operations, which is the consent of the main parties to the conflict.[87] It can be observed that the UN Security Council is ready to depart from the strict adherence of the basic principles of peacekeeping if circumstances on the ground so demand. Nonetheless, the UN Secretariat's DPKO on its website continues to stress that the three basic principles of consent of the parties, impartiality, and non-use of force except in self-defence and defence of the mandate guide any peacekeeping mission. Holding on to these principles still gives peacekeeping operations a heightened degree of legitimacy. When the Security Council authorizes peacekeeping contingents to proactively confront armed groups, it jeopardizes this authority.

However, the adoption of more robust measures is a corollary of the UN practice of deploying missions into more violent settings. Both the establishment of the FIB and the RPF were reactions to eruptions of violent conflicts with severe consequences for the civilian population and recurrent accusations of inaction on the part MONUSCO and UNMISS, respectively, to protect the people.[88] Contemporary UN peacekeeping missions no longer play the inter-positional role between conflicting states. They are increasingly set up in intrastate conflict scenes. Here, they are increasingly given a stabilization mandate.[89] This usually involves an offensive mandate and often focuses on the re-establishment of governmental authority and institutions. This approach often requires robust operations against internal insurgents or violent non-state actors.[90] Such a scenario places the UN mission close to the state party to the conflict and challenges the neutral role of the mission. Recommendations made by the High-Level Independent Panel on Peace Operations in 2015 allow us to presume that the inclusion of robust elements into peacekeeping operations is not excluded for future missions. Although the Panel stresses that 'mandating enforcement tasks to degrade, neutralize or defeat a designated enemy ... should be exceptional, time-limited and undertaken with full awareness of the risks and responsibilities for the United Nations mission as a whole', it continues by stating that peacekeeping principles 'must be interpreted progressively and with flexibility in the face of new challenges, and they should never be an excuse for failure to protect civilians or to defend the mission proactively'.[91]

[87] UN, 'Adopting Resolution 2304 (2016), Security Council Extends Mission in South Sudan Authorizes Expanded Peacekeeping Force to Bolster Civilian Protection Efforts' (*UN Meetings Coverage*, 12 August 2016) <https://www.un.org/press/en/2016/sc12475.doc.htm>.

[88] UN Internal Oversight Services, 'Evaluation of the Implementation and Results of Protection of Civilians Mandates in United Nations Peacekeeping Operations' (7 March 2014) UN Doc A/68/787.

[89] See MINUSTAH in Haiti, MONUSCO in the DRC, MINUSMA in Mali, and MINUSCA in the Central African Republic.

[90] C de Coning, C Aoi, and J Karlsrud, *UN Peacekeeping Doctrine in a New Era: Adapting to Stabilisation, Protection and New Threats* (Routledge 2017).

[91] UNGA/UNSC, 'Report of the High-level Independent Panel on Peace Operations on Uniting Our Strengths for Peace: Politics, Partnership and People' (17 June 2015) UN Doc GA A/70/95, SC S/2015/446, 14.

3. Conclusion

The Security Council, in its Chapter VII resolutions, uses increasingly detailed wording on how its efforts to maintain or restore international peace and security are to be implemented by multinational military operations. Within the context of UN peacekeeping missions, this has led to frictions with the basic principles of peacekeeping. Where the Council spells out that 'using all necessary means' includes 'undertaking robust action'[92] or 'neutralizing'[93] armed groups, the principles of limited use of force and impartiality are at stake. In general, UN Security Council practice has a strong impact on the development of multinational military operations, be they under UN command or led by states or regional organizations. Absent a clear legal basis for the model of authorization resolutions in the UN Charter, the Security Council has mandated a diverse range of military deployments. Even though each constitutive resolution is unique and tailored to the mission in question, the Security Council, through the drafting of its resolutions, has shaped the legal framework applicable to multinational military operations.

This is particularly true for peacekeeping missions as a primary UN responsibility. Some core tasks of peacekeepers that continuously find their way into mission mandates, like the protection of civilians, have evolved to comprehensive concepts. Multinational military forces need to be trained according to this UN-specific guidance. Having said this, centralized guidance on how to implement certain mission tasks is all the more valuable where the composition of the deployed forces is multinational and where a common understanding of the mandate is not a given.

Beyond UN peacekeeping missions, the Council's tendency to adopt more detailed mandates and to elaborate on their way of implementation may result in inconsistencies with the branch of IHL. While the Council frequently refers to IHL, it largely does so by reaffirming or clarifying existing law. Only rarely does it take decisions that deviate from IHL rules. Whereas in very few instances concerns were raised that the Security Council authorized military enforcement action that allowed going beyond what is permitted under IHL, most Council resolutions deviating from IHL have a narrowing rather than a broadening effect. As such, obligations that derive from Security Council mandates may put constraints on how force is used.

However, its pronouncements are not of such a nature as to mingle *jus ad bellum* and *jus in bello*, nor to alter the normative substance of IHL. Being a political organ, the Security Council is entitled to take action but not obliged to do so. As a consequence, the Council has put some IHL issues on his agenda while omitting

[92] UNSC Res 2304 (12 August 2016) UN Doc S/RES/2304.
[93] UNSC Res 2098 (n 53).

others.[94] Its choice of topics might have an impact on the development of IHL insofar as special emphasis is put on certain issues in the legal debate. However, when taking binding decisions under Chapter VII, the Council is cautious not to deviate from the substantive content of IHL norms. For the very few cases where it does so, it is unlikely that such practice affects the legal framework of IHL. Even if the Security Council moved towards adopting resolutions that could not be brought in conformity with *jus in bello* rules and this would be considered to be within its competences, the legal consequence of Article 103 UN Charter is 'priority of the Charter, not the invalidity of treaties conflicting with it'.[95] Moreover, many rules of this branch of international law belong to customary international law; some may even be classified as *jus cogens*.[96]

While not modifying the *jus in bello*, UN Security Council resolutions nevertheless increasingly determine the normative framework of multinational military missions beyond its primary function of justifying the infringement of the sovereignty and the territorial integrity of the state on whose territory the military operation is carried out. Multinational military missions can increasingly draw concrete instructions regarding their implementation from the resolution constituting it. This leaves less room for interpretation and, in turn, narrows the margin of discretion of states to implement the Council's enforcement measures.

[94] R Cryer, 'The Security Council and International Humanitarian Law' in SC Breau and A Jachec-Neale (eds), *Testing the Boundaries of International Humanitarian Law* (British Institute of International and Comparative Law 2006) 274.

[95] Sir H Waldock, 'Third Report on the Law of Treaties' (1964) II Yearbook of the International Law Commission 4, 36.

[96] R Nieto-Navia, 'International Peremptory Norms (Jus Cogens) and International Humanitarian Law' in L Chand Vohrah and others (eds), *Man's Inhumanity to Man: Essays on International Law in Honour of Antonio Cassese* (Kluwer Law International 2003) 627.

14

The Coordinating and Steering Function of Status of Forces Agreements

Dieter Fleck

1. Introduction

1.1 General

The law applicable to multinational extraterritorial military operations is largely characterized by generic rules that are rooted in general international law[1] and the national laws of sending states and the host state. An assessment of pertinent rules is all the more important, as many military operations on foreign territory today are conducted below the threshold of an armed conflict, that is, in situations in which international humanitarian law does not apply. The principles and rules to be considered here have often been developed for broader purposes and their applicability to the conduct of military operations in peacetime and times of crises may not have been fully anticipated at the time of their adoption. There may be uncertainties or even differences of opinion as to their applicability for special military tasks.

Status of forces agreements (SOFAs) are well-established instruments to jointly clarify such uncertainties and support cooperation between sending states and the host state. They are designed to facilitate smooth cooperation and avoid frictions that might become counterproductive for an effective execution of the mission. Considering that today military operations have to be prepared and conducted in an environment of civil-military cooperation and many, if not most, extraterritorial military operations are multinational in character, sending states may (and will be well-advised to) conclude SOFAs as multilateral instruments to facilitate, and if possible, to ensure, smooth cooperation among themselves.

As many participating states will adhere to different legal systems, it may be difficult to ensure that the rights and obligations provided for are fully rooted in the

[1] See TD Gill and D Fleck (eds), *The Handbook of the International Law of Military Operations* (2nd edn, OUP 2015); TD Gill and others (eds), *Leuven Manual of the International Law Applicable to Peace Operations, Prepared by an International Group of Experts at the Invitation of the International Society for Military Law and the Law of War* (CUP 2017); D Fleck (ed), *The Handbook of the Law of Visiting Forces* (2nd edn, OUP 2018).

Dieter Fleck, *The Coordinating and Steering Function of Status of Forces Agreements* In *The 'Legal Pluriverse' Surrounding Multinational Military Operations.* Edited by Robin Geiß and Heike Krieger, Oxford University Press (2020).
DOI: 10.1093/oso/9780198842965.003.0015

applicable legal systems. The classical method to do this—formal ratification and enactment by each party—is often not available due to a lack of time. Recourse to jurisdiction or third-party settlement of disputes is often not desired (and sometimes formally excluded) by the parties. This makes international cooperation and conflict settlement by negotiations at the lowest possible level a key feature of SOFA implementation.

1.2 A brief history of SOFAs

Before and during the Second World War, military deployments in foreign territories were mostly connected with support by the sending state in an armed conflict in which the host state was involved. During the First World War, British and other Allied Forces were engaged in military action in France, and during the Second World War, US forces were stationed in the United Kingdom and later in France and Belgium, before Germany was occupied. In all these cases the host state was hardly in a strong bargaining position, with the effect that the sending state was authorized to exercise its rights under its 'law of the flag' in a largely unlimited manner.

That situation had changed by 1951, when with the NATO SOFA[2] the first permanent visiting forces agreement was negotiated and concluded in a multilateral setting. With this new multilateral treaty, which was designed to remain in force with few exceptions even in the event of hostilities, NATO member states had developed a reciprocal and lasting solution for deployments on their territories. This result became possible due to widely compatible legal orders in the participating states, a shared confidence in the rule of law, and a prevailing interest in defining applicable rights and responsibilities in a balanced manner. The NATO SOFA was, however, not sufficient to solve issues arising in larger deployments of a longer-lasting nature and consequently had to be supplemented, for example in the Federal Republic of Germany,[3] or for a number of specific deployments in other countries, when co-use of infrastructure and equipment, for example for technical cooperation and training, required additional regulation.

[2] Agreement Between the Parties of the North Atlantic Treaty Regarding the Status of Forces (NATO SOFA) (19 June 1951) 199 UNTS 67.

[3] Agreement to Supplement the Agreement between the Parties of the North Atlantic Treaty regarding the Status of their Forces with respect to Foreign Forces stationed in the Federal Republic of Germany (Supplementary Agreement to NATO SOFA) (3 August 1959, amended by the Agreements of 21 October 1971 and 18 March 1993), Protocol of Signature to the Agreement to Supplement the Agreement between the Parties of the North Atlantic Treaty regarding the Status of their Forces with respect to Foreign Forces stationed in the Federal Republic of Germany (Protocol of Signature to the Supplementary Agreement to NATO SOFA) (3 August 1959, as amended on 21 October 1971, 18 May 1982, 18 March 1993, and 16 May 1994) 481 UNTS 262, BGBl 1961 II 1218, 73 II 1022, 94 II 2594.

Also, within the former Warsaw Pact, SOFAs were used for deployments of Soviet Forces in the German Democratic Republic or on the territory of other allied states and likewise for the comparatively rare occasions when other Warsaw Pact Forces were stationed abroad. Reciprocity issues became more and more important for military cooperation within the Western and Eastern alliances. Furthermore, SOFAs of different size, specification, and duration were concluded to arrange for the stationing conditions, for example of U.S. forces in Japan and the Republic of Korea, the United States and multinational forces in Afghanistan, and, last but not least, peace operations conducted or authorized by the UN or regional organizations.[4]

Such post-Second World War experience on the stationing of military forces on foreign territory has led to emphasize certain principles and procedures of cooperation between sending states and the host state, most importantly for the members of sending states' forces to respect the law of the host state and a certain readiness of sending states to share jurisdiction over these forces with the host state. An experienced expert has summarized key developments in this era with the following words:

> The strict application of sovereign immunity to foreign forces is not compatible with modern notions of international military cooperation. The modern concept of restricted immunity is based upon two basic principles. The first is that there should be functional immunity of visiting forces and personnel for acts *iure imperii* (in the scope of official duty on behalf of the foreign sovereign), but not for acts *iure gestionis* (acts or omissions outside such scope or personal in nature). The second is the limitation of immunity from the application of host nation law to matters of a procedural, rather than substantive nature.[5]

The two basic principles that were mentioned here describe certain trends in state practice rather than a major shift in legal theory. Such trends were more or less limited to cooperation between like-minded states. It is important to note that they did not result in a fundamental change of the status of foreign visiting forces as organs of their respective sending states, and they remained fully subject to detailed regulation in the particular SOFA.[6]

A new development for the law of visiting forces came with the expansion of UN peace operations and the need to stress the immunity of Blue Helmets including locally recruited personnel. Different from military cooperation within alliances,

[4] Fleck (n 1).

[5] PJ Conderman, 'Status of Armed Forces on Foreign Territory Agreements (SOFA)' in R Wolfrum (ed), *Max-Planck-Encyclopedia of Public International Law* (OUP 2012) available at <http://www.mpepil.com> (*MPEPIL*) para 34. All URLs accessed 27 December 2018.

[6] See Fleck, 'The Immunity of Visiting Forces and their Headquarters' in *The Handbook of the Law of Visiting Forces* (n 1) 75–89.

reciprocity of deployments was never an issue for such operations. The UN have, however, developed and maintained an interest in standardized and transparent solutions, which has led to the development of the UN Model SOFA and the endorsement of its rules by the General Assembly.[7]

With the end of the Cold War, traditional peacekeeping changed. Many UN missions today include peace enforcement and peacebuilding tasks. New mandates given by the Security Council under Chapter VII of the UN Charter have led to deployments that would, in extreme situations, no longer be sufficiently based on the consent of the host state and in which the use of force in self-defence, protection of civilians, and defence of the mandate becomes increasingly necessary. After a period of improvisation, the policy of the Secretary-General since the mid-1990s is now to prepare SOFAs for each peace operation, while recognizing that political exigencies may sometimes militate against specific negotiations. Generally speaking, however, the consent of the host state, impartiality, and non-use of force except in self-defence or defence of the mandate remain fundamental principles of all peace operations. The UN Model SOFA provides widely accepted standards for deployment and this may facilitate cooperation between the UN, troop-contributing states, and the host state even in situations in which a specific SOFA has not formally come into place.

For military cooperation among the member states of the European Union, the EU SOFA was concluded,[8] using the experience with the NATO SOFA. More recently, the European Union also prepared Model SOFAs for its peace operations[9] and civilian crisis management missions,[10] using the UN Model SOFA as standard regulation.

New requirements and changing political interests may influence trends for further development. States and international organizations deploying military forces abroad will use SOFAs to further define rights and responsibilities of their forces. Specific emphasis may be put on human rights protection in cooperation with the host state and specific obligations of visiting forces in the protection of the natural

[7] Model Status of Forces Agreement for Peacekeeping Operations (UN Model SOFA) (9 October 1990) UN Doc A/45/594, reprinted with short commentary in B Oswald, H Durham, and A Bates, *Documents on the Law of UN Peace Operations* (OUP 2010) 34–50.

[8] Agreement between the Member States of the European Union concerning the status of military and civilian staff seconded to the institutions of the European Union, of the headquarters and forces which may be made available to the European Union in the context of the preparation and execution of the tasks referred to in Article 17(2) of the Treaty on European Union, including exercises, and of the military and civilian staff of the Member States put at the disposal of the European Union to act in this context (EU SOFA) (17 November 2003) available at <http://eur-lex.europa.eu/LexUriServ/LexUriServ.do?uri=OJ:C:2003:321:0006:0016:EN:PDF>, not yet in force.

[9] Draft Model Agreement on the Status of the European Union-led forces between the European Union and a Host State (EUFOR Model SOFA) (20 July 2007) 11848/07 and Corr 1 (5 September 2007).

[10] Draft Model Agreement on the Status of the European Union Civilian Crisis Management Mission in a Host State (SOMA) (15 December 2008) 17141/08.

environment, in line with the UN human rights due diligence policy.[11] Where a SOFA is not (yet) enacted as law in the participating states, it cannot legally affect the rights and obligations of the parties. In such cases participants may (and will), however, apply SOFA rules as policy commitments, even if their practice is not fully regulated and certain deviations cannot be ruled out.

1.3 Purpose and outline of this chapter

It is the purpose of this chapter to examine the role of SOFAs in a mission-oriented manner. The chapter will first discuss to what extent SOFAs are declaratory of pre-existing international rules (section 2) or rather constitutive for special regulations (section 3). Furthermore, specific issues of SOFA implementation shall be considered (section 4): What action is to be taken to put them into force in each of the participating states? Are SOFA provisions sufficiently shared by those who have to implement them? Are there sufficient mechanisms for the settlement of disputes? How may a coordinating or even steering function be derived from SOFA implementation?

As current military operations are often influenced by dynamic changes, exhaustive and all-encompassing considerations should not be expected here. A comprehensive examination of current challenges has to start with examples of some practical impact, and at some point, the question whether an assessment based on such examples is indicative for the overall evaluation or rather for an exception from existing principles will be difficult to answer. Nevertheless, some general conclusions may be drawn (section 5).

2. SOFAs as Declaratory Instruments

Different from what a plain reading of the title might suggest, a SOFA rarely provides a new treaty regulation of the legal status of foreign military forces in the host state. From a strict legal point of view such specific regulation would not even be necessary, as the status of foreign military forces as organs of their sending states is derived from these states' sovereign immunity under customary international law. The immunity principle is well recognized in practice and jurisdiction.[12] A SOFA may confirm the immunity status for declaratory purposes, to ensure broad common understanding, considering that even absent such regulation

[11] See 'Human rights due diligence policy on United Nations support to non-United Nations security forces', Identical letters dated 25 February 2013 from the Secretary-General addressed to the President of the General Assembly and to the President of the Security Council, UN Doc A/67/775–S/2013/110.
[12] Fleck, Chapter 5.2 in Gill and Fleck (n 1) 110–27.

military forces like other state organs have 'official act' immunity (immunity *ratione materiae*) under customary international law.[13] The immunity of sending states' forces precludes the host state from interfering in acts of the sending state. It extends to acts and omissions committed within the performance of official duties, a condition that in case of doubt is to be confirmed by the commanding officer for the act in question. Members of the armed forces of a sending state that have committed a wrongful act may be requested to leave the host state, but their immunity before authorities and courts of the host state remains.

The immunity of foreign military forces depends on the sovereignty of the sending state, not on any specially agreed condition for the conduct of its military forces.[14] It may be noted here that extraterritorial military operations are representing the most numerous examples for immunity *ratione materiae*, a fact that is often neglected in scholarly works dealing with the legal roots of state immunity and its possible limitations.[15] The immunity of foreign forces may be limited with respect to international crimes.[16] But this does not affect the situation of visiting forces in general, in which force may have been used, and wrongful acts or even crimes may have been committed. The International Law Commission, in its current project on *Immunity of State Officials from Foreign Criminal Jurisdiction*, has confirmed the principle of immunity *ratione materiae*, underlining that an 'act performed in an official capacity' means 'any act performed by a State official in the exercise of State authority' and emphasizing that immunity *ratione materiae* with respect to acts performed in an official capacity 'continues to subsist after the individuals concerned have ceased to be State officials'.[17] Exemptions from immunity, which should be recognized in well-defined cases of international crimes, and procedural aspects were discussed in 2017.[18] The final outcome is still work in progress.

[13] See Fleck, 'Introduction' in *The Handbook of the Law of Visiting Forces* (n 1) 3–8.

[14] D Fleck, 'Are Foreign Military Personnel Exempt from International Criminal Jurisdiction under Status of Forces Agreements?' (2003) 1 Journal of International Criminal Justice 651–70, at 662–63.

[15] See, eg, H Fox and P Webb, *The Law of State Immunity* (3rd edn, OUP 2015); A Peters and others (eds), *Immunities in the Age of Global Constitutionalism* (Brill/Nijhoff 2014); J Foakes, *The Position of Heads of State and Senior Officials in International Law* (OUP 2014); M Wood, 'The Immunity of Official Visitors' (2012) 16 Max Planck Year Book of United Nations Law 35; and C Tomuschat, 'The International Law of State Immunity and its Development by National Institutions' (2011) 44 Vanderbildt Journal of Transnational Law 1105–40. A notable exception is the chapter by A Sari, 'The Status of Armed Forces in Public International Law: Jurisdiction and Immunity' in A Orakhelashvili (ed), *Research Handbook on Jurisdiction and Immunities in International Law* (Edward Elgar 2015).

[16] See D Akande and S Shah, 'Immunities of State Officials, International Crimes, and Foreign Domestic Courts' (2010) 21(4) European Journal of International Law 815–52, at 851–52.

[17] ILC, Draft Articles 2 and 6 provisionally adopted by the Drafting Committee at the sixty-seventh session (29 July 2015) UN Doc A/CN.4/L.865, see Sixth report on immunity of State officials from foreign criminal jurisdiction, by Concepción Escobar Hernández, Special Rapporteur (12 June 2018) UN Doc A/CN.4/722 and Report on the work of the seventieth session (2018) A/73/10 Chapter XI.

[18] Draft Article 7 (Crimes under international law in respect of which immunity *ratione materiae* shall not apply) (10 July 2017) UN Doc A/CN.4/L.893, listing '(a) crime of genocide; (b) crimes against humanity; (c) war crimes; (d) crime of apartheid; (e) torture; (f) enforced disappearance'.

A good understanding of state immunity remains of great relevance for planning and conducting military operations and in particular for the cooperation between sending states and the host state.[19] Hence immunity of foreign military forces must be respected, even absent specific confirmation in a SOFA. While this applies to any military mission of a sending state in any host state, it is of particular importance for international peace operations conducted with the consent of the host state and governed by the principles of impartiality and minimum use of force, except in self-defence and defence of the mandate.[20]

3. SOFAs as Constitutive for Certain Forms of Cooperation

In specific cases a SOFA may provide certain limitations to the immunity rule where this may be appropriate, for example to share criminal jurisdiction between the sending state and the host state, or to ensure compliance with local rules and procedures that otherwise would not apply to foreign military forces. A prominent example for this is the NATO SOFA[21] with its Article VII regulation on concurrent jurisdiction of the sending state and the receiving (or host) state.[22] This regulation is designed for the stationing of allied forces in allied territory predominately in peacetime, with a view to facilitate military cooperation between allies and partners, for example for training and exercises. It is hardly fitting, however, for the conduct of military operations outside the alliance, for example for official visits or instruction missions in third countries, and certainly will not be adequate in peace operations. In the latter cases no limitation of the immunity principle applies, as expressly confirmed, for example, by the UN Model SOFA.[23]

The settlement of claims normally requires substantial and procedural regulation in a SOFA. Claims provisions may include third party claims for any case of death, injury, loss, or damage caused in the performance of official duty for which the sending state is liable. Furthermore, they may include provisions for voluntary (*ex gratia*) payments by the sending state for losses or damages resulting from acts or omissions outside the performance of official duties. Liabilities may also be waived between the parties and the host state may accept certain responsibilities for the processing of claims and for cost-sharing. Finally, adequate solutions should be established for the settlement of disputes on the nature of claims and their compensation. Unless otherwise provided in treaty law, national courts

[19] See J Voetelink, *Status of Forces: Criminal Jurisdiction over Military Personnel Abroad* (Asser Press/Springer 2015); J Voetelink, 'The Status of Foreign Forces in Afghanistan Post 2014' (2015) 108 Militair Rechtelijk Tijdschrift 1–19.

[20] D Fleck, 'The Legal Status of Personnel Involved in United Nations Peace Operations' (2013) 95(891/892) International Review of the Red Cross 613–36.

[21] See n 2.

[22] This regulation is mirrored by Article 17 EU SOFA (n 6).

[23] See n 7 Sections 46–49.

would not have jurisdiction on disputes between the host state and a sending state; nor could a third-party claim against a sending state successfully be brought before a national court of the host state. Hence the SOFA should provide for a review of claims decisions upon request of the claimant. Claims regulations in SOFAs may thus represent a comprehensive *lex specialis* under both substantial and procedural aspects. Successful implementation of these rules is an excellent example for the steering and coordinating potential SOFAs have.

Specific provisions may be required for the employment of civilian contractors hired by the forces of a sending state, the United Nations, or a regional organization in the host state. As civilian contractors would not enjoy immunity in the host state absent formal agreement, special regulation may become necessary to ensure their adequate protection and compliance with recognized working standards.[24] It may not be possible to secure equal treatment of all contractors, as this depends on the individual contract. But pertinent SOFA principles may be used to coordinate such contracts.

Further examples for constitutive SOFA elements are arrangements on logistic support (goods and services), driving permits and vehicles, the provision of infrastructure, or assistance by customs or fiscal authorities of the host state. Such arrangements are not just declaratory of customary principles and rules. They need to be specially concluded between participating states. In particular, the financial consequences involved need to be settled, to provide for reliable forms and procedures of cooperation. Finally, for an effective settlement of any disputes between the host state and sending states, competent authorities need to be specified and appropriate procedures to be determined. Ideally, there will be a common SOFA text for all states participating in one operation. For peace operations this is ensured by the standing practice of the UN Secretariat to conclude the SOFA with binding effect for all contingents. For military operations of NATO and the EU, too, a common SOFA applies to all participating states.

4. The Implementation of SOFA Rules

The implementation of SOFAs requires cooperation between the sending state concerned and the host state and it is exactly for this purpose that SOFAs are concluded irrespective of whether their content is declaratory or constitutive in nature. Competent authorities of the host state and the sending states' forces must be

[24] The UN Model SOFA (n 7) para 28 provides for immunities of locally recruited personnel concerning official acts, exemption from taxation and national service obligations in accordance with the Convention on the Privileges and Immunities of the United Nations (13 February 1946) 1 UNTS 16, 15 UNTS 1, 21 UNTS 1418.

made aware of their rights and obligations. They must work together to ensure that the mission will be smoothly fulfilled in the interest of all participating parties.

4.1 Negotiation

As is the case for any international negotiation, each party has to nominate its delegation for which a chief negotiator and further representatives and experts must be selected. To ensure a good representation of all interests involved and relevant expertise, it may be advisable for the sending state to involve the ministry of defence (for members of its force and the civilian component), the ministry of the interior (in the event of police participation), the ministry of foreign affairs (including the sending state's embassy in the host state), and other ministries as required. The host state, in turn, may see a requirement to involve also other ministries, such as finance, justice, and environment. The presence of foreign military forces in a country may be perceived differently by different parts of the government and even more so by different parts of society. While no general rule can be developed here, a solution will need to be found within the legal order and political requirements of the host state.

The involvement of parts of the government and of civil society may be direct or indirect. A number of experts will have to be consulted without including them in the negotiating team. Competing interests and differences of opinion need to be harmonized and any head of delegation will be well advised to carefully explore them and develop proposals for solution at appropriate level of decision-making, before relevant topics are negotiated with a foreign party.

It will be useful to prepare a collection of issues based on internal consultations, and to search for models used in established practice that may provide solutions for current and future problems. A common understanding of relevant treaty or customary law will help both sides to conduct negotiations successfully. Hence it should be an important part of legal preparations to identify relevant treaty obligations and perceptions of customary law, which are binding for the other party. It may be helpful to organize mutual briefings on the respective obligations at the beginning of SOFA negotiations, thus creating an inventory of legal information, which may facilitate cooperation. Human rights and environmental law may be the focus of such considerations. They may have practical importance for the conduct of operations in the host state and well deserve to be considered as important parts of SOFA talks, based on respect for the law of the host state. Military operations involving more than one sending state will require special attention to be paid to those sending states' different legal perspectives and the question whether they need to be reflected in the SOFA text.

To ensure that negotiating procedures will be effective and lead to success in good time, both sides should prepare and agree on a programme and work plan for their negotiations. Even if it may be difficult to develop a realistic timetable, it is better to work on well-prepared assumptions than to take the risk that surprise becomes the rule. Heads of delegations might devote some time with their counterparts to prepare the contents and methods of the work ahead. They may also encourage smaller workshops and informal meetings in addition to formal sessions in plenary.

To avoid SOFAs becoming dead letter texts, practical implementation measures should be considered right from the beginning and throughout the negotiation process. For this purpose, the incorporation of SOFA provisions into the domestic law of the host state needs to be examined. The competent authorities on each side should be identified.

4.2 Enactment

While a SOFA should include a clear provision on its entry into force, it will be difficult to provide a certain date for that, considering that a lengthy process may be required to make its provisions binding both under the law of the host state and that of the sending state. As with any international agreements, SOFAs require ratification under the rules and regulations of the state parties. Certain SOFA provisions may affect the national law of the parties and thus require legislative acts in one or both states. For this purpose, national legislation may have to be prepared and discussed in parliament, finally adopted, and enacted. Even absent a strict legal requirement it may be important for political reasons to seek parliamentary approval of the outcome of SOFA negotiations, in particular in the host state.

The NATO SOFA (Article XVIII(2)) provided that the agreement should come into force '[t]hirty days after four signatory States have deposited their instruments of ratification', a process which took two years until 1953. By that time many other signatory states had still not ratified. For each of them the agreement entered into force at a later date, that is, 'thirty days after the deposit of its instrument of ratification'. SOFAs for UN peacekeeping operations, which are usually negotiated between the UN Secretariat (acting also on behalf of sending states) and the host state, usually state that the SOFA shall enter into force immediately upon signature by or on behalf of the UN Secretary-General and the Host Government.[25] Yet it is open to doubt whether this seemingly easy solution will in fact bind all participating states under their national legislation. The situation is different for SOFAs that do not go beyond the scope of executive agreements, that is, agreements on matters

[25] See para 59 of the UN Model SOFA and, eg, the Agreement Concerning the United Nations Mission in Sudan (UNMIS SOFA) (28 December 2005) <https://unmis.unmissions.org/Portals/UNMIS/Documents/General/sofa.pdf>, para 62.

falling within the authority of the participating governments without requiring parliamentary approval.

As the entry into force of a SOFA will generally require a lengthy process, practical solutions should be investigated for deployments that may become necessary prior to the entry into force. For the UN missions in Ethiopia and Eritrea (UNMEE), the Security Council had requested both governments to conclude, as necessary, SOFAs within thirty days; pending conclusion the UN Model SOFA should apply provisionally.[26] While such a solution is binding under Article 25 of the UN Charter, it may be more difficult without a Security Council decision to arrange for provisional application of SOFA rules in an effective and legally binding manner.[27] A distinction should be made here between validity under international law and legal effects at the national level. While state parties agreeing on the provisional application of their treaty commitments will be bound to such commitments under international law, they must still fulfil the constitutional requirements under their domestic legal order before a provisionally applied treaty will also prevail at the national level. To avoid any difficulties, parties should explore this issue in a result-oriented manner. In any case in which deployment is to start before the SOFA enters into force, it should be provided in the text that its provisions will apply retroactively from the beginning of deployment.

4.3 Settlement of disputes

It follows from the character of SOFA rules that any evolving dispute is to be settled by negotiation rather than judicial decision. A typical settlement of dispute clause would provide that any arising dispute will be resolved by negotiation at the lowest possible level and submitted to higher authorities only in the event that no solution could be reached. To ensure that this can be done effectively, points of contact for the communication of open issues and potential controversies should be established.

The NATO SOFA (Article XVI) provides that differences shall be settled by negotiation 'without recourse to any outside jurisdiction' and 'differences which cannot be settled by direct negotiation shall be referred to the North Atlantic Council'. It has never been necessary in NATO's history to invoke the North Atlantic Council for this purpose, as NATO member states have been able to solve all open issues in bilateral or multilateral cooperation among themselves.

More specific provisions on the settlement of disputes are included in the UN Model SOFA (Sections 51–54), calling for a standing claims commission to be

26 UNSC Res 1320 (15 September 2000) UN Doc S/RES/1320, para 6.

27 See Article 25 of the Vienna Convention on the Law of Treaties (adopted 23 May 1969, entered into force 27 January 1980) 1155 UNTS 331.

established by the parties and the possibility of review by a tribunal of three arbitrators, which would take final and binding decisions. It may be left open whether such specific provisions are necessary: in practice, most disputes could be settled in negotiations between representatives of the UN Secretary-General and the host state. In any case, as spelled out in the UN Model SOFA (paragraph 56), the SOFA should provide for 'appropriate measures to ensure close and reciprocal liaison at every appropriate level'.

In practice—and irrespective of the character, purpose, and mandate of a visiting force—there will be hardly any alternative to settlement by negotiation in case of any arising dispute. Hence judicial control may even be expressly excluded in the SOFA text.[28] It is only in exceptional cases that judgments by national or international courts may be sought. Even in such case the question remains open whether decisions reached by negotiation would not be more effective and sustainable.

5. Conclusion

The following insights may be summarized here:

- SOFAs are significant tools of cooperation between sending states and the host state, irrespective of whether their content is declaratory or constitutive in nature.
- A common understanding of relevant treaty law and customary law will help parties to conduct negotiations successfully.
- Respect for human rights and environmental law deserve to be considered as important parts of SOFA negotiations.
- Practical implementation measures should be considered right from the beginning and throughout the negotiation process. For this purpose, the requirement of and forms for incorporating SOFA provisions in domestic law needs to be examined.
- SOFAs require ratification under the rules and regulations of the state parties. For the SOFA to enter into force, legislative acts may be necessary in one or all states parties. It may be important not only for legal but also for political reasons to seek parliamentary approval of the outcome of SOFA negotiations, in particular in the host state.

[28] See, eg, L'accord entre le Gouvernement de la République française et le Gouvernement du Royaume du Maroc relatif au statut de leurs forces (signed 16 May 2005) available at <http://www.legifrance.gouv.fr/affichTexte.do?cidTexte=JORFTEXT000020530679>, which provides in Article 18: 'Tout différend né de l'interprétation ou de l'application du présent accord est réglé exclusivement par voie de négociation entre les Parties.'

- Special arrangements may become necessary to ensure provisional application of a SOFA prior to its formal entry into force.
- Any SOFA should include provisions on the settlement of disputes by negotiation at the lowest possible level.

Where these aspects are well considered and professional preparation is secured, SOFAs can have a coordinating function that considerably contributes to enhancing interoperability. SOFAs will not fully bridge remaining differences in the legal systems of participating states; but as far as they are formally ratified and enacted by the state(s) concerned they can have an effective steering function. In any event, international cooperation in SOFA implementation may help to make the military mission a success.

15
Accountability and Multinational Military Operations

*Paulina Starski**

1. Introduction

Multinational military operations (MMOs) might involve the concerted action of states—(ad hoc) 'coalitions of the willing'[1]—participating in a joint military operation in one of three ways: (1) every state retains command over its troops ('national command model'); (2) a 'multinational integrated command' is established; or (3) national contingents are subjected to the lead or domination of one state ('framework nation' or 'lead nation' model).[2] Furthermore, such coalitions may act with the authorization of an international organization (IO), within its institutional setting under its lead[3] or under the lead of one IO which in turn is authorized by another IO. The plurality of actors involved and the intricate web of different spheres of authority and control characterizing MMOs pose considerable challenges in terms of accountability. This chapter is dedicated to illustrating these challenges and critically reflecting on the specific schemes international law offers to address the 'pluriverse' of 'accountability problems' arising when states and IOs act together militarily.

After sketching out the conceptual contours of 'accountability' and mapping the 'accountability problem' surrounding MMOs (section 2), this contribution will, in its main part (section 3), turn to the rules on the 'international legal responsibility' of states and IOs—a legal scheme which realizes 'accountability'—before offering some final observations (section 4).

* The author's research on attribution and different spheres of control which are addressed within this contribution form part of her research project on 'The Unwilling or Unable State as a Challenge to International Law' founded by the Fritz Thyssen Foundation as well as the Daimler and Benz Foundation.

[1] See M Tondini, 'Coalitions of the Willing' in A Nollkaemper and I Plakokefalos (eds), *The Practice of Shared Responsibility in International Law* (CUP 2017) 701 et seq.

[2] US, 'The Army in Multinational Operations' (2010) <https://www.globalsecurity.org/military/library/policy/army/fm/3-16/fm3-16.pdf>, all URLs accessed 27 December 2018, 2–3; A Ryan, 'The Strong Lead-nation Model in an Ad-hoc Coalition of the Willing' (2002) 9 International Peacekeeping 23–44.

[3] B Boutin, 'Attribution of Conduct in International Military Operations' (2017) 18 Melbourne Journal of International Law 154–79, 155.

Paulina Starski, *Accountability and Multinational Military Operations* In *The 'Legal Pluriverse' Surrounding Multinational Military Operations*. Edited by Robin Geiß and Heike Krieger, Oxford University Press (2020).

DOI: 10.1093/oso/9780198842965.003.0016

2. Mapping the 'Accountability Problem'

'Accountability' is an 'essentially contested concept',[4] permeating manifold 'disciplines' and 'discourses'.[5] It can be defined as a 'social relationship in which an actor feels an obligation to explain and to justify his conduct to some significant other'.[6] Within the decentralized international legal order, one genuinely legal institution realizing 'accountability'[7] is 'international legal responsibility'. 'Responsibility'—derived from the Latin term *respondeo* ('I answer')[8]—involves the 'answerability for a wrongful act, which consists of an obligation to call into account a subject for its conduct and to make it respond to any moral or legal charges'.[9] One sub-system of 'international legal responsibility' is formed by the customary rules on the international responsibility of states reflected[10] in the International Law Commission's (ILC)[11] Articles on the Responsibility of States for Internationally Wrongful Acts (ASR), the other comprises the rules governing legal responsibility in the setting of IOs which have been restated in the 2011 ILC Articles on the Responsibility of International Organizations (ARIO).[12] While it remains controversial whether the ARIO reflect customary international law,[13] they are referenced by scholarship[14] and jurisprudence[15] regularly which justifies to take them as a general guideline for the present purpose. According to Article 2 ASR, 'an internationally wrongful act' which incurs the responsibility of a state consists of 'an action or omission' that 'is attributable to the State under international law' and 'constitutes a breach of an

[4] WB Gallie, 'Essentially Contested Concepts' (1956) 56 Proceedings of the Aristotelian Society 167 et seq. Also, A Reinisch, 'Governance Without Accountability?' [2002] 44 German Yearbook of International Law 270, 273.

[5] ILA, 'New Delhi Conference, Third Report' (2002) 2.

[6] M Bovens, 'Public Accountability' in Ewan Ferlie and others (eds), *The Oxford Handbook of Public Management* (OUP 2007) 182, 183.

[7] On different emanations of 'accountability' M Zwanenburg, *Accountability of Peace Support Operations* (Martinus Nijhoff 2005) 63.

[8] T Erskine, 'Introduction: Making Sense of "Responsibility" in International Relations' in T Erskine (ed), *Can Institutions have Responsibilities* (Palgrave Macmillan 2004) 1, 7.

[9] J Crawford and J Watkins, 'International Responsibility' in S Besson and J Tasioulas (eds), *The Philosophy of International Law* (OUP 2010) 283.

[10] J Crawford, 'State Responsibility' (*MPEPIL Online*, September 2006) <http://opil.ouplaw.com/view/10.1093/law:epil/9780199231690/law-9780199231690-e1093?prd=EPIL> para 31; K Larsen, 'Attribution of Conduct in Peace Operations: The "Ultimate Authority and Control" Test' (2008) 19 European Journal of International Law 509, 517 (regarding Articles 4, 8, 6 ASR).

[11] ILC, 'Report' (Fifty-third session) UN GAOR, 56th Sess, Supp No 10, 43 (2001) UN Doc A/56/10.

[12] ILC, 'Report' (Sixty-third session, 26 April–3 June and 4 July–12 August 2011, Supp No 10) UN Doc A/66/10, 54–68.

[13] Larsen (n 10) 518; H Krieger, 'A Credibility Gap: The Behrami and Saramati Decision of the European Court of Human Rights' (2009) 13 Journal of International Peacekeeping 159, 169.

[14] D van der Toorn, 'Attribution of Conduct by State Armed Forces Participating in UN-authorised Operations: The Impact of Behrami and Al-Jedda' (2008) 15 Australia International Law Journal 9, 19.

[15] See *Nuhanović v de Staat der Nederlanden* Case no 200.020.174/01 (Gerechtshof's-Gravenhage, Judgment, 5 July 2011) para 5.8; *Mustafić-Mujić et al v Netherlands* Case no 12/03329 (Hoge Raad, 1st Chamber, Judgment, 6 September 2013) 13 et seq; *Nuhanović v Netherlands* Case no 12/03324 (Hoge Raad, 1st Chamber, Judgment, 6 September 2013) 14 et seq.

international obligation of the State'. Article 4 ARIO contains a corresponding rule, the only difference being its reference to IOs.

While the terms 'responsibility' and 'liability' are frequently employed interchangeably, the concept of 'liability' has remained opaque.[16] For the purpose of this chapter, it shall denote the specific legal consequences that international legal responsibility of states/IOs renders.[17]

Determining which actors within MMOs 'should be held responsible, on which ground, and to which extent'[18] on the basis of the regime on the international responsibility of states/IOs, and towards whom, is challenging due to several factors: first, the main feature of such operations is the plurality of actors—in themselves legal constructs—each exercising different degrees of control. Such operations are conventionally embedded in complex institutional settings like the United Nations (UN), the European Union (EU), or the North Atlantic Treaty Organization (NATO). None of these institutions displays self-standing military capacity being dependent on national military contingents. Frequently, the institutional set-up displays a complex structure since an IO might 'act militarily' via more or less 'independent' sub-units and may beyond that be authorized by another IO, as the triad of UN-NATO-Kosovo Force (KFOR) exemplifies.[19] Secondly, violations of international law and harmful outcomes are the results of complex, causally connected courses of action in which various actors play a role. Thirdly, the rules of 'international legal responsibility', as reflected within the ASR/ARIO, are ambiguous. In light of these difficulties, alternative schemes—for example, the regimes on the international criminal responsibility of individuals (potentially concurrent with the responsibility of states/IOs)[20] and on civil liability as well as domestic (public or private) 'responsibility mechanisms' and 'softer' instruments like institutional oversight, investigations, and reporting[21]—are important devices to realize accountability, although remaining beyond the scope of this contribution.

[16] V Roeben, 'Responsibility in International Law' (2012) 16 Max Planck Yearbook of United Nations Law 99, 110.

[17] In the same vein B Boutin, *The Role of Control in Allocating International Responsibility in Collaborative Military Operations* (PhD thesis, Amsterdam 2015) 207; A Nollkaemper and D Jacobs, 'Shared Responsibility in International Law: A Conceptual Framework' (2013) 34 Michigan Journal of International Law 359, 414.

[18] Boutin (n 17) 3.

[19] On KFOR see J Cerone, 'Minding the Gap: Outlining KFOR Accountability in Post-Conflict Kosovo' (2001) 12 European Journal of International Law 469 et seq.

[20] *Case Concerning Application of the Convention on the Prevention and Punishment of the Crime of Genocide (Bosnia and Herzegovina v Serbia and Montenegro)* (Judgment) [2007] ICJ Rep 43, para 173; A Nollkaemper, 'Concurrence Between Individual Responsibility and State Responsibility in International Law' (2003) 52 International and Comparative Law Quarterly 615.

[21] R Murphy and S Wills, 'United Nations Peacekeeping Operations' in A Nollkaemper and I Plakokefalos (eds), *The Practice of Shared Responsibility in International Law* (CUP 2017) 585, 606 et seq.

3. Multinational Military Operations and the Rules of International Legal Responsibility

The challenges that MMOs pose in terms of international legal responsibility gravitate around two theoretical concepts: the 'attribution of conduct'—which have been already elaborated upon by the author in an earlier piece[22] (section 3.1)—and the 'attribution of responsibility'[23] (section 3.2). Both might generate a 'parallel' or 'joint responsibility' of several actors for one harmful outcome which raises questions regarding the distribution of secondary obligations (section 3.3). In addressing these aspects, this contribution will exemplarily focus on UN peacekeeping missions (UNPKMs) and MMOs acting under UN mandate.

3.1 Multinational military operations and 'attribution of conduct'

After depicting the contours of the notion of 'attribution of conduct' (section 3.1.1), the following paragraphs will analyse two specific categories of MMOs through the prism of 'attribution rules' (section 3.1.2) and discuss the possibility of a 'multiple attribution of conduct' (section 3.1.3).

3.1.1 'Attribution of conduct'

Attributing conduct is a legal operation[24] essentially connected with the idea of legal personality.[25] 'Attribution rules' determine the cases in which conduct of individuals constitutes conduct of juridical persons[26] like the state,[27] IOs,[28] or supranational organizations.[29] Establishing to which entity a certain conduct 'belongs'

[22] These aspects have already been elaborated by the author in 'Zurechnungsprobleme bei multinationalen militärischen Einsätzen' in S Graf von Kielmansegg, H Krieger, and S Sohm (eds), *Multinationalität und Integration im militärischen Bereich—die wehrrechtliche Perspektive* (Nomos 2018) 163–208.

[23] ILC, 'ARIO' (n 12) Article 1, para 4, n 1; J Crawford, *The International Law Commission's Articles on State Responsibility* (CUP 2002) 145; JD Fry, 'Attribution of Responsibility' in A Nollkaemper and I Plakokefalos (eds), *Principles of Shared Responsibility* (CUP 2014) 98, 102 et seq.

[24] ILC, 'Articles on the Responsibility of States for Internationally Wrongful Acts with commentaries' (2001) II Yearbook of the ILC 31, Article 2, para 6.

[25] P Groarke, 'The Legal Concept of the Person: A Relational Account' (2010) 51(2) Heythrop Journal 298, 304 et seq.; C Ahlborn, 'To Share or Not to Share? The Allocation of Responsibility between International Organizations and their Member States' (2013) SHARES Research Paper 28, Amsterdam Center for International Law 2013–226, 1, 5 et seq with further references. On legal personality H Kelsen, *Pure Theory of Law* (first published 1934, translation from the 2nd edn, 1960 by Max Knight, University of California Press 1967) 172 et seq.

[26] Ahlborn (n 25) 1, 5.

[27] Comprehensively U Häfelin, *Die Rechtspersönlichkeit des Staates* (Mohr 1959).

[28] For UN see *Reparation for injuries suffered in the service of the United Nations* (Advisory Opinion) [1949] ICJ Rep 174, 178 et seq.

[29] C Walter, 'Subjects of International Law' (*MPEPIL Online*, May 2007) <http://opil.ouplaw.com/view/10.1093/law:epil/9780199231690/law-9780199231690-e1476> para 5.

determines which rules define its legality and is a prerequisite for the entity's legal responsibility.[30] It is also a precondition for establishing the jurisdiction of adjudicative bodies. The ASR/ARIO entail specific attribution rules: pursuant to Article 4 ASR,[31] 'state conduct' equals 'conduct of its organs'. Article 6 ARIO echoes Article 4 ASR; establishing that conduct of its organs constitutes conduct of an IO. Article 7 ARIO[32] governs a 'secondment' constellation:[33] the conduct of an 'organ' placed at the disposal of an IO by a state or another IO is attributable to the IO under certain conditions.[34] The term 'at the disposal of' indicates a transfer of power.[35] Conduct of the seconded organ is attributable to the IO if it is functionally endowed with some of the tasks of the IO[36] and the latter exercises 'effective control' over it.[37]

3.1.2 Close-up on the 'attribution of conduct' problem

The operation of these 'attribution rules'—particularly Article 7 ARIO—will be addressed here, first with a view to UNPKMs (section 3.1.2.1), and then concerning MMOs merely mandated by the UN Security Council (UNSC) (section 3.1.2.2).

3.1.2.1 UN peacekeeping missions

In the case of UNPKMs,[38] troop-contributing nations (TCNs) place their military contingents at the disposal of the UN either by ways of contingent treaties or

[30] Article 2 lit a ASR, Article 4 lit a ARIO. See ILC, 'ASR' (n 24) Article 2, para 1.

[31] Crawford (n 10) para 18.

[32] In the earlier ARIO drafts Article 5 (ILC, 'Draft Articles on Responsibility of International Organizations' (27 May 2004) UN Doc A/CN4/L648, Article 5) or Article 6 (ILC, 'Draft Articles on Responsibility of International Organizations, Report of the International Law Commission, Sixty-first session' (4 May–5 June and 6 July–7 August 2009) General Assembly, Official Records, Sixty-fourth session Supp No 10, UN Doc A/64/10, 21, Article 6).

[33] Generally, P Palchetti, 'The Allocation of Responsibility for Internationally Wrongful Acts Committed in the Course of Multinational Operations' (2013) 95 International Review of the Red Cross 727, 731.

[34] Responsibility (not attribution) is addressed by agreements between the seconding state and the respective IO, Article 9 of the 'Model Memorandum of Understanding', in UN (ed), *COE Manual, UN Doc A/C.5/69/18* (UN 2014) 185 et seq.

[35] B Kondoch and M Zwanenburg, 'International Responsibility and Military Operations' in TD Gill and D Fleck (eds), *The Handbook of the International Law of Military Operations* (2nd edn, OUP 2015) 559, 563. But even if the IO endows the seconded organ with organ status within its institutional setting Article 7 ARIO is regarded to be applicable by the ILC ('ARIO' (n 12) 86, Article 6, para 6; 87, Article 7, para 1).

[36] M Kuhn, *Die Europäische Sicherheits- und Verteidigungspolitik im Mehrebenensystem* (Springer 2012) 167. cf A Sari, 'UN Peacekeeping Operations and Article 7 ARIO: The Missing Link' (2012) 9 International Organizations Law Review 77, 79.

[37] Critical Sari (n 36) 77, esp 80 et seq.

[38] Peacekeeping missions of the 1st to 3rd are to be distinguished from 4th generation missions, see A Surholt, *Amtshaftung für Handlungen in Auslandseinsätzen der Bundeswehr* (Nomos 2014) 99; A Sari, 'Jurisdiction and International Responsibility in Peace Support Operations: The Behrami and Saramati Cases' (2008) 8 Human Rights Law Review 151, 154; ILC, 'Report of the International Law Commission, Official Records of the General Assembly, Fifty-ninth Session' Supp No 10, UN Doc A/59/10, Article 4 of the Draft Articles on Responsibility of International Organisations, 103 et seq. On the UNMIK A Paulus, 'Art 29' in B Simma (ed), *The Charter of the United Nations* vol I (2nd edn, OUP 2002) para 48. Since the UN employ their own officials within UN Interim Administrations the Article 7 ARIO problem does not arise.

informally.[39] Such treaties are based on an *Exchange of Letters* and accompanied by *Memoranda of Understanding* (MoU)[40] referring to *Regulations*[41] adopted at UN level. The UNPKM itself is established as a subsidiary organ of one of the main UN organs. Functionally, national contingents fulfil a UN obligation—namely peace-keeping.[42] The UN takes the view that conduct of national contingents becoming operative within UNPKMs would be attributable to it since the mission qualified as a subsidiary UN organ and the UN exercised 'command and control'[43] or '(exclusive) operational command'[44] over them.[45] Others assume a rebuttable presumption of attributability to the UN.[46] In any case, an 'attribution automatism' does not correspond with the rationale of Article 7 ARIO:[47] while it is true that conduct of the UNPKM itself as a subsidiary organ of a main UN organ is attributable to it automatically (Article 6 ARIO), conduct of soldiers as organs of the TCN is only attributable to the UN if it exercises 'effective control', the exact contours of which are controversial.

The first challenge is to delineate the relationship between Article 4 ASR and Article 7 ARIO: the ILC suggests a 'reciprocal reading' of 'effective control':[48] conduct is attributable to the entity—either the IO to which an organ is seconded or the state/IO seconding it—which exercised 'effective control' over it.[49] However, since a state's armed forces qualify as its organs par excellence,[50] conduct of the soldier

[39] See, eg, 'Contingent Agreement between the UN and Finland regarding UNEF-I' 271 UNTS 136.

[40] See UN, 'Model Memorandum of Understanding' (n 34).

[41] See, eg, 'Regulations for the United Nations Emergency Force' (ST/SGB/UNEF/1) (20 February 1957) 271 UNTS 168.

[42] UN, *United Nations Peacekeeping Operations: Principles and Guidelines* (UN 2008) available at <http://www.un.org/en/peacekeeping/documents/capstone_eng.pdf> 13; UN, *Handbook on United Nations Multidimensional Peacekeeping Operations* (UN 2003) 57.

[43] Letter of the UN Legal Counsel to the Director of the UN Office of Legal Affairs, Codification Division, cited in ILC, 'General Assembly' (n 38) 112, para 5.

[44] UNGA, 'Report of the Secretary General on financing of United Nations peacekeeping operations' (20 September 1996) UN Doc A/51/389, para 17.

[45] See ILC, 'Responsibility of International Organizations' (25 June 2004) Un Doc A/CN.4/545; ILC, 'Responsibility of International Organizations' (17 February 2011) UN Doc A/CN.4/637/Add 1, s II.B.3, para 3; ILC, 'ARIO' (n 12) 88, Article 7, para 6. The UN assumed responsibility for conduct of peacekeeping forces and paid compensation, see ILC, 'Second report on responsibility of international organizations by Mr. Giorgio Gaja, Special Rapporteur' (2 April 2004) UN Doc A/CN.4/541, para 34 et seq. The UN conclude treaties on the legal status of troops with host states—*status of forces agreements* (SOFAs) or *status of mission agreement* (SOMAs)—and exercise diplomatic protection with regard to peacekeeping forces parallel to the respective nation states, UN, *Handbook on United Nations Multidimensional Peacekeeping Operations* (UN 2003) 13; 'Model Status-of-Forces Agreement for Peacekeeping Operations' (9 October 1990) UN Doc A/45/594.

[46] Kondoch and Zwanenburg (n 35) 563; Palchetti (n 33) 734; A Breitegger, 'Sacrificing the Effectiveness of the European Convention on Human Rights on the Altar of the Effective Functioning of Peace Support Operations: A Critique of Behrami & Saramati and Aljedda' (2009) 11 International Community Law Review 153, 159.

[47] Larsen (n 10) 516; Palchetti (n 33) 730 et seq.

[48] See also A Spagnolo, 'The "Reciprocal" Approach in Article 7 ARIO: A Reply to d'Argent' (2014) 1 Questions of International Law, Zoom-in 33 et seq.

[49] The ILC is imprecise on this point: 'ARIO' (n 12) 88 et seq, Article 7, para 7; UNGA (n 44) para 17 et seq, 6.

[50] See Larsen (n 10) 512.

acting as part of an MMO is according to Article 4 ASR—as a 'fall-back' rule—attributable to the state irrespective of any 'effective control' considerations.[51] In light of this, Article 7 ARIO might be read as implying that 'effective control' on part of the IO to which a state organ is seconded might in certain circumstances 'cut' the chain of attribution based on Article 4 ASR.[52]

Secondly, while it appears sensible to base attribution on 'effective control' in the secondment constellation—as responsibility should lie with the entity which controlled a course of action[53] thereby being endowed with the actual capacity to ensure its conformity with international law[54]—the question remains what 'control' exactly is and what renders it 'effective'. In that regard it is both a virtue and a vice that the 'effective control' notion permeates international law in different contexts:[55] Pursuant to Article 8 ASR, conduct of individuals is attributable to the state if they have acted 'on the instructions of, or under the direction or control of'[56] the state which has been translated by the International Court of Justice (ICJ) into a standard of 'effective control'.[57] Alternative standards like 'overall control' introduced by the International Criminal Tribunal for the Former Yugoslavia (ICTY)[58] have remained insulated.[59] Although the customary nature[60] of the 'effective control' standard and its significance outside the state responsibility context has remained controversial,[61] at least regarding the attribution of individual conduct to the state, no alternative standard can be identified which would more convincingly reflect international legal practice. Despite the differences between the

[51] P d'Argent, 'State Organs Placed at the Disposal of the UN, Effective Control, Wrongful Abstention and Dual Attribution of Conduct' (2014) 1 Questions of International Law, Zoom-in 17, 26 et seq.

[52] This might not be the case when several actors exercise 'effective control', see (n 135) et seq and accompanying text.

[53] On the failure to control see Boutin (n 17) 180 et seq.

[54] See also N Gal-Or and C Ryngaert, 'From Theory to Practice: Exploring the Relevance of the Draft Articles on the Responsibility of International Organizations (DARIO)' (2012) 13 German Law Journal 511, 529.

[55] It has also gained relevance within the *jus in bello* (Article 42 1907 Hague Regulations (UKTS (1910) 9)). It determines the superior responsibility in the context of international criminal law, see ICTY, *Mucić et al* (Judgment) IT-96-21 (20 February 2001) para 196. The ECtHR refers to this standard in order to delineate its jurisdiction and the applicability of the *Banković and others v Belgium and others* App no 52207/99 (ECtHR, Judgment, 12 December 2001) para 71.

[56] See ILC, 'ASR' (n 24) 20, 47, Article 8, para 1 et seq.

[57] *Military and Paramilitary Activities in and against Nicaragua (Nicaragua v United States of America)* (Merits) [1986] ICJ Rep 14 et seq.

[58] As a standard of attribution for hierarchically organized groups—ICTY, *Prosecutor v Tadić* IT-94-1, (1999) 38 ILM 1518, para 90 et seq; ibid para 137, 121.

[59] *Application of the Convention on the Prevention and Punishment of the Crime of Genocide (Bosnia and Herzegovina v Serbia and Montenegro)* (Judgment) [2007] ICJ Rep 43, 209 et seq, paras 402–07; Larsen (n 10) 514 et seq.

[60] In the opposite direction M Hirsch, *The Responsibility of International Organizations Toward Third Parties: Some Basic Principles* (Springer 1995) 76 et seq. On 'effective control' as a legal logical necessity H Krieger, 'Die Verantwortlichkeit Deutschlands nach der EMRK für seine Streitkräfte im Auslandseinsatz' (2002) 62 Zeitschrift für ausländisches öffentliches Recht und Völkerrecht (ZaöRV) 669, 677 et seq.

[61] Regarding self-defence against non-state actors P Starski, 'Right to Self-Defense, Attribution and the Non-State Actor' (2015) 75 ZaöRV 455 et seq.

constellations addressed by Article 8 ASR and Article 7 ARIO,[62] the ILC assumes a congruent reading of 'effective control' in both normative settings.[63] Yet, uncertainties remain in terms of its specific substance. The ICJ merely clarified that supportive and facilitating activities concerning financing and equipment fall short of it.[64] Unanimity exists, however, in terms of the factual focus of this notion: 'effective control' is 'factual control that is exercised over the specific conduct taken'[65] which is to be assessed considering the 'full factual circumstances' as well as the 'particular context' on a case-by-case basis,[66] giving factual causalities priority over formal links.[67] Hence, 'effective control' can only be determined with respect to the specific conduct causally[68] leading to a harmful outcome.

Since control is decisive that is 'concretely and actually exercised, beyond the formal delegation of operational authority',[69] not over the mission as such but over conduct that is alleged to be wrongful,[70] an exercise of 'effective control' in the sense of Article 7 ARIO is particularly given if a course of action is *factually* steered by ways of instructions.[71] Therefore, as a preliminary starting point the specific chains of command characterizing MMOs should be analysed, while keeping in mind that the existence of command powers does not constitute 'effective control' if the commanding actor does not exercise 'factual control'.

Within UNPKMs, TCNs transfer 'operational control' (OPCON)[72]—'authority delegated to a commander to direct forces assigned so that the commander may accomplish specific missions or tasks which are usually limited by function, time, or location; to deploy units concerned, and to retain or assign tactical control of those units'[73]—and occasionally also 'operational command' (OPCOM)—'authority granted to a commander to assign missions or tasks to subordinate commanders,

[62] cf ILC, 'ARIO' (n 12) 88, Article 7 para 5, but more cautiously para 4; Palchetti (n 33) 733; T Dannenbaum, 'Translating the Standard of Effective Control into a System of Effective Accountability' (2010) 51 Harvard International Law Journal 113, 155 et seq.

[63] Larsen (n 10) 515. For the contrary view Palchetti (n 33) 733. Critical F Messineo, 'Attribution of Conduct' in A Nollkaemper and I Plakokefalos (eds), *Principles of Shared Responsibility* (CUP 2014) 60, 92.

[64] See *Military and Paramilitary Activities in and against Nicaragua (Nicaragua v United States of America)* (Merits) (Judgment) [1986] ICJ Rep 14, 64, para 115.

[65] ILC, 'ARIO' (n 12) 87 et seq, Article 7, para 4. On the drafting history of Article 7 ARIO Messineo (n 63) 88 et seq. Regarding its 'factual' focus ILC, 'General Assembly' (n 38) ch V, para 72, sub-paras 3, 6, 8.

[66] ILC, 'ARIO' (n 12) 87 et seq, Article 7, para 4. See United Kingdom, UN Doc A/C.6/64/SR.16, para 23.

[67] See ILC, 'ARIO' (n 12) 87 et seq, Article 7, para 4.

[68] Boutin (n 3) 156.

[69] Boutin (n 17) 83; Dannenbaum (n 62) 151.

[70] Boutin (n 17) 85.

[71] A Cassese, 'The Nicaragua and Tadić Tests Revisited in Light of the ICJ Judgment on Genocide in Bosnia' (2007) 18 EJIL 649, 667.

[72] See *Capstone*-doctrine of the DKPO, UN, Peacekeeping Operations (n 42) 68.

[73] No uniform terminology has yet been established. The relevant terms all stem from the military context, however, within the legal discourse they are regularly given a distinct meaning. For the NATO terminology see NATO AAP-6, 'Glossary of Terms and Definitions' (NATO 2008). Cp DPKO Training Unit, 'Glossary of UN Peacekeeping Terms' (1998) <http://www.un.org/Depts/dpko/glossary>.

to deploy units, to reassign forces, and to retain or delegate operational and/or tactical control as the commander deems necessary'—to the UN.[74] OPCON/OPCOM is exercised by a UN Force Commander who assigns tasks to contributed troops organized in national contingents and headed by National Contingent Commanders acting on behalf of the UN.[75] 'Full command' or 'organic command'[76] in the sense of a subjection of the acting soldier in every military respect remains with the TCN.

Many instances show that the 'umbilical cord' between the soldiers and their states 'is not fully cut':[77] first, the state-soldier-nexus remains visible since soldiers continue to wear their national uniforms. Secondly, it is up to the national commanders to waive the immunity of their soldiers[78] which remain subject to national criminal prosecution and disciplinary measures.[79] Host states agree with TCNs—complementary to the treaties concluded between the host state and the UN—on the status of their soldiers. TCNs influence the Rules of Engagement (RoE) governing the specific deployment modalities[80] and regularly declare caveats[81] to the effect that diverging RoE might de facto apply within one UNPKM.[82] These institutional bonds between TCNs and their contingents do not render an attribution of conduct to the UN based on Article 7 ARIO impossible. Quite the contrary, they rather reflect the nature of an 'organ secondment': just as the fact that soldiers continue to serve 'national functions' does not prejudice the application of Article 7 ARIO,[83] it is not necessary that all institutional links to the seconding state are cut.[84] This follows *argumentum e contrario* from Article 6 ARIO.[85]

[74] See n 73.

[75] PC Cammaert and B Klappe, 'Authority, Command, and Control in United Nations-Led Peace Operations' in TD Gill and D Fleck (eds), *The Handbook of the International Law of Military Operations* (OUP 2010) 159.

[76] Boutin (n 17) 30 referring to *Attorney General v Nissan* [1969] UKHL 3 [1970] AC 179, 223.

[77] M Zwanenburg, 'North Atlantic Treaty Organization-Led Operations' in A Nollkaemper and I Plakokefalos (eds), *The Practice of Shared Responsibility in International Law* (CUP 2017) 639, 649.

[78] Within SOFAs between the UN and host states the authority to decide upon a waiver of immunity is assigned to the sending states, 'UNMIK Regulation No 2000/47, on the Status, Privileges and Immunities of KFOR and UNMIK and Their Personnel in Kosovo' (18 August 2000) UNMIK/REG/200/47.

[79] UN, 'Comprehensive Review of the Whole Question of Peacekeeping Operations in All Their Aspects' (21 November 1994) UN Doc A/49/681, 3. See Article 47 lit b 'Model Status-of-Forces Agreement for Peacekeeping Operations' (9 October 1990) UN Doc A/45/594.

[80] C Leck, 'International Responsibility in United Nations Peacekeeping Operations' (2009) 10 Melbourne Journal of International Law 346, 358; Krieger (n 13) 172.

[81] M Zwanenburg, 'International Military Forces' (*MPEPIL Online*, September 2015) <http://opil.ouplaw.com/view/10.1093/law:epil/9780199231690/law-9780199231690-e311?rskey=C9UhCf&result=9&prd=EPIL> para 23. Critical UN, 'The future of United Nations peace operations' (2 September 2015) UN Doc A/70/357–S/2015/682, para 98.

[82] Krieger (n 13) 172.

[83] I Couzigou, 'International Organisations and States within an Agency Relationship' [2014] Netherlands International Law Review 335, 348; Surholt (n 38) 124.

[84] See ILC, 'ARIO' (n 12) 87, Article 7, para 1.

[85] In constellations in which the institutional bonds between an organ and the entity seconding it are fully cut it appears persuasive to assume that only Article 6 ARIO is applicable, ILC, 'ARIO' (n 12) 87, Article 7, para 1. See also d'Argent (n 51) 17, 25.

Nevertheless, the national bonds of troop contingents are extensive: international orders have to be implemented by national commanders. On the one hand, soldiers will regularly be ordered to cooperate with international commanders and to obey their command,[86] which seemingly creates an uninterrupted chain of command from the UN to the soldier. On the other hand, general national orders to obey international orders are reversible.[87] Contingent treaties regularly entail clauses which allow TCNs to revoke the secondment of their troops anytime[88] which safeguard the TCN's legal ability to comply with constitutional requirements. Additionally, national commanders are regularly constitutionally obliged to examine the conformity of international orders with national and international law.[89] While national commanders may not make strategic decisions, the UN does not have the power to effectively implement an order against the will of a national commander.[90] The uninterrupted chain of command depends on the good will or at least passiveness of the TCN. Furthermore, UN command structures 'are straightforward in theory, but seldom so in practice'.[91] States have occasionally intervened in the operational management of their troops contrary to the formal command structures.[92] If the benchmark of 'effective control' was the ability to prevent harmful outcomes—as suggested by some[93]—these aspects would certainly render injurious conduct of soldiers acting as part of an MMO attributable to the TCN. Even if this line is not followed,[94] considering these intricately entangled layers of control it cannot be excluded per se that the 'attribution scheme' might point towards TCNs.[95]

This is particularly possible in constellations of *ultra vires* acts—conduct following national orders which contradict UN commands (provided that this

[86] For Germany see 'Anweisung zur Zusammenarbeit' and 'instruction to cooperate', based on § 7 *Soldatengesetz* (Military Statute) (adopted 19 March 1956) as amended 30 May 2005 (BGBl I, 1482) and 8 June 2017 (BGBl I, 1570); *Zentrale Dienstvorschrift* (Joint Service Regulation) 1/50 of the German Federal Army.

[87] In terms of the NATO setting Krieger (n 13) 173.

[88] UN (n 42) 68; M Bothe, 'Peacekeeping Forces' (*MPEPIL Online*, August 2016) <http://opil.ouplaw.com/view/10.1093/law:epil/9780199231690/law-9780199231690-e365> para 28 et seq.

[89] See E Vad, 'Auslandseinsätze deutscher Streitkräfte' (1997) Humanitäres Völkerrecht - Informationsschriften 74, 79.

[90] See also Dannenbaum (n 62) 148 et seq.

[91] Leck (n 80) 352.

[92] See for instance UN, 'Report of the Office of Internal Oversight Services' (7 March 2014) UN Doc A/68/787.

[93] *Mustafić-Mujić et al v the Netherlands* Case no 200.020.173/01 (Gerechtshof's-Gravenhage, Judgment, 5 July 2011) para 5.9 [ILDC 1742 (NL 2011)]; *Mustafić-Mujić et al v de Staat der Nederlanden* Case no 12/03329 (n 15). See *Nuhanović v de Staat der Nederlanden* Case no 200.020.174/01 (n 15) para 5.9; *Nuhanović v de Staat der Nederlanden* Case no 12/03324 (n 15); Case no C/09/295247 / HA ZA 07-2973 (Rechtbank Den Haag, Judgment, 16 July 2014); *Stichting Mothers of Srebrenica v de Staat der Nederlanden* Case no 200.158.313/01 and 200.160.317/01 (Gerechtshof Den Haag, Judgment, 27 June 2017).

[94] 'Effective control' *ex post* oriented and prima facie qualitatively different from an 'ability to prevent', A Nollkaemper, 'Dual Attribution' (2011) 9 Journal of International Criminal Justice 1143 et seq.

[95] C Ryngaert, 'Apportioning Responsibility between the UN and Member States in UN Peace-Support Operations' (2012) 45 Israel Law Review 151, 155; Gal-Or and Ryngaert (n 54) 530.

deviation eradicates 'effective control' on part of the UN)[96] as well as in cases of off duty conduct lying beyond the official mission context (eg sexual abuse).[97] Beyond that, international orders might give national commanders some leeway: Frequently, they will merely set a frame of action which has to be specified by national implementing orders.[98] While it remains debatable whether these 'national implementation margins' suffice to interrupt the chain of attribution to the UN, the overlap of 'factual control' should not be ignored.[99]

Accordingly, international legal documents reflect that TCNs acting as part of UNPKMs are not released from their international obligations which implies that violations of international rules remain attributable to them: General Comment 31 of the UN Human Rights Committee (HRC) suggests that parties to the International Covenant on Political and Civil Rights (ICCPR)[100] remain bound by their obligations extraterritorially when exercising 'effective control' 'regardless of the circumstances in which such power or effective control was obtained, such as forces constituting a national contingent of a State Party assigned to an international peace-keeping or peace-enforcement operation'.[101] The Committee found that Belgium was bound to fulfil the obligations stemming from the ICCPR when acting abroad, be it within peacekeeping missions or military operations under the auspices of NATO.[102] Previously, the Committee expressed its concerns about 'the behaviour of Belgian soldiers in Somalia' and acknowledged 'that the State Party has recognized the applicability of the Covenant in this respect'.[103] With regard to activities of Dutch peacekeepers in Srebrenica, the Committee assumed the applicability of some Covenant provisions.[104] Furthermore, it welcomed Italy's affirmation of the Covenant's applicability 'to the acts of Italian troops and police officers who are stationed abroad, whether in the context of peace or armed conflict',[105] while expressing its worries concerning Germany's state report since

[96] See ILC, 'ARIO' (n 12) 94, Article 8, para 4 et seq. But see Dannenbaum (n 62) 159 with Palchetti (n 33) 735 et seq.

[97] UN, *United Nations Juridical Yearbook* (UN 1986) 300 cited by ILC, 'Fifty-sixth Session Geneva, 3 May–4 June and 5 July–6 August 2004'; ILC, 'Report Gaja' (n 45) para 55.

[98] Spagnolo (n 48) 40.

[99] See Messineo (n 63) 78.

[100] Covenant on Political and Civil Rights (adopted 16 December 1966, entered into force 23 March 1976) 999 UNTS 171.

[101] UN Human Rights Committee (UNHRC), 'General Comment No. 31 [80]' (29 March 2004) UN Doc CCPR/C/21/Rev.1/Add.13, para 10.

[102] UNHRC, 'UN Human Rights Committee: Concluding Observations: Belgium, 12 August 2004' (21 and 24 July 2004) UN Doc CCPR/CO/81/BEL, para 6.

[103] UNHRC, 'UN Human Rights Committee: Concluding Observations: Belgium, 19 November 1998' (2 November 1998) UN Doc CCPR/C/79/Add.99, para 14.

[104] UNHRC, 'UN Human Rights Committee: Concluding Observations: Netherlands, 27 August 2001' (19 and 23 July 2001) UN Doc CCPR/CO/72/NET, para 8.

[105] UNHRC, 'UN Human Rights Committee: Concluding Observations: Italy, 24 April 2006' (2 November 2005) UN Doc CCPR/C/ITA/CO/5 para 3. Also, regarding Polish armed forces: UNHRC, 'UN Human Rights Committee: Concluding Observations: Poland, 2 December 2004' (4 November 2004) UN Doc CCPR/CO/82/POL, para 3.

it omitted to state how it safeguarded the fulfilment of Germany's human rights obligations within MMOs—without excluding UNPKMs.[106] In the case of *Kurbogaj v Spain*,[107] dealing with conduct of UN mandate in Kosovo (UNMIK) officials,[108] the Committee dismissed the complaint since the local remedies in Spain had not been exhausted. This could be interpreted as an acknowledgment of the fact that conduct by UNMIK is not exclusively attributable to the UN, which enjoys immunity before national courts[109]—this should apply even more so to the military components of UNPKMs.

One constructive way to ensure that TCNs remain bound by their human rights commitments when acting as part of UNPKMs while not releasing the UN from its international responsibility would be a 'multiple attribution of conduct' based on a 'dual effective control'.[110] These concepts—discussed below—might more adequately reflect the realities of UNPKMs.

3.1.2.2 Missions with UN mandate

While the UNSC fulfils its core task of peacekeeping by mandating an MMO, the institutional embedding of such operations is not comparable to UNPKMs. The acting states do not transfer any command or control powers onto the UN. The specific mandate might, however, oblige the acting states to coordinate their endeavours with the UN and to report regularly. Constellations in which the UN would 'effectively control' MMOs under UN mandate on the ground are hardly imaginable (although Article 7 ARIO forbids schematic assessments).[111] Most strikingly, however, the European Court of Human Rights (ECtHR) came to a different conclusion in its *Behrami/Saramati* judgment,[112] dealing inter alia with the legality of an incarceration by a KFOR soldier. Identifying which entity was acting in a legal sense—a prerequisite for establishing the Court's jurisdiction *ratione personae*, which is limited to European Convention on Human Rights (ECHR) parties—[113] the ECtHR attributed the conduct in question to the UN, assuming its 'ultimate authority and control'. The Court's finding rested on five argumentative pillars: (1) the UNSC possessed the competence to delegate its powers onto other entities; (2) the

[106] UNHRC, 'UN Human Rights Committee: Concluding Observations: Germany, 4 May 2004' (30 March 2004) UN Doc CCPR/CO/80/DEU, para 11; UN Doc CCPR/CO/80/DEU/Add.1.

[107] *Azem Kurbogaj and Ghevdet Kurbogaj v Spain* Communication No 1374/2005 (HRC, 11 August 2006) UN Doc CCPR/C/87/D/1374/2005.

[108] UNMIK is a subsidiary organ of the UNSC Paulus (n 38) para 48.

[109] Charter of the United Nations (adopted 26 June 1945, entered into force 24 October 1945) 892 UNTS 119 (UNC) Article 105 and Convention on the Immunities and Privileges of the UN (adopted 13 February 1946, entered into force 17 September 1946) 1 UNTS 15.

[110] Surholt (n 38) 131.

[111] UN, 'Report of the Secretary-General' (20 September 1996) UN Doc A/51/389, para 17.

[112] *Behrami and Saramati v France and others* App no 71412/01 (ECtHR, Grand Chamber Decision, 2 May 2007).

[113] See European Charter of Human Rights (adopted 4 November 1950, entered into force 3 September 1953) 213 UNTS 221 (ECHR) Article 1.

establishment of a military component in Kosovo would qualify as a delegation of transferable powers; (3) the UNSC did not merely authorize the operation but delegated its powers; (4) the mandate defined the powers of KFOR/NATO exercising 'operational control' precisely, and they comprised incarcerations; (5) the operating entities were obliged to report to the UNSC.[114]

The ECtHR's motives behind its 'attribution operation' become apparent[115] in between the lines[116] of its *rationes decidendi*: the Court regarded a judicial review of Chapter VII UN Charter resolutions as an encroachment upon the key competences of the UNSC.[117] Since ECHR rights are only derogable in exceptional circumstances (some of them not being derogable at all)[118] and principally apply in armed conflict situations, the Court seemed to assume that ECHR parties would become reluctant to participate in military operations under UN mandate in light of the legal restraints of the ECHR,[119] posing a serious impediment to an effective fulfilment of UN tasks.[120] Besides, by rejecting its jurisdiction the ECtHR could rather conveniently evade addressing the potential normative conflict between the UN Charter/UNSC resolutions and the ECHR in light of Articles 24 and 103 UN Charter.[121] The ECtHR has confirmed its 'ultimate authority' approach in subsequent decisions,[122] while qualifying it in *Al-Jedda v UK*. Here, it rejected the attribution of the conduct of the *Multi-National Force Iraq* (MNFI)—mandated by UNSC resolution 1511—to the UN due to its lack of 'ultimate control' (and 'effective control').[123] It is, however, questionable whether the differences between the KFOR and the MNFI merited such a distinction following the inner logic of the *Behrami/Saramati* judgment.

The ICJ has missed the opportunity to issue an *obiter dictum* on the attribution problem surrounding MMOs in the course of the proceedings initiated by former Yugoslavia regarding the NATO intervention in Kosovo.[124] But it seems most

[114] *Behrami and Saramati v France* (n 112) paras 140, 129, 134.

[115] G Hafner, 'The ECHR Torn between the United Nations and the States: The Behrami and Saramati Case' in A Fischer-Lescano (ed), *Frieden in Freiheit* (Nomos 2008) 103, 119.

[116] Critical Larsen (n 10) 521 et seq; Palchetti (n 33) 737 et seq.

[117] *Behrami and Saramati v France* (n 112) para 149.

[118] See Article 15 ECHR.

[119] But see Krieger (n 13) 169.

[120] D Sarooshi, *The United Nations and the Development of Collective Security* (OUP 1999) 164 et seq.

[121] See Breitegger (n 46) 174.

[122] *Kasumaj v Greece* App no 6974/05 (ECtHR, Judgment, 5 July 2007); *Gajic v Germany* App no 31446/92 (ECtHR, Judgment, 28 August 2007); *Berić and others v Bosnia and Herzegovina* App no 36357/04 (ECtHR, Judgment, 16 October 2007), as well as *Stephens v Cyprus, Turkey and the UN* App no 45267/06 (ECtHR, Judgment, 11 November 2008). See MC Lopez, 'Towards Dual or Multiple Attribution' (2013) 10 International Organizations Law Review 204 et seq.

[123] *Al-Jedda v UK* App no 27021/08 (ECtHR, Grand Chamber Judgment, 7 July 2011) para 84. On this Lopez (n 122) 211 et seq. See also the more restrictive approach in *Nada v Switzerland* App no 10593/08 (ECtHR, Grand Chamber Judgment, 12 September 2012) para 120.

[124] In its application Yugoslavia assumed that the actions of KFOR would be attributable to the TCN, *Legality of Use of Force (Serbia and Montenegro v Netherlands)* Memorial of Federal Republic of Yugoslavia 327 et seq, available at <http://www.icj-cij.org/files/case-related/110/8334.pdf>. The ICJ did not have to decide upon this point since it could declare that it had no jurisdiction over the case.

unlikely it would have followed the ECtHR's 'ultimate authority' approach: contrary to the factual orientation of attribution rules, the 'ultimate authority' of the UN assumed in the *Behrami/Saramati* judgment is merely virtual,[125] and the Court's distinction between 'authorization' and 'delegation' remains obscure.[126] The UN has almost no legal or factual means to steer and influence mandated MMOs on the ground beyond terminating the mandate. The legality of mandating UNSC resolutions which the ECtHR regarded as decisive is—according to the logic of general attribution principles—irrelevant.[127] The Court's reasoning conflicts with its *Bosphorus* judgment where it clarified that a transfer of sovereign rights onto other entities would not absolve ECHR parties from their Convention obligations.[128] Along these lines an even stronger case could be made for reviewing conduct of ECHR parties determined by acts of an IO onto which no sovereign powers have been transferred.[129] Most importantly, the 'ultimate authority' standard renders significant repercussions for the legal position of individuals whose rights are infringed in the course of MMOs:[130] though the complaint system of the ECHR would offer effective protection and judicial redress, it is unavailable since the Convention remains inapplicable *ratione personae*.[131] This is because the entity to which the conduct in question is attributable—the UN—is not bound by the ECHR and enjoys immunity in (national) courts.[132] International courts, on the other hand, which would be competent to adjudicate cases initiated by individuals against the UN do not exist.[133]

This leaves us with the following result: in most constellations of mandated MMOs, conduct of national contingents will not be attributable to the UN due to a lack of 'effective control' on its part.[134]

[125] PJ Kuijper, 'Introduction to the Symposium on Responsibility of International Organizations and of (Member) States' (2010) 7 International Organizations Law Review 9.

[126] *Behrami and Saramati v France* (n 112) para 43.

[127] Breitegger (n 46) 165 et seq.

[128] *Bosphorus v Ireland* App no 45036/98 (ECtHR, Grand Chamber Judgment, 30 June 2005) para 149 et seq.

[129] P Boudeau-Livinec, G Piero Buzzini, and S Villalpando, 'International Decision: Behrami & Nehrami v. France; Saramati v. France, Germany & Norway' (2008) 102 American Journal of International Law 323, 326 et seq; M Milanović and T Papić, 'As Bad as it Gets: The European Court of Human Right's Behrami and Saramati Decision and General International Law' (2009) 58 International and Comparative Law Quarterly 267, 274 et seq; Sari (n 38) 158.

[130] Critical Breitegger (n 46) 168.

[131] See only CA Bell, 'Reassessing Multiple Attribution: The International Law Commission and the Behrami and Saramati Decision' (2010) 42 International Law and Politics 533 et seq.

[132] See n 109; *Stitching Mothers of Srebrenica and others v the Netherlands* App no 65542/12 (ECtHR, Decision, 11 June 2013) esp paras 141 et seq.

[133] See Dannenbaum (n 62) 125 et seq.

[134] Particular problems occur in the context of 'joint operations', ILC, 'ARIO' (n 12) 89, Article 7, para 9.

3.1.2.3 'Multiple attribution of conduct'

Attributing conduct exclusively to one entity stands at odds with overlapping spheres of control characterizing MMOs. In this regard, a 'multiple attribution of conduct'[135] might represent the reality of complex command structures more adequately. This concept suggests that conduct of one agent simultaneously constitutes conduct of several entities. Hence, 'multiple attribution' does not arise in constellations in which separate actions of subjects cause one harmful outcome[136] or were (separate) organs of two subjects acting together.

A 'multiple attribution of conduct' would be compatible with the principle of independent responsibility[137] permeating the ASR/ARIO: this principle merely suggests that the responsibility of an actor is to be determined individually with respect to its own conduct,[138] while not excluding the materialization of instances of 'parallel responsibility'. Quite to the contrary: in cases of a multiplicity of actors responsible for the commission of one internationally wrongful act, Article 47 ASR/ Article 48 ARIO allow injured parties to invoke the responsibility of each actor individually while at the same time preventing their overcompensation.[139] This presupposes the possibility of a joint responsibility of different entities for the same internationally wrongful act[140] resulting from their individual conduct, which would be the effect of a 'multiple attribution of conduct'.[141]

Multiple attribution might, however, be difficult to reconcile with 'effective control' if it is understood as *exclusive* control.[142] One point is obvious: the stricter 'effective control' is understood, the less imaginable a multiple attribution of conduct becomes.[143] But it is also apparent that within MMOs, no actor ever attains absolute 'exclusive control'. Control over soldiers may be transferred partially yet effectively.[144]

In addition to this observation of factual circumstance, legal as well as policy aspects argue in favour of a multiple attribution of conduct.[145]

[135] Messineo (n 63) 62; Murphy and Wills (n 21) 604; C Ryngaert, 'The Responsibility of Member States of International Organizations: Concluding Observations' (2015) 12 International Organizations Law Review 502, 509.

[136] But see ILC, 'ASR' (n 24) 125, Article 47, para 6.

[137] Ahlborn (n 25) 1, 26.

[138] ILC, 'ASR' (n 24) 64, ch IV of part I, para 1.

[139] ILC, 'ASR' (n 24) 125, Article 47, para 9.

[140] ILC, 'ASR' (n 24) Article 48 ARIO, para 1.

[141] The discussion of whether 'multiple attribution' results in one wrongful act or several wrongful acts appears to be rather 'esoteric' Messineo (n 63) 79.

[142] Messineo (n 63) 91; also Couzigou (n 83) 350.

[143] Kondoch and Zwanenburg (n 35) 569.

[144] Boutin (n 17) 101.

[145] See *Nuhanović v de Staat der Nederlanden* Case no 200.020.174/01 (Gerechtshof's-Gravenhage, Judgment, 5 July 2011) para 5.9. This view was not shared by previous instances, *Nuhanovic v the Netherlands* Case no 265615/HA ZA 06-1671 (District Court, The Hague, Judgment, 10 September 2008) para 4.14.1 [engl. translation: ILDC 1092 (NL 2008)]. Some scholars assume that 'effective control' could be divided Krieger (n 13) 170 et seq. Assuming the possibility of a 'multiple attribution' Leck (n 80) 361 et seq; Sari (n 38) 159; Ahlborn (n 25) 5 et seq. Critical Palchetti (n 33) 739, 741.

Article 7 ARIO necessarily presupposes—in conjunction with Article 6 ARIO—that institutional bonds between the seconded organ and the seconding entity remain: neither is 'the umbilical cord' fully cut[146] nor necessarily the chain of attribution.[147] ILC Special Rapporteur Gaja did not regard the 'exclusiveness of control, which for instance the United Nations never has over national contingents' relevant 'but the extent of effective control' which would allow for a 'dual attribution of certain conducts'.[148] In its ARIO commentary, the ILC stressed that 'dual or even multiple attribution of conduct cannot be excluded'.[149] While the ILC speaks of an 'exclusive' 'effective control' in the context of the ASR,[150] it simultaneously purports that the same conduct could be exceptionally attributable to two states.[151] More importantly, the ILC pointed out that when the seconded organ acts 'exclusively for the purposes of'[152] the receiving state, 'its conduct is attributed to the latter State alone',[153] implying that the seconded organ could be under the control of both.[154]

The concept of 'multiple attribution of conduct' already found its way into jurisprudence and international legal materials: Dutch courts derived it from Article 48 in conjunction with Article 7 ARIO,[155] and the ECtHR hinted at it in its *Al-Jedda* judgment[156] by stressing that it did not assume that 'as a result of the authorization contained in Resolution 1511, the acts of soldiers within the Multi-National Force became attributable to the United Nations or—more importantly, for the purposes of this case—ceased to be attributable to the troop-contributing nations'.[157] In its *Opinion on Human Rights in Kosovo*, the Venice Commission clarified that an exclusive attribution of KFOR operations either to NATO or to the TCN would not be the only constructive option possible: there might be 'difficult intermediate cases, such as when soldiers are acting on the specific orders of their national commanders which are, however, themselves partly in execution of directives issued by the KFOR commander and partly within the exercise of their remaining scope of discretion'.[158] In light of the fact that the UN rather unambiguously assumes that any actions of peacekeeping forces are (generally) attributable to it, 'multiple attribution' seems to be implicitly present in statements of the HRC affirming the

[146] Zwanenburg (n 77) 649.
[147] For the contrary view Messineo (n 63) 88 et seq.
[148] ILC, 'Report Gaja' (n 45) para 48.
[149] ILC, 'ARIO' (n 12) 86, ch II, para 4.
[150] ILC, 'ASR' (n 24) 44, Article 6, para 1.
[151] ILC, 'ASR' (n 24) 124, Article 47, para 3.
[152] ILC, 'ASR' (n 24) 6, para 1.
[153] ILC, 'ASR' (n 24) Article 6, para 1.
[154] Boutin (n 17) 101.
[155] See n 145. In particular *Nuhanović v de Staat der Nederlanden* Case no 12/03324 (n 15) para 3.9.4; *Mustafić-Mujić et al v de Staat der Nederlanden* Case no 12/03329 (n 15) para 3.9.4.
[156] Lopez (n 122) 215.
[157] *Al-Jedda v UK* (n 123) para 80.
[158] European Commission for Democracy through Law, 'Opinion on Human Rights in Kosovo' No 280/2004 (8-9 October 2004) CDL-AD (2004) 033, 18, para 79.

responsibility of the parties to the ICCPR for its observance even when acting within UNPKMs.[159]

Furthermore, 'multiple attribution of conduct' is a feasible concept from a policy perspective: first, it might be an effective means to facilitate the establishment of a fair and just liability regime—both from the perspective of IOs as well as TCNs. In constellations in which following the 'traditional' doctrine an exclusive attribution of would have to be assumed—either to the UN to the TCN—'multiple attribution' would trigger a joint responsibility of actors. Secondly, and most important, it is—at least in the constellation of UNPKMs—an effective means for the effectuation of human rights and the strengthening of the position of victims. In particular, it would prevent the troubling consequences that the *Behrami/Saramati* judgment rendered.[160] Attributing injurious conduct (also) to the TCN in constellations of UNPKMs opens up the gate to national courts and international human rights courts.[161]

The key remaining problem that scholarship should direct its attention to is the exact contours of 'effective control' when understood non-exclusively, and the specific conditions under which Article 7 ARIO disrupts the chain of attribution between the soldier and the TCN.[162] 'Multiple attribution' requires viewing 'control' as a continuum, present in different degrees.[163] That inevitably induces uncertainties since it remains to be established when the threshold of 'effective control' is overstepped—yet, it reflects the realities of MMOs more adequately.

3.2 Multinational military operations and 'attribution of responsibility'

The 'attribution of conduct' paradigm is complemented by instances of 'attributed responsibility'[164]—neither of them is exclusive.

[159] See n 101 et seq.

[160] See n 112 et seq and accompanying text; Krieger (n 13) 171.

[161] European Commission for Democracy through Law (Venice Commission), 'Opinion on Human Rights in Kosovo: Possible Establishment of Review Mechanisms' No. 280/2004 (8-9 October 2004), CDL-AD (2004) 033, 18 para 75.

[162] See already n 48 et seq and accompanying text. Hinting at the possibility of a 'reciprocal reading' of 'effective control', Spagnolo (n 48) esp 40 et seq; Gal-Or and Ryngaert (n 54) 531. Also *Nuhanović v de Staat der Nederlanden* Case no 12/03324 (n 15) para 3.9.4; *Mustafić-Mujić et al v de Staat der Nederlanden* Case no 12/03329 (n 15) para 3.9.4. See critically P d'Argent, 'State Organs Placed at the Disposal of the UN, Effective Control, Wrongful Abstention and Dual Attribution of Conduct' (2014) 1 Questions of International Law, Zoom-in 26 et seq.

[163] C Eagleton, *International Organization and the Law of Responsibility* vol 76 (Brill 1950) 319, 386.

[164] Actors involved in MMOs may assume responsibility by ways of adopting certain conduct (Article 11 ASR, Article 9 ARIO), P d'Argent, 'Reparation, Cessation, Assurances and Guarantees of Non-Repetition' in A Nollkaemper and I Plakokefalos (eds), *Principles of Shared Responsibility* (CUP 2014) 210, 238 et seq. On UN practice Murphy and Wills (n 21) 597 et seq.

'Attributed responsibility'[165] ties into conduct attributable to a state/IO—being aid or assistance (Articles 14, 58 ARIO, Article 16 ASR[166]), direction and control (Articles 15, 59 ARIO, Article 17 ASR), coercion (Articles 16, 60 ARIO, Article 18 ASR), or—specifically in cases involving IO—adopting a binding decision leading to the circumvention of international obligations (Articles 17, 61 ARIO)—with regard to the wrongful act of another state/IO. While seemingly particularly apt to grasp the realities of MMOs,[167] on closer inspection these provisions pose considerable theoretical and practical challenges of which—focusing on Article 15 ARIO—only some shall be addressed here. These intricacies explain why their application in the MMO context has remained largely outside the spotlight of the discourse and has been rejected by states.[168]

Pursuant to Article 15 ARIO, the responsibility of an IO which directs and controls a state/IO in the commission of a wrongful act is triggered under strict conditions: it requires (1) its 'knowledge of the circumstances of the internationally wrongful act' (lit (a)); (2) its intention to support or facilitate the commission of a wrongful act;[169] (3) a causal relationship between 'directing and controlling' and the commission of the wrongful act; and (4) an 'obligation synchrony' meaning that the conduct of the state/IO must simultaneously constitute a breach of the international obligations of the directing and controlling IO (lit (b)).[170] On the macro-level, Article 15 ARIO appears to stand at odds with the principle of individual and independent responsibility[171] by establishing a 'derived',[172] 'derivative',[173] 'indirect',[174] 'ancillary',[175] or 'dependent' responsibility. On a closer look, however, it seems compatible with the principle if read substantively: Article 15 ARIO establishes that the deliberate participation of an IO in the wrongful conduct of a state/IO 'constitutes a separate wrong'.[176] Interpreted as such, it encompasses an individual and separate wrongful act—the 'second-tier wrongful act'—which is 'contingent'[177] on another wrongful act[178]—the 'first tier wrongful act'[179]—both

[165] Fry (n 23) 98 et seq.
[166] They cover the 'complicity' constellation; generally, H Aust, *Complicity and the Law of State Responsibility* (CUP 2011).
[167] For UNPKMs see Kuijper (n 125) 14; on KFOR/NATO/UN A Pellet, 'L'imputabilité d'éventuels actes illicites: Responsabilité de l'OTAN ou des États membres' in C Tomuschat (ed), *Kosovo and the International Community* (Kluwer Law 2002) 193, 199.
[168] See Boutin (n 17) 171; Kuijper (n 125) 21.
[169] ILC, 'ASR' (n 24) 66 Article 16, para 5.
[170] In contrast, Articles 17, 60 ARIO are characterized by an 'obligation asynchrony' or 'asymmetry'.
[171] On the principle of independent responsibility, see ILC, 'ASR' (n 24) ch IV of part I, 64, para 1.
[172] See, eg, Boutin (n 17) 173.
[173] ILC, 'ASR' (n 24) intro part I, ch IV, para 7.
[174] Zwanenburg (n 77) 648.
[175] J Crawford, *State Responsibility: The General Part* (CUP 2013) 395.
[176] Boutin (n 17) 173 et seq.
[177] M den Heijer, 'Shared Responsibility Before the European Court of Human Rights' (2013) 60 Netherlands International Law Review 411, 422.
[178] Boutin (n 17) 173 et seq.
[179] The 'directing and controlling entity' does not become the 'perpetrator' of the 'first-tier wrongful act', see also Fry (n 23) 109 et seq.

resulting in one harmful outcome. Irrespective of the possibility of such a reading, Article 15 ARIO inevitably dilutes the distinction between primary and secondary rules,[180] being full of conceptual ambiguities.[181] Its application on the micro-level is likewise problematic: first, it is unclear how 'direction and control' are to be understood. It is not the directing and controlling of the state/IO agent which is relevant but direction and control exercised over the state/IO in the commission of its wrongful act.[182] Drawing parallels to Article 8 ASR is hence problematic. which is also supported by the fact that—at least in its wording—Article 15 ARIO establishes a cumulative requirement of direction and control, while Article 8 ASR presents them as alternatives.[183] How 'direction and control' are to be understood particularly in the military context is yet to be explored by scholarship, considering the 'nuances of (...) command arrangements'.[184] If the ILC commentary on Article 17 ASR—the state responsibility counterpart of Article 15 ARIO—is consulted, direction and control would have to be actual[185] and operative.[186] Mere oversight,[187] incitement,[188] or influence would be insufficient. Control would involve 'domination over the commission of wrongful conduct',[189] which would effectively compromise 'a state's freedom to decide'.[190] This implies that factual direction and control is required, not only normative.[191] Since TCNs retain spheres of discretion—even within UNPKMs[192]—it is difficult to assume that their freedom to decide has been compromised completely.[193] The ILC implies, however, that an IO could direct and control another state or IO by issuing a decision binding upon it[194]—which would effectively lead to an overlap with Article 17 ARIO. A binding decision rather constitutes a case of legal, not factual control. *Boutin* argues that 'coalitions operating under a multinational command that is not fully integrated',

[180] Boutin (n 17) 173 (referring to V Lowe, 'Responsibility for the Conduct of Other States' (2002) 101 Kokusaihō gaikō zasshi 1, 4; Kuijper (n 125) 23. But see Fry (n 23) 104.

[181] cf ILC, 'ASR' (n 24) ch IV of part I, para 7; ILC, 'ASR' (n 24) 67, Article 16, para 9 with ILC, 'ASR' (n 24) 64, ch IV of part I, para 5; ILC, 'ASR' (n 24) 61, Article 17, para 1. See Fry (n 23) 118 et seq.

[182] See Fry (n 23) 109; Boutin (n 17) 181.

[183] See A Reinisch, 'Aid or Assistance and Direction and Control between States and International Organizations in the Commission of Internationally Wrongful Acts' (2010) 7 International Organizations Law Review 63, 75. But see ILC, 'ARIO' (n 12) 38, Article 15, para 3. The ILC referred here to contentions made by France in the course of the proceedings on the *Legality of Use of Force (Yugoslavia v France)* (Preliminary Objections of the French Republic) available at <http://www.icj-cij.org/files/case-related/107/10873.pdf> 26, para 15 et seq, para 46: France stated that NATO would be 'responsible for the "direction" of KFOR' and 'the United Nations for "control" of it'.

[184] See, eg, Boutin (n 17) 202.

[185] ILC, 'ASR' (n 24) Article 17, para 6.

[186] ILC, 'ASR' (n 24) Article 17, para 7.

[187] ibid.

[188] ILC, 'ASR' (n 24) 65, ch IV of part I, para 9.

[189] ILC, 'ASR' (n 24) Article 17, para 7.

[190] Crawford (n 175) 399.

[191] Fry (n 23) 118.

[192] See n 38 et seq and accompanying text.

[193] According to the ILC 'legal control' appears sufficient, 'ARIO' (n 12) 39, Article 15, para 5.

[194] ILC, 'ARIO' (n 12) 39, Article 15, para 5.

in which 'participants agree for some States to have a prevailing influence over the chain of command' might be covered by Article15 ARIO,[195] but the term 'prevailing influence' remains rather vague.

The ILC's classification of the NATO-KFOR-UN triangle as a case of control by one IO (UN) and direction by another (NATO) likewise raises more questions than providing answers.[196] Questions as to the delimitation of 'effective control' in the sense of Article 7 ARIO and Article 15 ARIO,[197] hence between 'attribution of conduct'—also considering the possibility of a 'multiple attribution of conduct'—and 'attribution of responsibility' remain to be answered. Furthermore, the necessary causal links between the 'first-tier wrongful act' and 'direction and control' still need to be explored. Leaving this problem aside, it will be difficult to establish the knowledge of a directing and controlling IO that a state/IO is committing a wrongful act even if one operates with the notion of constructive knowledge.[198]

In any case, 'attributed responsibility' is not a panacea for the responsibility challenge MMOs pose: first, establishing the first-tier wrongful act as well as the second-tier wrongful act requires deciding upon the attribution of conduct in the TCN-IO context. Secondly, 'attributed responsibility' does not bind the directing and controlling entity to the norms that apply to the entity committing the first-tier wrongful act, presupposing a synchrony of obligations. Therefore, in cases of violations of the ECHR by Convention parties, for example, the UN could not incur 'attributed responsibility' since it is not a party to the Convention.

3.3 Multinational military operations and the 'distribution of secondary obligations'

'Multiple attribution of conduct' as well as 'attributed responsibility' led to the responsibility of a plurality of actors for one harmful outcome, which raises questions as to the allocation of secondary obligations. Here, merely the duty to make reparations shall briefly be addressed. It is triggered when a wrongful act caused an injury (Article 31(1) ASR/Article 31(1) ARIO).[199] The ILC requires a sufficient causal link and a proximate cause.[200] In this context, the discussion so far has largely focused on the concept of 'joint and several responsibility'. Its main feature is that each subject within a group of actors is responsible and liable, and the injured subject may claim full reparation for the damage incurred from each

[195] Boutin (n 17) 155 et seq.
[196] ILC, 'ARIO' (n 12) 38 Article 15, para 3.
[197] Reinisch (n 183) 76 et seq.
[198] *Anglo-Norwegian Fisheries Case* (Merits) [1951] ICJ Rep 166, 152, separate opinion of J Alvarez ('ought to have known').
[199] D'Argent (n 164) 220.
[200] ILC, 'ASR' (n 24) 92, Article 31, para 10.

responsible actor[201] while internal compensatory schemes among the responsible subjects might apply. On the international plane, no general or coherent rules on 'joint and several responsibility' in this domestic sense can be identified.[202] Its provenance warrants to employ this term cautiously.[203] While the rule that each responsible actor is obliged to make full reparation could be derived from the general principle that responsibility of each actor is to be determined individually[204] and 'not diminished (...) by the fact that one or more other States' or IOs 'are also responsible for the same act',[205] the possibility of an apportionment remains to be discussed, especially regarding instances of 'attributed responsibility'. This concerns internal compensatory schemes as well, which are even more uncertain: although 'it is natural for that State to seek a contribution from the others on some basis' in cases '[w]here two or more States engage in a common activity and one of them is held responsible for damage arising',[206] no rules enjoying *lex lata* status can be identified in terms of rights of recourse.[207]

One way to allocate obligations of reparation internally (but potentially also externally) could be to determine the causal contributions of the responsible actors to the harmful outcome.[208] Indeed, the ILC has stated that 'unless some part of the injury can be shown to be severable in causal terms from that attributed to the responsible State, the latter is held responsible for all the consequences, not being too remote, of its wrongful conduct'.[209] This appears to imply that in certain instances apportionment would be imaginable.[210] Apportionment based on the causality of the contributions is particularly difficult, not only because legally relevant causality is never merely factual but essentially normative.[211] In the constellation of 'multiple attribution of conduct', this would effectively translate into distinguishing between different degrees of 'effective control' exercised over an agent since there would be only one conduct that is attributed to several actors. In the Article 15 ARIO constellation as an example of 'attributed responsibility', two instances of conduct and two wrongful acts would be interconnected by the same harm or damage that they have caused.[212] The aspect of control would surface here in different guises within the respective relationships (state/IO, state/acting agent). A price tag would have

[201] D'Argent (n 164) 244 et seq.
[202] Crawford (n 23) 272–73.
[203] See ILC, 'ASR' (n 24) 124, Article 47 ASR, para 3; Crawford (n 175) 329.
[204] See Article 48 ARIO, Article 47 ASR, ILC, 'Third Report on State Responsibility by Special Rapporteur James Crawford, UN Doc A/CN.4/510 and Add 1-4' in *Yearbook of the International Law Commission* (UN 2000) 3, para 276(d).
[205] ILC, 'ASR' (n 24) 124, Article 47, para 1. Also, D'Argent (n 164) 238.
[206] ILC, 'Third Report on State Responsibility by Special Rapporteur James Crawford, UN Doc A/CN.4/510 and Add 1-4' in *Yearbook of the International Law Commission* (UN 2000) 3, 75, para 276.
[207] Boutin (n 17) 215.
[208] Cf D'Argent (n 164) 220.
[209] ILC, 'ASR' (n 24) 93, Article 31, para 13.
[210] Boutin (n 17) 216.
[211] D'Argent (n 164) 223.
[212] Boutin (n 17) 177.

to be attached to these different degrees of control. An alternative option would be to apply qualitative schemes by establishing quasi-normative, moral, or policy-oriented categories of responsibility, indicating which entity is to be regarded more responsible. Irrespective of the questionable sensibility of such an approach, it is very much a construct of unripe scholarly imagination.

4. Conclusion

The 'pluriverse' of MMOs gravitates around three basic sub-problems in terms of legal accountability:[213] the 'attribution of conduct', the 'attribution of responsibility', and the allocation of secondary obligations stemming from responsibility. In these dimensions, the plurality of actors involved and the various overlapping spheres of control pose a major challenge. Obviously, 'control' lacks a general definition and occurs in many guises. It is, however, one of the fundaments of allocating responsibility: 'control breeds responsibility'.[214] MMOs confront us with a 'responsibility conundrum' exactly because—as *Boutin* has aptly pointed out—'control in the military sense and control in the legal sense has not been sufficiently explored'.[215] In the end, MMOs are an example of the high complexities of the world today: harmful outcomes are the product of a multitude of actors, actions, and omissions. In order to preserve international law's effectivity, the regime of international legal responsibility as a potentially powerful scheme to implement accountability must fit and be reactive to these realities. In that regard, there is yet a long path to travel—particularly for scholarship. A first and important step is, however, not only to accept that the 'duality of responsibility' is a 'constant feature of international law'[216] but moreover that specific conduct 'may well "belong" to more than one collective entity at once'.[217]

[213] Fry (n 23) 19.
[214] CC Hyde, *International Law, Chiefly as Interpreted and Applied by the United States* vol 2 (2nd edn, Little Brown and Company 1947) 922.
[215] Boutin (n 17) 156.
[216] *Application of the Convention on the Prevention and Punishment of the Crime of Genocide (Bosnia and Herzegovina v Serbia and Montenegro)* (Judgment) [2007] ICJ Rep 43, para 173.
[217] Messineo (n 63) 63.

16

Protecting the Environment during Multinational Military Operations

Onita Das

1. Introduction

Today, states increasingly operate as part of coalitions in the form of multinational military operations (MMOs) as seen in recent combat operations such as Kosovo, Iraq, Afghanistan, Syria, and elsewhere. These operations are commonly carried out under United Nations (UN) auspices or by a regional organization such as the North Atlantic Treaty Organization (NATO) and involve multinational forces embracing a broad spectrum of responsibilities—from conflict prevention, taking part in hostilities, to undertaking peacekeeping and peacebuilding duties.[1] MMOs have their advantages as they allow states to pool their resources, to aim for efficient employment of capabilities within the participating forces, and increase the cost effectiveness of often very expensive operations.[2] These operations, however, are not without drawbacks. In addition to general interoperability issues,[3] with their multinational dimension, MMOs face problems of legal interoperability, that is, challenges in relation to the applicability of relevant international legal norms during operations. Among other issues, such challenges may affect the protection of the environment[4] during MMOs.

As MMOs rapidly become the norm in contemporary armed conflict, they inevitably have an impact on the environment. Damage to the environment during military operations could be due to it being a military target or as part of collateral damage. MMOs in Kosovo, Iraq, and Afghanistan demonstrate that damage

[1] V Bernard, 'Multinational Operations and the Law—Great Expectations, Great Responsibilities' (2013) 95 International Review of the Red Cross 475, 475.

[2] M Zwanenburg, 'International Humanitarian Law Interoperability in Multinational Operations' (2013) 95 International Review of the Red Cross 681, 682.

[3] See J Derleth, 'Enhancing Interoperability: The Foundation for Effective NATO Operations' (*NATO Review Magazine*, 25 September 2013) <https://www.nato.int/docu/review/2015/also-in-2015/enhancing-interoperability-the-foundation-for-effective-nato-operations/EN/index.htm>. All URLs accessed 16 September 2019.

[4] '"Environment" includes natural resources, both abiotic and biotic, such as air, water, soil, fauna and flora and the interaction between the same factors and characteristics of the landscape.' Suggested definition in MG Jacobsson, Special Rapporteur, 'Preliminary Report on the Protection of the Environment in Relation to Armed Conflicts' (30 May 2014) UN Doc A/CN.4/674, 24.

Onita Das, *Protecting the Environment during Multinational Military Operations* In *The 'Legal Pluriverse' Surrounding Multinational Military Operations*. Edited by Robin Geiß and Heike Krieger, Oxford University Press (2020).
DOI: 10.1093/oso/9780198842965.003.0017

to the environment during such operations impacts not only the environment but also the war-torn population, negatively affecting their security, livelihood, and well-being. For example, the NATO-led high-altitude aerial bombing campaign in Kosovo hit a wide range of industrial complexes and public infrastructure, causing significant environmental damage.[5]

It is well known, however, that while International Humanitarian Law (IHL) seeks to protect the environment in armed conflict (AC),[6] protection is arguably limited and inadequate,[7] and protecting the environment faces further challenges from the changing nature of military operations. In 2011, the UN International Law Commission (ILC) decided to examine the international legal framework governing environmental protection in AC. Under the former UN Special Rapporteur Marie Jacobsson, the ILC addressed the topic through a temporal perspective, that is, reviewing legal measures taken to protect the environment before, during, and after ACs. The commission produced three reports with its findings.[8] Taking guidance from the ILC reports, this chapter explores the relevant legal frameworks providing environmental protection during MMOs, with a focus on 'during conflict'. Therefore, this chapter first considers the applicability of IHL during MMOs to protect the environment; secondly, it reviews the IHL provisions that offer environmental protection during MMOs and their limitations; thirdly, it explores the applicability of other legal bodies within the international law framework for the protection of the environment; and finally, it concludes on the way forward to meet the challenges presented by legal interoperability issues during MMOs to better protect the environment.

2. Legal Interoperability Challenges: Applicability of IHL during MMOs

Illustrating the complexity of legal interoperability in MMOs, one of the first hurdles to overcome concerning environmental protection in conflict is the issue of conflict classification. Conflict classification is required in order to apply the

[5] O Das, *Environmental Protection, Security and Armed Conflict: A Sustainable Development Perspective* (Edward Elgar 2013) 162.

[6] AC here is set in the context of MMOs. AC, conflict, and warfare are used interchangeably throughout the chapter.

[7] See, eg, UNEP, *Protecting the Environment during Armed Conflict: An Inventory and Analysis of International Law* (UNEP 2009) 4–5; M Bothe and others, 'International Law Protecting the Environment during Armed Conflict: Gaps and Opportunities' (2010) 92(879) International Review of the Red Cross 569, 569–79.

[8] Pre-conflict: Jacobsson, 'First Report' (n 4) and UN Doc A/CN.4/674/Corr.1; In-conflict: MG Jacobsson, Special Rapporteur, 'Second report on the protection of the environment in relation to armed conflicts' (28 May 2015) UN Doc A/CN.4/685; Post-conflict: MG Jacobsson, Special Rapporteur, 'Third report on the protection of the environment in relation to armed conflicts' (3 June 2016) UN Doc A/CN.4/700.

relevant rules of IHL to protect the environment. The second obstacle to environmental protection during MMOs is the issue of diverging legal obligations of multinational forces.

With regard to which IHL provisions apply, it is necessary to first determine if there is an AC and if the actor in a particular MMO is party to that conflict. Unfortunately, the classification of conflict is challenging due in part to there being no universal conflict classification process to determine what amounts to an AC or if there is one, what type it is.[9] Furthermore, any such classification is based on the factual circumstances of the particular situation.[10] Although the threshold for determining an AC is vague, in many cases it is clear that there is no conflict or that the multinational force concerned is not a party to the AC. For example, European Union Force Bosnia and Herzegovina (EUFOR) also known as Operation Althea in Bosnia, clearly did not operate in an AC situation.[11] However, in other cases the situation is less clear-cut.

Lack of clarity arises from the complexity of contemporary warfare which often involves a complex hybrid of internal and international elements. This includes the intermingling of civilian and military missions, participation of various non-state parties, or internal conflicts involving external actors—blurring the lines of interstate, that is, international armed conflicts (IACs) or civil conflicts, that is, non-international armed conflicts (NIACs). The conflict in Kosovo, for instance, started off as a low-intensity internal conflict but rapidly became an IAC when NATO launched military operations against the Federal Republic of Yugoslavia (FRY).[12] This demonstrates the difficulty of drawing a clear distinction between conflicts which are IACs or NIACs—with the law on armed conflict (LOAC)[13] clearly applying to either scenario. Determining the type of conflict matters because the classification ascertains which rules apply. This goes hand in hand with interpretation, which constitutes yet another problem of MMOs.

In less straightforward situations, different troop-contributing nations (TCNs) to an MMO may come to varied interpretations on the classification of a conflict and whether they are a party to it. This leads to differing conclusions concerning the application of IHL. The NATO-led International Security Assistance Force (ISAF) operation in Afghanistan is an example where some TCNs claimed that

[9] D Murray, *Practitioner's Guide to Human Rights Law in Armed Conflict* (Chatham House/OUP 2016) 53.

[10] ibid.

[11] F Naert, 'The Application of International Humanitarian Law and Human Rights Law in CSDP Operations' in E Cannizzaro and others (eds), *International Law as Law of the European Union* (Martinus Nijhoff 2011) 196.

[12] CE Bruch and JE Austin, 'The Kosovo Conflict: A Case Study of Unresolved Issues' in JE Austin and CE Bruch (eds), *The Environmental Consequences of War: Legal, Economic, and Scientific Perspectives* (CUP 2000) 648.

[13] IHL and LOAC are used interchangeably throughout the chapter.

AC existed only in some parts of Afghanistan,[14] some states considered there to be an NIAC 'between ISAF and the Afghan government on the one hand and one or more organised armed groups on the other',[15] while some states denied any existence of conflict in the country.[16] In relation to participation, some TCNs (eg the Netherlands and Germany) were even of the initial view that they were not involved in an AC.[17] While it could reasonably be expected that each TCN 'faced with roughly the same facts on the ground to come to the same conclusion on the application of the Conventions. In practice, however, each state makes this determination on its own.'[18] According to Zwanenburg, '[i]n multinational operations, there is no central authority that determines the law that applies to the operation.'[19] With each individual TCN left to determine the applicability of IHL to its own forces, diverging legal obligations within an MMO emerge. The lack of centralized interpretation and determination of applicable IHL is problematic.

An additional issue is that TCNs are not all parties to the same treaties. While the Geneva Conventions are universally ratified and their provisions deemed to be of customary nature, the Additional Protocols to the Geneva Convention are not. The United States, for example, is not a party to the Additional Protocols. In a complex MMO alliance it would thus have different obligations to other TCNs who are party to them. Diverging legal obligations among the multinational forces means varied environmental protection obligations, and ultimately, further decreasing or negating entirely protection for the environment 'in conflict' during MMOs.

3. MMOs, IHL, and Protection of the Environment

There is little specific legal protection for the environment during times of warfare. However, a number of treaty provisions and customary principles converge in IHL and these arguably address a broad range of threats to the environment arising from AC. This section explores the relevant rules and principles of IHL that seek to afford direct or indirect protection for the environment in conflict during MMOs.

[14] O Engdahl, 'Multinational Peace Operations Forces Involved in Armed Conflict: Who Are the Parties?' in K Mujezinović Larsen and others, *Searching for a 'Principle of Humanity' in International Humanitarian Law* (CUP 2013) 233.

[15] See Zwanenburg (n 2) 687.

[16] Engdahl (n 14) 233.

[17] FJ Hampson, 'Afghanistan 2001–2010' in E Wilmshurst (ed), *International Law and the Classification of Conflicts* (OUP 2012) 255.

[18] Zwanenburg (n 2) 688.

[19] ibid (footnote omitted).

3.1 IHL provisions

3.1.1 IAC

3.1.1.1 Direct environmental protection

With regard to IACs, the Convention on the Prohibition of Military or Any Other Hostile Use of Environmental Modification Techniques (ENMOD)[20] and two provisions within the 1977 Protocol Additional to the Geneva Conventions of 12 August 1949 relating to the Protection of Victims of International Armed Conflicts (AP I)[21] were expressly formulated to protect the environment during AC.

ENMOD does not specifically deal with damage to the environment during AC, but protects the environment from being used as a weapon by prohibiting military or any other hostile use of 'environmental modification techniques having widespread, long-lasting or severe effects as a means of destruction, damage or injury to any other State Party'.[22] Environmental modification techniques are considered techniques that cause change 'through the deliberate manipulation of natural processes—the dynamics, composition or structure of the Earth, including its biota, lithosphere, hydrosphere and atmosphere, or of outer space'.[23] According to Jacobsen, '[t]his means that the Convention covers a very narrowly defined environmental modification technique'.[24]

In addition, ENMOD has a threshold, applying only if the environment is manipulated causing either widespread, long-lasting, *or* severe effects.[25] This means that acts manipulating the environment are only considered unlawful if the environmental damage encompasses several hundred square kilometres, lasts over a period of months (approximately a season), or involves 'serious or significant disruption or harm to human life, natural and economic resources or other assets'.[26] Due to the alternative ('or') conditions, ENMOD's threshold for application appears lower in comparison to AP I's cumulative threshold (discussed later),[27] but ENMOD's actual scope is rather limited.[28] ENMOD only covers the 'deliberate manipulation of natural processes' and if that manipulation causes damage to another state party to the Convention.[29] In the context of the first Gulf War for example, Schmitt argues that Iraq's actions[30] were relatively universally considered not to

[20] (Adopted 10 December 1976, entered into force 5 October 1978) 167 ILM 88.
[21] (Adopted 8 June 1977, entered into force 7 December 1978) 1125 UNTS 3.
[22] Article I ENMOD.
[23] Article II ENMOD.
[24] Jacobsson, 'Second Report' (n 8) 38.
[25] Article I ENMOD.
[26] See Understanding to ENMOD.
[27] Differences in texts between ENMOD and AP I 'are not an oversight but intentional'. See Bothe (n 7) 572.
[28] MN Schmitt, 'Humanitarian Law and the Environment' (2000) 28(3) Denver Journal of International Law and Policy 265, 280.
[29] Article I ENMOD.
[30] From deliberately pumping Kuwaiti oil into the Persian Gulf to sabotaging more than 700 Kuwaiti oil wells. See Das (n 5) 143–47.

have violated ENMOD's provisions—'the environment was a target of sorts, but its processes were not manipulated such that it constituted a weapon'.[31] Considering the significant environmental damage caused by Iraqi forces,[32] this demonstrates ENMOD's limited application. In any event, Iraq is a signatory but not a party to the Convention.[33] While ENMOD is unlikely to be applicable in MMOs due to its narrow scope, it would also face difficulty in application because not all TCNs are likely to be party to it.

In AP I, Articles 35(3) and 55[34] specifically address damage to the natural environment. Article 35(3) prohibits the employment of 'methods and means of warfare which are intended, or may be expected, to cause widespread, long-term and severe damage to the natural environment'. The prohibition is absolute and 'continues to apply in the absence of any direct threat to the population or to the flora and fauna of the enemy State. It is the natural environment itself that is protected'.[35]

Similarly, Article 55 refers specifically to environmental damage but with a further anthropocentric link. Article 55(1) provides that, '[c]are shall be taken in warfare to protect the natural environment against widespread, long-term and severe damage. This protection includes a prohibition of the use of methods or means of warfare which are intended or may be expected, to cause such damage to the natural environment and thereby to prejudice the health or survival of the population'. Article 55(1) sets out an obligation to care included within a prohibition limiting the means and methods of warfare. However, the required risk assessment of the environmental damage under this provision is, according to the United Kingdom and France, to be assessed objectively and based on information available at the time.[36] Article 55(2) AP I protects the natural environment against attacks via reprisals, by prohibiting such attacks even where the natural environment is a military objective.[37] As Article 55 is set out in Section I, Part IV (Civilian Population), this gives the implication that the environment is considered a civilian object.[38] Christiansen argues that AP I, in recognizing 'the environment as a civilian object—as opposed to a military object (…) provides instant protection'.[39]

[31] Schmitt (n 28) 280 (footnote omitted).

[32] See Das (n 5) 143–47.

[33] ICRC, 'Treaties, State Parties and Commentaries: Iraq' <http://www.icrc.org/applic/ihl/ihl.nsf/vwTreatiesByCountrySelected.xsp?xp_countrySelected=IQ&nv=4>.

[34] Both provisions are complementary. See Y Sandoz and others, *Commentary on the Protocol Additional to the Geneva Conventions of 12 August 1949, and relating to the Protection of Victims of International Armed Conflicts (Protocol I)* (Martinus Nijhoff 1987) 389–420 (Article 35 commentary) and 661–64 (Article 55 commentary).

[35] ibid 420.

[36] Jacobsson, 'Second Report' (n 8) 39.

[37] ibid 43.

[38] ibid (citing JM Henckaerts and L Doswald-Beck (eds), *Customary International Humanitarian Law*, vols I and II (CUP 2005) 525).

[39] SM Christiansen, *Climate Conflicts—A Case of International Environmental and Humanitarian Law* (Springer 2015) 200 (footnote omitted).

Although these AP I provisions theoretically provide specific protection to the environment during AC, protection is obstructed by the stringent criteria of Articles 35(3) and 55(1). For any environmental damage to be prohibited, the damage must reach the high triple threshold criteria of AP I: 'widespread, long-term *and* severe'—the requirements are cumulative.[40] In addition to the provisions' narrow scope, there is some ambiguity as to the interpretation of the three conditions, making these provisions difficult to apply in practice.[41] These cumulative criteria are also reflected in Rule 45 of the ICRC study on customary IHL (ICRC study), which the ICRC states has achieved customary status for IAC situations but regarding NIACs, it has merely *arguably* reached customary status.[42] The ICRC also recognizes that the United States is a 'persistent objector' to this part of the rule,[43] arguably casting some doubt as to its customary nature. In addition, commentary on Rule 45 highlights the continued uncertainty of interpretation of 'widespread, long-term *and* severe' and its very high threshold as demonstrated by the difficulty in finding NATO in violation during its FRY bombing campaign and also causing disagreement as to whether the first Gulf War environmental damage reached this threshold.[44]

As of May 2018, there are 174 states party to AP I,[45] but the most important military power in the world today—the United States—is glaringly absent and so are a couple of other military powers such as Turkey or Pakistan. Also, despite the significant number of state parties to AP I, based on recent ILC reports, states have made no declarations regarding the interpretation of the above three conditions in light of environmental damage resulting from modern conflicts.[46] The uncertainty and difficulty in implementation and enforcement contributes to divergent interpretations among TCNs in MMOs and continues to leave environmental protection during AC in an unsatisfactory position.

In addition, despite ENMOD and AP I providing the most direct environmental protection in AC, not all states are contracting parties. This is particularly

40 Sandoz (n 34) 417 (Scholars maintain this threshold criteria is open to interpretation. 'Long-term' is interpreted as a period of decades but thus far, there is no agreement on the interpretation of 'widespread' and 'severe').

41 ibid (it appears the authors of AP I did not intend 'acts of warfare which cause short-term damage to the natural environment' and 'battlefield damage incidental to conventional warfare' to be prohibited by these provisions. The article 'is primarily directed to … such damage as would be likely to prejudice, over a long term, the continued survival of the civilian population or would risk causing major health problems').

42 ICRC, 'Rule 45. Causing Serious Damage to the Natural Environment' <https://ihl-databases.icrc.org/customary-ihl/eng/docs/v1_rul_rule45>.

43 ibid.

44 ibid. See also ICRC, 'Practice Relating to Rule 45. Causing Serious Damage to the Natural Environment' <https://ihl-databases.icrc.org/customary-ihl/eng/docs/v2_rul_rule45>.

45 The list of API State Parties is available at <https://ihl-databases.icrc.org/applic/ihl/ihl.nsf/Treaty.xsp?documentId=D9E6B6264D7723C3C12563CD002D6CE4&action=openDocument>.

46 See, eg, Jacobsson, 'First Report' (n 4); Jacobsson, 'Second Report' (n 8); Jacobsson, 'Third Report' (n 8).

problematic during MMOs, where TCNs have diverging legal obligations and as such, while some states are bound to protect the environment under these provisions, others are not. Even for legally bound states, differing interpretations as to the applicability of the provisions can be reached by each state. This further decreases the already limited environmental protection afforded by these IHL provisions, if not negating it entirely. It is therefore necessary to consider other means to bind those parties. This is where the relevant provisions within the Hague Regulations of 1899[47] and 1907[48] and the fourth Geneva Convention (GC IV) of 1949,[49] and customary IHL, come in. Both the Hague and Geneva Conventions are part of customary international law (CIL) and, accordingly, binding on all states.

3.1.1.2 Indirect environmental protection

The Hague Regulations do not expressly protect the environment in AC but contain provisions that limit the means and methods of warfare resulting in indirect protection. This provides some environmental protection during any 'in conflict' phase of an MMO. Article 23(g) Hague IV, for example, prohibits the destruction or seizure of enemy property 'unless such destruction or seizure be imperatively demanded by the necessities of war'. This limits the damage to property of the conflict state and potentially prevents or minimizes environmental harm that may be caused by such destruction or seizure.[50]

The law of occupation also applies to MMOs and is important as the spectrum of MMOs extends increasingly. In the context of environmental protection, Article 55 Hague IV provides that the occupying state may use and benefit from public property as well as reasonably exploit natural resources in the occupied territory. This provision requires the occupier to act as administrator and safeguard these resources but prohibits the occupier from permanently destroying or altering them.[51] Similarly, Article 53 GC IV prohibits the occupying power from destroying real or personal property except when militarily necessary. Although subject to military necessity, this provision does offer some scope for environmental protection.[52]

Provisions that indirectly touch on environmental protection during AC are also provided by AP I. In particular, Article 54 prohibits combatants from destroying

[47] Hague Convention (II) with Respect to the Laws and Customs of War on Land (adopted 29 July 1899, entered into force 4 September 1900) 32 Stat 1803.

[48] Hague Convention (IV) Respecting the Laws and Customs of War on Land (adopted 18 October 1907, entered into force 26 January 1910) 36 Stat 2277.

[49] Geneva Convention (IV) Relative to the Protection of Civilian Persons in Time of War (adopted 12 August 1949, entered into force 21 October 1950) 75 UNTS 287.

[50] UNEP (n 7) 16 (enemy property 'could include protected areas, environmental goods and natural resources').

[51] See also Article 55 Hague II.

[52] See, eg, *US v List (The 'Hostages Case')* (1949) 11 CCL No 10 Trials 1230, 1295–97 (retreating German army adopted scorched earth tactics in Norway and Finland). See ICRC, 'Article 53' (*Commentary of 1958*) <http://www.icrc.org/ihl.nsf/1a13044f3bbb5b8ec12563fb0066f226/a13817cda3424c3cc12563cd0042c6e6!OpenDocument> (on scope of property protected by Article 53).

the civilian population's means of survival, namely foodstuffs, agricultural areas, and irrigation works, subject to these objects being used in direct support of enemy forces. Article 56 deals with the danger to the environment as a consequence of destroying dams, dykes, or nuclear power stations. Article 52 provides general protection of civilian objects and Article 57 requires precaution in attacks during military operations, both of which have an indirect bearing on environmental protection. Ultimately, these provisions that afford some protection for the human population and the environment may contribute to alleviating the impact of warfare on the environment during MMOs. However, due to the possibility that not all TCNs in MMOs are party to AP I, in practice, these provisions may have limited applicability in protecting the environment.

3.1.2 NIAC

Although there are few IHL laws that protect the environment during IACs, there are even fewer IHL rules that do so in NIACs. Protection provided by Article 3 common to the four Geneva Conventions of 1949 (Common Article 3) is purely humanitarian and makes no mention of protecting specific objects or the environment during NIAC. Indirect environmental protection in NIACs is only provided by the customary principles of humanity, discrimination, distinction, proportionality, precautions in attack, and military necessity[53] which are applicable in IACs and NIACs, as well as a few provisions within the 1977 Protocol Additional to the Geneva Conventions of 12 August 1949 relating to the Protection of Victims of Non-International Armed Conflicts (AP II).[54]

Articles 14 and 15 AP II[55] anthropocentrically provide some form of environmental protection during NIACs. Article 14, protecting objects indispensable to the survival of the civilian population (eg food, food-producing agricultural areas, crops, livestock, irrigation works, drinking water installations, and supplies), indirectly protects water resources and the agricultural environment. Article 15 protects 'works and installations containing dangerous forces, namely dams, dykes and nuclear electrical generating stations', by prohibiting attacks on these installations even if these are military objectives, if such attacks may cause the release of dangerous forces and consequently cause severe losses among the civilian population. Additional environmental protection during NIACs is also provided by Rule 43 of the ICRC study which is applicable in both IACs and NIACs and considered to be part of CIL.[56] Rule 43 prohibits attacks on or destruction of the natural environment subject to the environment being a military objective or subject to

[53] See section 3.2.
[54] (Adopted 8 June 1977, entered into force 7 December 1978) 1125 UNTS 609.
[55] Very similar in scope to Articles 52, 54, and 56 AP I.
[56] JM Henckaerts, 'Annex. List of Customary Rules of International Humanitarian Law' (2005) 87(857) International Review of the Red Cross 198, 202, available at <https://www.icrc.org/eng/assets/files/other/customary-law-rules.pdf>.

imperative military necessity. It also prohibits excessive environmental damage in relation to the anticipated military advantage. Applicability of Rules 44 (due regard for the natural environment in military operations) and 45 (prohibition on causing serious damage to the natural environment) during NIACs are less certain as the International Committee of the Red Cross (ICRC) merely states that these rules *arguably* apply during NIACs.[57]

In MMOs, protection for the environment under these rules would depend on the understanding and interpretation of each TCN regarding the conflict situation they are participating in as well as the applicability of the relevant IHL. In addition, as most contemporary ACs are internal in nature, the scope of environmental protection under IHL is comparatively limited.[58] Nevertheless, the ILC recognizes significant development in the last twenty years with regard to a number of treaties that have incorporated NIACs in their scope of application.[59] In particular, the Convention on Prohibitions or Restrictions on the Use of Certain Conventional Weapons Which May Be Deemed to Be Excessively Injurious or to Have Indiscriminate Effects (Conventional Weapons Convention)[60] was amended to ensure that the Convention would also be applicable in NIACs.[61] In lieu of modern conflicts leaning more towards NIACs, perhaps states will see the benefit of amending other relevant international agreements to take into consideration NIACs and thereby increasing legal protection for the environment.[62]

3.2 IHL principles

Limits to the means and methods of warfare and as a result some form of environmental protection are also provided by the customary principles of warfare: humanity, distinction, precautions in attack, proportionality, and the rules of military necessity. These fundamental principles are applicable throughout an AC (international or non-international) and universally binding on all states.[63] Therefore, all TCNs in MMOs are bound by these principles.

The principle of humanity dictates that the infliction of suffering, injury, or destruction causing harm not actually necessary for achieving legitimate military objectives should be avoided.[64] This could be interpreted as including a duty to ensure

57 ibid.
58 UNEP (n 7) 28.
59 Jacobsson, 'Second Report' (n 8) 36 (see footnote 169).
60 (Adopted 10 October 1980, entered into force 2 December 1983) 1342 UNTS 137.
61 Amendment to the Conventional Weapons Conventions (21 December 2001) 2260 UNTS 82.
62 Due to difficulty in acquiring information on state and non-state actors' practice during NIACs, there is very little practice for the ILC to report on. See Jacobsson, 'Second Report' (n 8) 5.
63 See, eg, JM Henckaerts and L Doswald-Beck, *Customary International Humanitarian Law: Volume I: Rules* (CUP 2005).
64 This principle is set out as the 'laws of humanity' within the 1899 Martens Clause.

that war-related environmental damage should not be caused to the extent that it causes unnecessary suffering to the human population.[65]

The principle of distinction imposes upon combatants the legal obligation to distinguish between combatants and civilians and between military objectives and civilian objects.[66] The principle of distinction is codified by Article 48 AP I and supported by Articles 51 and 52 AP I. This principle also incorporates the principle of discrimination which specifies that only legitimate military objectives[67] must be targeted.[68] In an environmental context, this could include civilian targets that are environmental in nature or civilian targets (eg a chemical factory) which, if damaged or destroyed, could cause harm to the environment. Based on the prohibition of attacks against civilian objects[69] set out in various provisions, it is concluded that 'the natural environment is civilian in nature and therefore not in itself a military objective'.[70] However, as per other civilian objects, the natural environment may become a military objective and at that point may be subject to attack.[71]

The principle of proportionality sets crucial limits on warfare, requiring that the level of force employed by combatants in AC be proportionate and not excessive to the military objective.[72] Essentially, the effects of the means and methods of warfare used must not be disproportionate to the anticipated military advantage. The International Court of Justice (ICJ) stresses the importance of this principle in protecting the environment during AC.[73] Therefore, this principle could equally apply to any environmentally related military objective or any military objective during MMOs where the use of force may cause disproportionate damage to the environment.[74] While there is some debate as to what is proportionate, 'States generally accept the principle but avoid providing information on its precise application'.[75] According to Jacobsson, the interpretation of the principle should be conducted 'with a bona fide outcome in mind'.[76] In any event, what

[65] MN Schmitt, 'Green War: An Assessment of the Environmental Law of International Armed Conflict' (1997) 22 Yale Journal of International Law 61–62 (on applicability of this principle to the environment).

[66] Reaffirmed in Article 48 AP I and in *Legality of the Threat or Use of Nuclear Weapons* (Advisory Opinion) [1996] ICJ Rep 95, 257, para 78.

[67] Article 52(2) AP I: 'military objectives are limited to those objects which by their nature, location, purpose or use make an effective contribution to military action and whose total or partial destruction, capture or neutralization, in the circumstances ruling at the time, offers a definite military advantage'.

[68] Article 48 AP I.

[69] Civilian objects could include private land, crops, and natural resources. See Jacobsson, 'Second Report' (n 8) 48.

[70] ibid 49.

[71] ibid.

[72] 'Proportionality' does not expressly appear in any IHL treaty, but has an established place within the laws of war. For the essence of this principle, see Articles 51(5)(b) and 57(2) AP I and Article 8(2)(b)(iv) ICCSt.

[73] *Nuclear Weapons* (n 66) para 30.

[74] See Schmitt (n 65) 55–61 (on applicability of this principle to the environment).

[75] Jacobsson, 'Second Report' (n 8) 52.

[76] ibid.

constitutes 'proportionality' in terms of warfare is likely to change and develop over time.[77]

The principle of precautions in attack under IHL differs from and is not to be confused with the precautionary principle or approach under international environmental law (IEL). The obligation to take precautions in attacks is an important element of IHL aimed at protecting the civilian population, individual civilians, and civilian objects from the effects of attacks.[78] This principle is codified in Article 57(2) AP I which lists the types of or what is meant by such precautions that are required to be taken in the conduct of military operations. While Article 57(2) does not expressly mention the environment, the care required in such attacks to spare the civilian population or individual civilian from incidental loss of life, injury, and damage, could indirectly protect the environment (eg deciding not to bomb a chemical factory in order to prevent injury or loss of life to civilians would also spare the environment from any resulting pollution) and direct protection 'to the extent that the environment is considered a civilian object'.[79] Rule 44 of the ICRC study that addresses the obligation of due regard for the natural environment in military operations, on the other hand, requires all feasible precautions to be taken in the context of the environment specifically and also adds that lack of scientific certainty as to the effects of military operations on the environment does not negate the obligation to take such precaution.[80] Article 57 AP I, which also mentions taking 'feasible precautions',[81] does not provide a definition for it, but as Jacobsson notes, it 'has to be applied in the context of other legal rules'.[82] For example, 'feasible precautions' is defined in Protocol II of the Conventional Weapons Convention as 'those precautions which are practicable or practically possible taking into account all circumstances ruling at the time, including humanitarian and military considerations'.[83] In short, this principle only allows for the targeting of military objectives and requires military operations to take care in their attacks in order to avoid undue harm.

These customary IHL principles are, however, still subject to divergent understandings between states on how these principles are applicable. States, for instance, have diverging interpretations of what is a 'military objective' that may be legitimately targeted or attacked. The United States, for example, has a broader interpretation of what may constitute a military objective than many other states,

[77] ibid.
[78] ICRC, 'Rule 15. Precautions in Attack' (*Customary IHL*) <http://www.icrc.org/customary-ihl/eng/docs/v1_cha_chapter5_rule15>.
[79] Jacobsson, 'Second Report' (n 8) 50.
[80] ICRC, 'Rule 44. Due Regard for the Natural Environment in Military Operations' (*Customary IHL*) <http://www.icrc.org/customary-ihl/eng/docs/v1_rul_rule44>. See also Jacobsson, 'Second Report' (n 8) 53–55.
[81] States have expressed their interpretation of the term. See Jacobsson, 'Second Report' (n 8) 51 (see fn 235).
[82] ibid 50.
[83] See Article 3(10).

including its NATO allies.[84] The consequences are that while some states during a MMO may consider a certain object to be a civilian object, the United States may consider it to be a legitimate military target. This means less protection for the environment if broader interpretations of military objectives are taken.

In addition, all four fundamental IHL principles are subject to the principle of military necessity. Today, military necessity is recognized to permit 'only that degree and kind of force, not otherwise prohibited by the law of armed conflict, that is required in order to achieve the legitimate purpose of the conflict, namely the complete or partial submission of the enemy at the earliest possible moment with minimum expenditure of life and resources'.[85] In an environmental context, any military target or means and methods of warfare, whether it is an environmental target or means and methods that may affect the environment, is subject to this principle.[86] While there is a 'general duty for the military to avoid unnecessary damage to the environment and a general prohibition of environmental destruction not required by military necessity',[87] there is still a discretionary element to this principle. Military necessity is the reasonable judgement of a military commander in the heat of battle.[88] Therefore, reliance on this provision for environmental protection is subjective.[89]

These customary IHL principles are reflected in the recent ILC draft principles aimed at enhancing the protection of the environment in relation to AC.[90] The draft principles are understood to apply to both IACs and NIACs, covering the period before, during, and after conflict.[91] Draft Principle 9 aims at clarifying the protection of the natural environment in the context of the principle of distinction and the possible applicability of other bodies of law within the international law framework; Draft Principle 10 provides that LOAC including principles of

[84] Zwanenburg (n 2) 692–93.

[85] See UK: Ministry of Defence, *The Manual of the Law of Armed Conflict* (OUP 2004) Section 2.2 (Military Necessity). Similar interpretations are provided in other glossaries and military manuals. See, eg, NATO, Glossary of Terms and Definitions (AAP-6V) 2-M-5; US: Department of the Army, 'The Law of Land Warfare' (18 July 1956) Field Manual 27-10, para 3; France: Ministry of Defence, 'Manuel de Droit des Conflits Armés' (2001), 86 et seq.

[86] Schmitt (n 65) 52–55 (on applicability of this principle to the environment).

[87] MP Nevitt, 'Environmental Law in Military Operations' in GS Corn and others (eds), *U.S. Military Operations* (OUP 2016) 423.

[88] M Nishimura Hayashi, 'The Martens Clause and Military Necessity' in HM Hensel (ed), *The Legitimate Use of Military Force* (Ashgate Publishing 2008) 139–40.

[89] See *The Hostages* case (n 52) 1295–97: concluding that 'although, in retrospect, [the German] General Rendulic may have erred in his assessment of military necessity, he was not guilty of a criminal act because the doctrine of military necessity may be justified by one's reasonable assessment of the situation'.

[90] Part One (Preventive Measures) contains five principles applicable pre-conflict, Part Two contains five draft principles applicable during armed conflict and Part Three contains five draft principles applicable post-conflict. See M Lehto, 'First report on protection of the environment in relation to armed conflict' (30 April 2018) A/CN/.4/720, Annex, 65–67. For commentary on the Draft Articles, see ILC, 'Statement of the Chairman of the Drafting Committee, Mr Mathias Forteau' (67th session, 30 July 2015) A/CN.4/SR.3281.

[91] See Forteau, 'Statement of Chairman' (n 90) 4.

distinction, proportionality, military necessity, and precautions in attack shall be applied to protect the natural environment; Draft Principle 11 provides the need to take into consideration the environment when applying the principles of proportionality and military necessity; Draft Principle 12 prohibits reprisal attacks on the natural environment; and Draft Principle 13 designates protected important environmental and cultural zones by agreement, subject to the presence of any military objective.[92] While the ILC's draft principles are work in progress and not legally binding at present, they do provide suggested guiding principles and contribute to the discourse on environmental protection relevant to AC.

The relevant rules within IHL do theoretically protect the environment during AC to some extent and such protection could, if respected, lessen the negative impact on the environment and civilian population during MMOs. However, there are not only flaws in the existing laws of warfare providing environmental protection but also in the applicability of those laws during MMOs. The following section therefore considers the possibility of other legal frameworks providing environmental protection during MMOs, and section 5 explores the way forward in meeting challenges of legal interoperability during MMOs to better protect the environment.

4. Opportunities from a Legal Pluriverse: Application of Other Legal Regimes during MMOs

Jacobsson states that 'modern international law recognises that the international law applicable during armed conflict may be wider than the laws of warfare'.[93] The ILC, in its work on 'the Effects of Armed Conflicts on Treaties',[94] concludes that 'the existence of armed conflict does not necessarily terminate or suspend the operation of treaties'.[95] It should, however, be noted that the ILC's work on the effects of armed conflict on treaties only provides guidance on the regulation of inter-state treaty relations and does not set out what CIL norms or principles of international law continue to apply in times of AC.[96] Nonetheless, an array of treaties that provide important protection to the environment during peacetime may continue to operate during AC. However, whether or not a treaty continues to operate during AC is ascertained 'by a complex body of different considerations: express provisions and subject matter of the treaty, treaty interpretation according to Articles 31

[92] ibid 6–10 (for commentary on the reformulated principles).

[93] ILC, 'Report of the International Law Commission on the Work of its 63rd Session' (26 April–3 June and 4 July–12 August 2011) UN Doc A/66/10, Annex E, para 2.

[94] 'Draft Articles on the Effects of Armed Conflict on Treaties, with Commentaries' (adopted at the 63rd session of the ILC, 2011).

[95] ILC, 'Report of the International Law Commission on the Work of its 59th Session' (7 May–5 June and 9 July–10 August 2007) UNGA Supp A/62/10, paras 266–324.

[96] Jacobsson, 'Second Report' (n 8) 30.

and 32 of the Vienna Convention on the Law of Treaties (VCLT) of 23 May 1969, the nature and extent of the armed conflict, and the effect of the armed conflict in the treaty.'[97] In practice, this is to be determined on a case-by-case basis.[98] This section therefore explores other legal regimes that may provide protection to the environment during the 'in conflict' stage of MMOs.

4.1 International criminal law

The Annex of the ILC's draft articles on the 'effects of armed conflicts on treaties' (ILC's Annex) sets out an indicative list of treaty categories (including an international criminal justice category)[99] with the implication that they continue to operate (in whole or in part) during AC.[100] The Rome Statute,[101] which established the International Criminal Court (ICC), is specifically mentioned in the ILC's Annex[102] and contains an express provision within its definition of war crimes that offers protection to the environment during AC. Article 8(2)(b)(iv) of the Statute includes within acts of serious violations of the law and customs applicable in IAC the act of:

> Intentionally launching an attack in the knowledge that such attack will cause ... widespread, long-term and severe damage to the natural environment which would be clearly excessive in relation to the concrete and direct overall military advantage anticipated.

Such action damaging the environment may therefore constitute a war crime under the Statute. However, while the wording of the Rome Statute is similar to the relevant AP I provisions,[103] it seems that standards for protecting the environment during AC under this international criminal law (ICL) provision differs from the relevant provisions within IHL. According to Jacobsson, compromises were made with regard to several provisions within the Statute including Article 8(2)(b)(iv) 'so as to ensure that ICC judges do not apply the standard too strictly and put themselves in the military commanders shoes ex-post'.[104] Therefore, to attach accountability to serious violations (war crimes) in AC, Jacobsson clarifies that Article 8(2)(b)(iv) not only 'imports a standard of military necessity much higher

[97] Bothe (n 7) 580.
[98] ibid (citing ILC, Effects of Armed Conflicts on Treaties, 6 June 2008, Article 4).
[99] Draft Articles (n 94) Annex, Section (d) para 22.
[100] ibid Annex.
[101] Rome Statute of the ICC (adopted 17 July 1998, entered into force 1 July 2002) A/CONF.138/9 (ICCSt).
[102] Draft Articles (n 94) Annex, Section (d) para 22.
[103] See Articles 35(3) and 55 AP I.
[104] Jacobsson, 'Second Report' (n 8) 41.

than that traditionally understood by IHL', but that the terms 'clearly excessive' and 'overall military advantage' within the provision are also not the standards used within IHL.[105]

There are also jurisdictional limitations, namely that Article 8(2)(b)(iv) only protects the environment in IACs and the Statute does not provide a corresponding provision applicable in NIACs.[106] This omission of direct protection for the environment in NIACs restricts environmental protection during MMOs, as such operations very often take place in NIAC situations. Therefore, environmental protection in NIACs would have to be achieved indirectly. That means in order to secure any prosecution for environmental crimes under the Statute, as Hellestveit notes, 'it would have to be prosecuted for instance as a crime against humanity (murder or extermination), or as war crimes of direct targeting of the civilian population [8(2)(i)] or wanton destruction of property [8(2)(e)(xii)]'.[107] A further limitation is that not all parties are signatories to it.[108] The United States, for example, has neither signed nor ratified it. Therefore, while some states are bound by the Statute, other TCNs during MMOs are not, thereby contributing to the issue of diverse legal obligations in MMOs.

4.2 International environmental law

IEL is a body of international law that is relatively new compared to the IHL regime. However, IEL has developed extensively over the last few decades, providing an established framework of laws, standards, and mechanisms that regulate and protect the environment.[109] Increasing global environmental concerns, IEL's dynamic growth and the considerable environmental destruction in the first Gulf War sparked renewed debate on the applicability of IEL during AC.[110]

With a few exceptions,[111] most environmental treaties do not contain explicit provisions on whether they apply during AC. Most environmental treaties are

[105] ibid.
[106] See Article 8(2)(c) ICCSt.
[107] C Hellestveit, 'Some Perspectives on Challenges regarding Current Implementation of Existing Rules' in International Law and Policy Institute (ILPI), 'Protection of the Environment in Times of Armed Conflict' Report from the Expert Meeting on Protection of the Environment in times of Armed Conflict (Helsinki 14–15 September 2015), section 2.3.1.
[108] As of 5 June 2018, only 138 States have signed up. See UN Treaty Collection, 'Rome Statute of the International Criminal Court' <https://treaties.un.org/pages/ViewDetails.aspx?src=IND&mtdsg_no=XVIII-10&chapter=18&lang=en>.
[109] Bothe (n 7) 579.
[110] ILC, 'Memorandum by the Secretariat' (2 May–3 June and 4 July–5 August) UN Doc A/CN.4/550 + Corr.1 + Corr.2, 60, para 105.
[111] See eg, UN Convention of the Law of the Sea (UNCLOS) (adopted 10 December 1982, entered into force 16 November 1994) 1833 UNTS 3 specifies that the Area is used 'exclusively for peaceful purposes' (Article 141); Convention on the Law of the Non-navigational Uses of International Watercourses (adopted 21 May 1997, entered into force 17 August 2014) UN Doc A/51/869 expressly

silent on this issue.[112] This leaves the issue of applicability in AC in considerable uncertainty. Moreover, the *Nuclear Weapons* Advisory Opinion highlights the lack of consensus 'on the proposition that all environmental treaties apply both in peace and in time of armed conflict, subject to express provisions indicating the contrary'.[113] The ICJ did not resolve this issue but instead took the middle ground by stating that:

> [T]he issue is not whether the treaties relating to the protection of the environment are or are not applicable during an armed conflict, but rather whether the obligations stemming from these treaties were intended to be obligations of total restraint during military conflict.
> The Court does not consider that the treaties in question could have intended to deprive a State of the exercise of its right of self-defence under international law because of its obligations to protect the environment. Nonetheless, States must take environmental considerations into account when assessing what is necessary and proportionate in the pursuit of legitimate military objectives. Respect for the environment is one of the elements that go to assessing whether an action is in conformity with the principles of necessity and proportionality.[114]

The ICJ did, however, bring in IEL by observing that Principle 24 of the Rio Declaration together with Articles 35(3) and 55 AP I 'embody a general obligation to protect the natural environment against widespread, long-term and severe environmental damage; the prohibition of methods and means of warfare which are intended or may be expected, to cause such damage; and the prohibition of attacks against the natural environment by way of reprisals'.[115] Principle 24 of the Rio Declaration which urges states to 'respect international law by providing protection for the environment in times of armed conflict and cooperate in its further development, as necessary', does not clarify whether IEL is applicable during AC. In addition, the ICJ's 'general obligation' approach[116] with regard to the relevant provisions above, providing constraints to harming the environment during AC—including the threshold set out for environmental damage of 'widespread, long-term and severe' which echoes the threshold within IHL[117]—seems to embody LOAC with no reflection of IEL's prevention or precautionary principles.[118]

provides that international watercourses and related installations shall be protected according to the rules of international law applicable to IAC and NIAC (Article 29).

[112] Draft Articles (n 94) Annex, Section (g) para 52.
[113] ibid para 53 (citing Secretariat Memorandum (A/CN.4/550) paras 58–63).
[114] *Nuclear Weapons* (n 66) para 30.
[115] ibid para 31.
[116] ibid.
[117] See, eg, Articles 35(3) and 55 AP I.
[118] E Hey, *Advanced Introduction to International Environmental Law* (Edward Elgar 2016) 131–32.

Nevertheless, in its work on the 'effects of armed conflicts on treaties', notwithstanding the lack of general agreement on the specific legal question of the applicability of environmental treaties in AC, the ILC argues that the ICJ's views in *Nuclear Weapons* are significant in providing 'general and indirect support for the use of a presumption that environmental treaties apply in case of armed conflict'.[119] Though not completely clear with regard to how and to what extent environmental treaties apply, by requiring environmental considerations to be taken into account in the pursuit of military objectives and bringing in an element of IEL, the ICJ does to some extent suggest 'a framework for the application of IEL during conflict'.[120]

With regard to the applicability of IEL principles and concepts during AC, Jacobsson argues that 'environmental law principles and concepts that are of relevance to the present topic are imprecise and vague and seldom offer clear-cut answers and solutions'.[121] While IEL principles and concepts such as sustainable development, polluter pays, and precaution, for example, are important within IEL, there are still diverging views and uncertainty as to their applicability (eg being vague and imprecise) and customary law status.[122] While such principles and concepts may be applicable pre- and post-conflict[123] during MMOs (in many cases in a non-binding capacity unless they are already part of customary IEL), it is not at all certain to what extent such principles and concepts apply during the conflict phase.

In reality, although environmental treaties and customary IEL are binding, they may vary in their application during AC.[124] According to Bothe and others, '[t]his distinction may stem in part from the difficulty of determining whether a specific measure is customary international law and what its precise legal scope is'.[125] While IEL could be useful for additional environmental protection during MMOs, MMOs with their existing problems of diverging legal obligations in IHL applicability would very likely face the same problem with IEL. Therefore, it seems unlikely at present that TCNs in MMOs would choose to apply any ambiguous rules of IEL during conflict. In any event, while there is growing support amongst scholars that peacetime IEL should be applicable during AC,[126] states are still divided on this issue.[127]

[119] Draft Articles (n 94) Annex, Section (g), para (55) (footnote omitted).

[120] UNEP (n 7) 25.

[121] Jacobsson, 'First Report' (n 4) 32.

[122] See, eg, P Sands and others, *Principles of International Environmental Law* (3rd edn, CUP 2012) 206–29.

[123] Jacobsson, 'First Report' (n 4) 31–42 (merely sets out principles and concepts in international law that are 'candidates for continuing application during armed conflict' and does not address the extent of their applicability in AC).

[124] Bothe (n 7) 588.

[125] ibid.

[126] See, eg, S Vöneky, 'Peacetime Environmental Law as a Basis of State Responsibility for Environmental Damage Caused by War' in JE Austin and CE Bruch (eds), *The Environmental Consequences of War: Legal Economic and Scientific Perspectives* (CUP 2000) 194; Bothe (n 7) 569.

[127] See ILC, 'Report of the International Law Commission on the Work of its 66th session' (5 May–6 June and 7 July–8 August 2014) UN Doc A/69/10, Chapter XI: 'Protection of the Environment in relation to Armed Conflicts', 252–53.

4.3 International human rights law

It is indisputable that a damaged environment, as a result of conflict or otherwise, could interfere with the enjoyment of human rights. However, there is still uncertainty surrounding the universal acceptance of a substantive human right to a clean environment.[128] Therefore, at present, enjoyment of a clean environment is secured indirectly via other established human rights, such as the rights to food, health, and acceptable living conditions.[129]

International human rights law (IHRL) may provide additional guidance on conduct during any 'in conflict' stage of MMOs affecting the environment. After all, failing to protect the environment during AC could give rise to human rights violations. For example, Special Rapporteur Walter Kälin, in the 'Report on the situation of human rights in Kuwait under Iraqi occupation', expressed the view that the degradation of health as a consequence of Iraqi forces burning Kuwaiti oil wells may amount to human rights violations.[130] The report recognized that '[w]arfare often affects the natural environment; such consequences do not *per se* constitute human rights violations',[131] but went on to conclude that:

> [N]ot only in peacetime but also in times of armed conflict, the deliberate causing of large-scale environmental damage which severely affects the health of a considerable proportion of the population concerned, or creates risks for the health of future generations, amounts to a serious violation of the right to the enjoyment of the highest attainable standard of health as embodied in article 12 of the International Covenant on Economic, Social and Cultural Rights.[132]

This shows that IHRL can provide indirect environmental protection during AC. Nevertheless, the debate on whether IHRL applies during AC,[133] including in relation to protection of the environment, continues.[134] This is because as with IEL, questions arise as to its applicability during AC, be it international or non-international.[135] As Jha notes, '[t]here has been significant difficulty in resolving

[128] DK Anton and DL Shelton, *Environmental Protection and Human Rights* (CUP 2011) 139–44.

[129] Jacobsson, 'First Report' (n 4) 42.

[130] Report on the situation of human rights in Kuwait under Iraqi occupation, prepared by Mr Walter Kälin, Special Rapporteur of the Commission on Human Rights, in accordance with Commission resolution 1991/67 (16 January 1992) UN Doc E/CN.4/1992/26, paras 201–09.

[131] ibid para 208.

[132] ibid. See also L Doswald-Beck, *Human Rights in Times of Conflict and Terrorism* (OUP 2011) 486.

[133] See, eg, N Lubell, 'Challenges in Applying Human Rights Law to Armed Conflict' (2005) 87(860) International Review of the Red Cross 737; G Oberleitner, *Human Rights in Armed Conflict: Law, Practice and Policy* (CUP 2015).

[134] See, eg, UNEP (n 7) 48–50.

[135] UC Jha, *Armed Conflict and Environmental Damage* (Vij Books 2014) 252 (footnotes omitted).

this perceived incompatibility, particularly during NIAC, when it is unclear whether armed conflict is actually taking place'.[136] Droege and Tougas, on the other hand, argue that 'it is by now fairly uncontroversial that [IHRL] continues to apply during armed conflicts'.[137]

The ILC recognizes the possibility of a close link between human rights and IHL,[138] referring to the ICJ's statement in the *Legal Consequences of the Construction of a Wall in the Occupied Palestinian Territory* (Advisory Opinion).[139] In this case, the ICJ addresses the relationship between IHL and IHRL and the applicability of IHRL in extraterritorial circumstances:

> The protection offered by human rights conventions does not cease in case of armed conflict, save through the effect of provisions for derogation of the kind to be found in article 4 of the International Covenant on Civil and Political Rights. As regards the relationship between international humanitarian law and human rights law, there are thus three possible situations: some rights may be exclusively matters of international humanitarian law; others may be exclusively matters of human rights law; yet others may be matters of both these branches of international law. In order to answer the question put to it, the Court will have to take into consideration both these branches of international law, namely human rights law and, as *lex specialis*, international humanitarian law.[140]

The ILC report's reference to the ICJ's recurring statement and statements by other courts on the applicability of human rights in times of AC[141] indicates that protection of the environment through IHRL during AC depends on the circumstances.[142] Coupled with the fact that some states consistently reject the application of IHRL treaties in extraterritorial military operations,[143] this illustrates the need for further research, perhaps more examples of state practice or case law in

[136] ibid.

[137] C Dröge and ML Tougas, 'The Protection of the Natural Environment in Armed Conflict—Existing Rules and Need for Further Legal Protection' in R Rayfuse (ed), *War and the Environment: New Approaches to Protecting the Environment in Relation to Armed Conflict* (Koninklijke Brill NV 2014) 39.

[138] See Jacobsson, 'Second Report' (n 8) 27. See also Draft Articles (n 94) Annex, Section (f) para 49 (that 'non-derogable human rights provisions are applicable during armed conflict' (footnote omitted)).

[139] [2004] ICJ Rep 2004, para 106.

[140] ibid. The Court also quotes this passage in *Armed Activities on the Territory of the Congo (Democratic Republic of the Congo v Uganda)* (Judgment) [2005] ICJ Rep 2005, para 216.

[141] In the context of armed conflict and considerations of humanity, see, eg, *Corfu Channel Case* (Judgment) [1949] ICJ Rep 1949, 22; *Military and Paramilitary Activities in and against Nicaragua (Nicaragua v United States of America)* (Merits) [1986] ICJ Rep 1986, para 218. See also International Criminal Tribunal of Rwanda (ICTR), *Prosecutor v Clément Kayishema et al Trial Chamber* (Judgment) ICTR-95-1-T (21 May 1999) para 622 ('It should be stressed that in war time international humanitarian law coexists with human rights law, certain provisions of which cannot be derogated from').

[142] For a more detailed discussion see Jacobsson, 'Second Report' (n 8) 26–28.

[143] J Hartmann, 'The Copenhagen Process: Principles and Guidelines' in TD Gill (ed), *2013 Yearbook of International Humanitarian Law* (Springer 2015) 11.

applying IHRL in situations of AC.[144] At present, such uncertainty combined with problems of legal interoperability besieged by MMOs means it would be difficult to protect the environment in conflict via IHRL during MMOs.

5. Overcoming Legal Interoperability Challenges

While the IHL regime is considered *lex specialis* during conflict, there are gaps in the law as regards protecting the environment. Other bodies of international law (eg ICL, IEL, and IHRL) that are growing at a more dynamic pace could provide complementary protection to the environment during AC or at least fill the gaps left by IHL. However, applicability of these other regimes is far from certain and still being debated. This uncertainty is further compounded by the challenges of legal interoperability within MMOs, particularly the issue of diverse legal obligations regarding IHL applicability. There are, however, a number of ways that challenges to legal interoperability can be mitigated.

First, interoperability could be achieved through TCNs in a particular MMO setting forth common declarations to key provisions of IHL treaties. This could contribute to a more universal interpretation of a particular IHL provision. This first applies to IHL treaties where the TCNs are parties to or IHL provisions that are part of CIL. In addition, common interpretative declarations regarding particular provisions or terms within IHL, such as 'military objective' or 'military advantage', could prove useful to TCNs to guide them in respecting IHL in order to protect the environment during AC. Such harmonization would mean that there would be more uniformity in protecting the environment. Of course, the extent of such protection would depend on the interpretation agreed on. If states agree on a broader interpretation of what constitutes a 'military advantage' or 'military objective', environmental protection would be minimal. If states could agree on a narrower interpretation, however, the environment stands a chance of wider protection during MMOs.

Secondly, states participating in a MMO could set out a common framework, agreeing that some states apply some provisions or norms of law as a matter of policy. For instance, Fleck notes that '[i]n multinational military operations, non-parties to AP I have applied its protection standards for policy reasons, thus demonstrating that the alleged "great schism" between parties and non-parties to the Protocol which at times still dominates academic debates is not insurmountable in reality'.[145] For states not legally bound by certain provisions, taking the approach of applying the relevant norms as policy instead of law, can contribute to

144 See the respective chapters in this volume.

145 See D Fleck, 'Introduction' in D Fleck (ed), *The Handbook of International Humanitarian Law* (3rd edn, OUP 2013) xi (referring to the 1991 Gulf War where the United States fought alongside a coalition of twenty-six states where no common legal obligation of AP I existed. Yet, White House press

harmonizing 'divergent views on whether IHL is applicable in a particular situation'.[146] This could ensure that the environment is protected to the same degree among the TCNs in an MMO.

Thirdly, MMOs could integrate environmental protection considerations into their planning. This could include environmental considerations for any 'in conflict' situation. NATO, for example, through its Standardization Agreement (STANAG) No 7141,[147] incorporates environmental concerns within NATO operations. While NATO commanders are required to consider environmental protection during each stage of a military operation, these NATO environmental agreements are guidelines in reality, stopping 'short of requiring participating nations to fund or undertake specific actions that are not legally prescribed'.[148] Nevertheless, these guidelines do inform decision-making during NATO operations,[149] thus providing some protection for the environment during MMOs.

Finally, moving beyond policy and IHL, TCNs could set out specific environmental protection provisions in any legally binding agreements that govern the MMO concerned. In doing so, TCNs would be legally bound by the environmental protection terms set out in the agreements. Interestingly, incorporating environmental protection provisions is encouraged by the ILC as illustrated by Draft Principle 7 which provides that 'States and international organizations should, as appropriate, include provisions on environmental protection in agreements concerning the presence of military forces in relation to armed conflict'.[150] The ILC's Drafting Committee recognizes that the requirements under this draft principle do not correspond to any specific obligation under international law, but reflect an emerging trend among states and international organizations in relation to military operations.[151]

releases on aerial bombardment in Iraq commonly used the language of Article 51(5) AP I and the 'Chairman of the U.S. Joint Chiefs of Staff in his Report to Congress on Coalition operations in the Gulf, had gone even further in stating that the provisions of AP I were, for the main part, applied as if they constituted customary law'). See also Department of Defense, 'Conduct of the Persian Gulf War: final report to Congress' (April 1992) Govt Doc Number D 1.2:P 43/2, 700.

[146] Zwanenburg (n 2) 700 (refers to the Netherlands and the United States as examples).

[147] See NATO, *Standardization Agreement, STANAG 7141: Joint NATO Doctrine for Environmental Protection During NATO Led Military Activities* (7th edn, NATO 2018).

[148] Nevitt (n 87) 424.

[149] ibid.

[150] Lehto, 'First Report' (n 90) 65–67.

[151] For commentary on Draft Article 7, see 'Statement of the Chairman of the Drafting Committee: 68th session' (2 June 2016) available at <http://legal.un.org/docs/?path=../ilc/documentation/english/statements/2016_dc_chairman_statement_icil.pdf&lang=E>, 5–7. See also D Weir, 'Reframing the Remnants of War: The Role of the International Law Commission, Governments, and Society' in C Stahn and others (eds), *Environmental Protection and Transitions from Conflict to Peace* (OUP 2017) 451.

6. Conclusion

Flaws within IHL in protecting the environment during AC illustrate that it is no longer sufficient to only look towards IHL. Protection of the environment in the complex world of modern AC and MMOs may be better served by looking toward a legal pluriverse, that is, other international legal regimes (ICL, IEL, and IHRL), to complement protection provided by IHL as opposed to relying solely on the narrow scope of IHL rules and principles. Of course, more clarity is needed not only regarding environmental protection under IHL but also the applicability of these other bodies of international law in protecting the environment during AC and their relationship with IHL.

However, while looking towards a legal pluriverse to better protect the environment in times of AC is desirable, the complexities involved in MMOs highlight the challenges in relation to this. MMOs' legal interoperability problems, which includes conflict classification and diverse legal obligations—particularly divergent interpretations by TCNs in the application of IHL provisions—showcase the difficulty in protecting the environment during the 'in conflict' stage of MMOs via IHL, let alone through other legal regimes. Nevertheless, the environment must not be ignored. As seen from various military operations throughout the years, the environmental consequences can be extremely damaging. As MMOs become the norm, TCNs must strive to achieve effective legal interoperability in order to improve environmental protection during AC. This includes moving beyond existing IHL to do so.

17
Multinational Military Operations at Sea

Anna Petrig

1. Introduction

Multinational military operations have extended to the sea. With the deployment of three multinational forces to counter piracy off the coast of Somalia a decade ago, the first truly internationalized law enforcement operation at sea went into effect. At the time of writing, EU-led naval forces, with the support of NATO forces, are working towards the suppression of migrant smuggling and human trafficking in the Mediterranean and enforcing the arms embargo imposed by the Security Council on Libya. These operations mirror the changing security landscape, one in which criminal activity by non-state actors is steadily becoming a main security threat. This altered landscape has led to a new role for navies where they are increasingly engaged in policing the sea—that is, missions 'other than war'. This chapter describes the 'legal pluriverse' in which such multinational law enforcement operations at sea take place and proceeds in three steps. First, the legal paradigm governing these operations is identified, which is clearly peacetime law rather than the law of armed conflicts at sea (section 2). Secondly, the chapter takes stock of the rules authorizing multinational forces and/or contributing states to enforce the law at sea (section 3). In a last step, the legal bases imposing strictures on the exercise of these enforcement powers are carved out (section 4).

2. Changing Security Landscape, Changing Role for (Multinational) Naval Forces

It has been suggested, and will be explained in further detail now, that the security landscape has changed considerably since the turn of the millennium—and this holds true in the maritime setting as well (section 2.1). With classic interstate conflicts at sea fading from the spotlight and the suppression of transnational crime coming to the fore, the traditional war-related role of navies has slowly but steadily been supplanted by a new function: policing the sea. This new role is more often than not carried out by navies working together, either as naval coalitions or as highly integrated naval forces of regional organizations (section 2.2).

Anna Petrig, *Multinational Military Operations at Sea* In *The 'Legal Pluriverse' Surrounding Multinational Military Operations*. Edited by Robin Geiß and Heike Krieger, Oxford University Press (2020).
DOI: 10.1093/oso/9780198842965.003.0018

2.1 Maritime threats emanating from non-state actors

Before the end of the Cold War, the main scenario envisaged by maritime strategists was an interstate conflict at sea. In today's globalized world, by contrast, the maritime security challenges are considerably more diverse. In particular, illegal acts committed by non-state actors at sea have entered the limelight.[1] The concept of 'maritime security' began to emerge following a spate of terrorist attacks against vessels occurring in the wake of 9/11,[2] and the rise of Somali-based piracy after 2006 ultimately brought it to the forefront.[3] In its 2008 Report on Oceans and the Law of the Sea, the Secretary-General identified seven specific threats to maritime security: piracy and armed robbery; terrorist acts involving shipping, offshore installations, and other maritime interests; illicit trafficking in arms and weapons of mass destruction; illicit trafficking in narcotic drugs and psychotropic substances; smuggling and trafficking of persons by sea; illegal, unreported, and unregulated fishing; and intentional and unlawful damage to the marine environment.[4]

Most of these criminal phenomena occur in regional settings, yet their effects may go well beyond the *locus delicti* and affect distant societies. For example, Somali pirates (initially) operated within very limited geographical parameters, but the attacks affected a critical sea lane, and piracy—perceived as a threat 'to international navigation and the safety of commercial maritime routes, and to other vulnerable ships'—even prompted action by the Security Council.[5] The other security threats addressed in the Secretary-General's Report also illustrate what is referred to as globalization of security, meaning that states engage in constabulary action in distant theatres in order to defend their own security—especially in situations where the coastal or flag state is unwilling and/or unable to enforce the law itself.[6] Hence, the 'home game' of security, that is, law enforcement by a state in its own waters or against its own vessels, was expanded to an 'away game'[7] that aims at securing access to the sea, one of the global commons,[8] and protecting the maritime transportation systems as a whole rather than solely their own merchant fleet.[9]

[1] NATO Parliamentary Assembly, 'Maritime Security, NATO and EU Roles and Co-ordination' (Committee Report, 207 CDS 10Ebis, 19 November 2010) paras 6, 8, 15. <http://www.ft.dk/samling/20101/almdel/npa/bilag/5/925749.pdf>. All URLs accessed 27 December 2018.

[2] On these and other terrorist attacks against ships, see G Till, *Seapower: A Guide for the Twenty-First Century* (3rd edn, Routledge 2013) 292–93.

[3] C Bueger, 'What is Maritime Security?' (2015) 53 Marine Policy 159, 159.

[4] UNGA, 'Oceans and the law of the sea: Report of the Secretary-General' (10 March 2008) UN Doc A/63/63, paras 54–113.

[5] UNSC Res 1846 (2 December 2008) UN Doc S/RES/1846, preambular para 2.

[6] NATO Parliamentary Assembly (n 1) para 18.

[7] Till (n 2) 283.

[8] JG Gade and PS Hilde, 'NATO and the Maritime Domain' in JI Bekkevold and G Till (eds), *International Order at Sea* (Palgrave MacMillan 2016) 120.

[9] IT Luke, 'Naval Operations in Peacetime: Not Just "Warfare Lite"' (2013) 66 Naval War College Review 11, 13.

2.2 (Cooperating) navies as main actors in the 'away game'

As a general rule, only navies have the operational capacity to engage in the 'away game' and to sustain law enforcement operations at sea in distant theatres over longer periods of time. This is due to the simple fact that civilian agencies—in many states, the coast guard—rarely possess ocean-going vessels. This, taken together with the changing security landscape at sea, means that navies today are increasingly involved in missions 'other than war', which differ from traditional military tasks (ie conduct of hostilities) and pertain to the criminal rather than the military domain. In short, navies are conducting policing functions (ie law enforcement),[10] and for some navies, constabulary operations are even their principal employment.[11]

Depending on the division of tasks between civilian and military agencies under domestic law, navies traditionally fulfil certain constabulary tasks, such as the enforcement of customs, immigration and fisheries law.[12] These 'home game' enforcement activities are generally carried out in waters under the sovereignty of the enforcing state or against ships flying its flag—and by that state alone.[13] Maritime law enforcement operations discussed here differ in at least two respects. First, they take place in international waters (and, at times, even in the internal and territorial waters of third states as evidenced by the Somali counter-piracy operations) or against foreign-flagged vessels. Secondly, they are carried out collectively with other states and/or regional organizations in varying degrees of concertation and cooperation, as generally no single state has the resources necessary to counter contemporary maritime security threats.[14]

Such cooperation is encouraged by treaties aimed at suppressing transnational crime and by the law of the sea, which is said to have shifted from a paradigm of separation (preventing naval warfare by keeping maritime powers apart) to one of cooperation (bringing navies together to pursue matters of common interest).[15] Yet, cooperation duties are either qualified[16] or non-mandatory from the

[10] M Tondini, 'The Use of Force in the Course of Maritime Law Enforcement Operations' (2017) 4 Journal on the Use of Force and International Law 253, 253 and 256–57; Luke (n 9) 12; J Kraska and R Pedrozo, *International Maritime Security Law* (Martinus Nijhoff 2013) 49.

[11] S Haines, 'War at Sea: Nineteenth-Century Laws for Twenty-first Century Wars?' (2016) 98 International Review of the Red Cross 419, 424.

[12] Eg the Canadian Royal Navy: see B Lombardi, 'The Future Maritime Operating Environment and the Role of Naval Power' (Defence Research and Development Canada, DRDC-RDDC-2016-R085, May 2016) 69 <http://cradpdf.drdc-rddc.gc.ca/PDFS/unc229/p803867_A1b.pdf>.

[13] Cooperation between neighbouring states is not unusual (see, eg, Integrated Cross-border Law Enforcement Operations Act (Statutes of Canada 2012, chap 19, sec 368)); yet this is not truly internationalized law enforcement as contemplated here.

[14] NATO (n 1) para 18; Bueger (n 3) 163.

[15] J Kraska, 'Grasping "The Influence of Law on Sea Power"' (2009) 62 Naval War College Review 113, 113.

[16] Eg Article 100 of the United Nations Convention on the Law of the Sea (adopted 10 December 1982, entered into force 16 November 1994) 1833 UNTS 3 (UNCLOS) ('to the fullest extent possible'); Article 7 of the Protocol against the Smuggling of Migrants by Land, Sea and Air, supplementing the

outset.[17] What is more, mounting a multinational operation—the most far-reaching form of cooperation, defined as 'military actions conducted by forces of two or more nations, usually undertaken within the structure of a coalition or alliance'[18]—is determined by the political climate rather than cooperation duties under international law. In the past decade, such political will has been garnered on more than one occasion at the level of both the European Union and the North Atlantic Treaty Organization.

Counter-piracy operations off the coast of Somalia are the flagship in terms of cooperation between naval forces. No less than three multinational missions contributed to the counter-piracy efforts: the Combined Maritime Forces, a US-led international naval coalition contributing with *Coalition Task Forces 150* and *151* respectively; NATO's deployment of three consecutive operations—*Operation Allied Provider, Operation Allied Protector*, and *Operation Ocean Shield*—between 2008 and 2016; and (the first ever) EU-led naval forces, EUNAVFOR, engaging in *Operation Atalanta* since 2008. Thereby, the Shared Awareness and Deconfliction (SHADE) initiative contributed to 'de-confliction', that is, to the avoidance of redundant or conflicting activities of the (unprecedented) number of states and coalitions enforcing the law in one theatre.[19]

Counterterrorism operations are another field of activity of the Combined Maritime Forces (notably *Coalition Task Force 152*)[20] and NATO's *Operation Active Endeavour*, which evolved out of NATO's response to the 9/11 terrorist attacks and ended in 2016. During the operation's lifetime, NATO forces patrolled the Mediterranean in order to deter and disrupt terrorist activity and hailed more than 128,000 merchant vessels and boarded a total of 172 suspected ships.[21] The newly launched *Operation Sea Guardian* also features a counterterrorism component.[22]

United Nations Convention against Transnational Organized Crime (adopted 15 November 2000, entered into force 28 January 2004) 2241 UNTS 480 (Protocol on Migrant Smuggling) ('to the fullest extent possible').

[17] Eg Article 27 of the United Nations Convention against Transnational Organized Crime (adopted 15 November 2000, entered into force 29 September 2003) 2225 UNTS 209 ('*shall consider* entering into ... agreements or arrangements on direct cooperation between their law enforcement agencies' (emphasis added); UNODC, 'International Framework for Action—To Implement the Smuggling of Migrants Protocol' (2012) 110–11 <http://www.unodc.org/documents/human-trafficking/Migrant-Smuggling/Framework_for_Action_Smuggling_of_Migrants.pdf>.

[18] US Department of Defense, 'DOD Dictionary of Military and Associated Terms' (August 2017) 159 <http://www.jcs.mil/Portals/36/Documents/Doctrine/pubs/dictionary.pdf>.

[19] UNSC, 'Report of the Secretary-General on the situation with respect to piracy and armed robbery at sea off the coast of Somalia' (12 October 2017) UN Doc S/2017/859, paras 4–5, 37–40; UNSC Res 2383 (7 November 2017) UN Doc S/RES/2383, preambular para 13; R Geiß and A Petrig, *Piracy and Armed Robbery at Sea: The Legal Framework for Counter-Piracy Operations in Somalia and the Gulf of Aden* (OUP 2011).

[20] Combined Maritime Force, 'CTF 150: Maritime Security' <https://combinedmaritimeforces.com/ctf-150-maritime-security/>.

[21] NATO, 'Operation Active Endeavour' (last updated 27 October 2016) <http://www.nato.int/cps/en/natohq/topics_7932.htm>. Kraska and Pedrozo (n 10) 54.

[22] NATO, 'Operation Sea Guardian' (last updated 27 October 2016) <http://www.nato.int/cps/en/natohq/topics_136233.htm>.

At the time of writing, EUNAVFOR's *Operation Sophia* is contributing to the disruption of the business model of migrant smuggling and human trafficking networks in the Southern Central Mediterranean and to the enforcement of the arms embargo imposed by the Security Council on Libya.[23] In fulfilling this mandate, it receives support from NATO's *Operation Sea Guardian*.[24] As regards the enforcement of the arms embargo on Libya specifically, NATO deployed *Operation Unified Protector* in 2001, during the course of which a total of 3,100 vessels were hailed, around 300 boarded, and eleven denied transit to or from Libya.[25] This is just one of many examples where NATO took an active part in embargo enforcement.[26]

This new operational reality has found its way into strategic-doctrinal documents, namely NATO's Alliance Maritime Strategy of 2011[27] and the EU Maritime Security Strategy of 2014.[28] These documents evidence how the maritime dimension of security has risen in rank on their respective security agendas[29] and acknowledge the policing function navies have increasingly assumed in the past decade.[30] What is more, they may promote the deployment of additional multinational law enforcement operations in the future. This warrants further emphasis in section 3 that these operations are governed by peacetime law.

3. Multinational Law Enforcement at Sea: Governed by Peacetime Law

If the navies are policing the sea, their operations are governed by a law enforcement paradigm, that is, peacetime law. Doubts in that respect—and the idea that the law governing armed conflicts at sea could apply instead—may arise for a number of reasons, which are described in the following: because the measures

[23] Council Decision (CFSP) 2015/778 of 18 May 2015 on a European Union military operation in the Southern Central Mediterranean (EUNAVFOR MED) [2015] OJ L122/31, Article 1.

[24] NATO, 'Progress report on the implementation of the common set of proposals endorsed by NATO and EU Councils on 6 December 2016' (NATO, 14 June 2017) 3 <http://www.nato.int/nato_static_fl2014/assets/pdf/pdf_2017_06/20170619_170614-Joint-progress-report-EU-NATO-EN.pdf>; NATO, 'NATO and EU discuss future cooperation at sea' (30 June 2017) <http://www.nato.int/cps/en/natohq/news_145749.htm>.

[25] NATO, 'Operation UNIFIED PROTECTOR Final Mission Stats' (2 November 2011) <http://www.nato.int/nato_static_fl2014/assets/pdf/pdf_2011_11/20111108_111107-factsheet_up_factsfigures_en.pdf>.

[26] For further examples, see MD Fink, 'Maritime Embargo Operations: Naval Implementation of UN Sanctions at Sea under Articles 41 and 42 of the UN Charter' (2013) 60 Netherlands International Law Review 73.

[27] NATO, 'Alliance Maritime Strategy' (last updated 17 June 2011) <http://www.nato.int/cps/ua/natohq/official_texts_75615.htm>; Gade and Hilde (n 8) 123.

[28] Council Strategy (11205/14) of 24 June 2014 on European Union Maritime Security [2014].

[29] C Bueger and T Edmunds, 'Beyond Seablindness: A New Agenda for Maritime Security Studies' (2017) 93 International Affairs 1293, 1294, and 1297–98.

[30] Gade and Hilde (n 8) 123, note that AMS 'places near exclusive emphasis on non-traditional security challenges' and '[m]ore traditional security challenges of the type NATO faced during the Cold War are not mentioned'.

taken by the enforcers feature an (only apparent!) similarity with the exercise of belligerent rights (section 3.1); because military rather than civilian assets are deployed (section 3.2); because enforcement measures may take place in contexts where an armed conflict is ongoing (section 3.3); and ultimately because of the use of the term 'Maritime Security Operation', obscuring the nature of the operations subsumed under this operational rather than legal term (section 3.4).

3.1 No exercise of belligerent rights

For an untrained eye it may be difficult to determine from the outside whether a specific measure is authorized and confined by the law of naval warfare (hence, amounts to an exercise of belligerent rights) or by peacetime law, notably the law of the sea and further sources laid out in detail below (hence, amounts to a law enforcement measure). Not only are the measures similarly named, but in some cases may not be operationally distinguishable from each other, that is, the *practical* actions look alike under both regimes.[31] For example, under both legal regimes (wartime and peacetime law) ships may be stopped, boarded and searched, and cargo seized.[32]

From a *legal* point of view, however, it is of utmost importance to ascertain under which legal regime a specific measure is taken since the conditions for their authorization (eg against which ships they may be taken), the limitations to observe (eg in terms of use of force), and the legal consequences are regulated very differently under the law of naval warfare as compared to peacetime law. As long as multinational operations are deployed to suppress criminal acts at sea—most of which amount to offences defined under international law[33]—they are governed by the law enforcement paradigm.[34]

[31] R McLaughlin, 'Authorizations for Maritime Law Enforcement Operations' (2016) 98 International Review of the Red Cross 465, 490, states that 'to the untrained eye [maritime law enforcement powers] can represent a rough facsimile of many aspects of the law of naval warfare'; W Heintschel von Heinegg and MD Fink, 'Maritime Interception/Interdiction Operations' in TD Gill and D Fleck (eds), *The Handbook of International Law of Military Operations* (2nd edn, OUP 2015) 423.

[32] See E Papastavridis, *The Interception of Vessels on the High Seas: Contemporary Challenges to the Legal Order of the Oceans* (Hart Publishing 2013) Ch 3, describing 'The Right of Visit on the High Seas in Wartime' in a first step, to then turn to 'The Right of Visit on the High Seas in Peacetime'.

[33] Acts suppressed in the course of counter-piracy operations may, inter alia, fulfil Article 101 UNCLOS (n 16); Article 3 of the Convention for the Suppression of Unlawful Acts Against the Safety of Maritime Navigation (adopted 10 March 1988, entered into force 1 March 1992) 1678 UNTS 221 (SUA Convention) or Article 1 of the International Convention against the Taking of Hostages (adopted 17 November 1979, entered into force 3 June 1983) 1316 UNTS 205 (Hostage Convention). Acts suppressed in the course of operations to counter illegal migration in the Mediterranean may, inter alia, fulfil the offences defined in Article 3 *juncto* Article 6 Protocol on Migrant Smuggling (n 16), or Article 3 *juncto* Article 5 of the Protocol to Prevent, Suppress and Punish Trafficking in Persons, Especially Women and Children, supplementing the United Nations Convention against Transnational Organized Crime (adopted 15 November 2000, entered into force 25 December 2003) 2237 UNTS 319 (Protocol on Human Trafficking).

[34] Heintschel von Heinegg and Fink (n 31) 423; McLaughlin (n 31) 490.

3.2 Law of the sea foresees the use of warships

This finding is not altered by the fact that military personnel and warships are deployed to suppress criminal acts at sea. Rather, the law of the sea itself provides for the use of warships—next to other ships on government service, such as police and patrol boats—for law enforcement operations at sea.[35] In the Articles Concerning the Law of the Sea of 1956, which have had a profound impact on major law of the sea codifications, the International Law Commission even suggested to exclusively authorize warships when policing the sea because 'the use of other government ships does not provide for the same safeguards against abuse'—or, put differently, for reasons of legal certainty.[36] The drafters of the 1958 Convention on the High Seas and of the United Nations Convention on the Law of the Sea (UNCLOS) did not retain this limitation. Hence, both warships and other ships under government service can be employed for law enforcement operations at sea.

The choice between military and civilian assets namely hinges on the division of tasks between military (naval forces) and civilian agencies (eg coast guards or border patrols) under domestic law. The extent to which states are willing to rely on their navies for enforcement purposes varies.[37] Moreover, for law enforcement operations abroad specifically, the choice between military and civilian actors is influenced by operational considerations: only vessels of a considerable size and with specific equipment, that is, traditional warships such as frigates and destroyers,[38] have the capacity to remain in maritime areas far from the coast for longer periods of time and in adverse conditions. The fact that Japan's Coast Guard is one of a handful of coast guards possessing ocean-going vessels[39] explains why military (navies) rather than civil forces are the key actors in multinational law enforcement operations.[40] Yet, this does not alter the law enforcement character of the respective operations—as aptly stated in a NATO committee report: 'warships engaged in counter-piracy operations are treated as police or law enforcement forces'.[41]

[35] See, eg, UNCLOS (n 16) Articles 107, 110(1) and (2), 224.

[36] ILC, 'Articles concerning the Law of the Sea with commentaries' in 'Report of the International Law Commission covering the work of its eighth session' (23 April–4 July 1956) UN Doc A/3159, Article 45; see also 280 (comment on Article 33—Immunity of government ships) and 283 (comment on Article 45).

[37] Till (n 2) 316.

[38] A ship qualifies as a warship irrespective of its size and construction for so long as it fulfils the definitional criteria of a warship laid down in Article 29 UNCLOS (n 16): W Heintschel von Heinegg, 'Warships' (*Max Planck Encyclopedia of Public International Law*, October 2015) para 7 <http://opil.ouplaw.com/view/10.1093/law:epil/9780199231690/law-9780199231690-e443>.

[39] Till (n 2) 295.

[40] Tondini (n 10) 254 and 257; in more detail: Till (n 2) 316.

[41] Lord Jopling, 'Draft General Report—The Growing Threat of Piracy to Regional and Global Security' (Parliamentary Assembly NATO, 5 April 2009) para 39 <https://www.parlament.ch/centers/documents/en/atalanta-nato-2009-04-05-e.pdf>.

3.3 Law enforcement in situations of ongoing armed conflict

It is not unusual for multinational operations mandated with countering criminal activity to be deployed to regions where armed conflicts are ongoing. Not least because the Security Council authorizes enforcement measures specifically in situations where, due to an armed conflict, no effective government exists which is able to effectively enforce the law in its internal waters and territorial sea (failed/failing state situation). Furthermore, the Security Council regularly issues authorizations in the field of embargo enforcement. Such embargos are likely to be imposed upon a state involved in an armed conflict in order to interrupt arms flows and/or to cut revenues from oil, charcoal, or other resources.[42]

In some (but not all) of these resolutions, the Security Council stated that the exercise of the authorized measures must be in compliance with 'international humanitarian law and international human rights law, as applicable' (or similar wording),[43] thus giving the (false) impression that counter-piracy operations could fall within the ambit of wartime law. However, from the words 'as applicable' accrues that the Security Council did not declare international humanitarian law to be in fact applicable; rather, it seems that the Council aimed at stressing that the use of 'all necessary measures' to suppress illicit acts is not without limitations.[44]

Indeed, the simple fact that law enforcement measures are taken in a context where an armed conflict is ongoing does *not* automatically subject them to the law of armed conflicts. Rather, it would be necessary that the enforcers are a party to the armed conflict in question and that the measures are directed against conduct featuring a direct link with the armed conflict. This is not the case for either the enforcement measures aimed at suppressing Somali piracy[45] or for the operations enforcing the embargos imposed on Somalia and Libya, respectively.[46]

[42] Eg on Somalia: UNSC Res 2182 (21 October 2014) UN Doc S/RES/2182 recently renewed by UNSC Res 2385 (14 November 2017) UN Doc S/RES/2385; and Libya: UNSC Res 2292 (14 June 2016) UN Doc S/RES/2292, recently renewed by UNSC Res 2357 (12 June 2017) UN Doc S/RES/2357.

[43] Re Somali piracy: UNSC Res 1851 (16 December 2008) UN Doc S/RES/1851, para 6 (counter-piracy operations in Somali internal waters); re embargo enforcement: UNSC Res 2182 (n 42) para 16, and UNSC Res 2292 (n 42) para 4. By contrast, the resolutions pertaining to the migrant smuggling and human trafficking in the Mediterranean only refer to human rights law, but not to IHL as source limiting enforcement powers: UNSC Res 2240 (9 October 2015) UN Doc S/RES/2240 and consecutive UNSC Res 2316 (9 November 2016) UN Doc S/RES/2316, and UNSC Res 2380 (5 October 2017) UN Doc S/RES/2380.

[44] On limitations arising from, eg, international human rights law, see below section 5.2.

[45] For a detailed account, see Geiß and Petrig (n 19) 132–36.

[46] Re Somalia: M Frostad, 'United Nations Authorized Embargos and Maritime Interdiction: A Special Focus on Somalia' in G Andreone (ed), *The Future of the Law of the Sea: Bridging Gaps Between National, Individual and Common Interests* (Springer 2017) 226; re Libya: McLaughlin (n 31) 490; in general, see Heintschel von Heinegg and Fink (n 31) 423.

3.4 'Multinational law enforcement operations'

Multinational law enforcement operations mandated with the suppression of criminal activity at sea are often labelled as a 'Maritime Security Operation' (MSO). This obscures that they are governed by peacetime law, as the notion of an MSO is also used to refer to operations governed by the law of armed conflicts. Thus far, no uniform definition of the term exists. The Chiefs of European Navies, for example, describe MSO in the following terms:

> 2. MSO are defined as those measures performed by the appropriate civilian or military authorities and multinational agencies to counter the threat and mitigate the risks of illegal or threatening activities in the maritime domain, so that they may be acted upon in order to enforce law, protect citizens and safeguard national and international interests.
> 3. Developing these operations will focus on terrorism, proliferation, narcotic trafficking, illegal migration, piracy and armed robbery, but might also include smuggling, the protection of national resources, energy security, the prevention of environmental impact and safeguarding sovereignty.[47]

The *Dictionary of Military Terms and Associated Terms* of the US Department of Defense defines MSO in a crisper way as:

> Those operations to protect maritime sovereignty and resources and to counter maritime-related terrorism, weapons proliferation, transnational crime, piracy, environmental destruction, and illegal seaborne immigration.[48]

These (and other definitions)[49] are vague as regards the legal paradigm governing MSOs: are these law enforcement operations (criminal domain) or do they pertain to the conduct of naval warfare (military domain)? This ambiguity notably stems from references in MSO definitions to the 'safeguarding of sovereignty' (and similar wording), which is a potential goal of such operations going beyond the countering of illegal acts committed by private persons. Kraska encapsulates the qualification problem (and its consequences) when writing that MSOs 'lie between simple maritime law enforcement and the conduct of naval warfare; and the division among these categories is far from clear' and that MSOs 'may contemplate a greater use of force than law enforcement because the threats are deemed to go beyond mere infractions and harm national interests or affect international stability'.[50]

[47] Developing a European Interagency Strategy for Maritime Security Operations (Paper supported by the Chiefs of European Navies, 2006) 3, paras 2, 3.
[48] US Department of Defense (n 18) 147.
[49] Eg that of the Royal Navy cited by Till (n 2) 283.
[50] J Kraska, 'Military Operations' in DR Rothwell and others (eds), *The Oxford Handbook on the Law of the Sea* (OUP 2015) 873.

The newly established *Operation Sea Guardian*, for example, is an operation that potentially covers the full range of activities falling within an MSO. As per the words of NATO, it 'will respond to threats to maritime security that *straddle the boundary between defence and law enforcement*' and 'will contribute to mitigate gaps in the capacity of individual countries to enforce *civilian and/or military law at sea*'.[51] Hence, for each intervention under the umbrella of this broadly conceived operation, it is necessary (and crucial) to determine whether it amounts to law enforcement or not.

In sum, it is submitted here that the preferable term to denote operations aimed at suppressing criminal activity at sea is 'Multinational Law Enforcement Operations'. This term better reflects the binary approach (enshrined in law) between law enforcement on the one hand and conduct of hostilities on the other, and clearly shows that these operations belong to the former category.[52] Yet, it is acknowledged that in times of grey zone conflicts, for example, in the South China Sea, choosing between the two categories may be challenging.[53]

4. Authorizations to Enforce the Law at Sea: The Epitome of a 'Legal Pluriverse'

Now that the legal paradigm governing multinational operations mandated with the suppression of criminal acts by non-state actors has been identified—peacetime law—we can drill down on the legal bases authorizing multinational forces and/or contributing states to enforce the law at sea.[54] The brevity of this chapter does not allow for a full account of the rules governing enforcement jurisdiction at sea; rather, the intent is to explain how different legal sources interact and together form an intricate jurisdictional framework. After demonstrating that authorizations to enforce the law at sea are measure-specific rather than wholesale (section 4.1), the basic jurisdictional rules contained in UNCLOS, which are maritime zone-specific, are briefly explained (section 4.2). We then turn to more specific rules—contained in various legal sources, notably UNCLOS itself, treaties on transnational crime, and Security Council resolutions—which derogate from the basic jurisdictional rules for specific offences (section 4.3).[55] Finally, we conclude that jurisdiction at sea is not only measure-, maritime zone-, and offence-specific,

[51] NATO, 'Operation Sea Guardian' (n 22) (emphasis added).

[52] See Tondini (n 10) 253–54, using the term MLE to denote to policing operations by navies.

[53] See L Morris, 'Blunt Defenders of Sovereignty: The Rise of Coast Guards of East and Southeast Asia' (2017) 70 Naval War College Review 75.

[54] This chapter rests on the premise that states do not possess enforcement jurisdiction outside their territory, unless a permissive rule under international law confers them the authority to enforce the law: see, eg, D Guilfoyle, *Shipping Interdiction and the Law of the Sea* (CUP 2009) 7–8.

[55] What is more, it is necessary to implement the authorizations under international law into domestic law: McLaughlin (n 31) 468.

but also mandate-specific as the mandate of a given multinational operation may not extend to the whole range of enforcement measures that international law allows (section 4.4). Overall, the legal framework governing enforcement jurisdiction at sea is arguably the epitome of a 'legal pluriverse'.

4.1 Authorizations are measure-specific: no wholesale enforcement jurisdiction

First, it must be noted that jurisdiction to enforce the law in international waters or against foreign-flagged vessels is never wholesale; rather, states are generally only authorized to take *specific* types of enforcement measures.[56] This warrants a closer look into the gamut of measures that could potentially be taken by multinational naval forces.

It is not uncommon for a (multinational) law enforcement operation at sea to be referred to as a 'Maritime Interdiction Operation' (MIO), which NATO defines as '[a]n operation conducted to enforce prohibition on the maritime movement of specified persons or material within a defined geographic area'.[57] At times, this term is used interchangeably with 'Maritime Interception Operation'.[58] Either way, there is no agreed understanding of which enforcement measures fall within the ambit of the terms 'interdiction' and 'interception', respectively. Some sources adopt a broad understanding of the concept of 'interdiction', and use it to describe a two-step process comprised of 'boarding/searching' (boarding, inspection, and search of a ship) and 'seizure' (arresting the vessel and/or persons and seizing the cargo).[59] Other sources build on a narrower understanding of the terms 'interdiction' and 'interception', respectively, using them to denote 'boarding/searching' only (ie what Article 110 UNCLOS authorizes under the heading of 'right of visit').[60]

Leaving aside the lack of consensus on the concept of 'Maritime Interdiction/ Interception Operation', in substance it is an operational term rather than a legal

[56] Even the seemingly wholesale enforcement powers authorized by UNSC Res 1846 (n 5) ('to use … all necessary means') allow no more than those authorized under Article 105 UNCLOS (n 16): see Geiß and Petrig (n 19) 9, which mentions the example where the flag state grants consent to a third state to interdict its vessel: such permission to board seldom automatically includes permission to seize and is thus only a partial waiver of flag state jurisdiction.

[57] NATO, 'Maritime Interdiction Operation' (Official NATO Terminology Database, Record 9077) <https://nso.nato.int/natoterm/content/nato/pages/home.html>.

[58] Heintschel von Heinegg and Fink (n 31) 422, use the terms interchangeably after pointing out potential differences; US Navy, Marine Corps, and Coast Guard, 'The Commander's Handbook on the Law of Naval Operations' (Department of the Navy Office of the Chief of Naval Operations and Headquarters, US Marine Corps, Department of Homeland Security, and US Coast Guard August 2017) para 4.4.4. <http://www.jag.navy.mil/distrib/instructions/CDRs_HB_on_Law_of_Naval_Operations_AUG17.pdf>.

[59] Eg Guilfoyle (n 54) 4; 'The Commander's Handbook on the Law of Naval Operations' (n 58) para 4.4.4.

[60] Papastavridis (n 32) 1, eg, uses interception as a synonym for the right of visit.

one,[61] and more generic than specific, encompassing various types of enforcement measures. Hence, for an assessment of the legal rules that govern the powers of multinational naval forces, the concept is not particularly helpful. Rather, such evaluations can only be made with respect to a specific type of measure (eg arrest of a suspect or seizure of cargo) that states or multinational forces may take in the course of an operation. Thus, a closer look at the types of measures that law enforcement operations at sea potentially entail is advised.

To begin with, intelligence measures are necessary in order to identify and detect illegal conduct at sea. With regard to ships suspected of engaging in conduct prohibited by international law, the possible measures encompass their stopping, boarding, and inspection/searching. If suspicion is confirmed, the ships and/or cargo may be seized and/or destroyed or disposed of in another way (eg the selling of items prohibited by embargo measures). As regards persons on board suspected of engaging in illicit activity, measures range from arrest and detention to transfer for prosecution.

All mentioned measures belong to the category of enforcement jurisdiction, which must be distinguished from adjudicative jurisdiction.[62] The latter entails the authority to take measures related to the investigation and prosecution of alleged offences. Since multinational naval forces do not have adjudicative jurisdiction (rather, it remains within the ambit of states), it is not further discussed here.

4.2 Authorizations are maritime zone-specific: UNCLOS' basic jurisdictional rules

In order to decide whether an actor has the power to take a specific enforcement measure, the first source to consult is UNCLOS, which strikes a balance between the competing interests of different types of states and, as part of this endeavour, allocates enforcement jurisdiction to the port, coastal, flag, and/or boarding state.[63] Thereby, UNCLOS pursues a maritime zone-driven approach and formulates basic jurisdictional rules for each zone—notably internal waters, territorial sea, and the high seas[64]—which are to be followed unless derogated from by more specific rules, to which we turn in the following section.

[61] Heintschel von Heinegg and Fink (n 31) 423.

[62] This chapter rests on the threefold categorization of jurisdiction: to prescribe, enforce, and adjudicate: see Guilfoyle (n 54) 7–9. The jurisdictional rules of UNCLOS (n 16) do not always neatly distinguish between these two forms of jurisdiction: eg Article 27 UNCLOS (n 16) using the term 'criminal jurisdiction' to refer to both enforcement ('to arrest...') and adjudicative ('to investigate ...') jurisdiction.

[63] Guilfoyle (n 54) 4.

[64] There are additional maritime zones (eg the contiguous zone and the exclusive economic zone), which are not discussed here; for a more extensive account of enforcement powers in the different maritime zones, see N Klein, *Maritime Security and the Law of the Sea* (OUP 2011) Ch 3.

Put simply and starting closest to the shore and then moving seawards, these basic jurisdictional rules are as follows. The *internal waters*—comprising the waters situated landward of the baseline and ports—are considered to come within a state's territorial jurisdiction. As a consequence, ships entering these waters are, as a general rule, subject to the primary enforcement jurisdiction of the port state.[65] Seawards from the baseline lies the *territorial sea*, a belt of water of at most 12 miles breadth, over which the coastal state exercises sovereignty.[66] Hence, the coastal state is, as a general rule, allowed to take enforcement measures against vessels in these waters engaged in criminal activity.[67] Finally, on the *high seas*, the basic rule under the law of the sea is that the flag state has exclusive enforcement jurisdiction.[68]

In sum, the basic jurisdictional rules under the law of the sea are maritime zone-specific; for each zone, a different type of state (the port, coastal, or flag state) has, as a general rule, primary and exclusive enforcement jurisdiction. However, regarding jurisdiction at sea, this is not the end of the story: for specific offences, these basic jurisdictional rules are derogated from due to the presence of more specific rules, to which we turn now.

4.3 Authorizations are offence-specific: special rules derogating from UNCLOS' basic jurisdictional rules

Since the basic jurisdictional rules of UNCLOS do not apply if a specific authorization exists in relation to a specific type of offence, enforcement jurisdiction at sea is not only maritime zone-specific, but also offence-specific.[69] This makes jurisdiction at sea an intricate matter, especially when taken together with the fact that the specific rules derogating from the basic rules stem from various legal sources, three of which we turn to now: UNCLOS itself, multilateral treaties, and Security Council resolutions.[70]

[65] For a more detailed account, see EJ Molenaar, 'Port and Coastal States' in Rothwell and others (n 50) 280–303.

[66] UNCLOS (n 16) Article 2(3).

[67] UNCLOS (n 16) Article 25; RA Barnes, 'Article 25' in A Proelß (ed), *United Nations Convention on the Law of the Sea: A Commentary* (CH Beck/Hart 2017) 223, para 1; and RA Barnes, 'Article 27' in Proelß (ibid) 234, para 9.

[68] UNCLOS (n 16) Article 92(1); in detail: R Churchill and V Lowe, *The Law of the Sea* (3rd edn, Manchester University Press 1999) 208–20.

[69] Klein (n 64) 62, writes that jurisdiction is different 'according to what particular threat to maritime security is being addressed'; this is arguably imprecise because a threat often encompasses various offences (eg the threat of piracy may inter alia fulfil the offence of piracy as defined in Article 101 UNCLOS (n 16), hostage taking as defined in Article 1 Hostage Convention (n 33), and Article 3 SUA Convention (n 33) offences, armed robbery at sea, etc); and for these offences, jurisdiction to enforce is regulated differently.

[70] Since this chapter focuses on multinational operations, bilateral treaties as a source containing derogation rules are not discussed here; on this, see, eg, Guilfoyle (n 54) 246–54.

4.3.1 Derogations contained in UNCLOS

The first source of offence-specific authorizations overriding the UNCLOS basic jurisdictional rules is UNCLOS itself. Given the brevity of this chapter, these rules cannot be described in full, but it suffices to provide a few examples to illustrate the mechanism.

As regards the high seas, for instance, Article 92(1) stipulates that the flag state has exclusive jurisdiction (basic rule) 'save in exceptional cases expressly provided for . . . in this Convention' (derogation rule). Article 110 UNCLOS is an example of such a rule: it authorizes *every* state (and not just the flag state) to board a ship from which it can be reasonably expected that it engages in one of the listed offences, notably slavery and piracy. For the latter offence, Article 105 UNCLOS provides even more far-reaching powers and allows *every* state to seize a pirate ship and property on board and to arrest the suspects.

UNCLOS contains such specific jurisdictional rules derogating from the otherwise exclusive flag state jurisdiction only for a limited set of offences: notably for piracy, slave trade, and unauthorized broadcasting.[71] However, there are other offences where the states competent under the basic jurisdictional rules are not willing and/or able to enforce the law; in these cases, treaties other than UNCLOS and Security Council resolutions *may* remedy the situation by allocating jurisdiction to third states.

4.3.2 Derogations contained in treaties

It is UNCLOS itself that foresees the possibility that treaties derogate from its (jurisdiction) rules. First of all, Article 311(3) UNCLOS allows *inter se* agreements, provided they do not disturb the object and purpose of the treaty, do not affect the basic principles of UNCLOS, and do not affect the rights and obligations of third states under UNCLOS. Doctrine suggests that an agreement between a number of states to derogate *inter se* from jurisdictional rules (eg from the flag state principle) is permissible.[72] Secondly, basic jurisdictional rules of UNCLOS stipulate that specific treaty rules prevail. For example, Article 92(1) UNCLOS provides that flag state jurisdiction is exclusive 'save in exceptional cases expressly provided for in international treaties'.[73] This fits with the framework nature of UNCLOS, which limits itself to cornerstone rules (here, the maritime zone-specific basic jurisdictional rules) that are complemented by more detailed, subject-matter related external rules (here, offence-specific jurisdictional rules).[74] This mechanism allows UNCLOS 'to deal with change'[75]—notably, a changing security landscape.

[71] See UNCLOS (n 16) Articles 105, 109(4), and 110; UNCLOS (n 16) Article 108 (on drug trafficking) is not a jurisdictional rule but turns on cooperation.

[72] N Matz-Lück, 'Article 311' in Proelß (n 67) 2016, para 14.

[73] Churchill and Lowe (n 68) 209.

[74] RR Churchill, 'The 1982 United Nations Convention on the Law of the Sea' in Rothwell and others (n 50) 30.

[75] See I Buga, 'Between Stability and Change in the Law of the Sea Convention: Subsequent Practice, Treaty Modification, and Regime Interaction' in Rothwell and others (n 50) 46.

Indeed, a number of treaties dealing with transnational offences—such as the SUA Convention and its 2005 Protocol,[76] the Protocols on Human Trafficking and Migrant Smuggling, and the UN Drug Convention[77]—contain jurisdictional provisions. Yet, they chiefly pertain to prescriptive and adjudicative jurisdiction, and do not touch upon enforcement jurisdiction at all or transpire from a reluctance to encroach on the basic jurisdictional rules of the law of the sea in an all too general way. The SUA Convention illustrates this quite well: while it requires state parties to make the offences defined in the Convention 'punishable by appropriate penalties' under their domestic law (prescriptive jurisdiction) and to establish criminal jurisdiction if the offence features specific links with the state in question (adjudicative jurisdiction),[78] enforcement jurisdiction is explicitly excluded from the scope of the treaty.[79] The boarding provision added by the 2005 SUA Protocol remedied this lacuna only partially because it is still heavily predicated on flag state consent.[80] Furthermore, the clause is territorially confined to ships 'located seaward of any State's territorial sea' and thus inapplicable regarding armed robbery at sea (an offence essentially amounting to 'piracy' in the territorial waters). It was only through authorization of the Security Council—another source of derogation to which we turn now—that the respective enforcement powers to counter armed robbery in the territorial sea of Somalia were provided for.

4.3.3 Derogations contained in Security Council resolutions

In theory, the basic jurisdictional rules of UNCLOS together form a complete and well-balanced system with no jurisdictional loopholes. In practice, however, this jurisdictional framework often proves to be inadequate because it is based on the assumption that states actually *exercise* their jurisdiction. For a variety of reasons, however, this is not always the case. For instance, failed or failing states may lack the capacity to effectively control their ports and police their territorial sea. Further, the practice of flag of convenience entails that a significant number of ships are registered in states with a poor enforcement record;[81] and the flag state may at times even have an interest in the commission of the illegal act, which may, for example,

[76] Protocol of 2005 to the Suppression of Unlawful Acts Against the Safety of Maritime Navigation (adopted 14 October 2005, entered into force 28 July 2010) IMO Doc LEG/CONF.15/21 (2005 SUA Protocol).

[77] United Nations Convention against Illicit Traffic in Narcotic Drugs and Psychotropic Substances (adopted 20 December 1988, entered into force 11 November 1990) 1582 UNTS 95 (UN Drug Convention).

[78] SUA Convention (n 33) Articles 5 and 6.

[79] Article 9 leaves no doubt about it. See also Protocol on Migrant Smuggling (n 16) Articles 4, 8, 9.

[80] According to 2005 SUA Protocol (n 76) Article 8*bis*(5)(c), as a general rule, express flag state authorization is required; however, according to sub-para (d) and (e) a state (when becoming a party to the Protocol) may notify that its consent is presumed if after four hours no response is given or grant advance consent in general.

[81] AJ Marcopoulos, 'Flags of Terror: An Argument for Rethinking Maritime Security Policy Regarding Flags of Convenience' (2007) 32 Tulane Maritime Law Journal 277, 294–98.

hold true for a state subject to an embargo. This lack of enforcement by the competent state fosters the ideal climate for criminality to blossom. In exceptional cases, the Security Council has thus stepped in and authorized third states to enforce the law.

It did so regarding Somali-based piracy and authorized all states and regional organizations to '[e]nter into the territorial waters of Somalia' and to use therein 'all necessary means to repress acts of piracy and armed robbery at sea'.[82] In the (*nota bene* Chapter VII-based) resolution, the Council used every single opportunity to stress Somalia's sovereignty and to emphasize the request by and consent of the Somali Government to enforcement operations by third states in its territorial sea.[83] This evidences once more the overarching reluctance to encroach upon a coastal state's jurisdiction and to weigh security concerns over sovereignty concerns. It also explains why the Security Council has thus far refrained from authorizing enforcement action against migrant smuggling vessels in Libyan waters.[84] However, the Council did so for the high seas; concretely, it authorized states and regional organizations 'to inspect on the high seas off the coast of Libya vessels that they have reasonable grounds to suspect are being used for migrant smuggling or human trafficking from Libya' and to seize them.[85] While the Security Council broke with a cornerstone rule of the law of the sea—exclusive flag state jurisdiction—it tried to conceal this by relying on the concept of 'good faith efforts', which it introduced in the context of embargo enforcement authorizations.[86] That is, before using the authority provided by the respective resolution, enforcers must make 'good faith efforts to obtain the consent of the vessel's flag State'.[87]

Even if authorizations granted by the Security Council are limited in terms of their material, geographical, and temporal scope of application (they pertain to a specific offence occurring in a specific area and are generally only granted for one year, subject to renewal), reluctance to overtly break with the basic jurisdictional rules of UNCLOS transpires from these resolutions. This reluctance is underlined by the emphasis present in each of these resolutions that they shall not affect any rights or obligations under the law of the sea, including UNCLOS, and shall not be considered as establishing customary international law.[88]

[82] USNC Res 1846 (n 5) para 10 (most recently renewed by UNSC Res 2383 (n 19)).

[83] UNSC Res 1846 (n 5) preambular paras 3, 6–7 and paras 10–11.

[84] G Bevilacqua, 'Exploring the Ambiguity of Operation Sophia Between Military and Search and Rescue Activities' in Andreone (n 46) 176–78.

[85] UNSC Res 2240 (n 43) paras 7–8.

[86] See, eg, UNSC Res 2182 (n 42) para 16; UNSC Res 2292 (n 42) para 3.

[87] UNSC Res 2240 (n 43) para 7; B Wilson, 'The Mediterranean Migrant Crisis: Key Considerations for the UN Security Council' (2015) Harvard National Security Journal 1, 5, criticizes that this injects an unwarranted degree of uncertainty for the operations, including 'whether there is an expected time to allow for a flag response, whether a request needs to be in writing, and who is authorized to make and receive such requests'.

[88] UNSC Res 2240 (n 43) para 11; UNSC Res 1846 (n 5) para 11.

In sum, the UNCLOS doors are theoretically wide open for specific rules derogating from its basic jurisdictional rules; yet, in practice, the shift away from these cornerstone rules is a rather hesitant undertaking. Sovereignty and the freedom of the high seas, axioms on which the basic rules of UNCLOS rest, are values that are not easily put aside.

4.4 Authorizations are mandate-specific: may not extend to all measures authorized by international law

At first glance, the rules conferring enforcement jurisdiction, which have been discussed earlier, appear to be addressed to states only—with the exception of Security Council resolutions explicitly authorizing regional organizations to take enforcement measures at sea.[89] The EU, however, is a party to UNCLOS and to a good number of treaties aimed at the suppression of criminal phenomena;[90] the jurisdictional rules addressed to states thus apply *mutatis mutandis* to the EU.[91] Yet, this does not imply that EU-led naval forces can act upon *all* authorizations contained in these treaties without further ado. Rather, the EU's Common Foreign and Security Policy, under the roof of which EUNAVFOR's *Operation Atalanta* and *Operation Sophia* reside, remains intergovernmental rather than supranational in nature, and the establishment of an operation requires a Council Decision.[92] This decision defines the mandate, which does not necessarily extend to the use of all measures allowed under international law.[93]

By contrast, NATO is not a party to the treaties conferring power to enforce the law at sea. Yet, states are free to either exercise their enforcement powers together with other states (eg in naval coalitions such as the Combined Maritime Forces), or even to confer their enforcement powers to international organizations, such as NATO.[94] However, each operation and the scope of the mandate has to be decided

[89] UNCLOS (n 16) Article 92(1), eg, stipulates that 'every State' may seize a pirate ship; by contrast, UNSC Res 1846 (n 5) para 1, explicitly authorizes 'States and regional organizations' to counter piracy and armed robbery at sea in Somali territorial waters.

[90] Eg the Protocol on Migrant Smuggling (n 16), the Protocol on Human Trafficking (n 33), and the UN Drug Convention (n 77); however, the EU is not a party to the SUA Convention (n 33) or the 2005 SUA Protocol (n 76), which were both adopted under the auspices of the International Maritime Organization.

[91] For UNCLOS (n 16), this is spelled out explicitly in UNCLOS (n 16) Article 1(2)(2) *juncto* Article 305(1)(f).

[92] See G Butler and M Ratovich, 'Operation Sophia in Uncharted Waters: European and International Law Challenges for the EU Naval Mission in the Mediterranean Sea' (2016) 85 Nordic Journal of International Law 235, 238–39.

[93] See, eg, Council Decision (n 23) Article 2, which foresees different phases during which different types of enforcement measures can be taken by EUNAVFOR.

[94] Principle of attributed power: HG Schermers and NM Blokker, *International Institutional Law: Unity within Diversity* (5th edn, Martinus Nijhoff 2011) 157–59, paras 209–209A.

by the North Atlantic Council, in which all member states are represented.[95] At times, the mandate does not cover all phases of an operation and thus only extends to some of the measures that international law allows states to take. For example, NATO's counter-piracy operations in the Gulf of Aden were limited to disrupting and deterring pirate attacks and did not extend to the arrest, detention, and transfer of piracy suspects—as the EU-led operations do.[96]

5. Attaching Strictures: Moving Outside the 'Legal Universe'

Thus far, the focus has been on a complex legal framework conferring multinational forces and/or contributing states the power to enforce the law at sea. Now, we change perspective and ask what *strictures* attach to enforcement measures taken by multinational forces and/or contributing states, and where they stem from. Hence, this section turns on rules protecting persons subject to enforcement measures (ie suspects arrested, detained, and/or transferred for prosecution) whereby the emphasis is on procedural safeguards.[97]

Intuitively, one would think that the rules authorizing enforcement measures at sea (which imply coercion and, *ultimo*, the use of force) include limitations on their exercise. Yet, this is hardly the case. The primary reference point in terms of jurisdiction at sea is UNCLOS—a body of law known for its 'difficulty to configure persons as the beneficiaries of rights and the recipient of duties' and which does not confer any human rights to persons.[98] Treaties aimed at the suppression of transnational crimes—which also contain authorizations to enforce the law at sea—are not a rich source as regards procedural safeguards for suspects, either. For example, the SUA and Hostage Conventions entail a single procedural safeguard: the right to consular assistance (akin to Article 36 of the Vienna Convention on Consular Relations), a guarantee that was drafted with a view to apply to persons detained on land, and thus its applicability at sea is open to question.[99] Even the 2005 SUA Protocol—which stands out because it is arguably the sole treaty authorizing enforcement measures at sea containing a detailed list of safeguards limiting these powers—is not very helpful in terms of procedural safeguards. It obliges States Parties to 'ensure that persons on board against whom proceedings may be

[95] North Atlantic Treaty (adopted 4 April 1949, entered into force 24 August 1949) 34 UNTS 243, Article 9; Peter M Olson, 'A NATO Perspective on Applicability and Application of IHL to Multinational Forces' (2013) 95 International Review of the Red Cross 653, 654.

[96] A Petrig, *Human Rights and Law Enforcement at Sea: Arrest, Detention and Transfer of Piracy Suspects* (Brill Nijhoff 2014) 54–55; see also below.

[97] Of interest (but not discussed here) are the rules limiting the use of force or regulating the substantive treatment of suspects on board warships.

[98] Rather, UNCLOS (n 16) addresses persons either as objects of protection (eg Article 98) or repression (eg Article 105): I Papanicolopulu, 'The Law of the Sea Convention: No Place for Persons?' (2012) 27 International Journal of Marine and Coastal Law 867, 867, and 873.

[99] In detail: Petrig (n 96) 310–12.

commenced in connection with [any SUA offence] are afforded the protection of paragraph 2 of Article 10, regardless of location'. The latter provision, in turn, requires the enjoyment [by the suspects] of all rights and guarantees in conformity with ... applicable provisions of international law, including international human rights law'.[100] Hence, the provision simply refers to the applicable law; it does not, however, identify specific legal bases, let alone set its own standard. Such a referential approach is also followed by the Security Council when authorizing 'all necessary means' to suppress illegal acts at sea; while earlier resolutions generally remained moot in terms of strictures attached to the exercise of authorized enforcement measures, newer resolutions request that they be taken in compliance with *applicable* international law or human rights law more specifically.[101]

Since the legal bases authorizing enforcement powers are either conspicuously silent as regards the strictures imposed on their exercise or follow a purely referential approach, we must turn to the (referenced) external legal sources: first, we look at domestic law—a legal source that plays a pivotal role even in operations of a multinational character (section 5.1)—and, secondly, at international human rights law (section 5.2). However, there are acts and decisions taken in the course of a multinational law enforcement operation at sea which are not governed by law at all; for example, the decision to transfer a piracy suspect, which is a result of negotiations rather than a legal procedure (section 5.3).

5.1 Domestic law: pivotal even in multinational operations

Domestic law, which encompasses norms protecting persons seized at sea, plays a pivotal role—even in law enforcement operations that are *multinational* in nature. For this, there are at least three reasons.

First of all, as we have seen, the mandate of a specific multinational mission does not necessarily cover all phases of the operation. For example, NATO's counter-piracy operations in the Gulf of Aden followed a deter-and-disrupt strategy and operated a catch-and-release scheme. NATO, unlike the EU, did not conclude any transfer agreements for the purpose of prosecuting seized suspects in states of the region. If a contributing state nevertheless decided to arrest and detain a suspect with a view to his prosecution, it did so in its national capacity; thus, domestic

[100] Article 8*bis*(10)(a)(vii) *juncto* Article 10(2) introduced to the SUA Convention (n 33) by the 2005 SUA Protocol (n 76). By contrast, the Protocol establishes its *own* standard for the use of force and human treatment of persons on board: see Article 8*bis*(9) and 8*bis*(10)(1)(a)(ii) introduced to the SUA Convention (n 33) by the 2005 SUA Protocol (n 76).

[101] See eg UNSC Res 2240 (n 43) para 10; UNSC Res 2182 (n 42) 16; and UNSC Res 2292 (n 42) para 4; in detail: A Petrig, 'The Role Accorded to Human Rights in Security Council Maritime Resolutions' in K Neri (ed), *Le Conseil de sécurité des Nations Unies et la mer/ The United Nations Security Council and the Sea* (Editoriale Scientifica 2018) Part II.

law governed the deprivation of liberty, including the procedural safeguards to be granted to arrested or detained suspects.[102]

Secondly, even if the mandate of a multinational law enforcement operation at sea covers arrest, detention, and transfer for prosecution—such as EUNAVFOR's *Operation Atalanta*[103]—some contributing states (eg France and Spain) prefer to revert back to national control if specific situations arise, notably if a ship flying their flag comes under attack. As soon as a contributing state reverts back to national control—which requires nothing more than sending a message to the EUNAVFOR Operational Headquarters—enforcement measures are taken under national authority and domestic law therefore applies.[104]

Thirdly, in multinational operations at sea, contributing states retain a certain degree of command and control. For example, the arrest, detention, and transfer of piracy suspects is neither a process controlled entirely by EUNAVFOR nor do these matters fall solely within the competence of the respective contributing state.[105] Hence, domestic law remains important, yet opinions differ as to what *moment* domestic law comes to bear. Essentially, there are two approaches that states contributing to counter-piracy operations in the Gulf of Aden follow. According to the first approach, termed here the 'ordinary suspect approach', domestic law applies from the very moment a suspect is arrested by naval personnel of the respective state. Spain, for example, applies its ordinary criminal procedural rules as soon as its troops arrest a suspect, while France enacted a specific law governing policing measures at sea, which foresees various procedural safeguards.[106]

States following the second approach, referred to here as the 'extraordinary suspect approach', take the stance that suspects deprived of their liberty are not 'ordinary' criminal suspects (such as those arrested by these states within their territory) to which domestic law and the respective procedural safeguards apply. Norway, for example, uses the term 'EU detainees', while Italy's *Corte di Cassazione*

102 Petrig (n 96) 54–55.

103 Council Joint Action 2008/851/CFSP of 10 November 2008 on a European Union military operation to contribute to the deterrence, prevention and repression of acts of piracy and armed robbery off the Somali coast [2008] OJ L301/33, Article 2 (as amended by Council Decision 2010/766/CFSP of 7 December 2010 amending Joint Action 2008/851/CFSP on a European Union military operation to contribute to the deterrence, prevention and repression of acts of piracy and armed robbery off the Somali coast [2010] OJ L327/49, Article 1).

104 Petrig (n 96) 84.

105 This makes attribution of conduct violating international law an intricate issue; see *Re 'MV Courier'* [2014] 4 A 2948/11 (Oberverwaltungsgericht Nordrhein-Westfalen) where the core question was whether the decision to transfer a piracy suspect to Kenya is attributable to Germany or rather to EUNAVFOR *Operation Atalanta*.

106 Loi française n° 2011-13 du 5 janvier 2011 relative à la lutte contre la piraterie et à l'exercise des pouvoirs de police en l'Etat de mer (2011); see (Loi française n° 2011-13); see L Briand, 'Lutte contre la piraterie maritime: la France renforce son arsenal législatif. À propos de la loi n° 2011-13 du 5 janvier 2011 relative à la lutte contre la piraterie et à l'exercice des pouvoirs de police en l'État en mer' (2011) Gazette du Palais 8–12.

refers to arrest occurring at sea as '*sui generis* apprehension';[107] and Germany has argued that its troops do not act within a criminal prosecution framework (*nicht strafverfolgend tätig*) when seizing piracy suspects, and their detention thus qualifies as 'international law custody' (*völkerrechtlicher Gewahrsam*).[108] These states only apply domestic law to suspects in the (rare!) case that they decide to prosecute a piracy suspect in their domestic courts. Before such a decision is taken, however, suspects are in 'legal limbo': the EU cannot guarantee procedural safeguards (eg the right to be brought promptly before a judge) and the seizing state is not willing to do so. If suspects are ultimately released, their deprivation of liberty was never subject to judicial control; and, in cases of transfer, these states argue that it suffices if the suspects are brought before a judge in the receiving state—a problematic view, as we will see in the next section (5.2).[109]

In sum, domestic law (partially or entirely) governs enforcement measures taken at sea by states contributing to multinational operations. Yet, in each of the aforementioned situations, a common problem remains: domestic legal acts regulating law enforcement (and providing for procedural safeguards) may not apply to a state's navy because the personal scope of application only covers traditional law enforcement agencies—that is, the police. For example, this holds true for both the Danish Administration of Justice Act and the German Code of Criminal Procedure.[110] At the same time, specific rules governing law enforcement measures carried out by naval forces may not exist (yet). Or they are contained in classified, or at least non-public, military documents (such as Standard Operating Procedures or Rules of Engagement) not living up to the quality of law standard developed by the European Court of Human Rights, which requires that the legal basis providing for deprivation of liberty and governing the relevant procedure must be 'sufficiently accessible, precise and foreseeable in its application, in order to avoid all risk of arbitrariness'.[111] Hence, there is a clear lack of coordination between the option under the international law of the sea to use warships and military personnel for law enforcement at sea (and an operational reality where navies indeed increasingly police the sea) and domestic law. This results in normative uncertainty, if not normative gaps, vis-à-vis the strictures attaching to the exercise of enforcement powers.

[107] S Dominelli, 'Transfer of Suspected Pirates and Human Rights: Axiomatic Theories, State Practice, and Judicial Interventions—A European Perspective on Some Possible Shortcomings of the Current International Legal Framework' (2017) 3 Diritto Marittimo 647, 666.

[108] C Kreß, 'Die moderne Piraterie, das Strafrecht und die Menschenrechte: Gedanken aus Anlass der deutschen Mitwirkung an der Seeoperation ATALANTA' in D Weingartner (ed), *Die Bundeswehr als Armee im Einsatz: Entwicklungen im nationalen und internationalen Recht* (Nomos 2010) 104.

[109] On the two approaches, see Petrig (n 96) 118–26.

[110] ibid 58–59 (Denmark) and 123–24 (Germany).

[111] *Ismoilov and others v Russia* App no 2947/06 (ECtHR, Judgment, 24 April 2008) para 137; Petrig (n 96) 231 and 240.

5.2 International law: human rights law not yet refined for the maritime context

As regards strictures imposed on actors enforcing the law, international human rights law is an obvious body of law to turn to. However, the procedural safeguards contained in human rights treaties were mainly drafted (and interpreted) with a view to applying to domestic and land-based law enforcement activities carried out by organs of that respective state. None of these assumptions are fulfilled in the context of multinational military operations tasked with the suppression of criminality at sea: not only do they take place extraterritorially, but in the maritime environment as well, and—most importantly—in close cooperation with different states and/or regional organizations.

Today, it seems difficult for states to maintain that human rights do not apply at all in the maritime context;[112] however, the requirements for triggering their application in an extraterritorial maritime environment are not yet entirely clear.[113] Further, a series of questions arises from the cooperative approach taken to law enforcement at sea, namely *which state* bears the responsibility to grant specific rights. The following example on the right to be brought promptly before a judge in a case of arrest or detention[114] illustrates this.

While much has been written on the notion of 'promptness',[115] another key issue has received considerably less attention: whether suspects seized at sea must be brought before the judge of the *seizing* state or whether it suffices that judicial control takes place in a *third* state (generally the state to which the suspect is transferred for prosecution). In the *Courier* case, where the legality of an arrest carried out by the German Navy while contributing to EUNAVFOR's *Operation Atalanta* was at issue, the German Administrative Court of Cologne supported the view of the Federal Government of Germany: the right to liberty was respected, even though the suspect was not brought before a German judge, because he was brought before a Kenyan judge (seven days after his arrest).[116] The Court supported

[112] France argued this way in *Medvedyev and Others v France* App no 3394/03 (ECtHR, Grand Chamber Judgment, 29 March 2010) para 49; today, however, it has a specific law governing enforcement measures at sea, including procedural safeguards, see (n 106).

[113] Geiß and Petrig (n 19) 103–14; K Neri, 'The Applicability of the European Convention on Human Rights to State Enforcement and Control at Sea' in G Andreone (ed), *Jurisdiction and Control at Sea: Some Environmental and Security Issues* (Giannini Editore 2014) 153–68.

[114] European Convention on Human Rights Convention for the Protection of Human Rights and Fundamental Freedoms (adopted 4 November 1950, entered into force 3 September 1953) ETS 5, Article 5(3) (ECHR); Article 9(3) of the International Covenant on Civil and Political Rights (adopted 16 December 1966, entered into force 23 March 1976) 999 UNTS 171 (ICCPR).

[115] In *Rigopoulos v Spain* App no 37388/97 (ECtHR, Fourth Section Judgment, 12 January 1999); and *Medvedyev and Others v France* (n 112) paras 131–34, the Court bestowed the notion of 'promptness' with a broad meaning; see also *Ali Samatar and Others v France* App nos 17110/10 and 17301/10 (ECtHR, Judgment, 4 December 2014) paras 45–59; *Hassan and Others v France* App nos 46695/10 and 54588/10 (ECtHR, Judgment, 4 December 2014) paras 89–104.

[116] *Re 'MV Courier'* [2011] 25 K 4280/09 (Verwaltungsgericht Köln, 25. Kammer) paras 20–26 (Germany's argument) and paras 39–49 (Court's view); this aspect was not appealed.

its findings with reference to the *Rigopoulos* and *Medvedyev* cases decided by the European Court of Human Rights. Yet, these and newer cases pertaining to the right to liberty in the maritime context[117] differ on a crucial point from the scenario at hand: the suspects were *not* transferred to a third state, but rather brought (with some delay) before the courts of the seizing state. Hence, they do not answer the question whether a judge of the seizing state must intervene or whether a 'judge is a judge'—regardless of the state to which she or he belongs. The latter proposition cannot be maintained for a number of reasons. First, the *preventive* purpose of Article 5(3) of the European Convention on Human Rights (ECHR)—to prevent arbitrary detention, abuse of power, and ill-treatment by the very intervention of a judge—cannot be achieved if judicial control (by the receiving state) takes place after deprivation of liberty (by the seizing state) ended. Secondly, from the principle of equal sovereignty of states, it follows that state A (eg Germany) cannot ensure that a suspect transferred to Kenya is indeed brought before a judge in state B (eg Kenya). What is more, a Kenyan judge cannot review the legality of an arrest carried out by German forces without violating the principle of *par in parem non habet iudicium*. Rather, arrest and detention at sea (by the seizing state) and deprivation of liberty on land (by the receiving state) are two separate spheres, each of which falls within the purview of a different jurisdiction. Thirdly, and finally, the very idea behind the right to see a judge is to subject the power of arrest and detention to judicial control—that is, that authorizations to enforce the law must always be glued together with respective limitations preventing boundless state action.[118]

This is just one of several situations where actors involved in multinational counter-piracy operations advocated for modification of an otherwise well-established procedural safeguard.[119] This underlines the need for further refinement of international human rights law for application to maritime law enforcement operations. What is arguably even more concerning than the modification of specific rights is the fact that some measures taken in the course of multinational operations are not governed by law at all—as is the case for the transfer of piracy suspects to third states for prosecution, to which we turn now.

[117] *Ali Samatar and Others v France* (n 115); *Hassan and Others v France* (n 115).

[118] In more detail: A Petrig, 'Arrest, Detention and Transfer of Piracy Suspects: A Critical Appraisal of the German *Courier* Case Decision' in G Andreone, G Bevilacqua, G Cataldi, and C Cinelli (eds), *Insecurity at Sea: Piracy and Other Risks to Navigation* (Giannini Editore 2013) 161–67.

[119] Actors involved in counter-piracy operations in the Gulf of Aden further suggested that no individual *non-refoulement* assessment is necessary in light of the transfer agreements concluded with states of the region, which request that suspects are granted certain human rights: see Petrig (n 96) 359–68.

5.3 No law at all: enforcement measures outside the 'legal universe'

For the offence of piracy, international law grants both universal enforcement and adjudicative jurisdiction. Despite these comprehensive authorizations, in the counter-piracy operations off the coast of Somalia, it has proven difficult to implement the basic tenet of every law enforcement operation—to bring apprehended suspects to justice—because patrolling states have been reluctant to prosecute seized suspects in their domestic courts. In light of this, EUNAVFOR concluded several transfer agreements with regional states, whereby the latter declared their general willingness to accept piracy suspects for prosecution—subject, however, to their consent in each individual case.[120]

The most obvious legal mechanism to bring an alleged offender from the jurisdiction of the arresting state to the jurisdiction of the prosecuting state is extradition. Despite being the traditional and common *modus operandi* to acquire jurisdiction over a criminal suspect in a transnational setting, extradition has thus far never been used to bring a piracy suspect from a patrolling state's warship within the jurisdiction of the prosecuting state;[121] rather, states have opted for so-called 'transfers'. The practice of Denmark contributing to NATO's counter-piracy operations and EUNAVFOR's *Operation Atalanta* demonstrates that the decision to transfer is issued through a process that fundamentally differs from extradition. A transfer is the result of negotiation and cooperation between two states or between a state and EUNAVFOR, rather than a surrender taking place in execution of a decision issued by an administrative and/or judicial body in a formalized procedure described in a legal act. Further, unlike in extradition proceedings, no judicial review of a decision to transfer is possible and suspects cannot exercise any procedural rights (eg formulate a *non-refoulement* claim).[122]

This example suggests that not only is the law at times unclear when applied to extraterritorial, multinational law enforcement operations at sea, but some acts and decisions are neither within the realm of legal procedures nor are they governed by law.

6. Conclusion

The security landscape has changed considerably in recent years. With criminal activity by non-state actors becoming one of the main maritime security threats,

[120] TR Salomon, *Die internationale Strafverfolgungsstrategie gegenüber somalischen Piraten* (Springer 2017) 9–16.
[121] Petrig (n 96) 41–42; there has been one single instance of extradition, but it was a unique case because the suspects were already on the European mainland.
[122] ibid 127.

navies are increasingly engaged in policing operations rather than assuming naval warfare-related tasks. Such operations are not 'warfare lite',[123] but rather determined by peacetime law. While this determination is rather straightforward, identifying the respective authorization to enforce the law is more complex: the basic rules of the law of the sea, which are maritime zone-specific, are derogated from by more specific rules for specific offences. These derogation rules flow from various legal sources—namely UNCLOS itself, other treaties, and Security Council resolutions (the latter likewise making jurisdiction at sea a volatile system). What is more, the mandate of a specific multinational operation may not allow for the exercise of all enforcement powers permitted under international law. Jurisdiction at sea is thus maritime zone-, offence-, and mandate-specific. Overall, the legal framework governing enforcement jurisdiction at sea is arguably the epitome of a 'legal pluriverse', yet the powers are more clearly defined than the strictures attaching to their exercise. The sources from which limitations stem are diverse as well, although a number of ambiguities and normative gaps can be identified. They are notably due to the multinational character of enforcement operations, the fact that they take place in an extraterritorial maritime environment, and the navies occupying the role of lead actor rather than the police. Moreover, as the example of decisions to transfer piracy suspects illustrated, some phases of multinational law enforcement operations simply take place outside the 'legal universe' altogether.

As has been accurately pointed out, '[c]hoosing the right regime of authority for action and fully understanding the implications of that choice can make the difference between strategic success and failure' of maritime enforcement operations.[124] Yet, this alone is not enough: choosing the right source of authority and observing the relevant strictures when acting upon such authorizations ultimately determines the *legality* and the *legitimacy* of multinational law enforcement operations at sea.

[123] See title of Luke (n 9).
[124] ibid 11.

PART V

COMPLEX OPERATIONAL ENVIRONMENTS

Diversity of Actors and Its Impact on the Legal Pluriverse Surrounding Multinational Military Operations

18

Receiving States, Sending States, and the Impact of Their Domestic Laws

Aurel Sari

1. Introduction

The legal environment of multinational military operations consists of a mix of international and domestic norms. Rules of international law govern matters such as the right of multinational forces to be present in foreign territory, while rules of domestic law address questions such as the exercise of discipline over their members. On closer inspection, however, it does not take long to realize that there is hardly any aspect of multinational deployments that is covered *solely* by either international or domestic norms. Matters such as the presence of foreign troops, dispute settlement, discipline, the wearing of uniform, and contracting all engage rules of both international and domestic law, including the domestic laws of sending states, receiving states, and, potentially, third states. Multinational military operations are subject to a multitude of regulatory regimes.

The abundance of applicable legal regimes is a source of complexity and uncertainty. For example, disparities between the domestic laws of sending states and the institutional rules of sending organizations present problems for legal interoperability.[1] Another set of difficulties arises between sending states and receiving states. Both have a strong interest in asserting their authority: invariably, sending states will extend the applicability of their domestic laws to any forces they deployed abroad in order to maintain control over their personnel, while receiving states will seek to ensure that foreign troops present in their territory respect local law. Whereas achieving legal interoperability between sending states and organizations is mostly a question of coordination, between sending and receiving states, the challenge is to resolve jurisdictional conflicts and competition.

The present chapter focuses on this second set of difficulties and explores the exercise of jurisdiction in the context of multinational military operations from the perspective of sending and receiving states. Both categories of states may claim to be competent under international law to regulate the conduct of military

[1] See DS Goddard, 'Understanding the Challenge of Legal Interoperability in Coalition Operations' (2017) 9 Journal of National Security Law and Policy 211.

Aurel Sari, *Receiving States, Sending States, and the Impact of Their Domestic Laws* In *The 'Legal Pluriverse' Surrounding Multinational Military Operations*. Edited by Robin Geiß and Heike Krieger, Oxford University Press (2020).
DOI: 10.1093/oso/9780198842965.003.0019

contingents in certain matters, based on the territorial principle and the organic jurisdiction principle (sections 2 and 3). This overlap of competence may lead sending states and receiving states to exercise their authority in relation to the same subject matter (section 4). A number of principles, legal regimes, and instruments are available in international law to resolve the legal and practical challenges that this concurrent exercise of jurisdiction presents. We will review three of these applicable to consensual deployments:[2] the reserved domain of domestic jurisdiction, the law of state and functional immunity, and status of forces agreements (section 5).

2. Receiving States: The Territorial Principle

The modern international legal order was erected on the principle of state sovereignty. However, with the progressive de-territorialization of international law,[3] sovereignty is no longer the gold standard of legal argument, as it increasingly competes with other ideals and principles, such as human rights.[4] However, in certain fields, sovereignty retains its normative currency. In particular, it continues to serve as the primary justification for the exercise of authority by states within their own territory. As Max Huber noted in his arbitral award in the *Island of Palmas* case, sovereignty in essence refers to the exclusive competence of a state to exercise the functions of a state within its territory.[5] Despite the changed structure of international law, a state's capacity to exercise jurisdiction within its borders is still widely regarded as a manifestation of its sovereignty to this day.[6]

Since sovereignty is territorial in nature, the state's competence to exercise jurisdiction—that is, its capacity to regulate human conduct and to determine the consequence of events by prescribing and enforcing rules of law[7]—is itself primarily territorial in character.[8] In fact, the territorial principle furnishes states with

[2] Different rules and considerations apply during non-consensual deployments, including in times of armed conflict. See A Sari, 'The Status of Armed Forces in Public International Law: Jurisdiction and Immunity' in A Orakhelashvili (ed), *Research Handbook on Jurisdiction and Immunities in International Law* (Edward Elgar 2015) 319, 361–62.

[3] C Brölmann, 'Deterritorialization in International Law: Moving Away from the Divide Between National and International Law' in Andre Nollkaemper and Janne Elisabeth Nijman (eds), *New Perspectives on the Divide between National and International Law* (OUP 2007) 84.

[4] A Peters, 'Humanity as the A and Ω of Sovereignty' (2009) 20 European Journal of International Law 513. In the present context, see also L Raible, 'Title to Territory and Jurisdiction in International Human Rights Law: Three Models for a Fraught Relationship' [2018] Leiden Journal of International Law 1.

[5] *Island of Palmas Case* (1928) 2 RIAA 829, 838.

[6] *SS Lotus (France v Turkey)* PCIJ Rep Series A, No 10, 19 (a state's 'title to exercise jurisdiction rests in its sovereignty'). cf J Crawford, *Brownlie's Principles of Public International Law* (9th edn, OUP 2019) 191 ('The competence of states in respect of their territory is usually described in terms of sovereignty and jurisdiction').

[7] MS McDougal, 'Jurisdiction' (1980) 62 International Law Studies 634, 634.

[8] *Banković and Others v Belgium and Others* App no 52207/99 (ECtHR, Grand Chamber Judgment, 12 December 2001) para 59; *Legal Consequences of the Construction of a Wall in the Occupied Palestinian Territory* (Advisory Opinion) [2004] ICJ Rep 136, para 109.

the most comprehensive legal basis to assert their authority.[9] It is common to distinguish the exercise of prescriptive jurisdiction from the exercise of adjudicative and enforcement jurisdiction. The former refers to the state's capacity to create and to extend the application of legal norms through legislative and administrative action, while the latter two refer to its capacity to subject legal and natural persons to the judicial process of its courts and tribunals, and to compel compliance with its laws and regulations through judicial, executive, or administrative measures. The territorial principle enables states to exercise all three forms of jurisdiction—prescriptive, adjudicative, and enforcement—over all persons and objects located in their territory and over any activities and events taking place therein.[10]

When foreign armed forces are present on the territory of another state, territorial sovereignty entitles the local authorities, in principle, to subject the force and its individual members to their laws and legal processes in all matters, whether criminal or civil.[11] While local laws and regulations are applicable primarily to acts performed by the foreign force and its members inside the receiving state's territory, the territorial principle may also extend to acts or events that occurred partly outside its borders. For example, under the objective territorial principle,[12] members of foreign forces may be held responsible by the local authorities for conspiring abroad to commit a crime against local law inside the receiving state.[13] In addition, the receiving state may also be bound by treaty to establish its jurisdiction over foreign military personnel who have committed certain offences in third countries, for instance torture,[14] but who are now present on its territory.

Given that the territorial principle permits receiving states to exercise, in principle, the full spectrum of their jurisdictional competences over foreign forces, it would seem unnecessary for the local authorities to rely on other bases of jurisdiction to assert their authority.[15] Nevertheless, such other bases of jurisdiction may complement the territorial principle by enabling receiving states to exercise prescriptive jurisdiction extraterritorially, that is beyond their borders, in particular in the field of criminal law. Pursuant to the nationality principle, a receiving

[9] See C Ryngaert, *Jurisdiction in International Law* (2nd edn, OUP 2015) 49–100.

[10] *Laker Airways v Sabena and KLM*, 731 F.2d 909 (DC Cir 1984) 921 (territoriality is the 'most pervasive and basic principle underlying the exercise by nations of prescriptive regulatory power').

[11] Eg *Holmes v Laird*, 459 F.2d 1211 (DC Cir 1972) 1216.

[12] W Berge, 'Criminal Jurisdiction and the Territorial Principle' (1931–1932) 30 Michigan Law Review 238. See also PD Szigeti, 'The Illusion of Territorial Jurisdiction' (2017) 52 Texas International Law Journal 369.

[13] Eg *DPP v Doot* [1973] AC 807 (HL); *R v Fan* (1991) 56 ACR 189 (Court of Criminal Appeal, New South Wales); *HM Advocate v Megrahi* (2000) JC 555 (HCJ). See JDA Blackmore, 'The Jurisdictional Problem of the Extraterritorial Conspiracy' (2006) 17 Criminal Law Forum 71.

[14] Article 5(2) of the Convention Against Torture and Other Cruel, Inhuman or Degrading Treatment or Punishment (adopted 10 December 1984, entered into force 26 June 1987) 1465 UNTS 112. cf Joint Separate Opinion of Judges Higgins, Kooijmans and Buergenthal, *Case Concerning the Arrest Warrant of 11 April 2000 (Democratic Republic of the Congo v Belgium)* [2002] ICJ Rep 3, para 41.

[15] On these alternative bases of jurisdiction, see M Akehurst, 'Jurisdiction in International Law' (1972–1973) 46 British Yearbook of International Law 145, 156–66; Ryngaert (n 9) 101–42.

state may extend the reach of its criminal laws to acts committed by its nationals abroad,[16] thereby allowing its competent authorities to prosecute foreign service personnel holding its nationality for such acts if they are present within its borders. Similarly, a receiving state may establish its prescriptive jurisdiction over acts committed by foreign troops against its security or other vital interests pursuant to the protective principle;[17] over acts committed against its nationals pursuant to the passive personality principle;[18] as well as over certain international crimes, such as war crimes, under the principle of universal jurisdiction.[19] In all of these cases, the local authorities may claim the right to exercise adjudicative and enforcement jurisdiction over the foreign personnel concerned pursuant to the territorial principle once they are in the territory of the receiving state.

Classic formulations of the principle of territorial jurisdiction have often been framed in categorical terms. In the case of *The Schooner Exchange*, Chief Justice Marshall famously declared on behalf of the United States Supreme Court that the 'jurisdiction of the nation within its own territory is necessarily exclusive and absolute'.[20] More than a century later, Max Huber referred to the 'exclusive competence of the State in regard to its own territory' in the *Island of Palmas* case.[21] Statements to similar effect abound in the classical works on international law.[22] Even though broad assertions of territorial sovereignty might suggest that a state's competence to exercise jurisdiction within its own borders is both exclusive and absolute in scope, the relevant authorities in fact readily accept that territorial jurisdiction is subject to certain restrictions.[23] In practice, the right to exercise territorial jurisdiction is heavily curtailed by rules of customary international law and by applicable international agreements.[24] For instance, the law of state immunity bars local courts from exercising their jurisdiction over foreign states and their property in matters not of a commercial character, including over property of a military character or

[16] Eg Article 94 of the Swiss Military Penal Code, the Militärstrafgesetz vom 13. Juni 1927 (adopted 13 June 1927, entered into force 1 January 1928) AS 43 359 (MStG) penalizes Swiss nationals who enlist in foreign armed forces, irrespective of the place of their recruitment.

[17] Eg *R v Desmond Ellis* [1992] 95 Cr App R 52 (CCC). See MB Kirzek, 'The Protective Principle of Extraterritorial Jurisdiction: A Brief History and an Application of the Principle to Espionage as an Illustration of Current United States Practice' (1988) 6 Boston University International Law Journal 337.

[18] Eg *US v Roberts*, 1 F Supp.2d 601 (ED La 1998).

[19] Eg Article 129 of the Convention Relative to the Treatment of Prisoners of War (Geneva Convention III) (adopted 12 August 1949, entered into force 1 December 1950) 75 UNTS 135. See Y Dinstein, 'The Universality Principle and War Crimes' in MN Schmitt and others (eds), *The Law of Armed Conflict: Into the Next Millennium* (Naval War College 1998) 17.

[20] *The Schooner Exchange v McFaddon*, 11 US 116 (US SupCrt 1812) 136. See also *Church v Hubbart*, 6 US 187 (US SupCrt 1804) 234.

[21] *Island of Palmas* (n 5) 838 and 839.

[22] Eg H Wheaton, *Elements of International Law* (Carey, Lea & Blanchard 1836) 98; GF de Martens, *Precis Du Droit Des Gens Moderne De L'Europe* (Giullaumin Et Cie Libraries 1864) 227; JC Bluntschli, *Das moderne Völkerrecht der Civilisirten Staten als Rechtsbuch dargestellt* (CH Beck 1868) 85–86.

[23] Eg *The Schooner Exchange* (n 20) 136. See also *Longa v Netherlands* App no 33917/12 (ECtHR, 9 October 2012) para 69.

[24] Eg *Smallwood v Clifford*, 286 F.Supp 97 (D.DC 1968) 100.

property used or intended for use in the performance of military functions,[25] as well as over warships and naval auxiliaries.[26] Customary international law also accords immunity to state officials and agents from local jurisdiction in relation to acts carried out in the performance of their official duties. The International Law Commission is thus currently in the process of formulating a set of draft articles on the immunity of state officials from foreign criminal jurisdiction.[27]

3. Sending States: Organic Jurisdiction

Since the right to exercise jurisdiction that the territorial principle confers on receiving states is neither exclusive nor absolute in scope, it does not comprehensively prevent sending states from exercising their own jurisdiction in the territory of the receiving state. Indeed, state practice shows that national service laws and regulations routinely entitle the competent military authorities of sending states to take disciplinary measures against members of their forces and exercise other forms of jurisdiction over them during their deployment abroad,[28] whether in the context of bilateral or multilateral deployments. This should not come as a surprise. Military forces are the ultimate guarantor of the security and independence of the state to which they belong.[29] In order to enable them to carry out their responsibilities, national forces are subject to a unique system of internal governance and administration that is characterized by a superior-subordinate relationship, the exercise of command and control, and specialized disciplinary and justice procedures.[30] The primary purpose of this system of internal governance and administration is to maintain the combat effectiveness of the force.[31] It makes little difference in this respect whether the force is stationed at home or deployed abroad. The need to preserve the effectiveness of military contingents dictates that they should remain under their national chain of command and their distinct administrative arrangements wherever they are.[32]

[25] Article 21(1)(b) of the United Nations Convention on Jurisdictional Immunities of States and Their Property, Annex to GA Res. 59/38 (2 December 2004) UN Doc A/RES/59/38; [2005] 44 ILM 801 (UN State Immunity Convention).

[26] Article 16(2) UN State Immunity Convention.

[27] See the analytical guide to the work of the International Law Commission at <http://legal.un.org/ilc/guide/4_2.shtml>. All URLs accessed 27 December 2018.

[28] Eg Article 9 of the Defence Force Discipline Act 1982, Act No 152 of 1982 (Australia); Article L121-1 Code de Justice Militaire (Nouveau) (France); Articles 83–86 Code de Justice Militaire, Loi no 95-042/AN-RM du 20 avril 1995 (Mali); Article 10 Wet militaire strafrechtspraak, Rijkswet van 14 juni 1990, Stb. 370 (the Netherlands). See R Liivoja, *Criminal Jurisdiction over Armed Forces Abroad* (CUP 2017) 169–263.

[29] See Parliamentary Assembly of the Council of Europe, Recommendation 1742 on Human Rights of Members of the Armed Forces (11 April 2006) Doc 10861, para 1.

[30] *Smith v Secretary of State for Defence* [2010] UKSC 29 (UK Supreme Court) para 192.

[31] Supreme Court of Canada, *R v Généreux* [1992] 1 SCR 259, 293–95.

[32] Generally, see G Nolte (ed), *European Military Law Systems* (De Gruyter 2003).

However, despite the consistency with which sending states assert their jurisdiction over their armed forces abroad, it is not immediately clear what principle of international law entitles them to do so. Whereas the presence of foreign forces in the receiving state brings them squarely within its territorial jurisdiction, it also removes them from the territorial authority of the sending state, so that any exercise of jurisdiction by sending states over their armed forces abroad will by definition be extraterritorial in nature.[33] Domestic courts have occasionally suggested that the exercise of authority by a sending state over territory that belongs to the receiving state but in practice is occupied and administered by the sending state, such as territory leased or otherwise made available for the establishment of military bases and installations,[34] represents an exercise of territorial jurisdiction.[35] This approach is misguided, because it uses the term 'territorial jurisdiction' loosely to refer to any exercise of governmental authority over a given geographical area regardless of the legal principle on which it is based. Understood in this way, the term merely describes a factual situation—the exercise of power over territory. By contrast, territorial jurisdiction in the strict sense, as traditionally understood, means state jurisdiction based on the principle of territoriality, and thus stands for the competence that every state enjoys under international law over its national territory as a result of its sovereignty.[36] It follows from this definition that the competence to exercise territorial jurisdiction derives from territorial sovereignty and therefore rests with the territorial sovereign alone.[37] Sending states do not exercise territorial jurisdiction over their forces deployed in foreign territory, even if they exercise *de facto* or *de jure* control over portions of that territory.[38]

What other principles may justify the exercise of jurisdiction by sending states, then? As far as prescriptive jurisdiction is concerned, sending states may rely on several grounds to extend the application of their laws to their forces abroad, in

[33] R Higgins, *Problems and Process: International Law and How We Use It* (Clarendon Press 1994) 73.

[34] Eg Agreement for the Lease to the United States of Lands in Cuba for Coaling and Naval Stations (23 February 1903) 6 Bevans 1113 and Agreement Providing Conditions for the Lease of Coaling or Naval Stations (US–Cuba) (2 July 1903) 6 Bevans 1120. Generally, see J Woodliffe, *The Peacetime Use of Foreign Military Installations under Modern International Law* (Martinus Nijhoff 1992).

[35] *US v Corey*, 232 F.3d 1166 (9th Cir 2000); *Rasul v Bush*, 542 US 466 (US SupCrt 2004) 480–82. Similar claims have been made with regard to the exercise of jurisdiction over embassies and over foreign ships interdicted on the high seas: *US v Erdos*, 474 F.2d 157 (4th Cir 1973); *US v Cardales*, 168 F.3d 548 (1st Cir 1999) at 553. See J Yoon, 'International Law: Closing the Gap on Extraterritorial Jurisdiction One Way or the Other' (2001–2002) 14 Florida Journal of International Law 503.

[36] See *Al Odah v US*, 321 F.3d 1134 (DC Cir 2003) 1142–43.

[37] Occupying powers thus do not exercise territorial sovereignty over occupied territory. cf *R (Al-Skeini and Others) v Secretary of State for Defence* [2005] EWCA Civ 1609 (CA) especially paras 113–28; *R (Al-Skeini and Others) v Secretary of State for Defence* [2007] UKHL 26 (HL) especially paras 82–83, 129.

[38] cf dissenting opinion of J Jackson, joined by CJ Vinson, and JJ Frankfurter and Burton, in *Vermilya-Brown Co, Inc v Connell*, 335 US 377 (US SupCrt 1948) 392 and, more recently, dissenting opinion of J Scalia, joined by CJ Rehnquist, and J Thomas, in *Rasul v Bush*, 542 US 466 (US SupCrt 2004) 500–01. This may be contrasted with the case of the Akrotiri and Dhekelia Sovereign Base Area in Cyprus, over which the United Kingdom has retained sovereignty: Article 1 of the Treaty concerning the Establishment of the Republic of Cyprus (16 August 1960) 382 UNTS 9.

particular the nationality, the protective and the passive personality principle. Moreover, even though the territorial principle is not available to sending states in its pure form, in some cases they may nevertheless rely on the subjective and objective territorial principle to assert their jurisdiction over crimes commenced or completed by their troops inside the receiving state.[39] However, none of these traditional bases of jurisdiction, whether taken on their own or in combination, confer on sending states sufficient authority to regulate all questions relating to their armed forces abroad. In particular, they do not account for the competence of sending states to subject members of their forces, including those of foreign nationality, to military service laws and regulations.[40] For instance, it is difficult to see which traditional principle of jurisdiction would entitle a sending state to issue orders to military personnel who do not hold its nationality, to prescribe their working hours,[41] or to require them to wear uniform when not on duty.[42] That the relevant service laws and regulations of the sending state continue to apply to its personnel during their deployment abroad is evident, otherwise such deployments would be tantamount to releasing them from their military duties. This is obviously not the case.

Similarly, the traditional bases of jurisdiction do not satisfactorily explain the sending state's competence to exercise extraterritorial adjudicative and enforcement jurisdiction over members of its forces in the receiving state. As the Permanent Court of International Justice has ruled in the *Lotus* case, a state 'may not exercise its power in any form in the territory of another State', except if a permissive rule to the contrary derived from customary international law or an international agreement entitles it to do so.[43] International law offers many historic and contemporary examples of such permissive rules, including the capitulations granted by the Ottoman Empire and China to Western states,[44] the powers conferred on the commanders of civilian aircraft in flight over foreign territory,[45] and the agreement enabling the Scottish High Court of Justiciary to hear the *Lockerbie* case in the Netherlands.[46] However, as the *Lotus* judgment suggests, the exercise

[39] See n 12.

[40] Eg *US v Weiman*, 11 CMR 216 (CMA 1953).

[41] For examples of the rules governing working hours and overtime, see G Nolte and H Krieger, 'Comparison of European Military Law Systems', in Nolte (n 32) 19, 101–04.

[42] Eg The Queen's Regulations for the Army (1975) 1AC 13206 (UK) para 5, 363.

[43] *SS Lotus* (n 6) 18–19. See also *Corfu Channel Case (Albania v UK)* (Merits) [1949] ICJ Rep 4, 35; *Military and Paramilitary Activities in and against Nicaragua (Nicaragua v United States of America)* (Merits) [1986] ICJ Rep 14, paras 202–09.

[44] See E Pears, 'Turkish Capitulations and the Status of British and Other Foreign Subjects Residing in Turkey' (1905) 21 Law Quarterly Review 408; J Escarra, 'Le régime des concessions étrangères en Chine' (1929) 27-II Recueil des Cours 1.

[45] Articles 5–10 of the Convention on Offences and Certain Other Acts Committed on Board Aircraft (Tokyo Convention) (14 September 1963) 704 UNTS 219. See AW Knauth, 'The Aircraft Commander in International Law' (1947) 14 Journal of Air Law and Commerce 157.

[46] Agreement between the Government of the United Kingdom of Great Britain and Northern Ireland and the Government of the Kingdom of the Netherlands Concerning a Scottish Trial in the Netherlands (Lockerbie Agreement) (18 September 1998) 2062 UNTS 82. See DR Andrews, 'A Thorn

of extraterritorial adjudicative and enforcement jurisdiction in such cases is exceptional and must be based either on a rule of customary international law to this effect or on the consent of the territorial state expressed in an international agreement or through other means.[47]

The traditional bases of jurisdiction are too narrow to satisfy this requirement. For instance, the nationality principle does not cover military personnel who are not nationals of the sending state, while the protective, passive personality and universal principle are inapplicable to minor and therefore relatively insignificant infringements of discipline. It may be contended that the authority to exercise adjudicative and enforcement jurisdiction over military forces abroad derives from the receiving state's consent to the presence of the foreign force. As Chief Justice Marshall held in *The Schooner Exchange*, the grant of free passage to foreign troops necessarily implies that their commander may 'use that discipline, and to inflict those punishments which the general government of his army may require'.[48] However, the receiving state's consent does not account for sending states' underlying legal capacity to exercise command and control abroad, nor does it explain the exercise of jurisdiction in circumstances where such consent is lacking.

The answer lies elsewhere. International law recognizes the 'inalienable right' of every state to freely organize itself and to choose its own form of government.[49] This right not only guarantees each state's freedom to determine its own political system without foreign interference, but it also points to an absence of international norms substantively governing its choice as to how it constitutes itself.[50] Amongst other things, the right recognizes each state's competence to establish organs and subdivisions at the central, regional, and local level in order to carry out governmental functions, to transfer such functions to international organizations,[51] and to regulate and control its organs and officials. This latter competence of the state to

on the Tulip—A Scottish Trial in the Netherlands: The Story behind the Lockerbie Trial' (2004) 36 Case Western Reserve Journal of International Law 207.

[47] Eg *Miquiabas v Philippine Ryukyus Command US Army* (1948) 80 Phil. 262 (Supreme Court of the Philippines); *US v Robinson*, 843 F.2d 1 (1st Cir 1988) 4; *US v Carter*, 16 USCMA 277 (USCMA 1966).

[48] *The Schooner Exchange* (n 20) 140. cf *Longa* (n 23) para 72.

[49] Article 3 of the Convention on Rights and Duties of States adopted by the Seventh International Conference of American States (Montevideo Convention) (16 December 1933) 165 LNTS 19; Principle 3, UNGA Res 2625 (XXV) 'Friendly Relations Declaration' (24 October 1970) UN Doc A/RES/25/2625.

[50] This is not to say that no rules of international law apply to the internal organization of the state. International law requires state government to be effective (cf dissenting opinion of J Alvarez, *Anglo-Iranian Oil Co. Case (United Kingdom v Iran)* [1952] ICJ Rep 93, 39–40). States may even commit themselves to a certain form of government (eg Article 8 of the State Treaty for the Re-establishment of an Independent and Democratic Austria (Austrian State Treaty) (15 May 1955) 217 UNTS 224). Rather, international law leaves it to the discretion of states to choose the means and forms of exercising governmental authority. cf A Ræstad, 'La Reconnaissance, la Determination et la Signification en Droit International du Domaine Laisse par ce dernier a la Competence Exclusive de l'Etat' (1932) 3 Nordisk Tidsskrift for International Ret 108, 113; A Verdross, 'Domestic Jurisdiction Under International Law' (1971) 3 University of Toledo Law Review 119, 119–20.

[51] *Maastricht-Urteil* (1993) BVerfGE 89, 155; (1994) 33 ILM 388 (Bundesverfassungsgericht).

exercise jurisdiction over its organs and officials has been termed 'organic jurisdiction'.[52] Most of the time, states exercise authority over their organs within their own territory, in which case this form of jurisdiction overlaps with, and is obscured by, the territorial principle.[53] While some commentators have therefore questioned whether organic jurisdiction 'amounts to anything more than territorial or personal jurisdiction of the State',[54] the distinction nature and function of the concept emerges clearly in circumstances where states exercise jurisdiction over their own officials and agents located abroad.

Since national armed forces constitute an organ of the state to which they belong,[55] and remain an organ of their state even where they participate in multinational operations,[56] the right of each state to freely organize itself extends to the organization and administration of its armed forces.[57] It is consequently up to each state, subject to any applicable rules of international law,[58] to determine the strength and composition of its military,[59] to fill its ranks through conscription or through voluntary recruitment,[60] or to decide not to maintain a standing army at all.[61] Moreover, each state is competent to regulate the activities of its forces, for example by subjecting their deployment to constitutional limits,[62] by adopting rules governing such matters as their terms of service, and issuing binding instructions to them through their chain of command. When deployed abroad, national armed forces are therefore not only the object of their sending state's extraterritorial jurisdiction, but they also exercise extraterritorial jurisdiction themselves over subordinate units and personnel.[63] While it is tempting to describe this exercise of

[52] On the principle of organic jurisdiction, see F Seyersted, 'Jurisdiction over Organs and Officials of States, the Holy See and Intergovernmental Organisations' (1965) 14 International and Comparative Law Quarterly 31, 33–43.

[53] ibid 34.

[54] H Fox, 'Employment Contracts as an Exception to State Immunity: Is All Public Service Immune?' (1995) 66 British Yearbook of International Law 97, at 120.

[55] *Transaero, Inc. v La Fuerza Aerea Boliviana*, 30 F.3d 148 (DC Cir 1994) 153; *Shooting Range Extension Case* (1984) 86 ILR 533 (Verwaltungsgerichtshof Kassel) 534.

[56] cf *Attorney-General v Nissan* [1970] AC 179 (HL) 198.

[57] Dissenting opinion of J Fernandes in *Right of Passage over Indian Territory (Portugal v India)* (Merits) [1960] ICJ Rep 6, 125.

[58] Such as rules prohibiting the use of certain weapons: eg Convention on Prohibitions or Restrictions on the Use of Certain Conventional Weapons Which May Be Deemed to Be Excessively Injurious or to Have Indiscriminate Effects (10 October 1980) 162 UNTS 1342.

[59] *Nicaragua* (n 43) para 269.

[60] cf Case C-186/01, *Dory v Germany* [2003] ECR I-2479 (ECJ). See Martin Trybus, 'Case C-186/01, Alexander Dory v Federal Republic of Germany, Judgment of the Court of 11 March 2003, not yet reported' (2003) 40 Common Market Law Review 1269.

[61] Such as Iceland. See M Bjorgulfsdottir, 'The Paradox of a Neutral Ally: A Historical Overview of Iceland's Participation in NATO' (1989) 13 Fletcher Forum of World Affairs 71.

[62] For Germany, see D König, 'Putting an End to an Endless Constitutional Debate? The Decision of the Federal Constitutional Court on the "Out of Area" Deployment of German Armed Forces' (1995) 38 German Yearbook of International Law 103. For the United Kingdom, see House of Lords Select Committee on the Constitution, Waging War: Parliament's Role and Responsibility (2005–2006) HL 236-I and HL 236-II.

[63] McDougal (n 7) 634.

extraterritorial prescriptive, adjudicative, and enforcement jurisdiction by and over foreign forces in *sui generis* terms as 'service jurisdiction', the latter form of jurisdiction represents merely one particular manifestation of the principle of organic jurisdiction among others.[64]

4. Concurrent Jurisdiction: The Interplay of Domestic Laws

The fact that receiving states and sending states may both claim to be competent to exercise their authority over members of multinational forces means that their respective jurisdictional competences overlap. Jurisdiction over foreign forces is therefore concurrent under general international law, at least in principle. This presents certain difficulties.

Sending states may for good reasons object to the applicability of local laws and standards to their national contingents. For example, it would be inappropriate for receiving states to impose their employment and labour law on foreign troops. Matters pertaining to wages, overtime, holiday entitlements, promotion, or dismissal directly affect the relationship between each sending state and its troops and therefore should be governed by its own standards, rather than those of the receiving state.[65] Sending states may also object to the exercise of local adjudicative and enforcement jurisdiction. They may do so for operational reasons: the launch of criminal proceedings against their service personnel would prevent them from fully discharging their duties and may have an adverse effect on the overall effectiveness of the force.[66] They may do so to protect the individual rights of their troops, for instance where local procedural safeguards and conditions of detention do not meet international standards. Moreover, sending states may wish to shield their personnel from liability in proceedings relating to acts they performed in the course of their official duties, given that in such cases they act on behalf of their respective sending states in an official, rather than a private, capacity.[67]

Conversely, there are good reasons why receiving states may wish to assert their authority over foreign forces and resist the exercise of jurisdiction by sending states. While a receiving state may agree to the exercise of disciplinary and policing powers by the service authorities over other members of the foreign force, it may insist that they do not impose and execute punishments that contradict its public policy. The death penalty offers one example.[68] Similarly, while receiving

[64] Another example of the exercise of such extraterritorial jurisdiction by and over a state organ are the activities and prerogatives of consular officials and diplomatic agents.

[65] cf *R v Birkenhead Borough Justices, Ex parte Smith* [1954] 1 WLR 471 (QBD) 474.

[66] *The Schooner Exchange* (n 20) 139.

[67] As France did in *Case concerning the Differences between New Zealand and France arising from the Rainbow Warrior Affair* (1986) 19 RIAA 199, 211.

[68] *Short v Netherlands* (1990) 76 Rechtspraak van de Week 358, (1990) 29 ILM 1378, 30 March 1990 (Supreme Court of the Netherlands). See SJ Lepper, 'Short v the Kingdom of the Netherlands: Is It Time

states may be inclined not to impose their own labour standards on such matters as the promotion or dismissal of foreign personnel, they may not exercise such restraint when it comes to child labour, gender discrimination, or the employment of local civilians.[69] In all matters that potentially or actually affect third parties, receiving states generally will be reluctant to relinquish their regulatory authority. For example, receiving states will insist that foreign forces observe the applicable road safety and traffic regulations,[70] as this is clearly in the public interest.[71] They will also be reluctant to cede their adjudicative and enforcement jurisdiction in circumstances where foreign personnel commit crimes against local residents. More serious crimes, especially those of a sexual nature, are particularly sensitive.[72] This is true even for incidents that occur in the performance of official functions.[73]

While international law thus recognizes, in the form of the territorial and the organic principle, that receiving states and sending states have a legitimate interest in asserting their jurisdiction, their interests are diametrically opposed. Both states will seek to maximize their own jurisdiction and minimize the jurisdiction of the other party. It is therefore imperative, in the interests of legal certainty and the maintenance of amicable relations between sending and receiving states, to resolve, or at least mitigate as far as possible, any jurisdictional conflicts between them.

Of course, the mere existence of a jurisdictional competence does not necessarily mean that the state concerned will have exercised it. It is useful to recall the classic case of *R v Keyn* in this regard.[74] The case turned on the question whether the English Central Criminal Court had jurisdiction to try Ferdinand Keyn, the captain of a German ship, on the charge of manslaughter for a collision that took place between his and a British ship in British territorial waters in 1876. On appeal, the majority accepted that international law may have entitled the United Kingdom to try a foreign national for acts committed on a foreign ship present in British waters, but decided that this alone did not actually confer jurisdiction on the English courts in the absence of an Act of Parliament to this effect.[75] In other words, while

to Renegotiate the NATO Status of Forces Agreement' (1991) 24 Vanderbilt Journal of Transnational Law 867.

---

[69] cf *Holland v Lampen-Wolfe* [2000] 1 WLR 1573 (HL).

[70] Eg *Urey v Lummis* [1962] 1 WLR 826 (High Court, Queen's Bench Division).

[71] See J Vandiver, 'US Army Howitzer Shipment Halted by German Police' (Stars and Stripes, 11 January 2018) <http://www.stripes.com/news/europe/us-army-howitzer-shipment-halted-by-german-police-1.506232>.

[72] AB Norman, 'The Rape Controversy: Is a Revision of the Status of Forces Agreement with Japan Necessary' (1995) 6 Indiana International & Comparative Law Review 717.

[73] As illustrated by the Cavalese and the Calipari incidents. See A Ciampi, 'Public Prosecutor v Ashby. Judgement No 161/98' (1999) 93 American Journal of International Law 219; N Ronzitti, 'L'immunità funzionale degli organi stranieri dalla giurisdizione penale: Il caso *Calipari*' (2008) 91 Rivista di Diritto Internazionale 1033.

[74] *R v Keyn* [1876] 2 Ex D 63 (Court for Crown Cases Reserved). See AWB Simpson, *Leading Cases in the Common Law* (Clarendon Press 1996) 227–58.

[75] *Keyn* (n 74) 207.

international law may have permitted the United Kingdom to assert its jurisdiction, Parliament did not in fact make use of that right. As this case shows, the extent to which the laws of one sending state apply to its service personnel abroad, and thus the extent to which they overlap and may come into conflict with the laws of the receiving state, depends on the extraterritorial scope of application of those laws themselves. The precise scope of the jurisdictional overlap cannot be determined in the abstract but must be assessed in each individual case with reference to the applicable laws and regulations.

For example, section 42(1) of the Armed Forces Act 2006[76] expressly extends the applicability of English criminal law to British forces deployed abroad in the following terms:

> A person subject to service law, or a civilian subject to service discipline, commits an offence under this section if he does any act that –
> (a) is punishable by the law of England and Wales; or
> (b) if done in England or Wales, would be so punishable.

As a result of this Act, members of the British armed forces are subject to domestic criminal law wherever they are deployed.[77] It is on the basis of this provision that British service personnel have been tried in the United Kingdom for kidnapping, sexual assault, theft, and assault occasioning actual bodily harm committed in Germany,[78] and for murder[79] and manslaughter[80] committed in Afghanistan. By contrast, the provisions of the Health and Safety at Work etc Act 1974, which are applicable to the Ministry of Defence inside the United Kingdom, are applicable extraterritorially only to the extent that an Order in Council provides for this.[81] The Health and Safety at Work etc Act 1974 (Application Outside Great Britain) Order 2001 extends the application of the Act to offshore facilities and to certain activities taking place within the territorial waters of the United Kingdom or other designated areas. This means that the Act does not apply to British forces and activities outside these geographical zones, for instance in Iraq, Germany, or the British Sovereign Base Areas of Akrotiri and Dhekelia.

[76] Armed Forces Act 2006 (c 52).

[77] *R v Mohammed Gul* [2012] EWCA Crim 280 (Court of Appeal) para 190; *R v Mohammed Gul* [2013] UKSC 64 (UK Supreme Court) para 30.

[78] *R v Mayende and Others* [2015] EWCA Crim 1566 (Court Martial Appeal Court).

[79] See *R v Blackman* [2014] EWCA Crim 1029 (Court Martial Appeal Court).

[80] *R v Blackman* [2017] EWCA Crim 190 (Court Martial Appeal Court). See E Stuart-Cole, 'Blackman (Marine A): Inculpable or Incapable? R v Blackman (Alexander Wayne) [2017] EWCA Crim 190' (2017) 81 Journal of Criminal Law 262.

[81] Section 84 of The Health and Safety at Work etc Act 1974 (c 37).

5. Resolving Jurisdictional Conflicts

It must also be stressed that the mere existence of a jurisdictional competence does not mean that the state concerned is entitled to exercise it. Whether receiving states are entitled to rely on the territorial principle and sending states on the organic principle to exercise their authority depends on other applicable norms of international law that either permit or prohibit the exercise of their respective jurisdictional competences over a force.[82] Below, we will examine three sets of such rules.

5.1 The reserved domain of domestic jurisdiction

International law does not regulate every aspect of state conduct, but preserves a reserved domain of domestic jurisdiction within which states are free to act at their discretion to the extent that no applicable rules of international law govern their activities.[83] This reserved domain is not just an ever-decreasing sphere of state activity as yet unregulated by international norms, but also a reserve of matters which, because of their political sensitivity, international law protects from outside intervention.[84] While there exists no universally accepted list of matters that come within this reserved domain, it is widely accepted that it includes each state's right to freely decide its form of government and internal organization.[85] Since this right includes the exercise of jurisdiction by a state over its own organs,[86] it follows that the exercise of organic jurisdiction over the armed forces, including the exercise of command and control, falls within the reserved domain of domestic jurisdiction. This, in turn, implies that international law recognizes and safeguards the exclusive competence of each state to organize, administer, and control its armed forces.

This conclusion is supported by state practice. While states sometimes delegate limited powers of command and control over their armed forces to other states and to international organizations, in particular in the context of peace support and other multinational operations,[87] they never relinquish the ultimate authority

[82] cf *R v Mohammed Gul* [2013] UKSC 64 (UK Supreme Court) paras 42–58.

[83] *Nationality Decrees Issued in Tunis and Morocco, Advisory Opinion* (1923) PCIJ Series B, No 4, 23–24. See JL Brierly, 'Matters of Domestic Jurisdiction' (1925) 6 British Yearbook of International Law 8; Q Wright, 'Domestic Jurisdiction as a Limit on National and Supra-National Action' (1961) 56 Northwestern University Law Review 11; B Cheng, 'Jurimetrics: The Meaning and Measurement of Legal Sovereignty and Domestic Jurisdiction' (1991) 1 University of Miami Yearbook of International Law 30.

[84] cf JL Brierly, 'The General Act of Geneva, 1928' (1930) 11 British Yearbook of International Law 119, 129 ('It is a mistake, I think, to say that international law has no rule for matters of domestic jurisdiction; its rule is that they are matters of domestic jurisdiction').

[85] Eg Ræstad (n 50), 113. cf *Customs Régime between Germany and Austria (Protocol of March 19th, 1931), Advisory Opinion* (1931) PCIJ Series A/B, No 41, 45.

[86] See above.

[87] See B Cathcart, 'Command and Control in Military Operations' in TD Gill and D Fleck (eds), *The Handbook of the International Law of Military Operations* (2nd edn, OUP 2015) 259; Christopher Leck,

for the command and administration of their troops,[88] known as full or supreme command.[89] Sending states thus always retain supreme command over their forces during their presence abroad,[90] including all lesser powers of command and control included in the concept of supreme command, unless and to the extent that they expressly delegate some of these powers to another state or international organization.

Interference by one state with matters falling within the reserved domain of domestic jurisdiction of another state is prohibited when it is dictatorial or coercive in nature, that is to say when it implies 'a peremptory demand for positive conduct or abstention—a demand which, if not complied with, involves a threat of or recourse to compulsion in some form'.[91] The exercise of adjudicative and enforcement jurisdiction is coercive in nature by definition.[92] However, even the exercise of prescriptive jurisdiction may be considered dictatorial if it constitutes an attempt by one state to unilaterally regulate the conduct of the target state, with binding effect and backed by sanctions,[93] in an area where international law entitles that state to freedom of action.[94] Consequently, any exercise of jurisdiction by a receiving state over the internal governance and administration of a foreign force and its components represents, in principle, an unlawful interference into the domestic jurisdiction of the sending states concerned.[95] The very notion of a reserved domain implies that sending states' authority in these matters must be exclusive.

While the principle of the reserved domain thus limits the receiving state's right to exercise its territorial jurisdiction, the principle operates at a high level of generality. It is one thing to say that only sending states may issue military orders to their personnel and that the local authorities are incompetent to do so, but this does not imply that foreign forces may carry out their orders in total disregard of local law. Moreover, the dividing line between matters falling within the internal governance and administration of a force and matters that do not is not always easy to discern. For instance, regulating the external appearance of foreign military vehicles,

'International Responsibility in United Nations Peacekeeping Operations: Command and Control Arrangements and the Attribution of Conduct' (2009) 10 Melbourne Journal of International Law 346.

---

[88] *Jaloud v Netherlands* (2015) 60 EHRR 29, para 143.

[89] NATO Military Committee, MC 57 (Final) (11 October 1957) 10 ('Full Command is the military authority and responsibility of a superior officer to issue orders to subordinates, and covers every aspect of military operations and administration. It exists only within national services').

[90] cf *Shooting Range Extension Case* (n 55) 534.

[91] H Lauterpacht, 'The International Protection of Human Rights' (1947) 70-I Recueil des Cours 1, 20. See UNGA Res 2131 (XX) 'Declaration on the Inadmissibility of Intervention in the Domestic Affairs of States' (21 December 1965) UN Doc A/RES/20/2131; *Nicaragua* (n 43) paras 202–09.

[92] cf *Arrest Warrant Case* (n 14) para 70.

[93] cf *FTC v Compagnie De Saint-Gobain-Pont-a-Mousson*, 636 F.2d 1300 (DC Cir 1980) 1313–14.

[94] *Legal Status of Eastern Greenland (Denmark v Norway)* (1933) PCIJ Series A/B, No 53, 48 ('Legislation is one of the most obvious forms of the exercise of sovereign power').

[95] DJ Gerber, 'Beyond Balancing: International Law Restraints on the Reach of National Laws' (1984) 10 Yale Journal of International Law 185, 212.

such as their camouflage pattern, evidently falls within the reserved domain of each sending state. However, would a highway code requiring convoys, including convoys of foreign military vehicles, to display removable warning signs amount to prohibited intervention? What if the highway code required permanent alterations, such as the fixing of warning beacons? As this example illustrates, the point at which reasonable regulation turns into prohibited intervention is contextual and somewhat fluid. The prohibition to interfere with matters falling within a sending state's reserved domain of domestic jurisdiction therefore offers only imprecise guidance on what the limits of the lawful exercise of the receiving state's territorial jurisdiction are.

5.2 Immunity from jurisdiction

National armed forces constitute organs of their sending states[96] and as such benefit from the principle of state immunity.[97] In fact, acts performed by or concerning the armed forces are widely cited as examples of public acts to which immunity from foreign jurisdiction attaches under international law.[98] However, not every activity undertaken by the military is necessarily sovereign in character. Just like other state organs, the armed forces too are capable of entering into transactions of a private character to which state immunity does not apply.[99]

While the applicability of the principle of state immunity to foreign armed forces is not in doubt, it is less clear whether their immunities are governed by the general rules of state immunity or by special rules of international law. States often enter into so-called 'status of forces agreements' to regulate the exercise of jurisdiction over visiting forces in express terms, including their exemptions from local jurisdiction.[100] A strong argument can be made that consistent and widespread state practice relating to such agreements over the last century has given rise to certain customary rules in this area. For example, it is widely accepted that the scope of the immunities enjoyed by foreign forces from local jurisdiction depends on the operational environment in which they are deployed. Similarly, state practice in this field suggests that torts committed by foreign forces inside the territory of the receiving state continue to attract immunity from local jurisdiction under customary

[96] *Transaero, Inc v La Fuerza Aerea Boliviana*, 30 F.3d 148 (DC Cir 1994) 153.

[97] *Jurisdictional Immunities of the State (Germany v Italy; Greece intervening)* [2012] ICJ Rep 99, para 52. See also Draft Articles on the Jurisdictional Immunities of States and their Property, with Commentaries, Report of the International Law Commission on the work of its forty-third session (29 April–19 July 1991), [1991] II(2) YILC 13, 15–16.

[98] *Victory Transport Inc. v Comisaria General*, 336 F.2d 354 (2nd Cir 1964) 360; *McElhinney v Williams and Secretary of State for Northern Ireland* [1995] 3 IR 382 (Irish Supreme Court) 402.

[99] Eg *Trendtex Trading Corporation v Central Bank of Nigeria* [1977] QB 529 (CA) 558. As Hoffmann LJ held in *Littrell v USA (No 2)* [1995] 1 WLR 82 (CA) at 95, there is no 'bright line' by which sovereign activities performed by the armed forces may be distinguished from non-sovereign transactions.

[100] See below.

international law, notwithstanding the so-called 'territorial tort' exception. This point has been confirmed by case law.[101] The maritime domain offers other examples of specialized rules, such as the duty of local authorities not to exercise their powers on board warships without the consent of the commander.[102]

Given the existence of such special rules and considerations, Article 31 of the European Convention on State Immunity of 1972 stipulates that '[n]othing in this Convention shall affect any immunities or privileges enjoyed by a Contracting State in respect of anything done or omitted to be done by, or in relation to, its armed forces when on the territory of another Contracting State'.[103] The Convention thus explicitly defers to the *lex specialis* rules applicable in this area.[104] Although the more recent United Nations Convention on Jurisdictional Immunities of States and Their Property[105] lacks an explicit provision to this effect, its drafting history suggests that it was meant to adopt a similar stance.[106] State practice thus suggests that foreign forces benefit from distinct jurisdictional immunities under customary international law which in certain respects may be broader than the general rules of state immunity.[107]

In addition to benefitting from state immunity, members of foreign forces also enjoy immunity from the adjudicative and enforcement jurisdiction of another state for acts performed in their official capacity. As the International Criminal Tribunal for the Former Yugoslavia held in the *Blaškić* case, state officials acting in an official capacity are instruments of their state, and their official action must be attributed to that state itself.[108] The applicability of the principle of functional immunity to foreign military personnel is well established. In the case of *Underhill v Hernandez*, the US Circuit Court for the Second Circuit held that military personnel 'are not in any case amenable to the civil or criminal laws of a foreign state, in respect to acts done in their capacity as agents, for which they would be punishable or civilly responsible if done in their private capacity'.[109] The Mixed Courts of Egypt have also accepted that members of friendly forces are immune from local jurisdiction whenever they commit an offence in the performance of their

[101] *McElhinney v Ireland* (2002) 34 EHRR 322, para 38.

[102] See *Orfanidis v Ministère Public* (1943) 12 AD 141 (Egypt, Mixed Court of Cassation). See also *Japan v Smith and Stinner* (1952) 19 ILR 221 (High Court of Osaka) 222, on the functional immunity of foreign sailors.

[103] European Convention on State Immunity (adopted 16 May 1972, entered into force 11 June 1976) 1495 UNTS 182.

[104] See Explanatory Report on the European Convention on State Immunity, reprinted in A Dickinson, R Lindsay, and JP Loonam (eds), *State Immunity: Selected Materials and Commentary* (OUP 2004) 64.

[105] United Nations Convention on Jurisdictional Immunities of States and Their Property (2 December 2004) Annex to GA Res 59/38; (2005) 44 ILM 801.

[106] See Sari (n 2), 351–54.

[107] But see *Re Canada Labour Code* (1992) 2 SCR 50 (Supreme Court of Canada).

[108] *Prosecutor v Tihomir Blaskić (Judgement on the Request of Croatia for Review of the Decision of Trial Chamber II of 18 July 1997)* (1997) 110 ILR 607 (ICTY Appeals Chamber) para 38.

[109] *Underhill v Hernandez*, 65 F. 577 (Circuit Court of Appeals 2nd Cir 1895) 58.

duties.[110] In more recent times, the Italian Court of Cassation confirmed in the *Lozano* case that the principle of functional immunity applies to foreign troops as a matter of customary international law,[111] noting that the principle has found widespread recognition in the literature and case law.[112] Nonetheless, some questions remain unsettled. In particular, one line of cases questions whether functional immunity in domestic courts extends to acts performed in violation of international law.[113] In this respect, it is also worth noting that the draft articles on the immunity of state officials from foreign criminal jurisdiction provisionally adopted by the International Law Commission are without prejudice to the immunities enjoyed by persons connected with the military forces of a state under 'special rules of international law'.[114] Like the European and United Nations conventions on state immunity, the draft articles thus defer to any applicable *lex specialis* rules.

5.3 Status of forces agreements: tailor-made regimes

Neither the reserved domain of domestic jurisdiction nor the rules of functional and state immunity are capable of conclusively resolving all difficulties that arise with regard to the exercise of jurisdiction over foreign troops. Rather than leave the legal position of foreign forces to be resolved with reference to broad principles and uncertain rules of customary international law, states have therefore turned to international agreements to define the status of foreign troops on a case-by-case basis.[115] During the course of the twentieth century, status of forces agreements have become widespread.[116] However, their proliferation has not given rise to a uniform legal regime. Sending and receiving states enter into different legal arrangements depending on the reasons for the presence of the foreign force, its operational environment and the broader political context. Nevertheless, despite the absence of uniformity, international treaty practice in this area is remarkably

[110] Eg *Ministère Public v Triandafilou* (1942) 11 AD 165 (Egypt, Court of Cassation).

[111] *Italy v Mario Luiz Lozano* (2008) Judgment, 31171/2008, Oxford Reports on International Law in Domestic Courts 1085 (IT 2008) 24 July 2008 (Corte Suprema di Cassazione).

[112] The cases the Court of Cassation referred to include *Jones v Saudi Arabia* [2007] 1 AC 270 (House of Lords), *Al-Adsani v UK* (2002) 24 EHRR 11 and *Kalogeropoulou and Others v Greece and Germany* (2002) 129 ILR 537.

[113] In particular, see *Ferrini v Germany* (2003) 128 ILR 658 (Italy, Court of Cassation). See C Focarelli, 'Denying Foreign State Immunity for Commission of International Crimes: The Ferrini Decision' (2005) 54 International and Comparative Law Quarterly 951.

[114] Article 1(2) of the Text of draft articles 1, 3 and 4 provisionally adopted by the Drafting Committee at the Sixty-fifth session of the International Law Commission (4 June 2013) UN Doc A/CN.4/L.814.

[115] *Astrup v President of the Council of Ministers* (1973) 77 ILR 556 (Italy, Constitutional Court) 557.

[116] See A Sari, 'The Immunities of Visiting Forces', in T Ruys, N Angelet and L Ferro (eds), *The Cambridge Handbook of Immunities and International Law* (Cambridge University Press 2019) 559, 564–68.

consistent, as states and international organizations typically adopt similar arrangements in similar circumstances. Two types of legal regimes stand out.[117]

Status of forces agreements adopted for the purposes of peacekeeping and other security assistance operations that take place in challenging legal and operational environments are typically weighed in favour of sending states and organizations by conferring more extensive jurisdictional privileges and immunities on foreign forces. This approach is exemplified by the UN Model Status of Forces Agreement (UN Model SOFA) of 1990.[118] The UN Model SOFA confirms that UN officials and experts on mission enjoy the legal status provided for in the Convention on the Privileges and Immunities of the United Nations of 1946.[119] These two groups therefore enjoy immunity for official acts, which may be waived by the UN Secretary-General. By contrast, military members of national contingents are subject to the exclusive jurisdiction of their sending state in all criminal matters, meaning that they are completely exempt from the criminal jurisdiction of the receiving state. This immunity is not subject to waiver by the UN Secretary-General. These arrangements have served as a model for other status of forces agreements adopted for the purposes of multinational operations deployed in similar circumstances.[120]

By contrast, status of forces agreements adopted in the context of structured military cooperation between political allies are often modelled on the NATO Status of Forces Agreement (NATO SOFA) of 1951.[121] The NATO SOFA is based on the principle of reciprocity. It aims to balance the competing interests and jurisdictional competences of sending and receiving states in an equitable manner.[122] The NATO SOFA does so by recognizing that both states have exclusive jurisdiction over offences which violate their own law, but not the law of the other state. In cases where an act is subject to concurrent jurisdiction, the NATO SOFA establishes a system of priorities. Sending states enjoy the primary right to exercise jurisdiction over their service personnel in relation to offences arising out of the performance of their official duties and any offences directed solely against the sending state's security, property or personnel. Receiving states enjoy primary jurisdiction

[117] Other arrangements include the grant of immunities equivalent to those accorded to administrative and technical staff under the Vienna Convention on Diplomatic Relations of 1961: eg Agreement between Australia and the Kyrgyz Republic on the Status of Australian Forces in the Kyrgyz Republic (14 February 2002) [2002] ATS 14.

[118] Model Status-of-Forces Agreement for Peace-keeping Operations: Report of the Secretary-General (9 October 1990) UN Doc A/45/594.

[119] Convention on the Privileges and Immunities of the United Nations (adopted 13 February 1946, entered into force 17 September 1946) 1 UNTS 1.

[120] Eg Agreement between Australia, Papua New Guinea, New Zealand, Fiji and Vanuatu concerning the Neutral Truce Monitoring Group for Bougainville (5 December 1997) [1997] ATS 30.

[121] Agreement between the Parties to the North Atlantic Treaty Regarding the Status of Their Forces (19 June 1951) 199 UNTS 67.

[122] A Sari, 'The NATO SOFA at Sixty: Heading for Retirement or Has Life Just Begun?' (2012) NATO Legal Gazette 2, 5–6.

in all other cases. These arrangements are widely perceived to have struck a fair balance between the competing interests of sending states and receiving states,[123] since they accord priority of jurisdiction to the state which has the greater interest in exercising it. As such, the NATO SOFA has served as a model for a substantial number of bilateral[124] and multilateral[125] status of forces agreements.

6. Conclusion

Multinational military operations give rise to an overlap of competences between sending and receiving states. As we have seen, international law recognizes that both states have a legitimate interest in regulating the activities of the military contingents involved, either on the basis of the territorial principle or on the basis of the principle of organic jurisdiction. This opens the door for conflicts of jurisdiction and regulatory competition. Although conflicts of jurisdiction are a familiar feature of international relations, they are particularly acute in the present context, as they pit two core elements of sovereign statehood against each other: the receiving state's right to assert its authority within its territory versus the sending state's right to exercise command and control over its armed forces. Addressing the problem of concurrent jurisdiction is therefore one of the most pressing legal challenges faced by multinational deployments.

International law has not conclusively resolved this dilemma. Although certain principles and regimes, such as the law of state immunity, limit the extent to which sending states and receiving states may exercise their competences in parallel, the rules in question often offer only partial and imprecise guidance on how to deal with concurrent jurisdiction. There is a continuing need, therefore, for sending and receiving states to enter into tailor-made agreements that allocate the right to exercise jurisdiction among the parties in express terms and against the background of the specific legal, operational and political context of each particular deployment.[126] Even so, the legal framework of multinational deployments remains complex. For instance, the fact that the extraterritorial application of domestic laws

[123] cf Y Jung and JS Hwang, 'Where Does Inequality Come From—An Analysis of the Korea-United States Status of Forces Agreement' (2002–2003) 18 American University International Law Review 1103.

[124] Eg Exchange of Notes constituting an Agreement between the United Kingdom and Belize concerning the Continuing Presence in Belize after Independence of United Kingdom Armed Forces (1 December 1981) 1285 UNTS 206.

[125] Eg Convention between Denmark, Germany, and Poland on the Multinational Corps Northeast (5 September 1998) BGBl (1999) II 675.

[126] To similar effect, see WT Worster, 'Immunities of United Nations Peacekeepers in the Absence of a Status of Forces Agreement' (2008) 47 Military Law and the Law of War Review 277, 365.

is not always settled remains a source of uncertainty for all parties that status of forces agreements and other rules of international law do not address.[127] The close interaction between international and domestic norms in this area highlights that the generic rules of international law only go so far: specific legal problems require specific legal solutions.

[127] A Ramo, 'U.S. Military Accountability for Extraterritorial Environmental Impacts: An Examination of Okinawa, Environmental Justice, and Judicial Militarism' (2014) 28 Tulane Environmental Law Journal 53.

19

Legal Challenges in Multinational Military Operations

The Role of National Caveats

Jochen Katze and Maral Kashgar

1. Introduction

Multinational or combined military operations are defined as 'an operation conducted by forces of two or more nations acting together'.[1] Germany mostly participates in operations conducted by the North Atlantic Treaty Organization (NATO) or the European Union (EU), often mandated by and under varying degrees of supervision of the United Nations (UN). This chapter primarily uses NATO doctrine when describing principles and procedures related to national caveats. Due to their background, the authors focus on the German perspective. However, caveats are used by most troop-contributing nations (TCN) to a greater or lesser extent.

The very nature of a multinational military operation (MMO), that is its multinationality, poses a considerable challenge to its formation. Every single TCN has its own international and national legal obligations and policies, which may diverge from the laws and policies of other TCNs. Without an instrument enabling the TCNs to harmonize their differing standpoints, the TCNs' diverging national laws and policies have a high potential of hampering the establishment of a common operational framework for an MMO, especially a common Operation Plan (OPLAN) and Rules of Engagement (RoE) regulating the use of military force.

This obstacle to the forming of MMOs has been overcome to a certain degree by the use of so-called 'national caveats', which allow TCNs to agree to a common OPLAN and RoE while adhering to their national laws and policies. For this reason, national caveats are explicitly acknowledged by NATO doctrine when stating that it is recognized that nations will issue restrictions and/or amplifying instructions in order to ensure compliance with their national laws.[2]

[1] NATO, 'NATO Glossary of Terms and Definitions—AAP 6' (2017) <http://nso.nato.int/nso/zPublic/ap/aap6/AAP-6.pdf>, all URLs accessed 27 December 2018. For further details see also introduction.

[2] N Lange, 'MC 362/1—NATO Rules of Engagement' (*Centre d'Etude de Droit Militaire et de Droit de la Guerre Studiecentrum voor Militair Recht en Oorlogsrecht*) <http://www.ismllw-be.org/session/2015-05-05-LANGE%20N.pdf>, sec 05.

Jochen Katze and Maral Kashgar, *Legal Challenges in Multinational Military Operations* In *The 'Legal Pluriverse' Surrounding Multinational Military Operations*. Edited by Robin Geiß and Heike Krieger, Oxford University Press (2020).
DOI: 10.1093/oso/9780198842965.003.0020

Despite the enabling effect for participation, national caveats are a mixed blessing for the functioning of an MMO because they have the potential to severely limit the flexibility of the multinational commander in deploying the forces under his or her control. Therefore, national caveats have been criticized for significantly impeding the effective functioning of an MMO and thus for hampering its success.[3]

The aim of this chapter is to explain why national caveats are necessary (section 2), how they work (section 3), and how they impede the operations (section 4). The chapter closes with a short overview of how they are dealt with in practice (section 5).

2. The Rationale behind National Caveats

A multinational alliance faces two interrelated challenges in the process of forming an MMO.

2.1 The TCNs' responsibility for their national forces despite the transfer of command and control over them to the MMO

One of the first steps necessary for the formation of the force for an MMO is the TCNs' relinquishment of part of their authority over their national forces to the MMO. Besides the fact that this affects a key area of their national sovereignty, the TCNs remain responsible for the acts of their contributed forces to a crucial degree, despite the very loss of their command and control over them.[4] This dilemma constitutes the basic predicament which TCNs encounter when forming the force for an MMO.

2.1.1 Transfer of command and control over the national forces

The transfer of authority (TOA) over the national forces is necessary for the effective functioning of a multinational military force, as it empowers the multinational commander to employ her or his forces for the MMO mission.[5] To facilitate this process, NATO has defined various levels of command and control that apply to NATO-led operations.[6] 'Operational command' means that the multinational commander will have the authority 'to assign missions or tasks to subordinate commanders, to deploy units, to reassign forces, or to retain or

[3] Eg J Fussnecker, 'The Effects of International Human Rights Law on the Legal Interoperability of Multinational Military Operations' [2014] The Army Lawyer 7.

[4] On this topic see also Paulina Starski's contribution in this book (Chapter 15).

[5] NATO, 'AJP 3 (B)—Allied Joint Doctrine for the Conduct Operations' (16 March 2011) <http://nso.nato.int/nso/zPublic/ap/ajp-3(b).pdf>, no 0201.

[6] ibid no 0194 for an overview of defined command and control relationships.

delegate operational and/or tactical control as the commander deems necessary'.[7] Operational command usually stays with the TCN. 'Operational control', on the other hand, refers to the authority of a commander 'to direct forces assigned so that the commander may accomplish specific missions or tasks which are usually limited by function, time, or location; to deploy units concerned, and to retain or assign tactical control of those units'.[8] This is the level of command and control usually bestowed on multinational commanders.

Despite the limitations in command and control of a multinational commander, principally, he or she has sufficient authority over the national contingents to deploy them independently of the TCNs in order to achieve the mission.

2.1.2 Remaining state responsibility for the acts of the contributed forces[9]

TCNs will however need to ensure that their armed forces act in accordance with their international and national legal obligations and policies.[10] This state concern has been playing an increasingly important role as there seems to be a tendency in the judiciary of attributing the conduct of forces in an MMO to the TCNs rather than to the international organization mandating or conducting the operation.

For example, the Regional Court of Bonn ruled on 11 December 2013, that a claim for compensation with respect to injuries incurred on the occasion of the airstrikes on kidnapped fuel trucks in Kunduz Province, Afghanistan, was admissible. According to the court's reasoning, claims for compensation regarding potentially wrongful acts of German authorities were to be tried in German courts. The court attributed the airstrikes to Germany without going into much detail on the issue of whether the airstrikes were an act of German authorities. Ultimately, however, it rejected the claim on the merits, as is did not determine the existence of a wrongful act.[11]

Paradoxically, in the same case, the Administrative Court of Cologne argued and decided against attribution to Germany in its judgment on 9 February 2012.[12] Here, the applicant sought a declaration of unlawfulness of the airstrike. The Administrative Court, however, dismissed the action as inadmissible for several reasons. The court primarily held that German jurisdiction was not applicable to the case because the airstrike did not constitute state action which was attributable to German authorities. Looking at the United Nations mandate under which the German forces were acting and the chain of command—operational control within the ISAF forces as a NATO led operation—the Administrative Court found

[7] ibid no 0194, 'operational command': it does not include responsibility for administration which will remain with the TCN.
[8] ibid no 0194 'operational control'.
[9] On this topic see also Paulina Starski's contribution in this book (Chapter 15).
[10] cf Fussnecker (n 3) 9.
[11] Landgericht (Regional Court) Bonn, Urteil vom 11. Dezember 2013, Az 1 O 460/11.
[12] Verwaltungsgericht (Administrative Court) Köln, Urteil vom 09. Februar 2012, Az 26 K 5534/10.

that the German forces were subject to NATO control and that their actions were finally attributable to the United Nations.

In another, more recent case, the Higher Administrative Court of the Land of North Rhine Westphalia adopted a judgment on 18 September 2014, in which it departed from the approach taken by the Administrative Court of Cologne. This case concerned a Somali and eight other persons who were captured by the German naval contingent of the EU-led multinational military operation *ATALANTA* and transferred to Kenia for criminal prosecution for piracy. Despite the fact that Germany had transferred its command and control over its naval forces participating in the *ATALANTA* operation to the EU, the court held that the transfer of the applicant was attributable to Germany rather than to the EU. Contrary to the Administrative Court of Cologne in the *Kunduz* case, the Higher Administrative Court disregarded the actual chain of command within the operation. Instead, it focused on the German influence on the decision to transfer the applicant and held that its interference showed its effective control over the decision to transfer, so that the transfer had to be attributed to Germany. It further argued that the EU, at the time of transfer, did not have legal personality, which was established only after conclusion of the Lisbon Treaty with its Article 47 TEU.[13]

The European Court of Human Rights (ECtHR) seems to follow the same path of attributing military action to the TCN regardless of the forces being in the chain of command of an MMO, by deviating from the principles that it had laid down in its *Behrami/Saramati* decision. One famous example for this change in opinion is certainly the *Al Jedda* judgment.[14]

The District Court in The Hague, on the other hand, struck another balance in its *Srebrenica* judgment of 16 July 2014. This case dealt with the conduct of the Dutch contingent in the United Nations Protection Force (UNPROFOR) in relation to the genocide in Srebrenica. In a nutshell, the Dutch court limited the attribution of state action to TCNs to cases of *ultra vires* conduct. In the current case, it attributed parts of the Dutch conduct to the Netherlands, as some national orders were conflicting with UN orders.[15]

One cannot help but note a degree of inconsistency in the jurisprudence on state responsibility in relation to MMOs and the increasing tendency of European courts to holding TCNs accountable for the acts of their contributed troops despite their loss of control over them due to a multinational chain of command. Regardless of whether one approves of the described developments in judicial practice, it cannot

[13] Oberverwaltungsgericht (Higher Administrative Court) Münster, Urteil vom 18. September 2014, Az 4a 2948/11.

[14] *Al-Jedda v the United Kingdom* App no 27021/08 (ECtHR, Grand Chamber Judgment, 7 July 2011); *Behrami and Saramati v France, Germany and Norway* App nos 71412/01 and 78166/01 (ECtHR, Grand Chamber Decision, 2 May 2007).

[15] The Hague District Court, Case no C/09/295247 / HA ZA 07-2973, Judgment of 16 July 2014, available at <http://deeplink.rechtspraak.nl/uitspraak?id=ECLI:NL:RBDHA:2014:8748>.

be dismissed that it may promote the use of extensive national caveats by TCNs and—in the long run—even may have a counterproductive impact on TCNs' willingness to contribute troops to MMOs at all.

2.2 The finding of a common operational framework

A second difficulty to overcome is that the TCNs must agree upon common OPLAN and RoE in order to standardize the rules on the use of force which include aspects of kinetic operations, detention, seizure, and other executive measures necessary to achieve the mission goal.[16] In a NATO-led MMO, common RoE and OPLAN are approved and authorized by the North Atlantic Council and thus reached by consensus, that is, they must be accepted by all twenty-eight member states. This means that twenty-eight different legal and political positions must be reconciled.

The first difficulty posing a challenge to the establishment of a common operational framework concerns the different legal obligations of the TCNs. They may not be parties to the same international treaties, and thus not be bound by the same rules.[17] For instance, while the United States and Canada are not bound by the European Convention on Human Rights (ECHR), the European NATO states are. The application of the ECHR is particularly relevant with respect to the general prohibition of security or administrative detentions in Article 5 ECHR. Having regard to the restrictive approach of the ECtHR on overriding obligations under Article 103 UN Charter, ECHR state parties may be reluctant to conduct detention operations.[18]

[16] cf Fussnecker (n 3) 10.

[17] W Baron, 'Command Responsibility in a Multinational Setting: How to Deal with Different Interpretations of International (Humanitarian) Law. Some Experiences from Practice' (2005) 44 Military Law and Law of War Review 138, 139.

[18] See *Al-Jedda v the United Kingdom* (n 14), para 100 with reference to further case law of the ECtHR in this matter. Note however the recent judgment of the Grand Chamber in the *Case of Hassan v The United Kingdom*, in which the ECtHR expressly deviated from this position in the case of international armed conflicts. The Court first recognized the 'important differences of context and purpose between arrests carried out during peacetime and the arrest of a combatant in the course of an armed conflict', and emphasized that 'detention under the powers provided for in the Third and Fourth Geneva Conventions is [not] congruent with any of the categories set out in [Article 5, para 1] subparagraphs (a) to (f)', (para 96). Then, it held that

> [b]y reason of the co-existence of the safeguards provided by international humanitarian law and by the Convention in time of armed conflict, the grounds of permitted deprivation of liberty set out in subparagraphs (a) to (f) of that provision should be accommodated, as far as possible, with the taking of prisoners of war and the detention of civilians who pose a risk to security under the Third and Fourth Geneva Conventions. The Court is mindful of the fact that internment in peacetime does not fall within the scheme of deprivation of liberty governed by Article 5 of the Convention without the exercise of the power of derogation under Article 15 (see paragraph 97 above). It can only be in cases of international armed conflict, where the taking of prisoners of war and the detention of civilians who pose a threat to security

The International Covenant on Civil and Political Rights (ICCPR), on the other hand, to which all NATO states are parties, does not prohibit security detentions.[19] Thus, the question of detention may pose difficulties in agreeing upon the operational framework of an MMO or, if agreed upon, executing it.[20]

Further, TCNs may take different approaches as to the question of which bodies of law apply during an MMO. For instance, during a non-international armed conflict (NIAC), some TCNs may argue that the gaps in international humanitarian law (IHL) applicable to NIACs must be filled with international human rights law (IHRL). Other TCNs may however take the position that IHL derogates IHRL during times of armed conflict as *lex specialis*.[21] There may even be differences as to the qualification of the situation which leads to the application of different legal regimes. For instance, until 2009, Germany as a TCN to the International Security Assistance Force (ISAF) refused to characterize the situation in Afghanistan as an armed conflict and therefore would only allow its national forces to use force compatible with IHRL.[22] Other ISAF states such as the United States, on the other hand, applied IHL because they classified the situation as an armed conflict.[23]

Another substantial difference which often exists between TCNs—usually between the United States and European states—is the interpretation and application of the right to self-defence in military operations. While it is common ground between TCNs that self-defence is defined as 'the use of force to defend against attack or imminent attack',[24] most European states have a significantly narrower understanding of what constitutes an 'imminent attack' as compared to the United States.[25] Due to this diverging interpretation, it may occur that one TCN can immediately respond to an attack in self-defence while another TCN requires an authorization by RoE for an offensive operation.[26] US forces will apply their national Standing RoE (SROE) when exercising their right of self-defence, which state

> are accepted features of international humanitarian law, that Article 5 could be interpreted as permitting the exercise of such broad powers.

Hassan v The United Kingdom App no 29750/09 (ECtHR, Grand Chamber Judgment, 16 September 2014) para 104.

---

[19] D Cassel, 'International Human Rights Law and Security Detention' (2009) 40(3) Case Western Reserve Journal of International Law 383–402.

[20] cf also A Cole, 'Legal Issues in Forming the Coalition' in MN Schmitt (ed), *The War in Afghanistan: A Legal Analysis* (2009) 85 International Law Studies Series. US Naval War College 141, 149 et seq.

[21] Fussnecker (n 3) 12.

[22] ibid 12–13; T Noetzel, 'Germany's Small War in Afghanistan: Military Learning amid Politico-Strategic Inertia' (2010) 31 Contemporary Security Policy 486.

[23] LR Blank, 'Complex Legal Frameworks and Complex Operational Challenges: Navigating the Applicable Law Across the Continuum of Military Operations' (2012) 26 Emory International Law Review 87, 89; Fussnecker (n 3) 12–13 with further references.

[24] WS Williams, 'Multinational Rules of Engagement: Caveats and Friction' [2013] The Army Lawyer 24, 26 with further references.

[25] ibid.

[26] ibid; see also NATO, 'Legal Deskbook' (2010) <https://info.publicintelligence.net/NATO-LegalDeskbook.pdf>, part XII, sec B 3, 256—Self-defence.

that the immanency of an attack is to be determined based on all the facts and circumstances known to US forces at the time and may be made on every level. 'Imminent' does not mean 'immediate' or 'instantaneous'.[27] The NATO definition of self-defence essentially refers to the famous *Caroline* case, requiring the need to defend being 'instant, manifest and overwhelming'.[28] However, NATO recognizes that allied forces will act in accordance with their national law when acting in self-defence.[29] The differences in national positions on self-defence are the key reason for the existence of offensive RoE in case of a hostile act or hostile intent.[30] By employing authorized offensive RoE, commanders can ensure a uniform reaction of forces with different interpretations on the right of self-defence in given situations.

There are two options to deal with the legal and political differences in finding a common operational framework: either the states negotiate on the operational framework until it is down-watered to a degree acceptable to each TCN. This would however put the effectiveness of the operational framework into question. Or the TCNs agree upon an operational framework which deserves this title while retaining a 'backdoor' open for ensuring compliance with their national laws and policies by their national contingents. This backdoor' is called 'national caveat' and is a recognized—though not very well-liked—feature in military doctrine.

3. Definition and Functioning of National Caveats

As indicated above, national caveats prevent the paralysis of the multinational planning process on the strategic level and enable TCNs to agree on effective RoE which are not based on the lowest common denominator regarding the use of force. The key value of national caveats lies in their integrating function as they allow states to participate in an MMO even when they do not support every aspect of it and even if they cannot execute every task.[31] This function is of high political importance beyond the operational value of the contributed forces. As the NATO Allied Doctrine for the Conduct of Operations states:

> In practice, international consensus and legitimacy, rather than military preference or operational necessity, may drive multinational involvement and a

[27] Williams (n 24), 26.
[28] NATO Legal Deskbook (n 26) part XII, sec B 3, 256—Self-defence.
[29] ibid.
[30] For definitions see NATO Legal Deskbook (n 26) 255.
[31] Baron (n 17) 142.

> commander must occasionally be prepared to accept the former at the expense of the latter.[32]

Therefore, NATO recognizes 'that nations will issue restrictions and/or amplifying instructions in order to ensure compliance with their national law'.[33] The NATO doctrine on operational level planning specifically lists caveats as a parameter to be considered for planning.[34]

In NATO operations, caveats are defined as:

> any limitation[s], restriction[s] or constraint[s] by a nation on its military forces or civilian elements under NATO command and control or otherwise available to NATO, that does not permit NATO commanders to deploy and employ these assets fully in line with the approved operational plan.[35]

Such restrictions can have legal or political reasons, or—more profanely—be based on technical and/or training limitations, for example, the ability of helicopters to fly at night.

In NATO, national caveats should be declared upfront by a national government and communicated to the multinational commander in the context of the TOA, prior to the deployment of the national contingent.[36] They may, inter alia, impose restrictions on the conduct of certain kinds of operations or on the fulfilment of certain tasks, they may limit the freedom of movement within the joint operations area,[37] or restrict the use of certain means, for example, riot control agents. Such restrictions and limitations therefore lead to differing national RoE of the TCNs which diverge from the previously approved RoE of the MMO. As an aggravating factor in practice, national caveats sometimes remain undeclared and emerge during an ongoing operation.[38] This may happen—especially in case of the more technical reasons—because the need for declaring a restriction or caveat only manifested as the operations developed. Of course, this increases the difficulties for the multinational commander to operate effectively.

32 NATO AJP-3(B) (n 5) no 0204.

33 MC 362/1—NATO Rules of Engagement Section 05 (n 2). cf also NATO Parliamentary Assembly, 'Resolution 336 on reducing national caveats' (15 November 2005) <http://www.ft.dk/samling/20051/almdel/NPA/bilag/80/229913.pdf>, para 10, which reads: '*Recognizing* that sovereign nations have the right to define the terms by which they participate in a mission'.

34 NATO, 'AJP-5—Allied Joint Doctrine for Operational Level Planning' (26 June 2013) <https://nso.nato.int/nso/nsdd/_CommonList.html>, no 0372, lit h.

35 NATO AAP 06 (n 1) 'caveat/restriction'.

36 NATO Parliamentary Assembly—Resolution 336 (n 36); Williams (n 24) 25. See also section 5.

37 NATO AAP 06 (n 1) 'caveat/restriction'.

38 Williams (n 24) 25.

4. How Caveats Impede Multinational Military Operations

Despite their integrating function on the political and strategic level, national caveats pose a significant challenge to military effectiveness. This is clearly recognized by military doctrine, listing caveats as a limitation to freedom of action.[39]

During the Kosovo Force (KFOR) operation, for instance, the detrimental effect of national caveats came to light after KFOR failed to counter the civil unrests and attacks against Serb minorities in March 2004.[40] The actual NATO RoE, which might have proven effective, were of little use because each national contingent of KFOR was operating under its own national RoE.[41] It has been assessed that France, for example, took a very narrow approach to the NATO RoE,[42] limiting the priority of the mandate[43] to force protection, protection of the local population, and protection of KFOR installations and equipment.[44] Therefore, French forces failed to protect property of the Serb population, inter alia, leading to the destruction of many homes.[45] The German contingent, on the other hand, could not be appropriately deployed in countering the riots because the German forces were not allowed to use riot control agents (RCA)—tear gas in non-military terms—against the violent crowds due to Germany's national legislation implementing the Chemical Weapons Convention (CWC). This implementing legislation restricted the use of RCA beyond the scope of the CWC. Thus, when an Albanian mob attacked and burnt down Serb homes, churches, and monasteries in Prizren, the German KFOR contingent based in Prizren failed to comply with the requests for help of the United Nations Interim Administration Mission in Kosovo (UNMIK) police and other KFOR contingents.[46] This German legislation was changed after the 2004 incidents and the national interpretation of ROE was revised.[47]

[39] NATO AJP 5 (n 34).

[40] R Murphy, 'United Nations Peacekeeping and the Use of Force—the Failure to Protect in Kosovo' (2005) 5 Baltic Yearbook of International Law 77. From 17 to 18 March 2004, violent unrests in Kosovo led to the killing of nineteen and the wounding of more than 900 people. Many houses and property of the targeted Serb minority in Kosovo were destroyed, including churches and monasteries. For details see Human Rights Watch, 'Failure to Protect: Anti-Minority Violence in Kosovo, March 2004' (25 July 2004) <http://www.hrw.org/node/11989/section/1>.

[41] Murphy (n 40) 89.

[42] The KFOR RoE allowed the use of deadly force for the protection of property with designated special status under the protection of KFOR forces. Parts of a KFOR RoE soldiers card are reprinted in ibid, 87–89.

[43] For the United Nations mandate of KFOR see UNSC Res 1244 (10 June 1999) UN Doc S/RES/1244.

[44] Murphy (n 40) 98.

[45] ibid.

[46] A Szandar and A Ulrich, 'Die Hasen vom Amselfeld' (2004) 19 Der Spiegel 24–29; T Paterson, 'German troops "hid like rabbits" in Kosovo riots' *The Telegraph* (London, 9 May 2004) <http://www.telegraph.co.uk/news/1461366/German-troops-hid-like-rabbits-in-Kosovo-riots.html>.

[47] Murphy (n 40) 90.

Another MMO certainly struggling with national caveats was the NATO-led ISAF mission in Afghanistan.[48] Many TCNs had imposed some form of limitation on how and where their national forces could be deployed.[49] Germany, for instance, generally did not allow its forces to operate outside of northern Afghanistan and the area of Kabul.[50] This restriction derived from the national parliamentary mandate of the German Bundestag for the ISAF mission[51] and is a good example for a politically motivated caveat. For the German ISAF forces, it was nonetheless binding for constitutional reasons.

In consequence, German Operational Mentoring and Liaison Teams (OMLT) were significantly hampered in supporting their partner units. An OMLT consists of roughly thirty instructors and specialists who train and support an Afghan Kandak (battalion). In particular, they coordinate artillery and air support. Whenever the supported Kandak was ordered to operate outside of the northern territory, the German OMLT could not accompany them. This diminished not only the operational effectiveness for the specific operation but was also counterproductive to the overall training effort.[52]

Additionally, Germany initially restricted the use of force by its troops for mission accomplishment.[53] This restriction was certainly a result of Germany's initial reluctance to qualify the conflict in Afghanistan as an armed conflict which would have allowed its forces to operate on the basis of and in accordance with IHL.[54] This approach, for instance, led to the 'Baghlan bomber escape', where German forces had to let get away a high-ranking Taliban commander suspected of having killed more than seventy people in an attack.[55] Had Germany acknowledged that its forces were participating in an armed conflict with the consequence of applying IHL, its forces would have been permitted to kill the Baghlan bomber while he was fleeing.[56] Such limitations inevitably had an adverse impact on the success of the military operation.

[48] See V Morelli and P Belkin, 'NATO in Afghanistan: A test of the Transatlantic Alliance' (*Congressional Research Service, Report for Congress*, 3 December 2009) <http://fas.org/sgp/crs/row/RL33627.pdf>, 10–11.

[49] Williams (n 24) 25.

[50] Morelli and Belkin (n 48) 10–11.

[51] Eg see German Parliament resolution from 16 November 16, no 7, BT Drs 18/10347, available at <https://www.bundestag.de/ausschuesse/ausschuesse18/a12/auslandseinsaetze/auslandseinsaetze/isaf_bisherige_mandate/247448>.

[52] Auerswald and Saideman, 'NATO at war: Understanding the Challenges of Caveats in Afghanistan' <https://shape.nato.int/resources/1/.../nato%20at%20war.pdf>, 22.

[53] Noetzel (n 22) 492. See also S Koelbl and A Szandar, 'Not Licensed to Kill: German Special Forces in Afghanistan Let Taliban Commander Escape' (*Spiegel Online*, 19 May 2008) <http://www.spiegel.de/international/world/not-licensed-to-kill-german-special-forces-in-afghanistan-let-taliban-commander-escape-a-554033.html>; Der Spiegel, 'Changing the Rules in Afghanistan: German Troops Beef Up Fight against Taliban' (*Spiegel Online*, 9 July 2009) <http://www.spiegel.de/international/germany/changing-the-rules-in-afghanistan-german-troops-beef-up-fight-against-taliban-a-635192.html>.

[54] Fussnecker (n 3) 486–508.

[55] Koelbl and Szandar (n 53).

[56] Fussnecker (n 3) 17–18.

A further example worth mentioning is Operation Medusa, a Canadian-led NATO offensive against the Taliban in southern Afghanistan in January 2007, in which the Canadian forces had difficulties in getting the necessary support from other ISAF troops due to national caveats prohibiting their use in offensive operations which jeopardized the whole operation.[57]

The reluctance of several ISAF TCNs to take part in detention operations is a similarly conflicted issue. This reluctance was mostly attributed to the legal risks stemming from the application of human rights law, especially the ECHR.[58]

Germany regarded UN Security Council resolutions 1386 (2001) and 1510 (2003) as a sufficient legal basis for German ISAF forces to temporarily apprehend persons for mission accomplishment. Apprehended persons were—whenever possible—to be released within ninety-six hours or to be handed over to Afghan authorities. Handover was subject to German Ministry of Defence approval if there was a risk of the death penalty under Afghan law for the apprehended person.[59] There was detailed national guidance on the humane treatment of apprehended persons, including reporting obligations to the International Committee of the Red Cross (ICRC).[60] Accordingly, no caveats were declared regarding detention operations. However, the authority was rarely used. Between 26 April 2007 and 27 February 2015, no persons were detained by German personnel.[61] Germany took the view that Afghan authorities exercised criminal jurisdiction in Afghanistan, so the apprehension of insurgents was their responsibility. Operations were planned and conducted together with Afghan partners who would carry out necessary detentions.[62]

5. Handling of National Caveats

For handling and reducing the complicating and limiting effects of national caveats, awareness of national caveats must start early during the force generation process. TCNs therefore should, and usually do, inform the multinational commander about national caveats at the same time as when they declare their contribution to a specific MMO. In NATO operations, these caveats are then recorded in a 'Force

[57] Williams (n 24) 25. See also Spiegel staff, 'Afghanistan-Einsatz: Bundesregierung weist Vorwurf der unterlassenen Hilfeleistung zurück' (*Spiegel online*, 17 November 2006) <http://www.spiegel.de/politik/ausland/afghanistan-einsatz-bundesregierung-weist-vorwurf-der-unterlassenen-hilfeleistung-zurueck-a-449106.html>.

[58] Cole (n 20) 150, see also this article, no 2.

[59] Response of the German Government on a parliamentary inquiry form 29 August 2007, BT Drs 16/6282, available at <dipbt.bundestag.de/doc/btd/16/062/1606282.pdf>, 7.

[60] ibid 6.

[61] Response of the German Government on a parliamentary inquiry form 27 February 2015, BT Drs 18/4168, available at <dip21.bundestag.de/dip21/btd/18/041/1804168.pdf>, 21.

[62] Response of the German Government on a parliamentary inquiry form 12 July 2010, BT Drs 17/255, available at <http://dipbt.bundestag.de/extrakt/ba/WP17/268/26893.html>, 7.

Tracking Database' at the level of the joint force commander forming an information pool available to the multinational planners who do consider known national caveats early in the planning process. Other tools may be developed in the headquarters on different operational levels to keep track of national caveats and other restrictions placed on the national contingents of a multinational force. This is time-consuming and requires a lot of effort but is essential to ensure proper troop-to-task decisions.

With known caveats, a certain routine develops over time. *Ad hoc* caveats issued during an ongoing operation, on the other hand, pose even more significant difficulties. Given that they are unforeseen, there may be no adequate alternatives available to the military commander during the planning process. This makes it all the more difficult for the military commander to master the situation on the field. Such caveats may not only endanger the success of the respective operation, but they may also increase the risk for the forces affected by them and their allies.

At the TCN level, the National Contingent Commanders (NCC) are responsible for the communication as well as the implementation of national caveats.[63] NATO Doctrine describes the role of the NCC as follows:

> a. In general terms, the role of the NCC is to integrate his own national contingent into the Alliance force, promoting cohesion, trust and understanding while implementing his own nations' policies and caveats. He would also act as a national figurehead; a conduit back to his nation (…)
> b. The NCC will implement national caveats, although he will usually delegate elements to his national commanders within each component so that issues can be resolved early at lower levels, thus minimizing the overall impact on coalition cohesion.[64]

The NCC usually serves as part of the multinational force and primarily performs multinational duties, for example as the commander of a multinational unit or of the headquarter staff. Whenever caveats or other restrictions for his contingent become an issue, he acts in his national capacity and cannot be overruled by the multinational chain of command in this matter. Therefore, the NCC is sometimes referred to as the 'Red Card Holder'. Depending on the size of the contingent and the type of the caveat, this function is often delegated to lower-level commanders or subject-matter experts within the contingent.

6. Conclusion

Above examples show that despite their integrating function on the strategic and political level, national caveats often have a detrimental impact on the effective and

[63] NATO AJP 3(B) (n 5) ch 2, sec II, no 0222.
[64] ibid.

flexible functioning of an MMO.[65] They may also have political repercussions if they begin to upset the balance in sharing the burden of the operation between the coalition partners. This risk to the cohesion of a coalition should not be underestimated, as the frequent discussions on the topic in alliance fora suggest.

Because national caveats have added complexity and confusion to the already complex legal and operational situation,[66] there have been attempts on the international level to get a grip on existing national caveats and to limit their use. After the Kosovo riots in March 2004, the NATO Parliamentary Assembly adopted 'Resolution 336 on Reducing National Caveats', in which it highlighted the adverse effect of national caveats on NATO's ability to appropriately respond to the civil unrests.[67] In expressing its concerns about a similar effect of national caveats on the NATO mission in Afghanistan,[68] the Parliamentary Assembly urged the member states

a. to eliminate the use of undeclared caveats and allow the restrictions on a national contingent to be taken into consideration during the force planning process;
b. to minimize the use of declared caveats and regularly reconsider the specific caveats to determine which can be eliminated, given changes in the operating environment or in the available resources of the national contingent.[69]

However, resolution 336, being a political document with no legally binding force, did not have much effect. Multinational commanders will therefore have to continue planning with national caveats.

In order to avoid the paralysis of an MMO by national caveats, it is crucial for TCNs to minimize their differences in laws and policies and to harmonize their application of the RoE.[70] The tool of national caveats should be used with great caution. Otherwise, their integrating function on the political and strategic level will be undermined by the frictions on the operational and tactical level, leaving behind fictitious agreements upon the operational framework for an MMO, which ultimately results in a fictitious MMO.

65 Fussnecker (n 3) 7; Morelli and Belkin (n 48) 10–11.
66 cf G Corn, 'Mixing Apples and Hand Grenades: The Logical Limit of Applying Human Rights Norms to Armed Conflict' (2010) 85 Journal of International Humanitarian Legal Studies 52, 56.
67 NATO PA Resolution 336 (n 36) para 3.
68 ibid paras 5–9.
69 ibid para 12.
70 cf Williams (n 24) 27–28.

20
The Involvement of Private Security Companies in Multinational Military Operations

Hin-Yan Liu

1. Introduction

The involvement of Private Security Companies (PSCs) adds an array of legal dimensions to the complexity surrounding multinational military operations.[1] For the purposes of this chapter, a PSC is taken as a private, usually for-profit, company offering security-related services which include potentially lethal activities involving the possession and use of weapons and firearms.

At the core of the legal disruption[2] introduced by the PSC is the dissociation between state action and the obligations under international humanitarian and human rights law (IHL and IHRL, respectively).[3] Hitherto, the state's organizational monopoly on the use of legitimate force[4] and the international nature of these legal fields has rendered this conflation as relatively unproblematic. The introduction of the PSC, however, has left this heuristic increasingly untenable.[5] First, the law has failed to unambiguously marginalize, let alone criminalize, the provision

[1] For some examples of PSC involvement in multinational operations, see: TE Ricks, 'The U.N.'s Mercenary Problem' (*Foreign Policy*, 23 June 2016) <https://foreignpolicy.com/2016/06/23/the-u-n-s-mercenary-problem/>, all URLs accessed 27 December 2018; C Spearin, 'UN Peacekeeping and the International Private Military and Security Industry' (2011) 18 International Peacekeeping 196; O Bures, 'Private Military Companies: A Second Best Peacekeeping Option?' (2005) 12 International Peacekeeping 533; M Malamud, 'Private Military and Security Companies in UN Missions' (2014) 26 Peace Review 571; D Lilly, 'The Privatization of Peacekeeping: Prospects and Realities' (UNIDIR 2000) Disarmament Forum 3; J Genser and C Garvie, 'Contracting for Stability: The Potential Use of Private Military Contractors as a United Nations Rapid-Reaction Force' (2016) 16 Chicago Journal of International Law 439.

[2] Legal disruption is defined here as an innovation which either reveals the incompleteness of extant law or which wrenches open gaps in current legal doctrine and procedure.

[3] It is trivial to note that both IHL and IHRL are status-based in that only certain categories of actors, primarily states, are subject to fulfilling those obligations.

[4] M Weber, *From Max Weber: Essays in Sociology* (Routledge and Kegan Paul 1946) 78. To be clear, Weber explicitly envisaged the possibility for the state to delegate this monopoly.

[5] Whether the PSC has simply revealed existing regulatory gaps by using different actors or has created the legal shortcoming does not matter for the purposes of this chapter since the effect is similar.

Hin-Yan Liu, *The Involvement of Private Security Companies in Multinational Military Operations* In *The 'Legal Pluriverse' Surrounding Multinational Military Operations*. Edited by Robin Geiß and Heike Krieger, Oxford University Press (2020).
DOI: 10.1093/oso/9780198842965.003.0021

of martial services by private corporations.[6] Secondly, recent challenges[7] have been made against the prevalent notion that a strong international norm against mercenary activity exists.[8] Finally, with principled and consistent objections difficult to formulate against the private provision of organized force,[9] reliance has been placed in residual categories that focus upon conduct in hostilities: excessive uses of force and human rights violations by private security contractors on the field.[10] Taken together, the opprobrium directed against organized private violence as manifested in the PSC can be difficult to articulate coherently, thereby leaving ample space for the PSC industry to argue for their legitimacy.

Against this backdrop of diluting objections to private military and security actors exist practical realities that undermine the real ability to conduct humanitarian intervention where necessary. Lack of political will, coupled with decreasing military expenditure and capacity, has increased the willingness to contemplate private actors in this sphere that used to be reserved to state action. Indeed, Kofi Annan famously contemplated the imperative for engaging PSCs in peace operations in the absence of competing alternatives:

> Some have even suggested that private security firms, like the one which recently helped restore the elected President to power in Sierra Leone, might play a role in providing the United Nations with the rapid reaction capacity it needs. When we had need of skilled soldiers to separate fighters from refugees in the Rwandan refugee camps in Goma, I even considered the possibility of engaging a private firm. But the world may not be ready to privatize peace.[11]

There are significant pressures for employing PSCs in multinational military operations, including peace operations, in an environment of increasing military outsourcing.[12] These are primarily the perceived capacity to fulfil important humanitarian functions which have been neglected by traditional actors, and increased market pressures arising from the end of major conflicts in the Middle East. Given the myriad of ambiguities surrounding PSCs, this chapter focuses upon the legal complexities involved in their employment in multinational military operations.

[6] HY Liu, *Law's Impunity: Responsibility and the Modern Private Military Company* (Hart Publishing 2015).

[7] HY Liu and C Kinsey, 'Challenging the Strength of the Anti-Mercenary Norm' (2018) 3 Journal of Global Security Studies 93.

[8] S Percy, 'Mercenaries: Strong Norm, Weak Law' (2007) 61 International Organization 367; S Percy, *Mercenaries: The History of a Norm in International Relations* (OUP 2007).

[9] T Lynch and AJ Walsh, 'The Good Mercenary?' (2000) 8 Journal of Political Philosophy 133.

[10] This has channelled legal challenges almost exclusively to conduct *jus in bello*, largely obviating questions of *jus ad bellum*. Liu (n 6) ch 6.

[11] UN, 'Secretary-General Reflects on "Intervention" in Thirty-Fifth Annual Ditchley Foundation Lecture' (28 June 1998) SG/SM/6613, 8.

[12] For an overview of the modern PSC and their activities in recent conflicts, see Liu (n 6) ch 2.

The following section discusses legal complexities arising from jurisdictional issues, commencing with the non-binding Montreux Document relating to the international legal obligations of states in relation to the PSC. The chapter then discusses the potential for contractual mechanisms to cut through these complexities, as was the animating impetus behind the industry self-regulatory mechanism of the International Code of Conduct. Yet, despite the appearance of legal clarity and simplicity, this chapter demonstrates that greater legal complexities are introduced through the reliance on contractual mechanisms. In the concluding sections, this chapter suggests that the legal form that the PSC adopts, as well as the activities that it engages in, circumvent the presumptions that underlie the legal structures that address state control and responsibility in relation to the use of organized force. The chapter then concludes by suggesting that many of the legal complexities which are discussed here would be solved by reasserting the foundational principle of privileged belligerency. Reinstating this principle would neutralize the disruptive effects of the PSC in dissociating legitimate organized violence and state action, and the PSC constituting a liminal entity between civilian private actors and martial state actors.

2. Jurisdictional Legal Complexity

It is worth clarifying at the outset the core international legal questions arising from PSC involvement in multinational military operations. That PSC contractors lose civilian protections upon direct participation in hostilities is uncontroversial,[13] but this only opens the possibility for prosecution for acts of unprivileged belligerency rather than being an offence as such.[14] This conclusion obviates many of the convoluted questions of mercenary status for PSC contractors because the effect of being categorized as a mercenary is the denial of privileged belligerency status in international armed conflicts.[15] For non-international armed conflicts, where the status of combatant immunity has no direct equivalent, Article 6(5) of Additional Protocol II (AP II) provides an exculpation clause that insulates individuals from the domestic legal consequences of fighting.[16] The point is that the legal categories of privileged belligerency and civilian immunity from direct attack in armed conflict serve as heuristics. These shorthand approaches can only be justified, however,

[13] N Melzer, 'Interpretive Guidance on the Notion of Direct Participation in Hostilities Under International Humanitarian Law' (2008) 90 International Review of the Red Cross 991 (adopted by the Assembly of the International Committee of the Red Cross on 26 February 2009).

[14] TD Gill and D Fleck, 'Private Contractors and Security Companies' in TD Gill and D Fleck (eds), *The Handbook of the International Law of Military Operations* (OUP 2011) 489.

[15] Examined in depth, Liu (n 6) 146–83.

[16] For a discussion see ibid 52–55. See also Rule 159 because many major military powers are not party to Additional Protocol II, JM Henckaerts and L Doswald-Beck, *Customary International Humanitarian Law*, vol I: Rules (CUP 2009) 611–14.

where these mutually exclusive legal statuses remain intact. Where more liminal entities, such as the PSC in this context, disrupt the mutual exclusivity of privileged belligerency and civilian immunity, more complex legal assessments become necessary.

This is the other part of the legal disruption[17] introduced by the PSC: it is inherent within the prospect for PSC contractors to directly participate in hostilities, dissociating this relationship by actively introducing civilians into situations of armed conflict. This adds to the already mentioned core legal disruption of the PSC, breaking the bond between state action and IHL and IHRL obligations. In this sense, the PSC represents significant challenges to the legal order by posing significant challenges for legal regulation on at least two distinct levels, which greatly exacerbates legal complexity where they interact—such as with PSC involvement in multinational military operations.

2.1 Status of forces agreements: suspending territorial state jurisdiction for PSC contractors

The formally civilian nature of the PSC introduces questions for status of forces agreements (SOFAs): whether PSC contractors are covered by SOFAs, and in what ways, represent continuing issues for example for the United States.[18] While the United States has historically not sought jurisdictional protections for their contractors, in Iraq there was the probably unprecedented SOFA which exempted PSC contractors from domestic criminal jurisdiction.[19] If, however, the territorial state's jurisdiction is not supposed to apply according to the SOFA, the obvious subsequent legal question is: which one does?[20] In that specific setting, the Military Extraterritorial Jurisdiction Act 2000 (MEJA) extended US federal criminal law to Department of Defense (DoD) contractors.[21] Effectively, the SOFA had suspended the ordinary application of the territorial state's criminal jurisdiction and replaced

[17] See n 2 above, on the concept of legal disruption.

[18] International Security Advisory Board, 'Report on Status of Forces Agreements' (*US Department of State*, 2015) 20–23 <https://www.state.gov/documents/organization/236456.pdf>.

[19] ibid 21. SOFAs are a core concern for the United States: it was the refusal of Iraqi authorities to grant immunity from domestic law to remaining US troops after the end of 2011 (when the existing SOFA terminated) that ultimately precipitated the US withdrawal T Arango and M Schmidt, 'Iraqis Say No to Immunity for Remaining American Troops' *New York Times* (New York, 4 October 2011) <http://www.nytimes.com/2011/10/05/world/middleeast/iraqis-say-no-to-immunity-for-remaining-american-troops.html?>; P van Buren, 'Immunity: Disastrous Decisions in 2007 Return to Haunt 2012' (*Huffington Post*, 4 November 2011) <http://www.huffingtonpost.com/peter-van-buren/blackwater-shootings-2007_b_1066135.html>; International Security Advisory Board (n 18) 41–42.

[20] International Security Advisory Board (n 18) 22.

[21] Public Law 106–523. Section 3267(1). This Act was subsequently broadened in 2004 to remove the DoD nexus requirement. For the latest amendment drive, see C Doyle, 'Civilian Extraterritorial Jurisdiction Act: Federal Contractor Criminal Liability Overseas' (*Congressional Research Service*, 15 February 2012) <http://www.fas.org/sgp/crs/misc/R42358.pdf>.

it with an incomplete patchwork of home state criminal jurisdiction. Crucially, however, this home state criminal jurisdiction hinged, somewhat arbitrarily considering the context, upon the formal legal status of the contractual partner, because MEJA ultimately required employment or accompaniment of the armed forces to apply. In other words, where a PSC contractor was alleged to have engaged in criminal activities, they were beyond the reach of domestic Iraqi courts. The question of whether they were within the remit of US federal criminal courts depended on whether the PSC employing the contractor had a contract either with the armed forces or with a different governmental agency (in the latter case, they also fell outside of that residual jurisdiction).

Looking ahead at US policy on SOFA coverage for contractors, the US State Department advocates for an ad hoc basis: if the armed forces are highly dependent upon contractor services and where the contractors are deeply integrated into core military operations, then 'contractor protection is worth insisting on'.[22] While such contingency is perhaps prudent, given the imponderables of PSC contractor activities and the limited control and oversight of contractors,[23] the unequal and inconsistent application of territorial and home state criminal jurisdiction make for fairly arbitrary standards from a rule of law perspective. For example, two different sets of criminal law may apply to two different contractors who are performing the same role for the same PSC operating in the same theatre under the same conditions, merely because of a different contractual basis (where one is contracted to provide services to the armed forces while the other acts for a different governmental agency). In the extreme scenario, there may be no residual criminal jurisdiction that the contractor is amenable to, opening the prospect for impunity for alleged crimes.[24]

The question of SOFA coverage for PSC contractors is important because it effectively confers combatant privilege albeit on the basis of bilateral agreement underpinned by IHL. For non-international armed conflicts, SOFAs suspending the criminal jurisdiction of the territorial state mirror the aforementioned Article 6(5) AP II[25] which retroactively extends amnesty to persons who participated in the armed conflict. This conferral of effective combatant privilege to civilian contractors may undermine the legitimacy of IHL. The reason for this is the fact that it is inconsistent and piecemeal by nature, that it is conferred arbitrarily because it depends on the post-conflict political climate, and because of the sense of injustice invoked by legally immunizing armed actors from criminal prosecution where breaches of IHL have been alleged.[26]

22 International Security Advisory Board (n 18) 51–52.
23 ibid.
24 Liu (n 6).
25 See n 16 above.
26 Liu (n 6) ch 1.

2.2 International obligations of states related to the PSC: the Montreux Document

Questions of state control and responsibility become especially pertinent in the context of multinational military operations.[27] The crux of this set of legal problems arises from the different possible nexuses between the PSC and the different states involved, namely: the contracting state, the territorial state, the home state, and other states.[28] Thus, the legal obligations of a state are unclear as a matter of principle. This is because the state is not simply responsible for a set of actions or omissions, as it would be for its own armed forces. Rather, state responsibility is instead contingent upon the relationship it has with the specific PSC in question. This relationship may depend upon state actions, such as contracts for PSC services, but may equally be somewhat arbitrary and largely beyond state control, such as the home state which is where the PSC is legally incorporated. It should also be noted that states face significant legal hurdles in restricting the outflow of their citizens or subjects in the context of PSC activities.[29] This curtails their control towards the PSC, given the limitations of domestic neutrality legislation and the strength of the countervailing freedom of movement norm.[30] In the context of multinational military operations, these difficulties can exacerbate legal complexities. For example, a PSC may contract to perform different services which are subject to different conditions to different states which are part of the same multinational military operation. Or, the same state may hire different PSCs to perform a range of services in a way which intersects with the international legal obligations of other states in the same multinational military operation. Thus, both states and PSCs become nodes in complex legal networks whose precise configuration is highly contingent upon the details of how that network is connected.[31] This suggests in turn that the legal complexities of each multinational military operation must be unwound and understood independently, thereby introducing significant legal uncertainties around each concrete deployment.

The Montreux Document, which was agreed on by seventeen states on 17 September 2008, contains rules and good practices relating to PSCs operating in

[27] State control and responsibility for PSCs have been thoroughly examined in, for example, H Tonkin, *State Control Over Private Military and Security Companies in Armed Conflict* (CUP 2011); HY Liu, 'Leashing the Corporate Dogs of War: The Legal Implications of the Modern Private Military Company' (2010) 15 Journal of Conflict and Security Law 141.

[28] UNGA, 'Montreux Document on Pertinent International Legal Obligations and Good Practices for States related to Operations of Private Military and Security Companies during Armed Conflict' (17 September 2008) UN Doc A/63/467–S/2008/636, 9.

[29] Liu and Kinsey (n 7) 96 et seq.

[30] Liu and Kinsey (n 7).

[31] HY Liu, 'The Opposite of Autonomy in Weapons Systems', keynote presented at the Beyond Killer Robots: Networked Artificial Intelligence Disrupting the Battlefield conference held at the University of Copenhagen, 27–28 September 2018.

armed conflict.[32] It should be noted that the process culminating in the Document has been somewhat controversial. As a former member of the UN Working Group on the Use of Mercenaries observed, the entire process was carried out in secrecy, absent the involvement of any UN human rights special procedure or department, had only been endorsed by representatives of seventeen governments while simultaneously permitting strong PSC industry lobby participation, and was presented to both the UN General Assembly and the Security Council without following UN criteria or approaches.[33] As to the content of the Montreux Document, the first part reconfirms existing international legal obligations of the state concerning PSCs, while the second part sets forth some good practices with the status of recommendations. As to the relevance and application of the Montreux Document, it remains curtailed to situations of armed conflict so the multinational military operation in question must be above a certain threshold of intensity.

The Montreux Document sets forth four different categories of states, enumerated at the outset of each subsection of the Document, depending upon their relationship with the PSC, and sets out their pertinent international legal obligations and good practices both in fairly general terms and along repetitive themes.[34] This repetitiveness indicates that the relevant international obligations are overlapping in two different forms. First, there is an overlap between different states which may possess similar obligations in any given situation (such as a contracting state and a territorial state, both of which 'have an obligation, within their power, to ensure respect for international humanitarian law').[35] Secondly, there is the overlap whereby the same state can possess different types of obligations in the same situation (eg where the contracting state is also either the home state or the territorial state). Furthermore, the repetitive nature of themes running across the obligations of different types of states for the purpose of the Montreux Document runs roughshod over the actual or projected capacities possessed by the state in relation to ensuring IHL and IHRL compliance by the PSC. The situation of the home state is a case in point: a PSC may take its headquarters in a certain state for a number of different reasons, such as tax, geographical location, or the presence of international organizations (factors cited by Aegis for its move from London to Basel).[36] Yet, unless the home state is willing and able to take significant legal measures, such as Switzerland's outlawing of mercenary services in reaction to PSCs like Aegis

[32] Montreux Document (n 28), 17 September 2008, A/63/467–S/2008/636. The date is important, being the first anniversary of the controversial Nisour Square massacre where Blackwater contractors killed seventeen civilians at a busy traffic junction, BBC, 'US Contractors in Iraq Shootout' (*BBC News*, 17 September 2007) <http://news.bbc.co.uk/2/hi/middle_east/6998458.stm>.

[33] J Gómez del Prado, 'Private Military and Security Companies and the UN Working Group on the Use of Mercenaries' (2008) 13 Journal of Conflict and Security Law 429, 433.

[34] Montreux Document (n 28).

[35] ibid 7 and 8, respectively.

[36] Swissinfo, 'Mercenary Services Outlawed by Parliament' (*swissinfo.ch*, 24 September 2013) <http://www.swissinfo.ch/eng/politics/Mercenary_services_outlawed_by_parliament.html?cid=36968406>.

establishing themselves there, there are few legal tools available to the home state. Two factors further militate against home state control: the formal status of a PSC as a corporate legal person limits state interference, and the regulatory race-to-the-bottom whereby PSCs could relocate to the most advantageous jurisdiction analogous to flags of convenience under international maritime law.

The layering and overlapping of state obligations in relation to the PSC may minimize the likelihood of *lacunae* by increasing the likelihood that relevant state obligations would be triggered in any given situation. Overlooked in these efforts, however, is the possibility that increasing the number of (partially-) responsible parties may trigger the legal equivalent of the bystander effect,[37] or circumscribe the obligation of each party in such a way as to diminish the intended effect of asserting state obligations in the first place. The obligations recognized in the Montreux Document are further diluted beyond this division into different types of states because the obligations are couched in aspirational and conditional terms, for example to 'ensure respect for [IHL]' and '[an obligation], within their power' (Statements 3, 9, 14, and 18).

While explicitly not having legally binding status, the good practices section of the Montreux Document may shed more light on the underlying logic. For contracting states, there is the good practice to determine which services may or may not be contracted out.[38] This suggests that the default position permits, and perhaps encourages, outsourcing which forecloses prior questions as to whether martial services should be outsourced at all.[39] With regard to selection of PSCs, the document suggests inter alia that its capacity to fulfil its activities should be assessed, that transparency and supervision needs to be ensured, and that perhaps the lowest price should not be the sole criterion for selection.[40] A cynical observation would be that these recommendations should form the basis for solid legal obligation where private companies are engaged to perform services in armed conflict in conditions of admittedly limited control and oversight.

2.3 Compounding legal uncertainties: state obligations relating to PSCs in multinational military operations

Dismantling the connection between state action and concomitant state responsibility in the context of military operations has made applicable international legal obligations highly ambiguous as far as the PSC is concerned. Significant questions remain over the obligations of different states in how they relate to even a

[37] The bystander effect is the social psychological phenomenon whereby individuals are less inclined to offer help in the presence of others.
[38] Montreux Document (n 28).
[39] Liu (n 6) ch 6.
[40] Montreux Document (n 28).

single PSC as a result of the ambiguous, overlapping and, indeterminate nature of the international legal obligations and good practices set forth in the Montreux Document. Seemingly set along a single dimension, international legal obligations take on the character of a zero-sum game where such obligations are apportioned between different candidate states.[41] As an example of the complexities that can arise on the one-dimensional single PSC dimension, one state may hire a PSC based in another state to perform martial services on the territory of a third state. This is a complicated situation[42] where the ambiguities of legal obligations espoused by the Montreux Document cause problems for determining the substance and extent of each state's obligation. The ambiguities and overlaps between the obligations stipulated for contracting, territorial, and home states thus blur the lines of obligation that each is accorded.

Multinational military operations involving PSCs significantly increase the complexity of state obligations because of the interaction effects which compound the ambiguities inherent in the Montreux Document. The single dimension of legal obligation discussed above is replaced by a dense network of state obligations, which in turn are further connected to other legal complexities inherent within international military operations discussed elsewhere in this book.[43] Thus, even on a single plane involving a single PSC, the legal complexities triggered by such a PSC are manifold because of the multiple and interlocking state obligations as espoused by the Montreux Document. Furthermore, deeper connections are forged along this single plane that reach backwards to entangle these legal complexities with those that are extant in the very nature of multinational military operations.

If the legal complexities along a single plane are confounding, additional PSCs take this literally to another order of magnitude because their involvement shifts the complexity from a single two-dimensional plane to a three-dimensional space. It may be tempting to think that the legal issues arising from the involvement of one PSC are the same as those arising where there are two PSCs in a

[41] This division of responsibility is analogous to the apportioning of responsibility in the Autonomous Weapons Systems context, see M Schulzke, 'Autonomous Weapons and Distributed Responsibility' (2013) 26 Philosophy & Technology 203. The difficulty with this style of argumentation is that it treats responsibility as a uni-dimensional concept, whereas it is either a multi-dimensional concept or an umbrella concept overarching several similar concepts. For a differentiated typology of responsibilities, see HY Liu, 'Refining Responsibility: Differentiating Two Types of Responsibility Issues Raised by Autonomous Weapons Systems' in N Bhuta and others (eds), *Autonomous Weapons Systems—Law, Ethics Policy* (CUP 2016) and Liu (n 6).

[42] Complicated refers to a high level of difficulty and sophistication, while complexity invokes adaptive systems with emergent effects.

[43] The terminology applied here treats the 'dimension' as one-dimensional, the 'plane' and 'lattice' as two-dimensional, and the 'network' as three-dimensional. If legal complexities are a function of the number of possible connections between nodes in the network (it may be helpful to think of the nodes as states and PSCs), then it becomes clear that the complexities increase drastically in the step-jumps between one-dimensional complexity and two-dimensional complexity, and so on.

military operation. But '[y]ou think that because you understand "one" that you must therefore understand "two" because one and one make two. But you forget that you must also understand "and"'.[44] The combinations which are possible transform into permutations that vastly increase the range of possible outcomes, leading directly to deep ambiguities surrounding the legal obligations of states. Thus, adding a second PSC introduces a dense, intricate network of overlapping and ambiguous state obligations that are permutations (rather than mere combinations as they would be in a lattice). Some point examples include: the same PSC could be hired for different purposes by different states operating on the same territorial state; different PSCs could be hired for the same purpose by different states to operate on the territory of the same state; different PSCs could be hired for different purposes by the same state to operate on the territory of different states, and so on.

As legal questions concern the relationship or the interconnection between two nodes along a dimension, in the lattice, or within the network, the legal complexity increases by leaps and bounds with each shift. The ambiguity that shrouds the legal relations between a PSC and a state are thus also affected by the larger legal context in which these are embedded (whether the legal model applied is the single dimension, the two-dimensional plane, or the three-dimensional space) since it will be the overall framework that sets the tone for the legal complexity of that multinational military operation. If this is true, then it may be worth placing limits upon the configuration of such frameworks as a means of limiting the legal complexity that must be endured in any given operation.

Furthermore, these permutations of state obligations are isolated from the legal arrangements underpinning the multinational military operation, which then increase legal murkiness. How the role and function of PSCs relate to the military operation which they are embedded within, as well as how subcontracting for services is conducted through contractual chains of PSCs, is largely determined by the nature of the contract securing the engagement of the PSC. It is worth noting that the legal complexity introduced by contractual mechanisms reverses the difficulties by establishing legal obligations and good practices as set forth in the Montreux Document. Whereas the legal obligations of states are overlapping and ambiguous, contractual obligations tend to be clear and precise. Yet, contractual obligations lean towards being shrouded by opacity, rendering them inaccessible to all but the parties to the contract itself, while international legal obligations and good practices are open and accessible to the public at large. This opens up yet another area of legal complexity in utilizing PSCs in multinational operations, to which we now turn.

[44] DH Meadows, *Thinking in Systems: A Primer* (Chelsea Green Publishing 2008) 12.

3. Contractual Legal Simplicity?

The contractual nature of PSC involvement in multinational military operations may cut through layers of legal complexity: all questions of legal obligation can be boiled down to what is expressly stipulated in the contract.[45] This apparent simplicity undergirds impulses to regulate the PSC through contractual means.[46] The Montreux Document suggests as good practice for states '[t]o include contractual clauses and performance requirements that ensure respect for relevant national law, international humanitarian law and human rights law by the contracted PMSC'.[47] In a similar vein, the International Code of Conduct (ICoC) requires that 'Signatory Companies will make compliance with this Code an integral part of contractual agreements with Personnel and subcontractors'.[48] Anne-Marie Buzatu expressed faith that the ICoC has invested into contractual mechanisms in no uncertain terms: 'The ICoC uses contractual mechanisms to impose human-rights compliant standards *directly on the companies themselves, regardless of where they are operating*'.[49] There are three immediate problems associated with attempts to protect the values embodied in IHL and IHRL through contract law mechanisms. First, the advantage of clarity and precision in contractual requirements is lost because the ambiguities inherent within IHL and IHRL are incorporated in an intact fashion. Secondly, it is clear that IHL and IHRL do not apply to private entities like the PSC, which dilutes the imperative to respect such laws in the contractual setting

[45] But see the following section on 'contractual legal complexity'. The simplicity embodied in contractual mechanisms can be illusionary, however, because additional legal complexities can arise in the content of the contractual provisions themselves. For example, a PSC may be contracted to do different things under different contracts, or conversely where different states hire the same PSC on the basis of different contracts. Contractual obligations and liabilities are thus heavily contingent upon contractual provisions, but these are themselves confined to arrangements made by the parties to the contract, creating opacity for oversight and enforcement. For a detailed argument, see HY Liu, 'Contract Law as Cover: Curtailing the Scope of Private Military and Security Contractor Responsibilities' in J Berndtsson and C Kinsey (eds), *Ashgate Research Companion to Security Outsourcing in the 21st Century* (Ashgate 2016).

[46] L Dickinson, 'Contract as a Tool for Regulating Private Military Companies' in S Chesterman and C Lehnardt (eds), *From Mercenaries to Market: The Rise and Regulation of Private Military Companies* (OUP 2007).

[47] Montreux Document (n 28) Part II.

[48] Swiss Federal Department of Foreign Affairs, 'International Code of Conduct for Private Security Service Providers' paras 18–23. The ICoC is a PSC trade-organization that champions industry self-regulation over competing forms of regulatory oversight. Despite its name, the members are companies (with a limited number of state and NGO observers), and thus wields relatively little power over its member companies beyond expulsion from the club. The ICoC process takes departure from the Montreux Document process, and is its successor. See also, Liu (n 6) ch 6.

[49] AM Buzatu and B Buckland, 'Private Military & Security Companies: Future Challenges in Security Governance' (2010) Working Paper DCAF Horizon 2015 Working Paper No. 3 23, emphasis in the original. Buzatu, who has been influential in the development of the ICoC through her work at the Geneva Centre for the Democratic Control of Armed Forces (which is itself under mandate from the Swiss Government convening the ICoC initiative to facilitate its development), had emphasized her view that contract law mechanisms are integral to the protection of human rights in the PMSC context because of the direct legal enforceability of contractual provisions. Personal communication, 19 October 2010, Washington DC.

since the direct translation of IHL and IHRL into contractual terms becomes nonsensical.[50] Finally, there is a loss of normative context in 'contractualization':[51] IHL and IHRL are foundational principles deeply rooted in normative and philosophical discourses but are thus reduced to mere contractual requirements that are fulfilled for no greater reason than merely because the contract required it. This lack of normative grounding is theoretically problematic per se but is also troubling in practical terms since the meaning of IHL and IHRL in contractual provisions is isolated from the supporting discourses which elevate their importance in public law settings.

Deploying contractual tools as a means of simplifying the web of overlapping and ambiguous legal obligations may appear to be a sensible strategy but for the problems associated with the nature of contract law. This apparent simplicity is, however, misleading because the logic of contract law is that only contractual terms are enforceable or relevant, thereby rendering all other obligations or good practices as tangential and extraneous. In the contexts of the Montreux Document, it would indeed be good practice for states to incorporate contractual terms that ensure respect for relevant IHL and IHRL laws, but because this is not legally required it remains as merely an aspirational option. Furthermore, because the contract with the PSC would presumably dictate concrete tasks and functions that the PSC is to perform for the contracting state, the possibility for these conflicting with requirements to respect IHL and IHRL may be high.[52] An example might be the tension between the contractual terms requiring that a PSC protect military convoys and to adhere to IHL and IHRL in its operations. A PSC that succeeds in protecting those convoys with excessive use of force may have its failure to respect IHL and IHRL overlooked in the enforcement of that contract. After all, the 'core mission' of the PSC may be perceived as the protection of the military convoys, and the requirement to adhere to IHL and IHRL principles in the process as aspirational, subsidiary objectives.

4. Contractual Legal Complexity

In the good practices section of the Montreux Document, the nature of legal obligations makes a turn towards contractual considerations. I have written at length elsewhere about the incongruity of adopting contract law mechanisms to enforce

[50] There is a tautology here: because IHL and IHRL do not apply to private entities like the PSC, it becomes legally impossible for the PSC to violate IHL and IHRL. Thus, because the PSC cannot violate IHL and IHRL, it cannot breach the contractual obligations that inscribe IHL and IHRL requirements into the contract. Taken together, this means that there is no added value or protection provided by incorporating IHL and IHRL provisions into a contract with a PSC.

[51] Liu (n 45).

[52] JA Hessbruegge, *Human Rights and Personal Self-Defense in International Law* (OUP 2017).

values expressed in IHL and IHRL with regard to the PSC.[53] Thus, this section will only outline that argument before proceeding to address contractual complexities related to the PSC in the context of multinational military operations. That contract law distorts, or even disconnects, the legitimacy of a PSC to engage in a military operation on behalf of a state arises from the freedom of contract. This is both because the contract is the point of divergence away from the governing principles of IHL and IHRL that bind state action, and because the doctrine of privity[54] shrouds contractual arrangements from the view and reach of third parties.

The crux of contract law is the freedom of contract: 'The basic ideal of contract law, freedom of contract, indicates that contract law is an area in which *parties can set their own rules, creating rights and obligations that apply only to the contracting parties, and only because of the contract that they have entered*'.[55] The failure to exclude martial services from the scope of contract law means that it is possible, in a general sense, to contract a PSC to perform security or martial services in a multinational military operation. In an apparent tautology, the nature of the contractual obligation to perform martial services also means that it is the contract itself which empowers the PSC to engage in the multinational military operation: This is diametrically opposed to public international law arrangements which authorize, legitimate, underpin, and hold to account state involvement in multinational military operations. Thus, while the vertical public law requirement for using coercive powers would need to be fulfilled for state participation, PSCs become embroiled through horizontal private law mechanisms embodied in the contract. This observation itself undermines the legitimacy of PSC participation in multinational military operations that have elements of the use of force or coercive activity.[56] This is further exacerbated in the context of a multinational military operation if the coercive powers underpinning that operation are stipulated in vague wording or broad phrasing such as 'all necessary means'. Put differently, state participation in multinational military operations must exercise organized violence for the good of international peace and security and do so in a restrained manner in accordance with IHL and IHRL principles. PSC participation in multinational military operations, however, is dictated by whatever is expressly stipulated (and which furthermore can be enforced) by the contract, which needs to encompass neither the principles

[53] Liu (n 45); Liu (n 6) 194–217.

[54] The doctrine of privity stipulates that the terms of a contract can neither impose obligations nor confer benefits to a third party, see Law Commission, 'Privity of Contracts: Contracts for the Benefit of Third Parties' (Law Commission 1996) LC242 para 2.1; perhaps shockingly, the Law Commission notes that the privity doctrine had the effect of immunising parties to the contract from third party tort claims arising from negligence in performing the contract prior to *Donoghue v Stevenson* [1932] AC 562 (House of Lords).

[55] B Bix, *Contract Law: Rules, Theory, and Context* (CUP 2012) 110. Emphasis added.

[56] While Max Weber accorded the monopoly on the use of legitimate organized violence to the state, he also conceded the state's ability to delegate that monopoly, Weber (n 4) 78. The claim here is that delegation through contractual mechanisms is not only narrow and weak, but also sterilises the legitimacy of that violence.

of furthering international peace and security, nor mandate adherence to the requirements of IHL and IHRL. While it is trite to observe that the state must adhere both to legal obligations under *jus ad bellum* and *jus in bello*, this reveals the stark contrast where the PSC is concerned since only contractual terms are relevant.[57] Not only is reductionism inherent within the translation of public international law to contract law, but the prospect for divergence in this conversion process becomes clear.[58] Further problems arise because PSCs, as non-state entities, have no legal obligations imposed directly by IHL and IHRL.[59] Exclusively relying upon contractual mechanisms for alignment, control, oversight, and accountability of PSCs in multinational military operations becomes a perilous procedure, because the freedom of contract allows for broad discretion in concluding contractual terms: good practices and codes of conduct may provide guidance, but these need neither be adhered to nor enforced by the contractual party if breached.[60]

The doctrine of privity suggests that the PSC is an agent to its contracting party.[61] The idea was raised above that ambiguities pervade the international obligation of states towards PSCs as expressed in the overlapping and imprecise obligations set forth in the Montreux Document, and that contractual obligations might cut through this murkiness since contractual parties seek to set forth clear expectations for behaviour and performance. The doctrine of privity, however, suggests that any gains in the clarity of contractual obligations[62] will be lost by the opacity of contractual mechanisms that bar third parties from access, oversight, and enforcement of contractual terms. In other words, legal obligations may become clear in a contractual setting, but this clarity is only accessible for the PSC and the hiring party. The question then transmutes to whether or not gains in terms of contractual clarity between the parties can offset the problems associated with legal ambiguities in public international law obligations of states.

[57] Liu (n 6) ch 6.

[58] The International Code of Conduct (ICoC) seeks to embody IHL and IHRL principles into contractual mechanisms for direct enforcement, critically discussed above.

[59] Even the UN's 'Respect, Protect, Remedy' framework and guiding principles does not contemplate corporate use of force as the core of corporate activities and profits, JG Ruggie, *Just Business: Multinational Corporations and Human Rights* (W W Norton & Company 2013).

[60] Since only contractual parties may enforce a contract there is a subtle transition that results in a narrowing of PSC operations for narrow and private reasons which are discordant with those that undergird a multinational military operation.

[61] But see J Cockayne, 'Make or Buy? Principle-Agent Theory and the Regulation of Private Military Companies' in S Chesterman and C Lehnardt (eds), *From Mercenaries to Market: The Rise and Regulation of Private Military Companies* (OUP 2007).

[62] There is an incentive for contractual terms to be clear and precise to facilitate performance that is absent in other legal fields. Yet, open-ended contracts and cost-plus contracts have emerged which introduce uncertainties into what, exactly, are the contractual requirements.

5. PSCs Circumvent Legal Presumptions

The myriad of legal complexities introduced by the PSC in multinational military operations are such that they significantly undermine legal predictability.[63] At the root of the legal disruption triggered by the PSC is its organization of violence for profit by a private entity through the mechanisms of contract law. Thus, this configuration of the PSC bypasses many legal presumptions that underpin the legitimate use of organized force. For example, one of the reasons why IHL and IHRL are doctrinally limited to state action is that states had monopolized the legitimate use of force,[64] such that the control of organized violence could be collapsed into the control of state action.

Converging with this is the position of the PSC in relation to state responsibility for international wrongs,[65] which tightly couples responsibility to state control.[66] Article 5 of the Articles on the Responsibility of States for Internationally Wrongful Acts (ILC Articles) on the conduct of persons or entities exercising elements of governmental authority,[67] and Article 8 ILC Articles on the conduct directed or controlled by a state, are most relevant in terms of binding state responsibility to PSC activity.[68] The point, however, is that absent exceptional arrangements, PSCs contracted to perform martial services to the state will not cross the high thresholds that trigger state responsibility where international wrongs are at stake.[69] This conclusion may be exacerbated by *lex specialis* overriding these articles on state responsibility provided for by Article 55 ILC Articles. Thus, both IHL and IHRL may employ tighter attribution standards. Moreover, even beyond attribution, states' positive obligations to ensure or protect individuals under IHL and IHRL may be implicated by the actions of the PSC.

This observation actually reveals that the state is not in control of PSC action, and this becomes important because it breaks the coupling between organized violence and state action. In other words, there is no state responsibility for international wrongdoing perpetrated by a PSC because the state is not in control of that PSC. Thus, laws regulating organized use of force by regulating state action

[63] Taking this argument to its logical conclusion, see Liu (n 6).
[64] Aside from Weber's well-known claim, Weber (n 4), the historical progression towards this configuration has been charted by C Tilly, *Coercion, Capital and European States, A.D.990-1990* (Blackwell 1992).
[65] UNGA Res 56/83, 'Responsibility of States for internationally wrongful acts' (28 January 2002) UN Doc A/RES/56/83.
[66] See also, Tonkin (n 27).
[67] 'The conduct of a person or entity which is not an organ of the State under article 4 but which is empowered by the law of that State to exercise elements of the governmental authority shall be considered an act of the State under international law, provided the person or entity is acting in that capacity in the particular instance.'
[68] 'The conduct of a person or group of persons shall be considered an act of a State under international law if the person or group of persons is in fact acting on the instructions of, or under the direction or control of, that State in carrying out the conduct.'
[69] Liu (n 6).

overlook, or fail to comprehend, the prospect of a PSC deploying organized violence. At the core of the legal disruption triggered by the PSC is thus this dissociation of the state's monopoly of the legitimate use of organized force.

In the context of multinational military operations, this conflation with state action causes additional legal problems because there is not just one state involved. The additional complexity inherent within a web of interlocking international legal obligations makes oversight of PSCs that much more remote. Put differently, the state monopoly on the use of force is challenged in both directions: upstream because the monopolies of several states are combined; and downstream in that these monopolies are delegated to some extent to PSCs. Since IHL still attempts to govern the conduct of hostilities, and IHRL to protect individuals against state power, the locus of legal control still subsists at the intermediary level of the state. The legal difficulty is that, because of the horizontality of contractual mechanisms and the formal equality between contracting parties, the state no longer exercises the levels of control necessary for the state to meaningfully be responsible for its conduct.[70] Connecting these with legal complexities upstream may introduce too much uncertainty to be justifiable.

6. Conclusion: Reinstating Privileged Belligerency?

The legal disruption introduced by the PSC is its blending of private for-profit contractual activities with a sphere of activity traditionally held in public law and state action. Laws constraining the use of organized force have adopted the heuristic of containing state action.[71] Organizing such force through a corporate structure and deploying it through contractual mechanisms subverts the applicability of the ecosystem of legal constraints that have responded to the organized violence hitherto deployed by the state and enables PSCs to act in contexts of armed conflict with impunity.[72]

Overcoming this legal disruption can take one of two avenues: either the legal framework is structurally overhauled in order to accommodate for organized corporate violence alongside those that constrain the organized violence of states; or to reassert the previous status quo, in other words to re-establish the state's monopoly on the legitimate use of force that can be delegated only where state control and responsibility are entirely retained.

70 Liu (n 45).

71 The invocation of IHL and IHRL in this context is telling because of their nexus in containing *state* violence.

72 Liu (n 6) ch 6. Prior to questions of conduct in hostilities are also the largely overlooked questions *jus ad bellum* for the PSC.

The legal complexity of multinational military operations creates an even stronger impetus to overcome the legal disruption introduced by PSCs, to avoid opening even larger lacuna and creating yet more ambiguity in obligations, standards, and good practices. This complexity also speaks against attempts to define and develop legal frameworks to address the challenges wrought by the PSC because there will inevitably be oversights and further lacunae, whether these are structural features or the outcomes of the interaction between various legal areas.

Instead, what is needed is less complexity and less uncertainty in multinational military operations. Thus, given even the select subset of legal conundrums raised by the prospect of PSCs functioning in such contexts, it may be prudent to reinstate the institution of privileged belligerency.[73] Reasserting the distinction between combatants and non-combatants advances compliance with IHL, but perhaps more importantly in this context, resolves the legally disruptive aspects of the PSC. This is because the institution of privileged belligerency will re-collapse the legitimate use of organized force with state action and eliminate the liminal position of the PSC as introducing militarized civilians into situations of armed conflict. In other words, the institution of privileged belligerency would re-establish the familiar legal paradigms of IHL and IHRL, which would re-introduce legal predictability and stability as a consequence. This need not eliminate the PSC from participation in multinational military operations: rather, PSC status, activities, and engagement must all conform unambiguously to the clear tenets imposed by IHL. While far from being a regulatory panacea for the use of force, privileged belligerency would neutralize both forms of legal disruption precipitated by the PSC in one simple step.

Furthermore, this need not eliminate the presence of the PSC in multinational military operations: rather, this changes the legal basis upon which their involvement is grounded. Thus, as long as states are willing to legally empower a PSC with the exercise of governmental authority or where the PSC is in fact acting on the instructions of, or under the direction or control of, the state in satisfaction of Articles 5 and 8 ILC Articles,[74] then the PSC does not disrupt legal regulation in a significant manner. Thus, it is also the contractual mechanisms by which PSCs become involved in multinational military operations that are legally disruptive because these subvert the command and control structures that the law presumes, expects, and requires in order to function effectively.

[73] Privileged belligerency, also known as lawful combatancy, asserts the distinction between combatants and non-combatants and is one of the two pillars of IHL, see Y Dinstein, *The Conduct of Hostilities under the Law of International Armed Conflict* (CUP 2010) 33–61.

[74] Responsibility of States for internationally wrongful acts (n 65).

It remains unclear why the PSC has been able to blend civilian status with participation in armed conflict without attracting legal opprobrium to the point of outlaw.[75] In the context of multinational military operations at least, where legal complexity is already very high, redrawing the line between civilian and combatant seems to be a prudent step towards reducing legal uncertainty and to increase the clarity and applicability of IHL and IHRL.

[75] The significant size and continuation of the PSC industry suggests that the alleged anti-mercenary norm is small to non-existent, Liu and Kinsey (n 7).

21
Asymmetric Actors in Asymmetric Conflicts

Robert Frau

1. Introduction: Three Understandings of 'Asymmetry'

'Asymmetry' is not a legal term of art with a set definition.[1] In recent years, this term has been used to describe a range of ongoing conflicts; highlighting for example the different military capabilities of the belligerents or their nature as states or non-state actors. This chapter proposes three distinct meanings of 'asymmetry': the term is understood to include legal, factual, and methodological asymmetries. These three asymmetries describe several challenges to the law of armed conflict. One can apply these three understandings of asymmetry to actors and conflicts. In detail, asymmetry manifests itself in divergent applicability of the law, divergent application in practice, and different influence in the creation of new law, that is, methodological asymmetry. These asymmetries give rise to different challenges to the law, its enforcement, and its development.

In this sense, asymmetry, or to be more precise, the three asymmetries, constitute the legal pluriverse surrounding military operations. Legal asymmetries define the parameters of the legal pluriverse. Put differently, legal asymmetries constitute the dimensions of this pluriverse, while factual asymmetries describe the way actors behave within that space. Methodological asymmetries refer to the way the pluriverse is expanding or changing, and describes the interaction between assumed or real practical needs due to factual asymmetries and the legal framework.

The purpose of the chapter is to highlight the challenges posed by asymmetries. It attempts to describe the most relevant aspects of asymmetry and endeavours to propose answers.

[1] W Heintschel von Heinegg, 'Asymmetric Warfare' [2010] The Max Planck Encyclopedia of Public International Law 2; R Geiß, 'Asymmetric Conflict Structures' (2006) 88 International Review of the Red Cross 757, 759; E Lieblich and O Alterman, *Transnational Asymmetric Armed Conflict under International Humanitarian Law: Key Contemporary Challenges* (Institute for National Security Studies 2015) 25.

Robert Frau, *Asymmetric Actors in Asymmetric Conflicts* In *The 'Legal Pluriverse' Surrounding Multinational Military Operations*. Edited by Robin Geiß and Heike Krieger, Oxford University Press (2020).
DOI: 10.1093/oso/9780198842965.003.0022

2. Legal Asymmetry

For the purpose of this chapter, 'legal asymmetry' depicts divergent legal standards. In other words, the law sets different standards for different actors or provides different rules for comparable factual phenomena. Following this approach, 'asymmetric actors' may be understood to describe two or more actors who are treated by the law unequally. Likewise, 'asymmetric conflicts' may describe the fact that a different legal framework is applicable in each armed conflict. In this sense, legal asymmetries institute the dimension of the legal pluriverse surrounding military operations.

Current challenges posed by legal asymmetry encompass the type of armed conflict and recognition of governments, weapons law, questions related to status and enforcement by and against non-state actors.

2.1 Nature of armed conflict

The asymmetries start at the very initiation of international humanitarian law (IHL). The existence of the legal category 'non-international armed conflicts', describing conflicts between two actors of a different nature, is only one example of conflicts that are asymmetric by law and in practice. Another example are the different definitions of non-international armed conflicts as contained in Common Article 3 of the Geneva Conventions (GC) and Article 1 of the Additional Protocol II (AP II), and as further developed in the jurisprudence of the International Criminal Tribunal for Rwanda (ICTR) and the Rome Statute of the International Criminal Court (ICC).[2] Here, a state actor involved in a non-international armed conflict may even deny the applicability of IHL with the excuse that the conflict is not intense enough to be considered an issue for international law.[3]

In addition, in recent conflicts another asymmetry was created by state practice: in the non-international armed conflicts in Libya or Syria, several states recognized the (former) non-state actor, for example, the Libyan National Transitional Council or the Free Syrian Army, as a legitimate and lawful representative of the state in question. The (former) widely recognized government thus became a non-state actor. In the view of some states, accordingly, not the nature of the conflict

[2] cf only A Paulus and M Vashakmadze, 'Asymmetrical War and the Notion of Armed Conflict—A Tentative Conceptualization' (2009) 91 International Review of the Red Cross 95, 98 et seq, with further references.

[3] ibid 99; S Herr, 'Constraining the Conduct of Non-State Armed Groups' in AP Jakobi and KD Wolf (eds), *The Transnational Governance of Violence and Crime—Non-State Actors in Security* (Palgrave Macmillan 2013) 42.

changed, but the character of the belligerents. If one follows the politics of said states, this change in policy has a legal bearing to it.[4]

Moreover, if states get involved in such non-international armed conflicts, the consequences may be disastrous: if state A gets involved on the side of the (former) government against the insurgents, in its view helping the state actor, state B may recognize the (former) non-state actor as the new representative of the state in question, and, being asked by the non-state actor turned government, becomes involved on its side of the conflict. Even taking into account that recognition of governments is not decisive in international law in general and IHL in particular, the challenges are obvious. What is the applicable legal framework for the international community? What is the applicable law in the relation between state A and state B? In these scenarios, the different legal frameworks lead to divergent legal standards and initiate a debate that finds no common ground. How can the international community help in finding a peaceful solution if not even the question of the type of armed conflict is resolved?

Ultimately, premature recognition of a (former) non-state actor due to a political decision raises difficult legal questions. A solution would be to refrain from untimely declarations of recognition. If policy does not allow for such a cautious approach, states that recognize a new government may assert that their declaration has no impact on the nature of the armed conflict.

2.2 Obligations

In non-international armed conflicts, the parties to the conflict differ in their very nature. One party is a state actor, the other is a non-state actor.[5] Under general international law, this makes one belligerent a subject of international law on its own while the other belligerent enjoys only—if at all—derived subjectivity. While a state is able to enter agreements under international law in any instance, the issue is somewhat more difficult with regard to non-state actors. In recent years, scholarship has addressed the question of how to bind non-state actors to IHL, if they may be bound at all. This, of course, is a major legal asymmetry: While the state party to a non-international armed conflict is certainly bound, the non-state actor may not be bound at all.[6] Several attempts have been made to explain IHL's binding effect on organized armed groups. In the mind of the present author, these approaches fail

[4] For another example cf A Zimmermann, 'Abiding by and Enforcing International Humanitarian Law in Asymmetric Warfare: The Case of "Operation Cast Lead"' (2011) XXXI Polish Yearbook of International Law 47, 50 et seq.

[5] For the sake of length, non-international armed conflicts between non-state actors are left out of the analysis.

[6] This view is held by Paulus and Vashakmadze (n 2) 111.

to establish obligations for non-state actors. Two proposals should be mentioned before the approach taken here is explained.

2.2.1 Approaches to binding non-state actors

First, the doctrine of legislative jurisdiction maintains that non-state actors are bound by IHL because these groups are active on the territory of a state that has ratified the Geneva Conventions, their Additional Protocols, or other relevant treaties.[7] However, this approach does not pay due regard to the fact that the state may transform the treaty-law obligations into domestic law. An international treaty as such is not automatically part of a domestic legal order. This of course depends on the constitutional law of the state in question. For present purposes, it is sufficient to note that the doctrine of legislative jurisdiction may answer this question for some states, but it fails to provide a solution for every state in the world.[8] Moreover, an insurgent group attempts to overthrow the government and it is not very likely that the insurgent group adheres to the international treaties signed by that government.[9]

Secondly, international law does not bind because one subject of international law expects another subject to adhere to the law or because it makes political sense for an actor to respect international law. Reciprocity and political expectations may ease compliance with the law and help to enforce it. Nevertheless, the character of an international law obligation as being a *legal* obligation cannot be explained by this approach.[10]

The present author submits that fundamental criticism with regard to traditional international law, or to conventional approaches to bind non-state actors, cannot be maintained.[11] Broken down for this analysis, international (humanitarian) law provides for obligations of non-state actors. This can be deduced from the following observations.

[7] E David, 'IHL and Non-State Actors: Synopsis of the Issue' (2003) 37 Proceedings of the Bruges Colloquium: Relevance of International Humanitarian Law to Non-State Actors 35; S Sivakumaran, 'Binding Armed Opposition Groups' (2006) 55 International and Comparative Law Quarterly 369, 381 et seq.

[8] This approach is also rejected by Samuel Estreicher, but for different reasons. cf S Estreicher, 'Privileging Asymmetric Warfare? Part III: The Intentional Killing of Civilians under International Humanitarian Law' (2012) 12 Chicago Journal of International Law 589, 596 et seq.

[9] Herr (n 3) 43; R Frau, 'Überlegungen zur Bindung nichtstaatlicher Gewaltakteure an internationale Menschenrechte' (2013) 26 Humanitäres Völkerrecht—Informationsschriften 13, 16, both with further references.

[10] cf also T Pfanner, 'Asymmetrical Warfare from the Perspective of Humanitarian Law and Humanitarian Action' (2005) 87 International Review of the Red Cross 149, 161; B Simma, 'Reciprocity' (2008) The Max Planck Encyclopedia of Public International Law; Geiß (n 1) 763 et seq; Paulus and Vashakmadze (n 2) 109, 121 et seq.

[11] The approach taken here is stated in more detail in R Frau, 'Entwicklungen bei der gewohnheitsrechtlichen Einbindung nichtstaatlicher Gewaltakteure' in D Weingärtner and H Krieger (eds), *Streitkräfte und nicht-staatliche Akteure* (Nomos 2013) with regard to non-state actors and IHL and in Frau (n 9) with regard to human rights law.

2.2.2 Non-state actors as subjects of international law

2.2.2.1 Binding non-state actors to general international law

International law is based on the consent of states. They create international law and by their will entities become subjects of international law. Subjectivity, or personality, under international law means the capacity to possess rights and duties under international public law.[12] Granting subjectivity does not stop at creating a new legal person. By virtue of creation, this new subject is put under obligation to respect certain fundamental rules of international law. In other words, the creation of a new subject of international law always entails rights and/or duties for the new actor. Included in this basic package, as it were, are the rules about creating international law. If (new) subjects of international law were not bound by rules defining the system, international law as a legal system would not work. Thus, new subjects of international law are not created as a mere hull, but as actors already equipped with some basic rights and duties. To put it differently, new actors are not shady ghosts, nothing more than a structure, which is not stopped by the walls of international law, but they are actors of flesh—the rights; and blood—the duties. Or, vice versa, if international law grants an entity rights or puts an entity under duties under international law, this grant automatically entails a limited legal personality under international law; either limited with regard to the rights and duties in question (partial subjectivity[13]) or with regard to the subjects recognizing this status (relative subjectivity[14]).

Broken down to IHL, this means the following. States consent to rules relating to non-international armed conflicts. More precisely, state parties to the Geneva Conventions and/or AP II agree to regulate a situation by way of international law. Given the fact that such a situation only involves one of the state parties, one would expect that domestic law applied, as the classical concept of international law would suggest. The reasons for applying international law—protection of civilians, political advantages, etc—can be left aside. Decisive is the fact that states elevate this once purely domestic matter to the international sphere, rendering an internal conflict a non-international armed conflict. States agree to open their sovereignty to a certain extent, that is, the miniature convention of Common Article 3 GC (or even AP II). Simultaneously, states decide to bind the non-state party to the conflict to this miniature convention as well, as can be seen by the wording of Common Article 3 GC ('each Party to the conflict shall be bound to apply, as a minimum, the following provisions'). In the end, when the specific criteria of a provision are fulfilled, the non-state actor is bound by international law. In case of Article 1(1) AP II this happens to be a 'de-facto authority',[15] in cases of Common

[12] cf J Crawford (ed), *Brownlie's Principles of Public International Law* (8th edn, OUP 2012) 115; C Walter, 'Subjects of International Law' (2007) The Max Planck Encyclopedia of Public International Law 21.

[13] Walter (n 12) 23, para 23.

[14] ibid para 24.

[15] L Zegveld, *Accountability of Armed Opposition Groups in International Law* (CUP 2002) 15.

Article 3 GC the existence of a non-international armed conflict is sufficient.[16] The exact contents of the rights and obligations of a new subject are dealt with later.

2.2.2.2 Concerns regarding this approach

It has been held that the concrete consent of the non-state actor is absolutely necessary to bind such an actor to an international treaty.[17] Otherwise, it is claimed, one could not expect respect for the law from actors that had no say in its creation. Leaving aside the aspect that this is exactly the way domestic legal systems work, this criticism is not convincing.

To begin with, IHL is not about democracy. It is about finding a balance between military necessity and humanitarian considerations. IHL is about protection from the dangers of hostilities. Moreover, it may be troubling to sustain one's appreciation of international democracy with regard to actors such as the Islamic State in Iraq and Syria 2014, whose democratic legitimization is non-existent. But this is merely a political argument.

If these concerns are phrased not politically, but legally, these concerns touch upon the prohibition to create rights or obligations for someone without his/her consent as enshrined for example in Article 34 of the Vienna Convention on the Law of Treaties (VCLT) (*pacta tertiis nec nocent nec prosunt*). However, such concerns have no merit. This is due to the mere fact that without granting rights and conferring obligations to a non-state actor, this non-state actor would not exist as a subject of international law. There would simply be no one to benefit from this principle, no one to which this principle could be applied.

Consequently, the applicability of IHL in non-international armed conflicts entails the partial and relative subjectivity of a non-state actor, that is, subjectivity regarding particular fields of law and subjectivity with relations to particular other subjects of international law, which simultaneously confers certain rights and duties on this actor.

2.2.2.3 Additional ways to bind non-state actors to IHL

In addition to this approach, IHL provides two easy mechanisms to bind non-state actors.

First, a state party may recognize the organized armed group as belligerents. Consequently, the applicability of IHL is not in question anymore and the conflict has to be treated as if it were an international armed conflict.[18] Recognition

[16] M Sassòli, 'Transnational Armed Groups and International Humanitarian Law' (2006) Series 9, Program on Humanitarian Policy and Conflict Research, Harvard Occasional Paper, 4 et seq.

[17] cf C Ryngaert, 'Non-State Actors and International Humanitarian Law' (2008) Institute for International Law KU Leuven Working Paper, 6 et seq <https://www.law.kuleuven.be/iir/nl/onderzoek/working-papers/WP146e.pdf>. All URLs accessed 27 December 2018.

[18] Y Dinstein, *The Conduct of Hostilities under the Law of International Armed Conflict* (2nd edn, CUP 2010) 68.

of belligerency is part of IHL.[19] Issues of *pacta tertiis* are not being raised by state practice, jurisprudence, or scholarship. Granted, there is no treaty which regulates belligerency, but the concerns circle around the same issue: someone is bound by the decision of someone else without the first subject having the possibility to object. This shows that concerns about the undemocratic character of the proposed approach have no basis in IHL.[20]

Secondly, the non-state actor may bind itself by way of unilateral declaration.[21] This is most prominently the case with the Permanent Observer of Palestine to the Office of the United Nations at Geneva, which unilaterally declared in 1989 to be bound by the Geneva Conventions and the first two Additional Protocols.[22]

Geneva Call,[23] a non-governmental organization that strives for the adherence of non-state actors to the Anti-Personnel Mine Ban Treaty, takes a more tailored approach. This is achieved by signing a 'Deed of Commitment', in which the non-state actor declares to be bound by specific regulations. Altogether, non-state actors are convinced to sign such deeds with regard to: for Adherence to a Total Ban on Anti-Personnel Mines and for Cooperation in Mine Action; for the Protection of Children from the Effects of Armed Conflict; or for the Prohibition of Sexual Violence in Situations of Armed Conflict and towards the Elimination of Gender Discrimination. This does not mean that consent by non-state actors is in any case necessary to bind them. It is, however, an alternative way to bind them. The advantage is ownership of the obligations by non-state actors.

2.2.3 Obligations of non-state actors arising from IHL

The present analysis holds that non-state actors gain legal personality under international law by being entitled and obliged by treaty as well as customary law. This entails most importantly an obligation to comply with the two cardinal principles.

[19] ibid.

[20] It must be noted that the recognition as belligerents is not the same as the proposal above, recognizing the subjectivity of non-state actors by crossing the threshold of applicability. First, recognition of belligerents entails a political recognition as well and may legitimize the non-state actor. Secondly, recognition of belligerents has other legal consequences: pivotal is the change from international armed conflict to non-international armed conflict. Important are also the consequences for other states, who become neutrals in this international armed conflict; important is also that the belligerents may be recognized without a violation of the prohibition to intervene in domestic affairs of another state.

[21] As a disclaimer it should be noted that issuing a unilateral declaration does not automatically entail an obligation under international law. The obligation that follows could also be a national law obligation or a mere non-legal obligation, meaning a promise outside of any legal realm. This is left out by A Clapham, 'Weapons and Armed Non-state Actors' in S Casey-Maslen (ed), *Weapons under International Human Rights Law* (CUP 2014) 163, 184 et seq.

[22] cf <https://www.eda.admin.ch/dam/eda/fr/documents/aussenpolitik/voelkerrecht/geneve/890913-GENEVE_e.pdf>. Of course, the State of Palestine has since then ratified the Geneva Conventions as well as the three Additional Protocols, cf <https://ihl-databases.icrc.org/ihl>.

[23] cf E Decrey Warner, 'Armed Non-state Actors and Weapons' in *Current Perspectives on Regulating Means of Warfare. Proceedings of the 8th Bruges Colloquium*, No 37, 2008, p. 64 et seq; see <https://genevacall.org/>.

Thus, by law an asymmetry exists regarding by whom and the way that obligations are created. This will be picked up later in the section on methodology.

2.3 Weapons law

An important legal asymmetry can be identified in weapons law. Some treaties outlawing specific weapons are applicable only in international armed conflicts. In contrast, within the law of non-international armed conflict, the same weapons may only be prohibited by general rules, for example, the two cardinal principles.

Starting with explicit references to non-international armed conflicts in weapons law, only for states which have ratified the Amendment of Article 1[24] of the Certain Conventional Weapons Convention (CCW),[25] the CCW applies in international, internationalized (Article 1(4) AP I), and in non-international armed conflicts. Protocol V to the CCW on Explosive Remnants of War[26] is applicable in these situations (Article 1(3)), as is the Amended Protocol II on Mines, Booby-Traps and Other Devices[27] (Article 1(2)). If a state has not ratified these instruments, the CCW may apply in its original version, being applicable only in international armed conflicts and internationalized armed conflicts (Article 1 CCW).

In contrast, other treaties use the language of 'never under any circumstances' to extend their application. This is widely regarded as encompassing internal conflicts (and peacetime).[28] According to each respective Article 1(1), the Biological Weapons Convention of 1972,[29] the Chemical Weapons Convention of 1993,[30]

[24] Amendment to Article 1 of the Convention on Prohibitions or Restrictions on the Use of Certain Conventional Weapons which may be deemed to be Excessively Injurious or to have Indiscriminate Effects (adopted 21 December 2001, entered into force 18 May 2004) 2260 UNTS 82.

[25] Convention on the Prohibition of the Development, Production, Stockpiling and Use of Chemical Weapons and on their Destruction (adopted 13 January 1993, entered into force 29 April 1997) 1974 UNTS 45 (CWC).

Convention on Prohibitions or Restrictions on the Use of Certain Conventional Weapons Which May Be Deemed to Be Excessively Injurious or to Have Indiscriminate Effects (adopted 10 October 1980, entered into force 2 December 1993) 1342 UNTS 137 (CCW). For the drafting history cf D Turns, 'At the "Vanishing Point" of International Humanitarian Law: Methods and Means of Warfare in Non-international Armed Conflicts' (2002) 45 German Yearbook of International Law 115, 122 et seq.

[26] Protocol on Explosive Remnants of War to the Convention on Prohibitions or Restrictions on the Use of Certain Conventional Weapons which may be deemed to be Excessively Injurious or to have Indiscriminate Effects (Protocol V) (adopted 28 November 2003, entered into force 12 November 2006) 2399 UNTS 100.

[27] Protocol on Prohibitions or Restrictions on the Use of Mines, Booby-Traps and Other Devices, annexed to the Convention on Prohibitions or Restrictions on the Use of Certain Conventional Weapons which may be deemed to be Excessively Injurious or to have Indiscriminate Effects (Protocol II) (adopted on 3 May 1996, entered into force 3 December 1998) 2048 UNTS 93. (Amended Protocol II on Prohibitions or Restrictions on the Use of Mines, Booby-Traps and Other Devices).

[28] Turns (n 25) 126.

[29] Convention on the Prohibition of the Development, Production and Stockpiling of Bacteriological (Biological) and Toxin Weapons and on their Destruction (adopted 10 April 1972, entered into force 26 March 1975) 1015 UNTS 163 (BWC).

[30] CWC (n 25).

Anti-Personnel Mine Ban Treaty,[31] and the Cluster Munitions Convention[32] apply in 'any circumstance'.

Intensified are legal asymmetries by the way non-state actors are addressed. Where treaty law prohibits the use of a specific weapon in non-international armed conflicts, it does almost only prohibit the use by state actors. Treaty law has basically failed at addressing non-state entities as actors with regard to weapons. Some scholars blame the characteristics of international law for this. William Boothby, for example, seems to exclude non-state actors entirely from the spectrum of treaty law, even if a treaty explicitly refers to non-state actors.[33] Boothby follows Yoram Dinstein, who refuses to accept the doctrine of legislative jurisdiction and finds solace in binding non-state actors by way of customary law.[34] Andrew Clapham goes one step further and blames the structure of international law in general.[35] In his opinion, the traditional approach, which 'sees international law as excluding armed non-state actors from its list of suitable subjects',[36] is 'dangerous'. Nevertheless, weapons law addresses the use of specific weapons by non-state actors.

One can establish a matrix, differentiating the different kinds of obligations with regard to non-state actors. One can distinguish between rules addressing non-state actors directly, rules that impose duties on states to regulate the activities of non-state actors, and rules that apply to all by way of applicability of IHL.

Direct duties for non-state actors can be found within the framework of the amended CCW. The Amendment to the CCW borrows the language of Common Article 3 GC and states, '[i]n case of armed conflicts not of an international character occurring in the territory of one of the High Contracting Parties, each party to the conflict shall be bound to apply the prohibitions and restrictions of this Convention and its annexed Protocols'. Another explicit reference to non-state actors can be found in XII preambular paragraph to the Convention on Cluster Munitions (CMC). States are 'resolved also that armed groups distinct from the armed forces of a State shall not, under any circumstances, be permitted to engage in any activity prohibited to a State Party to this Convention'. Yet in the operative parts of the CMC, direct duties for non-state actors are missing.

Only one treaty puts states under an obligation to counter activities by non-state actors. Article 1(1)(b) of the Anti-Personnel Mine Ban Treaty reads: '1. Each State

[31] Convention on the Prohibition of the Use, Stockpiling, Production and Transfer of Anti-Personnel Mines and on their Destruction (adopted 18 September 1997) 2056 UNTS 211 (Anti-Personnel Mine Ban Treaty).

[32] Convention on Cluster Munitions (adopted 30 May 2008, entered into force 1 August 2010) 2688 UNTS 39 (CMC).

[33] W Boothby, *Weapons and the Law of Armed Conflict* (OUP 2009) 318.

[34] Y Dinstein, 'The interaction between Customary International Law and Treaties' in *Collected Courses of the Hague Academy of International Law*, vol 322 (Brill 2007) 344.

[35] Clapham (n 21) 169.

[36] ibid.

Party undertakes never under any circumstances: (…) b) To develop, produce, otherwise acquire, stockpile, retain or transfer to anyone, directly or indirectly, anti-personnel mines'. As a side note, the Arms Trade Treaty (ATT)[37] similarly does not include direct obligations for non-state actors. It obliges state parties to counter the diversion of weapons to unauthorized end users (Article 11 ATT).[38]

Overall, treaty law applicable to weapons use by non-state actors is fragmentary at best. The Anti-Personnel Mine Ban Treaty undertakes a rather faint-hearted approach to the issue. Only after the turn of the millennium, states put non-state actors under direct obligations. Weapons law thus reveals another asymmetry by law.

2.4 Status

Another legal asymmetry can be identified with regard to status of fighters in armed conflicts. In the law of international armed conflict, a combatant enjoys combatant immunity, that is he or she does not have to fear sanctions for lawful acts of war. This is an incentive to adhere to IHL: as long as a regular combatant keeps within the boundaries of the law and does not commit war crimes, there is no prosecution by either side to the conflict. In contrast, the law of non-international armed conflict does not know combatant immunity. Thus, the individual fighter in a non-international armed conflict has no established benefit from following the law. This asymmetry has been subject to debate.[39] It makes enforcement of IHL by non-state actors to a conflict more difficult, just because an incentive for individual fighters is missing.[40] If one takes a utilitarian perspective, the individual in question can hardly be blamed. Nevertheless, an amendment to the law of non-international armed conflict introducing some kind of combatant immunity seems unlikely.

As an alternative incentive, Article 6(5) AP II suggests the granting of amnesties after a non-international armed conflict. It provides that, '[a]t the end of hostilities, the authorities in power shall endeavour to grant the broadest possible amnesty to persons who have participated in the armed conflict, or those deprived of their liberty for reasons related to the armed conflict, whether they are interned or detained'. Although an amnesty may sound good, it cannot, however, stand a comparison with combatant immunity. Initially, amnesties are not mandatory. Whether a belligerent grants an amnesty depends on several circumstances that

[37] The Arms Trade Treaty of 2 April 2013, UN Doc. A/CONF.217/2013/L.3 (ATT). On the ATT's application with regard to Drones cf R Frau, 'Der Einsatz von Drohnen—Eine völkerrechtliche Betrachtung' [2013] Vereinte Nationen 99, 101.

[38] Clapham (n 21) 165 et seq interprets the ATT more extensively.

[39] cf the contributions in International Institute of Humanitarian Law (ed), *Non-State Actors and International Humanitarian Law. Organized Armed Groups: A Challenge for the 21st Century* (Franco Angeli Edizioni 2010); Lieblich and Alterman (n 1) 55 et seq.

[40] Herr (n 3) 42.

are contingent on the duration of a conflict, political support, the willingness of the winning party to the conflict, financial and personal resources after a conflict, and similar factors.

Also, while combatant immunity is a part of the hard core of the law of international armed conflict, amnesties give rise to criticism under international criminal law: domestic criminal prosecution is an aspect that the ICC has to take into account (Article 17(2) ICCSt). Before a case is admissible before this international forum, the ICC will evaluate prior domestic prosecution. Consequently, an unsophisticated amnesty after a conflict may create an easy way to the ICC. In other words, an amnesty may be promised during a conflict in order to give an incentive to individual fighters to adhere to IHL. Even if the amnesty is granted as promised, this amnesty may nevertheless not shield individuals from prosecution. This is even the case in scenarios where a war-torn society opts for an amnesty rather than criminal prosecution of war criminals in order to come to terms with the past. The ICC may still exercise jurisdiction if the Security Council refers a situation to the ICC. That the Security Council is prepared to refer a situation to the ICC is evidenced by the referral of the conflicts in Darfur, Sudan,[41] and Libya.[42] Most recently, the UN Security Council decided, in resolution 2178 (2014),[43] that states are under an obligation to 'provide the ability to prosecute and penalize' acts of international terrorism, especially by 'foreign terrorist fighters'. This shows the readiness of the Security Council to address situations of non-international armed conflicts, here labelled as terrorism, by way of international criminal law.

To conclude, there are divergent reactions to lawful acts of war, depending on the status of the individual in question. How this legal asymmetry should be addressed, if at all, remains unsolved and a major obstacle to enforcing IHL.

2.5 Further obligations

Treaty law applicable in international armed conflicts provides several rules for the treatment of detainees and interned persons, as well as for the treatment of wounded, sick, shipwrecked, missing, and dead persons. In contrast, AP II addressed those groups, but does so in very general and very few provisions. Again, while the rules for state parties to a conflict are detailed and impose specific obligations, rules for non-state parties are rather vague and require a thoughtful approach. This may be explained by the fact that organized armed groups should not be legitimatized to intern persons. However, this is to the detriment of the interned

[41] UNSC Res 1593 (31 March 2005) UN Doc S/RES/1593.

[42] UNSC Res 1970 (26 February 2011) UN Doc S/RES/1970.

[43] UNSC Res 2178 (24 September 2014) UN Doc S/RES/2178; UNSC Res 2199 (12 February 2015) UN Doc S/RES/2199, para 11.

persons. For them, their rights and guarantees are not as indisputable as in an international armed conflict.

2.6 Human rights

Human rights law is primarily addressing states. Whether it is also addressed to other actors in general, and organized armed groups in particular, has provoked a controversy.[44] This is due to the fact that only states are explicitly addressed in human rights instruments. Also, where individual complaints against human rights violations exist,[45] such a complaint may only rectify the violation by a state party, in other words by a state.

The present author holds it possible to bind organized armed groups to human rights law if one is prepared to take a different approach to this legal framework.[46] In addition to the arguments made earlier regarding the binding nature of the Geneva Conventions as well as other treaties to non-state actors, to be applied *mutatis mutandis* to human rights law, the following observations shall be made.

2.6.1 Vantage point

Traditionally, human rights law is understood from the perspective of states. This is consequential for interstate relations where obligations root exclusively in the consent of a state. However, human rights do not depend on the consent of a state but are supposed to 'derive from the inherent dignity of the human person'.[47] Thus, human rights supposedly exist independently from the consent of a state. If one follows through with this view, then one needs to take the perspective of the beneficiaries of human rights or, in other words, a human dignity approach.

This means, in more detail, that the hurt individual could not care less who violated his or her 'rights'. Decisive is the fact that this person was hurt by an entity far more powerful than he or she is. In this sense, restricting the applicability of human rights to violations stemming from states may seem arbitrary.

This approach is backed by recent jurisprudence of the European Court of Human Rights. The Court recently dropped its 'all-or-nothing' approach to either apply the entire European Convention or not at all.[48] The Court holds the view that

[44] cf only the stupendous work by A Clapham, *Human Rights Obligations of Non-State Actors* (OUP 2006) and M Schoiswohl, 'De Facto Regimes and Human Rights Obligations: The Twilight Zone of Public International Law?' (2001) 6 Austrian Review of International and European Law 45.

[45] Convention for the Protection of Human Rights and Fundamental Freedoms (adopted 4 November 1950, entered into force 3 September 1953) ETS 5, Article 34.

[46] cf Frau (n 9) for a more detailed explanation.

[47] Second preambular paragraph to the International Covenant on Civil and Political Rights (adopted 16 December 1966, entered into force 23 March 1976) 999 UNTS 171 (ICCPR).

[48] *Banković and Others v Belgium and Others* App no 52207/99 (ECtHR, Grand Chamber Judgment, 12 December 2001) para 75.

the Convention's rights may be 'divided and tailored' to a specific situation.[49] Truth be told, the Court phrased this reasoning in light of a state's responsibility and not for the possible responsibility of non-state actors. Nonetheless, it may be possible to tailor the applicability not only to specific rights, but to the obliged entities as well, as long as these entities are quasi-states or exercise 'all or some of the public powers normally to be exercised by that Government'.[50]

2.6.2 Human rights as *jus cogens*

Moreover, some human rights belong to the *jus cogens* of international law. As such, they are binding on any subject of international law. In essence, human rights of a peremptory nature are the basic human rights with *erga omnes* effects as identified by the International Court of Justice (ICJ),[51] namely the protection from slavery, racial discrimination and genocide, as well as protection from torture,[52] and maybe even the guarantee to a fair criminal trial.[53]

2.6.3 Human rights in armed conflict

IHL and international human rights law (IHRL) are not mutually exclusive.[54] However, the exact interplay is subject to debate.[55] Some authors argue for a merging of the regimes,[56] while others describe the relationship with the traditional concepts of *lex specialis* (humanitarian law) and *lex generalis* (human rights law),[57] or with the related concept of *renvoi*, meaning IHL making references to IHRL, and vice versa.[58] However, for the present purpose this dispute is of little importance, for the practical effects remain the same, regardless of the line of arguments. Therefore, the lawyer is responsible for working out

> with precision areas and questions where the coordinated application of provisions of both branches of the law leads to satisfactory—if not innovative—solutions, securing progress of the law or filling its gaps. (…) The point is not one of derogation by priority (…) but rather one of complex case-by-case mutual

[49] *Al-Skeini and Others v UK* App no 55721/07 (ECtHR, Grand Chamber Judgment, 7 July 2011) para 137.

[50] The phrasing is taken from *Banković* (n 48) para 71.

[51] *Case concerning the Barcelona Traction, Light and Power Company, Ltd. (Belgium v Spain)* (Judgment) [1970] ICJ Rep 3, 3 ff, para 34.

[52] ICTY, *Prosecutor v Furundžija* (Trial Chamber Judgment) IT-95-17/1-T (10 December 1998) paras 153 et seq.

[53] K Doehring, *Völkerrecht* (2nd edn, CF Müller 2004) 986.

[54] cf only A Orakhelashvili, 'The Interaction between Human Rights and Humanitarian Law: Fragmentation, Conflict, Parallelism, or Convergence?' (2008) 19 European Journal of International Law 161.

[55] R Kolb, 'Human Rights and Humanitarian Law' (2013) Max Planck Encyclopedia of Public International Law; Lieblich and Alterman (n 1) 43 et seq.

[56] Further references are provided Kolb (n 55) 30.

[57] Dinstein (n 18) 44 et seq.

[58] Kolb (n 55) 35 et seq.

> reinforcement and complement always on concrete issues. Thus, rather than stressing mutual exclusiveness, be it specialty or priority, it would be better to focus on two aspects: a) gap filling and development of the law by coordinated application of norms of HRL in order to strengthen IHL and vice versa; b) interpretation allowing an understanding of one branch in the light of the other normative corpus in all situations where this is necessary, i.e. in armed conflict or occupation.[59]

This is also the view of the ICJ.[60] It subscribed itself to such a reasoning when it was faced with problems regarding the right of life (Article 4(1) ICCPR) in armed conflict. The Court held that even if the other criteria required by Article 4(1) ICCPR are met, Article 4(2) ICCPR explicitly prohibits a derogation from the right to life. For present purposes, it is decisive to note that IHL and human rights law are not mutually exclusive. Human rights law complements IHL where IHL does not provide regulations. Consequently, from the applicability of IHL follows the applicability of human rights law at least as far as human rights law complements IHL.

2.6.4 International responsibility and criminal law

This view finds support in Article 10 of the ILC Articles on the Responsibility of States for Internationally Wrongful Acts,[61] which provides that the conduct of an insurrectional movement which becomes the new government of a state or the conduct of a movement which succeeds in establishing a new state in part of the territory of a pre-existing state or in a territory under its administration shall be considered an act of that state under international law. This holds true for such acts that have been committed before the insurrectional movement was successful.[62] In turn, this requires a prior obligation of the insurrectional movement. Without a primary obligation, the secondary responsibility for a violation would be nonsensical.

Supplementary support may be found in the crimes of international criminal law. In short, crimes against humanity sanction violations of human rights law by individual perpetrators.[63] From this, a binding force of human rights law to individuals or non-state actors does not follow. Nevertheless, an act needs to be committed in a wider context in order to be a crime against humanity. For example, the ICC Statute requires the act to be committed, inter alia, 'as part of a widespread or systematic attack directed against any civilian population' (Article 7 ICCSt).

[59] ibid 44; Dinstein (n 18) 60, seems to subscribe to this view.
[60] *Legality of the Threat or Use of Nuclear Weapons* (Advisory Opinion) [1996] ICJ Rep 226, para 25.
[61] UNGA Res 56/83 (28 January 2002) UN Doc A/RES/56/83.
[62] ILC, 'Report of the Commission to the General Assembly on the work of its fifty-third session—Draft Articles on Responsibility of States for Internationally Wrongful Acts' (2001) UN Doc A/CN.4/SER.A/2001/Add.1 (Part 2), para 4.
[63] Critical K Ambos, *Treatise on International Criminal Law*, vol 2 (OUP 2014) 47 et seq.

Non-state actors may implement such an attack.[64] Thus, crimes against humanity give evidence to the growing importance and legal significance of human rights law or the legal protection regarding specific human rights to actors other than states.[65]

2.6.5 Intermediate result

Nevertheless, one needs to be aware that the binding nature of human rights law with regard to organized armed groups is not as certain as the binding nature on states. Even if one is prepared to consider organized armed groups to be bound by human rights law, no accountability mechanism exists to counter violations. Here, the legal asymmetry augments the legal pluriverse in that different legal standards may be established.

2.7 Enforcement

Related to the issue of combatant immunity or criminal prosecution of lawful acts of war is the feature of enforcement by non-state actors. Recently, non-state actors have started to establish courts to deal with war crimes.[66] Whether these courts really deal with war crimes rather than internal enemies and 'traitors' can be left unaddressed here. However, this shows already one of the difficulties of or bias toward such rebel courts. In order to comply with human rights law, such courts must be measured against applicable treaty law. Article 14(1) ICCPR, for example, provides for a 'competent, independent and impartial tribunal established by law', while Common Article 3(1)(d) GC demands a 'regularly constituted court affording all the judicial guarantees which are recognized as indispensable by civilized peoples'. Aside from the question of legality, the issue of legitimacy remains. How can such courts be democratically legitimized? This issue becomes exacerbated if such courts are established while the conflict is still ongoing. A belligerent non-state actor is more likely to allocate its resources to the conflict instead of establishing a criminal code along with a code of criminal procedure as well as the relevant institutions and training of personnel.

While a state actor has means at hand to enforce IHL, a non-state actor will in most cases lack this capacity. Again, an asymmetry can be found.

[64] Likewise ibid 57.

[65] ibid.

[66] cf J Somer, 'Jungle Justice: Passing Sentence on the Equality of Belligerents in Non-International Armed Conflict' (2007) 89 International Review of the Red Cross 655; S Sivakumaran, 'Courts of Armed Opposition Groups—Fair Trails of Summary Justice?' (2009) 7 Journal of International Criminal Justice 489; J Willms, 'Courts of Armed Groups—A Tool for Inducing Higher Compliance with International Humanitarian Law?' in H Krieger (ed), *Inducing Compliance with International Humanitarian Law* (CUP 2015).

3. Factual Asymmetry

Factual asymmetry is a mere description of facts of armed conflict, for example, inequality in arms, in training, in financial or political support, or similar factors. Thus, inequality or asymmetry is not determined by law but by reality. Current challenges posed by factual or political asymmetry encompass the conduct of hostilities, especially precautions in attack, as well as reciprocity as an issue of enforcement.[67]

3.1 Actors and conflicts

First of all, one needs to be aware that in no conflict, both parties are in every regard equal.[68] May it be military strength, the number of troops, internal or external political support, financial and personal resources, availability of weapons, or in any other regard, no two parties will be alike. In that way, even international armed conflicts between two states who are equal by law, will involve unequal actors in terms of factual properties. In other words, they are asymmetric actors. That of course leads to an asymmetry of conflicts. No two conflicts are the same. These deliberations are not new and merely describe reality. Nevertheless, they have relevance for other fields.

3.2 Conduct of hostilities

The divergent military capacities lead to different ways of fighting a war. While one belligerent may have very sophisticated weaponry at its disposal, the other may have to rely on older or even outdated technology. Notwithstanding these factual differences, IHL applies equally. Most importantly, the basic principles are open to such asymmetries. Regardless of how sophisticated and modern the war fighting capabilities are, the prohibition to cause superfluous injury and unnecessary suffering and the principle of distinction remain the ground on which hostilities have to be conducted. Or, in the words of the ICJ, these 'cardinal principles'[69] 'constitute intransgressible principles of international customary law'[70]—regardless of any factual asymmetry.

[67] For an in-depth analysis cf Lieblich and Alterman (n 1) 53 et seq.
[68] Pfanner (n 10) 151.
[69] *Nuclear Weapons* (n 60) para 78.
[70] ibid para 79.

This plays a role for the application of 'feasible precautions' in actual conflicts. According to treaty law[71] as well as customary law,[72] belligerents have to take all feasible precautions. Feasible precautions are to be understood as 'those precautions which are practicable or practically possible taking into account all circumstances ruling at the time, including humanitarian and military considerations'.[73] Of course, what is practicable or practically possible depends on the military capabilities of the adversaries. If one has better equipment available, it may be practically possible to use the more modern weapon.[74] In essence, this is vital for the protection of civilians. Depending on the precautions taken, incidental damage to civilian objects or incidental harm to civilians may be spared.[75] Ultimately, IHL already takes into account a factual asymmetry of adversaries. This holds true, *mutatis mutandis*, for other obligations in IHL. One ought to mention the belligerents' obligation to take precautions against the effects of attacks.[76]

3.3 Enforcement

The above-mentioned legal asymmetries pose challenges for the enforcement of IHL.[77] Divergent legal standards can hardly convince the weaker party to adhere to IHL. In addition, the lack of organizational or hierarchical structure or authority of one belligerent may weaken its enforcement mechanisms.[78]

Asymmetry runs counter to reciprocity, understood to be an expectation towards the other actor.[79] If one actor adheres to IHL, it expects the other actor to do likewise. In this way, reciprocity plays a major factor in the real-life enforcement of IHL,[80] even if one keeps in mind that the adherence to IHL is not dependent on the adherence to IHL by the other party to the conflict.[81] Where expectations

[71] Protocol Additional to the Geneva Conventions of 12 August 1949 and relating to the Protection of Victims of International Armed Conflicts (Protocol I) (opened for signature 8 June 1977, entered into force 7 December 1978) 1125 UNTS 3, Article 57.

[72] JM Henckaerts and L Doswald-Beck, *Customary International Humanitarian Law* (CUP 2009) 51 et seq.

[73] Protocol II on Prohibitions or Restrictions on the Use of Mines, Booby-Traps and Other Devices (adopted 10 October 1980) 1342 UNTS 168, Article 3(4); Protocol III on Prohibitions or Restrictions on the Use of Incendiary Weapons (adopted 10 October 1980) 1342 UNTS 171, Article 1(5); Amended Protocol II on Prohibitions or Restrictions on the Use of Mines, Booby-Traps and Other Devices (n 27) Article 3(10).

[74] That is not to say that a belligerent is under an obligation to use the best of his equipment at all times.

[75] cf S Estreicher, 'Privileging Asymmetric Warfare? Part II: The "Proportionality" Principle under International Humanitarian Law' (2011) 12 Chicago Journal of International Law 143, 151 et seq.

[76] S Estreicher, 'Privileging Asymmetric Warfare? Part I: Defender Duties under International Humanitarian Law' (2011) 11 Chicago Journal of International Law 425, 435 et seq.

[77] cf Geiß (n 1) 770 et seq.

[78] cf also Paulus and Vashakmadze (n 2) 109; Herr (n 3).

[79] Pfanner (n 10) 160 et seq.

[80] cf Simma (n 10) 1

[81] Henckaerts and Doswald-Beck (n 72) Rule 140.

are not fulfilled, conversely, reciprocity fails as a motivation to adhere to IHL.[82] Consequently, reciprocity has a major impact on the enforcement of international law, that is increasing asymmetry may equal decreasing reciprocity.

In light of these difficulties, one needs to be aware that there is no way around organized armed groups or non-state actors in order to improve the enforcement of IHL.

4. Methodological Asymmetry

Both legal and factual asymmetry lead to the last manifestation of asymmetry, namely methodological asymmetry, referring to the way that new rules are created and the divergent roles that actors play in that regard. Current challenges posed by methodological asymmetry cover the creation of new treaty law or of new customary law.[83]

With regard to treaty law, one has to establish that only states are able to ratify international agreements. Even if willing, for non-state actors or organized armed groups it remains impossible to accede to a treaty regime. This holds true for IHL proper, weapons law, human rights law, or international criminal law.

The exclusion of non-state actors in the creation of new rules is deemed 'undemocratic' and leads some authors to understand the non-compliance of non-state actors. However, the debate about 'democratic participation' by non-state actors in the creation of new rules misinterprets the nature of international law. Nevertheless, for policy reasons it seems beneficiary to include non-state actors in the process of law-making, giving them a sense of ownership of the rules they have to adhere to. It is, however, practically difficult to give a say to an actor that only comes into existence *uno actu* with the commencement of a non-international armed conflict.

As already stated, other options to engage non-state actors are being realized as well.[84] The most prominent example is Geneva Call. Its approach offers a public forum to declare adherence to specific weapons prohibitions. This may be (politically) advantageous for an organized armed group, especially if the adversary, a state, refuses to sign the Anti-Personnel Mine Ban Treaty.

As another way to counter the methodological asymmetry, the practice of organized armed groups may be taken into account to a greater extent if customary law is identified. In order to establish the *opinio juris* required for the customary character of a rule (Article 38(1)(b) ICJ Statute), non-state actors may hold views

[82] Geiß (n 1) 770 et seq.
[83] cf for this aspect C Schaller, *Humanitäres Völkerrecht und nichtstaatliche Gewaltakteure - Neue Regeln für asymmetrische bewaffnete Konflikte?* (Stiftung Wissenschaft und Politik 2007) 29 et seq.
[84] The ICRC is, of course, of outmost importance. cf also Herr (n 3) 46.

that help in shaping the law. The field of methodological asymmetry seems like a subject that merits further attention.

5. Conclusion

Asymmetry comes in many forms. Different asymmetries constitute the legal pluriverse surrounding extraterritorial military operations. It is submitted that a threefold approach to asymmetry helps in understanding the difficult legal challenges and identifying possible answers. In detail, 'asymmetry' is understood to include legal, factual, and methodological asymmetries. Asymmetry manifests itself in divergent applicability of the law, divergent application in practice, and different influence in the creation of new law, that is, methodological asymmetry. These asymmetries give rise to different challenges to the law, its enforcement, and its development. Understood to mean different aspects of military operations, asymmetries help to describe the legal pluriverse, identify relevant problems, and may even help to find answers to these problems.

More to the point, legal asymmetries define the applicable legal framework and constitute different legal obligations on different actors. In addition, the law establishes different status groups with divergent legal obligations, which reach from obligations under international humanitarian law to human rights law and end in international criminal law. Within this legal framework, factual differences add to the complex legal pluriverse. Actors, who are not equal in all terms, may fight in a different fashion. Their available resources shape the conduct of hostilities. In this sense, no two conflicts are alike. When creating new treaty or customary law, states may review the practice of past conflicts and act accordingly. Here, treating state and non-state actors differently perpetuates asymmetries, which is not in itself detrimental to the *raison d'être* of IHL.[85] Thus, within the legal pluriverse surrounding military operations, asymmetries constitute the parameters, describe the way actors act during conflicts, and are decisive for the further development of the law within the legal pluriverse.

This chapter has identified some areas in which asymmetries pose rather major problems: first, while the nature of a specific conflict depends *de jure* on the facts on the ground, state practice (or rather policy) obfuscates the legal differentiation, thus creating different legal frameworks, depending on the state's policy. It would be advisable to keep political and legal aspects of such recognition separate. Secondly, when drafting new weapon ban treaties, states need to accept the reality of non-international armed conflicts and non-state actors that may use specific weaponry. To counter possible legal loopholes, states should extend the scope of

[85] Cf Paulus and Vashakmadze (n 2) 95 et seq.

application of such treaties to non-international armed conflicts. Most importantly, they should create rights and obligations for non-state actors, that is, prohibit organized armed groups from using the weapon addressed by a treaty. Thirdly, there is the need to institute a benefit for the individual fighter who adheres to IHL but does not belong to a state party to a conflict. How this is to be achieved, however, is too difficult to be solved here. Fourthly, with regard to feasible precautions one needs to be aware that the technical abilities of a state are not per se better than those of a non-state actor. This needs to be addressed first and foremost by the belligerents who have to take feasible precautions during the conduct of hostilities. Here, every belligerent is under an IHL obligation to adhere to the best of its abilities to the law. Fifthly, human rights law may be applied to non-state actors if one is prepared to take a different approach to human rights law. It is, however, difficult to agree to this finding with absolute certainty, given the fact that human rights instruments address states. Sixthly, with regard to establishing new treaties or identifying customary law, one needs to be aware of the category of non-state actors who play a major role in real-life application of IHL, but only a marginal role in its creation or identification. It may be advantageous to analyse the practice of organized armed groups who fulfil certain criteria, that is, adhere to IHL instead of disregarding IHL as such. This way, organized armed groups may be incentivized to adhere to IHL if the benefit is a say in the creation of new rules. In turn, this may create a new asymmetry between different 'classes' of organized armed groups. It would, however, reduce the gap between states and (some) non-state actors, thus diminishing the methodological asymmetry.

Overall, within the legal pluriverse surrounding military operations, asymmetries constitute the parameters, describe the way actors act during conflicts, and are decisive for the further development of the law within the legal pluriverse.

22
Human Rights Obligations of Armed Groups

Andreas Th Müller

1. Introduction

The 'legal pluriverse' surrounding multinational military operations (MMOs) is not only characterized by a multiplicity of actors within these missions,[1] but also one of the theatres where they operate. In addition to state actors, MMOs will often be confronted with non-state actors engaging in military activities. While such armed groups might support or even join MMOs, they even more typically find themselves on the opposite side. In both constellations, it is relevant to understand whether, and to what extent, armed groups are bound by international human rights law (IHRL).

Before addressing this question, which pertains to the broader topic of human rights obligations of non-state actors,[2] the inherently problematic character of the enterprise to be undertaken deserves to be highlighted. On the one hand, the protection of human dignity and human rights is a comprehensive task that should not depend on the quality of the actors interfering with human rights.[3] On the other hand, IHRL remains a state-centred body of law.[4]

As a consequence, the risk of a human rights protection gap arises.[5] To be sure, international law's silence in regard to non-state actors does not as such pose a problem. In the traditional division of labour between international law and domestic law, human rights violations of non-state actors fall within the responsibility of the latter. Inasmuch as domestic law lives up to this task, there is no need

[1] See in particular the contributions in Part V of this book.

[2] See, eg, P Alston (ed), *Non-State Actors and Human Rights* (OUP 2005); A Clapham, *Human Rights Obligations of Non-State Actors* (OUP 2006); A Bianchi (ed), *Non-State Actors and International Law* (Routledge 2009); M Noortmann, A Reinisch, and C Ryngaert (eds), *Non-State Actors in International Law* (Hart Publishing 2015).

[3] See Clapham (n 2) 534.

[4] See R McCorquodale, 'Non-State Actors and International Human Rights Law' in S Joseph and A McBeth (eds), *International Human Rights Law* (Edward Elgar 2010) 97.

[5] M Nowak and K Januszewski, 'Non-State Actors and Human Rights' in M Noortmann, A Reinisch, and C Ryngaert (eds), *Non-State Actors in International Law* (Hart Publishing 2015) 113, 116 ('accountability gap'); see also D Murray, *Human Rights Obligations of Non-State Armed Groups* (Hart Publishing 2016), 10 ('legal vacuum').

Andreas Th Müller, *Human Rights Obligations of Armed Groups* In *The 'Legal Pluriverse' Surrounding Multinational Military Operations*. Edited by Robin Geiß and Heike Krieger, Oxford University Press (2020).
DOI: 10.1093/oso/9780198842965.003.0023

for international law to become active. It suffices to target states for their failure to prevent and remedy human rights violations by non-state actors. Alas, in case of powerful armed groups—which are symptomatic of, and further entrench, situations of limited or diminishing statehood—states may not be capable of securing these groups' human rights compliance, which leads to the risk of the human rights protection gap. This risk is arguably on the rise due to the proliferation of internal armed conflicts and the number of armed groups taking part therein.[6]

This raises the question whether international law should not step in to close or alleviate this gap, lest the affected persons might be left without any protection at all. But what would 'should step in' entail? Are we facing a dysfunction of the existing international legal order that can only be remedied *de lege ferenda*? Or is this rather a problem of the proper interpretation and construction of international law *de lege lata*? The present contribution is primarily concerned with the latter alternative and aims at identifying, and analysing, various strategies that seek to tackle the above-identified human rights protection gap within the realm of international law as it stands.

To this effect, first the concept of 'armed groups' is to be examined (section 2). Subsequently, it must be clarified that recognition of direct human rights obligations of armed groups signifies accepting their partial international legal personality (section 3). Against this background, various strategies of international law attempting to cope with the human rights protection gap are analysed (section 4). Finally, this contributor's own approach will be developed (section 5).

2. What are 'Armed Groups'?

There exists no generally agreed-upon definition of armed groups. The term is not commonly used in international treaties,[7] but is prevalent in international legal writing.[8] Three core elements can be identified, namely that a group (1) must be armed, (2) has a certain degree of organization, and (3) acts in opposition to the government and/or other armed groups.

(1) First, the concept of armed groups is reasonably understood in a functional sense as a group which relies on means capable of causing physical violence, that is, substantial harm to persons or objects.[9] The use of arms does not only

[6] See Nowak and Januszewski (n 5) 137.

[7] However, see as an exception Article 4(1) of the Optional Protocol to the Convention on the Rights of the Child on the Involvement of Children in Armed Conflict of 25 May 2000 (opened for signature 25 May 2000, entered into force 12 February 2002) (CRC Optional Protocol); see section 4.1.

[8] For the terminological variations see, eg, Murray (n 5) ('non-state armed groups'); S Sivakumaran, 'Binding Armed Opposition Groups' (2006) 55 ICLQ 369; JJ Paust, 'Armed Opposition Groups' in M Noortmann, A Reinisch, and C Ryngaert (eds), *Non-State Actors in International Law* (Hart Publishing 2015) 273.

[9] See, eg, Paust (n 8) 273.

include the use of conventional weaponry, but also the employment of nuclear, biological and chemical arms as well as the launching of cyber-attacks to the extent that these are prone to cause substantial damage to persons or objects. Hence, if the use of physical violence, for example, in the fight against the state's law-enforcement authorities, reaches a significant level,[10] transnational criminal organizations engaging in trafficking in human beings or trade in narcotics might also qualify as armed groups.

(2) Furthermore, in order to coordinate a considerable number of persons and to assemble and apply armed force to a relevant extent, armed groups require a certain degree of organization. In that regard, they are to be distinguished from 'brigands, banditti and marauders'[11] as a rather *ad hoc* type, loosely coordinated group of persons. This does not necessarily presuppose the exercise of territorial control by such a group. The degree of organization needed to control territory over a qualified amount of time, however, is a cogent indicator for the existence of a sufficiently organized group.

(3) Finally, an armed group operates in opposition[12] to a government and/or other armed groups and is thus distinct from the government.[13] As their oppositional character is, as it were, part of their DNA, there is no need to specifically highlight this aspect even though it is preferred by some scholars.[14]

It is characteristic for such groups that they cannot be 'managed' by the state in the manner IHRL expects this from a state enjoying the monopoly on the use of force. This factor is the principal cause for the human rights protection gap.

As the concept of armed groups stems from the realm of IHRL, it must be distinguished from similar concepts in international humanitarian law such as national liberation movements, rebels, guerrilla forces, insurgents, or belligerents.[15] To be sure, there are important overlaps and interrelations between the two bodies of law, but in principle they each continue to operate with their specific scope of application.

[10] See ibid 290.

[11] ibid 273.

[12] See ibid 273 et seq; Clapham (n 2) 275; McCorquodale (n 4) 99; Sivakumaran (n 8) 369 et seq; NS Rodley, 'Can Armed Opposition Groups Violate Human Rights' in KE Mahoney and P Mahoney (eds), *Human Rights in the Twenty-first Century* (Martinus Nijhoff Publishers 1993) 297; see also P Alston, 'The "Not-a-Cat" Syndrome: Can the International Human Rights Regime Accommodate Non-State Actors?' in P Alston (ed), *Non-State Actors and Human Rights* (OUP 2005) 3; J Hessbruegge, 'Human Rights Violations Arising from Conduct of Non-State Actors' (2005) 11 Buffalo Human Rights Law Review 21, 22.

[13] See Article 4(1) CRC Optional Protocol (n 7).

[14] See references in n 12.

[15] See Article 1(4) of the First Additional Protocol to the Geneva Conventions (opened for signature 8 June 1977, entered into force 7 December 1978) 1125 UNTS 3; A Cassese, 'The State of Rebels under the 1977 Geneva Protocol on Non-International Armed Conflicts' (1981) 30 ICLQ 416; Clapham (n 2) 271 et seq; Paust (n 8) 279 et seq.

In spite of these clarifications, identifying and delimiting armed groups is not a matter of hard science. They rather call for a value judgment balancing the different factors. The larger and the better organized a group is, the more control it exercises over the life and limb of human beings, the more extensively and effectively it relies on the use of arms to pursue its objectives, the more appropriate it is to qualify it as an armed group. The connection to the human rights protection gap is obvious: all these factors contribute to increasing the likelihood that such group cannot be effectively controlled by any state, and that therefore the state-centred human rights law becomes dysfunctional.

3. Acceptance of Self-standing Human Rights Obligations as Generator of International Legal Personality of Armed Groups

The mere fact of identifying certain organized collectives of persons as armed groups does not imply that they have international legal personality. But what about going a step further and recognizing that armed groups have certain obligations under international law? This question is sometimes avoided or circumvented in international law scholarship arguing that there exists no necessary link between the existence of international human rights obligations for such groups and their international legal subjectivity.[16] If one conceives of international legal personality as a bundle of international rights and obligations,[17] however, the connection is obvious. If and to the extent that an entity bears rights and/or obligations under international law, it enjoys international legal personality and acquires the status of a subject under international law. Hence, to affirm that armed groups are, under international law, bound by human rights obligations means to accept their international legal personality to this extent.[18]

This opens the floor for the multifaceted debate regarding human rights obligations of non-state actors. Even though IHRL traditionally solely considers states to be its addressees, it has long been recognized that non-state actors can be bound by human rights obligations as well.

First of all, direct human rights obligations of individuals may exist (so-called 'Drittwirkung' or 'Horizontalwirkung').[19] For instance, the right to the protection of personal data under Article 8 of the EU Charter of Fundamental Rights

[16] See, for instance, Sivakumaran (n 8) 373.

[17] In this regard see, eg, H Kelsen, *Pure Theory of Law* (University of California Press 1967) 172 et seq; see in a similar vein J Klabbers, 'The Concept of Legal Personality' (2005) 11 Jus Gentium 35, 47.

[18] In view of such limited international legal personality, armed groups may be characterized as 'asymmetric actors'; see in this regard Robert Frau's contribution in this book (Chapter 21).

[19] See in general JH Knox, 'Horizontal Human Rights Law' (2008) 102 AJIL 1; Murray (n 5) 162 et seq.

also binds individuals.[20] According to Article 28 of the Banjul Charter, every individual shall have the duty to respect and consider his fellow beings without discrimination. In addition, inasmuch as Articles 6 and 7 of the Rome Statute of the International Criminal Court provide for the prosecution and punishment of individuals for grave human rights violations as genocide or crimes against humanity, it is reasonable to assume that this secondary obligation presupposes a primary obligation of individuals not to violate the respective human rights guarantees in the first place.[21]

Furthermore, it is broadly recognized that intergovernmental organizations can be directly bound by human rights obligations. This may occur via treaty obligations such as in the case of the EU's accession to the UN Convention on the Rights of Persons with Disabilities[22] or of its planned accession to the European Convention on Human Rights.[23] This may also be realized by the unilateral embracing of human rights obligations on the part of intergovernmental organizations or by customary law.[24]

On the other hand, the preparedness to accept direct international human rights obligations of other non-state actors such as transnational corporations is rather limited. Most commentators prefer the traditional conception of indirect obligation of such actors through the vehicle of the territorial or extraterritorial jurisdiction of states in combination with voluntary human rights compliance on the part of transnational corporations.[25]

It is in the context of this wider panorama of human rights obligations of non-state actors that the discussion of self-standing obligations of armed groups under IHRL must be placed. In view of the fact that individuals and intergovernmental organizations are nowadays, at least partly, recognized as addressees of IHRL and thus as (partial) subjects of international law, it is not far-fetched to accept human

[20] See C-131/12 *Google Spain and Google Inc v AEPD and González* [2014] ECLI:EU:C:2014:317, para 97. However, it remains true that international human rights law recognizes horizontal human rights obligations only on an exceptional basis; see Hessbruegge (n 12) 31.

[21] See in a similar vein Hessbruegge (n 12) 30; see, however, M Milanović, 'Is the Rome Statute Binding on Individuals? (And Why We Should Care)' (2011) 9 Journal of International Criminal Justice 25 et seq.

[22] Official Journal of the European Union (OJ) 2010 L 23/35.

[23] See Article 6(2) of the Treaty on European Union [2012] OJ 326/01; see, however, *Opinion 2/13* [2014] ECLI:EU:C:2014:2454.

[24] See *Interpretation of the Agreement of 25 March 1991 between the WHO and Egypt* (Advisory Opinion) [1980] ICJ Rep 73, para 37; see Nowak and Januszewski (n 5) 157, with further references. See also the discussion in G Verdirame, *The UN and Human Rights. Who Guards the Guardians?* (CUP 2011) 55 et seq, concluding that 'much—probably most—human rights law binds the UN and other international organisations already through custom' (ibid 89).

[25] As regards this approach see in particular UN Human Rights Council 'United Nations Guiding Principles on Business and Human Rights' (16 June 2011) UN Doc A/HRC/17/31, the so-called 'Ruggie Principles'.

rights obligations also in regard to armed groups. The recent practice of the UN Human Rights Council points in this direction, too.[26]

At the same time, one should not treat the acceptance of armed groups to the circle of subjects of international law lightly. Such acceptance might offer unwanted legitimacy to such groups. In addition, the expansion of the pool of human rights obligors does not necessarily translate into improving the overall human rights compliance. It can also create legal uncertainty by blurring the responsibilities of the actors involved. In addition, even if conceding that certain human rights violations cannot be properly addressed through holding states responsible for inaction to avoid or suppress human rights violations by private actors, it should not be forgotten that in many cases activating individual responsibility for serious human rights violations (via crimes against humanity or other core crimes)[27] might offer a better solution than seeking the attribution of individual acts to armed groups whose status in international law remains fragile. Finally, even if remaining gaps in human rights protection are to be deplored, this does not absolve of the question whether the necessary change is not to be effectuated by creating appropriate international norms rather than by reinterpreting, and perhaps overstretching, the existing ones.[28]

4. International Law Strategies of Coping with the Human Rights Protection Gap

Nonetheless, international law as it currently stands already provides for a variety of strategies which permit, at least under certain conditions and for certain contexts, to affirm self-standing international human rights obligations of armed groups and thus help coping with the above-identified human rights protection gap. In this regard, one can distinguish between heteronomous and autonomous strategies of making IHRL applicable to armed groups. Whereas in the former case the armed group becomes the object of state action, in the latter case, it is the armed group that creates human rights obligations for itself.

[26] See in particular the special sessions held by the HRC on 'the so-called Islamic State in Iraq and the Levant' (ISIS) and on Boko Haram in 2014 and 2015, respectively; Res A/HRC/RES/S-22/1 of 1 September 2014 and Res A/HRC/RES/S-23/1 of 21 May 2015. As concerns the HRC practice on the matter see further Geneva Academy—Academy of International Humanitarian Law and Human Rights, 'Human Rights Obligations of Armed Non-State Actors: An Exploration of the Practice of the UN Human Rights Council' (*Academy In-Brief No. 7*, December 2016) <http;//www.geneva-academy.ch/joomlatools-files/docman-files/InBrief7_web.pdf>. All URLs accessed 27 December 2018.

[27] See section 5.2.

[28] See section 5.3.

4.1 Heteronomous strategies

Despite substantial transformations in the international legal order,[29] states remain the chief lawmakers in international law.[30] In particular, international treaties are mostly concluded amongst states. Inasmuch as such treaties can establish, on the international plane, rights, but also duties for non-state actors,[31] it would be well possible for a treaty to impose obligations to respect international human rights on either a particular armed group or on armed groups in general[32]—irrespective of the consent of the affected armed group(s).[33] Yet, human rights treaties generally abstain from making armed groups the addressees of the international human rights obligations enshrined therein. In contrast, major international humanitarian law instruments give rise to obligations for non-state armed groups,[34] but only for the purposes of humanitarian law, not IHRL.

Article 4(1) of the CRC Optional Protocol[35] deserves special mention in this regard due to its hybrid status, in a double sense: while as a protocol to the Convention on the Rights of the Child it has human rights origins, the subject matter of the protocol pertains to the field of armed conflict. In addition, when the provision states that 'armed groups that are distinct from the armed forces of a State should not, under any circumstances, recruit or use in hostilities persons under the age of 18 years', the (arguably conscious) use of the ambiguous term 'should' leaves unclear whether the provision contains a binding legal obligation.[36] In any event, paragraph 2 of the provision leads back to familiar ground since states are called upon to guarantee the compliance of armed groups through their domestic laws.

Another interesting example is the African Union Convention for the Protection and Assistance of Internally Displaced Persons in Africa of 23 October 2009, the so-called 'Kampala Convention'. While in its Articles 3 to 5 the Convention contains obligations for its states parties, Article 7(5) directly refers to members of armed groups, as defined in Article 1(e).[37] Thus, members of armed groups are made

[29] See in particular B Simma, 'From Bilateralism to Community Interest in International Law' (1994) 250 Recueil des Cours de l'Académie de Droit International 233, 234 et seq; T Meron, *The Humanization of International Law* (Martinus Nijhoff Publishers 2006).

[30] See A Peters, *Jenseits der Menschenrechte. Die Rechtsstellung des Individuums im Völkerrecht* (Mohr Siebeck 2014) 43.

[31] See notably *Jurisdiction of the Courts of Danzig* (Advisory Opinion) [1928] PCIJ Series B, No 15, 17 et seq: 'it cannot be disputed that the very object of an international agreement, according to the intention of the contracting Parties, may be the adoption of some definite rules creating individual rights and obligations and enforceable by the national courts'.

[32] See Hessbruegge (n 12) 28.

[33] See ibid 29; but see the discussion in the text accompanying n 70 regarding the *pacta tertiis* rule.

[34] See notably Common Article 3 to the Geneva Conventions; see Cassese (n 15) 424; Hessbruegge (n 12) 29.

[35] See n 7.

[36] See Nowak and Januszewski (n 5) 152; Hessbruegge (n 12) 32, with further references.

[37] 'Dissident armed forces or other organized armed groups that are distinct from the armed forces of the state.'

the direct addressees of human rights obligations and, to this extent, subjects of international law. This is a particularly remarkable example, since the Convention specifically regulates the activity of armed groups, although in terms of individual obligations of members of armed groups and not of the armed groups as such.

In this context, it is common to also refer to the 1999 Berlin Resolution of the Institute of International Law.[38] Accordingly, all parties to an armed conflict 'irrespective of their status', that is, including armed groups, 'have the obligation to respect international humanitarian law as well as fundamental rights'.[39] While the resolution has as such no legal effects, it may nonetheless be considered an indicator for a nascent *opinio juris* on the subject.

This brings to the fore the question of international custom. For the identification of both the *consuetudo* and the *opinio juris* elements, traditionally state practice and the relevant utterances of state organs are examined. From a contemporary perspective, the practice of international organizations may also be considered a significant factor in the formation of customary law. There are even indications, albeit not widely accepted, that non-state actors such as armed groups might themselves take part in the creation of customary rules.[40] In any event, according to the prevailing view amongst scholars, currently there exists no customary rule accepting armed groups as addressees of international human rights obligations.[41] Although a substantial part of IHRL has meanwhile acquired customary law status, the question of the addressees of these rules is to be deemed a conceptually separated one; the former concerns the scope of application *ratione materiae*, the latter the scope of application *ratione personae* of IHRL.

Furthermore, when it comes to heteronomous law-making vis-à-vis armed groups, the role of the UN Security Council must not be neglected. As the ICJ stated in its *Kosovo* Advisory Opinion, it 'has not been uncommon for the Security Council to make demands on actors other than United Nation Member States and inter-governmental organizations'.[42] To be sure, the language of the pertinent Security Council resolutions is often (not seldom deliberately) ambiguous as to whether such prescriptions represent political demands or legal obligations. Nonetheless, the Security Council, under its authority to adopt binding legal resolutions under Chapter VII of the UN Charter,[43] is authorized to impose legal

[38] 'The Application of International Humanitarian Law and Fundamental Human Rights, in Armed Conflicts in which Non-State Entities are Parties', Resolution adopted at the Berlin Session, 25 August 1999, <http://www.idi-iil.org/app/uploads/2017/06/1999_ber_03_en.pdf>.

[39] ibid Article II; see also Article X in regard to disturbances short of armed conflict: 'All parties are bound to respect fundamental human rights under the scrutiny of the international community.'

[40] See ICTY, *Decision on the Defence Motion for Interlocutory Appeal on Jurisdiction* (*Prosecutor v. Duško Tadić*) [1995] IT-94-1-AR72, paras 103, 107 et seq.

[41] There is also widespread scepticism with respect to relevant general principles of international law in this regard; see Sivakumaran (n 8) 375 et seq.

[42] *Accordance with International Law of the Unilateral Declaration of Independence in Respect of Kosovo* (Advisory Opinion) [2010] ICJ Rep 403, para 116.

[43] See also Article 25 of the UN Charter.

obligations on armed groups, thereby making them partial international legal subjects. This view is corroborated by the fact that the ICJ acknowledged in the *Kosovo* Advisory Opinion that according to this functional, peace-promoting logic, individuals can be the direct addressees of Security Council resolutions as well.[44]

However, in view of the rules of interpretation that the ICJ established in regard to Security Council resolutions,[45] the creation of additional obligations for non-UN members, notably for non-state actors, must be established by clear language of the resolution and must not be easily presumed.[46] Often, the Security Council reaffirms existing obligations in a declaratory fashion rather than creating new ones in a constitutive manner.[47] Hence, there is limited evidence that the Security Council has actually adopted resolutions creating self-standing human rights obligations of armed groups.[48] Resolution 1193 (1998), 'urg[ing] the Afghan factions to put an end to the discrimination against girls and women and to other violations of human rights',[49] and resolution 1214 (1998), 'demand[ing] that the Afghan factions put an end to discrimination against girls and women and other violations of human rights', come at least close to creating direct obligations for armed groups, even though the terms 'urge' and 'demand' are (in contradistinction to the term 'decide') normally not considered a strong indicator for the intention of the Security Council to create binding obligations under international law.[50]

4.2 Autonomous strategies

Alternatively, it is furthermore worth considering whether human rights obligations of armed groups can come into existence by virtue of acts of armed groups themselves.

[44] See W Schroeder and A Th Müller, 'Elements of Supranationality in the Law of International Organizations' in U Fastenrath and others (eds), *From Bilateralism to Community Interest. Essays in Honour of Judge Bruno Simma* (OUP 2011) 358, 374 et seq.

[45] See *Kosovo Advisory Opinion* (n 42) paras 94, 117, referring to *Legal Consequences for States of the Continued Presence of South Africa in Namibia (South West Africa) notwithstanding Security Council Resolution 276 (1970)* (Advisory Opinion) [1971] ICJ Rep 16, para 114.

[46] See the approach taken by the ICJ in the *Kosovo Advisory Opinion* (n 42) paras 117 et seq.

[47] See, eg, UNSC Res 1378 (14 November 2001) UN Doc S/RES/1378, operative para 2 where the Security Council 'call[ed] on all Afghan forces [...] to adhere strictly to their obligations under human rights and international humanitarian law'; see Clapham (n 2) 283, note 46.

[48] Given the pertinent rules of interpretation, the example given by McCorquodale (n 4) 112 for direct international human rights obligations of terrorist organizations on the basis of UNSC Res 1373 (28 September 2001) UN Doc S/RES/1373 where the Security Council 'declare[d] that acts, methods, and practices of terrorism are contrary to the purposes and principles of the United Nations and that knowingly financing, planning and inciting terrorist acts are also contrary to the purposes and principles of the United Nations' is not convincing.

[49] UNSC Res 1193 (28 August 1998) UN Doc S/RES/1193, operative para 14.

[50] See Clapham (n 2) 282 for further examples.

First, such obligations could arise from unilateral declarations.[51] At first glance, it might appear counterintuitive that an armed group should voluntarily accept additional obligations without any obvious trade-off. However, at closer inspection, such self-binding declarations may well create benefits from the group's point of view. If the armed group is involved in an armed conflict, the acceptance of human rights obligations may raise the preparedness of a government and its forces to respect the human rights of the individuals fighting on behalf of the armed group (although the government is in any event bound by the pertinent human rights obligations). In addition to the benefit of reciprocity, such self-binding declarations may help the group to gain legitimacy. Honouring human rights obligations may prove conducive to being accepted as a player at eye level with the state and to marshalling support from other actors.

An interesting variation of such unilateral commitments are the so-called 'Deeds of Commitment' administered by Geneva Call, a Geneva-based NGO dedicated to promoting respect by armed non-state actors (ANSAs) for international humanitarian law in armed conflict and other situations of violence.[52] The key tool used by Geneva Call are deeds of commitment which allow ANSAs to undertake to respect specific international humanitarian norms. So far, fifty-four ANSAs have signed one or several of the existing three deeds of commitment.[53] The signature by the ANSA leadership is countersigned by Geneva Call and the Government of the Republic and Canton of Geneva,[54] and the signed documents are deposited with the Canton of Geneva. The ANSAs committing themselves[55] qualify as armed groups in the meaning relevant to the present contribution,[56] and various commitments also have an international human rights substratum,[57] with the perspective of future deeds focusing more explicitly on human rights commitments.[58] Against this background, the 'Deeds of Commitment' contribute to promote the instrument of unilateral commitments, although without formally elevating them to the international plane. To be sure, the procedure followed seeks to imitate the

[51] See Sivakumaran (n 8) 387 et seq, albeit in regard to international humanitarian law obligations.

[52] See Geneva Call, 'Mission' <http://www.genevacall.org/who-we-are/>.

[53] See Geneva Call, 'Deed of Commitment' <http://www.genevacall.org/how-we-work/deed-of-commitment/>. To date, forty-two ANSAs have signed the Deed of Commitment banning anti-personnel mines, twenty-six have signed the Deed of Commitment protecting children in armed conflict, and twenty-four have signed the Deed of Commitment prohibiting sexual violence and gender discrimination.

[54] Due to the signatures in addition to the armed group's commitment, the act might be qualified as a 'bilateral arrangement' (see Clapham (n 2) 297). However, given the language of the deeds, where the armed group solemnly commits itself to the terms contained in the Deeds of Commitment, and in view of the fact that Geneva Call and the Geneva Government solely provide *counter*-signatures without embracing a similar obligation themselves, it is more convincing to construe the act as a unilateral commitment on the part of the armed group, with Geneva Call and the Geneva Government formally taking note of the commitment by virtue of their counter-signatures.

[55] See the list in <http://www.genevacall.org/how-we-work/armed-non-state-actors/>.

[56] See section 2.

[57] See Clapham (n 2) 293; see, eg, Article 5 of the Deed of Commitment banning anti-personnel mines.

[58] See ibid 293 et seq.

well-established procedures of self-commitment of sovereign states, but inasmuch as not the Swiss Government but a regional government engages in countersigning and depositing the commitments, the procedure remains on the sub-international or rather transnational level. In addition, all the deeds of commitment contain a savings clause according to which the commitment 'shall not affect [the committing armed group's] legal status, pursuant to the relevant clause in common Article 3 of the Geneva Conventions of August 12, 1949'.[59] A comparable initiative worth mentioning in the present context are the efforts of the Special Representative of the UN Secretary General for Children and Armed Conflict, relying mostly on the Convention on the Rights of the Child as well as the Geneva Conventions, to obtain unilateral commitments from a series of armed groups.[60]

In addition, another manifestation of autonomous endorsements of human rights obligations by armed groups occurs via bilateral agreements with governments, notably with the government the armed group is fighting against.[61] Such agreements are expressly provided for in international humanitarian law[62] and are, within this scope, recognized as binding.[63] Such agreements may contain commitments beyond international humanitarian law, particularly human rights law commitments.[64] Thus, the armed group may become the addressee of self-standing human rights obligations.

Moreover, another manner in which human rights obligations of an armed group might arise through its own conduct is the succession in existing state human rights obligations by virtue of achieving *de facto* control of part of this state's territory.[65] Yet, this type of 'succession' is controversial and must be distinguished from the generally accepted emergence of international obligations from the substitution of an armed group into the position of the former government.[66] Nonetheless, there also exists certain authority for the proposition that the exercise of *de facto* control in parts of an existing state by an armed group gives rise to direct international human rights obligations of that armed

[59] See, eg, Article 6 of the Deed of Commitment banning anti-personnel mines.

[60] See Alston (n 12) 18; Clapham (n 2) 289 et seq. For a recent example see the commitment by the Revolutionary Armed Forces of Colombia-People's Army (FARC-EP) to stop the recruitment and use of children under 18; Office of the Special Representative of the Secretary-General for Children and Armed Forces, 'Leila Zerrougui Welcomes Commitment by FARC-EP in Colombia to End Child Recruitment' (*United Nations*, 5 November 2015) <http://childrenandarmedconflict.un.org/commitment-colombia-to-end-child-recruitment/>.

[61] See Sivakumaran (n 8) 389.

[62] See notably Common Article 3(2) of the Geneva Conventions; as to concrete examples of such agreement see, eg, Sivakumaran (n 8) 391 et seq.

[63] See L Zegveld, *Accountability of Armed Opposition Groups in International Law* (CUP 2002) 28 et seq, 50; Clapham (n 2) 297.

[64] See Clapham (n 2) 272, note 7.

[65] See the discussion in Zegveld (n 63) 15, 148 et seq; Sivakumaran (n 8) 379 et seq.

[66] See section 5.2.

group vis-à-vis the individuals who are under its control.[67] The rationale of recognizing self-standing human rights obligations of armed groups is to acknowledge situations where the entity governing and administering territory and population is not the state anymore, but an armed group, thus creating a vertical relationship between the armed group and individuals submitted to its control analogous to that which formerly existed between those individuals and the state.[68] Although not autonomous in the sense of a conscious decision of the group to embrace such obligations, it is the armed group that brings about, and prolongs, the situation in which it controls individuals. The duty to respect the human rights of the affected population can therefore be construed as an indirect consequence of the group's decision to conquer and administrate territory.

4.3 Heteronomous and autonomous strategies compared

The chief advantage of the above-described heteronomous strategies is that they are solidly grounded in traditional mechanisms of international law-making. If direct human rights obligations of armed groups are created by interstate treaties, there will be hardly any doubt[69] as to their binding character, since from the point of view of international law the responsibility, but also the authority, to control what happens on a state's territory rests with that state. The problem is, however, that only a very limited number of pertinent examples exist, and it is not to be expected that this option will be generously used by states in the foreseeable future.

An alternative, also relatively solidly anchored in international law, is the creation of self-standing human rights obligations by the Security Council. This strategy promises more flexibility, notably because in lieu of the need to devise an abstract regime for armed groups, including the thorny task of agreeing on a 'one-size fits all' definition of the concept, resolutions of the Security Council focus on a particular situation and thus allow for tailor-made solutions. At the same time, to rely on such *ad hoc* approaches may prove detrimental in terms of legal certainty and create imbalances between situations where the Security Council has recognized an armed group as bearer of international human rights obligations

[67] See Hessbruegge (n 12) 40; McCorquodale (n 4) 108, with further references, notably to UN Committee against Torture, *Sadiq Shek Elmi v Australia*, Communication No 120/1998 (1999) UN Doc CAT/C/22/D/120/1998.
[68] See Murray (n 5) 151 et seq, 168 et seq.
[69] See, however, n 70 regarding the *pacta tertiis* rule.

and others where it has, or could, not. This is dissatisfactory since it entails discrimination with respect to the human rights protection of populations finding themselves in a comparable situation.

The general disadvantage of heteronomous strategies is that they generate, even if not in the technical meaning of the *pacta tertiis* rule, obligations to the detriment of a third party, that is, the armed groups.[70] In contrast to states, these groups have neither consented to a pertinent treaty nor do they have a say in the composition of the Security Council. From the point of view of international law, this fact does not absolve armed groups from being regulated by states concluding an international treaty. Nonetheless, lack of ownership[71] in regard to rules imposing obligations on armed groups may have a negative impact on their preparedness to comply with these obligations.[72] Vice versa, autonomous strategies make it more likely for armed groups to respect the obligations they themselves have agreed to—and purportedly negotiated and influenced before agreeing to them.[73]

However, the problem with agreements that include armed groups and, for that matter, also with unilateral commitments of armed groups, is their questionable status under international law. It is controversially discussed whether such agreements and commitments can give rise to international obligations in the strict sense. Moreover, particularly those who are prepared to recognize legal acts involving armed groups as international in character, face the further problem that opening the fore of international law to armed groups and permitting them to negotiate and exchange promises at eye level with states might offer unwarranted legitimacy to those actors.[74] To be sure, the existing examples of such agreements and commitments are eager to stress that they do not affect the legal status of the involved parties, notably of the armed groups.[75] However, the mere fact of having rights and obligations under international law makes such groups subjects of international law and thus involves a status upgrade for them that the involved states might find difficult to accept.[76]

[70] See Articles 34–36 of the Vienna Convention on the Law of the Treaties (opened for signature 23 May 1969, entered into force 27 January 1980) 1155 UNTS 331 (VCLT); see, however, Sivakumaran (n 8) 377; see also the discussion in Cassese (n 15) 423 et seq.

[71] Sivakumaran (n 8) 375.

[72] See ibid 370.

[73] See McCorquodale (n 4) 113; see also the interesting discussion, albeit in regard to international humanitarian law, in A Roberts and S Sivakumaran, 'Lawmaking by Nonstate Actors: Engaging Armed Groups in the Creation of International Humanitarian Law' (2012) 37 Yale Journal of International Law 107, 126 et seq.

[74] See Hessbruegge (n 12) 38; Rodley (n 12) 315.

[75] See Article 4(3) of the CRC Optional Protocol (n 7), Article II of the 1999 Berlin Resolution (n 38) as well as the references in n 59 and n 62.

[76] See Clapham (n 2) 294; Roberts and Sandesh (n 73) 132 et seq.

5. Armed Groups as Addressees of International Human Rights Obligations: A Functional Approach?

5.1 Filling the human rights protection gap through functional approaches

The preceding analysis has only revealed isolated instances of self-standing human rights obligations of armed groups. While there exist various strategies of creating independent human rights obligations of armed groups, at the current stage of development of international law, they do not add up to a comprehensive picture of making armed groups the addressees of IHRL. At the same time, the problem of the human rights protection gap persists. In view of the fact that in situations where powerful armed groups operate, states often have only limited ability to guarantee their compliance with human rights, the effectiveness of the human rights protection system could be seriously compromised if the challenge posed by armed groups were not properly addressed.

Against this background, those functional approaches that consider human rights protection a paramount goal of the contemporary international legal order argue in favour of recognizing the international legal personality of armed groups in regard to human rights obligations in order to avoid the human rights protection gap. To this effect, it is often referred to the *Reparation of Injuries* Advisory Opinion: 'The subjects of law in any legal system are not necessarily identical in their nature or in the extent of their rights, and their nature depends upon the needs of the community. Throughout its history, the development of international law has been influenced by the requirements of international life'.[77] From there, it seems only a small step to conclude that 'the needs of the community determine the nature of an entity as a participant of international law … [and thus] require that the actions of armed opposition groups be effectively regulated'.[78]

Thus, functional approaches typically make a double claim: first, that the international legal order was never as state-centric as some seek to characterize it;[79] and secondly, that the inertia of an international legal order accustomed to deal with states as addressees of international obligations, notably in the field of IHRL, should not and need not result in downplaying or even ignoring relevant international legal developments in regard to non-state actors.

[77] *Reparation for Injuries Suffered in the Service of the United Nations* (Advisory Opinion) [1949] ICJ Rep 174, 178.
[78] Sivakumaran (n 8) 373; see also Nowak and Januszewski (n 5) 119.
[79] See, eg, Paust (n 8) 274.

5.2 Activating the potential of state-focused thinking (and individual responsibility)

However, before arguing in favour of expanding the circle of subjects of international law in the name of the effectiveness of human rights protection, it is preferable to first identify, and activate, the potential which is offered by the traditional state-focused view on international law. Upon closer examination, international law provides various means to avoid, or at least to reduce, the threatening human rights protection gap.

The most obvious approach is to attribute acts of armed groups as far as possible to states under the established rules on state responsibility. For instance, pursuant to Article 10(1) of the ILC Articles on State Responsibility (ASR),[80] the conduct of an insurrectional movement which becomes the new government of a state shall be considered an act of that state under international law. In addition, the conduct of a movement, insurrectional or other, which succeeds in establishing a new state in part of the territory of a pre-existing state or in a territory under its administration shall be considered an act of the new state under international law (para 2).[81] Furthermore, according to Article 9 ASR, the conduct of a group of persons, for example an armed group, shall be considered an act of a state if the group is in fact exercising elements of the governmental authority in the absence or default of the official authorities and in circumstances such as to call for the exercise of those elements of authority.[82]

To be sure, these are rather exceptional circumstances and can therefore only cover part of the human rights violations of armed groups. Yet, in the light of Article 4 ASR, the qualified inaction of state organs, notably a violation of a state's due diligence in preventing or punishing human rights violations by armed groups, can entail responsibility of that state.[83] Moreover, according to Article 11 ASR, conduct is also attributable to a state if and to the extent that the state acknowledges and adopts the conduct in question as its own. Furthermore, pursuant to Article 8 ASR, the conduct of a group of persons is also considered an act of a state if the group is in fact acting on the instructions of or under the direction or control of that state in carrying out the conduct. Even though the effective control standard that is underlying this provision is a rather demanding one,[84] further situations of human rights abuses of armed groups may be brought under the regime of state responsibility.

[80] UNGA Res 56/83 (12 December 2001) Articles on Responsibility of States for Internationally Wrongful Acts (ASR).

[81] See Clapham (n 2) 285 et seq, with further references.

[82] As regards the three conditions see ILC, 'Commentaries to the Draft Articles on Responsibility of States for Internationally Wrongful Acts' <http://legal.un.org/ilc/texts/instruments/english/commentaries/9_6_2001.pdf>, 49; see also Hessbruegge (n 12) 62 et seq.

[83] See McCorquodale (n 4) 103 et seq; Nowak and Januszewski (n 5) 117, 142; Hessbruegge (n 12) 24.

[84] As regards the effective control test see in particular *Military and Paramilitary Activities in and against Nicaragua (Nicaragua v United States of America)* (Merits, Judgment) [1986] ICJ Rep 14, para 115; *Application of the Convention on the Protection and Punishment of the Crime of Genocide (Bosnia*

In this context, the 'effectiveness of human rights protection' argument may be introduced to the debate in a manner that is completely compatible with traditional international legal reasoning, inasmuch as the recognition of human dignity and the importance of human rights as paramount objectives of the international legal order become manifest in the process of legal interpretation, both teleological and systematic.[85] This suggests a rather extensive, state responsibility-promoting interpretation of the rules on attribution of conduct in case of human rights violations by armed groups.[86] Such an approach can help, even if not to eliminate, but at least to reduce the human rights protection gap.

If attribution to a state nonetheless fails, the protection gap can be further narrowed by relying on the individual (criminal) responsibility of members, and particularly leaders, of armed groups. Individuals associated with armed groups may be prosecuted for crimes against humanity even if their conduct cannot be attributed to any state. Article 7(1) of the Rome Statute makes this clear when it requires for a crime of humanity to be realized that the acts are committed 'as part of a widespread or systematic attack directed against any civilian population', clarifying in paragraph 2 that the acts must be set 'pursuant to or in furtherance of a State or organizational policy to commit such attack'. An organizational policy may also be devised, and implemented, by a non-state actor, namely an armed group. However, the ICC has so far not developed a stringent interpretation of this provision.[87] In addition, while the penalization of crimes against humanity seeks to protect underlying human rights guarantees,[88] the substantive scope of crimes against humanity is narrower than the scope of international human rights law.[89] Hence, while offering a potentially helpful remedy in some situations, individual criminal responsibility can only remedy for some instances of human rights violations committed by armed groups.

and Herzegovina v Serbia and Montenegro) (Judgment) [2007] ICJ Rep 43, paras 399 et seq; see also Commentaries (n 82) 47 in this regard.

---

[85] See Article 31, para 3 lit c VCLT (n 70).

[86] See also K Mastorodimos, *Armed Non-State Actors in International Humanitarian and Human Rights Law* (Ashgate 2016), 143, arguing that, when it comes to human rights violations, the threshold of attribution of armed groups conduct to states is lowered in comparison with general public international law standards.

[87] See the discussion of the case law in CK Hall and K Ambos, 'Article 7' in O Triffterer and K Ambos (eds), *Rome Statute of the International Criminal Court* (3rd edn, CH Beck/Hart Publishing/Nomos 2016) para 110.

[88] See the list of acts contained in Article 7(1) of the Rome Convention, referring to grave human rights violations such as murder, extermination, enslavement, deportation or forcible transfer, imprisonment, torture, rape, enforced disappearance, apartheid, etc.

[89] See Hessbruegge (n 12) 42.

5.3 Direct human rights obligations of armed groups in case of *de facto* control of territory?

As we have seen, pursuant to Article 9 ASR, under certain circumstances conduct of an armed group may be attributed to a state if the group is in fact exercising elements of governmental authority in the absence of the official authorities. Taking the rule of attribution beyond this scenario would arguably overstretch the concept of state responsibility. Yet, a growing number of scholars take the position that when an armed group exercises *de facto* control over a territory similar to that of a state government, human rights abuses occurring in this framework should be directly attributed to the armed group.[90]

This seems a plausible position. After all, the human rights protection gap is largest in case of prolonged *de facto* control of territory by an armed group. There is ample opportunity for human rights violations when an armed group is in full control of territory and population. In addition, recourse to the state formally in charge of the territory in question is normally illusory in this scenario. In terms of effective human rights protection, the only way out seems to be the imposition of direct human rights obligations on armed groups. In addition, there is also an argument from general international law promoting such approach: the international legal order as we know it is first and foremost a territorial legal order. When it comes for international law to assign jurisdiction, the paramount factor is still territoriality. Especially in case of a threatening vacuum of territorial responsibility, international law tends to assign jurisdiction rather generously, thus lowering the standard requirements in order to avoid the vacuum.[91]

Tempting as this reasoning may be at first sight, it is not free of weaknesses. The benevolence of international law in assigning jurisdiction relates to states. It is questionable whether this idea can be transposed to a situation where there is no state actor at all. Furthermore, while the objective of securing effective human rights protection may deserve praise, when it comes to the question of whether direct human rights obligations of armed groups exist under international law, it is hard to find a sound legal basis, even for the particular scenario of *de facto* control of territory by armed groups.

There exists no pertinent treaty law, and it is not easy to argue that such obligations are based in customary law.[92] The instances of relevant practice are ephemeral.[93] States are particularly reluctant to admit armed groups to the privileged

[90] See Rodley (n 12) 300, 318; Hessbruegge (n 12) 24, 39 et seq; arguably also Clapham (n 2) 280, 283 et seq; Nowak and Januszewski (n 5) 159; Geneva Academy, Human Rights Obligations of Armed Non-State Actors (n 26) 26 et seq; Mastorodimos (n 86) 161 et seq.

[91] As to this *horror vacui* of international law see B Simma and A Th Müller, 'Exercise and Limits of Jurisdiction' in J Crawford and M Koskenniemi (eds), *The Cambridge Companion to International Law* (CUP 2012) 134, 139.

[92] See however Hessbruegge (n 12) 40.

[93] See n 67.

status of (if only partial) international legal personality. Moreover, even if direct human rights obligations of armed groups are affirmed, it is hard to see how they are to be implemented and policed if the armed group does not comply with them voluntarily.

Hence, in the absence of a specific element of consent or acceptance, it seems advisable, at this stage of development of international law, to act with caution regarding a generalized recognition of direct human rights obligations of armed groups, even in the admittedly particularly challenging scenario of prolonged *de facto* control of territory by an armed group.[94] Put differently, while an armed group exercising *de facto* control to a certain extent approximates a state and thus a symmetric relationship to other states, it nonetheless remains for equally important aspects an asymmetric actor that should not easily be 'symmetrized'.

At the same time, this reluctant position does not prevent from applying a systematic and teleological interpretation to existing human rights obligations that strengthens human rights protections.[95] What is more, this does not prevent from intensifying the calls for a long-needed reform of international law to cope with the significant increase in number and importance of armed groups and their relevance for the human rights situation of millions of human beings.[96] Such *de lege ferenda* efforts invite to discuss and devise compliance mechanisms that adapt to the particular characteristics of armed groups.[97]

6. Conclusion

The main conclusion of the present contribution is that in an area which is so prone to wishful thinking as that of the (purported) obligation of armed groups by IHRL, a good measure of modesty and caution is advisable. While it is well understood that in contexts of limited statehood efforts to fill the existing vacuum are particularly attractive, one should resist the temptation of copy-and-paste-solutions, approximating armed groups (in *de facto* control of territory) to states without a sound basis in international law.

However, this should not detract from soberly identifying, and applying, the strategies offered by international law as it stands in order to avoid the threatening human rights protection gap. Sometimes, a generous interpretation of the rules of state responsibility and individual responsibility may contribute to relieve the burden of expectation vis-à-vis the direct obligation of armed groups. But there

[94] Also advising for caution see Zegveld (n 63) 151 et seq; Clapham (n 2) 284.

[95] See section 5.2.

[96] See also McCorquodale (n 4) 112; Alston (n 12) 4, 35 et seq.

[97] See notably Nowak and Januszewski (n 5) 160, proposing the creation of a World Court of Human Rights with extensive powers vis-à-vis states and other 'entities', defined as 'any inter-governmental organization or non-State actor, including any business corporation'.

are also areas where contemporary international law recognizes that armed groups are as such the addressees of human rights obligations. In the context of heteronomous strategies, we have seen some instances of treaty law addressing armed groups and at least the possibility, confirmed in the *Kosovo* Advisory Opinion, of Security Council resolutions creating human rights obligations for armed groups. In addition, unilateral commitments of armed groups as well as agreements between armed groups and governments, that is, autonomous strategies, are promising instruments as they may contribute to a higher degree of identification of armed groups with their human rights compliance record.

There still remains a wide field of situations where international law-making with respect to human rights obligations of armed groups is certainly to be hoped for but has hitherto not materialized. It is important to emphasize that the existing rules on international legal personality and the applicability of certain fields of international law (such as IHRL) to certain actors are not set in stone, but subject to change.[98] One may deplore the lack of both creativity and resolve to address the challenges posed by the existence and activities of powerful armed groups for the protection of human rights of myriads of human beings—and the (seemingly) insurmountable challenges this might create for MMOs which are on the one hand bound by IHRL, but on the other hand are opposed by armed groups that are not. Yet, this cannot be a justification in itself to apply reciprocity (be it in form of a race to the bottom or to the top). After all, asymmetric relations are not atypical in human rights law. International lawyers are well advised to exercise patience in this regard and must notably not substitute an excessive, the-end-justifies-the-means interpretation of the existing law for the reform of international law in the accepted channels.

[98] See ibid 118.

Index

Note: *For the benefit of digital users, indexed terms that span two pages (e.g., 52–53) may, on occasion, appear on only one of those pages.*

Abella, 123–24
Abkhazia, 4–5
Abu Ghraib, 85
accountability, definition, 301–2
acting upon invitation, 6, 106–7, 205
active hostilities, 128–29, 132–33
act of violence (isolated/sporadic), 28, 58–59
actors, 20–21, 23–24, 164, 170, 407, 428
  armed forces (of states), 3, 16, 17, 28–29, 43, 45, 46, 49, 51–52, 58, 62, 164, 168, 169
  changing character (of the belligerents), 425–26, 428, 437
  in multinational military operations, 2, 3, 23, 164, 407
  multinational (armed) forces, 43–45, 51–52, 57, 164
  non state (see *non-state armed groups*)
  private (see also *PSCs*), 24, 164, 406
  states, 3, 24, 51–52, 164, 426–27, 428–30, 434–35
ad hoc alliances, 15–16
Administrative Court of Cologne, 366–67, 395–96
Afghan Interim Authority, 158
Afghanistan, 5, 6, 7, 11–12, 13, 16, 56–57, 62–63, 68, 72, 80–81, 85, 109–10, 112–13, 121, 133–34, 153, 154, 157, 160–61, 169, 170, 176, 205, 289, 322–23, 324–25, 384, 395, 398, 402, 403, 405
Afghan Law, 403
Afghan National Police, 159
Afghan National Security Forces, 158
AFISMA, 14–15
Africa, 17
African Charter on Human and Peoples' Rights (Banjul Charter), 242–43, 447–48
African Commission on Human and Peoples' Rights, 132
African Mission in Burundi (AMIB), 14
African Union, 6, 7, 14, 17
  Mandate/operation/mission, 14, 17
  Peace and Security Council (PSC AU), 8, 14
  permanent standby brigades with military, police, and civilian components, 17
African Union Convention for the Protection and Assistance of Internally Displaced Persons in Africa (Kampala Convention), 450–51
agricultural environment, 330–31
air campaign, 15, 17, 30, 97–98
airlift duties, 15
air support, 97–98
Algerian war, 11–12
Al-Qaeda, 40–42, 46–48, 68, 96–97, 119, 122, 169, 236
Al-Quds Army, 179
American Convention on Human Rights (ACHR), 102–3, 105, 242–43
American Declaration, 211
AMIB, 14
AMIS, 6, 14
AMISEC, 14
AMISOM, 15, 17
amnesties after NIACs, 433–34
Amsterdam Treaty, 14–15
Annan, Kofi, 272
Anti-Personnel Mine Ban Treaty, 430, 431–33
Arab-Israeli Wars, 12, 12n69, 271
Argentina, 54–55, 58–59
armed conflict, 19–20, 21, 28–29, 32, 34–36, 37–38, 44–45, 46–48, 49, 50–52, 54–55, 56–57, 58–59, 62, 63–64, 68–69, 71–72, 93, 99, 100–1, 111–12, 117–18, 124, 184, 194–95, 196–97, 198, 200–1, 214–15, 223, 239, 242–43, 260–61, 263, 269, 271–72, 287, 323, 324, 325, 326, 328–29, 331, 334–36, 337–38, 340, 341–42, 349–50, 351, 352, 402, 425, 450, 453–54
  assistance in, 44–45
  classification, 50–51, 58, 164
  effects of, 36–37, 99
  end of an armed conflict, 49, 52, 62
  factual concept, 93–94, 164
  parties, 52, 62, 164, 166, 170
  spill-over armed conflicts, 27, 38–39, 42–43, 46
armed groups, definition, 445–47
armed robbery, 346, 359, 360

Armenian-Azerbaijani conflict over Nagorno-Karabakh, 131
armistice agreement, 54–55
arms embargo, 273, 345, 360
Arms Trade Treaty, 432–33
Articles Concerning the Law of the Sea of 1956, 350
associations of states, 15–16
asymmetry, 424, 442–43
factual, 424, 439–41
actors and conflicts, 439
conduct of hostilities, 439, 440, 442–43
enforcement, 440–41
in NIACs, 425–27, 428–30, 431, 433, 434
legal, 424, 425–38
enforcement by and against non-state actors, 425, 438
human rights law, 435–38, 442–43
obligations, 426–27, 428–29, 430–31, 432, 433, 434–35, 437
status of fighters in armed conflicts, 425, 433–34
type of armed conflict and recognition of governments, 425–27, 429–31, 442–43
weapons law, 425, 431–33, 435, 441, 442–43
legal pluriverse surrounding military operations, 424, 430–31, 442–43
meaning, 424, 442
methodological, 424, 441–43
creation of new rules, 441
roles that actors play while developing new rules, 441
threefold approach, 442
asymmetric actors, 424, 425–27, 428, 429, 430–31, 432, 433, 437–38, 439, 442
meaning, 425
asymmetric conflicts, 424, 425, 439, 442
meaning, 425
asymmetry in armed conflicts, 23–24, 27, 30n14, 32, 424, 425
attribution, 23, 303, 311–12, 316, 395, 396, 459, 460
'multiple attribution', 314, 319–21
Axis Powers, 11
AU Mission in Somalia, 15, 17
Australia, 6, 8, 11–12, 13, 82, 116–17

Ba'ath Party, 179
Bahrain, 8
Balkan, 131
Bangladesh, 13–14
Banjul Charter (*see African Charter on Human and Peoples' Rights*)
beginning and end of armed conflict, 49
Beleaguered government, 6
Belgium, 82, 288, 310–11
belligerent states, 54–55
Berlin Resolution of the Institute of International Law, 451
best practice recommendations, 2
binding non state actors to international law, 428–29, 430, 432
Biological Weapons Convention of 1972, 431–32
Boko Haram, 8, 109–10
Bonn Agreement, 158
borderless conflict, 16
border patrols, 351
border regions, 38–39
Bosnia-Herzegovina, 12–13, 15, 154, 279–80, 324
Brazil, 213

Camp Bucca, 179–81, 183, 191
Canada, 8, 22, 82, 110, 112–13, 115, 116–17, 119, 121–22, 397, 403
Canadian Federal Court of Appeal, 112–13
Cameroon, 8
capacity building, 3, 5
capital punishment (*see also* death penalty), 244–45, 403
Capstone Doctrine, 283
Caribbean, 17
Caroline case, 398–99
cases
Albekov and others v Russia, 259–60
Al-Jedda v United Kingdom, 312, 315–16, 396
Al-Sadoon v United Kingdom, 186–87
Al-Skeini v United Kingdom, 113–14, 180, 181, 182–83
Amnesty International v Canada, 117–18, 121
Banković and Others v Belgium and Others, 182, 185–86, 192
Behrami/Saramati, 311–12, 316, 396
Bosphorus v Ireland, 312
Courier, 366–67
Ergi v Turkey, 258
Esmukhambetov and others v Russia, 250–51, 258
Finogenov v Russia, 124–25, 252–53
Hamdan v Rumsfeld, 119
Hassan v United Kingdom, 22, 113–14, 182–83, 192
Isayeva v Russia, 239–40, 245, 252, 258
Jaloud v The Netherlands, 85, 86, 114
Kerimova and others v Russia, 257–58, 259–60
Khamzayev and others v Russia, 257–58
Kurbogaj v Spain, 310–11
Lozano, 388–89
Medvedyev and others v France, 366–67
R v Keyn, 383–84

Rigopoulus v Spain, 366–67
Serdar Mohammed, 121
Underhill v Hernandez, 388–89
ceasefire agreement, 54–55, 61, 63–64, 65–66, 267
Central African Republic, 14
Certain Conventional Weapons Convention (CCW), 278–79, 331, 333, 431, 432
cessation of active hostilities, 53–54, 60–61, 167
Chad, 8
changing character of actors (see also under *actors*), 425–26, 428, 437
Chechnya, 131, 239–40, 252, 256
Chemical Weapons Convention of 1993, 401, 431–32
Chiefs of European Navies, 353
child soldiers, 130–31
China, 82–83, 379–80
civilians, 27, 28–29n11, 33, 39–40, 95–96, 135, 137–38, 167, 168, 423
interned civilians, 166, 167
civil-military cooperation, 287
civilians taking a 'direct part in hostilities', 132–33, 170, 171
civil war, 28–29, 59–60
civil unrest, 401
Cluster Munitions Convention, 431–32
'Coalition of the Willing', 8, 13, 300
coalition warfare, 1–2, 4–5, 7
coast guard, 351
Cold War, 11–14, 15, 290, 346
collateral damage, 99, 196, 245–46, 273–74
Collateral Damage Estimation (CDE), 99
collateral risk to civilians and civilian property, 231
collective security arrangements/organization, 15–16
collective self-defence, 6, 16
Colombia, 5, 38–39n62, 153–54
Combined Chiefs of Staff (CCSS), 11
Combined Maritime Forces, 348, 361
combined joined task force, 157–58
Combined Security Transition Command for Afghanistan (CSTC-A), 159
COMISAF, 77
Common Foreign and Security Policy (CFSP), 14–15, 361
common operational framework, 397, 399
Common Security and Defence Policy (CSDP), 14–15
community, 206–7, 208, 219
Comoros, 14
conduct of hostilities, 20–21, 22, 27, 28–29, 32–35, 39–43, 45–46, 49, 50, 51–52, 53, 54–55, 61–62, 64–65, 91, 94–95, 132, 166, 169, 171, 174, 198, 219, 347, 354, 406–7, 439, 442–43
classification of hostilities, 42–43
decline in hostile, 63–64
'direct participation in hostilities', 34–35, 51–52, 81, 99–100, 132–33, 174
ending of hostilities, 55, 64–65, 66–67, 68
places where hostilities take place, 32, 34–36, 39–40, 42–43, 45, 46
resumption of hostilities, 64–65, 66–67
risk of resumption, 66–67
conflict prevention, 153–54, 322
Congo v. Uganda, 203, 210–11
consent of the host state, 290
constitutional law of states, 427
Convention Against Torture and Other Cruel, Inhuman or Degrading Treatment or Punishment, 112–13
Convention on the High Seas, 351
Convention on the Privileges and Immunities of the United Nations, 390
Convention on the Prohibition of Military or Any Other Hostile Use of Environmental Modification Techniques (ENMOD), 326–27, 328–29
Convention on the Rights of the Child, 450
cooperative implementation (references may overlap with references to *relationship between sending state and host state*), 287, 293–98
Copenhagen Process Principles and Guidelines on the Handling of Detainees in International Military Operations, 22, 138–39, 160–61, 164–65
corruption, 158–59
cost-effectiveness, 1–2, 4–5, 15–16
Côte d'Ivoire, 7
Council of Europe (CoE), 126–27, 133–34, 242–43, 244–45
counter-insurgency, 76, 80–81, 109–10
counter-piracy operations, 23, 348, 351, 352, 361, 363–64, 366–67, 368
counter-terrorism, 3, 23, 59–60, 76, 104–5, 109–10, 229, 348, 434
crimes against humanity, 437–38, 447–48, 449, 459
prerequisite for this crime, 437–38
criminal legal process, 130–31, 136
Croatia, 53–54
Cuba, 211
cultural attitudes, 18–19
custody, 52
customary international humanitarian law, 38–39, 53, 57, 58, 60, 93, 97, 138–39, 141, 142–43, 148, 331, 424, 430–31
ICRC Study on, 328, 333

customary international law, 2, 55–56, 93, 97, 110–11, 116, 117–18, 119, 138–39, 142–43, 167, 170–71, 176, 177–78, 275, 285–86, 291–92, 301–2, 360, 376–77, 379–80, 387–88, 389–90, 430–31, 432, 439, 440, 441–43, 447–48, 451, 460–61
customs enforcement, 347
Cyprus, 131

death penalty (*see also* capital punishment), 133–34, 382
decolonization, 11–12
'Deeds of Commitment', 430, 453–54
defragmentation, 188, 196–97
degree of organization, 58, 59, 62, 65–66
delimitation commissions, 13–14
democracy, 13, 429–30, 438, 441
democratic control of armed forces, 27
Democratic Republic of the Congo, 5, 38n62, 277, 282–83
Denmark, 368
Department of Peace and Conflict Research at Uppsala University in Sweden (UCDP), 62, 63–64
  deprivation or restriction of liberty, 32, 34–35, 56, 57, 105, 106–7, 131, 136, 148, 163, 165, 166, 174, 175–76, 182, 188, 189, 190, 191, 198, 363–64, 365
  due process, 106–7
  limits, 106
derogate principle, 102, 131, 136–37, 139, 148
detention, 20–21, 22, 56–57, 91, 99–100, 105, 106–7, 109–10, 119, 126, 131, 134–35, 136, 137–39, 147–48, 160–61, 163, 164–65, 166, 167, 169, 170–71, 172, 173, 174, 175–76, 177–78, 179, 182–83, 188–89, 190, 191, 213, 216–18, 364, 366, 382, 397, 398, 403
  administrative detention, 134–35, 136–38, 148
  arbitrary detention, 134–35, 148, 177, 366–67
  based on UNSC resolutions, 137, 139, 177–78
  civilians and protected persons, 167, 168, 169, 170–71, 174, 176
  conditions, 165
  combatants, 81, 167, 168, 169, 256, 433
  combatant immunity, 433–34, 438
  definition, 134–35
  detention as an obligation, 163
  different interests protected by IHL and IHRL, 199, 200, 217–18
  different legal systems, 287–88
  different levels of protection for individuals, 166
  due process, 106–7, 171, 175, 177
  grounds for, 136, 139, 173, 176
  inherent power of the IHL to intern, 175–76
  in IACs and NIACs, 134–35, 136–37, 138–39, 148, 163, 165, 166, 177–78
  IAC, 137–38, 166–74, 177–78
    NIAC, 166, 174–78
  in international military operations, 164–65
  in peace operations, 138–39
  in peacetime, 137–39
  internment, 134–35, 136–39, 148, 167, 169, 171, 172, 173, 175–76, 188–89
  legal basis, 163, 164–65, 166, 167, 169, 172, 173, 174, 175–76, 177–78
  limits, 106, 166, 172, 173
  operational level, 100, 106
  part of law enforcement, 163
  preventive detention, 189–90
  procedural safeguards, 163, 165, 167, 171, 172, 173, 174, 175–76, 177–78, 188, 191, 216–17, 362–65
  reasons for detention, 163
  retained personnel, 169
  security detention, 105, 106, 134–35, 136, 137–38, 163, 171, 172, 173, 174
  substantive and procedural norms, 134, 135, 171, 172, 173, 174, 175, 176, 177–78
  transfer of detainees, 133–34, 164–65, 170
  treatment of detainees, 163, 164–65, 166, 170, 173, 174, 175, 177–78, 434–35
  unlawful, 176
determining applicable rules, 17–18, 30–31, 43–44, 426, 432
different levels or types of control, 213–15
disarmament, 273
disaster relief operation, 3
discrimination, 382–83, 447–48, 452
dispute settlement, 287, 291
dissolution of coalitions, 12
Doctrine for the Conduct of Operations, 399
DoD Detainee Program, 119
domestic law, 19–20, 24, 43–44, 91, 135, 136, 138–39, 143–44, 169, 176, 177–78, 207, 287, 289, 293, 296, 297, 298, 359, 363–64, 365, 373, 409–10, 427, 428–29, 434, 444–45, 450
  applicability, 207
drones (armed), 36–37, 229
drug trafficking, 23, 158–59, 346, 445–46
due diligence, 248–49, 458
due process, 106–7, 117–18, 177
duty to investigate, 84–86

ECOMIG, 6
ECOWAS, 6

effective control (standard), 208–11, 212–13, 214–15, 219, 303–7, 309, 311–12, 313, 314, 316, 319, 320–21, 458
'dual effective control', 311
expanding the notion, 211–12
extraterritorial, 208–10, 211, 310–11
prior to alleged violation, 211–12
rationale, 209–10
Egypt, 8, 54–55, 271
Mixed Courts of Egypt, 388–89
elements of crimes, 72–73, 82–83
English Central Criminal Court, 383–84
environmental law, 17–18, 23, 295, 298
environmental protection, 23, 290–91, 322–24, 327, 330–31
equality of belligerents, 30
ethical guidelines, 18–19
Ethiopia, 14, 56–57
Eritrea, 56–57
EUNAVFOR, 348, 349, 361, 364, 366–67, 368
Europe, 17, 22
European Convention on Human Rights (ECHR), 102–3, 105, 106, 112–13, 126–27, 131, 134, 136–39, 142, 143–45, 146–48, 177, 180, 188, 192, 194–95, 205, 211–12, 216–18, 220, 240, 241–42, 246–47, 251, 260–61, 311–12, 319, 366–67, 397, 403, 447–48
extraterritorial application of the, 181, 192
interpretation of the, 137–38
Protocol No 13, 133–34
right to remedies, 143–44
European Convention on State Immunity, 388
European Court of Human Rights (ECtHR), 22, 23, 85, 100–1, 102–3, 105, 106, 113–14, 115, 121–22, 124–25, 126, 167, 180, 182–83, 188, 191, 192, 195, 196–97, 209, 211–12, 217–18, 221–22, 239–40, 243, 245–46, 248, 249–50, 252, 256–58, 259–61, 311–12, 315–16, 365, 366–67, 396, 435–36
European human rights law, 131, 177
European perspective, 126–27, 134, 139
European Security and Defence Policy (ESDP), 14–15
European Union (EU), 1–2n6, 5, 14–15, 17, 126–27, 131, 139–40, 290, 302, 347–48, 361, 363–64, 393, 396
SOFA, 290
European Union Charter of Fundamental Rights, 447–48
European Union Force Bosnia and Herzegovina (EUFOR), 324
European Union Maritime Security Strategy of 2014, 349
European Union Police Mission (EUROPOL), 159
EUTM, 7n35
exercise of control, 206–7, 209–11, 212–15, 219
expanding the notion, 211–12
factually and normatively, 214–15
prior to alleged violation, 211–12
exclusionary approaches, 22
extraterritorial applicability, 111–13, 119, 122, 198, 200–1, 205, 207, 211, 213–14, 219, 220
extraterritorial hostilities, 200–1, 202–3, 204–5, 208, 209, 214–19, 220, 221–22
extraterritorial (multinational) military operations, 198, 220, 287, 290–92
extraterritorial use of force, 22, 27, 36–38, 39–40, 43, 46–48, 91–93, 99, 293

Fact-finding assessments, 85
failed state, 352, 359–60, 444–45
Falkland Islands War, 54–55
Fallujah, 122
'final release' definition, 56, 57
First World War, 11, 13–14, 288
flag state, 283, 357, 358, 360
Force Intervention Brigade (FIB), 282–83
formal settlement between conflicting parties, 53–55, 61–62
fragmentation of applicable norms, 33
France, 5, 6, 7n35, 8, 11, 12–13, 46–48, 116–17, 288, 327, 364, 401
freedom of the high seas, 361
functional approach, 182
functioning as government, 55–56, 207, 435–36

Gaddafi, Muammar, 276
Gambia, 6
general close of military operations, 49–50, 52, 53–54, 55–56, 63, 64–65
General Comment on the Right to Life, 92–93, 132
general conclusion of peace, 53–54, 60–61, 64–65
Geneva, 453–54
Geneva Call NGO, 430, 441, 453–54
Geneva Conventions, 20, 30n13, 36, 49, 52, 53, 55–56, 57, 93, 99–100, 134, 135, 137–38, 148, 164, 165, 166, 167, 168, 169, 170–71, 172, 173, 174–75, 177, 183, 202–3, 239, 271, 325, 328–29, 427, 428–29, 430, 435
Common Article 2, 36

Geneva Conventions (*cont.*)
Common Article 3, 27, 29–30, 32–33, 34–35, 36–38, 43, 45, 46, 49–50, 58–59, 93–94, 99–100, 101, 117–18, 119, 122, 165, 174, 175–76, 177–78, 202, 330, 425, 428–29, 432, 438, 453–54
End of application, 52
protective provisions for individuals, 56–57
genocide, 396, 447–48
genocide prevention, 12–13
geographical scope of application of IHL, 20–21, 27–43, 45–48, 68
Divided areas of operation, 29
Entire state/territory, 33–35, 38–39, 45, 46, 53–54
External scope, 35–43, 45, 46
Internal scope, 28–35, 38–39
Locations where hostilities take place, 33–35, 42–43
nexus-doctrine, 27, 34–35, 38–40, 42–43, 45, 46
Georgia, 4–5, 131
German Operational Mentoring and Liaison Teams (OMLT), 402
Germany, 4–5n18, 8, 11, 20, 82, 288, 310–11, 324–25, 364–65, 366–67, 384, 393, 395, 396, 398, 401, 402, 403
German Bundestag, 402
German Ministry of Defence, 403
Higher Administrative Court of the Land of North Rhine Westphalia, 396
Regional Court of Bonn, 395
'global armed conflict'-doctrine, 40–43, 46–48
Degree of organization, 40–42
threshold of violence, 40–42
'global battlefield', 27, 39–42
global institutionalized system, 15–16, 17
global security governance, 1, 13–14, 15
good offices, 153–54
governance, 3, 13, 15
Grand Alliance, 11
'grave breaches', 235, 236
Grotius, Hugo, 70
Guantánamo, 36–37, 120
guerrilla forces, 446
Guidelines on Police Administration, 155
Guidelines on Police Command, 155
Guidelines on Police Operations, 155
Gulf Cooperation Council, 8
Gulf of Aden, 361–62, 363–64
Gulf War, 56–57, 326–27, 328, 337

Haditha, 80
Hague Regulations, 168, 172, 328–29
Haiti, 7, 153, 154, 156–57, 161
High Court of England and Wales, 180
High-Level Independent Panel on Peace Operations, 284
History (until the First World War, which is not included), 3–4, 9
ancient multinational military operations, 9
Battle of Waterloo, 10
Boxer Rebellion, 10–11
Colonial age, 10–11
Crimean War, 10
Dutch War, 9–10
French Empire, 9–10
French Revolution, 10
middle ages, 9–10
Napoleon, 3–4, 10, 19
Ottoman Empire, 9–10, 379–80
Persian Empire, 9
Second Boer War, 10–11
Thirty-Years' War, 9–10
Trojan War, 9
Westphalian system in 1648, 9–10
hors de combat, 81
host state, 20
House of Lords, 180
humanitarian assistance, 126, 127–28, 139–41, 147–48, 273
basis in other laws, 139–40
consent of the belligerent parties, 139–40, 205
definition, 139–40
difficulties in carrying out legal obligations, 141
denial as crime under international law, 141
humanitarian aid, 139–40
legal basis, 140
principle of impartiality, 139–40, 283–84, 285
principle of neutrality, 139–40
protection of refugees, 141
right of the civilian population, 140, 141
supporting requests for asylum, 141
humanitarian law (IHL), 17–18, 19–21, 22, 23, 27–31, 32–35, 36–37, 38–46, 48, 49, 50–52, 53–55, 57, 58–59, 91, 92, 93–94, 104, 107–8, 110–12, 116–17, 120, 126, 135, 136–38, 140, 142–43, 148, 164–65, 166, 174, 175–76, 192, 194–95, 208, 218–19, 223, 225, 240, 248–49, 253–54, 255–56, 257–58, 259, 261, 262–63, 287, 324–25, 352, 406–7, 410, 417–18, 420, 422, 423, 425, 426–27, 429–30, 433, 440–41, 446, 454
assisting/intervening state, 43–44
applicability, 45–46, 49, 50–52, 54–55, 58–59, 60–61, 68, 91, 92–95, 97–98, 105, 128–29, 199, 203, 220, 269, 425, 429–30, 432
binding non-state actors, 426–27, 428–30, 432

divergences in interpretation, 91, 95, 97–98, 103, 107–8, 137–38
doctrine of legislative jurisdiction, 427, 432
guarantee of certain (human) rights, 202, 208
history, 202
humanity, 33–34, 200
IHL as *lex specialis* to IHRL, 101, 105, 201, 203, 215–19, 436–37
impact on military operations, 91, 200
incidental physical injury, 199
lacunae filling, 202–3
mechanisms of compliance with IHL, 165, 427
Object and purpose, 30–31, 91, 107, 200, 429
permissive and protective rules, 33–34, 199
principle of proportionality, 98–99, 104–5
procedural aspects, 99
prerequisite of conduct, 218–19
prohibition of certain conduct, 218–19, 439
realism, 200
rights not regulated by IHL, 217–18
'status' versus 'activities'-based approach, 39–42
uniform rules, 220
'zones', 39–40n71
'humanization' of international legal obligations, 127–28
Human Rights Committee (HRC), 92–93, 100–1, 112–13, 209–10, 310–11, 315–16
human rights law (*see also* international human rights law), 17–18, 19–22, 23, 24, 30–31, 33–34, 36–37, 43–44, 45–46, 59–60, 68–69, 73–74, 75, 76, 80–81, 84–85, 91, 92, 103, 104, 107, 109–12, 114–15, 117, 120, 124, 126, 138–39, 140, 142–43, 148, 154, 160, 163, 164–65, 166, 177–78, 192, 198, 200–1, 221–22, 256, 295, 298, 340–42, 352, 362–63, 365, 366–67, 403, 406–7, 417–18, 420, 422, 423, 435, 444
abuse of its rationale, 200, 221
applicability, 91–93, 99, 100–1, 105, 106, 107–8, 128–29, 198, 199, 200, 203, 205, 206–7, 208–9, 210, 212–13, 214, 215–16, 219, 220–21, 435–36, 451
'authority and control', 105
binding non-state actors, 435, 438, 442–43, 444
binding states, 435, 438
derogation from their obligations, 102–3, 105, 106, 131, 136–37, 139, 148, 184, 217–18
divergences in interpretation, 91–92, 103, 104, 107–8
extraterritorial application (in armed conflicts/hostilities), 100–1, 105, 147–48, 198, 200–1, 202–3, 204–5, 207, 208, 211–12, 214, 219
history, 202, 204
human rights bodies, 91–93, 100–1, 104, 105, 107–8, 145–46, 147–48, 212–13, 220–21
human rights instruments, 127–28
'jurisdiction' as a prerequisite for, 91–92, 105, 106–7, 147–48, 201, 203, 208–12, 213–15, 219
exercise of state power, 209–11, 212–13
protection gap, 445, 446, 447, 449–56, 457
relationship of control, 209, 211–12
limitations on HR (other than life and liberty), 198–99, 200–1, 204–6, 208
limitations under law/prescribed by law, 207, 208
mechanism, 200, 201, 204, 219
monitoring mechanism, 221–22, 438
'necessity' to limit HR to attain other objectives, 205–6, 216–17
object and purpose, 107, 200
operational aspects, 100, 106, 107, 200
principle of proportionality, 104–5, 205–6, 216–17
rationale/concept, 204–5, 435
regional, 239–40
scope (see *applicability*)
serving community interests, 204–7, 208
violation, 435
human rights safeguards, 167
human trafficking, 267, 345, 346, 360, 445–46
Hussein, Saddam, 12–13

identification of intention, 30–31, 32
ILA, 50–51, 62
International Law Association Study Group on the Conduct of Hostilities in the 21st Century, 224
ILC, 23, 292, 301–2, 306–7, 315, 317–21, 323, 335–36, 341–42, 343, 351, 376–77, 388–89
'illegal/irregular/unlawful combatants', 100, 168, 169, 170
imminent attack, 398–99
immunity, 133–34, 387, 408–9, 410, 433–34, 438
immunity of foreign military forces, 287, 289–90, 291–92, 293, 387
ratione materiae, 291–92
Implementation Force (IFOR), 15
incidental damage, 440
India, 13–14, 56–57
individual protection, 56–57, 130–31, 144–46, 147–48
inefficiency in multinational military operations, 18–19

Institute de Droit International, 273
institutional legitimacy, 260–61
insurgency, 120–21, 284
insurrectional movement, 437, 446
intensity of violence, 49, 50–51, 58–59, 62–63, 66–67
Inter-American Commission on Human Rights, 58–59, 115, 211
Inter-American Court of Human Rights, 115
internal disturbances, 58, 93–94
international agreements, 2, 19–20
international armed conflict (IAC), 19–20, 32–33, 43, 46, 49, 50–51, 53–55, 56, 57, 64–65, 93–94, 95–96, 99–100, 105, 118, 126–27, 128–29, 134, 135, 136–39, 148, 165, 167, 184–85, 187, 188, 189–90, 191, 220, 235, 257–58, 324, 328, 334–35, 337, 424, 429–30, 431, 433, 434–35
  ending of international armed conflict, 52, 56, 61–62, 64
  definition, 50
  laws of international armed conflicts, 43, 51–52, 64–65, 93, 105, 431
international code of conduct, 2, 406, 408, 416–17, 418–19
  industry self-regulatory mechanism, 408, 416–17
International Committee of the Red Cross (ICRC), 28–29, 36–37n50, 37–40, 39n68, 43–44, 45–46, 50–51, 53, 60, 61–62, 64–65, 66–67, 68, 96–97, 126–27, 135, 137–38, 163, 165, 171, 172, 173, 175–76, 177–78, 330–31, 403
  Resolution Strengthening Legal Protection for Victims of Armed Conflict, 165
International Court of Justice (ICJ), 100–1, 112–13, 128–29, 132, 139–40, 145–46, 147, 187, 198, 203, 205–6, 210–11, 214, 215, 216–17, 218, 306–7, 312, 332–33, 337–39, 341–42, 436, 437, 439, 451–52
International Covenant on Civil and Political Rights (ICCPR), 19–20, 74, 92–93, 100–1, 102–3, 105, 112–13, 116, 117–18, 136, 154–55, 167, 184–85, 201, 202–3, 209–11, 213–14, 216–17, 219, 242–43, 310–11, 315–16, 398, 437, 438
International Covenant on Economic, Social and Cultural Rights, 202–3
International crimes, 292, 437–38
International Criminal Court (ICC), 72–73, 81–84, 226, 235, 236, 336, 425, 434, 437–38
International Criminal Law, 34–35, 148, 226, 235, 237, 336–37, 434, 437–38
International Criminal Tribunal for the Former Yugoslavia (ICTY), 32–35, 53–54, 58–59, 60–61, 62, 64, 65, 128–29, 172, 235, 306–7, 388–89
  Blaškić case, 388–89
  Gotovina case, 53–54, 64, 65
  Tadić case, 53–54, 58–59, 60–62, 123–24
International Criminal Tribunal for Rwanda (ICTR), 38–39n62, 425
International disturbances, 28
International Environmental Law, 333, 337, 338–39
international human rights law (*see also* human rights law), 17–18, 19–22, 23, 24, 30–31, 33–34, 36–37, 43–44, 45–46, 59–60, 68–69, 74, 91–92, 103, 104, 107, 110, 126, 138–39, 140, 142–43, 148, 163, 164–65, 166, 177–78, 198, 200–1, 203, 221–22, 295, 298, 340, 398, 406–7, 417–18, 420, 422, 423, 435
  abuse of its rationale, 200, 221
  applicability, 91–93, 99, 100–1, 105, 106, 107–8, 128–29, 198, 199, 200, 203, 205, 206–7, 208–9, 210, 212–13, 214, 215–16, 219, 220–21, 435–36
  'authority and control', 105
  binding non-state actors, 435, 438, 442–43
  binding states, 435, 438
  derogation from their obligations, 102–3, 105, 106, 131, 136–37, 139, 148, 217–18
  divergences in interpretation, 91–92, 103, 104, 107–8
  extraterritorial application (in armed conflicts/hostilities), 100–1, 105, 147–48, 198, 200–1, 202–3, 204–5, 207, 208, 211–12, 214, 219
  history, 202, 204
  human rights bodies, 91–93, 100–1, 104, 105, 107–8, 145–46, 147–48, 212–13, 220–21
  human rights instruments, 127–28
  'jurisdiction' as a prerequisite for, 91–92, 105, 106–7, 147–48, 201, 203, 208–12, 213–15, 219
    exercise of state power, 209–11, 212–13
    relationship of control, 209, 211–12, 213–14
  limitations on HR (other than life and liberty), 198–99, 200–1, 204–6, 208
  limitations under law/prescribed by law, 207, 208
  mechanism, 200, 201, 204, 219
  monitoring mechanism, 221–22, 438
  object and purpose, 107, 200
  operational aspects, 100, 106, 107, 200

principle of proportionality, 104–5, 205–6, 216–17
rationale/concept, 204–5, 435
serving community interests, 204–7, 208
violation, 435
international legal personality of armed groups, 445, 447, 449, 460–61, 462
international organization (IO), 1–2, 3, 16, 17, 23, 55, 128, 133–34, 152, 300, 312, 316, 317–19
international peace and security, 275, 279, 280, 285
International Police Coordination Board, 159
international security governance, 1, 13–14, 15
international treaties, 20, 30–31, 130–31, 176
scope, 30
internment, 167, 169, 171, 172, 173, 175–76
interrogation, 179
intervention, 6, 8, 13, 17, 27, 43–44, 63–64, 385, 386–87
on humanitarian grounds, 6, 15–16, 51–52
invitation, 6, 106–7
Iran, 56–57
Iraq, 6, 8, 12–13, 15–16, 17, 35–36, 40–42, 46–48, 56–57, 62–63, 68, 80, 85, 96–97, 109–10, 120–21, 133–34, 139–40, 166, 176, 179, 193, 205, 272, 280, 322–23, 326–27, 340, 384, 409–10
ISIL, 6, 16, 17, 40–42, 46–48, 96–97, 120–21, 429
Island of Palmas case, 374, 376–77
islamist factions, 6, 8
Israel, 12, 54–56, 85, 205–6, 271, 272
Israeli Supreme Court, 78
Italy, 11, 82, 310–11, 364–65
Italian Court of Cassation, 388–89

Japan, 289, 351
Joint-Coordination and Monitoring Board, 159
Joint Forward Interrogation Team (JFIT), 179
Joint Investigative Assessment Teams, 85
joint operations, 8
joint operations area, 400
Joint Terminal Attack Controller (JTAC), 97–98
Jordan, 8, 54–55, 271
Juba, 283–84
jurisdiction, 198, 201, 214–15, 373–75, 409–10, 460
adjudicative jurisdiction, 356, 359, 368, 374–76, 379–80, 382–83, 386, 388–89
concurrent jurisdiction, 382–84, 390–92
domestic jurisdiction, 385, 389–90
enforcement jurisdiction, 356, 357, 361, 374–76, 379–80, 382–83, 386, 388–89
nationality principle, 375–76, 378–79, 380
organic jurisdiction, 373–74, 377–82, 383, 385, 391
passive personality principle, 375–76, 378–79, 380
prescriptive jurisdiction, 359, 374–76, 378–79, 386
service jurisdiction, 381–82
territorial jurisdiction, 357, 373–77, 383, 385, 386–87, 391
universal jurisdiction, 375–76, 380
jus ad bellum, 17–18, 46, 93–95, 269–70, 272, 273–75, 276, 285–86, 418–19
jus cogens, 241–42, 285–86, 436
guarantee to a fair criminal trial, 436
protection from slavery, 436
protection from torture, 436
racial discrimination and genocide, 436
jus in bello, 68–69, 91, 93–94, 269–70, 272, 273–75, 276, 285–86, 418–19
just post bellum, 68–69, 83

Kabul, 158, 402
Kenya, 43–44, 366–67, 396
Kellenberg, Jakob, 28–29
KFOR, 15, 20, 302, 311–12, 315–16, 319, 401
kinetic use of force, 95
Korea, Republic of, 289
Kosovo, 7, 15, 20, 133–34, 154, 310–12, 322–23, 324
Kosovo Advisory Opinion, 451–52, 461–62
Kunduz bombing, 85
Kunduz Province, 395
Kurdistan Workers' Party (PKK), 239–40
Kuwait, 8, 12–13, 340

Lake Chad Basin Commission, 8
land mines, 259–60
language, 18–19
La Tablada case, 58–59
law enforcement, 20–21, 22, 39–40, 45–46, 68–69, 106, 110, 122–23, 124–25, 151–52, 156–57, 163, 221–22, 241, 250–51, 252, 253–54, 255, 262–63, 345, 346, 347, 349–50, 351, 352, 353, 354, 355, 363, 364–65, 368, 438, 440–41
paradigm of, 350
'lawful acts of war', 102–3, 434
law of the sea, 17–18, 23, 347–48, 349–50, 357, 359, 360, 368–69
law of state jurisdiction, 17–18, 106–7
laws of armed conflict, 2, 5, 20–22, 27, 32, 34–35, 49, 70, 72–74, 84–85, 269, 271, 324, 424
at sea, 345
law of occupation, 329

leadership differences, 18–19
legal certainty, 50–51, 68, 383
legal classification of armed conflicts, 27, 32, 45, 46–48
legal framework, 19–20, 21, 23, 24, 91, 165, 177–78, 426, 435, 442
legal interoperability, 21, 70, 71–73, 78, 79–80, 81, 84, 91–92, 95, 98–99, 100, 104–5, 106–8, 322, 323–24, 342
legal justification, 5–6, 7, 17–18
legal regimes (overlapping), 2, 17–18, 19, 30–31, 45–46, 68–69, 91, 92, 104, 134–35, 202–3, 412–13
legal requirements, 16, 19
legitimacy (of war), 3–5, 11–12, 13, 15–16, 20, 59–60, 102–3, 163, 406–7, 408, 410, 417–19, 422, 434–35, 438
legitimate target under IHL, 51–52, 95–96, 97–98
lethal force, 75, 243–44, 250–51, 252, 254, 282–83
level of control, 208–9, 211–12
lex specialis (IHL to IHRL), 85, 101, 105, 111–12, 198, 201, 203, 215–19, 436–37
  as a means of resolving conflict (doctrine), 215–16, 218
  as interpretative tool (doctrine), 215–17
    doctrines not being panacea for regulating the relationship between IHRL and IHL, 215–17
Liberation Tigers of Tamil Eelam (LTTE), 30n17, 65–66
Libya, 5, 6, 62–63, 68, 272–74, 276, 282, 345, 349, 352, 360, 425–26, 434
Lieber Code, 75
limited military intrusion, 52
Lisbon Treaty, 396
local law (*see also* domestic law), 373, 375, 382
Lockerbie case, 379–80
logistical support, 8
Lotus case, 379–80

MAES, 14
Malaysia, 6
Mali, 5, 6, 7n35, 8, 14, 27
Mandate, 7, 8, 15–16, 106–7
  different types of, 3, 5
  organizational modalities, 7
  under the UN Charta, 5
maritime environment, damage to, 346
Maritime Interception Operation, 355–56
Maritime Interdiction Operation (MIO), 355–56
maritime law enforcement operations, 23, 347, 350, 355–56, 363, 364, 365, 366–67, 368
maritime security, concept of, 346
Maritime Security Operation (MSO), 349–50, 352, 353
maritime zones, 356
  high seas, 357, 358, 360
  internal waters, 352, 356, 357
  international waters, 347, 355, 356
  territorial sea, 352, 356, 357, 359–60
martial law, 253–54
margin of appreciation, 233, 237, 254–55
means and methods of warfare, 228, 273–74, 331
means of attack, 248–49
Memorandum of Arrangement (MoA), 179
Memorandum of Understanding (MoU), 304–5
mercenaries, 166, 168, 406–7, 408–9, 412–13
Middle East, 12, 17, 407
military advantage, 226–27, 273–75, 276
military necessity, 33–34, 73–74, 81, 94–95, 104–5, 200, 224, 329, 331, 334
military objective, 81, 224, 225, 226, 230–31, 256
military operations, 91, 94–95, 100–1, 105, 107–8, 241, 250–51, 262–63
MISCA, 14
MINUSCA, 5, 14
MINUSMA, 7n35, 14, 27
MNJTF, 8
MONUSCO, 277, 281–82, 283, 284
motive of war, 3–5
monitoring ceasefire, 5
Montreux Document, 406, 408, 411–14, 415, 416–18, 419
Morocco, 8
Mozambique, 14
multilateralism, 16, 19–20
'multinational armed conflicts' 43, 46
Multi-National Force Iraq (MNFI), 312
multinational military operations outside peacekeeping, 17, 164
multi-purpose collective security organization, 15–16
mutual defence arrangement, 15, 16

national caveats, 24, 73–74, 393, 394, 396–97, 399–400, 401, 403–5
National Contingent Commanders (NCC), 307–8, 404
National Development Strategy, 159
national liberation movements, 446
NATO, 5, 7, 12–13, 14, 15, 71, 72, 78, 126–27, 133–34, 152, 157–58, 272–73, 288, 293, 296–97, 302, 310–12, 315–16, 319, 322–23, 324, 328, 333–34, 343, 345, 347–48, 349, 351, 354, 355, 361, 363–64, 368, 393, 394–96, 397, 400, 401, 402, 403–4

Alliance Maritime Strategy of 2011, 349
Doctrine, 404
history and development, 288
Parliamentary Assembly, 405
SOFA, 290, 293, 390–91
naval forces, 345, 351
naval operations, 30
naval warfare, 347–48, 349–50, 353, 368–69
neighbouring country, 38–39, 46
Netherlands, 82, 96–97, 99, 116–17, 146–47, 310–11, 324–25, 379–80, 396
District Court in The Hague, 396
New Zealand, 6, 11–12, 82
nexus-doctrine, 27, 34–35, 38–40, 45, 46
Nicaragua Case, 139–40
Niger, 8
Nigeria, 8, 109–10
non-international armed conflict (NIAC), 19–20, 21, 27–30, 32–33, 34–43, 45, 46, 48, 49, 51–52, 56–57, 58–63, 65–66, 67–69, 93–94, 95–97, 99–100, 105, 109–10, 126–27, 132–33, 134, 135, 136–37, 138–39, 148, 163, 165, 167, 174–77, 189–90, 214–15, 220, 235, 262–63, 324, 328, 330–31, 334–35, 337, 398, 424, 425, 428–29, 431, 433, 444–45
beginning of a no international armed conflict, 59–60, 65–66, 425
classification, 42–43, 58–59, 96–97, 425
collating evidence, 67–68
defining the enemy, 96–97, 99
definition, 36, 57, 58–59, 96–97, 425
determination in practice, 67–68
end of a non-international armed conflict, 49, 57, 60–63, 65–67
laws of NIACs, 35–36, 38–39, 43–45, 57, 59–60, 62–63, 93, 95–96, 105, 136–37, 138–39, 431
party to, 44–45, 51–52, 62, 67, 96–97
pre-existing, 44–45
non-neighbouring/non-belligerent state, 39–45, 46
non-refoulement, 368
non-state (armed or unarmed) actors/groups, 23–24, 27, 28–30, 32–33, 35–36, 40–44, 45, 46, 57, 58, 65–67, 164, 177–78, 345, 346, 354–55, 425–27, 429–30, 432–33, 434–36, 437–38, 441–42, 444
exercise of territorial control, 29–30, 32–33, 58, 60, 66–67, 435–36, 446
rules applying by way of applicability of IHL, 432
rules directly addressing non-state actors/groups, 432
rules imposing duties on states to regulate non-state actors/groups, 432–33
norm conflict, 198
North Atlantic Council, 297, 361, 397
North Atlantic Treaty, 13
Northern Ireland, 124–25
North Kivu, 282–83
Norway, 116–17, 364–65
Nuclear Weapons, 338–39
Nuclear Weapons Advisory Opinion, 111–12, 113–14, 198, 201, 203, 210–11, 214, 215–18, 219, 220, 337–38
'non-arbitrary' formula, 216–17
number of multinational military operations, 12–13

Obama, Barack, 76, 110
Organisation of African Unity, 14
obligations of conduct, 248–49, 278–79
obligations of result, 248
obligations, positive, 245, 246–47, 249–50, 254, 261, 444–45
obligation to avoid/minimize collateral damage, 256–57, 258
obligation to cancel or suspend an attack in cases of expected excessive collateral damage, 256–57
obligation to give effective advance warning of an attack, 248–49, 256–57
obligation to protect life, 182, 259–60
obligation to refrain from launching an attack, 256–57
obligation to select the military objective expected to cause the least collateral damage, 256–57
obligation to take precautions, 253–54, 256–57
obligation to verify objectives, 256–57
observer missions, 13–14
Öcalan, Abdullah, 186–87
occupation, 52, 55–57, 109–10, 120–21, 132–33, 137, 167, 172, 173, 174, 176, 203, 205–7, 210–11, 214–15, 218–19, 280
ending of occupation, 56
law of occupation, 206–7, 210–11
occupying power, 74, 173, 182–83, 207, 208–9
operating upon request, 106–7, 205
operation, 5, 13–14
hybrid operations, 8
operating on the ground, 20
Operation Active Endeavour, 348
operational command (OPCOM), 304–5, 307–8, 394–95
operational control (OPCON), 307–8, 311–12, 394–95
operational differences, 91, 92, 93, 107

Operation Allied Provider, 348
Operation Allied Protector, 348
Operation Astute, 6
Operation Atalanta, 17, 348, 361, 364, 366–67, 368, 396
Operation Desert Storm, 12–13
Operation Inherent Resolve, 157–58
Operation Medusa, 160–61, 403
Operation Ocean Shield, 348
Operation Sea Guardian, 348, 349, 354
Operation Serval, 8
Operation Sophia, 349, 361
Operation Unified Protector, 272–73, 349
operative scope of missions, 16
opinio juris, 39–40, 46–48, 50–51, 118, 176, 441–42, 451
Organization for the Security and Cooperation in Europe (OSCE), 152, 157–58
Organization of American States, 115
overall control (standard), 306–7

pacta tertiis rule, 429–30, 456
Pakistan, 13–14, 56–57, 68, 328
Palestine, 205–6, 430
Paradigm, 91, 132
party to a conflict, 171
peace agreements, 61–62, 65–66
peacebuilding, 153–54, 322
peace enforcement, 13–14, 282
'peaceful settlement' standard, 60–62
Peacekeeping, UN (UNPKM), 7n35, 7, 13–14, 17–18, 51–52, 100–1, 124, 157, 164, 277, 281–85, 289–90, 293, 294, 296–97, 303, 304, 308, 310–12, 315–16, 317–19, 322, 390, 407
peacemaking operations, 164, 290, 293
peace treaty, 54–55, 60–61
Permanent Court of International Justice, 379–80
piracy, 16, 17, 267, 345, 346, 352, 358, 359, 360, 363, 364–65, 368
PKK, 131, 252–53
Poland, 8, 13
police, 16, 22, 57
Police Internal Investigations Unit, 155
police primacy, 110
Portugal, 6
post-conflict situations, 3, 5, 13, 16, 62–63, 68–69
post-election insurgency, 6
post-invasion stabilization, 8, 13–14
precautionary principle, 333
precautions in attack, 20–21, 22, 23, 79, 223, 239–41, 243–45, 246, 247, 248–49, 250–53, 254–56, 257–58, 259, 260–61, 262–63, 277–78, 331, 333, 440
preparatory work of treaties, 37–38
primary operational responsibility, 14
principle of distinction, 80, 81–82, 95, 100, 148, 166, 216–17, 235–36, 257–58, 276–77, 331, 332, 334–35, 439
principle of humanity, 331–32
principle of impartiality, 139–40, 283–84, 285, 293
principle of legality, 243–45
principle of neutrality, 139–40
principle of proportionality, 39–40, 72–73, 80–81, 82, 98–99, 104–5, 148, 223–35, 243–46, 259, 273–75, 276, 331, 332–33
  procedural aspects, 99
prisoners of war (POW) status, 99–100, 105, 135, 137–38, 166, 167, 168, 169, 170, 188–89, 191–92, 214–15, 220
  individuals entitled to the same rights, 169, 170
private military and security companies (PSCs), 24, 406, 407, 408–9, 410, 411–15, 416–17, 419, 420–21, 422, 423
  bystander effect, 413
  capacity to fulfil humanitarian functions, 407, 416–17
  case-by-case decisions, 411, 414–15
  code of conduct (see *international code of conduct*)
  contractual obligations, 415, 416–19, 420–21, 422
    compliance with domestic law, IHL and IHRL, 416–17, 418–19, 420, 422
    diametrically opposed to public international law, 418–19, 420
    freedom of contract, 417–19
  control of, 411, 419, 420–21, 422
  definition of PSCs, 406
  dissociation between state action and the obligation under IHL and IHRL, 406–7, 409, 412–13, 416–17, 418–19
  dissociation of the state's monopoly of the legitimate use of force, 420–21, 422
  doctrine of privity, 417–18, 419
  excessive use of force and IHRL violations, 406–7, 417
future development, 421
  'good practices', 411–14, 415, 416–19
home state control, 412–13, 421, 422
impunity, 421
in multinational military operations, 414, 415, 416–17, 418–19, 420, 421, 422, 423
minimizing lacunae, 413, 422
multiple dimensions, 414–15, 421
multiple PSCs involved, 414–15

legal complexities involved in their employment, 407, 408–10, 411, 413–15, 418–19, 420, 421, 422
arbitrary standards, 410
international legal obligations/regulations, 408, 409, 410, 411–15, 417–18
jurisdictional issues, 408–15
legal consequences arising from involvement in multinational military operations, 408–9, 410, 411, 413–15, 417, 418–19
loss of civilian protection, 408–9
liminal entity between civilians and martial state actors, 408–9, 411, 423
potential and complexity of contractual mechanisms, 408, 414–15, 416–19, 420, 422
state obligations (overlapping), 413–15, 417, 419, 420–21, 422
State responsibility, 420–21, 422
status-of-force agreement, 409–10
sub contraction, 415
willingness of states to contemplate PSCs in 'state action spheres', 407, 413
undermining legal predictability, 420, 421, 422, 423
privileged belligerency, 406, 408–9, 422
Prizren, 401
prohibition against unnecessary suffering, 225
protection for victims of armed conflicts, 163
protection of combatants, 57, 135, 167, 168, 169, 401, 422, 423, 433
combatant status, 169, 170, 422, 433
loss of combatant status, 169
protection of civilian objects, 126–27, 440
protection of civilians (in armed conflicts), 13–15, 23, 28–29n11, 33, 39–40, 57, 81, 103–4, 126–28, 131–39, 141, 171, 273, 276, 278–79, 281–82, 285, 440
protection of the environment in armed conflict, 329
protection of human dignity, 127–28, 129–31, 147–48, 171, 435, 444, 459
protection of life and bodily integrity, 127–28, 129–30, 147–48, 171, 440
protection of the local population, 401
protection of prisoners, 33, 53, 56, 57, 105, 166, 169, 177–78
imprisonment, 57
Protocols on Human Trafficking and Migrant Smuggling, 359
Protocols to the Geneva Conventions, 20, 29–30, 49, 55–56, 325, 427, 430
Additional Protocol I, 52, 53, 55–56, 57, 78–79, 97, 99–100, 117–18, 165, 166, 169, 170, 202–3, 224, 269, 326, 328–29, 336–37
Additional Protocol II, 29–30, 32–33, 34–35, 43, 45, 46, 49, 57, 58, 60, 93–94, 99–100, 165, 174–76, 177–78, 330, 425, 428–29, 433–35
applicability, 174–75
End of application, 52
public emergency, 241–42, 253–54

Qatar, 8

Raqqa, 109–10
rebel courts, 438
rebels, 446
reciprocity, understood as expectation towards other actors, 440–41, 453
recognition of organized armed group as belligerent, 429–30, 446
're-establishment' definition, 56–57
regional arrangements in Chapter VIII, 5
regional organizations, 1–2, 6, 7–8, 13–14, 15–16, 64–65, 128, 133–34, 289, 294
Regional Protection Force (RPF), 282, 283–84
regional systems, 91–92, 126–27
relationship between actors in an extraterritorial hostility, 200–1, 204–5
relationship between GC and ECHR, 137–38
relationship between IHL and ECHR, 137–38, 148
relationship between IHL and IHRL, 100, 101, 104, 107, 123–24, 126, 167, 187, 199, 200, 201–3, 215–19, 220–22, 436–37
convergence of their provisions, 216–18
exclusive matters of IHL, 128–29, 201–3
exclusive matters of IHRL, 128–29, 201–2, 203
matters of both branches, 128–29, 138–39, 201–2, 203
primary framework, 131
relationship between sending state and host state, 287, 288, 289, 290, 291–92, 293–95, 296, 373
relationship between UNSC resolution and the ECHR, 137
religion, 18–19
reparations, 126, 127–28, 142–47, 148
Basic Principles, 142–43
case-by-case, 147
claim of the applicant as starting point, 147, 148
compelling reasons, 144
customary right of individuals, 142–43
ECtHR case law, 142, 143–44, 146–47, 148
equity, 145–47, 148
influence by IHRL, 142–43
just satisfaction, 143–46, 147

reparations (*cont.*)
monetary, 146–47
non-pecuniary damages, 145–47
prerequisites for, 143–44
procedural obligations, 146–47
situations where damages should be awarded, 144–45
state responsibility, 142–43
taking necessary measures, 144–45, 144–45n109, 146–47
violation of IHL, 142–43
Reparation of Injuries Advisory Opinion, 457
repatriation, 56–57
reprisals, 327
Report on ocean and the law of the sea, 346
Report on the situation of human rights in Kuwait under Iraqi occupation, 340
Resolute Support Mission (RSM), 157–58
Responsibility of International Organizations (ARIO), 301–2
Responsibility of States for Internationally Wrongful Acts (ASR), 301–2, 317–19, 420, 422, 437
'Responsibility to Protect' doctrine, 6, 141
Report of 2014, 141
Restatement of the Law: The Foreign Relations Law of the United States, 119
resumption of hostilities, 49
right of collective self-defence, 6
right to humanitarian assistance, 127–28, 139–41, 147–48
basis in other laws, 139–40
consent of the belligerent parties, 139–40
definition, 139–40
denial as crime under international law, 141
difficulties in carrying out legal obligations, 141
humanitarian aid (workers and agencies), 139–40
legal basis, 140
principle of impartiality, 139–40, 283–84, 285
principle of neutrality, 139–40
protection of refugees, 141
right of the civilian population, 140, 141
supporting requests for asylum, 141
right to liberty, 131, 134–35, 136, 171, 198, 200–1, 212–13, 217–19, 366–67
right to life, 91, 92–93, 102–3, 131, 132–34, 147–48, 192, 196, 198, 200–1, 210–11, 212–13, 214–15, 216–19, 220, 241–43, 249–51, 437
'arbitrary' death, 102–3, 132, 148, 182, 216–17
intentional and incidental death, 102–3
justification for deprivation of life, 102–3, 132
rationale, 212–13
supplementing and interpreting IHL, 132–33
under ICCPR, 216–17, 219
violation, 133–34, 136
right to reparations for victims of armed conflicts, 127–28, 142–47, 148
Basic Principles, 142–43
customary right of individuals, 142–43
ECtHR case law, 142, 143–44, 146–47, 148
equity, 145–47, 148
influence by IHRL, 142–43
just satisfaction, 143–46, 147
monetary, 146–47
non-pecuniary damages, 145–47
prerequisites for, 143–44
procedural obligations, 146–47
State responsibility, 142–43
taking necessary measures, 144–45, 144–45n109, 146–47
violation of IHL, 142–43
right to self-defence, 15–16, 46–48, 102–4, 274–75, 293
differing national views, 103–4
Rio Declaration, 338–39
riot control, 400
riot control agents (RCA), 401
riots, 28
robust mandates, 12–13, 16, 124
Rome Statute of the International Criminal Court, 81, 82–83, 84, 235, 336–37, 447–48, 459
rule of law, 3, 288
rules of engagement (RoE), 2, 20, 73–74, 77, 79–80, 122, 152, 308, 393, 397, 399, 400, 401, 405
rule of targeting, 223, 224, 230–31, 235
Russian Federation, 4–5, 82–83
Rwanda, 38–39n62, 407

'safe havens', 36–37
Saudi-Arabia, 8, 17
Schooner Exchange case, 376–77, 380
Scottish High Court of Justiciary, 379–80
Second World War, 11, 54–55, 116–17, 288
self-defence, 6, 46–48, 80–81, 102–4, 122–23, 124, 152, 159–60, 398–99
differing national views, 103–4
Serbia, 53–54
Serb minorities, 401
Shared Awareness and Deconfliction (SHADE), 348
shared responsibilities, 7, 23
Sierra Leone, 65–66, 407
situations of persistent instability, 21

Six-Day War, 271
slavery, 358
social role of law, 200
soft law, 2
Somalia, 5, 7, 15, 16, 17, 43–44, 68, 124–25, 310–11, 345, 346, 348, 352, 359, 360, 368
South Africa, 14
South Asia, 17
South China Sea, 354
South Ossetisa, 4–5
South Sudan, 282, 283–84
sovereignty, 182, 210, 269–70, 347, 357, 360, 361, 374–75, 376–77, 378, 391, 394
Soviet Union, 11–13, 275, 286
Spain, 82, 310–11, 364
special political missions, 153–54
Special Representative of the UN Secretary-General for Children and Armed Conflict, 453–54
spies, 166, 168
Srebrenica, 12–13, 310–11, 396
Sri Lanka, 30n17, 65–66
state immunity, 17–18, 376–77, 387, 389–90, 391–92
state of war, 54–55
state practice, 22, 38, 39–40, 46–48, 50–51, 54–55, 70, 72–73, 126–27, 170, 176, 377, 385–86, 387–88, 425–26, 451
state responsibility, 17–18, 20, 23, 142–43, 301–2, 396–97, 420–21, 435–36, 458, 460
status of an individual, 166, 168, 170, 434
status-of-forces agreements (SOFAs), 20, 23, 117, 152, 287–88, 289, 290–91, 293–95, 298–99, 373–74, 387–88, 389, 391–92, 406, 407, 409–10
  as constitutive for certain forms of cooperation, 293, 294–95, 298
  as declaratory instruments, 291–93, 294–95, 298
  being a lex specialis, 293–94
  common understanding of law, 298, 299
  common SOFA applying to all participating states, 294
  different types of SOFA, 289, 290, 294
  dispute settlement, 291
  employment of civilian contractors, 294
  enactment, 296–97
  executive agreement, 296–97
  function, 287, 290–91
  history, 288, 289–90
  immunity, 289–90, 291–92, 293, 294, 387
    limitations, 293
    ratione materiae, 291–92
  implementation, 287–88, 291, 294–95, 296, 298
  jurisdiction, 289, 293–94, 297–98
  NATO, 288, 290, 293, 296–97
  negotiation of a SOFA, 295–96
  permanent, 288
  private security companies, 407, 409–10
  procedural regulation, 293–94
  provisional application, 297
  ratification, 296–97, 298
  reciprocity of deployments, 288, 289–90
  settlement of dispute, 297–98, 299
  situation prior to entering into force, 297, 299
  steering function, 299
  substantial regulation, 293–94
  Warsaw Pact, 289
SUA Convention, 359, 362–63
subject under international law, 428–29, 430–31, 437
Sudan, 8, 14, 434
'support-based approach', 44–45
supreme command, 385–86
Supreme War Council, 11
Syria, 6, 15–16, 17, 28–29, 34–36, 40–42, 45–48, 62–63, 96–97, 109–10, 120–21, 139–40, 157–58, 271, 322, 425–26

Taguba Report, 85
Taliban, 6, 13, 40–42, 169, 402, 403
Targeting objects, 97
Targeting process, 95–98, 99, 104–5
Targeting 'fighters'/combatants and civilians, 39–40, 95–98, 105, 171
temporal scope of application of IHL, 20–21, 49, 50–51, 52, 53–54, 55, 56, 57, 58–59, 60, 61–63, 64, 67
  beginning of application, 58–60, 64
  criteria/threshold test, 62–63, 64–65, 66–67
  effectiveness over formal criteria, 55, 64–65
  ending of application, 52, 55, 57, 60–62, 63, 64, 65–67, 68
  in international armed conflicts, 50–57, 64
  in non-international armed conflicts, 57–63, 65
  intention and expectations of the conflict parties, 64–65
  risk of resumption of hostilities, 66–67
territorial control, 32–33, 58, 60, 66–67, 164, 172, 174–75, 182–83, 193–94, 208–12, 213, 214–15, 378, 454, 460, 461
  expanding the notion, 211–12, 437
territorial state, 24, 33–35, 43, 209–10, 437
territory, 30, 32–35, 36, 38–39, 40–44, 45, 46, 52, 53, 55–56, 58, 136–37, 164, 171, 172, 174–75, 209–10, 214–15, 437
terrorism, 6, 8, 13, 104–5, 434
theatre of operation, 267, 444

Timor-Leste, 6
torts (committed by foreign forces), 387–88
torture, 375
transfer of authority (TOA), 394–95, 400
transnational armed conflicts, 42–43, 46
transnational corporations, 448
transnational crime, 345, 347–48, 354–55, 362–63, 445–46
Treaty law, 427, 429–32, 433, 434–35, 438, 440, 441, 442–43
  application in any circumstances, 431–32
  ratification, 427, 431
  subsequent practice, 185, 186–87
  unilaterally declared binding, 430, 453
troop-contributing state/nation (TCN), 20, 23, 24, 29, 44–45, 49, 56–57, 121, 304–5, 307–9, 310–11, 315–16, 317–19, 324–25, 326–27, 328–30, 331, 337, 342–43, 364, 393, 394, 395, 396–97, 398, 399, 400, 403–4
truce, 54–55
Turkey, 131, 328

Uganda, 38–39n62
Ukraine, 4–5, 15–16, 131
ultra vires conduct, 309–10, 396
Umm Qasr, 179–80, 182–83
UNAMID, 6, 8, 17
UNAMSIL, 281–82
unilateral operations, 15–16
United Arab Emirates, 8
United Kingdom, 5, 8, 11, 13, 46–48, 54–55, 82, 116–17, 124–25, 133–34, 137, 166, 176, 179–80, 182–83, 184, 185–86, 190, 288, 327, 383–84
UK Law of War Manual, 83
United Nations (UN), 1–2, 7–8, 13–14, 17, 51–52, 64–66, 100–1, 103–4, 126–27, 204–5, 289–90, 294, 302, 322, 393
  Article 2(4) UN Charter, 269–70, 275
  Article 24 UN Charter, 312
  Article 39 UN Charter, 267, 279–80
  Article 42 UN Charter, 269, 275
  Article 43 UN Charter, 269
  Article 51 UN Charter, 6
  Article 103 UN Charter, 285–86, 312
  Basic Principles, 142–43
  Charter, 20, 239, 271, 274, 280
  Chapter VII, 5, 7, 12–13, 152, 204–5, 268, 275, 276, 277, 279–80, 285–86, 290, 312, 451–52
  High Commissioner for Refugees (UNHCR), 141
  immunity, 133–34
  Mandates/Missions/resolutions, 5, 7n35, 7–9, 13–14, 15–16, 17–18, 19–20, 23, 55, 100–1, 133–34, 137, 139, 204–5, 267, 290, 312, 354–55, 357, 361, 368–69, 452, 461–62
  Secretary-General, 272, 278–79, 346, 390
  Security Council (UNSC), 5, 7, 12–13, 15–16, 19–20, 23, 51–52, 121, 135, 137, 139, 156, 158, 267, 290, 297, 304, 311–12, 345, 346, 349, 351, 352, 358, 359–60, 362–63, 403, 434, 451–52, 455–56
UN Force Commander, 307–8
United Nations Convention on Jurisdictional Immunities of States and Their Property, 388
United Nations Convention on the Law of the Sea (UNCLOS), 351, 354–55, 356, 357–61, 368–69
United Nations Convention on the Rights of Persons with Disabilities, 447–48
United Nations Department of Field Support (DFS), 281–82
United Nations Department of Peace Operations (DPKO), 154–55, 157, 161, 281–82, 283–84
United Nations Drug Convention, 359
United Nations Model SOFA, 289–90, 293, 297–98, 390
United Nations Protection Force's (UNPROFOR), 12–13, 396
United States of America, 3–4, 6, 8, 11–13, 16, 22, 35–36, 40–42, 46–48, 55–56, 68, 78, 82–83, 85, 96–97, 99, 110, 111–13, 115, 116–17, 118, 119, 120, 121–22, 126–27, 169, 170, 179, 183, 236, 288, 289, 325, 328, 333–34, 337, 397, 398–99, 409–10
  Department of Defense, 409–10
  Department of Defense Law of War Manual, 111–12, 118
  Military Extraterritorial Jurisdiction Act 2000, 409–10
  United States Supreme Court, 36, 119, 376–77
Universal Declaration of Human Rights, 117–18, 154–55
universal norms, 17–18
UN Human Rights Council, 128, 221–22, 448–49
unity of purpose, 19
  UN Mandate in Afghanistan (ISAF), 13, 85, 133–34, 157–60, 161, 324–25, 395–96, 398, 402, 403
UN Mandate in Kosovo (UNMIK), 133–34, 310–11, 401

UNMISS, 281–82, 284
UN Missions in Ethiopia and Eritrea (UNMEE), 297
UN Mission in Sierra Leone, 65–66
use of force, 46–48, 53, 68–69, 91, 92–93, 94–95, 102–4, 109–10, 132–33, 155, 231, 241, 244–46, 247, 248, 268, 269, 271, 273, 274–75, 293, 332–33, 349–50, 362–63, 399, 402, 406–7, 420–21, 422
  Human-rights-based approach, 132–33
  limitations, 103–4
  measure of last resort, 104
  monopolization by states, 420–21, 422
  national views, 103–4
  prohibition of, 269–70
Uruguay, 213–14

Venice Commission, 315–16
  Opinion on Human Rights in Kosovo, 315–16
Vienna Convention on Consular Relations, 362–63
Vienna Convention on the Law of Treaties (VCLT), 30–31, 32, 34–35, 37–38, 45, 61, 128, 184–85, 335–36, 429
  applicability, 30n13
Vietnam, 11–12, 13, 54–55
Vietnam War, 54–55

Wall Advisory Opinion, 201, 203, 205–6, 210–11, 215–16, 218, 219, 341
Walzer, Michael, 77, 87
'war on terrorism', 16, 40–42
Warsaw Summit, 71, 158–59
water resources, 330–31
weapons trafficking, 23, 346
withdrawal or defeat of one party, 49, 62, 64–65
woman soldiers, 18–19
wounded and sick persons, 56

Yemen, 8, 17, 68, 139–40
Yugoslavia (FRY), 12–13, 15, 72, 133–34, 312, 324, 328